W9-AHP-706

THE NEW OXFORD BOOK OF EIGHTEENTH CENTURY VERSE

THE NEW OXFORD BOOK OF EIGHTEENTH CENTURY VERSE

Chosen and Edited by

ROGER LONSDALE

Oxford New York
OXFORD UNIVERSITY PRESS
1984

Oxford University Press, Walton Street, Oxford OX2 6DP

London New York Toronto
Delhi Bombay Calcutta Madras Karachi
Kuala Lumpur Singapore Hong Kong Tokyo
Nairobi Dar es Salaam Cape Town
Melbourne Auckland

and associated companies in
Beirut Berlin Ibadan Mexico City Nicosia

Oxford is a trade mark of Oxford University Press

British Library Cataloguing in Publication Data
The New Oxford book of eighteenth century verse.—
(Oxford books)
1. English poetry—18th century
I. Lonsdale, Roger
821'.5'08 PR1215
ISBN 0–19–214122–8

Library of Congress Cataloging in Publication Data
Main entry under title:
The New Oxford book of eighteenth century verse
Includes index
1. English poetry—18th century. I. Lonsdale, Roger H.
PR1215.N48 821'.5'08 83–17477
ISBN 0–19–214122–8

Set by Wyvern Typesetting Ltd.
Printed in Great Britain by
Thomson Litho Ltd,
East Kilbride, Scotland

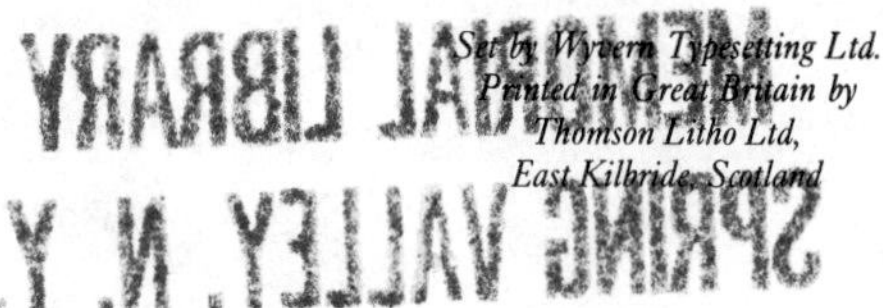

For Anne, Charles, and Kate

CONTENTS

CONTENTS

CONTENTS

CONTENTS

CONTENTS

CONTENTS

CONTENTS

CONTENTS

INTRODUCTION

(i)

IN the preface to his *Oxford Book of Eighteenth Century Verse* in 1926, David Nichol Smith suggested that attitudes to that century's poetry were 'still in process of readjustment':

> What is reasonably certain is that a new verdict, favourable or unfavourable, will be given by the twentieth century, and that in time we ourselves, or more probably our successors, will speak of the eighteenth century with as little sense of contention as we now speak of the seventeenth and the age of Elizabeth.

Almost sixty years later, Nichol Smith's prediction has surely been fulfilled. Indeed, the history and the nature of eighteenth-century poetry may well appear disappointingly uncontentious topics. Two generations of scholars have conscientiously explored and charted the territory. The general reader seems to know all too well what to expect from the age of Good Taste and Common Sense.

There have, of course, been readjustments. While Pope has been rehabilitated as a major satiric poet, we have been reminded that the early decades of the century have other representative voices; that, for example, Swift's deliberately 'unpoetic' intensity, and the blend of detailed natural description and religious sublimity in Thomson's blank verse, are also very much of their period. As for the later eighteenth century, what Northrop Frye has called 'a vague notion that the age of sensibility was the time when poetry moved from a reptilian Classicism, all cold and dry reason, to a mammalian Romanticism, all warm and wet feeling', tends to persist. The absence, after the death of Pope, of any comparably compelling figure before the appearance of Blake in the 1780s, may help to explain such vagueness. Yet the mid-century offers a variety of interesting individual voices, and the discovery in 1939 of Smart's extraordinary madhouse poem, 'Jubilate Agno', has only added to this diversity. The couplet survives with sombre dignity in Johnson's 'The Vanity of Human Wishes', more feverishly in Churchill's political satire in the 1760s, more lyrically and nostalgically in Goldsmith's 'The Deserted Village'. Since the 1740s, however, fashionable poetry had been increasingly preoccupied with other forms and interests. Literary historians have urged us to avoid labelling these decades 'pre-Romantic' (with the implication that their only achievement lay in perfunctory anticipations of Wordsworth) and to grant the Age of Sensibility its own personality. Its most representative poem is no doubt Gray's 'Elegy', in which confident and supremely eloquent generalities about life and death lead eventually to a much less assured projection of the isolated poet himself, burdened with mysterious sorrows.

Gray's later and more defiant version of the poet as 'The Bard' draws on a revealing blend of biblical, medieval, and Welsh sources to create the sublime if doomed figure who so awed contemporary readers. While Gray and his generation were increasingly fascinated by the lost sources of poetic power and authority, the pursuit of these elusive qualities could be frustrating and self-conscious. The search for inspiration led poets away from classical and French influences and back to the native tradition of Spenser, Shakespeare, and Milton, or further afield to the Orient, Scandinavia, the Middle Ages. William Collins, for example, imitated what he hoped was Persian poetry, invoked Shakespeare and Milton, vicariously indulged in Scottish superstitions, and celebrated the rare visionary powers of the true poet. By the 1760s, James Macpherson was 'discovering' a primitive epic in the Highlands, the ill-fated Thomas Chatterton was 'discovering' a cache of medieval lyrics in Bristol, and Thomas Percy was refurbishing ancient ballads to meet contemporary taste.

In tracing the changing sensibility of eighteenth-century poetry, literary historians have done much to persuade us to be sympathetic to its special conventions and aspirations, and not to judge it by criteria appropriate to quite different periods. Yet the very qualities welcomed in the new poets who emerged in the 1780s suggest the limitations of their predecessors: Crabbe's stern realism about rural life, and Burns's genial, colloquial vigour; Cowper's freshness of observation, disarming confidentiality and, always in the background, intimations of psychic instability; and Blake's enigmatic lyricism and radical conviction. We may have to concede, in fact, that emotional and stylistic inhibitions are what continue to strike many readers most forcibly about the verse of the earlier period. Commentators still generalize freely about the large areas of experience which, it is claimed, eighteenth-century poets ignored: interest in the non-rational, the insight of children, the isolation of the individual from conventional society, the exotic and savage, the poor and unlettered. The most sympathetic historians advise the reader that, from the poetry of an age of politeness and urbanity, he is not to expect earthy verisimilitude about everyday life, the expression of intimate or disturbing emotions, the energetic tones of a real speaking voice, or any but the most insipid eroticism.

Eighteenth-century poetic theory evidently made a virtue of such inhibitions. Throughout the period critics warned the poet to resist the temptation of dwelling on the local and the temporary surface of life, to avoid the homely, the crude, the capricious, and the abnormal. The ideal was apparently a 'polite' style which would succeed in muffling the 'low' and potentially disturbing immediacy of the real world. Theoretical preoccupation with general and universal experience made particularity of description and idiosyncratic subjectivity undesirable and irrelevant. The prescribed decorum of the relationship between poet and genteel reader led inevitably to reliance on predictable, usually classically influenced, forms and conventions, precisely adjusted style levels and specialized poetic diction.

Lucidity, elegance, and refinement are the positive qualities encouraged by such prescriptions, and these features of eighteenth-century verse have always appealed to readers who find in them the reflection of an age of apparent repose, moderation, and stability. Yet 'The Peace of the Augustans' has come increasingly to seem a dangerous delusion. Modern readers are inclined to view suspiciously poetry written, as we are so often assured it was, for the fashionable classes and accordingly subservient to the dictates of polite taste. Whereas Pope's later satire still engages urgently with the political and economic realities of his age as he perceived them, it is the evasive, escapist aspect of the poetry of the next two generations which can seem most striking. Just as the novel discovered its full potential between 1740 and 1760, the poets began retreating dispiritedly into a twilit, rural landscape to brood on Fancy and Melancholy and to contemplate their own sensibilities, turning their backs on public experience, and losing any capacity or desire to observe the actualities of contemporary life with any precision or immediacy, let alone to transform them imaginatively.

The ability of later eighteenth-century poets to ignore the social changes they were living through must seem ominous. Where do we find them responding to the agricultural and industrial revolutions, the effects of economic growth, increased social mobility, rapid urban development, changing sexual mores, the impact of British imperialism at home or abroad, or all the social tensions which would erupt in the last decade of the century? So evasive or so ignorant, it would seem, were the poets of such matters, so self-consciously elevated above the facts of everyday existence, that ideologically minded critics have had to resort to a process of deciphering the means by which the verse of the period contrives to gloss over, for example, the harsh realities of rural life, and the unjust relationships it complacently takes for granted.

(ii)

Since the landscape of eighteenth-century poetry is now apparently so well mapped and likely to afford so few unexpected perspectives, since the poets themselves were evidently so unanimous about their aims and means, it will seem outrageous to suggest that we still know very little about the subject. Yet given the sheer quantity of verse published in the century—the thousands of substantial, separately published poems, the hundreds of volumes of collected poems by individual authors, the innumerable miscellanies by several hands, all the verse which appeared in the poetry sections of hundreds of magazines and newspapers—this must literally be the case. How confident can we be that generations of historians and anthologists have efficiently sifted through this rubble in search of anything of value? With some honourable exceptions, they have in fact returned again and again to the same familiar material. Specialist studies have been written only of the most respectable and predictable genres, which are guaranteed to offer few or no surprises.

This situation is explicable only if we recognize the hypnotically influential way in which the eighteenth century succeeded in anthologizing itself. In one sense the process began with Pope's assault on what he could dismiss as Grub Street in *The Dunciad.* More directly influential have been Dodsley's *Collection of Poems* (1748–58), invariably trusted as definitively representative of the mid-century, and the much more massive compilations of English poetry which the booksellers began publishing towards the end of the century. So gratefully have most historians and anthologists relied on such huge collections as Robert Anderson's *Works of the British Poets* (13 vols., Edinburgh, 1792–5) and Alexander Chalmers's *Works of the English Poets* (21 vols., 1810), that the criteria governing the creation of this influential 'canon' have never been pondered. Some working principles of these editors were to have their own effect: Anderson (followed by Chalmers) admitted no anonymous authors, no women, no poets whose works had not already appeared in convenient collected editions, no living poets (so that Chalmers could replace eight of Anderson's poets with eight who had died by 1810). More significantly, however, these compilations were calculated to appeal to a respectable readership at a precise historical moment. For much of the century 'polite' taste had been steadily detaching itself from 'low', popular culture and by the 1790s, when Anderson made his crucial decisions, the divergence accelerated. In the decade of unprecedented social tension which followed the French Revolution, it need be no surprise that moderation, decorum, restraint and propriety were the criteria controlling admission to a compilation like Anderson's (endorsed by Chalmers in 1810), the very qualities which have helped to impart an air of remoteness and insubstantiality to much eighteenth-century poetry. There could be no place for the eccentric, the vulgar, the extravagant, the disturbing, the subversive.

Yet did such material exist to exercise the vigilance of the compilers? It is commonly assumed that the restraints imposed by polite taste were so pervasive that it never occurred to eighteenth-century poets to write in certain ways or on certain subjects, as if for several decades they simply failed to experience various basic human interests or emotions. In fact, throughout the century there were poets oblivious of, or indifferent to, the inhibitions of polite taste: the success of that taste lay less in governing what was written than in influencing what would be allowed to survive. Inevitably, many of the now totally forgotten poets of the period are precisely what we would have predicted: clumsy or insipid versifiers, feebly malignant dunces, slavish mimics of currently fashionable modes, opportunistic purveyors of doggerel on transient occasions, blank-verse moralists of stupefying turgidity, religiose maunderers of such lameness as hardly to qualify as pedestrian.

Yet the patient explorer will also encounter something much less predictable: the vigorous, humorous, idiosyncratic verse of authors, many of them anonymous, who felt impelled at least to try to describe with some immediacy and colloquial directness the changing world they lived in, often for anything but a polite readership. With varying degrees of competence and sophistication, they wrote about all aspects of mundane urban life, or, at a period when we are assured pastoral had declined into insipid Arcadianism or mutated into pompous georgic, continued writing realistically about rural superstitions, amusements, and hardships. In the 1740s when, if one were to believe some historians, all the poets had taken to gloomy meditations in graveyards, they were writing cheerfully about cricket, golf, and boxing. While many 'uneducated' poets tried feebly to imitate the poetic manners of their betters, there were others who wrote graphically if naively about their daily lives and resentfully about their poverty. Women, who also tended to see themselves as educationally deprived, wrote scathingly at times about their restricted lives and opportunities. Both sexes wrote, with surprising frequency, about the pains of matrimonial life. Poets wrote exuberant nonsense and garrulous autobiography and vigorous bawdy, described life in the army or the navy or prison, tried to convey the anguish of unemployment, campaigned with increasing fervour against the evils of war, imperialism, slavery and the treatment of the poor. In an age supposedly unanimous about the primacy of correctness and decorum, there was a surprising amount of stylistic restlessness: some poets wrote with unexpected plainness and simplicity throughout the century, others with an extravagance which at times can suggest literal derangement. Theoretically devoted to formal predictability, they wrote poems which seem to have no generic affiliations, or else perfunctorily claim to imitate Spenser or Milton, or shelter under the label of 'burlesque', while getting on with what they wanted to say.

(iii)

A single anthology can hardly illustrate all these assertions, especially when its aim is less to subvert traditional accounts of the nature and development of eighteenth-century poetry than to supplement them. I have tried to include all those writers who represent the familiar poetic interests and achievements of the century, while juxtaposing with them some much less familiar material. In this way I hope to suggest that there was greater diversity of style, form, and content in the period, particularly after the death of Pope, than is usually conceded. It is not necessary, in fact, to deviate far from the beaten track to demonstrate that polite taste exerted a less potent influence, indeed existed more precariously, than has often been asserted. Some historians mention the names of Edward Ward and John Wolcot at opposite ends of the century; but both were prolific, careless, uneven and indecorous writers, and the sheer size of their output has evidently made it easier to refer to them than to read their verse. Yet it is hard to see why Ward's earthy and at best graphic depictions of humble life should not enter our consciousness of what the 'Augustan' period could include, or why Wolcot's robust humour, mocking informality, and healthy scepticism about politics and sexual morality should not help to complicate our notions of 'pre-Romantic' verse.

About a quarter of the material in this anthology is, however, rather more obscure. Little or none of it seems to have been reprinted, or perhaps even read, since the eighteenth century itself ended. Without wishing to distort my representation of the period by laying undue emphasis on such verse, its inclusion may deserve further comment. I have tried to resist the temptation to include material merely because its style or content might seem to confound familiar generalizations about the period, or because it has purely documentary interest. Yet the problem, if it is allowed to be a problem, of what is 'literary' and what is 'non-literary' may well confront some readers at various points in this anthology. When such verse appears artless, unsubtle or inelegant, I hope that qualities of individuality and freshness will compensate. Such poems as those from the totally forgotten pens of Wright, Dower, Wilde and Hawthorn (nos. 138, 211, 418 and 420–1) may suggest that, when the poet has seen or felt something of his own, naivety or even clumsiness can impart to his verse a kind of immediacy about which conventional criticism and history have found little or nothing to say. In these and some other cases, the reader may well 'look round for poetry, and . . . be induced to enquire by what species of courtesy these attempts can be permitted to assume the title'. If so, I am content to let these and many other poets anticipate the supposedly revolutionary challenge to polite taste which Wordsworth would introduce with these words in 1798.

It would be misleading to suggest that only humble poets could look around them with freshness or immediacy or humour. T. S. Eliot thought of English verse after the death of Pope as the product of 'an age of retired country clergymen and schoolmasters'. If the reader feels confident about what he may expect from clerical poetry of the mid-eighteenth century, let him read the poems by Kenrick Prescot, 'J.T.', and Leonard Howard in this anthology (nos. 311, 315, 346). If he is convinced that excess of sensibility or devotion to stilted diction prevented poets from noticing what was going on around them, let him consider such poems as those by John Gerrard and James Graeme (nos. 358, 372) or a number of anonymous authors (e.g. nos. 320, 402–3, 409).

Mention of Wordsworth may call for some explanation of his and Coleridge's absence from the closing pages of this anthology. I have not consciously included any material written earlier than 1700 or later than 1799, with the exception of an extract from James Bissett's depiction of the classical gods as tourists in industrial Birmingham in 1800 as a postscript to a supposedly neo-classical era. Some of the most familiar poetry of Wordsworth and Coleridge theoretically qualifies for inclusion. Instead of reprinting such accessible poems as 'Tintern Abbey' and 'The Ancient Mariner', however, I have used the space to give some impression of the violent tensions in English society in the 1790s as perceived by the neglected poets of the decade. At the same time I have found various ways of reminding the reader of the emergence of Wordsworth and Coleridge in those heated years.

After several years of reading the 'submerged' poets of the period, I can only hope that this anthology succeeds to some extent in conveying my own conviction that the world of eighteenth-century poetry is at once less predictable and more familiar than we have been led to believe. Whether, in the absence of a single new figure who might focus all the neglected features of the period I have emphasized above, preconceptions about the age can be significantly changed I am inclined to doubt. One of the most interesting poets is the ubiquitous 'Anonymous', whose voice almost never registers in conventional literary history. If, inevitably, I would like to believe that this anthology is in various ways more representative of the full range of eighteenth-century verse than most collections, I have no desire that it should come to seem in any way definitive, aware as I am of the arbitrary decisions I have had to make, particularly among the poets so long buried beneath the debris of history. I would prefer it instead to be seen as making a case for further exploration and for further risking of judgement. As usual, readers will be struck by apparently inexplicable decisions in my selection from some of the better known poets: I am consoled only by the knowledge that limitations of space were always going to prevent illustration of the full range of, for example, Pope's achievement. Pope will, however, survive my attentions. I am more haunted by the lingering memory of some of the totally forgotten men and women whose literary bones I disturbed after they had slumbered peacefully for some two hundred years, who had something graphic or individual to say, however modestly, and for whom I had envisaged some kind of minor literary resurrection, but who necessarily fell back into the darkness of the centuries, perhaps irretrievably, at the last stage of my selection.

EDITORIAL PRINCIPLES

The arrangement is basically chronological, in that poets are introduced successively by the date of their earliest poem included in this anthology. Only when the date of composition is known to have been significantly earlier is it given priority over date of publication. Posthumously published poems are introduced not later than the date of the author's death. Since a poet's career may cover more than one decade, such an arrangement can be only approximately chronological. Pope poses a special problem since, emerging in the first decade of the century, his career would then carry the anthology forward to the 1740s. I have therefore divided the relatively large selection from his poems in the years in which he was preoccupied with translating Homer and wrote little original poetry. On balance, the chronological advantage seems to outweigh the inconvenience of this division.

Except for poems in dialect or in which archaic effects were deliberately sought, texts have been modernized: spelling and punctuation have been normalized, pervasive initial capitals and italics removed, and contractions expanded except when of metrical significance. (I have not, however, tried to impose an artificial consistency on the widely varying practice of poets and printers in the use of contractions.) While the original accidental features of a text can have their own interest and sometimes scholarly importance, it is worth remembering that the surviving manuscripts of many eighteenth-century poets make clear that they were content to leave such matters to the printer; that the original spelling and punctuation of some of the poems I have included would severely test the patience of many modern readers; that, while printing practice varied widely throughout the century, there was a widespread tendency from about 1750 for printers to reduce or eliminate the initial capitalization of nouns, and that most eighteenth-century readers thereafter would encounter English poetry in what was already a virtually modernized form. (I have followed the convention in recent modernizing of retaining initial capitals at least for personified qualities, but it is worth noting that the poets, or their printers, did not themselves consistently follow this principle.)

I have included few direct translations, because of limitations of space: a hundred pages devoted to the eighteenth century can be consulted in Charles Tomlinson's admirable *Oxford Book of Verse in English Translation* (1980). I have, however, included a number of imitations of poems in other languages, in which the original poem has been radically adapted to modern purposes: as, for example, in Thomas Morris's unusual account of a subaltern's life in the British army in Canada in imitation of Horace (no. 327).

For obvious reasons I have been able to give only excerpts from many of the century's longer poems. No anthologist can enjoy carving up the works of a major poet and in a number of important cases—poems by Swift, Pope, Johnson, Collins and Goldsmith—I could not bring myself to provide less than a complete text. Rather than offer a sequence of miscellaneous paragraphs from the final version of *The Seasons*, I have included the complete text of the first version of Thomson's 'Winter'. Totally neglected poets are a different matter: an excerpt gives them at least some chance of emerging from oblivion. I have tried to make the difference between excerpts and complete poems unambiguous: titles in square brackets are not the poet's but the editor's.

The date at the end of the poem is that of first publication. If the date of composition is verifiable and significantly different, this is also indicated. When the text followed is not that of the first edition, its source and date will be indicated in the endnotes. I have glossed on the page some words which seem likely to impede comprehension. Any other notes on the page are by the original author (included only selectively). Brief editorial notes on biographical and historical matters are confined to the end of the volume.

ACKNOWLEDGEMENTS

DURING my exploration of the poetry of the first half of the eighteenth century, I found David Foxon's monumental *English Verse 1701–1750* (Cambridge, 1975) an invaluable bibliographical guide, particularly to the existence and location of hitherto neglected material. My appreciation of Mr Foxon's expertise was only enhanced during my relatively unaided and much more laborious attempt to come to terms with the ever increasing output of verse in the later decades of the century. I am also grateful to Mr Foxon for his encouragement and willingness to answer particular queries.

Over a period of several years, many hundredweight, perhaps tons, of eighteenth-century verse were conveyed to the Upper Reading Room of the Bodleian Library for my inspection, and I am anxious to record my appreciation of the courteous and helpful service I received from the staff of the Library during this onerous process. I am inevitably indebted to the staff of other libraries: in particular to the British Library, but also to Balliol College Library, Birmingham Reference Library, the Brotherton Collection of Leeds University Library, the English Faculty Library, Oxford, Sheffield City Libraries, and the Special Collections Department of the University of Cincinnati Libraries. During visits to New Haven and Dublin I received generous assistance from Marjorie Wynne at the Beinecke Library at Yale and from Peter MacMahon at the National Library of Ireland.

For advice, information, or other assistance, I am grateful to James Basker, Antonia Forster, Harold Forster, Claude Rawson, Julian Roberts, Derek Roper and James Sambrook. Although I would not wish to implicate them in the way I have chosen to represent eighteenth-century poetry, I benefited at various times from the opportunity of discussing the subject with Irvin Ehrenpreis and Christopher Ricks. In the final stages of the compilation of this anthology I came to rely heavily on the vigilance, patience, and good sense of Mrs Judith Luna of the Oxford University Press.

This anthology has been completed during my tenure of a British Academy Readership. I am naturally grateful to the Academy for an appointment which dramatically accelerated my progress.

JOHN POMFRET

1667–1702

1 *The Choice*

IF heav'n the grateful liberty would give,
That I might choose my method how to live,
And all those hours propitious Fate should lend
In blissful ease and satisfaction spend:
Near some fair town I'd have a private seat,
Built uniform, not little, nor too great:
Better, if on a rising ground it stood,
Fields on this side, on that a neighbouring wood.
It should within no other things contain
But what were useful, necessary, plain:
Methinks 'tis nauseous, and I'd ne'er endure
The needless pomp of gaudy furniture.
A little garden, grateful to the eye,
And a cool rivulet run murm'ring by,
On whose delicious banks a stately row
Of shady limes or sycamores should grow;
At th' end of which a silent study placed
Should be with all the noblest authors graced:
Horace and Virgil, in whose mighty lines
Immortal wit and solid learning shines;
Sharp Juvenal, and am'rous Ovid too,
Who all the turns of love's soft passion knew;
He that with judgement reads his charming lines,
In which strong art with stronger nature joins,
Must grant his fancy does the best excel,
His thoughts so tender, and expressed so well;
With all those moderns, men of steady sense,
Esteemed for learning and for eloquence.
In some of these, as fancy should advise,
I'd always take my morning exercise:
For sure no minutes bring us more content
Than those in pleasing, useful studies spent.
I'd have a clear and competent estate,
That I might live genteelly, but not great:
As much as I could moderately spend;
A little more, sometimes t' oblige a friend.
Nor should the sons of poverty repine
Too much at fortune, they should taste of mine;

And all that objects of true pity were
Should be relieved with what my wants could spare:
For what our Maker has too largely giv'n
Should be returned in gratitude to heav'n.
A frugal plenty should my table spread,
With healthy, not luxurious, dishes fed:
Enough to satisfy, and something more
To feed the stranger, and the neighb'ring poor.
Strong meat indulges vice, and pampering food
Creates diseases, and inflames the blood.
But what's sufficient to make nature strong,
And the bright lamp of life continue long,
I'd freely take; and, as I did possess,
The bounteous Author of my plenty bless.
  I'd have a little vault, but always stored
With the best wines each vintage could afford.
Wine whets the wit, improves its native force,
And gives a pleasant flavour to discourse;
By making all our spirits debonair,
Throws off the lees, the sediment of care.
But as the greatest blessing heaven lends
May be debauched, and serve ignoble ends;
So, but too oft, the grape's refreshing juice
Does many mischievous effects produce.
My house should no such rude disorders know,
As from high drinking consequently flow.
Nor would I use what was so kindly giv'n
To the dishonour of indulgent heav'n.
If any neighbour came, he should be free,
Used with respect, and not uneasy be
In my retreat, or to himself or me.
What freedom, prudence, and right reason give,
All men may with impunity receive:
But the least swerving from their rule's too much;
For what's forbidden us, 'tis death to touch.
  That life may be more comfortable yet,
And all my joys refined, sincere, and great,
I'd choose two friends, whose company would be
A great advance to my felicity:
Well-born, of humours suited to my own,
Discreet, and men as well as books have known;
Brave, gen'rous, witty, and exactly free
From loose behaviour, or formality;
Airy and prudent, merry, but not light,
Quick in discerning, and in judging right.
Secret they should be, faithful to their trust;

In reas'ning cool, strong, temperate, and just;
Obliging, open, without huffing brave,
Brisk in gay talking, and in sober, grave;
Close in dispute, but not tenacious; tried
By solid reason, and let that decide;
Not prone to lust, revenge, or envious hate,
Nor busy meddlers with intrigues of state;
Strangers to slander, and sworn foes to spite,
Not quarrelsome, but stout enough to fight;
Loyal, and pious, friends to Caesar; true,
As dying martyrs, to their Maker too.
In their society I could not miss
A permanent, sincere, substantial bliss.
 Would bounteous heav'n once more indulge, I'd choose
(For who would so much satisfaction lose,
As witty nymphs, in conversation, give?)
Near some obliging, modest fair to live;
For there's that sweetness in a female mind,
Which in a man's we cannot hope to find;
That, by a secret but a pow'rful art,
Winds up the springs of life, and does impart
Fresh vital heat to the transported heart.
 I'd have her reason all her passions sway:
Easy in company, in private gay;
Coy to a fop, to the deserving free,
Still constant to herself, and just to me.
A soul she should have for great actions fit;
Prudence and wisdom to direct her wit,
Courage to look bold danger in the face,
No fear, but only to be proud, or base;
Quick to advise, by an emergence pressed,
To give good counsel, or to take the best.
I'd have th' expression of her thoughts be such,
She might not seem reserved, nor talk too much:
That shows a want of judgement, and of sense;
More than enough is but impertinence.
Her conduct regular, her mirth refined,
Civil to strangers, to her neighbours kind;
Averse to vanity, revenge, and pride,
In all the methods of deceit untried;
So faithful to her friend, and good to all,
No censure might upon her actions fall:
Then would e'en envy be compelled to say,
She goes the least of womankind astray.
 To this fair creature I'd sometimes retire;
Her conversation would new joys inspire,

Give life an edge so keen, no surly care
Would venture to assault my soul, or dare
Near my retreat to hide one secret snare.
But so divine, so noble a repast
I'd seldom, and with moderation, taste.
For highest cordials all their virtue lose
By a too frequent and too bold an use;
And what would cheer the spirits in distress,
Ruins our health when taken to excess.
  I'd be concerned in no litigious jar;
Beloved by all, not vainly popular.
Whate'er assistance I had power to bring
T' oblige my country, or to serve my king,
Whene'er they called, I'd readily afford,
My tongue, my pen, my counsel, or my sword.
Law-suits I'd shun, with as much studious care,
As I would dens where hungry lions are;
And rather put up injuries than be
A plague to him, who'd be a plague to me.
I value quiet at a price too great
To give for my revenge so dear a rate:
For what do we by all our bustle gain,
But counterfeit delight for real pain?
  If heav'n a date of many years would give,
Thus I'd in pleasure, ease, and plenty live.
And as I near approached the verge of life,
Some kind relation (for I'd have no wife)
Should take upon him all my worldly care,
While I did for a better state prepare.
Then I'd not be with any trouble vexed,
Nor have the ev'ning of my days perplexed;
But by a silent and a peaceful death,
Without a sigh, resign my aged breath:
And when committed to the dust, I'd have
Few tears, but friendly, dropped into my grave.
Then would my exit so propitious be,
All men would wish to live and die like me.

(1700)

THOMAS D'URFEY

1653–1723

2 *Dialogue, between Crab and Gillian*

Crab WHERE oxen do low and apples do grow,
Where corn is sown and grass is mown,
Where pigeons do fly and rooks nestle high,
    Fate give me for life a place;
Gill. Where hay is well cocked and udders are stroked,
Where duck and drake cry quack, quack, quack,
Where turkeys lay eggs and sows suckle pigs,
    Oh, there I would pass my days.
Crab On nought we will feed
Gill. But what we do breed;
Crab And wear on our backs
Gill. The wool of our flocks.
Crab And though linen feel
Gill. Rough, spun from the wheel,
'Tis cleanly, though coarse it comes.
Crab Town follies and cullies, and Mollies and Dollies,
For ever adieu and for ever;
Gill. And beaus that in boxes lie nuzzling their doxies,
In wigs that hang down to their bums.

Crab Adieu, the Pall Mall, the Park and Canal,
St. James's Square and flaunters there,
The gaming-house too, where high dice and low
    Are managed by all degrees.
Gill. Goodbye to the knight was bubbled last night,
That keeps a blowze and beats his spouse,
And now in great haste, to pay what he lost,
    Sends home to cut down the trees.
Crab And hey for the lad
Gill. Improves ev'ry clod,
Crab That ne'er set his hand
Gill. To bill or to bond,
Crab Nor barters his flocks
Gill. For wine or the pox,
To chouse him of half his days;
Crab But fishing and fowling, hunting and bowling,
    His pastimes are ever and ever,

chouse] cheat

Gill. Whose lips when ye buss 'em
  Smell like the bean-blossom;
Ah, he 'tis shall have my praise.

Crab To taverns where grow sour apple and sloe
A long adieu, and farewell too
The house of the great, whose cook has no meat
  And butler can't quench my thirst;
Gill. Goodbye to the Change, where rantipoles range,
Farewell cold tea and ratafie,
Hyde Park too, where Pride in coaches will ride,
  Although they be choked with dust.
Crab Farewell the law-gown,
Gill. The plague of the town,
Crab And friends of the Crown
Gill. Cried up or run down.
Crab And city jackdaws,
Gill. That fain would make laws
  To measure by yards and ells;
Crab Stockjobbers and swabbers, and toasters and roasters,
  For ever adieu and for ever;
Gill. We find what you're doing and home we're a-going,
  And so you may ring the bells.

(1701)

JOHN PHILIPS

1676–1709

3 from *The Splendid Shilling. An Imitation of Milton*

HAPPY the man, who, void of cares and strife,
In silken or in leathern purse retains
A Splendid Shilling: he nor hears with pain
New oysters cried, nor sighs for cheerful ale;
But with his friends, when nightly mists arise,
To Juniper's, Magpie, or Town-Hall repairs:
Where, mindful of the nymph whose wanton eye
Transfixed his soul, and kindled amorous flames,
Chloe, or Phillis, he each circling glass
Wisheth her health, and joy, and equal love.
Meanwhile he smokes, and laughs at merry tale,

2 rantipoles] ill-mannered women

Or pun ambiguous, or conundrum quaint.
But I, whom griping penury surrounds,
And hunger, sure attendant upon want,
With scanty offals and small acid tiff
(Wretched repast!) my meagre corpse sustain:
Then solitary walk, or doze at home
In garret vile, and with a warming puff
Regale chilled fingers; or from tube as black
As winter-chimney or well-polished jet,
Exhale mundungus, ill-perfuming scent.
Not blacker tube, nor of a shorter size,
Smokes Cambro-Briton (versed in pedigree,
Sprung from Cadwalader and Arthur, kings
Full famous in romantic tale) when he
O'er many a craggy hill and barren cliff,
Upon a cargo of famed Cestrian cheese,
High over-shadowing rides, with a design
To vend his wares, or at th' Arvonian mart,
Or Maridunum, or the ancient town
Ycleped Brechinia, or where Vaga's stream
Encircles Ariconium, fruitful soil,
Whence flow nectareous wines, that well may vie
With Massic, Setin, or renowned Falern.
  Thus while my joyless minutes tedious flow,
With looks demure and silent pace, a Dun,
Horrible monster! hated by gods and men,
To my aerial citadel ascends;
With vocal heel thrice thund'ring at my gates,
With hideous accent thrice he calls; I know
The voice ill-boding, and the solemn sound.
What should I do? or whither turn? Amazed,
Confounded, to the dark recess I fly
Of woodhole; straight my bristling hairs erect
Through sudden fear; a chilly sweat bedews
My shudd'ring limbs, and (wonderful to tell!)
My tongue forgets her faculty of speech,
So horrible he seems! His faded brow
Entrenched with many a frown, and conic beard,
And spreading band, admired by modern saints,
Disastrous acts forebode; in his right hand
Long scrolls of paper solemnly he waves,
With characters and figures dire inscribed,
Grievous to mortal eyes; (ye gods, avert

tiff] diluted punch   mundungus] bad-smelling tobacco   Cestrian] Cheshire
Arvonian mart] Aberavon   Maridunum] Carmarthen   Brechinia] Brecon
Vaga] the Wye   Ariconium] Hereford

Such plagues from righteous men!) Behind him stalks
Another monster, not unlike himself,
Sullen of aspect, by the vulgar called
A Catchpole, whose polluted hands the gods
With force incredible and magic charms
Erst have endued: if he his ample palm
Should haply on ill-fated shoulder lay
Of debtor, straight his body, to the touch
Obsequious (as whilom knights were wont)
To some enchanted castle is conveyed,
Where gates impregnable and coercive chains
In durance strict detain him, till, in form
Of money, Pallas sets the captive free.

(1701)

4 from *Blenheim*

[*War Poetry*]

Now from each van
The brazen instruments of death discharge
Horrible flames, and turbid streaming clouds
Of smoke sulphureous; intermixed with these
Large globous irons fly, of dreadful hiss,
Singeing the air, and from long distance bring
Surprising slaughter; on each side they fly
By chains connexed, and with destructive sweep
Behead whole troops at once; the hairy scalps
Are whirled aloof, while numerous trunks bestrow
Th' ensanguined field; with latent mischief stored
Show'rs of grenadoes rain, by sudden burst
Disploding murd'rous bowels, fragments of steel,
And stones, and glass, and nitrous grain adust.
A thousand ways at once the shivered orbs
Fly diverse, working torment and foul rout
With deadly bruise, and gashes furrowed deep.
Of pain impatient, the high-prancing steeds
Disdain the curb, and, flinging to and fro,
Spurn their dismounted riders; they expire
Indignant, by unhostile wounds destroyed.
Thus through each army death in various shapes
Prevailed; here mangled limbs, here brains and gore
Lie clotted; lifeless some: with anguish these
Gnashing, and loud laments invoking aid,

Unpitied and unheard; the louder din
Of guns, and trumpets' clang, and solemn sound
Of drums, o'ercame their groans.

(1705)

JONATHAN SWIFT

1667–1745

5 *To Their Excellencies the Lords Justices of Ireland. The Humble Petition of Frances Harris, Who Must Starve and Die a Maid If It Miscarries*

Humbly showeth:

THAT I went to warm myself in Lady Betty's chamber, because I was cold,
And I had in a purse, seven pound, four shillings and sixpence, besides farthings, in money, and gold;
So because I had been buying things for my Lady last night,
I was resolved to tell my money, to see if it was right.
Now you must know, because my trunk has a very bad lock,
Therefore all the money I have, which, God knows, is a very small stock,
I keep in a pocket tied about my middle, next my smock.
So when I went to put up my purse, as God would have it, my smock was unripped,
And, instead of putting it into my pocket, down it slipped:
Then the bell rung, and I went down to put my Lady to bed,
And, God knows, I thought my money was as safe as my maidenhead.
So when I came up again, I found my pocket feel very light,
But when I searched, and missed my purse, Lord! I thought I should have sunk outright.
'Lord! Madam,' says Mary, 'how d'ye do?'—'Indeed,' said I, 'never worse;
But pray, Mary, can you tell what I have done with my purse?'
'Lord help me,' said Mary, 'I never stirred out of this place!'
'Nay,' said I, 'I had it in Lady Betty's chamber, that's a plain case.'
So Mary got me to bed, and covered me up warm,
However, she stole away my garters, that I might do myself no harm.
So I tumbled and tossed all night, as you may very well think,
But hardly ever set my eyes together, or slept a wink.

So I was a-dreamed, methought, that we went and searched the folks round,
And in a corner of Mrs. Dukes' box, tied in a rag, the money was found.
So next morning we told Whittle, and he fell a-swearing;
Then my Dame Wadgar came, and she, you know, is thick of hearing;
'Dame,' said I, as loud as I could bawl, 'do you know what a loss I have had?'
'Nay,' said she, 'my Lord Collway's folks are all very sad,
For my Lord Dromedary comes a Tuesday without fail';
'Pugh!' said I, 'but that's not the business that I ail.'
Says Cary, says he, 'I have been a servant this five and twenty years, come spring,
And in all the places I lived, I never heard of such a thing.'
'Yes,' says the steward, 'I remember when I was at my Lady Shrewsbury's,
Such a thing as this happened, just about the time of gooseberries.'
So I went to the party suspected, and I found her full of grief;
(Now you must know, of all things in the world, I hate a thief).
However, I was resolved to bring the discourse slyly about.
'Mrs. Dukes,' said I, 'here's an ugly accident has happened out;
'Tis not that I value the money three skips of a louse;
But the thing I stand upon is the credit of the House;
'Tis true, seven pound, four shillings, and sixpence, makes a great hole in my wages,
Besides, as they say, service is no inheritance in these ages.
Now, Mrs. Dukes, you know, and everybody understands,
That though 'tis hard to judge, yet money can't go without hands.'
'The devil take me,' said she (blessing herself), 'if ever I saw't!'
So she roared like a Bedlam, as though I had called her all to naught;
So you know, what could I say to her any more?
I e'en left her, and came away as wise as I was before.
Well: but then they would have had me gone to the cunning man;
'No,' said I, ''tis the same thing, the chaplain will be here anon.'
So the chaplain came in. Now the servants say he is my sweetheart,
Because he's always in my chamber, and I always take his part;
So, as the devil would have it, before I was aware, out I blundered,
'Parson,' said I, 'can you cast a nativity, when a body's plundered?'
(Now you must know, he hates to be called parson, like the devil.)
'Truly,' says he, 'Mrs. Nab, it might become you to be more civil;
If your money be gone, as a learned divine says, d'ye see,
You are no text for my handling, so take that from me;
I was never taken for a conjurer before, I'd have you to know.'
'Lord,' said I, 'don't be angry, I'm sure I never thought you so;
You know I honour the cloth, I design to be a parson's wife,
I never took one in your coat for a conjurer in all my life.'
With that, he twisted his girdle at me like a rope, as who should say,

'Now you may go hang yourself for me', and so went away.
Well, I thought I should have swooned: 'Lord,' said I, 'what shall I do?
I have lost my money, and I shall lose my true-love too.'
Then my Lord called me; 'Harry,' said my Lord, 'don't cry,
I'll give something towards thy loss'; and says my Lady, 'so will I'.
'Oh but', said I, 'what if after all the chaplain won't come to?'
For that, he said (an't please your Excellencies) I must petition you.

The premises tenderly considered, I desire your Excellencies' protection,
And that I may have a share in next Sunday's collection:
And over and above, that I may have your Excellencies' letter
With an order for the chaplain aforesaid, or instead of him, a better;
And then your poor petitioner, both night and day,
Or the chaplain (for 'tis his trade) as in duty bound, shall ever pray.

(Wr. 1701; pub. 1709)

6 *Baucis and Philemon. Imitated from the Eighth Book of Ovid*

IN ancient times, as story tells,
The saints would often leave their cells,
And stroll about, but hide their quality,
To try good people's hospitality.
It happened on a winter night
(As authors of the legend write),
Two brother hermits, saints by trade,
Taking their tour in masquerade,
Disguised in tattered habits, went
To a small village down in Kent;
Where, in the strollers' canting strain,
They begged from door to door in vain;
Tried every tone might pity win,
But not a soul would let them in.
Our wand'ring saints, in woeful state,
Treated at this ungodly rate,
Having through all the village passed,
To a small cottage came at last,
Where dwelt a good old honest yeoman,
Called in the neighbourhood Philemon;
Who kindly did the saints invite
In his poor hut to pass the night;
And then the hospitable sire
Bid Goody Baucis mend the fire;

While he from out the chimney took
A flitch of bacon off the hook,
And freely from the fattest side
Cut out large slices to be fried;
Then stepped aside to fetch them drink,
Filled a large jug up to the brink,
And saw it fairly twice go round;
Yet (what was wonderful) they found
'Twas still replenished to the top,
As if they ne'er had touched a drop.
The good old couple was amazed,
And often on each other gazed;
For both were frightened to the heart,
And just began to cry, 'What art!'
Then softly turned aside to view
Whether the lights were burning blue.
The gentle pilgrims, soon aware on't,
Told them their calling and their errand:
'Good folks, you need not be afraid,
We are but saints,' the hermits said;
'No hurt shall come to you or yours;
But, for that pack of churlish boors,
Not fit to live on Christian ground,
They and their houses shall be drowned;
Whilst you shall see your cottage rise,
And grow a church before your eyes.'
  They scarce had spoke, when, fair and soft,
The roof began to mount aloft;
Aloft rose ev'ry beam and rafter;
The heavy wall climbed slowly after.
  The chimney widened and grew higher,
Became a steeple with a spire.
  The kettle to the top was hoist,
And there stood fastened to a joist,
But with the upside down, to show
Its inclination for below:
In vain; for some superior force
Applied at bottom stops its course:
Doomed ever in suspense to dwell,
'Tis now no kettle, but a bell.
  A wooden jack, which had almost
Lost by disuse the art to roast,
A sudden alteration feels,
Increased by new intestine wheels:
And, what exalts the wonder more,
The number made the motion slower.

The flier, tho't had leaden feet,
Turned round so quick you scarce could see't;
Now, slackened by some secret power,
Can hardly move an inch an hour.
The jack and chimney, near allied,
Had never left each other's side;
The chimney to a steeple grown,
The jack would not be left alone,
But up against the steeple reared,
Became a clock, and still adhered;
And still its love to household cares,
By an ill voice at noon, declares,
Warning the cook-maid not to burn
That roast meat, which it cannot turn.
  The groaning chair was seen to crawl,
Like an huge snail, half up the wall;
There stuck aloft in public view,
And with small change, a pulpit grew.
  The porringers, that in a row
Hung high, and made a glitt'ring show,
To a less noble substance changed,
Were now but leathern buckets ranged.
  The ballads pasted on the wall,
Of Joan of France, and English Moll,
Fair Rosamond, and Robin Hood,
The Little Children in the Wood,
Now seemed to look abundance better,
Improved in picture, size, and letter;
And, high in order placed, describe
The heraldry of ev'ry tribe.
  A bedstead of the antique mode,
Compact of timber many a load,
Such as our grandsires wont to use,
Was metamorphosed into pews;
Which still their ancient nature keep,
By lodging folks disposed to sleep.
  The cottage, by such feats as these,
Grown to a church by just degrees,
The hermits then desire their host
To ask for what he fancied most.
Philemon, having paused a while,
Returned 'em thanks in homely style;
Then said, 'My house is grown so fine,
Methinks, I still would call it mine.
I'm old, and fain would live at ease;
Make me the parson if you please.'

He spoke, and presently he feels
His grazier's coat fall down his heels;
He sees, yet hardly can believe,
About each arm a pudding-sleeve;
His waistcoat to a cassock grew,
And both assumed a sable hue;
But, being old, continued just
As threadbare, and as full of dust.
His talk was now of tithes and dues,
Could smoke his pipe, and read the news;
Knew how to preach old sermons next,
Vamped in the preface and the text;
At christ'nings well could act his part,
And had the service all by heart;
Wished women might have children fast,
And thought whose sow had farrowed last;
Against dissenters would repine,
And stood up firm for Right Divine;
Found his head filled with many a system;
But classic authors—he ne'er missed 'em.
Thus having furbished up a parson,
Dame Baucis next they played their farce on:
Instead of homespun coifs, were seen
Good pinners edged with colberteen;
Her petticoat, transformed apace,
Became black satin, flounced with lace.
Plain 'Goody' would no longer down,
'Twas 'Madam,' in her grogram gown.
Philemon was in great surprise,
And hardly could believe his eyes,
Amazed to see her look so prim,
And she admired as much at him.
Thus happy in their change of life,
Were several years this man and wife:
When on a day, which proved their last,
Discoursing o'er old stories past,
They went by chance, amidst their talk,
To the churchyard to fetch a walk;
When Baucis hastily cried out,
'My dear, I see your forehead sprout.'
'Sprout!' quoth the man; 'what's this you tell us?
I hope you don't believe me jealous:
But yet, methinks, I feel it true,
And really yours is budding too—
Nay,—now I cannot stir my foot;
It feels as if 'twere taking root.'

Description would but tire my Muse:
In short, they both were turned to yews.
Old Goodman Dobson of the Green
Remembers he the trees has seen;
He'll talk of them from noon to night,
And goes with folks to show the sight;
On Sundays, after ev'ning prayer,
He gathers all the parish there;
Points out the place of either yew,
Here Baucis, there Philemon, grew.
Till once a parson of our town,
To mend his barn, cut Baucis down;
At which, 'tis hard to be believed
How much the other tree was grieved,
Grew scrubby, died a-top, was stunted:
So the next parson stubbed and burnt it.

(Wr. 1706; pub. 1709)

7 *A Description of the Morning*

Now hardly here and there a hackney-coach
Appearing, showed the ruddy morn's approach.
Now Betty from her master's bed had flown,
And softly stole to discompose her own.
The slipshod prentice from his master's door
Had pared the dirt, and sprinkled round the floor.
Now Moll had whirled her mop with dext'rous airs,
Prepared to scrub the entry and the stairs.
The youth with broomy stumps began to trace
The kennel-edge, where wheels had worn the place.
The small-coal man was heard with cadence deep,
Till drowned in shriller notes of chimney-sweep.
Duns at his lordship's gate began to meet,
And Brickdust Moll had screamed through half the street.
The turnkey now his flock returning sees,
Duly let out a-nights to steal for fees.
The watchful bailiffs take their silent stands,
And schoolboys lag with satchels in their hands.

(1709)

7 kennel] gutter

8 *A Description of a City Shower*

CAREFUL observers may foretell the hour
(By sure prognostics) when to dread a show'r:
While rain depends, the pensive cat gives o'er
Her frolics, and pursues her tail no more.
Returning home at night, you'll find the sink
Strike your offended sense with double stink.
If you be wise, then go not far to dine,
You spend in coach-hire more than save in wine.
A coming show'r your shooting corns presage,
Old aches throb, your hollow tooth will rage.
Saunt'ring in coffee-house is Dulman seen;
He damns the climate, and complains of spleen.

Meanwhile the South, rising with dabbled wings,
A sable cloud athwart the welkin flings,
That swilled more liquor than it could contain,
And like a drunkard gives it up again.
Brisk Susan whips her linen from the rope,
While the first drizzling show'r is borne aslope;
Such is that sprinkling which some careless quean
Flirts on you from her mop, but not so clean.
You fly, invoke the gods; then turning, stop
To rail; she singing, still whirls on her mop.
Not yet the dust had shunned th' unequal strife,
But aided by the wind, fought still for life;
And wafted with its foe by violent gust,
'Twas doubtful which was rain, and which was dust.
Ah! where must needy poet seek for aid,
When dust and rain at once his coat invade?
Sole coat, where dust cemented by the rain
Erects the nap, and leaves a cloudy stain.

Now in contiguous drops the flood comes down,
Threat'ning with deluge this devoted town.
To shops in crowds the daggled females fly,
Pretend to cheapen goods, but nothing buy.
The Templar spruce, while ev'ry spout's a-broach,
Stays till 'tis fair, yet seems to call a coach.
The tucked-up sempstress walks with hasty strides,
While streams run down her oiled umbrella's sides.
Here various kinds, by various fortunes led,
Commence acquaintance underneath a shed.
Triumphant Tories and desponding Whigs
Forget their feuds, and join to save their wigs.

devoted] doomed

Boxed in a chair the beau impatient sits,
While spouts run clatt'ring o'er the roof by fits;
And ever and anon with frightful din
The leather sounds, he trembles from within.
So when Troy chair-men bore the wooden steed,
Pregnant with Greeks impatient to be freed
(Those bully Greeks, who, as the moderns do,
Instead of paying chair-men, run them through),
Laocoön struck the outside with his spear,
And each imprisoned hero quaked for fear.
  Now from all parts the swelling kennels flow,
And bear their trophies with them as they go:
Filth of all hues and odours seem to tell
What streets they sailed from, by the sight and smell.
They, as each torrent drives, with rapid force
From Smithfield or St. Pulchre's shape their course,
And in huge confluent join at Snow Hill ridge,
Fall from the Conduit prone to Holborn Bridge.
Sweepings from butchers' stalls, dung, guts, and blood,
Drowned puppies, stinking sprats, all drenched in mud,
Dead cats and turnip-tops come tumbling down the flood.

(1710)

9 *In Sickness. Written soon after the Author's coming to live in Ireland, upon the Queen's Death, October 1714*

'Tis true—then why should I repine
To see my life so fast decline?
But why obscurely here alone,
Where I am neither loved nor known?
My state of health none care to learn;
My life is here no soul's concern.
And those with whom I now converse
Without a tear will tend my hearse;
Removed from kind Arbuthnot's aid,
Who knows his art but not his trade,
Preferring his regard for me
Before his credit or his fee.
Some formal visits, looks, and words,
What mere humanity affords,
I meet perhaps from three or four,
From whom I once expected more;
Which those who tend the sick for pay

Can act as decently as they.
But no obliging, tender friend
To help at my approaching end;
My life is now a burthen grown
To others, ere it be my own.
  Ye formal weepers for the sick,
In your last offices be quick;
And spare my absent friends the grief
To hear, yet give me no relief;
Expired today, entombed tomorrow,
When known, will save a double sorrow.

(1735)

To Stella

March 13, 1723–4

[Written on the Day of her Birth, but not on the Subject, when I was sick in bed.]

Tormented with incessant pains,
Can I devise poetic strains?
Time was, when I could yearly pay
My verse on Stella's native day:
But now, unable grown to write,
I grieve she ever saw the light.
Ungrateful; since to her I owe
That I these pains can undergo.
She tends me like an humble slave;
And, when indecently I rave,
When out my brutish passions break,
With gall in ev'ry word I speak,
She with soft speech my anguish cheers,
Or melts my passions down with tears;
Although 'tis easy to descry
She wants assistance more than I;
Yet seems to feel my pains alone,
And is a stoic in her own.
When, among scholars, can we find
So soft and yet so firm a mind?
All accidents of life conspire
To raise up Stella's virtue higher;
Or else to introduce the rest
Which had been latent in her breast.
Her firmness who could e'er have known,

Had she not evils of her own?
Her kindness who could ever guess,
Had not her friends been in distress?
Whatever base returns you find
From me, dear Stella, still be kind.
In your own heart you'll reap the fruit,
Though I continue still a brute.
But, when I once am out of pain,
I promise to be good again;
Meantime, your other juster friends
Shall for my follies make amends;
So may we long continue thus,
Admiring you, you pitying us.

(1765)

11 *Stella's Birthday, 1725*

As, when a beauteous nymph decays,
We say, she's past her dancing days;
So poets lose their feet by time,
And can no longer dance in rhyme.
Your annual bard had rather chose
To celebrate your birth in prose;
Yet merry folks, who want by chance
A pair to make a country dance,
Call the old housekeeper, and get her
To fill a place for want of better;
While Sheridan is off the hooks,
And friend Delany at his books,
That Stella may avoid disgrace,
Once more the Dean supplies their place.
  Beauty and wit, too sad a truth,
Have always been confined to youth;
The god of wit and beauty's queen,
He twenty-one and she fifteen:
No poet ever sweetly sung,
Unless he were, like Phoebus, young;
Nor ever nymph inspired to rhyme,
Unless, like Venus, in her prime.
At fifty-six, if this be true,
Am I a poet fit for you?
Or, at the age of forty-three,
Are you a subject fit for me?
Adieu, bright wit, and radiant eyes;

You must be grave and I be wise.
Our fate in vain we would oppose,
But I'll be still your friend in prose:
Esteem and friendship to express
Will not require poetic dress;
And if the Muse deny her aid
To have them sung, they may be said.
  But, Stella, say, what evil tongue
Reports you are no longer young;
That Time sits with his scythe to mow
Where erst sat Cupid with his bow;
That half your locks are turned to grey?
I'll ne'er believe a word they say.
'Tis true, but let it not be known,
My eyes are somewhat dimmish grown;
For nature, always in the right,
To your decays adapts my sight,
And wrinkles undistinguished pass,
For I'm ashamed to use a glass;
And till I see them with these eyes,
Whoever says you have them, lies.
  No length of time can make you quit
Honour and virtue, sense and wit;
Thus you may still be young to me,
While I can better hear than see.
O ne'er may Fortune show her spite,
To make me deaf, and mend my sight.

(1727)

12 *A Beautiful Young Nymph Going to Bed*

CORINNA, pride of Drury Lane,
For whom no shepherd sighs in vain—
Never did Covent Garden boast
So bright a battered, strolling toast;
No drunken rake to pick her up,
No cellar where on tick to sup;
Returning at the midnight hour,
Four storeys climbing to her bow'r,
Then, seated on a three-legged chair,
Takes off her artificial hair;
Now, picking out a crystal eye,
She wipes it clean, and lays it by.
Her eyebrows from a mouse's hide,
Stuck on with art on either side,

Pulls off with care, and first displays 'em,
Then in a play-book smoothly lays 'em.
Now dextrously her plumpers draws,
That serve to fill her hollow jaws.
Untwists a wire, and from her gums
A set of teeth completely comes.
Pulls out the rags contrived to prop
Her flabby dugs and down they drop.
Proceeding on, the lovely goddess
Unlaces next her steel-ribbed bodice,
Which by the operator's skill,
Press down the lumps, the hollows fill;
Up goes her hand, and off she slips
The bolsters that supply her hips.
With gentlest touch, she next explores
Her chancres, issues, running sores,
Effects of many a sad disaster,
And then to each applies a plaster.
But must, before she goes to bed,
Rub off the daubs of white and red;
And smooth the furrows in her front,
With greasy paper stuck upon't.
She takes a bolus ere she sleeps,
And then between two blankets creeps.
With pains of love tormented lies;
Or if she chance to close her eyes,
Of Bridewell and the Compter dreams,
And feels the lash, and faintly screams;
Or, by a faithless bully drawn,
At some hedge-tavern lies in pawn;
Or to Jamaica seems transported,
Alone, and by no planter courted;
Or, near Fleet Ditch's oozy brinks,
Surrounded with a hundred stinks,
Belated, seems on watch to lie,
And snap some cully passing by;
Or, struck with fear, her fancy runs
On watchmen, constables and duns,
From whom she meets with frequent rubs;
But never from religious clubs,
Whose favour she is sure to find,
Because she pays them all in kind.
  Corinna wakes. A dreadful sight!
Behold the ruins of the night!

Compter] debtors' prison   cully] dupe

A wicked rat her plaster stole,
Half ate, and dragged it to his hole.
The crystal eye, alas, was missed;
And Puss had on her plumpers pissed.
A pigeon picked her issue-peas;
And Shock her tresses filled with fleas.
  The nymph, though in this mangled plight,
Must ev'ry morn her limbs unite.
But how shall I describe her arts
To recollect the scattered parts?
Or show the anguish, toil, and pain
Of gath'ring up herself again?
The bashful Muse will never bear
In such a scene to interfere.
Corinna in the morning dizened,
Who sees, will spew; who smells, be poisoned.

(Wr. 1731?; pub. 1734)

13 *The Day of Judgement*

WITH a whirl of thought oppressed,
I sink from reverie to rest.
An horrid vision seized my head,
I saw the graves give up their dead.
Jove, armed with terrors, burst the skies,
And thunder roars, and light'ning flies!
Amazed, confused, its fate unknown,
The world stands trembling at his throne.
While each pale sinner hangs his head,
Jove, nodding, shook the heav'ns, and said,
'Offending race of human kind,
By nature, reason, learning, blind;
You who through frailty stepped aside,
And you who never fell—though pride;
You who in different sects have shammed,
And come to see each other damned;
(So some folks told you, but they knew
No more of Jove's designs than you);
The world's mad business now is o'er,
And I resent these pranks no more.
I to such blockheads set my wit!
I damn such fools!—Go, go, you're bit.'

(Wr. 1731?; pub. 1774)

12 dizened] arrayed

14 *Verses on the Death of Dr. Swift, D.S.P.D., Occasioned by Reading a Maxim in Rochefoucauld*

As Rochefoucauld his maxims drew
From nature, I believe 'em true:
They argue no corrupted mind
In him; the fault is in mankind.
  This maxim more than all the rest
Is thought too base for human breast:
'In all distresses of our friends
We first consult our private ends,
While nature, kindly bent to ease us,
Points out some circumstance to please us.'
  If this perhaps your patience move,
Let reason and experience prove.
  We all behold with envious eyes
Our equal raised above our size;
Who would not at a crowded show
Stand high himself, keep others low?
I love my friend as well as you,
But would not have him stop my view;
Then let me have the higher post;
I ask but for an inch at most.
  If in a battle you should find,
One, whom you love of all mankind,
Had some heroic action done,
A champion killed, or trophy won;
Rather than thus be over-topped,
Would you not wish his laurels cropped?
  Dear honest Ned is in the gout,
Lies racked with pain, and you without:
How patiently you hear him groan!
How glad the case is not your own!
  What poet would not grieve to see
His brethren write as well as he?
But rather than they should excel,
He'd wish his rivals all in hell.
  Her end, when Emulation misses,
She turns to envy, stings and hisses;
The strongest friendship yields to pride,
Unless the odds be on our side.
  Vain human kind! Fantastic race!
Thy various follies who can trace?
Self-love, ambition, envy, pride,
Their empire in our hearts divide:

Give others riches, power, and station,
'Tis all on me an usurpation.
I have no title to aspire;
Yet, when you sink, I seem the higher.
In Pope, I cannot read a line,
But with a sigh, I wish it mine;
When he can in one couplet fix
More sense than I can do in six,
It gives me such a jealous fit,
I cry, 'Pox take him, and his wit.'
  Why must I be outdone by Gay,
In my own hum'rous biting way?
  Arbuthnot is no more my friend,
Who dares to irony pretend;
Which I was born to introduce,
Refined it first, and showed its use.
  St. John, as well as Pulteney, knows
That I had some repute for prose;
And till they drove me out of date,
Could maul a minister of state.
If they have mortified my pride,
And made me throw my pen aside,
If with such talents heav'n hath blest 'em,
Have I not reason to detest 'em?
  To all my foes, dear Fortune, send
Thy gifts, but never to my friend;
I tamely can endure the first,
But this with envy makes me burst.
  Thus much may serve by way of proem,
Proceed we therefore to our poem.
  The time is not remote, when I
Must by the course of nature die;
When I foresee my special friends
Will try to find their private ends,
Though it is hardly understood
Which way my death can do them good;
Yet thus, methinks, I hear 'em speak:
'See, how the Dean begins to break:
Poor gentleman, he droops apace,
You plainly find it in his face;
That old vertigo in his head
Will never leave him, till he's dead.
Besides, his memory decays,
He recollects not what he says;
He cannot call his friends to mind,
Forgets the place where last he dined;

Plies you with stories o'er and o'er:
He told them fifty times before.
How does he fancy we can sit
To hear his out-of-fashioned wit?
But he takes up with younger folks,
Who for his wine will bear his jokes:
Faith, he must make his stories shorter,
Or change his comrades once a quarter;
In half the time, he talks them round;
There must another set be found.
'For poetry, he's past his prime,
He takes an hour to find a rhyme:
His fire is out, his wit decayed,
His fancy sunk, his Muse a jade.
I'd have him throw away his pen;
But there's no talking to some men.'
And then their tenderness appears,
By adding largely to my years:
'He's older than he would be reckoned,
And well remembers Charles the Second.
'He hardly drinks a pint of wine;
And that, I doubt, is no good sign.
His stomach too begins to fail:
Last year we thought him strong and hale;
But now he's quite another thing;
I wish he may hold out till spring.'
Then hug themselves, and reason thus:
'It is not yet so bad with us.'
In such a case they talk in tropes,
And by their fears express their hopes;
Some great misfortune to portend,
No enemy can match a friend.
With all the kindness they profess,
The merit of a lucky guess
(When daily howd'y's come of course,
And servants answer, 'Worse and worse')
Would please 'em better than to tell
That, God be praised, the Dean is well.
Then he who prophesied the best
Approves his foresight to the rest:
'You know, I always feared the worst,
And often told you so at first.'
He'd rather choose that I should die
Than his prediction prove a lie.
Not one foretells I shall recover;
But all agree to give me over.

Yet should some neighbour feel a pain
Just in the parts where I complain;
How many a message would he send?
What hearty prayers that I should mend?
Inquire what regimen I kept;
What gave me ease, and how I slept?
And more lament, when I was dead,
Than all the sniv'llers round my bed.
My good companions, never fear,
For though you may mistake a year,
Though your prognostics run too fast,
They must be verified at last.
Behold the fatal day arrive!
'How is the Dean?' 'He's just alive.'
Now the departing prayer is read.
'He hardly breathes.' 'The Dean is dead.'
Before the passing-bell begun,
The news through half the town has run.
'O, may we all for death prepare!
What has he left? And who's his heir?'
'I know no more than what the news is,
'Tis all bequeathed to public uses.'
'To public use! A perfect whim!
What had the public done for him?
Mere envy, avarice, and pride!
He gave it all.—But first he died.
And had the Dean, in all the nation,
No worthy friend, no poor relation?
So ready to do strangers good,
Forgetting his own flesh and blood?'
Now Grub Street wits are all employed;
With elegies the town is cloyed:
Some paragraph in ev'ry paper,
To curse the Dean, or bless the Drapier.
The doctors, tender of their fame,
Wisely on me lay all the blame:
'We must confess his case was nice,
But he would never take advice;
Had he been ruled, for aught appears,
He might have lived these twenty years;
For when we opened him we found
That all his vital parts were sound.'
From Dublin soon to London spread,
'Tis told at court, the Dean is dead.
Kind Lady Suffolk in the spleen
Runs laughing up to tell the Queen.

The Queen, so gracious, mild, and good,
Cries, 'Is he gone? 'Tis time he should.
He's dead, you say? Why, let him rot;
I'm glad the medals were forgot.
I promised him, I own; but when?
I only was the Princess then;
But now as consort of the King,
You know 'tis quite a different thing.'
  Now, Chartres at Sir Robert's levee
Tells, with a sneer, the tidings heavy:
'Why, is he dead without his shoes?'
(Cries Bob) 'I'm sorry for the news;
Oh, were the wretch but living still,
And in his place my good friend Will;
Or had a mitre on his head,
Provided Bolingbroke were dead.'
  Now, Curll his shop from rubbish drains:
Three genuine tomes of *Swift's Remains*.
And then, to make them pass the glibber,
Revised by Tibbalds, Moore, and Cibber.
He'll treat me as he does my betters:
Publish my will, my life, my letters,
Revive the libels born to die,
Which Pope must bear, as well as I.
  Here shift the scene, to represent
How those I love my death lament.
Poor Pope will grieve a month; and Gay
A week; and Arbuthnot a day.
  St. John himself will scarce forbear
To bite his pen, and drop a tear.
The rest will give a shrug, and cry,
'I'm sorry; but we all must die.'
Indifference clad in wisdom's guise
All fortitude of mind supplies;
For how can stony bowels melt
In those who never pity felt;
When we are lashed, they kiss the rod,
Resigning to the will of God.
  The fools, my juniors by a year,
Are tortured with suspense and fear,
Who wisely thought my age a screen,
When death approached, to stand between:
The screen removed, their hearts are trembling,
They mourn for me without dissembling.
  My female friends, whose tender hearts
Have better learned to act their parts,

Receive the news in doleful dumps:
'The Dean is dead (and what is trumps?),
Then Lord have mercy on his soul.
(Ladies, I'll venture for the vole.)
Six deans, they say, must bear the pall.
(I wish I knew what king to call.)
Madam, your husband will attend
The funeral of so good a friend.'
'No, madam, 'tis a shocking sight,
And he's engaged tomorrow night!
My Lady Club would take it ill,
If he should fail her at quadrille.
He loved the Dean. (I lead a heart.)
But dearest friends, they say, must part.
His time was come, he ran his race;
We hope he's in a better place.'
  Why do we grieve that friends should die?
No loss more easy to supply.
One year is past; a different scene;
No further mention of the Dean,
Who now, alas, no more is missed
Than if he never did exist.
Where's now this fav'rite of Apollo?
Departed; and his works must follow,
Must undergo the common fate;
His kind of wit is out of date.
Some country squire to Lintot goes,
Inquires for Swift in verse and prose:
Says Lintot, 'I have heard the name;
He died a year ago.' The same.
He searcheth all his shop in vain:
'Sir, you may find them in Duck Lane:
I sent them with a load of books,
Last Monday, to the pastry-cooks.
To fancy they could live a year!
I find you're but a stranger here.
The Dean was famous in his time,
And had a kind of knack at rhyme;
His way of writing now is past;
The town hath got a better taste.
I keep no antiquated stuff;
But, spick and span I have enough.
Pray, do but give me leave to show 'em:
Here's Colley Cibber's birthday poem.
This ode you never yet have seen,
By Stephen Duck, upon the Queen.

Then here's a letter finely penned
Against the Craftsman and his friend;
It clearly shows that all reflection
On ministers is disaffection.
Next, here's Sir Robert's *Vindication*,
And Mr. Henley's last Oration;
The hawkers have not got 'em yet:
Your honour please to buy a set?
'Here's Woolston's tracts, the twelfth edition;
'Tis read by every politician;
The country members, when in town,
To all their boroughs send them down.
You never met a thing so smart;
The courtiers have them all by heart:
Those Maids of Honour (who can read)
Are taught to use them for their creed.
The rev'rend author's good intention
Hath been rewarded with a pension:
He doth an honour to his gown,
By bravely running priestcraft down;
He shows, as sure as God's in Gloucester,
That Jesus was a grand impostor,
That all his miracles were cheats,
Performed as jugglers do their feats.
The Church had never such a writer;
A shame he hath not got a mitre!'
Suppose me dead; and then suppose
A club assembled at the Rose,
Where, from discourse of this and that,
I grow the subject of their chat;
And, while they toss my name about,
With favour some, and some without,
One quite indiff'rent in the cause
My character impartial draws:
'The Dean, if we believe report,
Was never ill received at court.
As for his works in verse and prose,
I own myself no judge of those;
Nor, can I tell what critics thought 'em,
But, this I know, all people bought 'em;
As with a moral view designed
To cure the vices of mankind,
His vein, ironically grave,
Exposed the fool, and lashed the knave;
To steal a hint was never known,
But what he writ was all his own.

'He never thought an honour done him,
Because a duke was proud to own him;
Would rather slip aside, and choose
To talk with wits in dirty shoes;
Despised the fools with Stars and Garters
So often seen caressing Chartres.
He never courted men in station,
Nor persons had in admiration;
Of no man's greatness was afraid,
Because he sought for no man's aid.
Though trusted long in great affairs,
He gave himself no haughty airs;
Without regarding private ends,
Spent all his credit for his friends,
And only chose the wise and good—
No flatterers; no allies in blood—
But succoured virtue in distress,
And seldom failed of good success;
As numbers in their hearts must own,
Who, but for him, had been unknown.
'With princes kept a due decorum,
But never stood in awe before 'em:
And to her Majesty, God bless her,
Would speak as free as to her dresser;
She thought it his peculiar whim,
Nor took it ill as come from him.
He followed David's lesson just,
In princes never put thy trust.
And, would you make him truly sour,
Provoke him with a slave in power.
The Irish Senate if you named,
With what impatience he declaimed!
Fair Liberty was all his cry;
For her he stood prepared to die;
For her he boldly stood alone;
For her he oft exposed his own.
Two kingdoms, just as faction led,
Had set a price upon his head;
But not a traitor could be found,
To sell him for six hundred pound.
'Had he but spared his tongue and pen,
He might have rose like other men:
But power was never in his thought;
And wealth he valued not a groat.
Ingratitude he often found,
And pitied those who meant the wound:

But kept the tenor of his mind,
To merit well of human kind,
Nor made a sacrifice of those
Who still were true, to please his foes.
He laboured many a fruitless hour
To reconcile his friends in power;
Saw mischief by a faction brewing,
While they pursued each other's ruin;
But, finding vain was all his care,
He left the court in mere despair.
'And, oh, how short are human schemes!
Here ended all our golden dreams.
What St. John's skill in state affairs,
What Ormonde's valour, Oxford's cares,
To save their sinking country lent,
Was all destroyed by one event.
Too soon that precious life was ended,
On which alone our weal depended.
When up a dangerous faction starts,
With wrath and vengeance in their hearts;
By solemn league and covenant bound
To ruin, slaughter, and confound;
To turn religion to a fable,
And make the government a Babel;
Pervert the law, disgrace the gown,
Corrupt the senate, rob the crown;
To sacrifice old England's glory,
And make her infamous in story.
When such a tempest shook the land,
How could unguarded virtue stand?
'With horror, grief, despair the Dean
Beheld the dire destructive scene:
His friends in exile, or the Tower,
Himself within the frown of power;
Pursued by base envenomed pens
Far to the land of slaves and fens;
A servile race in folly nursed,
Who truckle most when treated worst.
'By innocence and resolution,
He bore continual persecution,
While numbers to preferment rose,
Whose merits were, to be his foes;
When ev'n his own familiar friends,
Intent upon their private ends,
Like renegadoes now he feels
Against him lifting up their heels.

'The Dean did by his pen defeat
An infamous destructive cheat;
Taught fools their int'rest how to know,
And gave them arms to ward the blow.
Envy hath owned it was his doing
To save that helpless land from ruin,
While they who at the steerage stood,
And reaped the profit, sought his blood.
'To save them from their evil fate,
In him was held a crime of state.
A wicked monster on the bench,
Whose fury blood could never quench,
As vile and profligate a villain
As modern Scroggs, or old Tresilian,
Who long all justice had discarded,
Nor feared he God, nor man regarded;
Vowed on the Dean his rage to vent,
And make him of his zeal repent;
But heav'n his innocence defends;
The grateful people stand his friends.
Not strains of law, nor judge's frown,
Nor topics brought to please the crown,
Nor witness hired, nor jury picked,
Prevail to bring him in convict.
'In exile with a steady heart,
He spent his life's declining part,
Where folly, pride, and faction sway,
Remote from St. John, Pope, and Gay.
'His friendship there to few confined,
Were always of the middling kind:
No fools of rank, a mongrel breed,
Who fain would pass for lords indeed,
Where titles give no right or power,
And peerage is a withered flower;
He would have held it a disgrace,
If such a wretch had known his face.
On rural squires, that kingdom's bane,
He vented oft his wrath in vain:
Biennial squires, to market brought,
Who sell their souls and votes for naught;
The nation stripped, go joyful back,
To rob the church, their tenants rack,
Go snacks with thieves and rapparees,
And keep the peace, to pick up fees;
In every job to have a share,
A jail or barrack to repair;

And turn the tax for public roads
Commodious to their own abodes.
  'Perhaps I may allow the Dean
Had too much satire in his vein;
And seemed determined not to starve it,
Because no age could more deserve it.
Yet malice never was his aim;
He lashed the vice, but spared the name.
No individual could resent,
Where thousands equally were meant.
His satire points at no defect
But what all mortals may correct;
For he abhorred that senseless tribe
Who call it humour when they jibe.
He spared a hump or crooked nose
Whose owners set not up for beaux.
True genuine dullness moved his pity,
Unless it offered to be witty.
Those who their ignorance confessed
He ne'er offended with a jest;
But laughed to hear an idiot quote
A verse from Horace learned by rote.
  'He knew an hundred pleasant stories,
With all the turns of Whigs and Tories;
Was cheerful to his dying day,
And friends would let him have his way.
  'He gave the little wealth he had
To build a house for fools and mad,
And showed by one satiric touch,
No nation wanted it so much.
That kingdom he hath left his debtor;
I wish it soon may have a better.'

(Wr. 1731; pub. 1739)

DANIEL DEFOE

1660–1731

15 from *Reformation of Manners*

[*London*]

NO city in the spacious universe
Boasts of religion more, or minds it less;
Of reformation talks and government,

Backed with an hundred Acts of Parliament,
Those useless scarecrows of neglected laws,
That miss th' effect by missing first the cause:
Thy magistrates, who should reform the town,
Punish the poor men's faults, but hide their own;
Suppress the players' booths in Smithfield Fair,
But leave the Cloisters, for their wives are there,
Where all the scenes of lewdness do appear.
  Satire, the arts and mysteries forbear,
Too black for thee to write or us to hear;
No man, but he that is as vile as they,
Can all the tricks and cheats of trade survey.
Some in clandestine companies combine,
Erect new stocks to trade beyond the line:
With air and empty names beguile the town,
And raise new credits first, then cry 'em down:
Divide the empty nothing into shares,
To set the town together by the ears.
The sham projectors and the brokers join,
And both the cully merchant undermine;
First he must be drawn in and then betrayed,
And they demolish the machine they made:
So conjuring chymists, with their charm and spell,
Some wondrous liquid wondrously exhale;
But when the gaping mob their money pay,
The cheat's dissolved, the vapour flies away:
The wond'ring bubbles stand amazed to see
Their money mountebanked to Mercury.
  Some fit out ships, and double freights ensure,
And burn the ships to make the voyage secure:
Promiscuous plunders through the world commit,
And with the money buy their safe retreat.
  Others seek out to Afric's torrid zone,
And search the burning shores of Serralone;
There in insufferable heats they fry,
And run vast risks to see the gold, and die:
The harmless natives basely they trepan,
And barter baubles for the souls of men:
The wretches they to Christian climes bring o'er,
To serve worse heathens than they did before.
The cruelties they suffer there are such,
Amboyna's nothing, they've outdone the Dutch.
  Cortez, Pizarro, Guzman, Penaloe,
Who drank the blood and gold of Mexico,
Who thirteen millions of souls destroyed,
And left one third of God's creation void;

By birth for nature's butchery designed,
Compared to these are merciful and kind.
Death could their cruellest designs fulfil,
Blood quenched their thirst, and it sufficed to kill:
But these the tender *coup de grâce* deny,
And make men beg in vain for leave to die;
To more than Spanish cruelty inclined,
Torment the body and debauch the mind:
The ling'ring life of slavery preserve,
And vilely teach them both to sin and serve.
In vain they talk to them of shades below:
They fear no hell, but where such Christians go.
Of Jesus Christ they very often hear,
Often as his blaspheming servants swear;
They hear and wonder what strange gods they be,
Can bear with patience such indignity.
They look for famines, plagues, disease and death,
Blasts from above and earthquakes from beneath:
But when they see regardless heaven looks on,
They curse our gods, or think that we have none.
Thus thousands to religion are brought o'er,
And made worse devils than they were before.

(1702)

LAWRENCE SPOONER

fl. 1703

16 from *A Looking-Glass for Smokers*

[*On Giving Up Smoking*]

BUT O! the freedom, pleasure and the ease
That I sustainèd, when this foul disease
I had shook off! It was a kind of life
From death's confines, an end of fearful strife
Betwixt my soul and body. Civil wars
In this respect were ended; locks and bars
That kept my prisoned soul were then broke ope.
My mind was pleasant, sprightly, full of hope:
I had no shame (as I had had before)
Because my neighbours saw me out of door
Defiling of the wholesome, precious air
With foreign fumes; nor did I greatly fear

That anyone should justly at me scoff,
When this defiling branch was loppèd off.

I now could rise in quiet from my bed
And feel no scorchèd throat nor aching head;
My mouth was moist, my lungs could not send forth
As heretofore a noisome, stinking breath.
I could perform my duties to my God,
Or go about my business well abroad,
And naught to hinder . . .

(1703)

LADY MARY CHUDLEIGH

1656–1710

17

To the Ladies

WIFE and servant are the same,
But only differ in the name:
For when that fatal knot is tied,
Which nothing, nothing can divide,
When she the word *Obey* has said,
And man by law supreme has made,
Then all that's kind is laid aside,
And nothing left but state and pride.
Fierce as an eastern prince he grows,
And all his innate rigour shows:
Then but to look, to laugh, or speak,
Will the nuptial contract break.
Like mutes, she signs alone must make,
And never any freedom take,
But still be governed by a nod,
And fear her husband as her god:
Him still must serve, him still obey,
And nothing act, and nothing say,
But what her haughty lord thinks fit,
Who, with the power, has all the wit.
Then shun, oh! shun that wretched state,
And all the fawning flatt'rers hate.
Value yourselves, and men despise:
You must be proud, if you'll be wise.

(1703)

SARAH FYGE EGERTON

1669?–1722

18

The Emulation

SAY, tyrant Custom, why must we obey
The impositions of thy haughty sway?
From the first dawn of life unto the grave,
Poor womankind's in every state a slave,
The nurse, the mistress, parent and the swain,
For love she must, there's none escape that pain.
Then comes the last, the fatal slavery:
The husband with insulting tyranny
Can have ill manners justified by law,
For men all join to keep the wife in awe.
Moses, who first our freedom did rebuke,
Was married when he writ the Pentateuch.
They're wise to keep us slaves, for well they know,
If we were loose, we soon should make them so.
We yield like vanquished kings whom fetters bind,
When chance of war is to usurpers kind;
Submit in form; but they'd our thoughts control,
And lay restraints on the impassive soul.
They fear we should excel their sluggish parts,
Should we attempt the sciences and arts;
Pretend they were designed for them alone,
So keep us fools to raise their own renown.
Thus priests of old, their grandeur to maintain,
Cried vulgar eyes would sacred laws profane;
So kept the mysteries behind a screen:
Their homage and the name were lost had they been seen.
But in this blessèd age such freedom's given,
That every man explains the will of heaven;
And shall we women now sit tamely by,
Make no excursions in philosophy,
Or grace our thoughts in tuneful poetry?
We will our rights in learning's world maintain;
Wit's empire now shall know a female reign.
Come, all ye fair, the great attempt improve,
Divinely imitate the realms above:
There's ten celestial females govern wit,
And but two gods that dare pretend to it.
And shall these finite males reverse their rules?
No, we'll be wits, and then men must be fools.

(1703)

WILLIAM CONGREVE

1670–1729

19 *A Hue and Cry after Fair Amoret*

FAIR Amoret is gone astray;
  Pursue and seek her, ev'ry lover;
I'll tell the signs by which you may
  The wand'ring shepherdess discover.

Coquet and coy at once her air,
  Both studied, though both seem neglected;
Careless she is with artful care,
  Affecting to seem unaffected.

With skill her eyes dart ev'ry glance,
  Yet change so soon you'd ne'er suspect 'em;
For she'd persuade they wound by chance,
  Though certain aim and art direct 'em.

She likes herself, yet others hates
  For that which in herself she prizes;
And, while she laughs at them, forgets
  She is the thing that she despises.

(1704)

20 *Song*

SEE, see she wakes, Sabina wakes!
  And now the sun begins to rise;
Less glorious is the morn that breaks
  From his bright beams than her fair eyes.

With light united, day they give,
  But diff'rent fates ere night fulfil:
How many by his warmth will live!
  How many will her coldness kill!

(1704)

21

Song

PIOUS Selinda goes to prayers,
  If I but ask the favour;
And yet the tender fool's in tears,
  When she believes I'll leave her.

Would I were free from this restraint,
  Or else had hopes to win her;
Would she could make of me a saint,
  Or I of her a sinner.

(1704)

22

Doris

DORIS, a nymph of riper age,
  Has every grace and art
A wise observer to engage,
  Or wound a heedless heart.
Of native blush and rosy dye
  Time has her cheek bereft,
Which makes the prudent nymph supply
  With paint th' injurious theft.
Her sparkling eyes she still retains,
  And teeth in good repair,
And her well-furnished front disdains
  To grace with borrowed hair.
Of size, she is not short nor tall,
  And does to fat incline
No more than what the French would call
  Aimable embonpoint.
Farther her person to disclose
  I leave—let it suffice,
She has few faults but what she knows,
  And can with skill disguise.
She many lovers has refused,
  With many more complied,
Which, like her clothes, when little used
  She always lays aside.
She's one who looks with great contempt
  On each affected creature,
Whose nicety would seem exempt
  From appetites of nature.

She thinks they want or health or sense,
  Who want an inclination;
And therefore never takes offence
  At him who pleads his passion.
Whom she refuses she treats still
  With so much sweet behaviour,
That her refusal, through her skill,
  Looks almost like a favour.
Since she this softness can express
  To those whom she rejects,
She must be very fond, you'll guess,
  Of such whom she affects.
But here our Doris far outgoes
  All that her sex have done;
She no regard for custom knows,
  Which reason bids her shun.
By reason, her own reason's meant,
  Or, if you please, her will:
For when this last is discontent,
  The first is served but ill.
Peculiar therefore is her way;
  Whether by nature taught,
I shall not undertake to say,
  Or by experience bought.
But who o'er-night obtained her grace,
  She can next day disown,
And stare upon the strange man's face
  As one she ne'er had known.
So well she can the truth disguise,
  Such artful wonder frame,
The lover or distrusts his eyes,
  Or thinks 'twas all a dream.
Some censure this as lewd and low,
  Who are to bounty blind;
For to forget what we bestow
  Bespeaks a noble mind.
Doris our thanks nor asks nor needs,
  For all her favours done:
From her love flows, as light proceeds
  Spontaneous from the sun.
On one or other still her fires
  Display their genial force;
And she, like Sol, alone retires
  To shine elsewhere of course.

(1710)

JOSEPH ADDISON

1672–1719

23 ## *A Letter from Italy, to the Right Honourable Charles Lord Halifax*

WHILE you, my lord, the rural shades admire,
And from Britannia's public posts retire,
Nor longer, her ungrateful sons to please,
For their advantage sacrifice your ease;
Me into foreign realms my fate conveys,
Through nations fruitful of immortal lays,
Where the soft season and inviting clime
Conspire to trouble your repose with rhyme.
  For wheresoe'er I turn my ravished eyes,
Gay gilded scenes and shining prospects rise,
Poetic fields encompass me around,
And still I seem to tread on classic ground;
For here the Muse so oft her harp has strung
That not a mountain rears its head unsung,
Renowned in verse each shady thicket grows,
And ev'ry stream in heavenly numbers flows.
  How am I pleased to search the hills and woods
For rising springs and celebrated floods!
To view the Nar, tumultuous in his course,
And trace the smooth Clitumnus to his source,
To see the Mincio draw his watry store
Through the long windings of a fruitful shore,
And hoary Albula's infected tide
O'er the warm bed of smoking sulphur glide.
  Fired with a thousand raptures I survey
Eridanus through flowery meadows stray,
The king of floods! that rolling o'er the plains
The tow'ring Alps of half their moisture drains,
And, proudly swoll'n with a whole winter's snows,
Distributes wealth and plenty where he flows.
  Sometimes, misguided by the tuneful throng,
I look for streams immortalized in song,
That lost in silence and oblivion lie
(Dumb are their fountains and their channels dry),
Yet run for ever by the Muse's skill,
And in the smooth description murmur still.
  Sometimes to gentle Tiber I retire,

And the famed river's empty shores admire,
That destitute of strength derives its course
From thrifty urns and an unfruitful source;
Yet, sung so often in poetic lays,
With scorn the Danube and the Nile surveys;
So high the deathless Muse exalts her theme!
Such was the Boyne, a poor inglorious stream,
That in Hibernian vales obscurely strayed,
And unobserved in wild meanders played;
Till by your lines and Nassau's sword renowned,
Its rising billows through the world resound,
Where'er the hero's godlike acts can pierce,
Or where the fame of an immortal verse.
  Oh, could the Muse my ravished breast inspire
With warmth like yours, and raise an equal fire,
Unnumbered beauties in my verse should shine,
And Virgil's Italy should yield to mine!
  See how the golden groves around me smile,
That shun the coast of Britain's stormy isle,
Or, when transplanted and preserved with care,
Curse the cold clime and starve in northern air.
Here kindly warmth their mounting juice ferments
To nobler tastes and more exalted scents:
Ev'n the rough rocks with tender myrtle bloom,
And trodden weeds send out a rich perfume.
Bear me, some god, to Baia's gentle seats,
Or cover me in Umbria's green retreats;
Where western gales eternally reside,
And all the seasons lavish all their pride:
Blossoms and fruits and flowers together rise,
And the whole year in gay confusion lies.
  Immortal glories in my mind revive,
And in my soul a thousand passions strive,
When Rome's exalted beauties I descry
Magnificent in piles of ruin lie.
An amphitheatre's amazing height
Here fills my eye with terror and delight,
That on its public shows unpeopled Rome,
And held uncrowded nations in its womb.
Here pillars rough with sculpture pierce the skies:
And here the proud triumphal arches rise,
Where the old Romans' deathless acts displayed
Their base degenerate progeny upbraid.
Whole rivers here forsake the fields below,
And wond'ring at their height through airy channels flow.
  Still to new scenes my wand'ring Muse retires,

And the dumb show of breathing rocks admires;
Where the smooth chisel all its force has shown,
And softened into flesh the rugged stone.
In solemn silence, a majestic band,
Heroes and gods and Roman consuls stand,
Stern tyrants, whom their cruelties renown,
And emperors in Parian marble frown;
While the bright dames, to whom they humbly sued,
Still show the charms that their proud hearts subdued.
  Fain would I Raphael's godlike art rehearse,
And show th' immortal labours in my verse,
Where from the mingled strength of shade and light
A new creation rises to my sight:
Such heav'nly figures from his pencil flow,
So warm with life his blended colours glow.
From theme to theme with secret pleasure tossed,
Amidst the soft variety I'm lost:
Here pleasing airs my ravished soul confound
With circling notes and labyrinths of sound;
Here domes and temples rise in distant views,
And opening palaces invite my Muse.
  How has kind heav'n adorned the happy land,
And scattered blessings with a wasteful hand!
But what avail her unexhausted stores,
Her blooming mountains and her sunny shores,
With all the gifts that heav'n and earth impart,
The smiles of nature and the charms of art,
While proud Oppression in her valleys reigns,
And Tyranny usurps her happy plains?
The poor inhabitant beholds in vain
The redd'ning orange and the swelling grain:
Joyless he sees the growing oils and wines,
And in the myrtle's fragrant shade repines:
Starves, in the midst of nature's bounty cursed,
And in the loaden vineyard dies for thirst.
  Oh Liberty, thou goddess heavenly bright,
Profuse of bliss and pregnant with delight,
Eternal pleasures in thy presence reign,
And smiling Plenty leads thy wanton train!
Eased of her load Subjection grows more light,
And Poverty looks cheerful in thy sight;
Thou mak'st the gloomy face of nature gay,
Giv'st beauty to the sun, and pleasure to the day.
  Thee, goddess, thee, Britannia's isle adores;
How has she oft exhausted all her stores,
How oft in fields of death thy presence sought,

Nor thinks the mighty prize too dearly bought!
On foreign mountains may the sun refine
The grape's soft juice, and mellow it to wine,
With citron groves adorn a distant soil,
And the fat olive swell with floods of oil:
We envy not the warmer clime that lies
In ten degrees of more indulgent skies,
Nor at the coarseness of our heav'n repine,
Though o'er our heads the frozen Pleiads shine:
'Tis Liberty that crowns Britannia's isle,
And makes her barren rocks and her bleak mountains smile.
  Others with towering piles may please the sight,
And in their proud aspiring domes delight;
A nicer touch to the stretched canvas give,
Or teach their animated rocks to live:
'Tis Britain's care to watch o'er Europe's fate,
And hold in balance each contending state,
To threaten bold presumptuous kings with war,
And answer her afflicted neighbours' pray'r.
The Dane and Swede, roused up by fierce alarms,
Bless the wise conduct of her pious arms:
Soon as her fleets appear their terrors cease,
And all the northern world lies hushed in peace.
  Th' ambitious Gaul beholds with secret dread
Her thunder aimed at his aspiring head,
And fain her godlike sons would disunite
By foreign gold or by domestic spite;
But strives in vain to conquer or divide,
Whom Nassau's arms defend and counsels guide.
  Fired with the name, which I so oft have found
The distant climes and different tongues resound,
I bridle in my struggling Muse with pain,
That longs to launch into a bolder strain.
  But I've already troubled you too long,
Nor dare attempt a more advent'rous song.
My humble verse demands a softer theme,
A painted meadow or a purling stream;
Unfit for heroes, whom immortal lays,
And lines like Virgil's or like yours, should praise.

(1704)

24 Ode

THE spacious firmament on high,
With all the blue ethereal sky,
And spangled heav'ns, a shining frame,
Their great original proclaim:
Th' unwearied sun, from day to day,
Does his Creator's power display,
And publishes to every land
The work of an almighty hand.

Soon as the evening shades prevail,
The moon takes up the wondrous tale,
And nightly to the list'ning earth
Repeats the story of her birth:
Whilst all the stars that round her burn,
And all the planets in their turn,
Confirm the tidings as they roll,
And spread the truth from pole to pole.

What though, in solemn silence, all
Move round the dark terrestrial ball?
What though nor real voice nor sound
Amid their radiant orbs be found?
In reason's ear they all rejoice,
And utter forth a glorious voice,
For ever singing, as they shine,
'The hand that made us is divine.'

(1712)

25 Song

OH the charming month of May!
Oh the charming month of May!
When the breezes fan the treeses
Full of blossoms fresh and gay—
Full, &c.

Oh what joys our prospects yield!
Charming joys our prospects yield!
In a new livery when we see every
Bush and meadow, tree and field—
Bush, &c.

Oh how fresh the morning air!
Charming fresh the morning air!
When the zephyrs and the heifers
Their odoriferous breath compare—
Their, &c.

Oh how fine our ev'ning walk!
Charming fine our ev'ning walk!
When the nightingale delighting
With her song suspends our talk—
With her, &c.

Oh how sweet at night to dream!
Charming sweet at night to dream!
On mossy pillows, by the trilloes
Of a gentle purling stream—
Of a, &c.

Oh how kind the country lass!
Charming kind the country lass!
Who, her cow bilking, leaves her milking
For a green gown upon the grass—
For a, &c.

Oh how sweet it is to spy!
Charming sweet it is to spy!
At the conclusion, her confusion,
Blushing cheeks, and downcast eye—
Blushing, &c.

Oh the cooling curds and cream!
Charming cooling curds and cream!
When all is over, she gives her lover,
Who on her skimming-dish carves her name—
Who on, &c.

(1713)

MATTHEW PRIOR

1664–1721

26 *To a Child of Quality of Five Years Old, the Author Supposed Forty*

LORDS, knights, and squires, the num'rous band
  That wear the fair Miss Mary's fetters,
Were summoned, by her high command,
  To show their passion by their letters.

My pen amongst the rest I took,
  Lest those bright eyes that cannot read
Should dart their kindling fires, and look
  The pow'r they have to be obeyed.

Nor quality, nor reputation,
  Forbid me yet my flame to tell,
Dear five years old befriends my passion,
  And I may write till she can spell.

For, while she makes her silkworms beds
  With all the tender things I swear;
Whilst all the house my passion reads
  In papers round her baby's hair;

She may receive and own my flame,
  For, though the strictest prudes should know it,
She'll pass for a most virtuous dame,
  And I for an unhappy poet.

Then too, alas! when she shall tear
  The lines some younger rival sends,
She'll give me leave to write, I fear,
  And we shall still continue friends.

For, as our diff'rent ages move,
  'Tis so ordained (would Fate but mend it!)
That I shall be past making love,
  When she begins to comprehend it.

(1704)

baby's] doll's

27

A Simile

DEAR Thomas, didst thou never pop
Thy head into a tin-man's shop?
There, Thomas, didst thou never see
('Tis but by way of simile)
A squirrel spend his little rage
In jumping round a rolling cage?
The cage, as either side turned up,
Striking a ring of bells a-top?
Moved in the orb, pleased with the chimes,
The foolish creature thinks he climbs:
But here or there, turn wood or wire,
He never gets two inches higher.
So fares it with those merry blades,
That frisk it under Pindus' shades.
In noble songs, and lofty odes,
They tread on stars, and talk with gods;
Still dancing in an airy round,
Still pleased with their own verses' sound;
Brought back, how fast soe'er they go,
Always aspiring, always low.

(1706)

28

An Ode

THE merchant, to secure his treasure,
Conveys it in a borrowed name:
Euphelia serves to grace my measure,
But Cloe is my real flame.

My softest verse, my darling lyre,
Upon Euphelia's toilet lay,
When Cloe noted her desire
That I should sing, that I should play.

My lyre I tune, my voice I raise,
But with my numbers mix my sighs:
And whilst I sing Euphelia's praise,
I fix my soul on Cloe's eyes.

Fair Cloe blushed, Euphelia frowned;
  I sung and gazed, I played and trembled;
And Venus to the Loves around
  Remarked how ill we all dissembled.

(1709)

29 *A Dutch Proverb*

FIRE, water, woman, are man's ruin,
Says wise Professor Vander Brüin.
By flames a house I hired was lost
Last year, and I must pay the cost.
This spring the rains o'erflowed my ground,
And my best Flanders mare was drowned.
A slave I am to Clara's eyes:
The gypsy knows her pow'r, and flies.
Fire, water, woman, are my ruin:
And great thy wisdom, Vander Brüin.

(1709)

30 from *Solomon on the Vanity of the World,* Book III

PASS we the ills, which each man feels or dreads,
The weight or fall'n, or hanging o'er our heads;
The bear, the lion, terrors of the plain,
The sheepfold scattered, and the shepherd slain;
The frequent errors of the pathless wood,
The giddy precipice, and the dang'rous flood:
The noisome pest'lence that, in open war
Terrible, marches through the midday air,
And scatters death; the arrow that by night
Cuts the dank mist, and fatal wings its flight;
The billowing snow, and violence of the show'r,
That from the hills disperse their dreadful store,
And o'er the vales collected ruin pour;
The worm that gnaws the ripening fruit, sad guest,
Canker or locust hurtful to infest
The blade; while husks elude the tiller's care,

And eminence of want distinguishes the year.
  Pass we the slow disease, and subtle pain,
Which our weak frame is destined to sustain;
The cruel stone, with congregated war
Tearing his bloody way; the cold catarrh,
With frequent impulse, and continued strife,
Weak'ning the wasted seats of irksome life;
The gout's fierce rack, the burning fever's rage,
The sad experience of decay; and age,
Herself the sorest ill; while death and ease,
Oft and in vain invoked, or to appease
Or end the grief, with hasty wings recede
From the vexed patient, and the sickly bed.
  Naught shall it profit that the charming fair,
Angelic, softest work of heav'n, draws near
To the cold shaking paralytic hand,
Senseless of beauty's touch or love's command,
Nor longer apt, or able to fulfil
The dictates of its feeble master's will.
  Naught shall the psaltry and the harp avail,
The pleasing song, or well repeated tale,
When the quick spirits their warm march forbear,
And numbing coldness has unbraced the ear.
  The verdant rising of the flow'ry hill,
The vale enamelled and the crystal rill,
The ocean rolling and the shelly shore,
Beautiful objects, shall delight no more,
When the laxed sinews of the weakened eye
In wat'ry damps, or dim suffusion lie.
Day follows night; the clouds return again
After the falling of the latter rain:
But to the aged-blind shall ne'er return
Grateful vicissitude: he still must mourn
The sun, and moon, and every starry light
Eclipsed to him, and lost in everlasting night.
  Behold where age's wretched victim lies:
See his head trembling, and his half-closed eyes:
Frequent for breath his panting bosom heaves:
To broken sleep his remnant sense he gives;
And only by his pains, awaking, finds he lives.
  Loosed by devouring time the silver cord
Dissevered lies: unhonoured from the board
The crystal urn, when broken, is thrown by;
And apter utensils their place supply.
These things and thou must share one equal lot:
Die and be lost, corrupt and be forgot;

While still another, and another race
Shall now supply, and now give up the place.
From earth all came, to earth must all return;
Frail as the cord, and brittle as the urn.

(Wr. by 1708; pub. 1718)

31

Jinny the Just

RELEASED from the noise of the butcher and baker,
Who, my old friends be thanked, did seldom forsake her,
And from the soft duns of my landlord the Quaker;

From chiding the footmen and watching the lasses,
From Nell that burned milk too, and Tom that broke glasses
(Sad mischiefs through which a good housekeeper passes!);

From some real care, but more fancied vexation,
From a life parti-coloured, half reason, half passion,
Here lies after all the best wench in the nation.

From the Rhine to the Po, from the Thames to the Rhone,
Joanna or Janneton, Jinny or Joan,
'Twas all one to her by what name she was known;

For the idiom of words very little she heeded,
Provided the matter she drove at succeeded,
She took and gave languages just as she needed;

So for kitchen and market, for bargain and sale,
She paid English or Dutch or French down on the nail,
But in telling a story she sometimes did fail;

Then begging excuse, as she happened to stammer,
With respect to her betters, but none to her grammar,
Her blush helped her out, and her jargon became her.

Her habit and mien she endeavoured to frame
To the different *goût* of the place where she came,
Her outside still changed, but her inside the same:

At the Hague in her slippers, and hair as the mode is,
At Paris all falbalowed fine as a goddess,
And at censuring London in smock-sleeves and bodice,

She ordered affairs, that few people could tell
In what part about her that mixture did dwell
Of Vrough or Mistress, or Mademoiselle.

For her surname and race let the heralds e'en answer,
Her own proper worth was enough to advance her,
And he who liked her little valued her grandsire;

But from what house so ever her lineage may come,
I wish my own Jinny but out of her tomb,
Though all her relations were there in her room.

Of such terrible beauty she never could boast
As with absolute sway o'er all hearts rules the roast,
When J—— bawls aloud to the Chair for a toast;

But of good household features her person was made,
Nor by faction cried up, nor of censure afraid,
And her beauty was rather for use than parade;

Her blood so well mixed and flesh so well pasted,
That though her youth faded her comeliness lasted,
The blue was worn off but the plum was well tasted.

Less smooth than her skin, and less white than her breast,
Was this polished stone beneath which she lies pressed;
Stop, reader, and sigh, while thou think'st on the rest.

With a just trim of virtue her soul was endued,
Not affectedly pious nor secretly lewd,
She cut even between the coquette and the prude.

And her will with her duty so equally stood
That, seldom opposed, she was commonly good,
And did pretty well, doing just what she would.

Declining all power, she found means to persuade,
Was then most regarded when most she obeyed,
The mistress in truth, when she seemed but the maid.

Such care of her own proper actions she took,
That on other folks' lives she had no time to look,
So censure and praise were struck out of her book;

Her thought still confined to its own little sphere,
She minded not who did excel or did err,
But just as the matter related to her;

Then too when her private tribunal was reared,
Her mercy so mixed with her judgement appeared
That her foes were condemned and her friends always cleared.

Her religion so well with her learning did suit
That in practice sincere, and in controverse mute,
She showed she knew better to live than dispute.

Some parts of the Bible by heart she recited,
And much in historical chapters delighted,
But in points about faith she was something short-sighted;

So notions and modes she referred to the schools,
And in matters of conscience adhered to two rules—
To advise with no bigots, and jest with no fools;

And scrupling but little, enough she believed;
By charity ample small sins she retrieved,
And when she had new clothes she always received.

Thus still whilst her morning unseen fled away
In ordering the linen, and making the tea,
That she scarce could have time for the Psalms of the day;

And while after dinner the night came so soon
That half she proposed very seldom was done,
With twenty 'God bless me's, how this day is gone!';

While she read and accounted and paid and abated,
Ate and drank, played and worked, laughed and cried, loved
and hated,
As answered the end of her being created;

In the midst of her age came a cruel disease,
Which neither her broths nor receipts could appease,
So down dropped her clay; may her soul be at peace.

Retire from this sepulchre all the profane,
Ye that love for debauch or that marry for gain,
Retire lest ye trouble the manes of Jane.

But thou, that know'st love above interest or lust,
Strew the myrtle and rose on this once beloved dust,
And shed one pious tear upon Jinny the Just.

Tread soft on her grave, and do right to her honour,
Let neither rude hand nor ill tongue light upon her,
Do all the small favours that now can be done her.

And when what thou liked shall return to her clay,
For so I'm persuaded she must do one day,
Whatever fantastic John Asgill may say;

When, as I have done now, thou shalt set up a stone
For something however distinguished or known,
May some pious friend the misfortune bemoan,
And make thy concern by reflection his own.

(Wr. by 1708; pub. 1907)

32 *Daphne and Apollo. Faithfully Translated from Ovid's Metamorphoses, Book 1st*

A. ABATE, fair fugitive, abate thy speed,
Dismiss thy fears, and turn thy beauteous head;
With kind regard a panting lover view;
Less swiftly fly, less swiftly I'll pursue.
Pathless, alas! and rugged is the ground,
Some stone may hurt thee, or some thorn may wound.
D. This care is for himself, as sure as death:
One mile has put the fellow out of breath.
He'll never do, I'll lead him t'other round;
Washy he is, perhaps not over-sound.
A. You fly, alas! not knowing whom you fly;
Nor ill-bred swain, nor rusty clown, am I:
I Claros isle and Tenedos command—
D. Thank you: I would not leave my native land.
A. What is to come, by certain art I know.
D. Pish! Partridge has as fair pretence as thou.
A. Behold the beauties of my locks—
D. —A fig!—
That may be counterfeit, a Spanish wig.
Who cares for all that bush of curling hair,
Whilst your smooth chin is so extremely bare?
A. I sing—
D. —That never shall be Daphne's choice:
Syphacio had an admirable voice.
A. Of ev'ry herb I tell the mystic pow'r;
To certain health the patient I restore;
Sent for, caressed—
D. —Ours is a wholesome air;
You'd better go to town, and practise there.
For me, I've no obstructions to remove:
I'm pretty well, I thank your father Jove;

And physic is a weak ally to love.
A. For learning famed, fine verses I compose.
D. So do your brother quacks and brother beaux.
Memorials only, and reviews, write prose.
A. From the bent yew I send the pointed reed,
Sure of its aim and fatal in its speed.—
D. Then, leaving me, whom sure you wouldn't kill,
In yonder thicket exercise your skill:
Shoot there at beasts; but for the human heart,
Your cousin Cupid has the only dart.
A. Yet turn, O beauteous maid! yet deign to hear
A love-sick deity's impetuous pray'r;
O let me woo thee as thou wouldst be wooed!
D. First, therefore, don't be so extremely rude:
Don't tear the hedges down, and tread the clover
Like a hobgoblin, rather than a lover.
Next, to my father's grotto sometimes come;
At ebbing-tide he always is at home.
Read the *Courant* with him, and let him know
A little politics, how matters go
Upon his brother rivers, Rhine and Po.
As any maid or footman comes or goes,
Pull off your hat, and ask how Daphne does:
These sort of folks will to each other tell
That you respect me; that, you know, looks well.
Then, if you are, as you pretend, the god
That rules the day, and much upon the road,
You'll find a hundred trifles in your way,
That you may bring one home from Africa:
Some little rarity, some bird or beast,
And now and then a jewel from the east,
A lacquered cabinet, some china ware,
You have them mighty cheap at Pekin fair.
Next, *nota bene*, you shall never rove,
Nor take example by your father Jove.
Last, for the ease and comfort of my life,
Make me your—Lord! what startles you?—your wife.
I'm now, they say, sixteen, or something more;
We mortals seldom live above fourscore:
Fourscore—you're good at numbers—let us see,
Seventeen, suppose remaining sixty-three;
Aye, in that span of time you'll bury me.
Meantime, if you have tumult, noise and strife
(Things not abhorrent to a married life),
They'll quickly end, you see; what signify
A few odd years to you that never die?

And, after all, you're half your time away,
You know your business takes you up all day;
And, coming late to bed, you need not fear,
Whatever noise I make, you'll sleep, my dear;
Or, if a winter evening should be long,
E'en read your physic-book, or make a song.
Your steeds, your wife, diaculum, and rhyme,
May take up any honest godhead's time.
Thus, as you like it, you may love again,
And let another Daphne have her reign.
Now love or leave, my dear; retreat or follow:
I Daphne, this premised, take thee, Apollo.
And may I split into ten thousand trees,
If I give up on other terms than these.

She said; but what the am'rous god replied,
So Fate ordains, is to our search denied;
By rats, alas! the manuscript is eat,
O cruel banquet! which we all regret.
Bavius, thy labours must this work restore;
May thy good-will be equal to thy pow'r!

(Wr. by 1715; pub. 1740)

33 *The Lady who Offers her Looking-Glass to Venus*

VENUS, take my votive glass;
Since I am not what I was,
What from this day I shall be,
Venus, let me never see.

(1718)

34 *A Better Answer to Cloe Jealous*

DEAR Cloe, how blubbered is that pretty face,
Thy cheek all on fire, and thy hair all uncurled:
Pr'ythee quit this caprice; and (as old Falstaff says)
Let us e'en talk a little like folks of this world.

How canst thou presume thou hast leave to destroy
The beauties, which Venus but lent to thy keeping?
Those looks were designed to inspire love and joy:
More ord'nary eyes may serve people for weeping.

32 diaculum] plaster

To be vexed at a trifle or two that I writ,
  Your judgement at once and my passion you wrong:
You take that for fact, which will scarce be found wit:
  Od's life! must one swear to the truth of a song?

What I speak, my fair Cloe, and what I write, shows
  The diff'rence there is betwixt nature and art:
I court others in verse, but I love thee in prose:
  And they have my whimsies, but thou hast my heart.

The god of us verse-men (you know, child) the sun,
  How after his journeys he sets up his rest:
If at morning o'er earth 'tis his fancy to run,
  At night he reclines on his Thetis's breast.

So when I am wearied with wand'ring all day,
  To thee, my delight, in the evening I come:
No matter what beauties I saw in my way;
  They were but my visits, but thou art my home.

Then finish, dear Cloe, this pastoral war;
  And let us, like Horace and Lydia, agree:
For thou art a girl as much brighter than her,
  As he was a poet sublimer than me.

(1718)

35 *A True Maid*

'No, no; for my virginity,
  When I lose that,' says Rose, 'I'll die':
'Behind the elms last night,' cried Dick,
  'Rose, were you not extremely sick?'

(1718)

36 *A Reasonable Affliction*

On his death-bed poor Lubin lies:
  His spouse is in despair;
With frequent sobs and mutual cries,
  They both express their care.

A different cause, says parson Sly,
  The same effect may give:
Poor Lubin fears that he shall die;
  His wife, that he may live.

(1718)

37 from *Alma: or, The Progress of the Mind,* Canto II

In Britain's isles, as Heylyn notes,
The ladies trip in petticoats;
Which, for the honour of their nation,
They quit but on some great occasion.
Men there in breeches clad you view:
They claim that garment as their due.
In Turkey the reverse appears;
Long coats the haughty husband wears,
And greets his wife with angry speeches,
If she be seen without her breeches.
In our fantastic climes, the fair
With cleanly powder dry their hair:
And round their lovely breast and head
Fresh flow'rs their mingled odours shed.
Your nicer Hottentots think meet
With guts and tripe to deck their feet:
With downcast looks on Totta's legs,
The ogling youth most humbly begs
She would not from his hopes remove
At once his breakfast and his love;
And, if the skittish nymph should fly,
He in a double sense must die.
We simple toasters take delight
To see our women's teeth look white;
And every saucy ill-bred fellow
Sneers at a mouth profoundly yellow.
In China none hold women sweet,
Except their snags are black as jet.
King Chihu put ten queens to death,
Convict on statute, *ivory teeth*.
At Tonquin, if a prince should die
(As Jesuits write, who never lie),
The wife, and counsellor, and priest,
Who served him most, and loved him best,
Prepare and light his funeral fire,
And cheerful on the pile expire.
In Europe 'twould be hard to find,
In each degree, one half so kind.
Now turn we to the farthest east,
And there observe the gentry dressed.
Prince Giolo, and his royal sisters,
Scarred with ten thousand comely blisters,

The marks remaining on the skin,
To tell the quality within.
Distinguished slashes deck the great:
As each excels in birth or state,
His oylet-holes are more and ampler:
The king's own body was a sampler.
Happy the climate, where the beau
Wears the same suit for use and show:
And at a small expense your wife,
If once well pinked, is clothed for life.
  Westward again, the Indian fair
Is nicely smeared with fat of bear.
Before you see, you smell your toast,
And sweetest she who stinks the most.
The finest sparks and cleanest beaux
Drip from the shoulders to the toes.
How sleek their skins! their joints how easy!
There slovens only are not greasy.
  I mentioned diff'rent ways of breeding:
Begin we in our children's reading.
To master John the English maid
A hornbook gives of gingerbread;
And, that the child may learn the better,
As he can name, he eats the letter.
Proceeding thus with vast delight,
He spells, and gnaws, from left to right.
But, show a Hebrew's hopeful son
Where we suppose the book begun,
The child would thank you for your kindness,
And read quite backward from our *finis*:
Devour he learning ne'er so fast,
Great A would be reserved the last.
  An equal instance of this matter
Is in the manners of a daughter.
In Europe, if a harmless maid,
By nature and by love betrayed,
Should, ere a wife, become a nurse,
Her friends would look on her the worse.
In China, Dampier's *Travels* tell ye
(Look in his index for Pagelli),
Soon as the British ships unmoor,
And jolly long-boat rows to shore,
Down come the nobles of the land:
Each brings his daughter in his hand,
Beseeching the imperious tar
To make her but one hour his care.

The tender mother stands affrighted
Lest her dear daughter should be slighted:
And poor miss Yaya dreads the shame
Of going back the maid she came.
  Observe how custom, Dick, compels
The lady that in Europe dwells:
After her tea, she slips away,
And what to do one need not say.
Now see how great Pomonque's queen
Behaved herself amongst the men:
Pleased with her punch, the gallant soul
First drank, then watered in the bowl;
And sprinkled in the captain's face
The marks of her peculiar grace.

(1718)

38 *A Letter to the Honourable Lady Miss Margaret Cavendish-Holles-Harley*

My noble, lovely, little Peggy,
Let this, my first epistle, beg ye,
At dawn of morn and close of even,
To lift your heart and hands to heaven:
In double beauty say your prayer,
Our Father first, then Notre Père.
And, dearest child, along the day,
In every thing you do and say,
Obey and please my lord and lady,
So God shall love, and angels aid ye.

If to these precepts you attend,
No second letter need I send;
And so I rest your constant friend,
M.P.

(Wr. 1720; pub. 1740)

ANONYMOUS

39 *Ignotum per Ignotius, or a Furious Hodge-Podge of Nonsense. A Pindaric*

OR yield or die's the word, what could he mean,
That tempted the corroborated scene?
Though frying-pans do bite their nails,
Let fritters pass in ancient heraldry,
And pudding boast its pedigree:
When toads do fight with bankrupt quails,
Green cheese in embryo and lockram shirts
Do poll for Knights o' the Shire,
All buttoned down the skirts,
And quibble votes for the intoxicated year.

The semicircular excursions ran
Forth to monopolise the three-legged can;
When Justice Lickspit kembed his head,
Triumphant hieroglyphic thrummed the law,
And spouting cataracts foresaw
That magazines on bulks lay dead.
The scouring eggshells all besmeared with blood,
Invelopèd in damned dry blows,
Detached the sudorific mud,
And brewed a pair of stiff mustachios.

It galled the winching brush to hear them say
That rigid southern hog-troughs danced the hay;
Though porringers themselves do beat,
And flyblown crow, on vane of weathercock,
Does threshing floors from hinges knock,
And squeamish bellows loathe their meat.
Yet grinning oaks still show their butter-teeth,
And fiery hogos from their sties
Do limping legacies bequeath,
And jest upon their blind forefathers' eyes.

(1705)

EDWARD WARD

1667–1731

40 from *A Journey to H[e]ll: or, A Visit Paid to the D[evi]l*, Part III

[*The Parish Poor-Officers*]

THESE souls, my lord, assembled at the bar,
That look so bluff and seem so fat and fair,
Were, upon earth, appointed to secure
Their parish rights, and to subsist the poor,
By well dispensing to the needy crew
Those charities by gift or claim their due,
That what good Christians for their succour spared
Might be amongst the hungry wretches shared.
Instead of this they basely proved unjust,
Filled their own bags, and falsified their trust;
Drowned half the parish charity in wine,
To fill the guts of the insatiate swine;
Could never meet, or public business do,
Without canary and a fowl or two;
Nor end the meanest trifle in debate
Without the pleasures of a tavern-treat.
If some poor crazy almsman, lame or sick,
Decreed to starve on ninepence for a week,
Petitioned these proud masters of the poor
To make the scanty sum but threepence more,
So many tavern consults must be held,
Before they to the pauper's suit would yield,
That pounds in wine of the poor's money flew,
Ere the dull sots determined what to do.
At last, perhaps, 'twas gen'rously agreed
He should have half the sum to serve his need;
Three halfpence weekly added to his store
To keep the wretch still miserably poor,
That want and sickness, meeting with old age,
Might hurry his starved carcase off the stage,
When due subsistence might his life preserve;
But 'twas their will that all the poor should starve,
For ev'ry one they hastened to the grave,
Themselves, not parish, did their pensions save.
Thus on the poor's just dues they swilled and fed,
And were their lords alive, and heirs when dead.

When Mars and Venus in conjunction were,
And, by their influence, moved some wanton pair
To taste love's joys without the parson's leave,
And mutual pleasures to each other give:
If the kind lass, too forward in her lust,
Received the blessing with too great a gust,
And in nine months brought forth a girl or boy,
The squalling fruits of their unlicensed joy,
Such a discov'ry proved a gainful matter
To these, the plagues of each poor fornicator;
Who the kind welcome news no sooner heard,
But the stern lobcocks in a gang appeared,
And, with their awful frowns and woeful threats,
Frighted the female sinner into fits:
Who, coming to her foolish self again,
Declares the father, where 'twas got, and when,
How many times she'd sinned, and what he said
To coax her to resign her maidenhead;
Whether the gem upon a bed was lost,
Or standing with her rump against a post;
Whether her kind consent was fairly won,
Or if the pleasing job by force was done;
Whether fair promises her heart ensnared,
Or money gained admission to her beard;
What she first thought on't, how she liked the sport;
Whether it pleased her well, or if it hurt;
Whether she cried, or had a greater will,
When once engaged, to struggle or lie still;
And whether, when attacked in love's surprise,
She opened not her legs, but shut her eyes.
Thus each old bawdy sot, with ruby face,
In gold-twine buttons and a band of lace,
Would take his turn th' offender to torment
With questions fulsome and impertinent:
Thus listen with a lank, lascivious ear
To bawdy secrets told them out of fear,
Shameful to own and scandalous to hear.

(1705)

lobcocks] bumpkins

41 *Dialogue between a Squeamish Cotting Mechanic and his Sluttish Wife, in the Kitchen*

Husband Is the fish ready? You're a tedious while;
Take care the butter does not turn to oil:
Lay on more coals, and hang the pot down low'r,
Or 'twill not boil with such a fire this hour.
Is that, my dear, the saucepan you design
To stew the shrimps and melt the butter in?
Nouns! withinside as nasty it appears
As if't had ne'er been scoured this fifty years.
Rare hussifs! how confounded black it looks!
God sends us meat, the devil sends us cooks.
Wife Why, how now, cot! Must I be taught by you?
Sure I without you know what I've to do.
Prithee go mind your shop, attend your trade,
And leave the kitchen to your wife and maid.
O'erlook your 'prentices, you cot, and see
They do their work, leave cookery to me.
Is't fit a man, you contradicting sot,
Should mind the kettle or the porridge-pot,
And run his nose in ev'ry dirty hole,
To see what platter's clean, what dish is foul?
Be gone, you prating ninny, whilst you're well,
Or, faith, I'll pin the dish-clout to your tail.
Husband I'll not be poisoned by a sluttish quean.
Hussy, I say, go scour the saucepan clean.
What though your mistress is a careless beast,
I love to have my victuals cleanly dressed!
Cot me no cots, I'll not be bound to eat
Such dirty sauce to good and wholesome meat.
I will direct and govern, since I find
You're both to so much nastiness inclined.
I'd have you know I neither fear or matter
Your threatened dish-clouts or your scalding water.
Wife Stand by, you prating fool, you damned provoker,
Or, by my soul, I'll burn you with the poker.
Must I be thus abused, as if your maid,
And called a slut before a saucy jade?
Gad, speak another word and, by my troth,
I'll spoil the fish and scald you with the broth.
The kitchen fire, alas! don't burn to please ye;
The saucepan is, forsooth, too foul and greasy.

Cotting] (of a man) meddling with women's matters

Minx, touch it not, I say it's clean enough:
Your scouring rubs the tin withinside off;
I'll have no melted butter taste of brass
To please the humour of a squeamish ass.
If cot-comptroller does not like its looks,
Let him spend sixpence at his nasty cook's,
Where rotten mutton, beef that's turnip-fed,
Lean measly pork on London muck-hills bred,
Will please the fool much better than the best
Of meat by his own wife or servant dressed.
Why don't you thither go before you dine,
Where you may see, perhaps, a noble loin
Of a bull-calf lie sweating at the fire,
Beneath fat pork, nursed up in t—d and mire,
And under that a chump of Suffolk beef,
Thrice roasted for some hungry clown's relief,
Till black as soot that from the chimney falls,
And hard as Severn salmon dried in Wales,
All basted with a flux of mingled fat,
Which greasily distils from this and that?
Such nice tid cleanly bits would please my dear;
Prithee go thither, do not plague us here.

Husband Hussy, what I direct you ought to do;
I'm lord and master of this house and you.
Do you not know that wise and noble prince,
King 'Hasuerus, made a law long since
That ev'ry husband should the ruler be
Of his own wife, as well as family?
How dare you then control my lawful sway,
When Scripture tells you woman should obey?
Therefore, I say, I'll have my fish well dressed,
After such manner as shall please me best,
Or, hussy, by this ladle, if I han't,
I'll make you show good reason why I shan't.
I'll have more coals upon the fire, I tell ye,
And have the saucepan cleaned, aye marry will I,
Or I'll acquaint your teacher, Mr. Blunder,
That all the art of man can't keep you under.

Wife Here, hussy, fetch some coals, 'tis long of you
That we have ev'ry day all this to do.
Pray clean the saucepan, you forgetful trull,
I must confess it looks a little dull.
You shall not say I love this jarring life,
You shall have no complaints against your wife.
But prithee, husband, leave us and be easy,
Ne'er doubt but I will cook your fish to please ye.

When men o'erlook us, we proceed in fear,
And ne'er can do so well when they are near;
Therefore I hope, my dear, you will not mind
A woman's passion, words you know are wind.
I would not for the world have Mr. Blunder
Know that we jar; the good old man would wonder
That you and I, who've been so long his hearers,
Should now want grace, and fall into such errors.

Husband Since you repent your failings, I'll be gone,
But prithee let the fish be nicely done.
I buy the best and, whether roast or boiled,
You know I hate to have my victuals spoiled.

Wife My dear, I'll take such care, that you shall find
It shall be rightly ordered to your mind.
I'm glad he's gone. Pox take him for a cot;
What wife would humour such a snarling sot?
Here, Kather'n, take my keys, slip gently by
The Fox, and fetch a dram for thee and I.
Lay down the saucepan; poh! it's clean enough
For such an old, ill-natured, stingy cuff.
Prithee ne'er value what thy master says;
You should not mind his cross-grained, foolish ways;
But when I bid you, hussy, you must run.
Now his back's turned, the kitchen is our own.
Bless me! how eas'ly can a woman blind
And cheat a husband, if he proves unkind:
He thinks, poor cuckold, that he bears the rule,
When heaven knows I do but gull the fool.

(1710)

42 *The Extravagant Drunkard's Wish*

HAD I my wish, I would distend my guts
  As wide as from the north to southern skies,
And have at once as many mouths and throats
  As old Briareus arms, or Argos eyes.
The raging sea's unpalatable brine,
  That drowns so many thousands in a year,
I'd turn into an ocean of good wine,
  And for my cup would choose the hemisphere;
Would then perform the wager Xanthus laid,
  In spite of all the river's flowing streams,
Swill till I pissed a deluge, then to bed,
  And please my thirsty soul with small-beer dreams.

41 cuff] miser

Thus drink and sleep and, waking, swill again,
  Till I had drunk the sea-gods' cellar dry,
Then rob the niggard Neptune, and his train
  Of Tritons, of that wealth they now enjoy;
Kiss the whole Nerides and make the jades
  Sing all their charming songs to please my ear,
And whether flesh or fish, thornbacks or maids,
  I'd make the gypsies kind through love or fear.
And when thus wicked and thus wealthy grown,
  For nothing good, I'd turn rebellious Whig,
Pull ev'ry monarch headlong from his throne,
  And with the Prince of Darkness make a league,
That he and I, and all the Whigs beside,
  Might rend down churches, crowns in pieces tear,
Exert our malice, gratify our pride,
  And settle Satan's kingdom ev'rywhere.

(1713)

ISAAC WATTS

1674–1748

43 *Few Happy Matches*

SAY, mighty Love, and teach my song
To whom thy sweetest joys belong,
  And who the happy pairs
Whose yielding hearts and joining hands
Find blessings twisted with their bands
  To soften all their cares.

Not the wild herd of nymphs and swains
That thoughtless fly into the chains
  As custom leads the way:
If there be bliss without design,
Ivies and oaks may grow and twine,
  And be as blest as they.

Not sordid souls of earthy mould
Who, drawn by kindred charms of gold,
  To dull embraces move:
So two rich mountains of Peru
May rush to wealthy marriage too,
  And make a world of love.

Not the mad tribe that hell inspires
With wanton flames; those raging fires
  The purer bliss destroy:
On Etna's top let furies wed,
And sheets of lightning dress the bed
  T' improve the burning joy.

Nor the dull pairs, whose marble forms
None of the melting passions warms,
  Can mingle hearts and hands:
Logs of green wood that quench the coals
Are married just like Stoic souls,
  With osiers for their bands.

Not minds of melancholy strain,
Still silent, or that still complain,
  Can the dear bondage bless:
As well may heavenly consorts spring
From two old lutes with ne'er a string,
  Or none besides the bass.

Nor can the soft enchantments hold
Two jarring souls of angry mould,
  The rugged and the keen:
Samson's young foxes might as well
In bonds of cheerful wedlock dwell
  With firebrands tied between.

Nor let the cruel fetters bind
A gentle to a savage mind,
  For Love abhors the sight:
Loose the fierce tiger from the deer,
For native rage and native fear
  Rise and forbid delight.

Two kindest souls alone must meet;
'Tis friendship makes the bondage sweet,
  And feeds their mutual loves:
Bright Venus on her rolling throne
Is drawn by gentlest birds alone,
  And Cupids yoke the doves.

(1706)

44 *The Day of Judgement. An Ode*

Attempted in English Sapphic

WHEN the fierce north wind with his airy forces
Rears up the Baltic to a foaming fury,
And the red lightning with a storm of hail comes
Rushing amain down,

How the poor sailors stand amazed and tremble!
While the hoarse thunder like a bloody trumpet
Roars a loud onset to the gaping waters
Quick to devour them.

Such shall the noise be, and the wild disorder,
(If things eternal may be like these earthly)
Such the dire terror when the great archangel
Shakes the creation;

Tears the strong pillars of the vault of heaven,
Breaks up old marble, the repose of princes;
See the graves open, and the bones arising,
Flames all around 'em.

Hark the shrill outcries of the guilty wretches!
Lively bright horror and amazing anguish
Stare through their eye-lids, while the living worm lies
Gnawing within them.

Thoughts like old vultures prey upon their heartstrings,
And the smart twinges, when their eye beholds the
Lofty Judge frowning, and the flood of vengeance
Rolling afore him.

Hopeless immortals! how they scream and shiver
While devils push them to the pit wide yawning
Hideous and gloomy, to receive them headlong
Down to the centre.

Stop here, my fancy (all away, ye horrid
Doleful ideas): come arise to Jesus,
How he sits god-like! and the saints around him
Throned, yet adoring!

O may I sit there when he comes triumphant
Dooming the nations: then ascend to glory,
While our hosannahs all along the passage
Shout the Redeemer.

(1706)

45 *Crucifixion to the World by the Cross of Christ*

WHEN I survey the wond'rous cross
On which the Prince of Glory died,
My richest gain I count but loss,
And pour contempt on all my pride.

Forbid it, Lord, that I should boast
Save in the death of Christ my God;
All the vain things that charm me most,
I sacrifice them to his blood.

See from his head, his hands, his feet,
Sorrow and love flow mingled down;
Did e'er such love and sorrow meet?
Or thorns compose so rich a crown?

His dying crimson like a robe
Spreads o'er his body on the tree;
Then am I dead to all the globe,
And all the globe is dead to me.

Were the whole realm of nature mine,
That were a present far too small;
Love so amazing, so divine,
Demands my soul, my life, my all.

(1707)

46 *The Adventurous Muse*

URANIA takes her morning flight
With an inimitable wing:
Through rising deluges of dawning light
She cleaves her wondrous way,
She tunes immortal anthems to the growing day;
Nor Rapin gives her rules to fly, nor Purcell notes to sing.

She nor inquires, nor knows nor fears,
Where lie the pointed rocks, or where th' ingulfing sand;
Climbing the liquid mountains of the skies
She meets descending angels as she flies,
Nor asks them where their country lies,
Or where the sea-marks stand.
Touched with an empyreal ray
She springs unerring upward to eternal day,
Spreads her white sails aloft, and steers
With bold and safe attempt to the celestial land.

Whilst little skiffs along the mortal shores
With humble toil in order creep,
Coasting in sight of one another's oars,
Nor venture through the boundless deep:
Such low pretending souls are they
Who dwell inclosed in solid orbs of skull,
Plodding along their sober way;
The snail o'ertakes them in their wildest play,
While the poor labourers sweat to be correctly dull.

Give me the chariot whose diviner wheels
Mark their own route, and unconfined
Bound o'er the everlasting hills,
And lose the clouds below, and leave the stars behind.
Give me the Muse whose generous force
Impatient of the reins
Pursues an unattempted course,
Breaks all the critic's iron chains,
And bears to paradise the raptured mind.

There Milton dwells: the mortal sung
Themes not presumed by mortal tongue;
New terrors and new glories shine
In every page, and flying scenes divine
Surprise the wond'ring sense, and draw our souls along.
Behold his Muse sent out t' explore
The unapparent deep where waves of Chaos roar,
And realms of night unknown before.
She traced a glorious path unknown,
Through fields of heav'nly war, and seraphs overthrown,
Where his advent'rous genius led:
Sovereign, she framed a model of her own,
Nor thanked the living nor the dead.
The noble hater of degenerate rhyme
Shook off the chains, and built his verse sublime,

A monument too high for coupled sounds to climb.
He mourned the garden lost below
(Earth is the scene for tuneful woe);
Now bliss beats high in all his veins,
Now the lost Eden he regains,
Keeps his own air, and triumphs in unrivalled strains.

Immortal bard! Thus thy own Raphael sings,
And knows no rule but native fire:
All heav'n sits silent while to his sovereign strings
He talks unutterable things;
With graces infinite his untaught fingers rove
Across the golden lyre:
From every note devotion springs,
Rapture and harmony and love
O'erspread the list'ning choir.

(1709)

47 *The Hurry of the Spirits, in a Fever and Nervous Disorders*

My frame of nature is a ruffled sea,
And my disease the tempest. Nature feels
A strange commotion to her inmost centre;
The throne of reason shakes. 'Be still, my thoughts;
Peace and be still.' In vain my reason gives
The peaceful word, my spirit strives in vain
To calm the tumult and command my thoughts.
This flesh, this circling blood, these brutal powers
Made to obey, turn rebels to the mind,
Nor hear its laws. The engine rules the man.
Unhappy change! When nature's meaner springs,
Fired to impetuous ferments, break all order;
When little restless atoms rise and reign
Tyrants in sovereign uproar, and impose
Ideas on the mind; confused ideas
Of non-existents and impossibles.
Who can describe them? Fragments of old dreams,
Borrowed from midnight, torn from fairy fields
And fairy skies, and regions of the dead,
Abrupt, ill-sorted. O 'tis all confusion!
If I but close my eyes, strange images
In thousand forms and thousand colours rise,
Stars, rainbows, moons, green dragons, bears, and ghosts,

An endless medley, rush upon the stage,
And dance and riot wild in reason's court
Above control. I'm in a raging storm,
Where seas and skies are blended, while my soul
Like some light worthless chip of floating cork
Is tossed from wave to wave: now overwhelmed
With breaking floods I drown, and seem to lose
All being; now high-mounted on the ridge
Of a tall foaming surge, I'm all at once
Caught up into the storm, and ride the wind,
The whistling wind; unmanageable steed,
And feeble rider! Hurried many a league
Over the rising hills of roaring brine,
Through airy wilds unknown, with dreadful speed
And infinite surprise; till some few minutes
Have spent the blast, and then perhaps I drop
Near to the peaceful coast; some friendly billow
Lodges me on the beach, and I find rest.
Short rest I find; for the next rolling wave
Snatches me back again; then ebbing far
Sets me adrift, and I'm borne off to sea
Helpless, amidst the bluster of the winds,
Beyond the ken of shore.

Ah, when will these tumultuous scenes be gone?
When shall this weary spirit, tossed with tempests,
Harrassed and broken, reach the port of rest,
And hold it firm? When shall this wayward flesh
With all th' irregular springs of vital movement
Ungovernable, return to sacred order,
And pay their duties to the ruling mind?

(Wr. 1712; pub. 1734)

48 *Praise for Mercies Spiritual and Temporal*

WHENE'ER I take my walks abroad,
How many poor I see!
What shall I render to my God
For all his gifts to me?

Not more than others I deserve,
Yet God hath given me more;
For I have food, while others starve,
Or beg from door to door.

How many children in the street
  Half-naked I behold?
While I am clothed from head to feet,
  And covered from the cold.

While some poor wretches scarce can tell
  Where they may lay their head,
I have a home wherein to dwell,
  And rest upon my bed.

While others early learn to swear,
  And curse and lie and steal,
Lord, I am taught thy name to fear,
  And do thy holy will.

Are these thy favours day by day
  To me above the rest?
Then let me love thee more than they,
  And try to serve thee best.

(1715)

49 *Against Idleness and Mischief*

How doth the little busy bee
  Improve each shining hour,
And gather honey all the day
  From every opening flower!

How skilfully she builds her cell!
  How neat she spreads the wax!
And labours hard to store it well
  With the sweet food she makes.

In works of labour or of skill
  I would be busy too:
For Satan finds some mischief still
  For idle hands to do.

In books or work or healthful play
  Let my first years be passed,
That I may give for every day
  Some good account at last.

(1715)

50 *The Sluggard*

'TIS the voice of the sluggard; I heard him complain,
'You have waked me too soon, I must slumber again.'
As the door on its hinges, so he on his bed,
Turns his sides and his shoulders and his heavy head.

'A little more sleep, and a little more slumber;'
Thus he wastes half his days and his hours without number;
And when he gets up, he sits folding his hands,
Or walks about saunt'ring, or trifling he stands.

I passed by his garden and saw the wild brier,
The thorn and the thistle grow broader and higher;
The clothes that hang on him are turning to rags;
And his money still wastes, till he starves or he begs.

I made him a visit, still hoping to find
He had took better care for improving his mind:
He told me his dreams, talked of eating and drinking;
But he scarce reads his Bible, and never loves thinking.

Said I then to my heart, 'Here's a lesson for me;
That man's but the picture of what I might be:
But thanks to my friends for their care in my breeding,
Who taught me betimes to love working and reading.'

(1715)

51 *Innocent Play*

ABROAD in the meadows to see the young lambs
Run sporting about by the side of their dams,
  With fleeces so clean and so white;
Or a nest of young doves in a large open cage,
When they play all in love without anger or rage,
  How much we may learn from the sight!

If we had been ducks, we might dabble in mud,
Or dogs, we might play till it ended in blood,
  So foul or so fierce are their natures.
But Thomas and William, and such pretty names,
Should be cleanly and harmless as doves or as lambs,
  Those lovely sweet innocent creatures.

Not a thing that we do, not a word that we say,
Should injure another in jesting or play,
  For he's still in earnest that's hurt.
How rude are the boys that throw pebbles and mire!
There's none but a madman will fling about fire,
  And tell you, ' 'Tis all but in sport.'

(1715)

52

Man Frail, and God Eternal

OUR God, our help in ages past,
  Our hope for years to come,
Our shelter from the stormy blast,
  And our eternal home.

Under the shadow of thy throne
  Thy saints have dwelt secure;
Sufficient is thine arm alone,
  And our defence is sure.

Before the hills in order stood,
  Or earth received her frame,
From everlasting thou art God,
  To endless years the same.

Thy word commands our flesh to dust,
  'Return, ye sons of men:'
All nations rose from earth at first,
  And turn to earth again.

A thousand ages in thy sight
  Are like an evening gone;
Short as the watch that ends the night
  Before the rising sun.

The busy tribes of flesh and blood
  With all their lives and cares
Are carried downwards by thy flood,
  And lost in following years.

Time like an ever-rolling stream
  Bears all its sons away;
They fly forgotten as a dream
  Dies at the opening day.

Like flow'ry fields the nations stand
  Pleased with the morning-light;
The flowers beneath the mower's hand
  Lie withering ere 'tis night.

Our God, our help in ages past,
  Our hope for years to come,
Be thou our guard while troubles last,
  And our eternal home.

(1719)

ANDREW MICHAEL RAMSAY

1686–1743

53 *Friendship in Perfection*

Philander YE glowing seraphs, that now breathe above
In that pure element of unstained love,
Where clasping round each other ye're entwined,
As if ye were but one compounded mind;
Can ye stoop down to tell me what's the name
Of that pure love which in your orb does flame?
Is't ever here below, or all above?
Can mortal passions fuel such a love?
Strephon Can mortal passions fuel such a love!
What means my dear Philander thus to rove?
Rip up, untwine my soul, and then you'll see
What crystal streams of friendship glide through me;
Unravel this my soul, and then you'll know
That love can find another way to flow
Than in seraphic channels: here's the soul
That moves in friendship's orb without control.
Philander Words spoke with such a passion do display
A soul pegged over-high, that cannot stay
On such a bended stretch; the tide's too high:
'Twill burst the banks ere long and soon run dry.
Strephon My love's my soul, and that from Fate is free:
'Tis that unchanged and deathless part of me.
My passion stands secure; the pow'rs above
Must first annihilate my soul, and then my love.
Philander But ah! dear Strephon, granting this were true,
It won't be long ere death part me from you.

By what mark then shall we each other know,
When stripped to naked souls we leave this ball below?
Strephon I'll tell thee what I'll do, should Fate deny
To let me take thee with me when I die:
I will suspend my bliss, not wing away
Unto the seats of that Eternal Day;
But, lest that I should lose thee in the crowd,
Stop short of heaven, I'd wait thee in a cloud.
Philander Oh no! dear Strephon, that you cannot do:
Your guardian angels won't such stops allow.
The chorus that's above will long to see
A soul like yours t' accent their harmony.
Strephon Well, granting it were so, I'd steal away
When they dissolved in hallelujahs lay;
Yes, slip beyond the screen, leave their blessed company,
Forsake the seraphs to converse with thee.
Thus turtle-like to my dear mate I'll fly,
And down before thee in the sunbeams play.
Then, teaching thee all that I learned above
Anent the seraphs' friendship and their love,
I'd charm thy soul: it should take wing and fly
Beyond the dull confinements of the sky,
And turn all light, all love, as well as I.

(Wr. by 1706; pub. 1728)

ANONYMOUS

54 *On the Death of Old Bennet the News-Crier*

ONE evening, when the sun was just gone down,
As I was walking through the noisy town,
A sudden silence through each street was spread,
As if the soul of London had been fled.
Much I enquired the cause, but could not hear,
Till Fame, so frightened that she did not dare
To raise her voice, thus whispered in my ear:
'Bennet, the prince of hawkers, is no more,
Bennet, my herald on the British shore;
Bennet, by whom I own myself outdone,
Though I an hundred mouths, he had but one.
He, when the list'ning town he would amuse,
Made Echo tremble with his bloody news;

No more shall Echo now his voice return,
Echo for ever must in silence mourn.
Lament, ye heroes, who frequent the wars,
The great proclaimer of your dreadful scars.
Thus wept the conqueror that the world o'ercame,
Homer was wanting to enlarge his fame:
Homer, the first of hawkers that is known,
Great news from Troy cried up and down the town.
None like him has there been for ages past,
Till our Stentorian Bennet came at last:
Homer and Bennet were in this agreed,
Homer was blind, and Bennet could not read.'

(1708)

WILLIAM KING

1662–1712

55 *The Beggar Woman*

A GENTLEMAN in hunting rode astray,
More out of choice than that he lost his way.
He let his company the hare pursue,
For he himself had other game in view:
A beggar by her trade; yet not so mean
But that her cheeks were fresh and linen clean.
'Mistress,' quoth he, 'and what if we two should
Retire a little way into the wood?'
She needed not much courtship to be kind,
He ambles on before, she trots behind;
For little Bobby, to her shoulders bound,
Hinders the gentle dame from ridding ground.
He often asked her to expose, but she
Still feared the coming of his company.
Says she, 'I know an unfrequented place,
To the left hand, where we our time may pass,
And the meanwhile your horse may find some grass.'
Thither they come, and both the horse secure;
Then thinks the squire, I have the matter sure.
She's asked to sit, but then excuse is made:
'Sitting,' says she, ''s not usual in my trade;
Should you be rude, and then should throw me down,
I might perhaps break more backs than my own.'

He smiling cries, 'Come, I'll the knot untie,
And, if you mean the child's, we'll lay it by.'
Says she, 'That can't be done, for then 'twill cry.
I'd not have us, but chiefly for your sake,
Discovered by the hideous noise 'twould make.
Use is another nature and 'twould lack,
More than the breast, its custom to the back.'
'Then,' says the gentleman, 'I should be loth
To come so far and disoblige you both:
Were the child tied to me, d'ye think 'twould do?'
'Mighty well, sir! Oh, Lord! if tied to you!'
With speed incredible to work she goes,
And from her shoulders soon the burthen throws;
Then mounts the infant with a gentle toss
Upon her generous friend, and, like a cross,
The sheet she with a dextrous motion winds,
Till a firm knot the wand'ring fabric binds.
The gentleman had scarce got time to know
What she was doing; she, about to go,
Cries, 'Sir, goodbye; ben't angry that we part,
I trust the child to ye with all my heart:
But, ere you get another, 'ti'n't amiss
To try a year or two how you'll keep this.'

(1709)

JOHN REYNOLDS

1667–1727

56 from *Death's Vision*

[*Mysteries Revealed after Death*]

I SEE why the touched needle scents about
Till it has found its darling quarter out;
And why, unconstant grown, it sometimes takes
New-sprung amours, and its dear north forsakes;
Why flow'ring vines, though fixed in distant soil,
Prompt wines in England to ferment and boil;
How blooming trees (as 'twere for future birth)
Unstain dyed clothes, and call their atoms forth;
Why dark'ned seas pretend to scatter light,
As if they truly lodged the sun by night;

I see (philosophy I longed to know,
But was too deep for poring minds below)
Why list'ning seas so daily watch the shore,
Crowd up the roads down which they ran before,
As if they yet remembered old command,
Or craved new leave to drown the guilty land;
Heav'n's shops and magazines unlocked I view,
What cool alembic drops the rain and dew;
What lathe so turns, what art japans the bow,
What looms prepare and weave the fleecy snow;
In what tight mills the icy balls are ground,
Why small or larger made, why white and round;
How the sun's banner stormy fight prepares,
And summons airy troops to blust'ring wars;
What wild ingredients are together crammed,
And into cloudy cannons closely rammed,
At whose dread roar fierce balls and fire are hurled,
Omens of that, that must calcine the world;
From what low birth proud meteors climb the air,
What combs and kindles their presaging hair;
How could I feast the students now below
(Might I for their relief and ease
Descend a *θεὸς ἀπὸ μηχανῆς*),
Solve their distracting problems quick and show
Rules of reflected and refracted light,
How all the tribes of sep'rate colours grow,
And all combined beget the single white.
Learned Death, that in one hour instructs me more
Than all my years on earth before!
Than all my academic aids could do,
Than cronies, books and contemplations too!
Death! that exalts me straight to high'st degree!
Commenced a more than Newton in abstruse philosophy.

(1709)

japans] lacquers *θεὸς ἀπὸ μηχανῆς*] *deus ex machina*, providential interposition

WILLIAM DIAPER
1685–1717

57

from *Brent, a Poem*

To Thomas Palmer Esq.

HAPPY are you, whom Quantock overlooks,
Blessed with keen healthy air and crystal brooks;
While wretched we the baneful influence mourn
Of cold Aquarius and his weeping urn.
Eternal mists their dropping curse distil
And drizzly vapours all the ditches fill:
The swampy land's a bog, the fields are seas
And too much moisture is the grand disease.
Here every eye with brackish rheum o'erflows
And a fresh drop still hangs at every nose.
Here the winds rule with uncontested right,
The wanton gods at pleasure take their flight;
No sheltering hedge, no tree or spreading bough
Obstruct their course, but unconfined they blow;
With dewy wings they sweep the watry meads
And proudly trample o'er the bending reeds.
We are to north and southern blasts exposed,
Still drowned by one, or by the other frozed.
Though Venice boast, Brent is as famed a seat,
For here we live in seas, and sail through every street;
And this great privilege we farther gain,
We never are obliged to pray for rain.
And 'tis as fond to wish for sunny days,
For though the god of light condense his rays
And try his pow'r, we must in water lie;
The marsh will still be such, and Brent will ne'er be dry.
Sure this is nature's gaol for rogues designed;
Whoever lives in Brent must live confined.
Moated around, the water is our fence;
None comes to us, and none can go from hence:
But should a milder day invite abroad
To wade through mire, and wallow in the mud,
Some envious rhine will quickly thwart the road;
And then a small round twig is all your hopes,
You pass not bridges, but you dance on ropes.

rhine] ditch

All dogs here take the water, and we find
No creature but of an amphibious kind:
Rabbits with ducks, and geese here sail with hens,
And all for food must paddle in the fens;
Nay, when provision fails, the hungry mouse
Will fear no pool to reach a neighb'ring house.
The good old hen clucks boldly through the stream
And chicken newly hatched assay to swim.
All have a moorish taste, cow, sheep and swine,
Eat all like frog, and savour of the rhine.
Bread is our only sauce, a barley-cake
Hard as your cheese, and as your trencher black.
Our choicest drink (and that's the greatest curse)
Is but bad water made by brewing worse;
Better to taste the ditch pure and unmixed
Than when to more unwholesome ale bewitched.

(Wr. 1709; pub. 1727)

58 from *Oppian's Halieuticks*, Book I

[*Eels and Tortoises*]

STRANGE the formation of the eely race,
That know no sex, yet love the close embrace.
Their folded lengths they round each other twine,
Twist am'rous knots, and slimy bodies join;
Till the close strife brings off a frothy juice,
The seed that must the wriggling kind produce.
Regardless they their future offspring leave,
But porous sands the spumy drops receive.
That genial bed impregnates all the heap,
And little eelets soon begin to creep.
Half-fish, half-slime they try their doubtful strength,
And slowly trail along their wormy length.
What great effects from slender causes flow!
Congers their bulk to these productions owe:
The forms, which from the frothy drop began,
Stretch out immense and eddy all the main.
Justly might female tortoises complain,
To whom enjoyment is the greatest pain;
They dread the trial, and foreboding hate
The growing passion of the cruel mate.
He amorous pursues, they conscious fly
Joyless caresses, and resolved deny.

Since partial heav'n has thus restrained the bliss,
The males they welcome with a closer kiss,
Bite angry, and reluctant hate declare.
The tortoise-courtship is a state of war.
Eager they fight, but with unlike design,
Males to obtain, and females to decline.
The conflict lasts, till these by strength o'ercome
All sorrowing yield to the resistless doom.
Not like a bride, but pensive captive, led
To the loathed duties of an hated bed.

(Wr. by 1717; pub. 1722)

AMBROSE PHILIPS

1674–1749

59 *A Winter-Piece*

To the Earl of Dorset

Copenhagen, March 9, 1709.

FROM frozen climes, and endless tracts of snow,
From streams that northern winds forbid to flow,
What present shall the Muse to Dorset bring,
Or how, so near the Pole, attempt to sing?
The hoary winter here conceals from sight
All pleasing objects that to verse invite.
The hills and dales, and the delightful woods,
The flow'ry plains and silver-streaming floods,
By snow disguised, in bright confusion lie,
And with one dazzling waste fatigue the eye.
No gentle-breathing breeze prepares the spring,
No birds within the desert region sing;
The ships unmoved the boist'rous winds defy,
While rattling chariots o'er the ocean fly.
The vast leviathan wants room to play,
And spout his waters in the face of day;
The starving wolves along the main sea prowl,
And to the moon in icy valleys howl.
For many a shining league the level main
Here spreads itself into a glassy plain;
There solid billows of enormous size,
Alps of green ice, in wild disorder rise.

And yet but lately have I seen, e'en here,
The winter in a lovely dress appear.
Ere yet the clouds let fall the treasured snow,
Or winds begun through hazy skies to blow,
At evening a keen eastern breeze arose,
And the descending rain unsullied froze.
Soon as the silent shades of night withdrew,
The ruddy morn disclosed at once to view
The face of nature in a rich disguise,
And brightened ev'ry object to my eyes.
For ev'ry shrub, and ev'ry blade of grass,
And ev'ry pointed thorn, seemed wrought in glass;
In pearls and rubies rich the hawthorns show,
While through the ice the crimson berries glow.
The thick-sprung reeds the wat'ry marshes yield
Seem polished lances in a hostile field.
The stag in limpid currents, with surprise,
Sees crystal branches on his forehead rise.
The spreading oak, the beech and tow'ring pine,
Glazed over, in the freezing ether shine:
The frighted birds the rattling branches shun,
That wave and glitter in the distant sun.
When, if a sudden gust of wind arise,
The brittle forest into atoms flies;
The crackling wood beneath the tempest bends,
And in a spangled show'r the prospect ends;
Or, if a southern gale the region warm,
And by degrees unbind the wintry charm,
The traveller a miry country sees,
And journeys sad beneath the dropping trees.
Like some deluded peasant Merlin leads
Through fragrant bowers and through delicious meads;
While here enchanted gardens to him rise,
And airy fabrics there attract his eyes,
His wand'ring feet the magic paths pursue;
And, while he thinks the fair illusion true,
The trackless scenes disperse in fluid air,
And woods and wilds and thorny ways appear:
A tedious road the weary wretch returns,
And, as he goes, the transient vision mourns.

(1709)

60 *To Miss Charlotte Pulteney in her Mother's Arms*

TIMELY blossom, infant fair,
Fondling of a happy pair,
Every morn and every night,
Their solicitous delight,
Sleeping, waking, still at ease,
Pleasing, without skill to please,
Little gossip, blithe and hale,
Tattling many a broken tale,
Singing many a tuneless song,
Lavish of a heedless tongue,
Simple maiden, void of art,
Babbling out the very heart,
Yet abandoned to thy will,
Yet imagining no ill,
Yet too innocent to blush,
Like the linlet in the bush,
To the mother-linnet's note
Moduling her slender throat,
Chirping forth thy petty joys,
Wanton in the change of toys,
Like the linnet green in May,
Flitting to each bloomy spray,
Wearied then, and glad of rest,
Like the linlet in the nest.
This thy present happy lot,
This, in time, will be forgot:
Other pleasures, other cares,
Ever-busy time prepares;
And thou shalt in thy daughter see
This picture, once, resembled thee.

(1725)

ALEXANDER POPE

1688–1744

61 *The Alley. An Imitation of Spenser*

IN ev'ry town where Thamis rolls his tide,
A narrow pass there is, with houses low,
Where ever and anon the stream is eyed,
And many a boat soft sliding to and fro.
There oft are heard the notes of infant woe,
The short thick sob, loud scream, and shriller squall:
How can ye, mothers, vex your children so?
Some play, some eat, some cack against the wall,
And as they crouchen low for bread and butter call.

And on the broken pavement, here and there,
Doth many a stinking sprat and herring lie;
A brandy and tobacco shop is near,
And hens, and dogs, and hogs are feeding by;
And here a sailor's jacket hangs to dry.
At ev'ry door are sunburnt matrons seen
Mending old nets to catch the scaly fry;
Now singing shrill, and scolding eft between,
Scolds answer foul-mouthed scolds; bad neighbourhood I ween.

The snappish cur (the passenger's annoy)
Close at my heel with yelping treble flies;
The whimp'ring girl, and hoarser screaming boy,
Join to the yelping treble shrilling cries;
The scolding quean to louder notes doth rise,
And her full pipes those shrilling cries confound:
To her full pipes the grunting hog replies;
The grunting hogs alarm the neighbours round,
And curs, girls, boys and scolds in the deep bass are drowned.

Hard by a sty, beneath a roof of thatch,
Dwelt Obloquy, who in her early days
Baskets of fish at Billingsgate did watch,
Cod, whiting, oyster, mackrel, sprat, or plaice:
There learned she speech from tongues that never cease.
Slander beside her like a magpie chatters,
With Envy (spitting cat), dread foe to peace;
Like a cursed cur, Malice before her clatters,
And, vexing ev'ry wight, tears clothes and all to tatters.

Her dugs were marked by ev'ry collier's hand,
Her mouth was black as bulldog's at the stall:
She scratchèd, bit, and spared ne lace ne band,
And 'bitch' and 'rogue' her answer was to all;
Nay, e'en the parts of shame by name would call:
Yea, when she passèd by or lane or nook,
Would greet the man who turned him to the wall,
And by his hand obscene the porter took,
Nor ever did askance like modest virgin look.

Such place hath Deptford, navy-building town,
Woolwich and Wapping, smelling strong of pitch;
Such Lambeth, envy of each band and gown,
And Twick'nham such, which fairer scenes enrich,
Grots, statues, urns, and Jo[hnsto]n's dog and bitch:
Ne village is without, on either side,
All up the silver Thames, or all adown;
Ne Richmond's self, from whose tall front are eyed
Vales, spires, meand'ring streams, and Windsor's tow'ry pride.

(Wr. by 1709; pub. 1727)

62 from *An Essay on Criticism*

Of all the causes which conspire to blind
Man's erring judgement, and misguide the mind,
What the weak head with strongest bias rules,
Is pride, the never-failing vice of fools.
Whatever nature has in worth denied,
She gives in large recruits of needless pride;
For as in bodies, thus in souls we find
What wants in blood and spirits, swelled with wind;
Pride, where wit fails, steps in to our defence,
And fills up all the mighty void of sense!
If once right reason drives that cloud away,
Truth breaks upon us with resistless day.
Trust not yourself; but your defects to know,
Make use of ev'ry friend—and ev'ry foe.
A little learning is a dang'rous thing;
Drink deep, or taste not the Pierian spring:
There shallow draughts intoxicate the brain,
And drinking largely sobers us again.
Fired at first sight with what the Muse imparts,
In fearless youth we tempt the heights of arts,
While from the bounded level of our mind,

Short views we take, nor see the lengths behind;
But more advanced, behold with strange surprise
New, distant scenes of endless science rise!
So pleased at first the tow'ring Alps we try,
Mount o'er the vales, and seem to tread the sky;
Th' eternal snows appear already past,
And the first clouds and mountains seem the last:
But, those attained, we tremble to survey
The growing labours of the lengthened way,
Th' increasing prospect tires our wand'ring eyes,
Hills peep o'er hills, and Alps on Alps arise!
  A perfect judge will read each work of wit
With the same spirit that its author writ,
Survey the whole, nor seek slight faults to find,
Where nature moves, and rapture warms the mind;
Nor lose, for that malignant dull delight,
The gen'rous pleasure to be charmed with wit.
But in such lays as neither ebb nor flow,
Correctly cold, and regularly low,
That shunning faults, one quiet tenor keep;
We cannot blame indeed—but we may sleep.
In wit, as nature, what affects our hearts
Is not th' exactness of peculiar parts;
'Tis not a lip, or eye, we beauty call,
But the joint force and full result of all.
Thus when we view some well-proportioned dome,
(The world's just wonder, and ev'n thine, O Rome!)
No single parts unequally surprise,
All comes united to th' admiring eyes;
No monstrous height, or breadth, or length appear;
The whole at once is bold and regular.

. . . . .

  Some to conceit alone their taste confine,
And glitt'ring thoughts struck out at ev'ry line;
Pleased with a work where nothing's just or fit,
One glaring chaos and wild heap of wit.
Poets, like painters, thus, unskilled to trace
The naked nature and the living grace,
With gold and jewels cover every part,
And hide with ornaments their want of art.
True wit is nature to advantage dressed,
What oft was thought, but ne'er so well expressed;
Something, whose truth convinced at sight we find,
That gives us back the image of our mind:
As shades more sweetly recommend the light,

So modest plainness sets off sprightly wit:
For works may have more wit than does 'em good,
As bodies perish through excess of blood.
  Others for language all their care express,
And value books, as women men, for dress:
Their praise is still,—the style is excellent;
The sense, they humbly take upon content.
Words are like leaves; and where they most abound,
Much fruit of sense beneath is rarely found.
False eloquence, like the prismatic glass,
Its gaudy colours spreads on ev'ry place;
The face of nature we no more survey,
All glares alike, without distinction gay:
But true expression, like th' unchanging sun,
Clears and improves whate'er it shines upon,
It gilds all objects, but it alters none.
Expression is the dress of thought, and still
Appears more decent as more suitable;
A vile conceit in pompous words expressed
Is like a clown in regal purple dressed;
For diff'rent styles with diff'rent subjects sort,
As several garbs with country, town and court.
Some by old words to fame have made pretence,
Ancients in phrase, mere moderns in their sense!
Such laboured nothings, in so strange a style,
Amaze th' unlearned, and make the learned smile.
Unlucky as Fungoso in the play,
These sparks with awkward vanity display
What the fine gentleman wore yesterday!
And but so mimic ancient wits at best,
As apes our grandsires, in their doublets dressed.
In words, as fashions, the same rule will hold,
Alike fantastic, if too new, or old;
Be not the first by whom the new are tried,
Nor yet the last to lay the old aside.
  But most by numbers judge a poet's song,
And smooth or rough, with them, is right or wrong:
In the bright Muse though thousand charms conspire,
Her voice is all these tuneful fools admire,
Who haunt Parnassus but to please their ear,
Not mend their minds; as some to church repair,
Not for the doctrine, but the music there.
These equal syllables alone require,
Though oft the ear the open vowels tire,
While expletives their feeble aid *do* join,
And ten low words oft creep in one dull line,

While they ring round the same unvaried chimes,
With sure returns of still expected rhymes.
Where'er you find 'the cooling western breeze',
In the next line, it 'whispers through the trees';
If crystal streams 'with pleasing murmurs creep',
The reader's threatened (not in vain) with 'sleep'.
Then, at the last and only couplet fraught
With some unmeaning thing they call a thought,
A needless Alexandrine ends the song,
That, like a wounded snake, drags its slow length along.
Leave such to tune their own dull rhymes, and know
What's roundly smooth, or languishingly slow;
And praise the easy vigour of a line,
Where Denham's strength and Waller's sweetness join.
True ease in writing comes from art, not chance,
As those move easiest who have learned to dance.
'Tis not enough no harshness gives offence,
The sound must seem an echo to the sense.
Soft is the strain when Zephyr gently blows,
And the smooth stream in smoother numbers flows;
But when loud surges lash the sounding shore,
The hoarse, rough verse should like the torrent roar.
When Ajax strives some rock's vast weight to throw,
The line too labours, and the words move slow:
Not so, when swift Camilla scours the plain,
Flies o'er th' unbending corn, and skims along the main.

(1711)

63 from *Windsor Forest*

To the Right Honourable George Lord Lansdowne

THY forests, Windsor! and thy green retreats,
At once the Monarch's and the Muses' seats,
Invite my lays. Be present, sylvan maids!
Unlock your springs, and open all your shades.
Granville commands; your aid, O Muses, bring!
What Muse for Granville can refuse to sing?
The groves of Eden, vanished now so long,
Live in description, and look green in song:
These, were my breast inspired with equal flame,
Like them in beauty, should be like in fame.
Here hills and vales, the woodland and the plain,
Here earth and water seem to strive again;

Not chaos-like together crushed and bruised,
But, as the world, harmoniously confused:
Where order in variety we see,
And where, though all things differ, all agree.
Here waving groves a chequered scene display,
And part admit and part exclude the day;
As some coy nymph her lover's warm address
Nor quite indulges, nor can quite repress.
There, interspersed in lawns and opening glades,
Thin trees arise that shun each other's shades.
Here in full light the russet plains extend:
There, wrapped in clouds the bluish hills ascend:
Ev'n the wild heath displays her purple dyes,
And midst the desert fruitful fields arise,
That crowned with tufted trees and springing corn,
Like verdant isles the sable waste adorn.
Let India boast her plants, nor envy we
The weeping amber or the balmy tree,
While by our oaks the precious loads are borne,
And realms commanded which those trees adorn.
Not proud Olympus yields a nobler sight,
Though gods assembled grace his tow'ring height,
Than what more humble mountains offer here,
Where, in their blessings, all those gods appear.
See Pan with flocks, with fruits Pomona crowned,
Here blushing Flora paints th' enamelled ground,
Here Ceres' gifts in waving prospect stand,
And nodding tempt the joyful reaper's hand;
Rich Industry sits smiling on the plains,
And peace and plenty tell, a Stuart reigns.

(1713)

64 from *The Rape of the Lock*

Canto I

WHAT dire offence from am'rous causes springs,
What mighty contests rise from trivial things,
I sing—This verse to Caryll, Muse! is due;
This, ev'n Belinda may vouchsafe to view:
Slight is the subject, but not so the praise,
If she inspire, and he approve my lays.
  Say what strange motive, goddess! could compel
A well-bred lord t' assault a gentle belle?

Oh say what stranger cause, yet unexplored,
Could make a gentle belle reject a lord?
In tasks so bold, can little men engage,
And in soft bosoms dwells such mighty rage?
  Sol through white curtains shot a tim'rous ray,
And oped those eyes that must eclipse the day;
Now lapdogs give themselves the rousing shake,
And sleepless lovers, just at twelve, awake:
Thrice rung the bell, the slipper knocked the ground,
And the pressed watch returned a silver sound.
Belinda still her downy pillow pressed,
Her guardian Sylph prolonged the balmy rest.
'Twas he had summoned to her silent bed
The morning-dream that hovered o'er her head.
A youth more glitt'ring than a birth-night beau
(That ev'n in slumber caused her cheek to glow),
Seemed to her ear his winning lips to lay,
And thus in whispers said, or seemed to say:
  'Fairest of mortals, thou distinguished care
Of thousand bright inhabitants of air!
If e'er one vision touched thy infant thought,
Of all the nurse and all the priest have taught,
Of airy elves by moonlight shadows seen,
The silver token, and the circled green,
Or virgins visited by angel-pow'rs,
With golden crowns and wreaths of heav'nly flowers,
Hear and believe! thy own importance know,
Nor bound thy narrow views to things below.
Some secret truths, from learned pride concealed,
To maids alone and children are revealed:
What though no credit doubting wits may give?
The fair and innocent shall still believe.
Know then, unnumbered spirits round thee fly,
The light militia of the lower sky;
These, though unseen, are ever on the wing,
Hang o'er the box, and hover round the Ring.
Think what an equipage thou hast in air,
And view with scorn two pages and a chair.
As now your own, our beings were of old,
And once inclosed in woman's beauteous mould;
Thence, by a soft transition, we repair
From earthly vehicles to these of air.
Think not, when woman's transient breath is fled,
That all her vanities at once are dead;
Succeeding vanities she still regards,
And though she plays no more, o'erlooks the cards.

Her joy in gilded chariots, when alive,
And love of ombre, after death survive.
For when the fair in all their pride expire,
To their first elements their souls retire:
The sprites of fiery termagants in flame
Mount up, and take a Salamander's name.
Soft yielding minds to water glide away,
And sip, with Nymphs, their elemental tea.
The graver prude sinks downward to a Gnome,
In search of mischief still on earth to roam.
The light coquettes in Sylphs aloft repair,
And sport and flutter in the fields of air.
'Know farther yet; whoever fair and chaste
Rejects mankind, is by some Sylph embraced:
For spirits, freed from mortal laws, with ease
Assume what sexes and what shapes they please.
What guards the purity of melting maids,
In courtly balls, and midnight masquerades,
Safe from the treach'rous friend, the daring spark,
The glance by day, the whisper in the dark,
When kind occasion prompts their warm desires,
When music softens, and when dancing fires?
'Tis but their Sylph, the wise celestials know,
Though Honour is the word with men below.
'Some nymphs there are, too conscious of their face,
For life predestined to the Gnomes' embrace.
These swell their prospects and exalt their pride,
When offers are disdained and love denied.
Then gay ideas crowd the vacant brain,
While peers and dukes, and all their sweeping train,
And garters, stars and coronets appear,
And in soft sounds, 'Your Grace' salutes their ear.
'Tis these that early taint the female soul,
Instruct the eyes of young coquettes to roll,
Teach infant cheeks a bidden blush to know,
And little hearts to flutter at a beau.
'Oft when the world imagine women stray,
The Sylphs through mystic mazes guide their way,
Through all the giddy circle they pursue,
And old impertinence expel by new.
What tender maid but must a victim fall
To one man's treat, but for another's ball?
When Florio speaks, what virgin could withstand,
If gentle Damon did not squeeze her hand?
With varying vanities, from ev'ry part,
They shift the moving toyshop of their heart;

Where wigs with wigs, with sword-knots sword-knots strive,
Beaus banish beaus, and coaches coaches drive.
This erring mortals levity may call,
Oh, blind to truth! the Sylphs contrive it all.
  'Of these am I, who thy protection claim,
A watchful sprite, and Ariel is my name.
Late, as I ranged the crystal wilds of air,
In the clear mirror of thy ruling star
I saw, alas! some dread event impend,
Ere to the main this morning sun descend.
But heav'n reveals not what, or how, or where:
Warned by thy Sylph, oh, pious maid, beware!
This to disclose is all thy guardian can.
Beware of all, but most beware of man!'
  He said; when Shock, who thought she slept too long,
Leaped up, and waked his mistress with his tongue.
'Twas then, Belinda! if report say true,
Thy eyes first opened on a billet-doux;
Wounds, charms, and ardours were no sooner read,
But all the vision vanished from thy head.
  And now, unveiled, the toilet stands displayed,
Each silver vase in mystic order laid.
First, robed in white, the nymph intent adores,
With head uncovered, the cosmetic powers.
A heav'nly image in the glass appears,
To that she bends, to that her eyes she rears;
Th' inferior priestess, at her altar's side,
Trembling, begins the sacred rites of pride.
Unnumbered treasures ope at once, and here
The various off'rings of the world appear;
From each she nicely culls with curious toil,
And decks the goddess with the glitt'ring spoil.
This casket India's glowing gems unlocks,
And all Arabia breathes from yonder box.
The tortoise here and elephant unite,
Transformed to combs, the speckled and the white.
Here files of pins extend their shining rows,
Puffs, powders, patches, bibles, billet-doux.
Now awful beauty puts on all its arms;
The fair each moment rises in her charms,
Repairs her smiles, awakens ev'ry grace,
And calls forth all the wonders of her face;
Sees by degrees a purer blush arise,
And keener lightnings quicken in her eyes.
The busy Sylphs surround their darling care;
These set the head, and those divide the hair,

Some fold the sleeve, whilst others plait the gown;
And Betty's praised for labours not her own.

Canto II

Not with more glories, in th' ethereal plain,
The sun first rises o'er the purpled main,
Than, issuing forth, the rival of his beams
Launched on the bosom of the silver Thames.
Fair nymphs and well-dressed youths around her shone,
But ev'ry eye was fixed on her alone.
On her white breast a sparkling cross she wore,
Which Jews might kiss, and infidels adore.
Her lively looks a sprightly mind disclose,
Quick as her eyes, and as unfixed as those:
Favours to none, to all she smiles extends;
Oft she rejects, but never once offends.
Bright as the sun, her eyes the gazers strike,
And, like the sun, they shine on all alike.
Yet graceful ease, and sweetness void of pride,
Might hide her faults, if belles had faults to hide:
If to her share some female errors fall,
Look on her face, and you'll forget 'em all.
  This nymph, to the destruction of mankind,
Nourished two locks, which graceful hung behind
In equal curls, and well conspired to deck
With shining ringlets the smooth iv'ry neck.
Love in these labyrinths his slaves detains,
And mighty hearts are held in slender chains.
With hairy springes we the birds betray,
Slight lines of hair surprise the finny prey,
Fair tresses man's imperial race insnare,
And beauty draws us with a single hair.
  Th' advent'rous baron the bright locks admired;
He saw, he wished, and to the prize aspired.
Resolved to win, he meditates the way,
By force to ravish, or by fraud betray;
For when success a lover's toil attends,
Few ask, if fraud or force attained his ends.
  For this, ere Phoebus rose, he had implored
Propitious heav'n, and every pow'r adored,
But chiefly Love—to Love an altar built,
Of twelve vast French romances, neatly gilt.
There lay three garters, half a pair of gloves;
And all the trophies of his former loves.
With tender billet-doux he lights the pyre,

And breathes three am'rous sighs to raise the fire.
Then prostrate falls, and begs with ardent eyes
Soon to obtain, and long possess the prize:
The pow'rs gave ear, and granted half his pray'r,
The rest, the winds dispersed in empty air.
   But now secure the painted vessel glides,
The sunbeams trembling on the floating tides,
While melting music steals upon the sky,
And softened sounds along the waters die.
Smooth flow the waves, the zephyrs gently play,
Belinda smiled, and all the world was gay.
All but the Sylph—with careful thoughts oppressed,
Th' impending woe sat heavy on his breast.
He summons straight his denizens of air;
The lucid squadrons round the sails repair:
Soft o'er the shrouds aerial whispers breathe,
That seemed but zephyrs to the train beneath.
Some to the sun their insect-wings unfold,
Waft on the breeze, or sink in clouds of gold.
Transparent forms, too fine for mortal sight,
Their fluid bodies half dissolved in light.
Loose to the wind their airy garments flew,
Thin glitt'ring textures of the filmy dew,
Dipped in the richest tincture of the skies,
Where light disports in ever-mingling dyes,
While ev'ry beam new transient colours flings,
Colours that change whene'er they wave their wings.
Amid the circle on the gilded mast,
Superior by the head, was Ariel placed;
His purple pinions opening to the sun,
He raised his azure wand, and thus begun:
   'Ye Sylphs and Sylphids, to your chief give ear;
Fays, fairies, genii, elves, and daemons hear!
Ye know the spheres and various tasks assigned
By laws eternal to th' aerial kind.
Some in the fields of purest ether play,
And bask and whiten in the blaze of day.
Some guide the course of wand'ring orbs on high,
Or roll the planets through the boundless sky.
Some less refined, beneath the moon's pale light
Pursue the stars that shoot athwart the night,
Or suck the mists in grosser air below,
Or dip their pinions in the painted bow,
Or brew fierce tempests on the wintry main,
Or o'er the glebe distil the kindly rain.
Others on earth o'er human race preside,

Watch all their ways, and all their actions guide:
Of these the chief the care of nations own,
And guard with arms divine the British throne.
 'Our humbler province is to tend the fair,
Not a less pleasing, though less glorious care;
To save the powder from too rude a gale,
Nor let th' imprisoned essences exhale,
To draw fresh colours from the vernal flow'rs,
To steal from rainbows, ere they drop in showers,
A brighter wash; to curl their waving hairs,
Assist their blushes, and inspire their airs;
Nay oft, in dreams, invention we bestow,
To change a flounce, or add a furbelow.
 'This day, black omens threat the brightest fair
That e'er deserved a watchful spirit's care;
Some dire disaster, or by force or slight,
But what, or where, the Fates have wrapped in night.
Whether the nymph shall break Diana's law,
Or some frail china jar receive a flaw,
Or stain her honour, or her new brocade,
Forget her pray'rs, or miss a masquerade,
Or lose her heart, or necklace, at a ball;
Or whether heav'n has doomed that Shock must fall.
Haste, then, ye spirits! to your charge repair;
The flutt'ring fan be Zephyretta's care;
The drops to thee, Brillante, we consign;
And, Momentilla, let the watch be thine;
Do thou, Crispissa, tend her fav'rite lock;
Ariel himself shall be the guard of Shock.
 'To fifty chosen Sylphs, of special note,
We trust th' important charge, the petticoat:
Oft have we known that sev'n-fold fence to fail,
Though stiff with hoops, and armed with ribs of whale;
Form a strong line about the silver bound,
And guard the wide circumference around.
 'Whatever spirit, careless of his charge,
His post neglects, or leaves the fair at large,
Shall feel sharp vengeance soon o'ertake his sins,
Be stopped in vials, or transfixed with pins;
Or plunged in lakes of bitter washes lie,
Or wedged whole ages in a bodkin's eye:
Gums and pomatums shall his flight restrain,
While clogged he beats his silken wings in vain;
Or alum-styptics with contracting power

drops] diamond ear-rings

Shrink his thin essence like a rivelled flower:
Or, as Ixion fixed, the wretch shall feel
The giddy motion of the whirling mill,
In fumes of burning chocolate shall glow,
And tremble at the sea that froths below!'
He spoke; the spirits from the sails descend;
Some, orb in orb, around the nymph extend,
Some thrid the mazy ringlets of her hair,
Some hang upon the pendants of her ear;
With beating hearts the dire event they wait,
Anxious and trembling for the birth of Fate.

(1712–14)

65 *Epistle to Miss Blount, on her Leaving the Town, after the Coronation*

As some fond virgin, whom her mother's care
Drags from the town to wholesome country air,
Just when she learns to roll a melting eye,
And hear a spark, yet think no danger nigh;
From the dear man unwilling she must sever,
Yet takes one kiss before she parts for ever:
Thus from the world fair Zephalinda flew,
Saw others happy, and with sighs withdrew;
Not that their pleasures caused her discontent,
She sighed not that they stayed, but that she went.
She went to plain-work, and to purling brooks,
Old-fashioned halls, dull aunts, and croaking rooks;
She went from op'ra, park, assembly, play,
To morning walks, and pray'rs three hours a day;
To pass her time 'twixt reading and bohea,
To muse, and spill her solitary tea,
Or o'er cold coffee trifle with the spoon,
Count the slow clock, and dine exact at noon;
Divert her eyes with pictures in the fire,
Hum half a tune, tell stories to the squire;
Up to her godly garret after sev'n,
There starve and pray, for that's the way to heav'n.
Some squire, perhaps, you take delight to rack,
Whose game is whisk, whose treat a toast in sack,
Who visits with a gun, presents you birds,
Then gives a smacking buss and cries,—No words!

65 bohea] black tea

Or with his hound comes hollowing from the stable,
Makes love with nods, and knees beneath a table;
Whose laughs are hearty, though his jests are coarse,
And loves you best of all things—but his horse.
  In some fair evening, on your elbow laid,
You dream of triumphs in the rural shade;
In pensive thought recall the fancied scene,
See coronations rise on ev'ry green;
Before you pass th' imaginary sights
Of lords, and earls, and dukes, and gartered knights,
While the spread fan o'ershades your closing eyes;
Then give one flirt, and all the vision flies.
Thus vanish sceptres, coronets, and balls,
And leave you in lone woods, or empty walls.
  So when your slave, at some dear, idle time
(Not plagued with head-aches, or the want of rhyme),
Stands in the streets, abstracted from the crew,
And while he seems to study, thinks of you:
Just when his fancy points your sprightly eyes,
Or sees the blush of soft Parthenia rise,
Gay pats my shoulder, and you vanish quite;
Streets, chairs, and coxcombs rush upon my sight;
Vexed to be still in town, I knit my brow,
Look sour, and hum a tune—as you may now.

(Wr. 1714; pub. 1717)

66 *Elegy to the Memory of an Unfortunate Lady*

WHAT beck'ning ghost, along the moonlight shade
Invites my steps, and points to yonder glade?
'Tis she!—but why that bleeding bosom gored,
Why dimly gleams the visionary sword?
Oh, ever beauteous, ever friendly! tell,
Is it, in heav'n, a crime to love too well?
To bear too tender or too firm a heart,
To act a lover's or a Roman's part?
Is there no bright reversion in the sky
For those who greatly think, or bravely die?
  Why bade ye else, ye pow'rs! her soul aspire
Above the vulgar flight of low desire?
Ambition first sprung from your blest abodes,
The glorious fault of angels and of gods:
Thence to their images on earth it flows,
And in the breasts of kings and heroes glows!

Most souls, 'tis true, but peep out once an age,
Dull, sullen pris'ners in the body's cage:
Dim lights of life that burn a length of years,
Useless, unseen, as lamps in sepulchres;
Like Eastern kings a lazy state they keep,
And close confined to their own palace sleep.
From these perhaps (ere nature bade her die)
Fate snatched her early to the pitying sky.
As into air the purer spirits flow,
And sep'rate from their kindred dregs below;
So flew the soul to its congenial place,
Nor left one virtue to redeem her race.
But thou, false guardian of a charge too good,
Thou, mean deserter of thy brother's blood!
See on these ruby lips the trembling breath,
These cheeks now fading at the blast of death:
Cold is that breast which warmed the world before,
And those love-darting eyes must roll no more.
Thus, if eternal justice rules the ball,
Thus shall your wives, and thus your children fall:
On all the line a sudden vengeance waits,
And frequent hearses shall besiege your gates.
There passengers shall stand, and pointing say
(While the long fun'rals blacken all the way),
'Lo! these were they, whose souls the Furies steeled,
And cursed with hearts unknowing how to yield.'
Thus unlamented pass the proud away,
The gaze of fools, and pageant of a day!
So perish all, whose breast ne'er learned to glow
For others' good, or melt at others' woe.
What can atone (oh ever-injured shade!)
Thy fate unpitied, and thy rites unpaid?
No friend's complaint, no kind domestic tear
Pleased thy pale ghost, or graced thy mournful bier.
By foreign hands thy dying eyes were closed,
By foreign hands thy decent limbs composed,
By foreign hands thy humble grave adorned,
By strangers honoured, and by strangers mourned!
What though no friends in sable weeds appear,
Grieve for an hour, perhaps, then mourn a year,
And bear about the mockery of woe
To midnight dances, and the public show?
What though no weeping loves thy ashes grace,
Nor polished marble emulate thy face?
What though no sacred earth allow thee room,
Nor hallowed dirge be muttered o'er thy tomb?

Yet shall thy grave with rising flow'rs be dressed
And the green turf lie lightly on thy breast:
There shall the morn her earliest tears bestow,
There the first roses of the year shall blow;
While angels with their silver wings o'ershade
The ground now sacred by thy reliques made.
  So peaceful rests, without a stone, a name,
What once had beauty, titles, wealth, and fame.
How loved, how honoured once, avails thee not,
To whom related, or by whom begot;
A heap of dust alone remains of thee;
'Tis all thou art, and all the proud shall be!
  Poets themselves must fall, like those they sung;
Deaf the praised ear, and mute the tuneful tongue.
Ev'n he, whose soul now melts in mournful lays,
Shall shortly want the gen'rous tear he pays;
Then from his closing eyes thy form shall part,
And the last pang shall tear thee from his heart,
Life's idle business at one gasp be o'er,
The Muse forgot, and thou beloved no more!

(1717)

67 *A Hymn Written in Windsor Forest*

All hail! once pleasing, once inspiring shade,
  Scene of my youthful loves and happier hours!
Where the kind Muses met me as I strayed,
  And gently pressed my hand, and said, 'Be ours!—
Take all thou e'er shalt have, a constant Muse:
  At Court thou may'st be liked, but nothing gain;
Stocks thou may'st buy and sell, but always lose;
  And love the brightest eyes, but love in vain!'

(Wr. 1717; pub. 1831)

68 *To Mr. Gay, Who wrote him a Congratulatory Letter On the Finishing his House*

Ah, friend! 'tis true—this truth you lovers know—
In vain my structures rise, my gardens grow;
In vain fair Thames reflects the double scenes
Of hanging mountains and of sloping greens:
Joy lives not here; to happier seats it flies,
And only dwells where Wortley casts her eyes.

What are the gay parterre, the chequered shade,
The morning bower, the ev'ning colonnade,
But soft recesses of uneasy minds,
To sigh unheard in to the passing winds?
So the struck deer in some sequestered part
Lies down to die, the arrow at his heart;
There, stretched unseen in coverts hid from day,
Bleeds drop by drop, and pants his life away.

(Wr. 1722?; pub. 1737–1803)

69 *On a Certain Lady at Court*

I KNOW the thing that's most uncommon
  (Envy be silent and attend!);
I know a reasonable woman,
  Handsome and witty, yet a friend.

Not warped by passion, awed by rumour,
  Not grave through pride, or gay through folly;
An equal mixture of good humour
  And sensible soft melancholy.

'Has she no faults, then (Envy says), sir?'
  Yes, she has one, I must aver:
When all the world conspires to praise her,
  The woman's deaf, and does not hear.

(Wr. *c.*1725; pub. 1732)

(*see also Nos. 165–72*)

BERNARD MANDEVILLE

1670–1733

70 *On Honour*

FAR from the thronged luxurious town,
Lives an enchantress of renown
Called Honour, who by secret charms
Pulls swains from yielding virgins' arms;
For her the husband leaves his wife,
Despises pleasure, health and life;

For her the Trojan refugee
Forgot the cave and went to sea;
By her the daughter of the sun,
Bewitching Circe, was outdone,
From whose bright looks, by arts unknown,
She drew Ulysses to her own.
In bloody fields she sits as gay
As other ladies at a play,
Whilst the wild sparks on which she dotes
Are cutting one another's throats.
And when these sweethearts, for their sins,
Have all the bones broke in their skins,
Of her esteem the only token
Is t' have certificates th' are broken,
Which in grave lines are cut on stone,
And in some church or chapel shown
To people that, neglecting prayer,
Have time to mind who's buried there.
Till some half-witted fellow comes
To copy what is writ on tombs;
And then, to their immortal glory,
Forsooth, they're said to live in story,
A recompense which, to a wonder,
Must please a man that's cut asunder.
'Tis thought the cruel-hearted jade
Is, and will ever be, a maid,
Because none e'er lay in her bed,
Unless they first were knocked o' th' head.

(1710)

JOHN SMITH
1662–1717

71 *A Solitary Canto to Chloris the Disdainful*

WHAT a pox do you mean with your pride and ill-nature,
Like a jilt to neglect thus your own and God's creature?
You idly mistake the design of a lover:
His bus'ness is action much more than to suffer.
'Tis a barb'rous return, a hellish disdain,
To requite all the pleasure I offer with pain.
Didst thou come of some rough-hewn Northumberland breed,

Wert thou got and brought forth on the banks of far Tweed,
There damned to the yoke and tyrannical rule
Of some jealous old hunks or suspicious young fool,
Yet methinks you might find some expedient or other,
Though you knew nothing of it—to bring us together;
And not thus to let a brisk likely young fellow
To bulk it, or use the hard ground for a pillow.
No, madam, in good faith, I came not to fool here,
Or court, you may guess, the north wind for a cooler:
My bus'ness is—Let me come in, and I warrant
You'll say I know how to deliver my errand.
What a devil, d'y'think I'll stand here like an ass,
And with knuckle lie drumming on pane of small glass,
Or coxcomb that fancies he shrewdly does nick it,
When his passion in sighs he conveys through the wicket?
All th' amorous rout of the curs in the town
Are in loud Irish howl serenading the moon,
But Cynthia the kind condescends to each span'el,
While in pity she graciously shines from the kennel.
Grave owls, night's winged lovers, fly over our head,
And with screaming in churchyards awaken the dead;
But you, cruel nymph, while your grace I'm imploring,
My ditty ne'er mind, but in blanket lie snoring.
Hark! how the winds roar, my misfortunes condoling,
While I lie at your door all the night caterwauling;
And as of complaining soft flute I make trial,
They dolefully whistle in consort through keyhole.
The ground's cased with ice, and the whole street a glass is
For the moon and the stars to behold their bright faces;
The season's so sharp, one would swear the cold reigns
In your blood, and has froze up your heart and your veins,
And like little St. Francis enamoured I grow
Of a damsel of ice or a mistress of snow.
Come, lay by this scorn you so fondly affect,
Your unchristian behaviour, and heath'nish neglect,
Lest the powers of love, their just vengeance to show,
Make you dote on an ass or some nauseous old beau,
Who, to balk and torment you, your court shall decline,
And scorn your addresses, as you have done mine.
Thy mother was courteous before thee, and nature
Entails her good qualities all on the daughter:
No longer then dream on those dull idle fancies
Of honour, ne'er found but in plays and romances,
Nor that Graecian jilt who a fair thread did twist off,
And stood with her sparks at close guard with her distaff.
Have I not set traps, and laid many a gin

With springes to noose you, and catch your heart in?
Ha'nt I wheedled, presented, and offered petitions,
In order to bring you to milder conditions?
Your chambermaid fee'd with my person and money,
To know how your pulse beat, and practise upon ye?
Been religiously drunk at all times and all places,
By spelling your name o'er in stum in beer-glasses?
Besides, what might plague you and touch your heart more near,
Thy spouse now solaces with doxy in corner,
Melodious stage-punk, whose bewitching sweet tongue
Does lewdly seduce his false heart with a song;
And if this one mortifying thought will not win ye,
Nor raise your dull spleen—why the devil is in ye.
In Turkey the wives and Mahometan beauties,
If their husbands neglect to do family duties,
Those heralds of Cupid conclude it but decent
T' ennoble their family's crest with a crescent;
And sure 'tis not fit Christian ladies should want
A freedom that love does to infidels grant.
I've lain down before you already too long,
In hopes I might take you—with fiddle and song;
Then prithee, dear Chloris, be gentle and coming,
While love is in humour and youth is a-blooming.
When age comes 'twill make me too wise to endure
The delays and fatigues of a tedious amour;
Believe me, I ne'er shall have patience hereafter
To stand like a cistern to catch your rain-water,
Nor at your door whimper, bewailing my fate,
While it falls in big drops from the eaves of my hat;
No, sweet Mrs. Chloris—pray excuse me for that.

(1713)

ANNE FINCH, COUNTESS OF WINCHILSEA
1661–1720

72 *A Nocturnal Reverie*

IN such a night, when every louder wind
Is to its distant cavern safe confined;
And only gentle Zephyr fans his wings,
And lonely Philomel, still waking, sings;
Or from some tree, famed for the owl's delight,

71 stum] unfermented wine

She, hollowing clear, directs the wand'rer right;
In such a night, when passing clouds give place,
Or thinly veil the heaven's mysterious face;
When in some river overhung with green,
The waving moon and trembling leaves are seen;
When freshened grass now bears itself upright,
And makes cool banks to pleasing rest invite,
Whence springs the woodbind and the bramble-rose,
And where the sleepy cowslip sheltered grows;
Whilst now a paler hue the foxglove takes,
Yet chequers still with red the dusky brakes;
When scattered glow-worms, but in twilight fine,
Show trivial beauties, watch their hour to shine;
Whilst Salisb'ry stands the test of every light,
In perfect charms and perfect virtue bright;
When odours, which declined repelling day,
Through temp'rate air uninterrupted stray;
When darkened groves their softest shadows wear,
And falling waters we distinctly hear;
When through the gloom more venerable shows
Some ancient fabric, awful in repose,
While sunburnt hills their swarthy looks conceal,
And swelling haycocks thicken up the vale;
When the loosed horse now, as his pasture leads,
Comes slowly grazing through th' adjoining meads,
Whose stealing pace and lengthened shade we fear,
Till torn-up forage in his teeth we hear;
When nibbling sheep at large pursue their food,
And unmolested kine rechew the cud;
When curlews cry beneath the village walls,
And to her straggling brood the partridge calls;
Their short-lived jubilee the creatures keep,
Which but endures whilst tyrant man does sleep;
When a sedate content the spirit feels,
And no fierce light disturbs, whilst it reveals,
But silent musings urge the mind to seek
Something too high for syllables to speak;
Till the free soul to a compos'dness charmed,
Finding the elements of rage disarmed,
O'er all below a solemn quiet grown,
Joys in th' inferior world and thinks it like her own:
In such a night let me abroad remain,
Till morning breaks, and all's confused again:
Our cares, our toils, our clamours are renewed,
Or pleasures, seldom reached, again pursued.

(1713)

73 *A Song on the South Sea*

OMBRE and basset laid aside,
New games employ the fair;
And brokers all those hours divide
Which lovers used to share.

The court, the park, the foreign song
And harlequin's grimace,
Forlorn; amidst the city throng
Behold each blooming face.

With Jews and Gentiles undismayed
Young tender virgins mix,
Of whiskers nor of beards afraid,
Nor all the cozening tricks.

Bright jewels, polished once to deck
The fair one's rising breast,
Or sparkle round her ivory neck,
Lie pawned in iron chest.

The gayer passions of the mind
How avarice controls!
Even love does now no longer find
A place in female souls.

(Wr. 1720; pub. 1938)

SAMUEL JONES

d. 1732

74 *Poverty, in Imitation of Milton*

HAIL, happy lot of the laborious man,
Securest state of life, great Poverty,
To thee thrice hail! ——
Millions of active arms to thee each dawn,
Of supplications feminine devoid,
Erect their noble nerves, ——
Smile cheerful on the sultry steeds of heaven,
Vying in labour with their painful driver.

To thee, the cold and tedious winter's night,
The profit of innumerable hands
Most sinewy all! o' th' world's vast altar burns.
To thee! consummate happiness of mind,
And health, and length of life, and innocence,
With all the remnants of discarded virtue,
Are like events to causes ever knit.
Despite of pompous ornament, with thee
The Author of the furniture of heaven,
Of which both Art's and Nature's eyes see little
In the low'st floorage of the earth-nigh chambers,
And Founder of the boundless wealth beneath,
Of which to men and devils much unknown,
Took up his more than blessed abode when Man.
In thee, that second to the first great All
Drunk up the deluge of original guilt,
And brought the face of heaven's high road to ken:
Beneath thy umbrage very frailties died for.
Hail then to th' image of our Saviour's life!
As near as human things with things divine
Can correspond.——
Most venerable Poverty! to thee all hail!

(1714)

75 *The Force of Love*

WHEN Cleomira disbelieves
Her shepherd, when he swears he lives
Or dies i' th' smiles or frowns she gives,

The echo mourns him to the plain,
And pity moves in ev'ry swain,
And makes the nymphs partake his pain.

But pity and the fair ones prove,
When Cleomira hates his love,
Like strange embraces to a dove.

For Cleomira's hate can turn
Fresh youth and beauty to an urn:
Death sure than it's much easier borne!

But Cleomira's love can bless,
And turn t' a grove a wilderness,
A dungeon to a pleasant place.

Without it, Pleasure's self will show
The ghost of sorrow haunting you
In all the blissful things you do:

And with it, Nature's self may fall,
Old Night and Death frail men appal,
Without dismaying you at all.

(1714)

76 *The Ploughman, in Imitation of Milton*

HAPPY'S the man whose pleasant labours with the lark
Salute the opening of the radiant east;
Who, cheerful as the sun, begins his task
Of cultivating Nature's plenteous gifts,
Without a certain hope, except in heav'n;
Who in his nostrils snuffs the morning dew,
And takes the physic of the op'ning ground;
Yet feels no guilty love annoy his rest,
No lust of lawless gain to make him rise
And hammer mischiefs for a sleeping man;
Who neither spurs nor spares his beast too far,
But makes him serve the purpose heav'n designed;
Whose team with bells to him impart a joy
Like that old soldiers feel when hostile fire
Deals death like fate, and makes the coward run
Or die, with apprehensions vast and strange:
Or as the lover feels, when Byblis first,
Agreed to crown him monarch of her joys,
Lies sheltered only in her shift below him.

(1714)

RICHARDSON PACK

1682–1728

77 *An Epistle from a Half-Pay Officer in the Country to his Friend in London, upon Reading the Address of the Two Houses, to thank her Majesty for the Safe, Honourable and Advantageous Peace*

CURSE on the star, dear Harry, that betrayed
My choice from law, divinity or trade,
To turn a rambling brother o' the blade!
Of all professions sure the worst is war.
How whimsical our fortune! how bizarre!
This week we shine in scarlet and in gold:
The next, the cloak is pawned—the watch is sold.
Today we're company for any lord:
Tomorrow not a soul will take our word.
Like meteors raised in a tempestuous sky,
A while we glitter, then obscurely die.
Must heroes suffer such disgrace as this?
O cursed effects of Honourable Peace!

I, who not long ago indulged my hours
In witty commerce or in soft amours,
And in rich Mulso, Volney or Champagne
Adored each night the beauties then in reign
(Till, arms submitting to the awful gown,
Our troops were forced to abdicate the town),
Must now retire, and languish out my days
Far from the roads of pleasure or of praise:
Quit sweet Hyde Park for dull provincial air,
And change the playhouse for a country fair;
With sneaking parsons beastly bumpers quaff,
At low conceits and vile conundrums laugh;
Toast to the Church and talk of Right Divine,
And herd with squires—more noisy than their swine.
Must heroes suffer such disgrace as this?
O cursed effects of Honourable Peace!

There was a time—oh yes! there was a time—
(Ere poverty made luxury a crime)
When marigolds in porridge were a jest,
And soups were used to introduce the feast.

Then French ragouts were orthodox and good,
And truffles held no heresy in food.
Nor to eat mackerel was judged high treason,
Though gooseberries as yet were not in season.
But under H[ar]ley's frugal dispensation,
These vanities require a reformation.
Scourged by his wand and humbled by his sway,
I've learned to suit my diet to my pay;
And now can sanctify with solemn face
A heavy dumpling with a formal grace.
In awkward plenty, slovenly I dine,
And nappy ale supplies the want of wine.
No nice desserts my learned palate please:
To fill up chinks—a slice of Suffolk cheese.
  And must then heroes nibble Suffolk cheese?
  O cursed effects of Honourable Peace!

  But ah! the hardest part is still behind—
The fair too, gentle Harry, prove unkind.
Think then how wretchedly my life must pass!
For what's this world, my friend, without a lass?
Poor be my lot, inglorious be my state,
Give me but woman, I'll absolve my fate.
But 'tis in vain——
Th' ungrateful sex, as senseless as unjust,
To feed their pride will even starve their lust:
And fooled by equipage and empty show,
Quit the tough soldier for the lathy beau.
I who so oft their forward zeal have showed,
And in their service spent my warmest blood,
Am now reduced (hard fate!) for want of pelf
To fight the Jesuit's battle by myself.
  Must heroes suffer such disgrace as this?
  O cursed effects of Honourable Peace!

(Wr. 1714; pub. 1719)

WILLIAM HARRISON

1685–1713

78 *In Praise of Laudanum*

I FEEL, O Laudanum, thy power divine,
And fall with pleasure at thy slumb'ring shrine:
Lulled by thy charms I 'scape each anxious thought,
And everything but Mira is forgot.

(1714)

THOMAS PARNELL

1679–1718

79 *A Hymn to Contentment*

LOVELY, lasting Peace of Mind!
Sweet delight of human kind!
Heavenly-born, and bred on high
To crown the fav'rites of the sky
With more of happiness below
Than victors in a triumph know!
Whither, O whither art thou fled,
To lay thy meek, contented head;
What happy region dost thou please
To make the seat of calms and ease?
  Ambition searches all its sphere
Of pomp and state, to meet thee there.
Increasing Avarice would find
Thy presence in its gold enshrined.
The bold advent'rer ploughs his way
Through rocks amidst the foaming sea,
To gain thy love; and then perceives
Thou wert not in the rocks and waves.
The silent heart, which grief assails,
Treads soft and lonesome o'er the vales,
Sees daisies open, rivers run,
And seeks, as I have vainly done,
Amusing thought; but learns to know
That Solitude's the nurse of woe.

No real happiness is found
In trailing purple o'er the ground;
Or in a soul exalted high,
To range the circuit of the sky,
Converse with stars above, and know
All nature in its forms below;
The rest it seeks, in seeking dies,
And doubts at last for knowledge rise.
  Lovely, lasting Peace, appear!
This world itself, if thou art here,
Is once again with Eden blessed,
And man contains it in his breast.
  'Twas thus, as under shade I stood,
I sung my wishes to the wood,
And, lost in thought, no more perceived
The branches whisper as they waved:
It seemed as all the quiet place
Confessed the presence of the Grace,
When thus she spoke—'Go rule thy will,
Bid thy wild passions all be still,
Know God—and bring thy heart to know
The joys which from religion flow:
Then ev'ry Grace shall prove its guest,
And I'll be there to crown the rest.'
  Oh! by yonder mossy seat,
In my hours of sweet retreat,
Might I thus my soul employ,
With sense of gratitude and joy:
Raised as ancient prophets were,
In heavenly vision, praise and pray'r;
Pleasing all men, hurting none,
Pleased and blessed with God alone.
Then while the gardens take my sight
With all the colours of delight;
While silver waters glide along
To please my ear, and court my song;
I'll lift my voice, and tune my string,
And thee, great Source of Nature, sing.
  The sun that walks his airy way,
To light the world and give the day;
The moon that shines with borrowed light;
The stars that gild the gloomy night;
The seas that roll unnumbered waves;
The wood that spreads its shady leaves;
The field whose ears conceal the grain,
The yellow treasure of the plain;

All of these, and all I see,
Should be sung, and sung by me:
They speak their Maker as they can,
But want and ask the tongue of man.
Go search among your idle dreams,
Your busy or your vain extremes;
And find a life of equal bliss,
Or own the next begun in this.

(1714)

80 *An Elegy, to an Old Beauty*

In vain, poor nymph, to please our youthful sight
You sleep in cream and frontlets all the night,
Your face with patches soil, with paint repair,
Dress with gay gowns, and shade with foreign hair.
If truth, in spite of manners, must be told,
Why really fifty-five is something old.
Once you were young; or one, whose life's so long
She might have borne my mother, tells me wrong.
And once (since envy's dead before you die),
The women own you played a sparkling eye,
Taught the light foot a modish little trip,
And pouted with the prettiest purple lip.
To some new charmer are the roses fled,
Which blew to damask all thy cheek with red;
Youth calls the Graces there to fix their reign,
And Airs by thousands fill their easy train.
So parting summer bids her flow'ry prime
Attend the sun to dress some foreign clime,
While with'ring seasons in succession, here,
Strip the gay gardens, and deform the year.
But thou, since nature bids, the world resign;
'Tis now thy daughter's daughter's time to shine.
With more address (or such as pleases more),
She runs her female exercises o'er,
Unfurls or closes, raps or turns the fan,
And smiles, or blushes, at the creature man.
With quicker life, as gilded coaches pass,
In sideling courtesy she drops the glass.
With better strength, on visit-days, she bears
To mount her fifty flights of ample stairs.
Her mien, her shape, her temper, eyes and tongue
Are sure to conquer—for the rogue is young;

And all that's madly wild, or oddly gay,
We call it only pretty Fanny's way.
  Let time, that makes you homely, make you sage;
The sphere of wisdom is the sphere of age.
'Tis true, when beauty dawns with early fire,
And hears the flatt'ring tongues of soft desire,
If not from virtue, from its gravest ways
The soul with pleasing avocation strays.
But beauty gone, 'tis easier to be wise;
As harpers better, by the loss of eyes.
  Henceforth retire, reduce your roving airs,
Haunt less the plays, and more the public prayers,
Reject the Mechlin head and gold brocade,
Go pray, in sober Norwich crape arrayed.
Thy pendant diamonds let thy Fanny take,
(Their trembling lustre shows how much you shake);
Or bid her wear thy necklace rowed with pearl,
You'll find your Fanny an obedient girl.
So for the rest, with less incumbrance hung,
You walk through life, unmingled with the young;
And view the shade and substance, as you pass,
With joint endeavour trifling at the glass,
Or Folly dressed, and rambling all her days,
To meet her counterpart, and grow by praise:
Yet still sedate yourself, and gravely plain,
You neither fret, nor envy at the vain.
  'Twas thus (if man with woman we compare)
The wise Athenian crossed a glittering fair.
Unmoved by tongues and sights, he walked the place,
Through tape, toys, tinsel, gimp, perfume and lace;
Then bends from Mars's hill his awful eyes,
And—'What a world I never want!' he cries;
But cries unheard; for Folly will be free.
So parts the buzzing gaudy crowd, and he:
As careless he for them, as they for him;
He wrapped in wisdom, and they whirled by whim.

(1721)

81 *A Night-Piece on Death*

By the blue taper's trembling light,
No more I waste the wakeful night,
Intent with endless view to pore
The schoolmen and the sages o'er:

Their books from wisdom widely stray,
Or point at best the longest way.
I'll seek a readier path, and go
Where wisdom's surely taught below.
  How deep yon azure dyes the sky,
Where orbs of gold unnumbered lie,
While through their ranks in silver pride
The nether crescent seems to glide.
The slumb'ring breeze forgets to breathe,
The lake is smooth and clear beneath,
Where once again the spangled show
Descends to meet our eyes below.
The grounds, which on the right aspire,
In dimness from the view retire:
The left presents a place of graves,
Whose wall the silent water laves.
That steeple guides thy doubtful sight
Among the livid gleams of night.
There pass, with melancholy state,
By all the solemn heaps of fate,
And think, as softly-sad you tread
Above the venerable dead,
'Time was, like thee they life possessed,
And time shall be, that thou shalt rest.'
  Those graves, with bending osier bound,
That nameless heave the crumbled ground,
Quick to the glancing thought disclose
Where Toil and Poverty repose.
  The flat smooth stones that bear a name,
The chisel's slender help to fame
(Which ere our set of friends decay
Their frequent steps may wear away),
A middle race of mortals own,
Men, half ambitious, all unknown.
  The marble tombs that rise on high,
Whose dead in vaulted arches lie,
Whose pillars swell with sculptured stones,
Arms, angels, epitaphs and bones,
These (all the poor remains of state)
Adorn the rich, or praise the great;
Who, while on earth in fame they live,
Are senseless of the fame they give.
  Ha! while I gaze, pale Cynthia fades,
The bursting earth unveils the shades!
All slow and wan, and wrapped with shrouds,
They rise in visionary crowds,

And all with sober accent cry,
'Think, mortal, what it is to die.'
  Now from yon black and fun'ral yew,
That bathes the charnel-house with dew,
Methinks I hear a voice begin
(Ye ravens, cease your croaking din,
Ye tolling clocks, no time resound
O'er the long lake and midnight ground);
It sends a peal of hollow groans,
Thus speaking from among the bones:
  'When men my scythe and darts supply,
How great a King of Fears am I!
They view me like the last of things:
They make, and then they dread, my stings.
Fools! if you less provoked your fears,
No more my spectre-form appears.
Death's but a path that must be trod,
If man would ever pass to God;
A port of calms, a state of ease
From the rough rage of swelling seas.
  'Why then thy flowing sable stoles,
Deep pendant cypress, mourning poles,
Loose scarfs to fall athwart thy weeds,
Long palls, drawn hearses, covered steeds,
And plumes of black, that, as they tread,
Nod o'er the scutcheons of the dead?
  'Nor can the parted body know,
Nor wants the soul, these forms of woe.
As men who long in prison dwell,
With lamps that glimmer round the cell,
Whene'er their suffering years are run,
Spring forth to greet the glitt'ring sun:
Such joy, though far transcending sense,
Have pious souls at parting hence.
On earth, and in the body placed,
A few, and evil, years they waste;
But when their chains are cast aside,
See the glad scene unfolding wide,
Clap the glad wing, and tow'r away,
And mingle with the blaze of day.'

(1721)

JOHN GAY

1685–1732

82 from *The Shepherd's Week*

TUESDAY; OR, THE DITTY

MARIAN

YOUNG Colin Clout, a lad of peerless meed,
Full well could dance, and deftly tune the reed;
In ev'ry wood his carols sweet were known,
At ev'ry wake his nimble feats were shown.
When in the ring the rustic routs he threw,
The damsels' pleasures with his conquests grew;
Or when aslant the cudgel threats his head,
His danger smites the breast of ev'ry maid,
But chief of Marian. Marian loved the swain,
The parson's maid, and neatest of the plain.
Marian, that soft could stroke the uddered cow,
Or lessen with her sieve the barley mow;
Marbled with sage, the hard'ning cheese she pressed,
And yellow butter Marian's skill confessed;
But Marian, now devoid of country cares,
Nor yellow butter nor sage cheese prepares.
For yearning love the witless maid employs,
And love, say swains, all busy heed destroys.
Colin makes mock at all her piteous smart,
A lass, that Cic'ly hight, had won his heart,
Cic'ly the western lass that tends the kee,[1]
The rival of the parson's maid was she.
In dreary shade now Marian lies along,
And, mixed with sighs, thus wails in plaining song:
  'Ah! woeful day! ah, woeful noon and morn!
When first by thee my younglings white were shorn,
Then first, I ween, I cast a lover's eye,
My sheep were silly, but more silly I.
Beneath the shears they felt no lasting smart,
They lost but fleeces, while I lost a heart.
  'Ah, Colin! canst thou leave thy sweetheart true?
What I have done for thee will Cic'ly do?
Will she thy linen wash or hosen darn,
And knit thee gloves made of her own-spun yarn?

[1] Kee, a west country word for kine or cows.

Will she with huswife's hand provide thy meat,
And ev'ry Sunday morn thy neckcloth plait,
Which, o'er thy kersey doublet spreading wide,
In service-time drew Cic'ly's eyes aside?
   'Where'er I gad I cannot hide my care,
My new disasters in my look appear.
White as the curd my ruddy cheek is grown,
So thin my features that I'm hardly known:
Our neighbours tell me oft in joking talk
Of ashes, leather, oatmeal, bran and chalk;
Unwittingly of Marian they divine,
And wist not that with thoughtful love I pine.
Yet Colin Clout, untoward shepherd swain,
Walks whistling blithe, while pitiful I plain.
   'Whilom with thee 'twas Marian's dear delight
To moil all day, and merry-make at night.
If in the soil you guide the crooked share,
Your early breakfast is my constant care.
And when with even hand you strow the grain,
I fright the thievish rooks from off the plain.
In misling days when I my thresher heard,
With nappy beer I to the barn repaired;
Lost in the music of the whirling flail,
To gaze on thee I left the smoking pail;
In harvest when the sun was mounted high,
My leathern bottle did thy drought supply;
Whene'er you mowed I followed with the rake,
And have full oft been sunburnt for thy sake;
When in the welkin gathering showers were seen,
I lagged the last with Colin on the green;
And when at eve returning with thy car,
Awaiting heard the jingling bells from far,
Straight on the fire the sooty pot I placed,
To warm thy broth I burnt my hands for haste.
When hungry thou stood'st staring, like an oaf,
I sliced the luncheon from the barley loaf,
With crumbled bread I thickened well thy mess.
Ah, love me more, or love thy pottage less!
   'Last Friday's eve, when as the sun was set,
I, near yon stile, three sallow gypsies met.
Upon my hand they cast a poring look,
Bid me beware, and thrice their heads they shook;
They said that many crosses I must prove,
Some in my worldly gain, but most in love.
Next morn I missed three hens and our old cock,
And off the hedge two pinners and a smock.

I bore these losses with a Christian mind,
And no mishaps could feel, while thou wert kind.
But since, alas! I grew my Colin's scorn,
I've known no pleasure, night, or noon, or morn.
Help me, ye gypsies, bring him home again,
And to a constant lass give back her swain.
'Have I not sat with thee full many a night,
When dying embers were our only light,
When ev'ry creature did in slumbers lie,
Besides our cat, my Colin Clout and I?
No troublous thoughts the cat or Colin move,
While I alone am kept awake by love.
'Remember, Colin, when, at last year's wake,
I bought the costly present for thy sake,
Couldst thou spell o'er the posy on thy knife,
And with another change thy state of life?
If thou forgett'st, I wot I can repeat,
My memory can tell the verse so sweet:
As this is graved upon this knife of thine,
So is thy image on this heart of mine.
But woe is me! Such presents luckless prove,
For knives, they tell me, always sever love.'
Thus Marian wailed, her eyes with tears brimful,
When Goody Dobbins brought her cow to bull.
With apron blue to dry her tears she sought,
Then saw the cow well served, and took a groat.

(1714)

83 from *Trivia: or, The Art of Walking the Streets of London*, Book II

Frosty Weather.

WINTER my theme confines; whose nitry wind
Shall crust the slabby mire, and kennels bind;
She bids the snow descend in flaky sheets,
And in her hoary mantle clothe the streets.
Let not the virgin tread these slipp'ry roads,
The gath'ring fleece the hollow patten loads;
But if thy footsteps slide with clotted frost,
Strike off the breaking balls against the post.
On silent wheel the passing coaches roll;
Oft look behind, and ward the threat'ning pole.
In hardened orbs the schoolboy moulds the snow,
To mark the coachman with a dext'rous throw.
Why do ye, boys, the kennel's surface spread,

To tempt with faithless pass the matron's tread?
How can ye laugh to see the damsel spurn,
Sink in your frauds and her green stocking mourn?
At White's the harnessed chairman idly stands,
And swings around his waist his tingling hands:
The sempstress speeds to Change with red-tipped nose;
The Belgian stove beneath her footstool glows;
In half-whipped muslin needles useless lie,
And shuttlecocks across the counter fly.
These sports warm harmless; why then will ye prove,
Deluded maids, the dang'rous flame of love?

The Dangers of Football.

Where Covent Garden's famous temple stands,
That boasts the work of Jones' immortal hands,
Columns with plain magnificence appear,
And graceful porches lead along the square:
Here oft my course I bend, when lo! from far,
I spy the furies of the football war:
The 'prentice quits his shop to join the crew,
Increasing crowds the flying game pursue.
Thus, as you roll the ball o'er snowy ground,
The gath'ring globe augments with every round.
But whither shall I run? the throng draws nigh,
The ball now skims the street, now soars on high;
The dext'rous glazier strong returns the bound,
And jingling sashes on the penthouse sound.

An Episode of the great Frost.

O roving Muse, recall that wond'rous year,
When winter reigned in bleak Britannia's air;
When hoary Thames, with frosted osiers crowned,
Was three long moons in icy fetters bound.
The waterman, forlorn along the shore,
Pensive reclines upon his useless oar,
Sees harnessed steeds desert the stony town,
And wander roads unstable, not their own:
Wheels o'er the hardened waters smoothly glide,
And rase with whitened tracks the slipp'ry tide.
Here the fat cook piles high the blazing fire,
And scarce the spit can turn the steer entire.
Booths sudden hide the Thames, long streets appear,
And num'rous games proclaim the crowded fair.
So when a gen'ral bids the martial train
Spread their encampment o'er the spacious plain,
Thick-rising tents a canvas city build,
And the loud dice resound through all the field.
'Twas here the matron found a doleful fate:
Let elegiac lay the woe relate,
Soft as the breath of distant flutes, at hours

When silent ev'ning closes up the flow'rs;
Lulling as falling water's hollow noise;
Indulging grief, like Philomela's voice.
  Doll ev'ry day had walked these treach'rous roads;
Her neck grew warped beneath autumnal loads
Of various fruit; she now a basket bore:
That head, alas! shall basket bear no more.
Each booth she frequent passed, in quest of gain,
And boys with pleasure heard her shrilling strain.
Ah Doll! all mortals must resign their breath,
And industry itself submit to death!
The cracking crystal yields, she sinks, she dies,
Her head, chopped off, from her lost shoulders flies;
'Pippins,' she cried, but death her voice confounds,
And 'pip-pip-pip' along the ice resounds.
So when the Thracian furies Orpheus tore,
And left his bleeding trunk deformed with gore,
His severed head floats down the silver tide,
His yet warm tongue for his lost consort cried;
'Eurydice' with quiv'ring voice he mourned,
And Heber's banks 'Eurydice' returned.

A Thaw.

  But now the western gale the flood unbinds,
And black'ning clouds move on with warmer winds.
The wooden town its frail foundation leaves,
And Thames' full urn rolls down his plenteous waves;
From ev'ry penthouse streams the fleeting snow,
And with dissolving frost the pavements flow.

How to know the Days of the Week.

  Experienced men, inured to city ways,
Need not the calendar to count their days.
When through the town with slow and solemn air,
Led by the nostril, walks the muzzled bear;
Behind him moves majestically dull,
The pride of Hockley-hole, the surly bull;
Learn hence the periods of the week to name:
Mondays and Thursdays are the days of game.
  When fishy stalls with double store are laid;
The golden-bellied carp, the broad-finned maid,
Red-speckled trouts, the salmon's silver jowl,
The jointed lobster, and unscaly sole,
And luscious scallops to allure the tastes
Of rigid zealots to delicious fasts;
Wednesdays and Fridays you'll observe from hence,
Days, when our sires were doomed to abstinence.
  When dirty waters from balconies drop,
And dext'rous damsels twirl the sprinkling mop,
And cleanse the spattered sash, and scrub the stairs;

Know Saturday's conclusive morn appears.

Remarks on the Cries of the Town.

Successive cries the seasons' change declare,
And mark the monthly progress of the year.
Hark, how the streets with treble voices ring,
To sell the bounteous product of the spring!
Sweet-smelling flow'rs, and elder's early bud,
With nettle's tender shoots, to cleanse the blood:
And when June's thunder cools the sultry skies,
Ev'n Sundays are profaned by mack'rel cries.
Walnuts the fruit'rer's hand, in autumn, stain,
Blue plums and juicy pears augment his gain;
Next, oranges the longing boys entice
To trust their copper fortunes to the dice.

Of Christmas.

When rosemary and bays, the poet's crown,
Are bawled in frequent cries through all the town,
Then judge the festival of Christmas near,
Christmas, the joyous period of the year.
Now with bright holly all your temples strow,
With laurel green and sacred mistletoe.
Now, heav'n-born Charity, thy blessings shed;
Bid meagre Want uprear her sickly head:
Bid shiv'ring limbs be warm; let plenty's bowl
In humble roofs make glad the needy soul.
See, see, the heav'n-born maid her blessings shed.
Lo! meagre Want uprears her sickly head;
Clothed are the naked, and the needy glad,
While selfish Avarice alone is sad.

(1716)

84 *The Birth of the Squire. An Eclogue*

In Imitation of the Pollio *of Virgil*

YE sylvan Muses, loftier strains recite;
Not all in shades and humble cots delight.
Hark! the bells ring; along the distant grounds
The driving gales convey the swelling sounds;
Th' attentive swain, forgetful of his work,
With gaping wonder leans upon his fork.
What sudden news alarms the waking morn?
To the glad Squire a hopeful heir is born.
Mourn, mourn, ye stags, and all ye beasts of chase,
This hour destruction brings on all your race:
See the pleased tenants duteous off'rings bear,
Turkeys and geese and grocer's sweetest ware;

With the new health the pond'rous tankard flows,
And old October reddens ev'ry nose.
Beagles and spaniels round his cradle stand,
Kiss his moist lip and gently lick his hand;
He joys to hear the shrill horn's echoing sounds,
And learns to lisp the names of all the hounds.
With frothy ale to make his cup o'erflow,
Barley shall in paternal acres grow;
The bee shall sip the fragrant dew from flow'rs,
To give metheglin for his morning hours;
For him the clust'ring hop shall climb the poles,
And his own orchard sparkle in his bowls.
  His sire's exploits he now with wonder hears,
The monstrous tales indulge his greedy ears;
How when youth strung his nerves and warmed his veins,
He rode the mighty Nimrod of the plains:
He leads the staring infant through the hall,
Points out the horny spoils that grace the wall;
Tells, how this stag through three whole counties fled,
What rivers swam, where bayed, and where he bled.
Now he the wonders of the fox repeats,
Describes the desp'rate chase, and all his cheats;
How in one day beneath his furious speed,
He tired seven coursers of the fleetest breed;
How high the pale he leaped, how wide the ditch,
When the hound tore the haunches of the witch![1]
These stories which descend from son to son,
The forward boy shall one day make his own.
  Ah, too fond mother, think the time draws nigh,
That calls the darling from thy tender eye;
How shall his spirit brook the rigid rules,
And the long tyranny of grammar schools?
Let younger brothers o'er dull authors plod,
Lashed into Latin by the tingling rod;
No, let him never feel that smart disgrace:
Why should he wiser prove than all his race?
  When rip'ning youth with down o'ershades his chin,
And ev'ry female eye incites to sin,
The milk-maid (thoughtless of her future shame)
With smacking lip shall raise his guilty flame;
The dairy, barn, the hayloft and the grove
Shall oft be conscious of their stolen love.
But think, Priscilla, on that dreadful time
When pangs and watry qualms shall own thy crime;

[1] The most common accident to sportsmen; to hunt a witch in the shape of a hare.

How wilt thou tremble, when thy nipple's pressed,
To see the white drops bathe thy swelling breast!
Nine moons shall publicly divulge thy shame,
And the young Squire forestall a father's name.
When twice twelve times the reaper's sweeping hand
With levelled harvest has bestrown the land,
On famed St. Hubert's feast, his winding horn
Shall cheer the joyful hound and wake the morn:
This memorable day his eager speed
Shall urge with bloody heel the rising steed.
O check the foamy bit, nor tempt thy fate,
Think on the murders of a five-bar gate!
Yet prodigal of life, the leap he tries,
Low in the dust his grovelling honour lies,
Headlong he falls, and on the rugged stone
Distorts his neck, and cracks the collar-bone;
O vent'rous youth, thy thirst of game allay,
May'st thou survive the perils of this day!
He shall survive; and in late years be sent
To snore away debates in Parliament.
The time shall come, when his more solid sense
With nod important shall the laws dispense;
A Justice with grave Justices shall sit,
He praise their wisdom, they admire his wit.
No greyhound shall attend the tenant's pace,
No rusty gun the farmer's chimney grace;
Salmons shall leave their covers void of fear,
Nor dread the thievish net or triple spear;
Poachers shall tremble at his awful name,
Whom vengeance now o'ertakes for murdered game.
Assist me, Bacchus, and ye drunken Powers,
To sing his friendships and his midnight hours!
Why dost thou glory in thy strength of beer,
Firm-corked, and mellowed till the twentieth year;
Brewed or when Phoebus warms the fleecy sign,
Or when his languid rays in Scorpio shine?
Think on the mischiefs which from hence have sprung!
It arms with curses dire the wrathful tongue;
Foul scandal to the lying lip affords,
And prompts the mem'ry with injurious words.
O where is wisdom, when by this o'erpowered?
The state is censured, and the maid deflowered!
And wilt thou still, O Squire, brew ale so strong?
Hear then the dictates of prophetic song.
Methinks I see him in his hall appear,
Where the long table floats in clammy beer,

'Midst mugs and glasses shattered o'er the floor,
Dead-drunk his servile crew supinely snore;
Triumphant, o'er the prostrate brutes he stands,
The mighty bumper trembles in his hands;
Boldly he drinks and, like his glorious sires,
In copious gulps of potent ale expires.

(1720)

85 *To a Young Lady With Some Lampreys*

WITH lovers 'twas of old the fashion
By presents to convey their passion:
No matter what the gift they sent,
The lady saw that love was meant.
Fair Atalanta, as a favour,
Took the boar's head her hero gave her;
Nor could the bristly thing affront her,
'Twas a fit present from a hunter.
When squires send woodcocks to the dame,
It serves to show their absent flame:
Some by a snip of woven hair
In posied lockets bribe the fair;
How many mercenary matches
Have sprung from di'mond-rings and watches!
But hold—a ring, a watch, a locket,
Would drain at once a poet's pocket;
He should send songs that cost him nought,
Nor ev'n be prodigal of thought.
Why then send lampreys? fie, for shame!
'Twill set a virgin's blood on flame.
This to fifteen a proper gift!
It might lend sixty-five a lift.
I know your maiden aunt will scold,
And think my present somewhat bold.
I see her lift her hands and eyes:
'What, eat it, niece? eat Spanish flies!
Lamprey's a most immodest diet:
You'll neither wake nor sleep in quiet.
Should I tonight eat sago-cream,
'Twould make me blush to tell my dream;
If I eat lobster, 'tis so warming
That ev'ry man I see looks charming;
Wherefore had not the filthy fellow
Laid Rochester upon your pillow?

I vow and swear, I think the present
Had been as modest and as decent.
  'Who has her virtue in her power?
Each day has its unguarded hour;
Always in danger of undoing,
A prawn, a shrimp may prove our ruin!
  'The shepherdess, who lives on salad,
To cool her youth controls her palate;
Should Dian's maids turn liqu'rish livers,
And of huge lampreys rob the rivers,
Then all beside each glade and visto,
You'd see nymphs lying like Calisto.
  'The man who meant to heat your blood,
Needs not himself such vicious food——'
  In this, I own, your aunt is clear,
I sent you what I well might spare:
For when I see you (without joking),
Your eyes, lips, breasts are so provoking,
They set my heart more cock-a-hoop
Than could whole seas of craw-fish soup.

(1720)

86 *Sweet William's Farewell to Black-Eyed Susan*

A Ballad

ALL in the Downs the fleet was moored,
  The streamers waving in the wind,
When black-eyed Susan came aboard.
  'Oh! where shall I my true love find?
Tell me, ye jovial sailors, tell me true,
If my sweet William sails among the crew.'

William, who, high upon the yard,
  Rocked with the billow to and fro,
Soon as her well-known voice he heard,
  He sighed and cast his eyes below:
The cord slides swiftly through his glowing hands,
And (quick as lightning) on the deck he stands.

So the sweet lark, high-poised in air,
  Shuts close his pinions to his breast
(If, chance, his mate's shrill call he hear)
  And drops at once into her nest.
The noblest captain in the British fleet
Might envy William's lip those kisses sweet.

'O Susan, Susan, lovely dear,
My vows shall ever true remain;
Let me kiss off that falling tear,
We only part to meet again.
Change, as ye list, ye winds; my heart shall be
The faithful compass that still points to thee.

'Believe not what the landmen say,
Who tempt with doubts thy constant mind:
They'll tell thee, sailors, when away,
In ev'ry port a mistress find.
Yes, yes, believe them when they tell thee so,
For thou art present wheresoe'er I go.

'If to far India's coast we sail,
Thy eyes are seen in di'monds bright,
Thy breath is Africk's spicy gale,
Thy skin is ivory, so white.
Thus ev'ry beauteous object that I view
Wakes in my soul some charm of lovely Sue.

'Though battle call me from thy arms,
Let not my pretty Susan mourn;
Though cannons roar, yet safe from harms
William shall to his dear return.
Love turns aside the balls that round me fly,
Lest precious tears should drop from Susan's eye.'

The boatswain gave the dreadful word,
The sails their swelling bosom spread,
No longer must she stay aboard:
They kissed, she sighed, he hung his head.
Her less'ning boat unwilling rows to land:
'Adieu!' she cries; and waves her lily hand.

(1720)

87 *My Own Epitaph*

LIFE is a jest, and all things show it;
I thought so once, but now I know it.

(1720)

88 from *Fables*

The Wild Boar and the Ram

AGAINST an elm a sheep was tied,
The butcher's knife in blood was dyed;
The patient flock, in silent fright,
From far beheld the horrid sight.
A savage Boar, who near them stood,
Thus mocked to scorn the fleecy brood:
'All cowards should be served like you.
See, see, your murd'rer is in view:
With purple hands and reeking knife,
He strips the skin yet warm with life.
Your quartered sires, your bleeding dams,
The dying bleat of harmless lambs,
Call for revenge. O stupid race!
The heart that wants revenge is base.'
'I grant,' an ancient Ram replies,
'We bear no terror in our eyes;
Yet think us not of soul so tame,
Which no repeated wrongs inflame;
Insensible of ev'ry ill,
Because we want thy tusks to kill.
Know, those who violence pursue
Give to themselves the vengeance due,
For in these massacres they find
The two chief plagues that waste mankind.
Our skin supplies the wrangling bar,
It wakes their slumb'ring sons to war;
And well revenge may rest contented,
Since drums and parchment were invented.'

(1727)

89 from *The Beggar's Opera*

Airs

(i)

A FOX may steal your hens, sir,
A whore your health and pence, sir,
Your daughter rob your chest, sir,
Your wife may steal your rest, sir,
A thief your goods and plate.

But this is all but picking,
With rest, pence, chest and chicken;
It ever was decreed, sir,
If lawyer's hand is fee'd, sir,
He steals your whole estate.

(ii)

MACHEATH AND POLLY

Mac. Were I laid on Greenland's coast,
And in my arms embraced my lass,
Warm amidst eternal frost,
Too soon the half-year's night would pass.
Polly Were I sold on Indian soil,
Soon as the burning day was closed,
I could mock the sultry toil,
When on my charmer's breast reposed.
Mac. And I would love you all the day,
Polly Every night would kiss and play,
Mac. If with me you'd fondly stray
Polly Over the hills and far away.

(iii)

Since laws were made for ev'ry degree,
To curb vice in others, as well as me,
I wonder we han't better company
Upon Tyburn tree!
But gold from law can take out the sting;
And if rich men like us were to swing,
'Twould thin the land, such numbers to string
Upon Tyburn tree!

(1728)

90 from *Polly. An Opera*

Air

THE sportsmen keep hawks, and their quarry they gain;
Thus the woodcock, the partridge, the pheasant is slain.
What care and expense for their hounds are employed!
Thus the fox and the hare and the stag are destroyed.
The spaniel they cherish, whose flattering way
Can as well as their masters cringe, fawn and betray.
Thus staunch politicians, look all the world round,
Love the men who can serve as hawk, spaniel or hound.

(1729)

91 from *Acis and Galatea. An English Pastoral Opera*

Air

O RUDDIER than the cherry,
O sweeter than the berry,
O nymph more bright
Than moonshine night,
Like kidlings blithe and merry.

Ripe as the melting cluster,
No lily has such lustre,
Yet hard to tame
As raging flame,
And fierce as storms that bluster.

(1732)

JOHN WINSTANLEY

1678?–1750

92 *Fanny's Removal in 1714*

ALAS! poor Fanny! wretched girl, alas!
Her fatal exit too is come to pass!
Among the many changes made of late,
Her turn is now, and she must share the fate
Of judges, privy counsellors and ministers of state.
The Fates decreed, 'tis folly to repine;
I heard her mistress cry, 'My slave is mine';
Then, flourishing the poker in her hand,
Said, 'Queen I am, this sceptre shall command';
With which poor Fanny out of door she banged.
Poor wench! alas! far happier had she been
If her past happy days she ne'er had seen,
Nor stood so fair in th' graces of her queen.
The time no later was than t' other day
(But royal favour will like time decay),
When Madam's most important nice affairs
Were done by Fanny, passed through Fanny's ears;
When fierce competitors for Madam's love
For Fanny's favour vehemently strove,

And gained a mighty point, if Fanny did approve.
And, cunning gypsy, she could coax with ease,
For of her mistress she had learned to please;
With all her courtiers, whether Whig or Tory,
Had curried favour, and could tell her story.
One was her charming dear, and one her honey;
But he most dear, be sure, who gave most money.
Such was her conduct, such her int'rest deemed,
More like a mistress than a maid she seemed.
  Thus Fanny lived, a day or two ago;
But now, alas! poor girl! it is not so:
Her cup of pleasant joy is dashed with bitter woe.
Her mistress will (and she will be obeyed,
For who against her will dare intercede?)
Turn Fanny off, and take another maid.
No matter why, for 'tis enough she'll do't;
Her power o'er her servant's absolute,
And, sure, no servant dare dispute the sway
Of her whom princes would be proud t' obey:
Besides, so mild, so good she is, that still
The world must needs conclude of Fanny ill,
Though Madam give no other reason than her will.
  Methinks I hear one say, 'What, Fanny gone?
Turned off! no sure! why then, the girl's undone:
But so all servants prove, they ne'er can tell
When mistresses or masters use them well.'
Another misses Fanny, and then cries,
'What, Madam! sh' as told tales, I warrant lies,
About I don't know who nor what, whereby
Some darling fav'rite's nose is put awry;
So I suppose your ladyship intends,
By turning her away, to make amends.'
Another, hearing Fanny is turned off
(Some wretched, senseless, self-conceited calf),
Condoles her thus, in ribaldry and scoff:
'Sad slut! I ne'er expected better on her!
She always primmed, and took so much upon her,
Praised men of manners, sense, true love, forsooth, and honour!'
One (something smart and perter than the rest)
Cries, 'Fanny's only gone to make a jest.'
Others, whose wond'rous parts profoundly range
Through all the dark mysterious turns of change,
Thinking that they the secret cause have got,
Conclude poor Fanny has been in a plot:
Cry, 'Madam! faith, 'tis well she's gone, for who
But we could tell the ills she'd bring you to?'

One very gravely cries, 'Now I remember
I saw her plodding with a smart pretender;
And 'tis as certain as that same's a sin,
Her only bus'ness was to bring him in.'
Another swears, 'By ——, that's true', for he
Something like that did hear, did someone see;
And then, a third goes on, 'The case is plain,
The jade was bribed—for her sole idol's gain';
'Damn her,' another cries, 'to th' pit of hell!
A b——, a w——, I always said she'd sell
Her mistress, self and all, to him would pay her well.'
Thus all condemn, few pity, none excuse her;
Some seem surprised a little, most abuse her;
Tax her with faults, high crimes and misbehaviour,
All which poor Fanny will forswear by'r Saviour:
And so, to clear herself in time, I leave her.

(Wr. 1714; pub. 1742)

93

Epigram on the First of April

NATURE is rising from the dead,
Frost and Scythian snows are fled;
Boreas to his cavern creeps,
And, tired with winter-blust'ring, sleeps.
Soft zephyrs from the ocean move,
The birthplace of the Queen of Love,
And o'er the meadows, hills and dales
Play with their sweet reviving gales;
Chasing all discontent and care,
And ev'ry sadness, but despair.
Ah! Chloe, when, my charming fair?

(1732)

94

Miss Betty's Singing-Bird

A PRETTY song, this coming spring,
A little chanting bird will sing;
The bird you've heard old women say
Comes often down the chimney-way,
Then flies or hops the house around,
Where tricks and pranks are to be found;

92 plodding] plotting

The same which does all stories tell,
When little girls do ill or well;
When they're obstrep'rous or loquacious,
Contrump'rous, boist'rous or audacious;
With what is given 'em discontent,
Or say things of their own invent;
Fling off their caps and cloaks i' th' street,
Beat little children that they meet;
Call Aunt a sow or ugly witch,
Cic'ly a hussy, slut or b—h,
Scratch, bite and pinch, or pull her quoif,
And lead her a most dreadful life;
Saunter an hour or two to school;
And when they come there play the fool,
The ramping hoyden or Miss Bumkin,
The girls they sit by ever thumping;
Call masters bastard or such name,
And ev'ry little miss defame;
When Aunt can scarce on them prevail
To wear a gown not rattle-tail,
Yet never want a daggled tail;
When they have got a knack of crying,
Their stays a-lacing or hair tying;
Go oft to bed with weeping eyes,
Yet sigh and slobber when they rise;
When raisins, sugar-plums nor figs
Will bribe them not to pull off wigs;
For which, their bawling and their yelping,
They surely get full many a skelping,
Are locked in vault, or hole o' th' stairs,
To sigh, and fret, and melt in tears,
To bawl and roar, and not let out
Till many a tear is dropped about,
And after to their mistress sent
For further flogging punishment;
Which chastisements, if proving vain,
They never more must go again
To Lecoudre or Delamain,
But carried be, from city far,
To Jerrico or Mullingar.
    These, and perhaps a bolder thing,
    This little prating bird will sing
    Of naughty girls this coming spring.
But, if they're modest, mild and witty,
And do things innocent and pretty;
Observing always what they're bid,

Never deserving to be chid,
Discreet and good, they will be then
By ladies loved, admired by men;
Indulged in ev'ry harmless way,
And suffered now and then to play;
Have all the finest, nicest clothes,
Rich ribbons, laces, stockings, shoes,
Gold snuffbox, watch and diamond pendant,
And cross with jewels at the end on't;
Oft coach abroad, to take the air
At park and strand, when weather's fair;
Go now and then on holidays
To concerts, puppet-shows and plays;
Be always fine, most nicely dressed,
In what's most curious, rich and best.
  All these this pretty bird will sing;
  All these and more will surely bring
  To girls, if good, this coming spring.

(1742)

95 *To the Revd. Mr. —— on his Drinking Sea-Water*

Methinks, dear Tom, I see thee stand demure
Close by old Ocean's side, with arms erect,
Gulping the brine; and, with gigantic quaff,
Pledge the proud whale, and from ten thousand springs
Dilute the hyp, concomitant unkind!
  For thee th' Euphrates, from her spicy banks,
Conveys her healing stream; for thee the Caspian
Filters his balsam; while the fragrant Nile
Tinges with balmy dew the greeting seas,
Conscious of thee; whose tow'ring pyramids
Would pride to lodge thy consecrated urn.
  For thee the sage Batavian, from his stern,
With face distorted and convulsive grin,
Disgorges eastern gums, in bowels pent,
And streaks the surge with salutary hue.
  For thee the Thames, impregnated with steam
Mercurial, wafts her complicated dose
From reeking vaults, full copiously supplied
By bums venereal, ruefully discharged
By Ward's mysterious drop or magic pill.

(1751)

95 Batavian] Dutchman

MARY MONCK

1690?–1715

96 *Masque of the Virtues against Love. From Guarini*

WE the White Witches are, that free
Enchanted hearts from slavery;
Love's dark abodes all tremble at our voice,
And at the awful noise
All the blind archers scud along,
And frighted to their shady myrtles throng.
We cloud the sun that shines in Caelia's eyes,
Hush the winds swelled by lovers' sighs,
And stop their tides of tears even when they highest rise.
We, by our magic's guiltless power,
Hearts long since dead to a new life restore.

All Love's black arts and fatal wiles,
How he the heedless wretch beguiles,
How in false smiles the face is dressed,
And how false pity heaves the breast,
Circe's spells, the Sirens' lays,
How one transforms, the other slays,
We open show
To mortal view;
Come love-sick minds, see how the force of charms
The tyrant of his rage disarms.
Yours be the advantage all; for we
Claim naught but th' honour of the victory.

(1716)

97 *On a Romantic Lady*

THIS poring over your *Grand Cyrus*
Must ruin you and will quite tire us.
It makes you think that an affront 'tis,
Unless your lover's an Orontes,
And courts you with a passion frantic,
In manner and in style romantic.
Now though I count myself no zero,
I don't pretend to be an hero,
Or a by-blow of him that thunders,

Nor are you one of the Sev'n Wonders,
But a young damsel very pretty,
And your true name is Mistress Betty.

(1716)

HENRY CAREY

1687?–1743

98 *The Ballad of Sally in our Alley*

Of all the girls that are so smart
  There's none like pretty Sally;
She is the darling of my heart,
  And she lives in our alley.
There is no lady in the land
  Is half so sweet as Sally;
She is the darling of my heart,
  And she lives in our alley.

Her father he makes cabbage-nets,
  And through the streets does cry 'em;
Her mother she sells laces long
  To such as please to buy 'em;
But sure such folks could ne'er beget
  So sweet a girl as Sally!
She is the darling of my heart,
  And she lives in our alley.

When she is by I leave my work
  (I love her so sincerely);
My master comes like any Turk
  And bangs me most severely;
But let him bang his bellyfull,
  I'll bear it all for Sally;
She is the darling of my heart,
  And she lives in our alley.

Of all the days that's in the week
  I dearly love but one day,
And that's the day that comes betwixt
  A Saturday and Monday;
For then I'm dressed all in my best
  To walk abroad with Sally;
She is the darling of my heart,
  And she lives in our alley.

My master carries me to church,
  And often am I blamed
Because I leave him in the lurch
  As soon as text is named;
I leave the church in sermon time
  And slink away to Sally;
She is the darling of my heart,
  And she lives in our alley.

When Christmas comes about again,
  O then I shall have money;
I'll hoard it up, and box and all
  I'll give it to my honey;
And would it were ten thousand pounds,
  I'd give it all to Sally;
She is the darling of my heart,
  And she lives in our alley.

My master and the neighbours all
  Make game of me and Sally;
And, but for her, I'd better be
  A slave and row a galley;
But when my seven long years are out,
  O, then I'll marry Sally!
O then we'll wed, and then we'll bed,
  But not in our alley.

(1715?)

99 from *Namby-Pamby: or, A Panegyric on the New Versification*

Naughty-paughty Jack-a-Dandy,
Stole a piece of sugar candy
From the grocer's shoppy-shop,
And away did hoppy-hop.

ALL ye poets of the age,
All ye witlings of the stage,
Learn your jingles to reform,
Crop your numbers and conform.
Let your little verses flow
Gently, sweetly, row by row;
Let the verse the subject fit,
Little subject, little wit.
Namby-Pamby is your guide,
Albion's joy, Hibernia's pride.

Namby-Pamby Pilly-piss,
Rhimy pimed on Missy-Miss;
Tartaretta Tartaree,
From the navel to the knee;
That her father's gracy-grace
Might give him a placy-place.
He no longer writes of Mammy
Andromache and her lammy,
Hanging-panging at the breast
Of a matron most distressed.
Now the venal poet sings
Baby clouts and baby things,
Baby dolls and baby houses,
Little misses, little spouses,
Little playthings, little toys,
Little girls and little boys.
As an actor does his part,
So the nurses get by heart
Namby-Pamby's little rhymes,
Little jingle, little chimes,
To repeat to little miss,
Piddling ponds of pissy-piss;
Cacking-packing like a lady,
Or bye-bying in the crady.
Namby-Pamby ne'er will die
While the nurse sings lullaby.
Namby-Pamby's doubly mild,
Once a man, and twice a child;
To his hanging-sleeves restored,
Now he foots it like a lord;
Now he pumps his little wits,
Sh—ing writes, and writing sh—ts,
All by little tiny bits.
Now methinks I hear him say,
Boys and girls, come out to play!
Moon does shine as bright as day. . . .

(1725)

100 *A Lilliputian Ode on their Majesties' Accession*

SMILE, smile,
Blest isle!
Grief past,
At last,

Halcyon
Comes on.
New King,
Bells ring;
New Queen,
Blest scene!
Britain
Again
Revives
And thrives.
Fear flies,
Stocks rise;
Wealth flows,
Art grows.
Strange pack
Sent back;
Own folks
Crack jokes.
Those out
May pout;
Those in
Will grin.

Great, small,
Pleased all.

God send
No end
To line
Divine
Of George and Caroline!

(1727)

101 *Roger and Dolly*

YOUNG Roger came tapping at Dolly's window,
Tumpaty, tumpaty, tump.
He begged for admittance, she answered him, 'No',
Glumpaty, glumpaty, glump.
'My Dolly, my dear, your true love is here',
Dumpaty, dumpaty, dump.
'No, Roger, no, as you came you may go',
Clumpaty, clumpaty, clump.

'O what is the reason, dear Dolly,' he cried,
    Pumpaty, pumpaty, pump.
'That thus I'm cast off and unkindly denied?'
    Frumpaty, frumpaty, frump.
'Some rival more dear I guess has been here',
    Crumpaty, crumpaty, crump.
'Suppose there's been two; pray, sir, what's that to you?'
    Numpaty, numpaty, nump.

O then with a sigh a sad farewell he took,
    Lumpaty, lumpaty, lump.
And all in despair he leaped into the brook,
    Flumpaty, flumpaty, flump.
His courage it cooled, he found himself fooled,
    Trumpaty, trumpaty, trump.
He swam to the shore and saw Dolly no more,
    Rumpaty, rumpaty, rump.

And then she recalled and recalled him again,
    Humpaty, humpaty, hump.
But he like a madman ran over the plain,
    Stumpaty, stumpaty, stump.
Determined to find a damsel more kind,
    Plumpaty, plumpaty, plump.
While Dolly's afraid she shall die an old maid,
    Mumpaty, mumpaty, mump.

(1737)

CAPTAIN H——

fl. 1716

102 *An Imitation of Martial, Book II Ep. 105*

SWEET spouse, you must presently troop and be gone,
  Or fairly submit to your betters;
Unless for the faults that are past you atone,
  I must knock off my conjugal fetters.

When at night I am paying the tribute of love—
  You know well enough what's my meaning—
You scorn to assist my devotions, or move,
  As if all the while you were dreaming.

At cribbage and put and all-fours I have seen
A porter more passion expressing
Than thou, wicked Kate, in the rapturous scene,
And the height of the amorous blessing.

Then say I to myself, 'Is my wife made of stone,
Or does the old serpent possess her?'
Better motion and vigour by far might be shown
By dull spouse of a German professor.

So, Kate, take advice and reform in good time,
And while I'm performing my duty,
Come in for your club, and repent of the crime
Of paying all scores with your beauty.

All day thou may'st cant, and look grave as a nun,
And run after Burgess the surly;
Or see that the family business be done,
And chide all thy servants demurely.

But when you're in bed with your master and king,
That tales out of school ne'er does trumpet,
Move, wriggle, heave, pant, clip round like a ring:
In short, be as lewd as a strumpet.

(1716)

LADY MARY WORTLEY MONTAGU
1689–1762

103 from *Six Town Eclogues*

Saturday

The Small-Pox

FLAVIA

THE wretched Flavia, on her couch reclined,
Thus breathed the anguish of a wounded mind.
A glass reversed in her right hand she bore,
For now she shunned the face she sought before.

102 put and all-fours] card games

'How am I changed! alas! how am I grown
A frightful spectre, to myself unknown!
Where's my complexion? where the radiant bloom,
That promised happiness for years to come?
Then, with what pleasure I this face surveyed!
To look once more, my visits oft delayed!
Charmed with the view, a fresher red would rise,
And a new life shot sparkling from my eyes!
Ah! faithless glass, my wonted bloom restore!
Alas! I rave, that bloom is now no more!
'The greatest good the gods on men bestow,
Ev'n youth itself, to me is useless now.
There was a time (oh! that I could forget!)
When opera-tickets poured before my feet;
And at the Ring, where brightest beauties shine,
The earliest cherries of the spring were mine.
Witness, O Lillie, and thou, Motteux, tell,
How much japan these eyes have made you sell.
With what contempt ye saw me oft despise
The humble offer of the raffled prize;
For at each raffle still the prize I bore,
With scorn rejected, or with triumph wore.
Now beauty's fled, and presents are no more.
'For me the patriot has the House forsook,
And left debates to catch a passing look;
For me the soldier has soft verses writ;
For me the beau has aimed to be a wit.
For me the wit to nonsense was betrayed;
The gamester has for me his dun delayed,
And overseen the card I would have paid.
The bold and haughty by success made vain,
Awed by my eyes, has trembled to complain:
The bashful squire, touched with a wish unknown,
Has dared to speak with spirit not his own:
Fired by one wish, all did alike adore;
Now beauty's fled, and lovers are no more.
'As round the room I turn my weeping eyes,
New unaffected scenes of sorrow rise.
Far from my sight that killing picture bear,
The face disfigure, or the canvas tear!
That picture, which with pride I used to show,
The lost resemblance but upbraids me now.
And thou, my toilette, where I oft have sat,
While hours unheeded passed in deep debate,

japan] Japanese work with painted and varnished design overseen . . . paid] underwritten her next bet

How curls should fall, or where a patch to place;
If blue or scarlet best became my face;
Now on some happier nymph your aid bestow;
On fairer heads, ye useless jewels, glow!
No borrowed lustre can my charms restore,
Beauty is fled, and dress is now no more.
  'Ye meaner beauties, I permit you shine;
Go, triumph in the hearts that once were mine;
But, midst your triumphs with confusion know,
'Tis to my ruin all your charms ye owe.
Would pitying heav'n restore my wonted mien,
Ye still might move unthought of and unseen:
But oh, how vain, how wretched is the boast
Of beauty faded, and of empire lost!
What now is left but weeping to deplore
My beauty fled, and empire now no more?
  'Ye cruel chymists, what withheld your aid?
Could no pomatums save a trembling maid?
How false and trifling is that art you boast;
No art can give me back my beauty lost!
In tears, surrounded by my friends I lay,
Masked o'er, and trembling at the light of day;
Mirmillo came my fortune to deplore
(A golden-headed cane well carved he bore):
"Cordials", he cried, "my spirits must restore!
Beauty is fled, and spirit is no more!"
Galen the grave, officious Squirt was there,
With fruitless grief and unavailing care:
Machaon too, the great Machaon, known
By his red cloak and his superior frown;
"And why," he cried, "this grief and this despair?
You shall again be well, again be fair;
Believe my oath" (with that an oath he swore);
False was his oath! my beauty is no more.
  'Cease, hapless maid, no more thy tale pursue,
Forsake mankind, and bid the world adieu.
Monarchs and beauties rule with equal sway,
All strive to serve, and glory to obey:
Alike unpitied when deposed they grow,
Men mock the idol of their former vow.
  'Adieu, ye parks—in some obscure recess,
Where gentle streams will weep at my distress,
Where no false friend will in my grief take part,
And mourn my ruin with a joyful heart;
There let me live in some deserted place,
There hide in shades this lost inglorious face.

Plays, operas, circles, I no more must view!
My toilette, patches, all the world, adieu!'

(Wr. 1716; pub. 1747)

104 *A Receipt to Cure the Vapours*

WHY will Delia thus retire,
  And idly languish life away?
While the sighing crowd admire,
  'Tis too soon for hartshorn tea.

All those dismal looks and fretting
  Cannot Damon's life restore;
Long ago the worms have ate him,
  You can never see him more.

Once again consult your toilette,
  In the glass your face review:
So much weeping soon will spoil it,
  And no spring your charms renew.

I, like you, was born a woman,
  Well I know what vapours mean:
The disease, alas! is common;
  Single, we have all the spleen.

All the morals that they tell us
  Never cured the sorrow yet:
Choose, among the pretty fellows,
  One of honour, youth and wit.

Prithee hear him every morning,
  At the least an hour or two;
Once again at night returning—
  I believe the dose will do.

(Wr. 1730?; pub. 1748)

LEONARD WELSTED

1688–1747

105

The Invitation

FREEMAN, I treat tonight, and treat your friends:
If, happily, from care your thought unbends,
If Lucy rules not with her jealous sway,
I shall expect you at the close of day.
  I give you the rough wholesome grape, that grows
In Tuscan vales, or where the Tagus flows;
Or, if the Gallic vine delight you more,
Of Hermitage I boast a slender store.
This is my wealth: if you have better wine,
Make me your guest; if not, I claim you mine.
  Already is my little sideboard graced;
The glasses marshalled; the decanters placed:
The room is cool; the summer-hearth is gay
With greens and flowers, th' exub'rance of the May.
Indulge the bliss this cheerful season brings;
Omit minuter hopes, and joyless things;
Let fame and riches wait. This happy morn,
With Brunswick, peace and liberty were born!
'Tis fit, my friend, we consecrate to mirth
The day, which gave th' illustrious monarch birth:
When the sun sets, we'll break into delight,
And give to gay festivity the night.
  Of what avail is fortune unenjoyed?
Or what is life, in anxious hours employed?
Let the dull miser pine with niggard care,
And brood o'er gold, devoted to his heir:
While we in honest mirth send time away,
Regardless what severer sages say.
In cheerful minds unbidden joys arise,
And well-timed levities become the wise.
  What virtue does not generous wine impart?
It gives a winning frankness to the heart;
With sprightly hope the drooping spirits arms;
Awakens love, and brightens beauty's charms;
High, florid thoughts th' inspiring juices breed;
Spleen they dispel, and clear the brow of need.
  Expect superfluous splendour from the great:
Ragousts, and costly follies served in plate,
And ortolans, from distant regions brought.

In foreign arts of luxury untaught,
I give you only lamb from Uxbridge fields:
And add the choicest herb the garden yields;
Silesian lettuce, with soft Lucca oil,
Delicious blessings of a different soil!
None do our band of fellowship compose,
But know the chasteness of the banquet-rose.
Belmour is ours; Loveless, with humour stored;
And careless Florio, if he keeps his word.
I should exceed your rule, were more allowed:
There's less of mirth than tumult in a crowd.
Remember, time posts on with subtle haste:
Now, as I write, the numbered minutes waste.
Then, Freeman, let us seize the present hour,
And husband the swift moments in our pow'r.
Good-humour bring along, and banish care:
You know your friends; you know your bill of fare.

(1719)

ALEXANDER PENNECUIK

d. 1730

106 from *A Marriage Betwixt Scrape, Monarch of the Maunders, and Blobberlips, Queen of the Gypsies*

BELOW fair Peebles, on the river's side,
The merry beggars were busking a bride,
A gang of strollers acting their freaks,
Gabbling and dancing as merry as Greeks.
In a thicket of trees myself I hid,
Where I heard and saw what the beggars did.

No shelly-coat goblin, or elf on the green,
E'er tripped more nimbly than the beggars' Queen;
Blobberlips the bride did dance and play
(For this, it seems, was her wedding-day).
She was matched to old Scrape, the maunders' King
(This made all the rag-regiment sing),
Who gave her a curch as wide as a hood,
A silver brooch and a silken snood,

106 maunders] beggars busking] dressing shelly-coat] dressed in shells (of water-spirits) curch] head-covering

A pearled cross-cloth, a woven belt,
A large leathren swag to hold the gelt;
A pair of scissors to clip the plasters
To keep open the wounds which show their disasters;
Needles to sew the passports when torn,
An elchin to cobble the shoes when worn;
A string of beads, a bitch and a kent
(To help her through the bogs and the bent),
A blanket, a pair of new-soled hose,
A mill with snitian to pepper her nose.
'You're Queen of the covey,' says he, 'though in rags;
My fair fuss, you shall carry the bags;
All night you shall lie on pillows of flags.
I've trussed you a lady's shirt from the hedge
(Auld lousy duds gars ay folk fidge).
On pad of bulrushes your buttocks I'll lay,
There sleep and sing till the cock crow day.
Then beg on the way, and rob all we meet,
Steal from the hedge both the shirt and the sheet.
I'll pour on thy pail a pot of good ale,
Laughing like us at ev'ry mail;
On stol'n eggs and butter we'll dine,
My *bona roba*, in a cloven pine;
With ducklings i' th' season, bacon and pease,
Capons, turkeys and fat dabs of cheese;
I'll learn you to filch a duck or a hen,
Fill the swag with lour, for a bousing ken.

'*And a-begging we will go,*
And a-begging we will go;
With a pock for our oatmeal,
Another for our rye;
A little bottle by our side,
To drink when we are dry.
And a-begging we will go,' &c.

Blubberlips kissed him ten times and mair;
Cries, 'Blessings lie lurking in his tufts of hair;
Lang grows his beard, thick, forked and fair:
I'll kemb his beard, his whiskers I'll plait;
With feathers of ravens brush his bald pate.

gelt] money elchin] elsin, awl kent] long staff bent] rushes mill] snuffbox snitian] snuff fuss] strapping woman flags] water plants trussed] stowed away duds] clothes gars] makes fidge] fidget mail] discomfort *bona roba*] wench swag] bag lour] money bousing ken] alehouse *pock*] poke, bag

He'll lie on the pad with his dell till she twang,
Let the constable, justice and the d—l go hang.
When we roost in barns, old Chuck will teach us
To cut bien whids and be perfect in crutches,
To clap our fambles, throw up our nab-cheats,
To filch from the hedge both the shirts and the sheets.
The cowlies on the straw with the morties will be glad,
But ilk an must maund on his awn pad:
The doxies turn up their keels and spelder,
Wapping till a kinch twang in the kelder.

'The covey coming by
Will bumbumbis cry,
Hedgehog, toad, beetle,
Dick the jewels,
There they lie.'

(1720)

EDWARD LITTLETON

1698?–1734

107 *The Spider*

ARTIST, that underneath my table
Thy curious feature hast displayed,
Who, if we may believe the fable,
Wast once a lovely, blooming maid;

Insidious, restless, watchful spider,
Fear no officious damsel's broom;
Extend thine artful structure wider,
And spread thy banners round my room.

Wiped from the great man's costly ceiling,
Thou'rt welcome to my dusty roof;
There thou shall find a peaceful dwelling,
And undisturbed attend the woof,

106 pad] bed dell] wench cut bien whids] tell good lies fambles] hands nab-cheats] hats cowlies] cullies, men morties] women doxies] wenches spelder] spread wapping] copulating kinch] child kelder] womb

Whilst I the wond'rous fabric stare at,
And think on hapless poet's fate,
Like thee confined to lonely garret,
And rudely banished rooms of state.

And as from out thy tortured body
Thou draw'st the slender strings with pain,
So does he labour like a noddy
To spin materials from his brain;

He, for some flutt'ring, tawdry creature
That made a fluster in his eye,
And that's a conquest little better
Than thine o'er captive butterfly.

Thus far 'tis plain you both agree,
Your deaths perhaps may better show it;
'Tis ten to one but penury
Ends both the spider and the poet.

(1720)

ALLAN RAMSAY

1686–1758

108 *Polwart on the Green*

At Polwart on the Green
If you'll meet me the morn,
Where lasses do convene
To dance about the thorn;
A kindly welcome you shall meet
Frae her wha likes to view
A lover and a lad complete,
The lad and lover you.

Let dorty dames say na,
As lang as e'er they please,
Seem caulder than the sna',
While inwardly they bleeze;

108 dorty] proud   bleeze] blaze

But I will frankly shaw my mind,
And yield my heart to thee;
Be ever to the captive kind,
That langs na to be free.

At Polwart on the Green,
Among the new-mawn hay,
With sangs and dancing keen
We'll pass the heartsome day,
At night if beds be o'er thrang laid,
And thou be twin'd of thine,
Thou shalt be welcome, my dear lad,
To take a part of mine.

(1720)

109 *Up in the Air*

NOW the sun's gane out o' sight,
Beet the ingle and snuff the light:
In glens the fairies skip and dance,
And witches wallop o'er to France,
Up in the air
On my bonny grey mare.
And I see her yet, and I see her yet,
Up in, &c.

The wind's drifting hail and sna'
O'er frozen hags like a foot ba',
Nae starns keek throw the azure slit,
'Tis cauld and mirk as ony pit,
The man i' the moon
Is carowsing aboon,
D'ye see, d'ye see, d'ye see him yet?
The man, &c.

Take your glass to clear your een,
'Tis the elixir hales the spleen,
Baith wit and mirth it will inspire,
And gently puffs the lover's fire,

twin'd of] parted from

109 ingle] fire hags] peat pits starns] stars keek] peep mirk] dark een] eyes

Up in the air,
It drives away care,
Ha'e wi' ye, ha'e wi' ye, and ha'e wi' ye lads yet,
Up in, &c.

Steek the doors, keep out the frost,
Come, Willy, gi'es about ye'r tost,
Til't lads, and lilt it out,
And let us ha'e a blythsom bowt,
Up wi't there, there,
Dinna cheat, but drink fair,
Huzza, huzza, and huzza lads yet,
Up wi't, &c.

(1720)

110 *An Ode to Mr. F[orbes]*

NOW gowans sprout and lavrocks sing,
And welcome west winds warm the spring,
O'er hill and dale they saftly blaw,
And drive the winter's cauld awa.
The ships lang gyzened at the pier
Now spread their sails and smoothly steer.
The nags and nowt hate wissened strae,
And frisking to the fields they gae,
Nor hynds wi' elson and hemp lingle,
Sit soling shoon out o'er the ingle.
Now bonny haughs their verdure boast,
That late were clade wi' snaw and frost.
With her gay train the Paphian Queen
By moonlight dances on the green;
She leads while Nymphs and Graces sing,
And trip around the fairy ring.
Meantime poor Vulcan hard at thrift,
Gets mony a sair and heavy lift,
Whilst, rinnen down, his haff-blind lads
Blaw up the fire, and thump the gads.

Now leave your fitsted on the dew,
And busk ye'r sell in habit new.

steek] shut

110 gowans] daisies lavrocks] larks gyzened] dried out nowt] cows elson] awl lingle] thread haughs] valleys gads] bars of metal fitsted] footstep

Be gratefu' to the guiding powers,
And blythly spend your easy hours.
O kanny F——! tutor time,
And live as lang's ye'r in your prime;
That ill-bred Death has nae regard
To king or cottar, or a laird,
As soon a castle he'll attack,
As waus of divots roofed wi' thack.
Immediately we'll a' take flight
Unto the mirk realms of night,
As stories gang, with gaists to roam,
In gloumie Pluto's gousty dome;
Bid fair good-day to pleasure syne
Of bonny lasses and red wine.

Then deem ilk little care a crime,
Dares waste an hour of precious time;
And since our life's sae unko short,
Enjoy it a', ye've nae mair for't.

(1721)

111 *Lass with a Lump of Land*

Gi'e me a lass with a lump of land,
And we for life shall gang thegither;
Tho' daft or wise I'll never demand,
Or black or fair it maksna whether.
I'm aff with wit, and beauty will fade,
And blood alane is no worth a shilling;
But she that's rich, her market's made,
For ilka charm about her is killing.

Gi'e me a lass with a lump of land,
And in my bosom I'll hug my treasure;
Gin I had anes her gear in my hand,
Should love turn dowf, it will find pleasure.
Laugh on wha likes, but there's my hand,
I hate with poortith, though bonny, to meddle;
Unless they bring cash, or a lump of land,
They'se never get me to dance to their fiddle.

cottar] peasant gousty] desolate syne] then unko] extremely
111 dowf] dull poortith] poverty

There's meikle good love in bands and bags,
  And siller and gowd's a sweet complexion;
But beauty, and wit, and vertue in rags,
  Have tint the art of gaining affection.
Love tips his arrows with woods and parks,
  And castles, and riggs, and moors, and meadows;
And nathing can catch our modern sparks,
  But well tochered lasses, or jointured widows.

(1726)

THOMAS TICKELL

1685–1740

112 *To the Earl of Warwick*

On the Death of Mr. Addison

If, dumb too long, the drooping Muse hath stayed,
And left her debt to Addison unpaid,
Blame not her silence, Warwick, but bemoan,
And judge, oh judge, my bosom by your own.
What mourner ever felt poetic fires!
Slow comes the verse, that real woe inspires:
Grief unaffected suits but ill with art,
Or flowing numbers with a bleeding heart.
  Can I forget the dismal night, that gave
My soul's best part forever to the grave!
How silent did his old companions tread,
By midnight lamps, the mansions of the dead,
Through breathing statues, then unheeded things,
Through rows of warriors, and through walks of kings!
What awe did the slow solemn knell inspire;
The pealing organ, and the pausing choir;
The duties by the lawn-robed prelate paid;
And the last words, that dust to dust conveyed!
While speechless o'er thy closing grave we bend,
Accept these tears, thou dear departed friend;
Oh gone forever, take this long adieu,
And sleep in peace, next thy loved Montagu!
  To strew fresh laurels let the task be mine,
A frequent pilgrim, at thy sacred shrine;

111 tint] lost   riggs] ridges   tochered] dowried

Mine with true sighs thy absence to bemoan,
And grave with faithful epitaphs thy stone.
If e'er from me thy loved memorial part,
May shame afflict this alienated heart;
Of thee forgetful if I form a song,
My lyre be broken, and untuned my tongue,
My grief be doubled, from thy image free,
And mirth a torment, unchastised by thee.
  Oft let me range the gloomy aisles alone
(Sad luxury! to vulgar minds unknown),
Along the walls where speaking marbles show
What worthies form the hallowed mould below:
Proud names, who once the reins of empire held;
In arms who triumphed; or in arts excelled;
Chiefs, graced with scars, and prodigal of blood;
Stern patriots, who for sacred freedom stood;
Just men, by whom impartial laws were given;
And saints, who taught, and led, the way to heaven.
Ne'er to these chambers, where the mighty rest,
Since their foundation, came a nobler guest,
Nor e'er was to the bowers of bliss conveyed
A fairer spirit, or more welcome shade.
  In what new region, to the just assigned,
What new employments please th' unbodied mind?
A winged Virtue through th' ethereal sky,
From world to world unwearied does he fly?
Or curious trace the long laborious maze
Of heaven's decrees where wondering angels gaze?
Does he delight to hear bold seraphs tell
How Michael battled, and the Dragon fell?
Or, mixed with milder cherubim, to glow
In hymns of love, not ill essayed below?
Or dost thou warn poor mortals left behind,
A task well suited to thy gentle mind?
Oh, if sometimes thy spotless form descend,
To me thy aid, thou guardian genius, lend!
When rage misguides me, or when fear alarms,
When pain distresses, or when pleasure charms,
In silent whisperings purer thoughts impart,
And turn from ill a frail and feeble heart;
Lead through the paths thy virtue trod before,
Till bliss shall join, nor death can part us more.
  That awful form (which, so ye heavens decree,
Must still be loved and still deplored by me)
In nightly visions seldom fails to rise,
Or, roused by fancy, meets my waking eyes.

If business calls, or crowded courts invite,
Th' unblemished statesman seems to strike my sight;
If in the stage I seek to soothe my care,
I meet his soul, which breathes in Cato there;
If pensive to the rural shades I rove,
His shape o'ertakes me in the lonely grove:
'Twas there of just and good he reasoned strong,
Cleared some great truth, or raised some serious song;
There patient showed us the wise course to steer,
A candid censor, and a friend severe;
There taught us how to live; and (oh! too high
The price for knowledge) taught us how to die.
  Thou hill, whose brow the antique structures grace,
Reared by bold chiefs of Warwick's noble race,
Why, once so loved, whene'er thy bower appears,
O'er my dim eyeballs glance the sudden tears!
How sweet were once thy prospects fresh and fair,
Thy sloping walks, and unpolluted air!
How sweet the glooms beneath thy aged trees,
Thy noontide shadow, and thy evening breeze!
His image thy forsaken bowers restore;
Thy walks and airy prospects charm no more,
No more the summer in thy glooms allayed,
Thy ev'ning breezes, and thy noonday shade.
  From other ills, however fortune frowned,
Some refuge in the Muse's art I found:
Reluctant now I touch the trembling string,
Bereft of him, who taught me how to sing,
And these sad accents, murmured o'er his urn,
Betray that absence, they attempt to mourn.
Oh! must I then (now fresh my bosom bleeds,
And Craggs in death to Addison succeeds)
The verse, begun to one lost friend, prolong,
And weep a second in th' unfinished song!
  These works divine, which, on his deathbed laid,
To thee, O Craggs, th' expiring sage conveyed,
Great, but ill-omened monument of fame,
Nor he survived to give, nor thou to claim.
Swift after him thy social spirit flies,
And close to his, how soon! thy coffin lies.
Blest pair! whose union future bards shall tell
In future tongues: each other's boast! farewell.
Farewell! whom joined in fame, in friendship tried,
No chance could sever, nor the grave divide.

(1721)

SAMUEL CROXALL

1690?–1752

113

Sylvia

WERE I invited to a nectar feast
In heaven, and Venus named me for her guest;
Though Mercury the messenger should prove,
Or her own son, the mighty God of Love;
At the same instant let but honest Tom
From Sylvia's dear terrestrial lodging come,
With look important say—*desires—at three*
Alone—your company—to drink some tea:
Though Tom were mortal, Mercury divine,
Though Sylvia gave me water, Venus wine,
Though heaven was here, and Bow Street lay as far
As the vast distance of the utmost star;
To Sylvia's arms with all my strength I'd fly,
Let who would meet the beauty of the sky.

(1721)

CHARLES MORDAUNT, EARL OF PETERBOROUGH

1658–1735

114

'I Said to my Heart'

I SAID to my heart, between sleeping and waking,
'Thou wild thing, that always art leaping or aching
For the black, or the fair, in what clime, in what nation,
Hast thou not felt a fit of pitapat-ation?'

Thus accused, the wild thing gave this sober reply:
'See the heart without motion, though Celia pass by;
Not the beauty she has, nor the wit that she borrows,
Give the eyes any joy, or the heart any sorrows.

'When our Sappho appears, whose wit's so refined,
I'm forced to applaud with the rest of mankind:
Whatever she says is with spirit and fire;
Every word I attend—but I only admire.

'Prudentia, as vainly, does put in her claim,
Ever gazing on heaven, though man's her chief aim.
'Tis love, not devotion, that turns up her eyes:
Those stars of this world are not yet for the skies.

'But Chloe so lively, so easy, so fair,
Her wit so genteel, without art, without care;
When she comes in my way, the motion and pain,
The leapings and achings, return all again.

'Oh, wonderful creature! Oh, woman of reason!
Never grave out of pride, nor gay out of season:
When so easy to guess who this angel should be,
Would you think Mrs. Howard ne'er thought it was she?'

(1723)

DAVID MALLET
1705?–1765

115 *William and Margaret*

'Twas at the silent, solemn hour,
When night and morning meet;
In glided Margaret's grimly ghost,
And stood at William's feet.

Her face was like an April morn,
Clad in a wintry cloud:
And clay-cold was her lily hand,
That held her sable shroud.

So shall the fairest face appear,
When youth and years are flown:
Such is the robe that kings must wear,
When death has reft their crown.

Her bloom was like the springing flower,
That sips the silver dew;
The rose was budded in her cheek,
Just opening to the view.

But love had, like the canker-worm,
  Consumed her early prime:
The rose grew pale, and left her cheek;
  She died before her time.

'Awake!' she cried, 'thy true love calls,
  Come from her midnight grave;
Now let thy pity hear the maid
  Thy love refused to save.

'This is the dumb and dreary hour,
  When injured ghosts complain;
When yawning graves give up their dead
  To haunt the faithless swain.

'Bethink thee, William, of thy fault,
  Thy pledge, and broken oath:
And give me back my maiden vow,
  And give me back my troth.

'Why did you promise love to me,
  And not that promise keep?
Why did you swear my eyes were bright,
  Yet leave those eyes to weep?

'How could you say my face was fair,
  And yet that face forsake?
How could you win my virgin heart,
  Yet leave that heart to break?

'Why did you say my lip was sweet,
  And made the scarlet pale?
And why did I, young, witless maid,
  Believe the flattering tale?

'That face, alas! no more is fair;
  Those lips no longer red:
Dark are my eyes, now closed in death,
  And every charm is fled.

'The hungry worm my sister is;
  This winding-sheet I wear:
And cold and weary lasts our night,
  Till that last morn appear.

'But hark!—the cock has warned me hence;
  A long and late adieu!
Come, see, false man, how low she lies,
  Who died for love of you.'

The lark sung loud; the morning smiled,
  And raised her glistering head:
Pale William quaked in every limb,
  And raving left his bed.

He hied him to the fatal place
  Where Margaret's body lay:
And stretched him on the grass-green turf,
  That wrapped her breathless clay.

And thrice he called on Margaret's name,
  And thrice he wept full sore:
Then laid his cheek to her cold grave,
  And word spake never more.

(1723)

ELIZABETH TOLLET

1694–1754

116 from *Hypatia*

WHAT cruel laws depress the female kind,
To humble cares and servile tasks confined!
In gilded toys their florid bloom to spend,
And empty glories that in age must end;
For am'rous youth to spread the artful snares,
And by their triumphs to enlarge their cares.
For, once engaged in the domestic chain,
Compare the sorrows, and compute the gain;
What happiness can servitude afford?
A will resigned to an imperious lord,
Or slave to avarice, to beauty blind,
Or soured with spleen, or ranging unconfined.
That haughty man, unrivalled and alone,
May boast the world of science all his own:
As barb'rous tyrants, to secure their sway,
Conclude that ignorance will best obey.

Then boldly loud, and privileged to rail,
As prejudice o'er reason may prevail,
Unequal nature is accused to fail.
The theme, in keen iambics smoothly writ,
Which was but malice late, shall soon be wit.
  Nature in vain can womankind inspire
With brighter particles of active fire,
Which to their frame a due proportion hold,
Refined by dwelling in a purer mould,
If useless rust must fair endowments hide,
Or wit, disdaining ease, be misapplied.
'Tis then that wit, which reason should refine,
And disengage the metal from the mine,
Luxuriates, or degen'rates to design.
Wit unemployed becomes a dang'rous thing,
As waters stagnate and defile their spring.
The cultivated mind, a fertile soil,
With rich increase rewards the useful toil:
But fallow left, an hateful crop succeeds
Of tangling brambles and pernicious weeds;
'Tis endless labour then the ground to clear,
And trust the doubtful earnest of the year.
  Yet oft we hear, in height of stupid pride,
Some senseless idiot curse a lettered bride.

(1724)

117 *Winter Song*

ASK me no more, my truth to prove,
What I would suffer for my love.
With thee I would in exile go
To regions of eternal snow,
O'er floods by solid ice confined,
Through forest bare with northern wind:
While all around my eyes I cast,
Where all is wild and all is waste.
If there the tim'rous stag you chase,
Or rouse to fight a fiercer race,
Undaunted I thy arms would bear,
And give thy hand the hunter's spear.
When the low sun withdraws his light,
And menaces an half-year's night,
The conscious moon and stars above
Shall guide me with my wand'ring love.

Beneath the mountain's hollow brow,
Or in its rocky cells below,
Thy rural feast I would provide,
Nor envy palaces their pride.
The softest moss should dress thy bed,
With savage spoils about thee spread:
While faithful love the watch should keep,
To banish danger from thy sleep.

(1755)

HENRY BAKER

1698–1774

118

The Rapture

YOU gods! to fold the charmer in my arms,
And press her panting bosom close to mine!
Whilst with tumultuous ardour turning round,
With equal warmth my rapture she returns,
Owns all the bliss, and gives me sigh for sigh!
To drink large draughts of pleasure from her lips,
And in her eyes behold immortal day,
Is ecstasy so great! delight so vast!
That was it lasting, could but nature bear
The rage of such unsufferable joy,
Thus blest, I scarce one thought should cast away
On heav'n's eternal happiness, or you!

(1725)

119

Love

LOVE's an headstrong wild desire
To possess what we admire:
Hurrying on without reflecting,
All that's just or wise neglecting.
Pain or pleasure it is neither,
But excess of both together;
Now, addressing, cringing, whining,
Vowing, fretting, weeping, pining,
Murm'ring, languishing and sighing,
Mad, despairing, raving, dying:

Now, caressing, laughing, toying,
Fondling, kissing and enjoying.
Always in extremes abiding,
Without measure, fond or chiding:
Either furious with possessing,
Or despairing of the blessing:
Now transported; now tormented;
Still uneasy; ne'er contented.
None can tell its rise or progress,
Or its ingress or its egress,
Whether by a look produced,
Or by sympathy infused.
Fancy does so well maintain it,
Weaker reason can't restrain it,
But is forced to fly before it,
Or else worship and adore it.

(1725)

120 *The Declaimer*

WOMAN! thoughtless, giddy creature,
Laughing, idle, flutt'ring thing:
Most uncertain work of nature,
Still, like fancy, on the wing.

Slave to ev'ry changing passion,
Loving, hating, in extreme:
Fond of ev'ry foolish fashion,
And, at best, a pleasing dream.

Lovely-trifle! dear-illusion!
Conquering-weakness! wished-for-pain!
Man's chief glory and confusion,
Of all vanity most vain!

Thus, deriding beauty's power,
Bevil called it all a cheat;
But in less than half an hour
Kneeled and whined at Celia's feet.

(1726)

HETTY WRIGHT

1697–1751

121 *Wedlock. A Satire*

THOU tyrant, whom I will not name,
Whom heaven and hell alike disclaim;
Abhorred and shunned, for different ends,
By angels, Jesuits, beasts and fiends!
What terms to curse thee shall I find,
Thou plague peculiar to mankind?
O may my verse excel in spite
The wiliest, wittiest imps of night!
Then lend me for a while your rage,
You maidens old and matrons sage:
So may my terms in railing seem
As vile and hateful as my theme.
  Eternal foe to soft desires,
Inflamer of forbidden fires,
Thou source of discord, pain and care,
Thou sure forerunner of despair,
Thou scorpion with a double face,
Thou lawful plague of human race,
Thou bane of freedom, ease and mirth,
Thou deep damnation upon earth,
Thou serpent which the angels fly,
Thou monster whom the beasts defy,
Whom wily Jesuits sneer at too;
And Satan (let him have his due)
Was never so confirmed a dunce
To risk damnation more than once.
That wretch, if such a wretch there be,
Who hopes for happiness from thee,
May search successfully as well
For truth in whores and ease in hell.

(Wr. *c.*1725; pub. 1862)

122 *To an Infant Expiring the Second Day of its Birth*

TENDER softness, infant mild,
Perfect, purest, brightest child;
Transient lustre, beauteous clay,
Smiling wonder of a day:

Ere the last convulsive start
Rends the unresisting heart;
Ere the long-enduring swoon
Weighs thy precious eyelids down;
Oh! regard a mother's moan,
Anguish deeper than thy own!
Fairest eyes, whose dawning light
Late with rapture blessed my sight,
Ere your orbs extinguished be,
Bend their trembling beams on me.
Drooping sweetness, verdant flow'r,
Blooming, with'ring in an hour,
Ere thy gentle breast sustains
Latest, fiercest, vital pains,
Hear a suppliant! Let me be
Partner in thy destiny!

(Wr. 1728; pub. 1733)

JOHN DYER
1700–1758

123 *To Clio. From Rome*

ALAS, dear Clio, every day
Some sweet idea dies away:
Echoes of songs, and dreams of joys,
Inhuman absence all destroys.

Inhuman absence—and his train,
Avarice, and toil, and care, and pain,
And strife and trouble. Oh! for love,
Angelic Clio, these remove!

Nothing, alas, where'er I walk,
Nothing but fear and sorrow talk;
Where'er I walk, from bound to bound,
Nothing but ruin spreads around,

Or busts that seem from graves to rise,
Or statues stern with sightless eyes,
Cold Death's pale people. Oh! for love,
Angelic Clio, these remove!

The tuneful song, O speed away,
Say every sweet thing love can say,
Speed the bright beams of wit and sense,
Speed thy white doves, and draw me hence.

So may the carved, fair, speaking stone,
Persuasive half, and half moss-grown,
So may the column's graceful height,
O'er woods and temples gleaming bright,

And the wreathed urn among the vines,
Whose form my pencil now designs,
Be, with their ashes, lost in air,
No more the trifles of my care.

(Wr. 1724–5; pub. 1855)

124

Grongar Hill

SILENT Nymph, with curious eye!
Who, the purple ev'ning, lie
On the mountain's lonely van,
Beyond the noise of busy man,
Painting fair the form of things,
While the yellow linnet sings;
Or the tuneful nightingale
Charms the forest with her tale;
Come with all thy various hues,
Come, and aid thy sister Muse;
Now while Phoebus riding high
Gives lustre to the land and sky!
Grongar Hill invites my song,
Draw the landscape bright and strong;
Grongar, in whose mossy cells
Sweetly-musing Quiet dwells;
Grongar, in whose silent shade,
For the modest Muses made,
So oft I have, the evening still,
At the fountain of a rill,
Sat upon a flow'ry bed,
With my hand beneath my head;
While strayed my eyes o'er Towy's flood,
Over mead and over wood,
From house to house, from hill to hill,
Till Contemplation had her fill.

About his chequered sides I wind,
And leave his brooks and meads behind,
And groves and grottoes where I lay,
And vistoes shooting beams of day:
Wide and wider spreads the vale,
As circles on a smooth canal.
The mountains round, unhappy fate!
Sooner or later, of all height,
Withdraw their summits from the skies,
And lessen as the others rise:
Still the prospect wider spreads,
Adds a thousand woods and meads,
Still it widens, widens still,
And sinks the newly-risen hill.

Now I gain the mountain's brow,
What a landscape lies below!
No clouds, no vapours intervene,
But the gay, the open scene
Does the face of nature show,
In all the hues of heaven's bow!
And, swelling to embrace the light,
Spreads around beneath the sight.

Old castles on the cliffs arise,
Proudly tow'ring in the skies!
Rushing from the woods, the spires
Seem from hence ascending fires!
Half his beams Apollo sheds
On the yellow mountain-heads!
Gilds the fleeces of the flocks,
And glitters on the broken rocks!

Below me trees unnumbered rise,
Beautiful in various dyes:
The gloomy pine, the poplar blue,
The yellow beech, the sable yew,
The slender fir that taper grows,
The sturdy oak with broad-spread boughs.
And beyond the purple grove,
Haunt of Phillis, queen of love!
Gaudy as the op'ning dawn,
Lies a long and level lawn,
On which a dark hill, steep and high,
Holds and charms the wand'ring eye!
Deep are his feet in Towy's flood,
His sides are clothed with waving wood,
And ancient towers crown his brow,
That cast an awful look below;

Whose ragged walls the ivy creeps,
And with her arms from falling keeps;
So both a safety from the wind
On mutual dependence find.
'Tis now the raven's bleak abode;
'Tis now th' apartment of the toad;
And there the fox securely feeds;
And there the pois'nous adder breeds,
Concealed in ruins, moss and weeds;
While, ever and anon, there falls
Huge heaps of hoary mouldered walls.
Yet time has seen, that lifts the low,
And level lays the lofty brow,
Has seen this broken pile complete,
Big with the vanity of state;
But transient is the smile of fate!
A little rule, a little sway,
A sunbeam in a winter's day,
Is all the proud and mighty have
Between the cradle and the grave.
And see the rivers how they run,
Through woods and meads, in shade and sun;
Sometimes swift, sometimes slow,
Wave succeeding wave, they go
A various journey to the deep,
Like human life to endless sleep!
Thus is nature's vesture wrought
To instruct our wand'ring thought;
Thus she dresses green and gay,
To disperse our cares away.
Ever charming, ever new,
When will the landscape tire the view!
The fountain's fall, the river's flow,
The woody valleys, warm and low;
The windy summit, wild and high,
Roughly rushing on the sky!
The pleasant seat, the ruined tow'r,
The naked rock, the shady bow'r;
The town and village, dome and farm,
Each give each a double charm,
As pearls upon an Ethiop's arm.
See on the mountain's southern side,
Where the prospect opens wide,
Where the evening gilds the tide;
How close and small the hedges lie!
What streaks of meadows cross the eye!

A step methinks may pass the stream,
So little distant dangers seem;
So we mistake the future's face,
Eyed through hope's deluding glass;
As yon summits soft and fair,
Clad in colours of the air,
Which to those who journey near,
Barren, brown and rough appear;
Still we tread the same coarse way,
The present's still a cloudy day.
O may I with myself agree,
And never covet what I see:
Content me with an humble shade,
My passions tamed, my wishes laid;
For while our wishes wildly roll,
We banish quiet from the soul:
'Tis thus the busy beat the air,
And misers gather wealth and care.
Now, ev'n now, my joys run high,
As on the mountain-turf I lie;
While the wanton Zephyr sings,
And in the vale perfumes his wings;
While the waters murmur deep;
While the shepherd charms his sheep;
While the birds unbounded fly,
And with music fill the sky,
Now, ev'n now, my joys run high.
Be full, ye courts, be great who will;
Search for Peace with all your skill:
Open wide the lofty door,
Seek her on the marble floor,
In vain you search, she is not there;
In vain ye search the domes of care!
Grass and flowers Quiet treads,
On the meads and mountain-heads,
Along with Pleasure, close allied,
Ever by each other's side:
And often, by the murm'ring rill,
Hears the thrush, while all is still,
Within the groves of Grongar Hill.

(1726)

125 *My Ox Duke*

'TWAS on a summer noon, in Stainsford mead
New mown and tedded, while the weary swains,
Louting beneath an oak, their toils relieved;
And some with wanton tale the nymphs beguiled,
And some with song, and some with kisses rude;
Their scythes hung o'er their heads: when my brown ox,
Old labourer Duke, in awkward haste I saw
Run stumbling through the field to reach the shade
Of an old open barn, whose gloomy floor
The lash of sounding flails had long forgot.
In vain his eager haste: sudden old Duke
Stopped; a soft ridge of snow-white little pigs
Along the sacred threshold sleeping lay.
Burnt in the beam, and stung with swarming flies,
He stood tormented on the shadow's edge:
What should he do? What sweet forbearance held
His heavy foot from trampling on the weak,
To gain his wishes? Hither, hither all,
Ye vain, ye proud! see, humble heaven attends;
The fly-teased brute with gentle pity stays,
And shields the sleeping young. O gracious Lord!
Aid of the feeble, cheerer of distress,
In his low labyrinth each small reptile's guide!
God of unnumbered worlds! Almighty power!
Assuage our pride. Be meek, thou child of man:
Who gives thee life, gives every worm to live,
Thy kindred of the dust.—Long waiting stood
The good old labourer, in the burning beam,
And breathed upon them, nosed them, touched them soft,
With lovely fear to hurt their tender sides;
Again soft touched them; gently moved his head
From one to one; again, with touches soft,
He breathed them o'er, till gruntling waked and stared
The merry little young, their tails upcurled,
And gambolled off with scattered flight. Then sprung
The honest ox, rejoiced, into the shade.

(Wr. 1735?; pub. 1855)

louting] lolling

126 from *The Fleece*, Book III

[*The Happy Workhouse and the Good Effects of Industry*]

O WHEN, through ev'ry province, shall be raised
Houses of labour, seats of kind constraint,
For those who now delight in fruitless sports
More than in cheerful works of virtuous trade,
Which honest wealth would yield, and portion due
Of public welfare? Ho, ye poor, who seek,
Among the dwellings of the diligent,
For sustenance unearned; who stroll abroad
From house to house with mischievous intent,
Feigning misfortune: Ho, ye lame, ye blind;
Ye languid limbs, with real want oppressed,
Who tread the rough highways, and mountains wild,
Through storms, and rains, and bitterness of heart;
Ye children of affliction, be compelled
To happiness: the long-wished daylight dawns,
When charitable rigour shall detain
Your step-bruised feet. Ev'n now the sons of trade,
Where'er their cultivated hamlets smile,
Erect the mansion:[1] here soft fleeces shine;
The card awaits you, and the comb, and wheel;
Here shroud you from the thunder of the storm;
No rain shall wet your pillow: here abounds
Pure bev'rage; here your viands are prepared;
To heal each sickness the physician waits,
And priest entreats to give your Maker praise.
Behold, in Calder's[2] vale, where wide around
Unnumbered villas creep the shrubby hills,
A spacious dome for this fair purpose rise.
High o'er the open gates, with gracious air,
Eliza's image stands. By gentle steps
Up-raised, from room to room we slowly walk,
And view with wonder and with silent joy
The sprightly scene, where many a busy hand,
Where spools, cards, wheels and looms, with motion quick
And ever-murm'ring sound, th' unwonted sense
Wrap in surprise. To see them all employed,
All blithe, it gives the spreading heart delight,
As neither meats, nor drinks, nor aught of joy

[1] This alludes to the workhouses at Bristol, Birmingham, etc.
[2] A river in Yorkshire, which runs below Halifax, and passes by Wakefield.

Corporeal, can bestow. Nor less they gain
Virtue than wealth, while, on their useful works
From day to day intent, in their full minds
Evil no place can find. With equal scale
Some deal abroad the well-assorted fleece;
These card the short, those comb the longer flake;
Others the harsh and clotted lock receive,
Yet sever and refine with patient toil,
And bring to proper use. Flax too, and hemp,
Excite their diligence. The younger hands
Ply at the easy work of winding yarn
On swiftly-circling engines, and their notes
Warble together as a choir of larks:
Such joy arises in the mind employed.
Another scene displays the more robust,
Rasping or grinding rough Brazilian woods,
And what Campeachy's disputable shore
Copious affords to tinge the thirsty web;
And the Caribbee isles, whose dulcet canes
Equal the honeycomb. We next are shown
A circular machine[1] of new design,
In conic shape: it draws and spins a thread
Without the tedious toil of needless hands.
A wheel, invisible beneath the floor,
To ev'ry member of th' harmonious frame
Gives necessary motion. One, intent,
O'erlooks the work: the carded wool, he says,
Is smoothly lapped around those cylinders,
Which, gently turning, yield it to yon cirque
Of upright spindles which, with rapid whirl,
Spin out in long extent an even twine.
  From this delightful mansion (if we seek
Still more to view the gifts which honest toil
Distributes) take we now our eastward course,
To the rich fields of Burstal. Wide around
Hillock and valley, farm and village, smile:
And ruddy roofs and chimney-tops appear
Of busy Leeds, up-wafting to the clouds
The incense of thanksgiving: all is joy;
And trade and business guide the living scene,
Roll the full cars, adown the winding Aire
Load the slow-sailing barges, pile the pack
On the long tinkling train of slow-paced steeds.

[1] A most curious machine, invented by Mr. Paul. It is at present contrived to spin cotton; but it may be made to spin fine carded wool.

As when a sunny day invites abroad
The sedulous ants, they issue from their cells
In bands unnumbered, eager for their work;
O'er high, o'er low, they lift, they draw, they haste
With warm affection to each other's aid;
Repeat their virtuous efforts, and succeed.
Thus all is here in motion, all is life.
The creaking wain brings copious store of corn;
The grazier's sleeky kine obstruct the roads;
The neat-dressed housewives, for the festal board
Crowned with full baskets, in the field-way paths
Come tripping on; th' echoing hills repeat
The stroke of axe and hammer; scaffolds rise,
And growing edifices; heaps of stone,
Beneath the chisel, beauteous shapes assume
Of frieze and column. Some, with even line,
New streets are marking in the neighb'ring fields,
And sacred domes of worship. Industry,
Which dignifies the artist, lifts the swain,
And the straw cottage to a palace turns,
Over the work presides. Such was the scene
Of hurrying Carthage, when the Trojan chief
First viewed her growing turrets. So appear
Th' increasing walls of busy Manchester,
Sheffield, and Birmingham, whose redd'ning fields
Rise and enlarge their suburbs. Lo, in throngs,
For ev'ry realm, the careful factors meet,
Whisp'ring each other. In long ranks the bales,
Like war's bright files, beyond the sight extend.
Straight, ere the sounding bell the signal strikes,
Which ends the hour of traffic, they conclude
The speedy compact; and well-pleased transfer,
With mutual benefit, superior wealth
To many a kingdom's rent or tyrant's hoard.

(1757)

GEORGE BERKELEY

1685–1753

127 *On the Prospect of Planting Arts and Learning in America*

THE Muse, disgusted at an age and clime
  Barren of every glorious theme,
In distant lands now waits a better time,
  Producing subjects worthy fame;

In happy climes, where from the genial sun
  And virgin earth such scenes ensue,
The force of art by nature seems outdone,
  And fancied beauties by the true;

In happy climes, the seat of innocence,
  Where nature guides and virtue rules,
Where men shall not impose, for truth and sense,
  The pedantry of courts and schools:

There shall be sung another golden age,
  The rise of empire and of arts,
The good and great inspiring epic rage,
  The wisest heads and noblest hearts.

Not such as Europe breeds in her decay;
  Such as she bred when fresh and young,
When heavenly flame did animate her clay,
  By future poets shall be sung.

Westward the course of empire takes its way;
  The first four acts already past,
A fifth shall close the drama with the day:
  Time's noblest offspring is the last.

(Wr. 1726; pub. 1752)

JONATHAN RICHARDSON

1667?–1745

128 *On My Late Dear Wife*

(i)

ADIEU, dear life! here am I left alone;
The world is strangely changed since thou art gone.
Compose thyself to rest, all will be well;
I'll come to bed 'as fast as possible'.

Jan. 18, 1726

(ii)

Slumb'ring disturbed, appeared the well-known face,
Lovely, engaging, as she ever was;
I kissed and caught the phantom in my arms,
I knew it such, but such a shade hath charms!
Devout, I thanked kind heaven that, with a wife,
Had brightened up my choicest years of life;
But now, alas! 'tis thus!—She sighed—Poor heart!
A melancholy phantom as thou art,
From thee more happiness I thus receive
Than all the living woman-kind can give.
    This as I was about to say,
    But scrupling, is my heart yet free?
    It is, as on our wedding day,
    For she was all the sex to me.
I waked, and found it was a shade indeed.
She and her future sighs, or smiles, were fled;
I now am sighing in my widowed bed.

Really dreamed, July 14–15, 1726

(iii)

I know not where, but gloomy was the place,
Methought I saw a gloomy phantom pass;
'Twas she, the much-loved form! nor spoke, nor stayed,
No motion of her eyes, or hand, or head,
But, gliding on, I lost her in the shade.
All solemn was, no argument of love
Appeared her inward sentiment to prove;

Confused and grieved, I stood; then spoke my heart:
Who could have thought such lovers thus would part!

Dreamed, Sept. 10–11
Written, Sept. 16, 1726

(iv)

On My Dreaming of My Wife

As waked from sleep, methought I heard the voice
Of one that mourned; I listened to the noise.
I looked, and quickly found it was my dear;
Dead as she was, I little thought her there.
I questioned her with tenderness, while she
Sighed only, but would else still silent be.
I waked indeed; the lovely mourner's gone,
She sighs no more, 'tis I that sigh alone.

Musing on her, I slept again, but where
I went I know not, but I found her there.
Her lovely eyes she kindly fixed on me,
'Let Miser not be nangry then,' said she,
A language love had taught, and love alone
Could teach; we prattled as we oft had done,
But she, I know not how, was quickly gone.

With her imaginary presence blessed,
My slumbers are emphatically rest;
I of my waking thoughts can little boast,
They always sadly tell me she is lost.
Much of our happiness we always owe
To error, better to believe than know!
Return, delusion sweet, and oft return!
I joy, mistaken; undeceived, I mourn;
But all my sighs and griefs are fully paid,
When I but see the shadow of her shade.

July 15, 1728

(Pub. 1776)

129 *Self-Consciousness Makes All Changes Happy. Ode*

'TIS not the gaudy stream of rosy flame
Decking the azure of the lofty sky,
Nor all the beauties, early autumn's claim,
Nor what the taste delights, or what the eye:

No such are now. Clouds rolling on the wind,
  Darkness and wet, above and on the ground;
And yet 'tis spring, 'tis summer, in my mind,
  Within, the warbling nightingale is found.

Philosophy divine, sweet innocence,
  Self-approbation, nobly built, secure,
More than the stars' benignant influence
  Delight; and, when those perish, will endure.

When empires tremble and the mountains nod,
  When ocean's usurpation tops the air,
When conflagration ruins worlds, their God
  Regards the heart sincere, sits smiling there.

Aug. 30, 1735

(Pub. 1776)

SAMUEL WESLEY
1691–1739

130 *On the Setting up Mr. Butler's Monument in Westminster Abbey*

WHILE Butler, needy wretch! was yet alive,
No gen'rous patron would a dinner give:
See him, when starved to death and turned to dust,
Presented with a monumental bust!
The poet's fate is here in emblem shown:
He asked for bread, and he received a stone.

(1726)

131 *An Epitaph*

HERE lie I, once a witty fair,
  Ill-loving and ill-loved;
Whose heedless beauty was my snare,
  Whose wit my folly proved.

Reader, should any curious stay
  To ask my luckless name,
Tell them the grave that hides my clay
  Conceals me from my shame.

Tell them I mourned for guilt of sin
More than for pleasure spent:
Tell them, whate'er my morn had been,
My noon was penitent.

(1736)

132 *Anacreontic, On Parting with a little Child*

DEAR, farewell, a little while,
Easy parting with a smile;
Ev'ry object in thy way
Makes thee innocently gay;
All that thou can'st hear or see,
All is novelty to thee.
Thoughts of parents left behind
Vex not yet thine infant mind;
Why should then their hearts repine,
Mournful theirs, and merry thine?
'Tis the world, the seeming wise
Toil to make their children rise;
While the heir that reaps their gains
Thankless thinks not of their pains.
Sportive youth in haste to live
Heeds not ills that years may give:
Age in woe and wisdom grey
Vainly mourns for them that play.

(1736)

JAMES THOMSON

1700–1748

133 *Winter*

SEE! Winter comes to rule the varied year,
Sullen and sad, with all his varied train,
Vapours, and clouds, and storms: be these my theme,
These, that exalt the soul to solemn thought,
And heavenly musing. Welcome, kindred glooms!
Wished, wintry horrors, hail! With frequent foot,
Pleased have I, in my cheerful morn of life,

When nursed by careless Solitude I lived,
And sung of nature with unceasing joy,
Pleased have I wandered through your rough domains;
Trod the pure, virgin snows, myself as pure,
Heard the winds roar, and the big torrent burst,
Or seen the deep, fermenting tempest brewed
In the red evening sky. Thus passed the time,
Till, through the opening chambers of the south,
Looked out the joyous Spring, looked out and smiled.
  Thee too, inspirer of the toiling swain!
Fair Autumn, yellow-robed! I'll sing of thee,
Of thy last, tempered days and sunny calms;
When all the golden Hours are on the wing,
Attending thy retreat and round thy wain,
Slow-rolling onward to the southern sky.
  Behold! the well-poised hornet hovering hangs,
With quivering pinions, in the genial blaze;
Flies off in airy circles, then returns,
And hums and dances to the beating ray:
Nor shall the man that musing walks alone,
And heedless strays within his radiant lists,
Go unchastised away. Sometimes a fleece
Of clouds, wide-scattering, with a lucid veil
Soft shadow o'er th' unruffled face of heaven;
And, through their dewy sluices, shed the sun
With tempered influence down. Then is the time
For those, whom Wisdom and whom Nature charm,
To steal themselves from the degenerate crowd,
And soar above this little scene of things:
To tread low-thoughted Vice beneath their feet,
To lay their passions in a gentle calm,
And woo lone Quiet in her silent walks.
  Now solitary, and in pensive guise,
Oft let me wander o'er the russet mead,
Or through the pining grove, where scarce is heard
One dying strain to cheer the woodman's toil:
Sad Philomel, perchance, pours forth her plaint
Far through the withering copse. Meanwhile, the leaves,
That late the forest clad with lively green,
Nipped by the drizzly night, and sallow-hued,
Fall, wavering, through the air; or shower amain,
Urged by the breeze that sobs amid the boughs.
Then list'ning hares forsake the rustling woods,
And, starting at the frequent noise, escape
To the rough stubble and the rushy fen.
Then woodcocks o'er the fluctuating main,

That glimmers to the glimpses of the moon,
Stretch their long voyage to the woodland glade,
Where, wheeling with uncertain flight, they mock
The nimble fowler's aim. Now Nature droops;
Languish the living herbs with pale decay,
And all the various family of flowers
Their sunny robes resign. The falling fruits,
Through the still night, forsake the parent-bough,
That, in the first grey glances of the dawn,
Looks wild, and wonders at the wintry waste.
  The year, yet pleasing but declining fast,
Soft o'er the secret soul, in gentle gales,
A philosophic melancholy breathes,
And bears the swelling thought aloft to heaven.
Then forming fancy rouses to conceive
What never mingled with the vulgar's dream:
Then wake the tender pang, the pitying tear,
The sigh for suffering worth, the wish preferred
For humankind, the joy to see them blessed,
And all the social offspring of the heart!
  Oh! bear me then to high, embowering shades,
To twilight groves, and visionary vales,
To weeping grottoes and to hoary caves;
Where angel-forms are seen, and voices heard,
Sighed in low whispers, that abstract the soul
From outward sense, far into worlds remote.
  Now, when the western sun withdraws the day,
And humid Evening, gliding o'er the sky,
In her chill progress checks the straggling beams,
And robs them of their gathered, vapoury prey,
Where marshes stagnate and where rivers wind,
Cluster the rolling fogs, and swim along
The dusky-mantled lawn: then slow descend,
Once more to mingle with their watry friends.
The vivid stars shine out in radiant files,
And boundless ether glows; till the fair moon
Shows her broad visage in the crimsoned east;
Now, stooping, seems to kiss the passing cloud,
Now o'er the pure cerulean rides sublime.
Wide the pale deluge floats with silver waves,
O'er the skied mountain to the low-laid vale;
From the white rocks, with dim reflection, gleams,
And faintly glitters through the waving shades.
  All night, abundant dews unnoted fall,
And, at return of morning, silver o'er
The face of mother-earth; from every branch

Depending, tremble the translucent gems,
And, quivering, seem to fall away, yet cling,
And sparkle in the sun, whose rising eye,
With fogs bedimmed, portends a beauteous day.
  Now giddy youth, whom headlong passions fire,
Rouse the wild game, and stain the guiltless grove
With violence and death; yet call it sport
To scatter ruin through the realms of Love,
And Peace, that thinks no ill: but these the Muse,
Whose charity unlimited extends
As wide as Nature works, disdains to sing,
Returning to her nobler theme in view.
  For see! where Winter comes, himself confessed,
Striding the gloomy blast. First rains obscure
Drive through the mingling skies with tempest foul;
Beat on the mountain's brow, and shake the woods
That, sounding, wave below. The dreary plain
Lies overwhelmed and lost. The bellying clouds
Combine and, deepening into night, shut up
The day's fair face. The wanderers of heaven,
Each to his home, retire; save those that love
To take their pastime in the troubled air,
And, skimming, flutter round the dimply flood.
The cattle from th' untasted fields return,
And ask, with meaning low, their wonted stalls,
Or ruminate in the contiguous shade:
Thither the household, feathery people crowd,
The crested cock with all his female train,
Pensive and wet. Meanwhile, the cottage-swain
Hangs o'er th' enlivening blaze and, taleful, there
Recounts his simple frolic: much he talks
And much he laughs, nor recks the storm that blows
Without, and rattles on his humble roof.
  At last the muddy deluge pours along,
Resistless, roaring; dreadful down it comes
From the chapped mountain and the mossy wild,
Tumbling through rocks abrupt, and sounding far:
Then o'er the sanded valley, floating, spreads,
Calm, sluggish, silent; till again constrained
Betwixt two meeting hills, it bursts a way,
Where rocks and woods o'erhang the turbid stream.
There gathering triple force, rapid and deep,
It boils, and wheels, and foams, and thunders through.
  Nature! great parent! whose directing hand
Rolls round the seasons of the changeful year,
How mighty, how majestic are thy works!

With what a pleasing dread they swell the soul,
That sees, astonished! and astonished sings!
You too, ye winds! that now begin to blow
With boisterous sweep, I raise my voice to you.
Where are your stores, ye viewless beings! say,
Where your aerial magazines reserved,
Against the day of tempest perilous?
In what untravelled country of the air,
Hushed in still silence, sleep you when 'tis calm?
  Late, in the louring sky, red, fiery streaks
Begin to flush about; the reeling clouds
Stagger with dizzy aim, as doubting yet
Which master to obey; while rising slow,
Sad, in the leaden-coloured east, the moon
Wears a bleak circle round her sullied orb.
Then issues forth the storm with loud control,
And the thin fabric of the pillared air
O'erturns at once. Prone on th' uncertain main
Descends th' ethereal force, and ploughs its waves
With dreadful rift: from the mid-deep appears,
Surge after surge, the rising, watry war.
Whitening, the angry billows roll immense,
And roar their terrors through the shuddering soul
Of feeble man, amidst their fury caught,
And dashed upon his fate. Then, o'er the cliff
Where dwells the sea-mew, unconfined they fly,
And, hurrying, swallow up the sterile shore.
  The mountain growls, and all its sturdy sons
Stoop to the bottom of the rocks they shade:
Lone on its midnight-side, and all aghast,
The dark, wayfaring stranger, breathless, toils,
And climbs against the blast—
Low waves the rooted forest, vexed, and sheds
What of its leafy honours yet remains.
Thus, struggling through the dissipated grove,
The whirling tempest raves along the plain;
And, on the cottage thatched or lordly dome
Keen-fastening, shakes 'em to the solid base.
Sleep, frighted, flies; the hollow chimney howls,
The windows rattle, and the hinges creak.
  Then too, they say, through all the burthened air
Long groans are heard, shrill sounds and distant sighs,
That, murmured by the demon of the night,
Warn the devoted wretch of woe and death!
Wild uproar lords it wide: the clouds commixed
With stars, swift-gliding, sweep along the sky.

All nature reels. But hark! the Almighty speaks:
Instant the chidden storm begins to pant,
And dies at once into a noiseless calm.
  As yet 'tis midnight's reign; the weary clouds,
Slow-meeting, mingle into solid gloom.
Now, while the drowsy world lies lost in sleep,
Let me associate with the low-browed Night,
And Contemplation, her sedate compeer;
Let me shake off th' intrusive cares of day,
And lay the meddling senses all aside.
  And now, ye lying Vanities of life!
You ever-tempting, ever-cheating train!
Where are you now? and what is your amount?
Vexation, disappointment and remorse.
Sad, sickening thought! and yet deluded man,
A scene of wild, disjointed visions past,
And broken slumbers, rises still resolved,
With new-flushed hopes, to run your giddy round.
  Father of light and life! Thou Good Supreme,
O! teach me what is good! teach me thyself!
Save me from folly, vanity and vice,
From every low pursuit! and feed my soul
With knowledge, conscious peace and virtue pure,
Sacred, substantial, never-fading bliss!
  Lo! from the livid east or piercing north,
Thick clouds ascend, in whose capacious womb
A vapoury deluge lies, to snow congealed:
Heavy, they roll their fleecy world along,
And the sky saddens with th' impending storm.
Through the hushed air the whitening shower descends,
At first thin-wavering; till at last the flakes
Fall broad and wide and fast, dimming the day
With a continual flow. See! sudden hoared,
The woods beneath the stainless burden bow;
Black'ning, along the mazy stream it melts.
Earth's universal face, deep-hid and chill,
Is all one dazzling waste. The labourer-ox
Stands covered o'er with snow, and then demands
The fruit of all his toil. The fowls of heaven,
Tamed by the cruel season, crowd around
The winnowing store, and claim the little boon
That Providence allows. The foodless wilds
Pour forth their brown inhabitants; the hare,
Though timorous of heart, and hard beset
By death in various forms, dark snares, and dogs,
And more unpitying men, the garden seeks,

Urged on by fearless want. The bleating kind
Eye the bleak heavens, and next the glistening earth,
With looks of dumb despair; then sad, dispersed,
Dig for the withered herb through heaps of snow.
  Now, shepherds, to your helpless charge be kind;
Baffle the raging year, and fill their pens
With food at will; lodge them below the blast,
And watch them strict: for from the bellowing east,
In this dire season, oft the whirlwind's wing
Sweeps up the burthen of whole wintry plains
In one fierce blast, and o'er th' unhappy flocks,
Lodged in the hollow of two neighbouring hills,
The billowy tempest whelms; till, upwards urged,
The valley to a shining mountain swells,
That curls its wreaths amid the freezing sky.
  Now, amid all the rigours of the year,
In the wild depth of winter, while without
The ceaseless winds blow keen, be my retreat
A rural, sheltered, solitary scene,
Where ruddy fire and beaming tapers join
To chase the cheerless gloom: there let me sit,
And hold high converse with the mighty dead,
Sages of ancient times, as gods revered,
As gods beneficent, who blessed mankind
With arts and arms, and humanised a world.
Roused at th' inspiring thought, I throw aside
The long-lived volume and, deep-musing, hail
The sacred shades that, slowly-rising, pass
Before my wondering eyes. First, Socrates,
Truth's early champion, martyr for his god;
Solon the next, who built his commonweal
On equity's firm base; Lycurgus then,
Severely good; and him of rugged Rome,
Numa, who softened her rapacious sons;
Cimon sweet-souled, and Aristides just;
Unconquered Cato, virtuous in extreme;
With that attempered hero,[1] mild and firm,
Who wept the brother, while the tyrant bled;
Scipio, the humane warrior, gently brave,
Fair learning's friend, who early sought the shade,
To dwell with Innocence and Truth retired;
And, equal to the best, the Theban, he
Who, single, raised his country into fame.
Thousands behind, the boast of Greece and Rome,

[1] *Timoleon.*

Whom Virtue owns, the tribute of a verse
Demand, but who can count the stars of heaven?
Who sing their influence on this lower world?
But see who yonder comes! nor comes alone,
With sober state and of majestic mien,
The Sister-Muses in his train. 'Tis he!
Maro! the best of poets and of men!
Great Homer too appears, of daring wing!
Parent of song! and, equal, by his side,
The British Muse; joined hand in hand they walk,
Darkling, nor miss their way to fame's ascent.
  Society divine! Immortal minds!
Still visit thus my nights, for you reserved,
And mount my soaring soul to deeds like yours.
Silence! thou lonely power! the door be thine:
See on the hallowed hour that none intrude,
Save Lycidas, the friend with sense refined,
Learning digested well, exalted faith,
Unstudied wit, and humour ever gay.
  Clear frost succeeds and, through the blue serene,
For sight too fine, th' ethereal nitre flies,
To bake the glebe and bind the slipp'ry flood.
This of the wintry season is the prime;
Pure are the days, and lustrous are the nights,
Brightened with starry worlds till then unseen.
Meanwhile the orient, darkly red, breathes forth
An icy gale that, in its mid-career,
Arrests the bickering stream. The nightly sky,
And all her glowing constellations, pour
Their rigid influence down. It freezes on
Till morn, late-rising, o'er the drooping world
Lifts her pale eye, unjoyous: then appears
The various labour of the silent night,
The pendant icicle, the frost-work fair
Where thousand figures rise, the crusted snow,
Though white, made whiter by the fining north.
On blithesome frolics bent, the youthful swains,
While every work of man is laid at rest,
Rush o'er the watry plains and, shuddering, view
The fearful deeps below; or with the gun
And faithful spaniel range the ravaged fields,
And, adding to the ruins of the year,
Distress the feathery or the footed game.
  But hark! the nightly winds, with hollow voice,
Blow blustering from the south. The frost subdued
Gradual resolves into a weeping thaw.

Spotted, the mountains shine; loose sleet descends,
And floods the country round; the rivers swell,
Impatient for the day. Those sullen seas,
That wash th' ungenial pole, will rest no more
Beneath the shackles of the mighty north,
But, rousing all their waves, resistless heave.
And hark! the length'ning roar continuous runs
Athwart the rifted main; at once it bursts,
And piles a thousand mountains to the clouds!
Ill fares the bark, the wretches' last resort,
That, lost amid the floating fragments, moors
Beneath the shelter of an icy isle,
While night o'erwhelms the sea, and horror looks
More horrible. Can human hearts endure
Th' assembled mischiefs that besiege them round:
Unlist'ning hunger, fainting weariness,
The roar of winds and waves, the crush of ice,
Now ceasing, now renewed with louder rage,
And bellowing round the main? Nations remote,
Shook from their midnight-slumbers, deem they hear
Portentous thunder in the troubled sky.
More to embroil the deep, leviathan
And his unwieldy train, in horrid sport,
Tempest the loosened brine; while through the gloom,
Far from the dire, unhospitable shore,
The lion's rage, the wolf's sad howl is heard,
And all the fell society of night.
Yet Providence, that ever-waking eye,
Looks down with pity on the fruitless toil
Of mortals lost to hope, and lights them safe
Through all this dreary labyrinth of fate.
   'Tis done! Dread Winter has subdued the year,
And reigns tremendous o'er the desert plains!
How dead the vegetable kingdom lies!
How dumb the tuneful! Horror wide extends
His solitary empire. Now, fond Man!
Behold thy pictured life: pass some few years,
Thy flow'ring Spring, thy shortlived Summer's strength,
Thy sober Autumn fading into age,
And pale, concluding Winter shuts thy scene,
And shrouds thee in the grave. Where now are fled
Those dreams of greatness? those unsolid hopes
Of happiness? those longings after fame?
Those restless cares? those busy, bustling days?
Those nights of secret guilt? those veering thoughts,
Flutt'ring 'twixt good and ill, that shared thy life?

All now are vanished! Virtue sole survives,
Immortal, mankind's never-failing friend,
His guide to happiness on high. And see!
'Tis come, the glorious Morn! the second birth
Of heaven and earth! awakening Nature hears
Th' almighty trumpet's voice, and starts to life,
Renewed, unfading. Now th' eternal Scheme,
That dark perplexity, that mystic maze,
Which sight could never trace, nor heart conceive,
To Reason's eye refined, clears up apace.
Angels and men, astonished, pause—and dread
To travel through the depths of Providence,
Untried, unbounded. Ye vain learned! see,
And, prostrate in the dust, adore that Power
And Goodness, oft arraigned. See now the cause,
Why conscious worth, oppressed, in secret long
Mourned, unregarded; why the good man's share
In life was gall and bitterness of soul;
Why the lone widow and her orphans pined,
In starving solitude; while Luxury,
In palaces, lay prompting her low thought
To form unreal wants; why heaven-born Faith
And Charity, prime grace! wore the red marks
Of Persecution's scourge; why licensed Pain,
That cruel spoiler, that embosomed foe,
Imbittered all our bliss. Ye good distressed!
Ye noble few! that here unbending stand
Beneath life's pressures, yet a little while,
And all your woes are past. Time swiftly fleets,
And wished Eternity, approaching, brings
Life undecaying, love without allay,
Pure, flowing joy, and happiness sincere.

(1726)

134 from *To the Memory of Sir Isaac Newton*

ALL intellectual eye, our solar round
First gazing through, he, by the blended power
Of gravitation and projection, saw
The whole in silent harmony revolve.
From unassisted vision hid, the moons,
To cheer remoter planets numerous poured,
By him in all their mingled tracts were seen.
He also fixed the wandering Queen of Night,

Whether she wanes into a scanty orb,
Or, waxing broad, with her pale shadowy light,
In a soft deluge overflows the sky.
Her every motion clear-discerning, he
Adjusted to the mutual main, and taught
Why now the mighty mass of waters swells
Resistless, heaving on the broken rocks,
And the full river turning; till again
The tide revertive, unattracted, leaves
A yellow waste of idle sands behind.
  Then breaking hence, he took his ardent flight
Through the blue infinite; and every star,
Which the clear concave of a winter's night
Pours on the eye, or astronomic tube,
Far-stretching, snatches from the dark abyss,
Or such as farther in successive skies
To fancy shine alone, at his approach
Blazed into suns, the living centre each
Of an harmonious system: all combined,
And ruled unerring by that single power
Which draws the stone projected to the ground.
  O unprofuse magnificence divine!
O wisdom truly perfect! thus to call
From a few causes such a scheme of things,
Effects so various, beautiful and great,
An universe complete! And O beloved
Of heaven! whose well-purged penetrative eye,
The mystic veil transpiercing, inly scanned
The rising, moving, wide-established frame.
  He, first of men, with awful wing pursued
The comet through the long elliptic curve,
As round innumerous worlds he wound his way,
Till, to the forehead of our evening sky
Returned, the blazing wonder glares anew,
And o'er the trembling nations shakes dismay.
  The heavens are all his own, from the wild rule
Of whirling vortices and circling spheres
To their first great simplicity restored.
The schools astonished stood; but found it vain
To keep at odds with demonstration strong,
And, unawakened, dream beneath the blaze
Of truth. At once their pleasing visions fled,
With the gay shadows of the morning mixed,
When Newton rose, our philosophic sun.
  Th' aerial flow of sound was known to him,
From whence it first in wavy circles breaks,

Till the touched organ takes the meaning in.
Nor could the darting beam, of speed immense,
Escape his swift pursuit and measuring eye.
Even light itself, which everything displays,
Shone undiscovered, till his brighter mind
Untwisted all the shining robe of day;
And, from the whitening undistinguished blaze,
Collecting every ray into his kind,
To the charmed eye educed the gorgeous train
Of parent-colours. First the flaming red
Sprung vivid forth; the tawny orange next;
And next delicious yellow; by whose side
Fell the kind beams of all-refreshing green.
Then the pure blue, that swells autumnal skies,
Ethereal played; and then, of sadder hue,
Emerged the deepened indigo, as when
The heavy-skirted evening droops with frost;
While the last gleamings of refracted light
Died in the fainting violet away.
These, when the clouds distil the rosy shower,
Shine out distinct adown the watry bow;
While o'er our heads the dewy vision bends
Delightful, melting on the fields beneath.
Myriads of mingling dyes from these result,
And myriads still remain—infinite source
Of beauty, ever-flushing, ever-new!
Did ever poet image aught so fair,
Dreaming in whispering groves by the hoarse brook?
Or prophet, to whose rapture heaven descends?
Even now the setting sun and shifting clouds,
Seen, Greenwich, from thy lovely heights, declare
How just, how beauteous the refractive law.
The noiseless tide of time, all bearing down
To vast eternity's unbounded sea,
Where the green islands of the happy shine,
He stemmed alone; and, to the source (involved
Deep in primeval gloom) ascending, raised
His lights at equal distances, to guide
Historian wildered on his darksome way.
But who can number up his labours? who
His high discoveries sing? When but a few
Of the deep-studying race can stretch their minds
To what he knew: in fancy's lighter thought,
How shall the Muse then grasp the mighty theme?
What wonder thence that his devotion swelled
Responsive to his knowledge? For could he,

Whose piercing mental eye diffusive saw
The finished university of things
In all its order, magnitude and parts,
Forbear incessant to adore that Power
Who fills, sustains and actuates the whole?

(1727)

135 *Hymn on Solitude*

HAIL, ever-pleasing Solitude!
Companion of the wise and good!
But from whose holy, piercing eye
The herd of fools and villains fly.
Oh! how I love with thee to walk!
And listen to thy whispered talk,
Which innocence and truth imparts,
And melts the most obdurate hearts.
A thousand shapes you wear with ease,
And still in every shape you please;
Now wrapt in some mysterious dream,
A lone philosopher you seem;
Now quick from hill to vale you fly,
And now you sweep the vaulted sky,
And nature triumphs in your eye:
Then straight again you court the shade,
And pining hang the pensive head.
A shepherd next you haunt the plain,
And warble forth your oaten strain.
A lover now with all the grace
Of that sweet passion in your face!
Then, soft-divided, you assume
The gentle-looking H[ertfor]d's bloom,
As, with her Philomela, she
(Her Philomela fond of thee),
Amid the long-withdrawing vale,
Awakes the rivalled nightingale.
A thousand shapes you wear with ease,
And still in every shape you please.
Thine is th' unbounded breath of morn,
Just as the dew-bent rose is born;
And while meridian fervours beat,
Thine is the woodland's dumb retreat;
But chief, when evening scenes decay,
And the faint landscape swims away,

Thine is the doubtful dear decline,
And that best hour of musing thine.
  Descending angels bless thy train,
The virtues of the sage and swain;
Plain Innocence in white arrayed,
And Contemplation rears the head;
Religion with her awful brow,
And rapt Urania waits on you.
  Oh, let me pierce thy secret cell!
And in thy deep recesses dwell:
For ever with thy raptures fired,
For ever from the world retired;
Nor by a mortal seen, save he
A Lycidas or Lycon be.

(1729)

136 *Rule, Britannia*

WHEN Britain first, at heaven's command,
  Arose from out the azure main,
This was the charter of the land,
  And guardian angels sung this strain—
    'Rule, Britannia, rule the waves;
    Britons never will be slaves.'

The nations, not so blest as thee,
  Must in their turns to tyrants fall;
While thou shalt flourish great and free,
  The dread and envy of them all.
    'Rule,' &c.

Still more majestic shalt thou rise,
  More dreadful from each foreign stroke;
As the loud blast that tears the skies
  Serves but to root thy native oak.
    'Rule,' &c.

Thee haughty tyrants ne'er shall tame;
  All their attempts to bend thee down
Will but arouse thy generous flame,
  But work their woe and thy renown.
    'Rule,' &c.

To thee belongs the rural reign;
  Thy cities shall with commerce shine;
All thine shall be the subject main,
  And every shore it circles thine.
    'Rule,' &c.

The Muses, still with freedom found,
  Shall to thy happy coast repair:
Blest isle! with matchless beauty crowned,
  And manly hearts to guard the fair.
    'Rule, Britannia, rule the waves;
    Britons never will be slaves.'

(1740)

137 from *The Castle of Indolence*, Canto I

In lowly dale, fast by a river's side,
With woody hill o'er hill encompassed round,
A most enchanting wizard did abide,
Than whom a fiend more fell is nowhere found.
It was, I ween, a lovely spot of ground;
And there a season atween June and May,
Half prankt with spring, with summer half imbrowned,
A listless climate made, where, sooth to say,
No living wight could work, ne carèd even for play.

Was naught around but images of rest:
Sleep-soothing groves, and quiet lawns between;
And flowery beds that slumbrous influence kest,
From poppies breathed; and beds of pleasant green,
Where never yet was creeping creature seen.
Meantime unnumbered glittering streamlets played,
And hurlèd everywhere their waters sheen;
That, as they bickered through the sunny glade,
Though restless still themselves, a lulling murmur made.

Joined to the prattle of the purling rills,
Were heard the lowing herds along the vale,
And flocks loud-bleating from the distant hills,
And vacant shepherds piping in the dale:
And now and then sweet Philomel would wail,
Or stock-doves plain amid the forest deep,
That drowsy rustled to the sighing gale;
And still a coil the grasshopper did keep:
Yet all these sounds yblent inclinèd all to sleep.

Full in the passage of the vale, above,
A sable, silent, solemn forest stood;
Where nought but shadowy forms were seen to move,
As Idless fancied in her dreaming mood.
And up the hills, on either side, a wood
Of blackening pines, ay waving to and fro,
Sent forth a sleepy horror through the blood;
And where this valley winded out, below,
The murmuring main was heard, and scarcely heard, to flow.

A pleasing land of drowsyhed it was:
Of dreams that wave before the half-shut eye;
And of gay castles in the clouds that pass,
For ever flushing round a summer sky:
There eke the soft delights, that witchingly
Instil a wanton sweetness through the breast,
And the calm pleasures always hovered nigh;
But whate'er smacked of noyance, or unrest,
Was far far off expelled from this delicious nest.

The landskip such, inspiring perfect ease;
Where Indolence (for so the wizard hight)
Close-hid his castle mid embowering trees,
That half shut out the beams of Phoebus bright,
And made a kind of checkered day and night.
Meanwhile, unceasing at the massy gate,
Beneath a spacious palm, the wicked wight
Was placed; and, to his lute, of cruel fate
And labour harsh complained, lamenting man's estate.

. . . .

Sometimes the pencil, in cool airy halls,
Bade the gay bloom of vernal landskips rise,
Or Autumn's varied shades imbrown the walls:
Now the black tempest strikes the astonished eyes;
Now down the steep the flashing torrent flies;
The trembling sun now plays o'er ocean blue,
And now rude mountains frown amid the skies;
Whate'er Lorrain light-touched with softening hue,
Or savage Rosa dashed, or learnèd Poussin drew.

Each sound too here to languishment inclined,
Lulled the weak bosom, and inducèd ease.
Aerial music in the warbling wind,
At distance rising oft, by small degrees,
Nearer and nearer came, till o'er the trees

It hung, and breathed such soul-dissolving airs
As did, alas! with soft perdition please:
Entangled deep in its enchanting snares,
The listening heart forgot all duties and all cares.

A certain music, never known before,
Here soothed the pensive melancholy mind;
Full easily obtained. Behoves no more,
But sidelong to the gently-waving wind
To lay the well-tuned instrument reclined;
From which, with airy flying fingers light,
Beyond each mortal touch the most refined,
The gods of winds drew sounds of deep delight:
Whence, with just cause, the harp of Aeolus it hight.

Ah me! what hand can touch the strings so fine?
Who up the lofty diapason roll
Such sweet, such sad, such solemn airs divine,
Then let them down again into the soul?
Now rising love they fanned; now pleasing dole
They breathed, in tender musings, through the heart;
And now a graver sacred strain they stole,
As when seraphic hands an hymn impart:
Wild warbling nature all, above the reach of art!

Such the gay splendour, the luxurious state,
Of Caliphs old, who on the Tygris' shore,
In mighty Bagdat, populous and great,
Held their bright court, where was of ladies store;
And verse, love, music still the garland wore:
When sleep was coy, the bard in waiting there
Cheered the lone midnight with the muse's lore;
Composing music bade his dreams be fair,
And music lent new gladness to the morning air.

Near the pavilions where we slept, still ran
Soft-tinkling streams, and dashing waters fell,
And sobbing breezes sighed, and oft began
(So worked the wizard) wintry storms to swell,
As heaven and earth they would together mell:
At doors and windows, threatening, seemed to call
The demons of the tempest, growling fell;
Yet the least entrance found they none at all;
Whence sweeter grew our sleep, secure in massy hall.

And hither Morpheus sent his kindest dreams,
Raising a world of gayer tinct and grace;
O'er which were shadowy cast Elysian gleams,
That played in waving lights from place to place,
And shed a roseate smile on nature's face.
Not Titian's pencil e'er could so array,
So fleece with clouds the pure ethereal space;
Ne could it e'er such melting forms display,
As loose on flowery beds all languishingly lay.

No, fair illusions! artful phantoms, no!
My muse will not attempt your fairy-land:
She has no colours that like you can glow;
To catch your vivid scenes too gross her hand.
But sure it is, was ne'er a subtler band
Than these same guileful angel-seeming sprights,
Who thus in dreams voluptuous, soft, and bland,
Poured all the Arabian heaven upon our nights,
And blessed them oft besides with more refined delights.

(1748)

JOHN WRIGHT

fl. 1708–1727

138 *The Poor Man's Province*

I ROSE betimes to go I knew not where,
By eventide I found that I was there;
And as I went I fell upon a strand,
Where all men do obey, but none command.
I asked the name of this unpleasant shore;
They said, 'It is the Province of the Poor,
And lies upon the coast of Want and Wrong,
Which you will find as you do pass along.'
I went on still an easy country-jog,
But presently I met a dismal fog,
Which grew so dark I could not see my way,
And made me fall upon my knees to pray.
Before I did begin, I looked about
To see if I could spy a cushion out;
But there, alas! was nothing to be found
But sighs and sobs upon the naked ground.

I thought 'twas something hard, but yet at last
I did conclude to stay, night came so fast;
And when I thought I would refresh my soul,
The country yielded neither fish nor fowl.
So nature being weary sought to please
Itself with sleep, but there was little ease;
For lying down upon a felt'red flock,
It yielded to me like a flinty rock.
The morning came, the sun went on his race,
But pinching wants appeared in ev'ry place.
There was a talk of plenty that was nigh,
But still the people had no cash to buy.
Abundance of good things went up and down,
And choice provisions passèd through the town;
Yet those that livèd there could do no more
Than just behold them running past the door.
Whilst I was forcèd here to make abode,
I found old rags and tatters alamode;
And those that got new clothes never had
A penny for their old, they were so bad.
Charcoal and billet never touch their fire,
Such costly things they must not once desire;
'Tis well if they can get some fuel in
By flaying of the earth, to burn its skin.
Rich carpets and fine hangings don't become
Their drooping cottages, yet they have some
Resemblance of such glory on their walls,
Where cobwebs hang, and spiders get their falls.
Instead of silver plate, an earthen dish,
And little there to put, except a wish
Of some such dainties as the rich enjoy,
Whilst hope and hunger do their peace destroy.
I saw no feasting all the time I stayed,
But now and then there is a visit paid,
To tell each other they are very poor,
A story which they knew too well before.
When straits are very great they often try
To beg or borrow, which will best comply
With those to whom they make their sad address,
But when they borrow much, they pay the less.
When they fall out, they'll speak as big as those
Who have it in their hands for to oppose;
But after all, no Chanc'ry suits they know,
For they are fain to end it all below.

felt'red flock] matted bed of coarse wool   billet] firewood

There is no trading here, for trade must trust,
And trust they can't, for then their starving must
Come next in place, so they are bound to live
Upon the crumbs which God doth daily give.
Would they be frugal, they have naught to spare,
So their condition doth impede their care;
To spin out nothing is the strangest pull,
And none can do't, for nothing hath no wool.
And some designing men, who love their gold,
Ride through this province, as I have been told,
To grind the faces of these wretched souls,
Whilst they themselves drink wine in lusty bowls.
When I was mounted for to come away,
Behind a bush I heard one of them say,
'Christ, and a crust, Lord, sanctify to me;
Can I be poor who have a right to thee?'
At this my heart began to leap indeed,
For now I thought grace might consist with need;
And if the Lord be pleased to make me one
Of his poor flock, I shall not be undone.

(1727)

CHRISTOPHER PITT

1699–1748

139 *On the Masquerades*

WELL—we have reached the precipice at last;
The present age of vice obscures the past.
Our dull forefathers were content to stay,
Nor sinned till nature pointed out the way:
No arts they practised to forestall delight,
But stopped, to wait the calls of appetite.
Their top-debauches were at best precise,
An unimproved simplicity of vice.
  But this blest age has found a fairer road,
And left the paths their ancestors had trod.
Nay, we could wear (our taste so very nice is)
Their old cast-fashions sooner than their vices.
Whoring till now a common trade has been,
But masquerades refine upon the sin:
An higher taste to wickedness impart,
And second nature with the helps of art.

New ways and means to pleasure we devise,
Since pleasure looks the lovelier in disguise.
The stealth and frolic give a smarter gust,
Add wit to vice, and elegance to lust.
  In vain the modish evil to redress,
At once conspire the pulpit and the press:
Our priests and poets preach and write in vain;
All satire's lost, both sacred and profane.
So many various changes to impart
Would tire an Ovid's or a Proteus' art;
Where lost in one promiscuous whim we see
Sex, age, condition, quality, degree.
Where the facetious crowd themselves lay down,
And take up every person but their own.
Fools, dukes, rakes, cardinals, fops, Indian queens,
Belles in tie-wigs, and lords in harlequins;
Troops of right-honourable porters come,
And gartered small-coal-merchants crowd the room;
Valets adorned with coronets appear,
Lackeys of state, and footmen with a star:
Sailors of quality with judges mix,
And chimney-sweepers drive their coach and six.
Statesmen so used at court the mask to wear,
With less disguise assume the visor here.
Officious Hei[degge]r deceives our eyes,
For his own person is his best disguise:
And half the reigning toasts of equal grace
Trust to the natural visor of the face.
Idiots turn conjurors, and courtiers clowns,
And sultans drop their handkerchiefs to nuns.
Starched Quakers glare in furbelows and silk;
Beaux deal in sprats, and duchesses cry milk.
  But guard thy fancy, Muse, nor stain thy pen
With the lewd joys of this fantastic scene,
Where sexes blend in one confused intrigue,
Where the girls ravish, and the men grow big;
Nor credit what the idle world has said
Of lawyers forced, and judges brought to bed,
Or that to belles their brothers breathe their vows,
Or husbands through mistake gallant a spouse.
Such dire disasters, and a numerous throng
Of like enormities, require the song:
But the chaste Muse, with blushes covered o'er,
Retires confused, and will reveal no more.

(1727)

FRANCIS HAWLING

fl. 1727

140 from *The Signal: or, A Satire against Modesty*

[*The Author Consults a Critic and Sells his Manuscript*]

How shall I tell the torments of that hour,
The insolence of delegated power?
Name not the tyranny of cruel knaves,
Name not the passiveness of abject slaves:
With less remorse, he sacrificed my fame;
More sordid, I consented to my shame,
Full of resentments I could not express,
And 'gainst the powers of shame and self-redress.
But to continue—with imperious will
He draws from left to right his murdering quill;
A thousand tender things he now erased,
Expression mutilates and sense defaced;
What's warm from life and just to nature's laws,
He blotted out—not crueller the cause.
I begged that one soliloquy he'd spare;
He cut me short with a forbidding air:
'Sir, I shall careful be of your renown,
But I'm the judge what 'tis will please the town.'
Yet still constrained by hope or awed by fear,
I yielded—life on any terms is dear—
With the rough power implicitly complied,
So near are modesty and shame allied.
The counsel up, retired, I meekly took
The miserable fragments of my book,
With loss of limbs beheld my mangled boy;
Despair reproached: 'twas mercy to destroy.
All mad with rage I down the back way run,
Resolved the Muse and them forever more to shun.
Old Mother Puff, the turning of the street,
Raised paste round blighted fruit and offal meat;
Two yards' tarpaulin, cast above her shed,
Sheltered her stall, her utensils and bed;
For ornament was pasted round the place
Guy Warwick, George and Dragon, Chevy Chase;
Three ragged slaves of Troy's famed siege there stood,
And 'bout two-thirds of the Children in the Wood.
Part of a tattered blanket, help of skewer,

Covered her feeble limbs from cold secure;
Two inch of pipe within her leathern jaws,
One side emitting fumes, which t' other draws;
With parched hands pendant o'er a charcoal pan,
She sat complaining of the times and man.
  'Goody!', quoth I, 'do you waste paper buy?'
'Sir—pray, a little louder—price?—which pie?'
Inclining of my head and she her ear:
'I've this, I say, to sell.'—'Um! yes, I hear;
You ask, if I mistake not, what I'll give.
Ah! master, it is very hard to live!'
Then drew her purse: 'Here's what I can afford,
If you'll be pleased to take 't.' I'm at a word:
'And is this all?—is that the most, my dame?'
'Indeed it is.'—'And what's this pie?'—'The same.'
Ware then for ware I took, my last appeal,
And ate out twelve months' labour at a meal.

(1727)

ANONYMOUS

141 [*The Dream*]

I DREAMED that, buried in my fellow clay,
Close by a common beggar's side I lay;
And as so mean a neighbour shocked my pride,
Thus, like a corpse of consequence, I cried:
'Scoundrel, begone, and henceforth touch me not;
More manners learn, and at a distance rot.'
'How, scoundrel!' in a haughtier tone cried he:
'Proud lump of dirt, I scorn thy words and thee.
Here all are equal, now thy case is mine:
This is my rotting-place, and that is thine.'

(1727)

WILLIAM SOMERVILE

1675–1742

142 from *The Bowling-Green*

Where fair Sabrina's wand'ring currents flow,
A large smooth plain extends its verdant brow;
Here ev'ry morn, while fruitful vapours feed
The swelling blade and bless the smoking mead,
A cruel tyrant reigns: like Time, the swain
Whets his unrighteous scythe, and shaves the plain.
Beneath each stroke the peeping flow'rs decay,
And all th' unripened crop is swept away.
The heavy roller next he tugs along,
Whiffs his short pipe, or rears a rural song;
With curious eye then the pressed turf he views,
And ev'ry rising prominence subdues.
Now when each craving stomach was well stored,
And 'Church and King' had travelled round the board,
Hither at Fortune's shrine to pay their court,
With eager hopes the motley tribe resort:
Attorneys spruce in their plate-buttoned frocks,
And rosy parsons, fat and orthodox;
Of ev'ry sect, Whigs, Papists and High-fliers,
Cornuted aldermen, and hen-pecked squires;
Foxhunters, quacks, scribblers in verse and prose,
And half-pay captains, and half-witted beaux.
On the green cirque the ready racers stand,
Disposed in pairs, and tempt the bowler's hand;
Each polished sphere does his round brother own,
The twins distinguished by their marks are known.
As the strong rein guides the well-managed horse,
Here weighty lead infused directs their course.
These in the ready road drive on with speed,
But those in crooked paths more artfully succeed.
So the tall ship, that makes some dang'rous bay,
With a side wind obliquely slopes her way.
Lo! there the silver tumbler fixed on high,
The victor's prize, inviting every eye!
The champions or consent or chance divide,
While each man thinks his own the surer side,
And the jack leads, the skilful bowler's guide.
Bendo stripped first; from foreign coasts he brought
A chaos of receipts, and anarchy of thought,

Where the tumultuous whims, to faction prone,
Still justled monarch Reason from her throne:
More dang'rous than the porcupine's his quill,
Inured to slaughter, and secure to kill.
Let loose, just heav'n, each virulent disease,
But save us from such murderers as these;
Might Bendo live but half a patriarch's age,
Th' unpeopled world would sink beneath his rage;
Nor need t' appease the just Creator's ire
A second deluge, or consuming fire.
He winks one eye, and knits his brow severe,
Then from his hand launches the flying sphere;
Out of the green the guiltless wood he hurled,
Swift as his patients from this nether world:
Then grinned malignant, but the jocund crowd
Deride his senseless rage, and shout aloud.
  Next, Zadoc, 'tis thy turn, imperious priest!
Still late at church, but early at a feast.
No turkey-cock appears with better grace,
His garments black, vermilion paints his face;
His wattles hang upon his stiffened band,
His platter feet upon the trigger stand,
He grasps the bowl in his rough brawny hand.
Then squatting down, with his grey goggle-eyes
He takes his aim, and at the mark it flies.
Zadoc pursues, and wobbles o'er the plain,
But shakes his strutting paunch and ambles on in vain;
For oh! wide-erring to the left it glides,
The inmate lead the lighter wood misguides.
He sharp reproofs with kind entreaties joins,
Then on the counter side with pain reclines;
As if he meant to regulate its course
By pow'r attractive and magnetic force.
Now almost in despair, he raves, he storms,
Writhes his unwieldy trunk in various forms:
Unhappy Proteus! still in vain he tries
A thousand shapes, the bowl erroneous flies,
Deaf to his pray'rs, regardless of his cries.
His puffing cheeks with rising rage inflame,
And all his sparkling rubies glow with shame.
  Bendo's proud heart, proof against Fortune's frown,
Resolves once more to make the prize his own;
Cautious he plods, surveying all the green,
And measures with his eye the space between.

trigger] trig, the place from which to deliver the bowl

But as on him 'twas a peculiar curse
To fall from one extreme into a worse,
Conscious of too much vigour, now for fear
He should exceed, at hand he checks the sphere.
Soon as he found its languid force decay,
And the too weak impression die away,
Quick after it he scuds, urges behind
Step after step, and now, with anxious mind,
Hangs o'er the bowl slow-creeping on the plain,
And chides its faint efforts, and bawls amain.
Then on the guiltless green the blame to lay,
Curses the mountains that obstruct his way;
Brazens it out with an audacious face,
His insolence improving with disgrace.
  Zadoc, who now with three black mugs had cheered
His drooping heart, and his sunk spirits reared,
Advances to the trig with solemn pace,
And ruddy hope sits blooming on his face.
The bowl he poised, with pain his hams he bends,
On well-chose ground unto the mark it tends:
Each adverse heart pants with unusual fear,
With joy he follows the propitious sphere.
Alas! how frail is ev'ry mortal scheme!
We build on sand, our happiness a dream.
Bendo's short bowl stops the proud victor's course,
Purloins his fame, and deadens all its force.
At Bendo from each corner of his eyes
He darts malignant rays, then mutt'ring flies
Into the bow'r; there, panting and half-dead,
In thick mundungus clouds he hides his head.

(1727)

143 *Hudibras and Milton Reconciled*

To Sir Adolphus Oughton

DEAR Knight, how great a drudge is he
Who would excel in poetry!
And yet how few have learnt the art
To inform the head, or touch the heart!
Some, with a dry and barren brain,
Poor rogues! like costive lapdogs strain;

142 mundungus] tobacco

While others with a flux of wit,
The reader and their friends besh–t.
Would you (Sir Knight) my judgement know?
He still writes worst who writes so-so.
In this the mighty secret lies:
To elevate, and to surprise.
Thus far my pen at random run;
The fire was out, the clock struck one.

When lo! strange hollow murmurs from without
Invade my ears. In ev'ry quarter roused,
The warring winds rush from their rocky caves
Tumultuous; the vapours dank or dry,
Beneath their standards ranged, with low'ring front
Darken the welkin. At each dreadful shock
Oaks, pines and elms down to their mother earth
Bend low their suppliant heads. The nodding tow'rs
Menace destruction, and old Edrick's house[1]
From its foundation shakes. The bellying clouds
Burst into rain, or gild their sable skirts
With flakes of ruddy fire; fierce elements
In ruin reconciled! redoubled peals
Of ceaseless thunder roar. Convulsions rend
The firmament. The whole creation stands
Mute and appalled, and trembling waits its doom.

And now perhaps (dear friend) you wonder,
In this dread scene of wind, rain, thunder,
What a poor guilty wretch could do.
Then hear (for, faith, I tell you true),
I pissed, thrice shook my giddy head,
Let a great f—t, and went to bed.

(1727)

144 from *The Chase*, Book II

[*Hare-Hunting*]

HARK! from yon covert, where those tow'ring oaks
Above the humble copse aspiring rise,
What glorious triumphs burst in ev'ry gale
Upon our ravished ears! The hunters shout,
The clanging horns swell their sweet-winding notes,
The pack wide-op'ning load the trembling air
With various melody; from tree to tree

[1] Called Edston, alias Edrickstow, from one Edrick the Saxon proprietor.

The propagated cry redoubling bounds,
And wingèd zephyrs waft the floating joy
Through all the regions near. Afflictive birch
No more the schoolboy dreads, his prison broke,
Scamp'ring he flies, nor heeds his master's call.
The weary traveller forgets his road,
And climbs th' adjacent hill; the ploughman leaves
Th' unfinished furrow; nor his bleating flocks
Are now the shepherd's joy; men, boys and girls
Desert th' unpeopled village; and wild crowds
Spread o'er the plain, by the sweet frenzy seized.
Look, how she pants! and o'er yon op'ning glade
Slips glancing by; while at the further end
The puzzling pack unravel wile by wile
Maze within maze. The covert's utmost bound
Slyly she skirts; behind them cautious creeps,
And, in that very track so lately stained
By all the steaming crowd, seems to pursue
The foes she flies. Let cavillers deny
That brutes have reason; sure 'tis something more,
'Tis heav'n directs, and stratagems inspires
Beyond the short extent of human thought.
But hold—I see her from the covert break:
Sad on yon little eminence she sits;
Intent she listens with one ear erect,
Pond'ring, and doubtful what new course to take,
And how t' escape the fierce bloodthirsty crew,
That still urge on, and still in volleys loud
Insult her woes, and mock her sore distress.
As now in louder peals the loaded winds
Bring on the gath'ring storm, her fears prevail;
And o'er the plain, and o'er the mountain's ridge,
Away she flies; nor ships with wind and tide,
And all their canvas wings, scud half so fast.
Once more, ye jovial train, your courage try,
And each clean courser's speed. We scour along,
In pleasing hurry and confusion tossed,
Oblivion to be wished. The patient pack
Hang on the scent unwearied, up they climb,
And ardent we pursue; our lab'ring steeds
We press, we gore; till once the summit gained,
Painfully panting, there we breathe awhile;
Then like a foaming torrent, pouring down
Precipitant, we smoke along the vale.

(1735)

JOHN BYROM

1692–1763

145 *Epigram on the Feuds between Handel and Bononcini*

SOME say, compared to Bononcini,
That Mynheer Handel's but a ninny;
Others aver that he to Handel
Is scarcely fit to hold a candle:
Strange all this difference should be
'Twixt Tweedle-dum and Tweedle-dee!

(1727)

146 *To Henry Wright of Mobberley, Esq. On Buying the Picture of F[ather] Malebranche*

WELL, dear Mr. Wright, I must send you a line;
The purchase is made, Father Malebranche is mine.
The adventure is past which I longed to achieve,
And I'm so overjoyed you will hardly believe.
If you will but have patience, I'll tell you, dear friend,
The whole history out from beginning to end.
Excuse the long tale; I could talk, Mr. Wright,
About this same picture from morning to night.

The morning it lowered like the morning in *Cato*,
And brought on, methought, as important a day too;
But about ten o'clock it began to be clear;
And the fate of our capital piece drawing near,
Having supped off to breakfast some common decoction,
Away trudges I in all haste to the auction;
Should have called upon you, but the Weaver Committee
Forbade me that pleasure;—the more was the pity.

The clock struck eleven as I entered the room,
Where Rembrandt and Guido stood waiting their doom,
With Holbein and Rubens, Van Dyck, Tintoret,
Jordano, Poussin, Carlo Dolci, et caet.
When at length in the corner perceiving the Père,
'Ha,' quoth I to his face, 'my old friend, are you there?'
And methought the face smiled, just as though it would say,
'What, you're come, Mr. Byrom, to fetch me away!'

Now before I had time to return it an answer,
Comes a shorthander by, Jemmy Ord was the man, sir:
'So, Doctor, good morrow.'—'So, Jemmy, bon jour.'
'Some rare pictures here.'—'So there are to be sure.'
'Shall we look at some of 'em?'—'With all my heart, Jemmy.'
So I walked up and down, and my old pupil wi' me,
Making still such remarks as our wisdoms thought proper,
Where things were hit off in wood, canvas or copper.

When at length about noon Mr. Auctioneer Cox,
With his book and his hammer, mounts into his box:
'Lot the first—number one'—then advanced his upholder
With Malebranche: so Atlas bore heaven on his shoulder.
Then my heart, sir, it went pit-a-pat, in good sooth,
To see the sweet face of the searcher of truth:
Ha, thought I to myself, if it cost me a million,
This right honest head then shall grace my pavilion.

Thus stood lot the first both in number and worth,
If pictures were prized for the men they set forth:
I'm sure to my thinking, compared to this number,
Most lots in the room seemed to be but mere lumber.
The head then appearing, Cox left us to see't,
And fell to discoursing concerning the feet:
'So long and so broad—'tis a very fine head—
Please to enter it, gentlemen'—was all that he said.

Had I been in his place, not a stroke of an hammer
Till the force had been tried both of rhetoric and grammar;
'A very fine head!'—had thy head been as fine,
All the heads in the house had veiled bonnets to thine:
Not a word whose it was—but in short 'twas a head—
'Put it up what you please'—and so somebody said,
'Half a piece'—and so on—For three pounds and a crown,
To sum up my good fortune, I fetched him me down.

There were three or four bidders, I cannot tell whether,
But they never could come two upon me together;
For as soon as one spoke, then immediately pop
I advanced something more, fear the hammer should drop.
I considered, should Cox take a whim of a sudden,
What a hurry it would put a man's Lancashire blood in!
'Once—twice—three pounds five'—so, *nemine con*,
Came an absolute rap—and thrice happy was John.

'Who bought it?' quoth Cox. 'Here's the money,' quoth I,
Still willing to make the securest reply:
And the safest receipt that a body can trust
For preventing disputes is—down with your dust!
So I bought it, and paid for't, and boldly I say
'Twas the best purchase made at Cadogan's that day;
The works the man wrote are the finest in nature,
And a most clever piece is his genuine portraiture.

For the rest of the pictures, and how they were sold,
To others there present I leave to be told:
They seemed to go off, as at most other sales,
Just as folks' money, judgement or fancy prevails;
Some cheap and some dear; such an image as this
Comes a trifle to me: and an old wooden Swiss
Wench's head, God knows who—forty-eight guineas—if her
Grace of Marlborough likes it—so fancy will differ.

When the business was over, and the crowd somewhat gone,
Whip into a coach I convey number one.
'Drive along, honest friend, fast as e'er you can pin.'
So he did, and 'tis now safe and sound at Gray's Inn.
Done at Paris, it says, from the life by one Gery
(Who that was I can't tell, but I wish his heart merry)
In the year ninety-eight; sixty just from the birth
Of the greatest divine that e'er lived upon earth.

And now if, some evening when you are at leisure,
You'll come and rejoice with me over my treasure,
With a friend or two with you, that will in free sort
Let us mix metaphysics and shorthand and port,
We'll talk of his book, or what else you've a mind,
Take a glass, read or write, as we see we're inclined:
Such friends and such freedom! What can be more clever?
Huzza! Father Malebranche and shorthand for ever.

(Wr. 1727; pub. 1782)

147 *Tom the Porter*

As Tom the porter went up Ludgate Hill,
A swinging show'r obliged him to stand still;
So, in the right-hand passage through the gate,
He pitched his burden down, just by the grate
From whence the doleful accent sounds away,
'Pity—the poor—and hungry—debtors—pray.'

To the same garrison, from Paul's Churchyard,
An half-drowned soldier ran to mount the guard.
Now Tom, it seems, the Ludgateer and he
Were old acquaintance formerly, all three;
And as the coast was clear, by cloudy weather,
They quickly fell into discourse together.
'Twas in December, when the Highland clans
Had got to Derbyshire from Prestonpans,
And struck all London with a general panic—
But mark the force of principles Britannic.

The soldier told 'em fresh the City news,
Just piping hot from stockjobbers and Jews:
Of French fleets landing, and of Dutch neutrality;
Of jealousies at Court among the quality;
Of Swarston-Bridge, that never was pulled down;
Of all the rebels in full march to town;
And of a hundred things beside, that made
Lord May'r himself and Aldermen afraid;
Painting with many an oath the case in view,
And asked the porter—what he thought to do.

'Do?' says he gravely—'What I did before;
What I have done these thirty years and more;
Carry, as I am like to do, my pack,
Glad to maintain my belly by my back;
If that but hold, I care not; for my part,
Come as come will, 't shall never break my heart;
I don't see folks that fight about their thrones
Mind either soldiers' flesh or porters' bones;
Whoe'er gets better when the battle's fought,
Thy pay nor mine will be advanced a groat.
—But to the purpose—now we are met here,
I'll join, if 't will, for one full mug of beer.'

The soldier, touched a little with surprise
To see his friend's indifference, replies:
'What you say, Tom, I own, is very good,
But—*our Religion*!' (and he da—ned his blood)
'What will become of *our Religion*?'—'True!'
Says the jail-bird—'and of *our Freedom* too?
If the Pretender' (rapped he out) 'comes on,
Our Liberties and Properties are gone!'

And so the soldier and the pris'ner joined
To work up Tom into a better mind;
He staring, dumb, with wonder struck and pity,
Took up his load and trudged into the City.

(1746)

148 *Careless Content*

I AM content, I do not care,
  Wag as it will the world for me;
When fuss and fret was all my fare,
  It got no ground, as I could see:
So when away my caring went,
I counted cost, and was content.

With more of thanks, and less of thought,
  I strive to make my matters meet;
To seek what ancient sages sought,
  Physic and food, in sour and sweet:
To take what passes in good part,
And keep the hiccups from the heart.

With good and gentle-humoured hearts,
  I choose to chat where'er I come,
Whate'er the subject be that starts;
  But if I get among the glum,
I hold my tongue to tell the troth,
And keep my breath to cool my broth.

For chance or change, of peace or pain,
  For Fortune's favour or her frown;
For lack or glut, for loss or gain,
  I never dodge, nor up nor down:
But swing what way the ship shall swim,
Or tack about with equal trim.

I suit not where I shall not speed,
  Nor trace the turn of ev'ry tide;
If simple sense will not succeed,
  I make no bustling, but abide:
For shining wealth or scaring woe,
I force no friend, I fear no foe.

Of *Ups* and *Downs*, of *Ins* and *Outs*,
  Of *they're i'th' wrong*, and *we're i'th' right*,
I shun the rancours and the routs,
  And wishing well to every wight,
Whatever turn the matter takes,
I deem it all but ducks and drakes.

With whom I feast I do not fawn,
  Nor, if the folks should flout me, faint;
If wonted welcome be withdrawn,
  I cook no kind of a complaint:
With none disposed to disagree,
But like them best, who best like me.

Not that I rate myself the rule
  How all my betters should behave;
But fame shall find me no man's fool,
  Nor to a set of men a slave:
I love a friendship free and frank,
And hate to hang upon a hank.

Fond of a true and trusty tie,
  I never lose where'er I link,
Though if a bus'ness budges by,
  I talk thereon just as I think:
My word, my work, my heart, my hand,
Still on a side together stand.

If names or notions make a noise,
  Whatever hap the question hath,
The point impartially I poise,
  And read or write, but without wrath;
For should I burn or break my brains,
Pray, who will pay me for my pains?

I love my neighbour as myself,
  Myself like him too, by his leave;
Nor to his pleasure, pow'r or pelf,
  Came I to crouch, as I conceive:
Dame Nature doubtless has designed
A man, the monarch of his mind.

Now taste and try this temper, sirs,
  Mood it and brood it in your breast;
Or if ye ween, for worldly stirs,
  That man does right to mar his rest,
Let me be deft and debonair,
I am content, I do not care.

(Wr. by 1763; pub. 1773)

149

On the Origin of Evil

EVIL, if rightly understood,
Is but the skeleton of good,
Divested of its flesh and blood.

While it remains without divorce
Within its hidden, secret source,
It is the good's own strength and force.

As bone has the supporting share
In human form divinely fair,
Although an evil when laid bare;

As light and air are fed by fire,
A shining good while all conspire,
But (separate) dark, raging ire;

As hope and love arise from faith,
Which then admits no ill, nor hath,
But, if alone, it would be wrath;

Or any instance thought upon
In which the evil can be none,
Till unity of good is gone;

So, by abuse of thought and skill,
The greatest good, to wit free-will,
Becomes the origin of ill.

Thus when rebellious angels fell,
The very heav'n, where good ones dwell,
Became th' apostate spirits' hell.

Seeking, against eternal right,
A force without a love and light,
They found and felt its evil might.

Thus Adam biting at their bait,
Of good and evil when he ate,
Died to his first thrice happy state;

Fell to the evils of this ball,
Which, in harmonious union all,
Were Paradise before his fall.

And when the life of Christ in men
Revives its faded image, then
Will all be Paradise again.

(Wr. by 1763; pub. 1772)

RICHARD SAVAGE

1697?–1743

150 from *The Bastard*

IN gayer hours, when high my fancy ran,
The Muse, exulting, thus her lay began:
'Blest be the Bastard's birth! through wond'rous ways
He shines eccentric like a comet's blaze.
No sickly fruit of faint compliance he;
He! stamped in nature's mint of ecstasy!
He lives to build, not boast, a gen'rous race:
No tenth transmitter of a foolish face.
His daring hope no sire's example bounds;
His first-born lights no prejudice confounds.
He, kindling from within, requires no flame;
He glories in a Bastard's glowing name.
'Born to himself, by no possession led,
In freedom fostered, and by fortune fed;
Nor guides nor rules his sov'reign choice control,
His body independent as his soul.
Loosed to the world's wide range—enjoined no aim,
Prescribed no duty, and assigned no name:
Nature's unbounded son, he stands alone,
His heart unbiased, and his mind his own.

'O Mother, yet *no* Mother!—'tis to you
My thanks for such distinguished claims are due.
You, unenslaved to nature's narrow laws,
Warm championess for freedom's sacred cause,
From all the dry devoirs of blood and line,
From ties maternal, moral and divine,
Discharged my grasping soul; pushed me from shore,
And launched me into life without an oar.
'What had I lost if, conjugally kind,
By nature hating, yet by vows confined,
Untaught the matrimonial bounds to slight,
And coldly conscious of a husband's right,
You had faint-drawn me with a form alone,
A lawful lump of life by force your own!
Then, while your backward will retrenched desire,
And unconcurring spirits lent no fire,
I had been born your dull, domestic heir,
Load of your life and motive of your care;
Perhaps been poorly rich and meanly great,
The slave of pomp, a cypher in the state;
Lordly neglectful of a worth unknown,
And slumb'ring in a seat, by chance my own.
'Far other blessings wait the Bastard's lot,
Conceived in rapture, and with fire begot!
Strong as necessity he starts away,
Climbs against wrongs, and brightens into day.'
Thus unprophetic, lately misinspired,
I sung; gay, flatt'ring hope my fancy fired;
Inly secure, through conscious scorn of ill,
Nor taught by wisdom how to balance will,
Rashly deceived, I saw no pits to shun,
But thought to purpose and to act were one;
Heedless what pointed cares pervert his way,
Whom caution arms not and whom woes betray;
But now exposed and shrinking from distress,
I fly to shelter, while the tempests press;
My Muse to grief resigns the varying tone,
The raptures languish, and the numbers groan.

(1728)

EDWARD CHICKEN

1698–1746

151 from *The Collier's Wedding*

At last the beef appears in sight,
The groom moves slow the pond'rous weight;
Then haste is made, the table clad,
No patience till the grace is said.
Swift to the smoking beef they fly;
Some cut their passage through a pie:
Out streams the gravy on the cloth;
Some burn their tongue with scalding broth:
But rolling spices make them fain,
They shake their heads, and sup again.
'Cut up that goose,' cries one below,
'Hand down a leg, or wing, or so.'
An honest neighbour tries the point,
Works hard but cannot hit a joint:
The bride sat nigh, she rose in prim,
And cut and tore her limb from limb.
Now geese, cocks, hens their fury feel,
Extended jaws devour the veal:
Each rives and eats what he can get,
And all is fish that comes to net.
No qualmish appetites here sit,
None curious for a dainty bit.
The bridegroom waits with active force,
And brings them drink 'twixt ev'ry course,
With napkin round his body girt,
To keep his clothes from grease and dirt;
With busy face he runs about
To fill the pots which are drunk out.
Old Bessy, dressed in all her airs,
Gives her attendance in the stairs;
There she receives the broken meat,
Just when it is not fit to eat.
Plates, knives and spoons about are tossed,
The old wife's care's that naught be lost:
By her the borrowed things are known,
She wishes folks may get their own.
Now all are full, the meat away,
The table drawn, the pipers play.
The bridegroom first gets on the floor,

And dances all the maidens o'er;
Then rubs his face, and makes a bow,
So marches off, what can he do?
He must not tire himself outright,
The bride expects a dance at night.
In ev'ry room, both high and low,
The fiddlers play, the bagpipes blow;
Some shout the bride, and some the groom,
They roar the very music dumb.
Hand over head, and one through other,
They dance with sister and with brother:
Their common tune is *Get her Bo*,
The weary lass cries, 'Music so';
Till tired in circling round, they wheel,
And beat the ground with toe and heel.
  A collier lad of taller size,
With rings of dust about his eyes,
Laid down his pipe, rose from the table,
And swore he'd dance while he was able.
He catched a partner by the hand,
And kissed her first to make her stand;
And then he bade the music play,
And said, 'Now lass, come dance away.'
He led her off; just when begun,
She stopped, cried 'Houts—some other tune';
Then whispered in the piper's ear,
So loud that ev'ryone might hear,
'I wish you'd play me *Jumping John*.'
He tried his reed, and tuned his drone,
The pipes scream out her fav'rite jig;
She knacked her thumbs and stood her trig,
Then cocked her belly up a little,
And wet her fingers with her spittle.
So off she goes; the collier lad
Sprung from the floor and danced like mad:
They sweep each corner of the room,
And all stand clear where'er they come.
They dance and tire the piper out,
And all's concluded with a shout.
  Old Bessy next was taken in,
She curled her nose, and cocked her chin;
Then held her coats on either side,
And kneeled, and cried, 'Up with the bride!
Come, piper,' says the good old woman,

knacked] snapped   trig] starting-point

'Play me *The Joyful Days are coming*;
I'll dance for joy, upon my life,
For now my daughter's made a wife.'
The old wife did what limbs could do;
'Well danced, old Bessy,' cried the crew.
The goody laughed and showed her teeth,
And said, 'Ah! sirs, I have no breath;
I once was thought right good at this';
So, curtseying, mumbled up his kiss.

(Wr. 1729?; pub. 173–?)

ANONYMOUS

152 from *The Comparison*

LET dirty streets be paved with flow'ry green
And, through the murky fog that hangs between,
Let an unclouded sun and azure skies be seen;
Where busy crowds pressed on and thronged the way,
Let groves and forests rise as thick as they;
Let cascades play and streams come murm'ring down,
Where noisy coaches rattled o'er the town;
Let stinking kennels be transformed to brooks,
Coxcombs (an easy change) to jays and rooks;
Prating coquets be turned to cackling geese,
And mobs huzzaing into buzzing bees;
Let birds in concert serenade each street,
Cows low at the Exchange and sheep at Guildhall bleat;
Let thrushes echo round from square to square,
And blackbirds whistle through each thoroughfare;
Let cuckoos 'Cuckoo' cry and oxen bellow,
Where 'Mackerel new' were cried and 'Medlars mellow';
Where 'Small-coal' murmured in a hollow note,
Let ravens croak and mutter through their throat;
Where 'Chimney-sweep' in shriller accents rung,
Let piping shepherds tune their rural song;
Where lamps and torches ill supplied the night,
Let Cynthia and the heavenly lamps give light;
Let owls and bitterns sound their midnight ditty,
Where watchmen's thumps resounded o'er the city,
Ere smoky towns shall vie with rural plains,
Or city cockneys rival country swains.

Let cars, sedans and chairs, and rolling sledges,
Transfixed, sprout up in shrubs and quickset hedges;

Let towers be metamorphosed into trees,
And smoke salute them in a fragrant breeze;
In groups of lofty rocks let Paul's be reared,
Such as to Indian Kings it once appeared,
And the wide subterranean vault below
Be changed to one which nature has made so,
Or in a mountain let the fabric end,
In trees its stately pinnacles ascend,
The spacious dome spread out in lofty green,
And sportive squirrels on the fanes be seen;
Let riv'lets gently by the side stream down,
And be a general conduit for the town;
Through every street descending fountains glide,
And form a murmuring current in Cheapside;
Let noise no more disturb fair Thames's shore,
Nor voices louder than her waters roar;
Her crowded banks be dressed with sportive willows,
Shading the shore and beck'ning to the billows;
Nor oars and scullers on her banks resound,
But boats, to ploughshares turned, divide the ground,
While all the noisy crowd that haunt the Strand
No longer plough the waves but plough the land;
Where jobbers with their airy bubbles bawl,
Let empty echoes to each other call;
In fine, let stalls and shops no longer stink,
And beaux (a painful task!) begin to think;
Let thy eternal din, O London! cease,
And all thy streets and palaces be peace,
Ere smoky towns shall vie with rural plains,
And city cockneys rival country swains.

(1729)

JAMES BRAMSTON

1694?–1743

153

from *The Art of Politics*

[*Time's Changes*]

LIKE South Sea stock, expressions rise and fall:
King Edward's words are now no words at all.
Did aught your predecessors' genius cramp?
Sure ev'ry reign may have its proper stamp.

All sublunary things of death partake;
What alteration does a cent'ry make?
Kings and comedians all are mortal found,
Caesar and Pinkethman are under ground.
What's not destroyed by time's devouring hand?
Where's Troy, and where's the maypole in the Strand?
Pease, cabbages and turnips once grew where
Now stands New Bond Street and a newer square;
Such piles of buildings now rise up and down,
London itself seems going out of town.
Our fathers crossed from Fulham in a wherry;
Their sons enjoy a bridge at Putney-ferry.
Think we that modern words eternal are?
Toupet and Tompion, Cosins and Colmar,
Hereafter will be called by some plain man
A wig, a watch, a pair of stays, a fan.
To things themselves if time such change affords,
Can there be any trusting to our words?

(1729)

154 from *The Man of Taste*

WHOE'ER he be that to a Taste aspires,
Let him read this, and be what he desires:
In men and manners versed, from life I write,
Not what was once but what is now polite.
Those who of courtly France have made the tour
Can scarce our English awkwardness endure.
But honest men, who never were abroad,
Like England only, and its Taste applaud.
Strife still persists, which yields the better *goût*:
Books or the world, the many or the few.
True Taste to me is by this touchstone known:
That's always best that's nearest to my own.
To show that my pretensions are not vain,
My father was a play'r in Drury Lane;
Pears and pistachio-nuts my mother sold,
He a dramatic poet, she a scold.
His tragic muse could countesses affright;
Her wit in boxes was my Lord's delight.
No mercenary priest e'er joined their hands,
Uncramped by wedlock's unpoetic bands:
Laws my Pindaric parents mattered not,
So I was tragi-comically got.

My infant tears a sort of measure kept,
I squalled in distichs, and in triplets wept.
No youth did I in education waste,
Happy in an hereditary Taste.
Writing ne'er cramped the sinews of my thumb,
No barb'rous birch e'er brushed my brawny bum.
My guts ne'er suffered from a college-cook,
My name ne'er entered in a buttery-book.
Grammar in vain the sons of Priscian teach,
Good parts are better than eight parts of speech:
Since these declined, those undeclined, they call,
I thank my stars that I declined 'em all.
To Greek or Latin tongues without pretence,
I trust to mother Wit and father Sense.
Nature's my guide, all sciences I scorn;
Pains I abhor, I was a *poet born*.
  Yet is my *goût* for criticism such,
I've got some French, and know a little Dutch.
Huge commentators grace my learned shelves,
Notes upon books outdo the books themselves.
Critics indeed are valuable men,
But hypercritics are as good again.
Though Blackmore's works my soul with raptures fill,
With notes by Bentley they'd be better still.
The *Boghouse Miscellany*'s well designed
To ease the body, and improve the mind.
Swift's whims and jokes for my resentment call,
For he displeases me, that pleases all.
Verse without rhyme I never could endure,
Uncouth in numbers, and in sense obscure.
To him as nature, when he ceased to see,
Milton's an universal blank to me.
Confirmed and settled by the nation's voice,
Rhyme is the poet's pride and people's choice:
Always upheld by national support
Of market, university and court.
Thomson, write blank; but know that, for that reason,
These lines shall live when thine are out of season.
Rhyme binds and beautifies the poet's lays,
As London ladies owe their shapes to stays.

(1733)

ANDREW BRICE

1690–1773

155 from *Freedom: A Poem, Written in Time of Recess from the Rapacious Claws of Bailiffs*

[*The Poet's Terror at the Bailiffs of Exeter*]

WHILE perils imminent by slender thread,
Like pointed dagger o'er my caskless head
Vibrissant, menace thus immediate fate,
Each distant buzz my harrassed soul confounds,
Their terrible irruption waiting. As
When, in a city sacked, victorious Rage
And Plunder range licentious; when mad Lust
Loose roams and hot Pollution every porch
Attacks; when mangling Slaughter prances through
The blood-gurged street; retired to close recess
The fainting virgin cowers at every noise
Remote, and her dishevelled tresses twist
The sanguinary hand already feels;—
So me, continual scared, each airy puff
In dreadful undulations from afar,
Or fluttering insect's nigh bombylious whirr,
With killing panic strikes, the shoulder-grasp
Avoidless as proclaiming. Pestered ears
Vain 'twere to dam, the terror to exclude,
Arresting every sense. My shrinking back
The clap by instinct shuns, and eyeballs make
Spontaneous retrospection; heart too warns,
Faint-throbbing constant, or to arms or flight.
To flight? Ah! where, at heel (I shuddering tell!)
Since the fierce terriers I ween pursue
Close as my shadow? Where I wistly glance
Direct, my path their apparitions skim,
Along the roof or glide, or whizzing flit
Beside my ears, me round or circling hem.
Like eager bulldog Brooks's spectrum shoots,
Ope-mouthed, his grinders frothed with blood, and things
Slavering of viscous foam. And Townsend seems,
With knobbed battoon uplift (huge Gazite's hand,
Monster less horrible! such weaver's beam

bombylious] buzzing

Might burthen) rushing on. Stern Rogers glares,
With aspect like Medusa's snake-locked front
Petrific, to a marbled Niobe
Me staring. Rice him (countenance imbossed
With boil-volcanoes, wherein Tophet-flames
Glow quenchless, worm perennial gnawing) backs.
Behind them Kent perhorrid lurks, conjoined
With Tucker, surly as on Russian snows
The cub-robbed bear, more vigilant to spring
Than libbard on his prey. On drivelled wall
Dried spawls fortuitous foul represent,
In fresco vile, cursed Elliot's phizz, than which
Not rough-carved lion at the prow, not masque
For th' island dev'l-got witch-teemed monster wrought,
Not Angelo's Doompiece famed (where demons vie
Deformèd visage), one so hideous shows.
And thousand bums minacious perdue seem
In every chink; while peals of hell-rung bans,
Ructant from Savery's throat and Newton's (sounds
Of desolation as if to denounce
Inthralment endless!) sorely terebrate
My sense auricular. Oh, torturing fear!
Anticipation of what pains, 'tis sung,
The damned endure! Ixion's twirlèd wheel,
Th' impendent threat'ning rock, the greedy beak
Which the fresh-growing liver ceaseless digs,
The plenty-mockèd thirst of Pelops' sire,
Frustrated labour of the Belides,
Vain toil of Sisyphus, and biting rods
By wood Alecto thrown, are felt in thee!
Yet torments light with those conferred, I doubt,
The upper hell, where Valglin sways, possess.
  Horror on horror! see! behind his grates
The steeled perdition, giant-cruelty,
Whose guilt-engrossing, transmigrated soul
A thousand alligators erst had taught
Larger voration! See! he whets his tusk
Scurvied with prisoners' blood, his orbs and rolls
That sparkle fiery malice, breathing fierce
Expectance of my coming! Hark! he clinks
The gyves excessive! Lo! and baleful damps
My nostril from his mirksome vault infest!
Distracting vision! which my frighted balls

drivelled] bespattered spawls] saliva bums minacious perdue] threatening bumbailiffs in ambush bans] curses ructant] belching terebrate] pierce wood] mad conferred] compared voration] devouring

Of light their strained cords burst to start from, then
Deep in their sockets shrink; crazed my whole frame
Of nature feels, unhinged and ev'ry bone
Clatt'ring within the flabby lean, their pith
Exhaust, and tide of every art'ry frore.

(1730)

STEPHEN DUCK

1705–1756

156 from *The Thresher's Labour*

SOON as the harvest hath laid bare the plains,
And barns well filled reward the farmer's pains,
What corn each sheaf will yield intent to hear,
And guess from thence the profits of the year,
Or else impending ruin to prevent
By paying, timely, threat'ning landlord's rent,
He calls his threshers forth: around we stand,
With deep attention waiting his command.
To each our tasks he readily divides,
And, pointing, to our different stations guides.
As he directs, to different barns we go;
Here two for wheat, and there for barley two.
But first, to show what he expects to find,
These words, or words like these, disclose his mind:
'So dry the corn was carried from the field,
So easily 'twill thresh, so well 'twill yield.
Sure large day's work I well may hope for now;
Come, strip, and try, let's see what you can do.'
Divested of our clothes, with flail in hand,
At a just distance, front to front we stand;
And first the threshall's gently swung, to prove
Whether with just exactness it will move:
That once secure, more quick we whirl them round,
From the strong planks our crabtree staves rebound,
And echoing barns return the rattling sound.
Now in the air our knotty weapons fly,
And now with equal force descend from high:
Down one, one up, so well they keep the time,
The Cyclops' hammers could not truer chime;

156 threshall] flail

Nor with more heavy strokes could Etna groan,
When Vulcan forged the arms for Thetis' son.
In briny streams our sweat descends apace,
Drops from our locks, or trickles down our face.
No intermission in our works we know;
The noisy threshall must for ever go.
Their master absent, others safely play;
The sleeping threshall doth itself betray.
Nor yet the tedious labour to beguile,
And make the passing minutes sweetly smile,
Can we, like shepherds, tell a merry tale:
The voice is lost, drowned by the noisy flail.
But we may think.—Alas! what pleasing thing
Here to the mind can the dull fancy bring?
The eye beholds no pleasant object here:
No cheerful sound diverts the list'ning ear.
The shepherd well may tune his voice to sing,
Inspired by all the beauties of the spring:
No fountains murmur here, no lambkins play,
No linnets warble, and no fields look gay;
'Tis all a dull and melancholy scene,
Fit only to provoke the Muse's spleen.
When sooty pease we thresh, you scarce can know
Our native colour, as from work we go:
The sweat, and dust, and suffocating smoke
Make us so much like Ethiopians look,
We scare our wives, when evening brings us home,
And frighted infants think the bugbear come.
Week after week we this dull task pursue,
Unless when winnowing days produce a new,
A new indeed, but frequently a worse:
The threshall yields but to the master's curse.
He counts the bushels, counts how much a day,
Then swears we've idled half our time away.
'Why look ye, rogues! D'ye think that this will do?
Your neighbours thresh as much again as you.'
Now in our hands we wish our noisy tools,
To drown the hated names of rogues and fools;
But wanting those, we just like schoolboys look,
When th' angry master views the blotted book.
They cry their ink was faulty, and their pen;
We, 'The corn threshes bad, 'twas cut too green.'

(1730)

HILDEBRAND JACOB

1693–1739

157

The Judgement of Tiresias

WHEN willing nymphs and swains unite
In quest of amorous delight,
Which sex does Venus most befriend,
Which party best obtains its end,
Which does the greatest pleasure prove,
And taste the sweetest joys of love?
'Twixt Jove and Juno, we are told,
This was a famed dispute of old.
Long the debate with equal strife
They held, like mortal man and wife:
The god in reason could not yield,
The goddess scorned to quit the field.
At length quoth Jove, thus rudely crossed,
His breath and patience almost lost,
'If by your sex's appetite,
Proud queen, we measure your delight,
'Tis plain the goddess does dispense
To them her kindest influence.'
Juno the inference denied
And, with decisive female pride,
Would have it still o' th' other side.
'I'll lay,' says Jupiter, 'I'm right
Three storms, with clouds as black as night,
Three peals of thunder mixed with hail,
And lightning shafts which never fail;
Win 'em, and use 'em at command
Against your foes by sea or land,
For vows forgot or rites neglected,
My friends of Crete alone excepted.'
' 'Tis done,' she cried, 'and Argus' eyes
I stake against your troubled skies,
Those watchful eyes you so much dread
When wand'ring from our nuptial bed.'
'Enough,' quoth Jove, 'by Styx's flood,
The wager's ratified and good!'
But who can this affair decide?
'Tiresias can,' the Thund'rer cried:
'Tiresias either sex has tried.'
Tiresias summoned straight appears,

And thus the knotty question clears:
'Parent of gods! tremendous Jove!
Great monarch of the realms above!
And you, dread queen! in Samos known,
Invoked by matrons when they groan;
The judgement you require, attend,
Nor may th' impartial judge offend.
An abler sure you ne'er had found
In heav'n, on earth, or under ground;
For I've done all that's done by man,
And suffered all poor woman can,
Have made myself the bold attack,
And fought like tigress on my back;
Now pressed the fair within my arms,
Now died beneath the hero's charms,
Still greatly blest; for what degree
'Twixt ecstasy and ecstasy?
And who will venture to compare
The mighty raptures none can bear?
The happy moment is the same
To active man or passive dame:
The diff'rence lies, with due submission,
Not in degree, but repetition.
That sex which oftest can renew
Those happy moments, still too few!
That sex does Venus most befriend,
That party best obtains its end.'

(1730)

158 *To Geron*

So prudent and so young a wife!
Old Geron, thou art blest for life.
So kindly careful of your health,
So close a steward of your wealth;
Still railing at th' expensive town,
Fond of your seat, when you are down;
At home in London before nine,
And ready dressed at noon to dine;
Though blooming, fair; beloved, a prude;
To beaux and coxcombs almost rude.
I cannot, happy man! conceive,
What the ill-natured world believe,

That all this care she's pleased to take
Is not for her old Geron's sake;
But for those twenty thousand pounds,
Rich jewels, and new-purchased grounds,
Unsettled yet by deed and free,
That you may leave to her—or me.

(1735)

159 *To Cloe*

CLOE, blooming sweet as May,
We must tempt Mama away;
Still the jealous dame destroys
All our schemes of future joys:
All the projects we have tried
Vainly yet have been applied.
At my bait she now must bite,
If I guess her temper right:
She shall have her lover too.
Trust me, Cloe, this will do.

(1735)

160 *The Alarm*

WHAT is't, good prying friend, you say?
A hair or two just turning grey!
Quick, boy! for the next barber send:
This sight my Cloe may offend;
I'll pass for twenty-five no more,
Though I have seen seven lustrums o'er.
Go, tap the oldest cask of wine;
Invite those merry blades to dine;
Bid Arrigoni bring his lute;
And brush my best embroidered suit!
  This mighty hurry, friend, forgive;
'Tis time to be in haste, to live!

(1735)

COLLEY CIBBER

1671–1757

161

The Blind Boy

O SAY what is that thing called light,
Which I can ne'er enjoy?
What is the blessing of the sight?
O tell your poor blind boy!

You talk of wond'rous things you see,
You say the sun shines bright!
I feel him warm, but how can he
Then make it day or night?

My day or night myself I make,
Whene'er I wake or play;
And could I ever keep awake,
It would be always day.

With heavy sighs I often hear
You mourn my hopeless woe.
But sure with patience I may bear
A loss I ne'er can know.

Then let not what I cannot have
My cheer of mind destroy.
Whilst thus I sing, I am a king,
Although a poor blind boy!

(1731?)

CHARLES WOODWARD

fl. 1731

162

The Midnight Ramble

PAUL'S clock struck twelve, 'twas time to go to bed;
The club broke up, each from the table fled.
Claret had topsy-turvy turned my brain;
From Brown's like mad I staggered to Bow Lane.
With many a stumble reeling to my door,
Upon the steps I trod upon a whore.

Starting, I gazed! The watchman coming by,
'Ad zounds,' said I, 'here does the devil lie:
I beg that you would bring your lantern nigh.'
'What? Who? My master, here,' replied the slave;
'I'll light you home, sir, if you'll give me leave.'
'Home, friend!' quoth I, 'I live at this same house:
This is my trap, I am a city mouse;
But some damned, venomous cat, I fear, doth lie
To snap me up as I am passing by.'
  The midnight representer of the moon
Displayed his light, and I distinguished soon
A poor geneva drab at full length laid,
As drunk as hell by juice of berry made,
And fall'n a victim to the midnight shade.
  I roused the boozy cat with point of sword;
She gaped and stared, but could not speak a word.
Quoth I, 'A coach, good honest watchman, call:
This poor unlucky bitch has got a fall.
I think she must be stunned; pray lend a hand,
Let's see if this poor toad can make a stand.'
With many a heavy lift, against the door
Upon her bum we raised this dismal whore.
The watchman called a coach, helped in my trull
And after headlong tumbled in—the fool.
The coachman asked me to what part of town
My honour would be drove, and where set down.
I told him, faith, I could not tell him where,
But where he proper thought to take the air:
Sufficed with that, he straightway shut the door,
And safely buttoned in myself and whore.
Both drunk and both asleep, we jolted on,
Nor waked before he stopped to set us down.
In Tothill Street he wisely stood to stop:
Starting I waked, when lo! a noted shop
That sold geneva was before my eyes,
Which at first glance did give a strange surprise,
For I'd been dreaming much of paradise.
  At first I fancied I had been in hell,
But thought it strange they there should liquor sell:
What first so made me think, and curse my fate,
A red-faced fellow in a chair of state,
Like Belzebub, in fiery triumph sat.
Others did to their matted beds retire,
And belched geneva which did soon take fire,

geneva] gin

By help of lighted coals a little higher.
With gaping throats they swallowed pints so fast,
By Jove, I thought they would have drank their last.
At length a fellow with a string and bladder,
With coat embroidered o'er with gin and slabber,
With awkward bow approached the coach's side,
And begged me to walk in and eke my bride.
With jolting of the coach, sleep and fresh air,
My Polly Peachum looked exceeding fair;
Besides, if you must know, she pukèd there.
The demons all arose and gave me place;
I sat me down and viewed my Polly's face,
Which did resemble much a wainscot-case.
I called for gin by quarts; they drank about,
And some of honour talked and made a rout,
Others to state affairs much bent their mind;
No tongue lay still, but all was unconfined.
At length a lusty strum called Bushel Nan,
With half a bellows to supply a fan,
Did whisk the smoke around at such a rate
That I was very glad to shift my seat.
I took fresh quarters nearer to the fire
And up behind the settle did retire;
There took a nod until the break of day,
And then each fiend broke up and went away.
Some to the markets went, baskets to carry,
And others reeling home both drunk and weary.
I for my own part left my Polly there,
And to Bow Lane jogged nodding in a chair.

(1731)

MARY BARBER

1690?–1757

163 *Written for My Son, and Spoken by Him at His First Putting on Breeches*

WHAT is it our mammas bewitches,
To plague us little boys with breeches?
To tyrant Custom we must yield
Whilst vanquished Reason flies the field.

162 strum] strumpet

Our legs must suffer by ligation,
To keep the blood from circulation;
And then our feet, though young and tender,
We to the shoemaker surrender,
Who often makes our shoes so strait
Our growing feet they cramp and fret;
Whilst, with contrivance most profound,
Across our insteps we are bound;
Which is the cause, I make no doubt,
Why thousands suffer in the gout.
Our wiser ancestors wore brogues,
Before the surgeons bribed these rogues,
With narrow toes, and heels like pegs,
To help to make us break our legs.
  Then, ere we know to use our fists,
Our mothers closely bind our wrists;
And never think our clothes are neat,
Till they're so tight we cannot eat.
And, to increase our other pains,
The hat-band helps to cramp our brains.
The cravat finishes the work,
Like bowstring sent from the Grand Turk.
  Thus dress, that should prolong our date,
Is made to hasten on our fate.
Fair privilege of nobler natures,
To be more plagued than other creatures!
The wild inhabitants of air
Are clothed by heaven with wondrous care:
Their beauteous, well-compacted feathers
Are coats of mail against all weathers;
Enamelled, to delight the eye,
Gay as the bow that decks the sky.
The beasts are clothed with beauteous skins;
The fishes armed with scales and fins,
Whose lustre lends the sailor light,
When all the stars are hid in night.
  O were our dress contrived like these,
For use, for ornament and ease!
Man only seems to sorrow born,
Naked, defenceless and forlorn.
  Yet we have Reason, to supply
What nature did to man deny:
Weak viceroy! Who thy power will own,
When Custom has usurped thy throne?

ligation] binding

In vain did I appeal to thee,
Ere I would wear his livery;
Who, in defiance to thy rules,
Delights to make us act like fools.
O'er human race the tyrant reigns,
And binds them in eternal chains.
We yield to his despotic sway,
The only monarch all obey.

(1731)

164 *On seeing an Officer's Widow distracted, who had been driven to Despair by a long and fruitless Solicitation for the Arrears of her Pension*

O WRETCH! hath madness cured thy dire despair?
Yes—All thy sorrows now are light as air:
No more you mourn your once loved husband's fate,
Who bravely perished for a thankless state.
For rolling years thy piety prevailed;
At length, quite sunk—thy hope, thy patience failed.
Distracted now you tread on life's last stage,
Nor feel the weight of poverty and age:
How blest in this, compared with those whose lot
Dooms them to miseries, by you forgot!
Now, wild as winds, you from your offspring fly,
Or fright them from you with distracted eye;
Rove through the streets; or sing, devoid of care,
With tattered garments and dishevelled hair;
By hooting boys to higher frenzy fired,
At length you sink, by cruel treatment tired,
Sink into sleep, an emblem of the dead,
A stone thy pillow, the cold earth thy bed.
O tell it not; let none the story hear,
Lest Britain's martial sons should learn to fear:
And when they next the hostile wall attack,
Feel the heart fail, the lifted arm grow slack;
And pausing cry—'Though death we scorn to dread,
Our orphan offspring, must they pine for bread?
See their loved mothers into prisons thrown,
And, unrelieved, in iron bondage groan?'
Britain, for this impending ruin dread;
Their woes call loud for vengeance on thy head:
Nor wonder, if disasters wait your fleets;

Nor wonder at complainings in your streets.
Be timely wise; arrest th' uplifted hand,
Ere pestilence or famine sweep the land.

(1734)

ALEXANDER POPE

1688–1744

(*see also Nos. 61–9*)

165 from *An Epistle to Richard Boyle, Earl of Burlington*

At Timon's villa let us pass a day,
Where all cry out, 'What sums are thrown away!'
So proud, so grand, of that stupendous air,
Soft and agreeable come never there.
Greatness, with Timon, dwells in such a draught
As brings all Brobdignag before your thought.
To compass this, his building is a town,
His pond an ocean, his parterre a down:
Who but must laugh, the master when he sees,
A puny insect, shiv'ring at a breeze!
Lo, what huge heaps of littleness around!
The whole, a laboured quarry above ground.
Two Cupids squirt before: a lake behind
Improves the keenness of the northern wind.
His gardens next your admiration call,
On ev'ry side you look, behold the wall!
No pleasing intricacies intervene,
No artful wildness to perplex the scene;
Grove nods at grove, each alley has a brother,
And half the platform just reflects the other.
The suff'ring eye inverted nature sees,
Trees cut to statues, statues thick as trees,
With here a fountain, never to be played,
And there a summer-house, that knows no shade;
Here Amphitrite sails through myrtle bow'rs;
There gladiators fight, or die, in flow'rs;
Unwatered see the drooping sea-horse mourn,
And swallows roost in Nilus' dusty urn.
My Lord advances with majestic mien,

Smit with the mighty pleasure to be seen:
But soft—by regular approach—not yet—
First through the length of yon hot terrace sweat,
And when up ten steep slopes you've dragged your thighs,
Just at his study-door he'll bless your eyes.
  His study! with what authors is it stored?
In books, not authors, curious is my Lord;
To all their dated backs he turns you round;
These Aldus printed, those Du Sueïl has bound.
Lo, some are vellum, and the rest as good
For all his Lordship knows, but they are wood.
For Locke or Milton 'tis in vain to look,
These shelves admit not any modern book.
  And now the chapel's silver bell you hear,
That summons you to all the pride of pray'r:
Light quirks of music, broken and uneven,
Make the soul dance upon a jig to heaven.
On painted ceilings you devoutly stare,
Where sprawl the saints of Verrio or Laguerre,
On gilded clouds in fair expansion lie,
And bring all paradise before your eye.
To rest, the cushion and soft dean invite,
Who never mentions hell to ears polite.
  But hark! the chiming clocks to dinner call;
A hundred footsteps scrape the marble hall:
The rich buffet well-coloured serpents grace,
And gaping Tritons spew to wash your face.
Is this a dinner? this a genial room?
No, 'tis a temple, and a hecatomb.
A solemn sacrifice, performed in state,
You drink by measure, and to minutes eat.
So quick retires each flying course, you'd swear
Sancho's dread doctor and his wand were there.
Between each act the trembling salvers ring,
From soup to sweet-wine, and God bless the King.
In plenty starving, tantalised in state,
And complaisantly helped to all I hate,
Treated, caressed, and tired, I take my leave,
Sick of his civil pride from morn to eve;
I curse such lavish cost, and little skill,
And swear no day was ever passed so ill.
  Yet hence the poor are clothed, the hungry fed;
Health to himself, and to his infants bread,
The lab'rer bears: what his hard heart denies,
His charitable vanity supplies.
  Another age shall see the golden ear

Imbrown the slope, and nod on the parterre,
Deep harvests bury all his pride has planned,
And laughing Ceres reassume the land.

(1731)

166 *An Essay on Man*

from *Epistle I*

THE bliss of man (could pride that blessing find)
Is not to act or think beyond mankind;
No pow'rs of body or of soul to share,
But what his nature and his state can bear.
Why has not man a microscopic eye?
For this plain reason, man is not a fly.
Say what the use, were finer optics giv'n,
T' inspect a mite, not comprehend the heav'n?
Or touch, if tremblingly alive all o'er,
To smart and agonise at ev'ry pore?
Or quick effluvia darting through the brain,
Die of a rose in aromatic pain?
If nature thundered in his opening ears,
And stunned him with the music of the spheres,
How would he wish that heav'n had left him still
The whisp'ring zephyr, and the purling rill?
Who finds not Providence all good and wise,
Alike in what it gives, and what denies?
Far as creation's ample range extends,
The scale of sensual, mental pow'rs ascends:
Mark how it mounts to man's imperial race,
From the green myriads in the peopled grass:
What modes of sight betwixt each wide extreme,
The mole's dim curtain, and the lynx's beam:
Of smell, the headlong lioness between,
And hound sagacious on the tainted green:
Of hearing, from the life that fills the flood,
To that which warbles through the vernal wood:
The spider's touch, how exquisitely fine!
Feels at each thread, and lives along the line:
In the nice bee, what sense so subtly true
From pois'nous herbs extracts the healing dew:
How instinct varies in the grov'ling swine,
Compared, half-reas'ning elephant, with thine:
'Twixt that, and reason, what a nice barrier,
For ever sep'rate, yet for ever near!

Remembrance and reflection how allied;
What thin partitions sense from thought divide;
And middle natures, how they long to join,
Yet never pass th' insuperable line!
Without this just gradation could they be
Subjected, these to those, or all to thee?
The pow'rs of all subdued by thee alone,
Is not thy reason all these pow'rs in one?
  See, through this air, this ocean, and this earth,
All matter quick, and bursting into birth.
Above, how high progressive life may go!
Around, how wide! how deep extend below!
Vast chain of being, which from God began,
Natures ethereal, human, angel, man,
Beast, bird, fish, insect! what no eye can see,
No glass can reach! from infinite to thee,
From thee to nothing!—On superior pow'rs
Were we to press, inferior might on ours;
Or in the full creation leave a void,
Where, one step broken, the great scale's destroyed:
From nature's chain whatever link you strike,
Tenth or ten thousandth, breaks the chain alike.
  And, if each system in gradation roll,
Alike essential to th' amazing whole,
The least confusion but in one, not all
That system only, but the whole must fall.
Let earth unbalanced from her orbit fly,
Planets and suns run lawless through the sky;
Let ruling angels from their spheres be hurled,
Being on being wrecked, and world on world,
Heav'ns whole foundations to their centre nod,
And nature tremble to the throne of God:
All this dread order break—for whom? for thee?
Vile worm!—oh madness, pride, impiety!
  What if the foot, ordained the dust to tread,
Or hand to toil, aspired to be the head?
What if the head, the eye, or ear repined
To serve mere engines to the ruling mind?
Just as absurd for any part to claim
To be another, in this gen'ral frame;
Just as absurd, to mourn the tasks or pains
The great directing Mind of All ordains.
  All are but parts of one stupendous whole,
Whose body nature is, and God the soul;
That, changed through all, and yet in all the same,
Great in the earth, as in the ethereal frame,

Warms in the sun, refreshes in the breeze,
Glows in the stars, and blossoms in the trees,
Lives through all life, extends through all extent,
Spreads undivided, operates unspent,
Breathes in our soul, informs our mortal part,
As full, as perfect, in a hair as heart;
As full, as perfect, in vile man that mourns,
As the rapt seraph that adores and burns;
To him no high, no low, no great, no small;
He fills, he bounds, connects, and equals all.
  Cease then, nor order imperfection name:
Our proper bliss depends on what we blame.
Know thy own point: this kind, this due degree
Of blindness, weakness, heav'n bestows on thee.
Submit—in this, or any other sphere,
Secure to be as blest as thou canst bear:
Safe in the hand of one disposing pow'r,
Or in the natal, or the mortal hour.
All nature is but art, unknown to thee;
All chance, direction, which thou canst not see;
All discord, harmony not understood;
All partial evil, universal good.
And, spite of pride, in erring reason's spite,
One truth is clear, 'Whatever is, is right.'

(1733)

from *Epistle II*

Know then thyself, presume not God to scan;
The proper study of mankind is man.
Placed on this isthmus of a middle state,
A being darkly wise, and rudely great:
With too much knowledge for the sceptic side,
With too much weakness for the stoic's pride,
He hangs between; in doubt to act, or rest,
In doubt to deem himself a god, or beast;
In doubt his mind or body to prefer,
Born but to die, and reas'ning but to err;
Alike in ignorance, his reason such,
Whether he thinks too little, or too much:
Chaos of thought and passion, all confused;
Still by himself abused, or disabused;
Created half to rise, and half to fall;
Great lord of all things, yet a prey to all;
Sole judge of truth, in endless error hurled:
The glory, jest, and riddle of the world!

(1733)

167 *An Epistle from Mr. Pope to Dr. Arbuthnot*

SHUT, shut the door, good John! fatigued, I said;
Tie up the knocker, say I'm sick, I'm dead.
The dog-star rages! nay 'tis past a doubt,
All Bedlam, or Parnassus, is let out:
Fire in each eye, and papers in each hand,
They rave, recite, and madden round the land.
What walls can guard me, or what shades can hide?
They pierce my thickets, through my grot they glide,
By land, by water, they renew the charge,
They stop the chariot, and they board the barge.
No place is sacred, not the church is free,
Ev'n Sunday shines no Sabbath-day to me:
Then from the Mint walks forth the man of rhyme,
Happy! to catch me, just at dinner-time.
Is there a parson, much bemused in beer,
A maudlin poetess, a rhyming peer,
A clerk, foredoomed his father's soul to cross,
Who pens a stanza, when he should engross?
Is there, who, locked from ink and paper, scrawls
With desp'rate charcoal round his darkened walls?
All fly to Twit'nam, and in humble strain
Apply to me, to keep them mad or vain.
Arthur, whose giddy son neglects the laws,
Imputes to me and my damned works the cause:
Poor Cornus sees his frantic wife elope,
And curses wit, and poetry, and Pope.
Friend to my life (which did not you prolong,
The world had wanted many an idle song),
What drop or nostrum can this plague remove?
Or which must end me, a fool's wrath or love?
A dire dilemma! either way I'm sped,
If foes, they write, if friends, they read me dead.
Seized and tied down to judge, how wretched I!
Who can't be silent, and who will not lie;
To laugh, were want of goodness and of grace,
And to be grave, exceeds all pow'r of face.
I sit with sad civility, I read
With honest anguish, and an aching head;
And drop at last, but in unwilling ears,
This saving counsel, 'Keep your piece nine years.'
'Nine years!' cries he, who, high in Drury Lane,
Lulled by soft zephyrs through the broken pane,
Rhymes ere he wakes, and prints before Term ends,

Obliged by hunger, and request of friends:
'The piece, you think, is incorrect? why take it,
I'm all submission; what you'd have it, make it.'
  Three things another's modest wishes bound,
My friendship, and a prologue, and ten pound.
  Pitholeon sends to me: 'You know his Grace,
I want a patron; ask him for a place.'
Pitholeon libelled me—'But here's a letter
Informs you, Sir, 'twas when he knew no better.
Dare you refuse him? Curll invites to dine,
He'll write a journal, or he'll turn divine.'
  Bless me! a packet. ''Tis a stranger sues,
A virgin tragedy, an orphan Muse.'
If I dislike it, 'Furies, death and rage!'
If I approve, 'Commend it to the stage.'
There (thank my stars) my whole commission ends,
The play'rs and I are, luckily, no friends.
Fired that the house reject him, ''Sdeath, I'll print it,
And shame the fools—Your interest, Sir, with Lintot.'
Lintot, dull rogue! will think your price too much:
'Not, Sir, if you revise it, and retouch.'
All my demurs but double his attacks:
And last he whispers, 'Do, and we go snacks.'
Glad of a quarrel, straight I clap the door:
Sir, let me see your works and you no more.
  'Tis sung, when Midas' ears began to spring
(Midas, a sacred person and a king),
His very minister who spied them first
(Some say his queen) was forced to speak or burst:
And is not mine, my friend, a sorer case,
When every coxcomb perks them in my face?
'Good friend, forbear! you deal in dang'rous things,
I'd never name queens, ministers, or kings;
Keep close to ears, and those let asses prick,
'Tis nothing'—Nothing? if they bite and kick?
Out with it, *Dunciad*! let the secret pass,
That secret to each fool, that he's an ass:
The truth once told (and wherefore should we lie?)
The queen of Midas slept, and so may I.
  You think this cruel? Take it for a rule,
No creature smarts so little as a fool.
Let peals of laughter, Codrus! round thee break,
Thou unconcerned canst hear the mighty crack.
Pit, box, and gallery in convulsions hurled,
Thou stand'st unshook amidst a bursting world.
Who shames a scribbler? break one cobweb through,

He spins the slight, self-pleasing thread anew;
Destroy his fib or sophistry; in vain,
The creature's at his dirty work again,
Throned in the centre of his thin designs,
Proud of a vast extent of flimsy lines.
Whom have I hurt? has poet yet, or peer,
Lost the arched eyebrow, or Parnassian sneer?
And has not Colley still his lord, and whore?
His butchers Henley, his freemasons Moore?
Does not one table Bavius still admit?
Still to one bishop Philips seem a wit?
Still Sappho——'Hold! for God's sake—you'll offend:
No names—be calm—learn prudence of a friend:
I too could write, and I am twice as tall,
But foes like these!'——One flatt'rer's worse than all;
Of all mad creatures, if the learned are right,
It is the slaver kills, and not the bite.
A fool quite angry is quite innocent;
Alas! 'tis ten times worse when they repent.
  One dedicates in high heroic prose,
And ridicules beyond a hundred foes;
One from all Grub Street will my fame defend,
And, more abusive, calls himself my friend.
This prints my letters, that expects a bribe,
And others roar aloud, 'Subscribe, subscribe.'
  There are, who to my person pay their court,
I cough like Horace, and, though lean, am short;
Ammon's great son one shoulder had too high,
Such Ovid's nose,—and 'Sir! you have an eye—'.
Go on, obliging creatures, make me see
All that disgraced my betters met in me:
Say, for my comfort, languishing in bed,
'Just so immortal Maro held his head';
And, when I die, be sure you let me know
Great Homer died three thousand years ago.
  Why did I write? what sin to me unknown
Dipped me in ink, my parents', or my own?
As yet a child, nor yet a fool to fame,
I lisped in numbers, for the numbers came.
I left no calling for this idle trade,
No duty broke, no father disobeyed.
The Muse but served to ease some friend, not wife,
To help me through this long disease, my life;
To second, Arbuthnot! thy art and care,
And teach the being you preserved to bear.
  But why then publish? Granville the polite,

And knowing Walsh, would tell me I could write;
Well-natured Garth inflamed with early praise,
And Congreve loved, and Swift endured my lays;
The courtly Talbot, Somers, Sheffield read,
Ev'n mitred Rochester would nod the head,
And St. John's self (great Dryden's friends before)
With open arms received one poet more.
Happy my studies, when by these approved!
Happier their author, when by these beloved!
From these the world will judge of men and books,
Not from the Burnets, Oldmixons, and Cookes.
  Soft were my numbers; who could take offence
While pure description held the place of sense?
Like gentle Fanny's was my flow'ry theme,
A painted mistress, or a purling stream.
Yet then did Gildon draw his venal quill;
I wished the man a dinner, and sat still:
Yet then did Dennis rave in furious fret;
I never answered, I was not in debt:
If want provoked, or madness made them print,
I waged no war with Bedlam or the Mint.
  Did some more sober critic come abroad?
If wrong, I smiled; if right, I kissed the rod.
Pains, reading, study are their just pretence,
And all they want is spirit, taste, and sense.
Commas and points they set exactly right,
And 'twere a sin to rob them of their mite.
Yet ne'er one sprig of laurel graced these ribalds,
From slashing Bentley down to piddling Tibbalds.
Each wight who reads not, and but scans and spells,
Each word-catcher that lives on syllables,
Ev'n such small critics, some regard may claim,
Preserved in Milton's or in Shakespeare's name.
Pretty! in amber to observe the forms
Of hairs, or straws, or dirt, or grubs, or worms;
The things, we know, are neither rich nor rare,
But wonder how the devil they got there.
  Were others angry? I excused them too;
Well might they rage; I gave them but their due.
A man's true merit 'tis not hard to find,
But each man's secret standard in his mind,
That casting-weight pride adds to emptiness,
This, who can gratify, for who can guess?
The bard whom pilfered pastorals renown,
Who turns a Persian tale for half-a-crown,
Just writes to make his barrenness appear,

And strains from hard-bound brains eight lines a year;
He, who still wanting, though he lives on theft,
Steals much, spends little, yet has nothing left;
And he, who now to sense, now nonsense leaning,
Means not, but blunders round about a meaning;
And he, whose fustian's so sublimely bad,
It is not poetry, but prose run mad:
All these, my modest satire bade translate,
And owned that nine such poets made a Tate.
How did they fume, and stamp, and roar, and chafe!
And swear, not Addison himself was safe.
  Peace to all such! but were there one whose fires
True genius kindles, and fair fame inspires,
Blest with each talent and each art to please,
And born to write, converse, and live with ease:
Should such a man, too fond to rule alone,
Bear, like the Turk, no brother near the throne,
View him with scornful, yet with jealous eyes,
And hate for arts that caused himself to rise;
Damn with faint praise, assent with civil leer,
And, without sneering, teach the rest to sneer;
Willing to wound, and yet afraid to strike,
Just hint a fault, and hesitate dislike;
Alike reserved to blame, or to commend,
A tim'rous foe, and a suspicious friend,
Dreading ev'n fools, by flatterers besieged,
And so obliging that he ne'er obliged;
Like Cato, give his little senate laws,
And sit attentive to his own applause;
While wits and Templars every sentence raise,
And wonder with a foolish face of praise.
Who but must laugh, if such a man there be?
Who would not weep, if Atticus were he?
  What though my name stood rubric on the walls,
Or plastered posts, with claps in capitals?
Or smoking forth, a hundred hawkers load,
On wings of winds came flying all abroad?
I sought no homage from the race that write;
I kept, like Asian monarchs, from their sight:
Poems I heeded (now be-rhymed so long)
No more than thou, great George! a birthday song.
I ne'er with wits or witlings passed my days,
To spread about the itch of verse and praise;
Nor like a puppy daggled through the town,
To fetch and carry sing-song up and down;
Nor at rehearsals sweat, and mouthed, and cried,

With handkerchief and orange at my side:
But sick of fops, and poetry, and prate,
To Bufo left the whole Castalian state.
  Proud as Apollo on his forkèd hill,
Sat full-blown Bufo, puffed by every quill;
Fed with soft dedication all day long,
Horace and he went hand in hand in song.
His library (where busts of poets dead
And a true Pindar stood without a head)
Received of wits an undistinguished race,
Who first his judgement asked, and then a place:
Much they extolled his pictures, much his seat,
And flattered every day, and some days eat:
Till grown more frugal in his riper days,
He paid some bards with port, and some with praise,
To some a dry rehearsal was assigned,
And others (harder still) he paid in kind.
Dryden alone (what wonder?) came not nigh,
Dryden alone escaped this judging eye:
But still the great have kindness in reserve,
He helped to bury whom he helped to starve.
  May some choice patron bless each grey goose quill!
May every Bavius have his Bufo still!
So when a statesman wants a day's defence,
Or envy holds a whole week's war with sense,
Or simple pride for flatt'ry makes demands,
May dunce by dunce be whistled off my hands!
Blessed be the great! for those they take away,
And those they left me—for they left me Gay;
Left me to see neglected genius bloom,
Neglected die, and tell it on his tomb;
Of all thy blameless life the sole return
My verse, and Queensb'ry weeping o'er thy urn!
  Oh let me live my own, and die so too!
('To live and die is all I have to do:')
Maintain a poet's dignity and ease,
And see what friends, and read what books I please.
Above a patron, though I condescend
Sometimes to call a minister my friend:
I was not born for courts or great affairs,
I pay my debts, believe, and say my pray'rs,
Can sleep without a poem in my head,
Nor know if Dennis be alive or dead.
  Why am I asked what next shall see the light?
Heav'ns! was I born for nothing but to write?
Has life no joys for me? or (to be grave)

Have I no friend to serve, no soul to save?
'I found him close with Swift'—'Indeed? no doubt'
(Cries prating Balbus) 'something will come out.'
'Tis all in vain, deny it as I will:
'No, such a genius never can lie still';
And then for mine obligingly mistakes
The first lampoon Sir Will or Bubo makes.
Poor guiltless I! and can I choose but smile,
When ev'ry coxcomb knows me by my style?
  Cursed be the verse, how well soe'er it flow,
That tends to make one worthy man my foe,
Give virtue scandal, innocence a fear,
Or from the soft-eyed virgin steal a tear!
But he who hurts a harmless neighbour's peace,
Insults fall'n worth, or beauty in distress,
Who loves a lie, lame slander helps about,
Who writes a libel, or who copies out;
That fop, whose pride affects a patron's name,
Yet absent, wounds an author's honest fame;
Who can your merit selfishly approve,
And show the sense of it without the love;
Who has the vanity to call you friend,
Yet wants the honour, injured, to defend;
Who tells whate'er you think, whate'er you say,
And, if he lie not, must at least betray;
Who to the dean and silver bell can swear,
And sees at Cannons what was never there;
Who reads, but with a lust to misapply,
Makes satire a lampoon, and fiction lie:
A lash like mine no honest man shall dread,
But all such babbling blockheads in his stead.
  Let Sporus tremble——'What? that thing of silk,
Sporus, that mere white curd of ass's milk?
Satire or sense, alas! can Sporus feel?
Who breaks a butterfly upon a wheel?'
Yet let me flap this bug with gilded wings,
This painted child of dirt, that stinks and stings;
Whose buzz the witty and the fair annoys,
Yet wit ne'er tastes, and beauty ne'er enjoys:
So well-bred spaniels civilly delight
In mumbling of the game they dare not bite.
Eternal smiles his emptiness betray,
As shallow streams run dimpling all the way.
Whether in florid impotence he speaks,
And, as the prompter breathes, the puppet squeaks;
Or at the ear of Eve, familiar toad,

Half froth, half venom, spits himself abroad,
In puns, or politics, or tales, or lies,
Or spite, or smut, or rhymes, or blasphemies.
His wit all see-saw, between that and this,
Now high, now low, now master up, now miss,
And he himself one vile antithesis.
Amphibious thing! that acting either part,
The trifling head, or the corrupted heart!
Fop at the toilet, flatt'rer at the board,
Now trips a lady, and now struts a lord.
Eve's tempter thus the rabbins have expressed,
A cherub's face, a reptile all the rest;
Beauty that shocks you, parts that none will trust,
Wit that can creep, and pride that licks the dust.
  Not Fortune's worshipper, nor Fashion's fool,
Not Lucre's madman, nor Ambition's tool,
Not proud, nor servile; be one poet's praise,
That, if he pleased, he pleased by manly ways;
That flatt'ry, ev'n to kings, he held a shame,
And thought a lie in verse or prose the same;
That not in Fancy's maze he wandered long,
But stooped to Truth, and moralised his song:
That not for fame, but Virtue's better end,
He stood the furious foe, the timid friend,
The damning critic, half-approving wit,
The coxcomb hit, or fearing to be hit;
Laughed at the loss of friends he never had,
The dull, the proud, the wicked, and the mad;
The distant threats of vengeance on his head,
The blow unfelt, the tear he never shed;
The tale revived, the lie so oft o'erthrown;
Th' imputed trash, and dullness not his own;
The morals blackened when the writings 'scape;
The libelled person, and the pictured shape;
Abuse, on all he loved, or loved him, spread,
A friend in exile, or a father dead;
The whisper, that to greatness still too near,
Perhaps yet vibrates on his Sovereign's ear—
Welcome for thee, fair Virtue! all the past:
For thee, fair Virtue! welcome ev'n the last!
  'But why insult the poor, affront the great?'
A knave's a knave, to me, in ev'ry state;
Alike my scorn, if he succeed or fail,
Sporus at court, or Japhet in a jail,
A hireling scribbler, or a hireling peer,
Knight of the Post corrupt, or of the Shire;

If on a pillory, or near a throne,
He gain his prince's ear, or lose his own.
  Yet soft by nature, more a dupe than wit,
Sappho can tell you how this man was bit:
This dreaded sat'rist Dennis will confess
Foe to his pride, but friend to his distress:
So humble, he has knocked at Tibbald's door,
Has drunk with Cibber, nay has rhymed for Moore.
Full ten years slandered, did he once reply?
Three thousand suns went down on Welsted's lie;
To please a mistress one aspersed his life;
He lashed him not, but let her be his wife;
Let Budgell charge low Grub Street on his quill,
And write whate'er he pleased, except his will;
Let the two Curlls of town and court abuse
His father, mother, body, soul, and Muse.
Yet why? that father held it for a rule,
It was a sin to call our neighbour fool;
That harmless mother thought no wife a whore,—
Hear this, and spare his family, James Moore!
Unspotted names, and memorable long!
If there be force in virtue, or in song.
  Of gentle blood (part shed in honour's cause,
While yet in Britain honour had applause)
Each parent sprung——'What fortune, pray?'——Their own,
And better got than Bestia's from the throne.
Born to no pride, inheriting no strife,
Nor marrying discord in a noble wife,
Stranger to civil and religious rage,
The good man walked innoxious through his age.
No courts he saw, no suits would ever try,
Nor dared an oath, nor hazarded a lie:
Unlearned, he knew no schoolman's subtle art,
No language, but the language of the heart.
By nature honest, by experience wise,
Healthy by temp'rance and by exercise,
His life, though long, to sickness passed unknown,
His death was instant, and without a groan.
O grant me thus to live, and thus to die!
Who sprung from kings shall know less joy than I.
  O friend! may each domestic bliss be thine!
Be no unpleasing melancholy mine:
Me, let the tender office long engage
To rock the cradle of reposing age,
With lenient arts extend a mother's breath,
Make languor smile, and smooth the bed of death,

Explore the thought, explain the asking eye,
And keep awhile one parent from the sky!
On cares like these if length of days attend,
May heav'n, to bless those days, preserve my friend,
Preserve him social, cheerful, and serene,
And just as rich as when he served a queen.
Whether that blessing be denied or giv'n,
Thus far was right, the rest belongs to heav'n.

(1735)

168 *Epistle to a Lady: Of the Characters of Women*

NOTHING so true as what you once let fall:
'Most women have no characters at all.'
Matter too soft a lasting mark to bear,
And best distinguished by black, brown, or fair.
  How many pictures of one nymph we view,
All how unlike each other, all how true!
Arcadia's Countess, here, in ermined pride,
Is there, Pastora by a fountain side.
Here Fannia, leering on her own good man,
And there, a naked Leda with a swan.
Let then the fair one beautifully cry
In Magdalen's loose hair and lifted eye,
Or dressed in smiles of sweet Cecilia shine,
With simp'ring angels, palms, and harps divine;
Whether the charmer sinner it, or saint it,
If folly grows romantic, I must paint it.
  Come then, the colours and the ground prepare!
Dip in the rainbow, trick her off in air,
Choose a firm cloud before it fall, and in it
Catch, ere she change, the Cynthia of this minute.
  Rufa, whose eye quick-glancing o'er the park
Attracts each light gay meteor of a spark,
Agrees as ill with Rufa studying Locke,
As Sappho's diamonds with her dirty smock,
Or Sappho at her toilet's greasy task,
With Sappho fragrant at an evening mask:
So morning insects, that in muck begun,
Shine, buzz, and fly-blow in the setting sun.
  How soft is Silia! fearful to offend,
The frail one's advocate, the weak one's friend:
To her, Calista proved her conduct nice,
And good Simplicius asks of her advice.

Sudden, she storms! she raves! You tip the wink,
But spare your censure—Silia does not drink.
All eyes may see from what the change arose,
All eyes may see—a pimple on her nose.
  Papillia, wedded to her doting spark,
Sighs for the shades—'How charming is a park!'
A park is purchased, but the fair he sees
All bathed in tears—'Oh odious, odious trees!'
  Ladies, like variegated tulips, show,
'Tis to their changes that their charms we owe;
Their happy spots the nice admirer take,
Fine by defect, and delicately weak.
'Twas thus Calypso once each heart alarmed,
Awed without virtue, without beauty charmed;
Her tongue bewitched as oddly as her eyes,
Less wit than mimic, more a wit than wise;
Strange graces still, and stranger flights she had,
Was just not ugly, and was just not mad;
Yet ne'er so sure our passion to create,
As when she touched the brink of all we hate.
  Narcissa's nature, tolerably mild,
To make a wash would hardly stew a child,
Has ev'n been proved to grant a lover's pray'r,
And paid a tradesman once to make him stare;
Gave alms at Easter, in a Christian trim,
And made a widow happy for a whim.
Why then declare good-nature is her scorn,
When 'tis by that alone she can be borne?
Why pique all mortals, yet affect a name?
A fool to pleasure, and a slave to fame:
Now deep in Taylor and the Book of Martyrs,
Now drinking citron with his Grace and Chartres.
Now conscience chills her, and now passion burns;
And atheism and religion take their turns;
A very heathen in the carnal part,
Yet still a sad, good Christian at her heart.
  See sin in state, majestically drunk,
Proud as a peeress, prouder as a punk;
Chaste to her husband, frank to all beside,
A teeming mistress, but a barren bride.
What then? let blood and body bear the fault,
Her head's untouched, that noble seat of thought:
Such this day's doctrine—in another fit
She sins with poets through pure love of wit.
What has not fired her bosom or her brain?
Caesar and Tall-boy, Charles and Charlemagne.

As Helluo, late dictator of the feast,
The nose of *haut-goût* and the tip of taste,
Critiqued your wine, and analysed your meat,
Yet on plain pudding deigned at home to eat;
So Philomedé, lect'ring all mankind
On the soft passion, and the taste refined,
Th' address, the delicacy—stoops at once,
And makes her hearty meal upon a dunce.
  Flavia's a wit, has too much sense to pray;
To toast our wants and wishes is her way;
Nor asks of God, but of her stars, to give
The mighty blessing, 'while we live, to live.'
Then all for death, that opiate of the soul!
Lucretia's dagger, Rosamonda's bowl.
Say, what can cause such impotence of mind?
A spark too fickle, or a spouse too kind.
Wise wretch! with pleasures too refined to please,
With too much spirit to be e'er at ease,
With too much quickness ever to be taught,
With too much thinking to have common thought:
Who purchase pain with all that joy can give,
And die of nothing but a rage to live.
  Turn then from wits; and look on Simo's mate,
No ass so meek, no ass so obstinate;
Or her that owns her faults, but never mends,
Because she's honest, and the best of friends;
Or her whose life the church and scandal share,
For ever in a passion, or a pray'r;
Or her who laughs at hell, but (like her Grace)
Cries, 'Ah! how charming if there's no such place!';
Or who in sweet vicissitude appears
Of mirth and opium, ratafie and tears,
The daily anodyne, and nightly draught,
To kill those foes to fair ones, time and thought.
Woman and fool are two hard things to hit,
For true no-meaning puzzles more than wit.
  But what are these to great Atossa's mind?
Scarce once herself, by turns all womankind!
Who, with herself, or others, from her birth
Finds all her life one warfare upon earth:
Shines in exposing knaves and painting fools,
Yet is whate'er she hates and ridicules.
No thought advances, but her eddy brain
Whisks it about, and down it goes again.

haut-goût] strong relish or flavour   ratafie] fruit-flavoured cordial or liqueur

Full sixty years the world has been her trade,
The wisest fool much time has ever made.
From loveless youth to unrespected age,
No passion gratified except her rage,
So much the fury still outran the wit,
The pleasure missed her, and the scandal hit.
Who breaks with her, provokes revenge from hell,
But he's a bolder man who dares be well:
Her ev'ry turn with violence pursued,
Nor more a storm her hate than gratitude.
To that each passion turns, or soon or late;
Love, if it makes her yield, must make her hate:
Superiors? death! and equals? what a curse!
But an inferior not dependant? worse.
Offend her, and she knows not to forgive;
Oblige her, and she'll hate you while you live:
But die, and she'll adore you—then the bust
And temple rise—then fall again to dust.
Last night, her lord was all that's good and great,
A knave this morning, and his will a cheat.
Strange! by the means defeated of the ends,
By spirit robbed of pow'r, by warmth of friends,
By wealth of follow'rs! without one distress,
Sick of herself through very selfishness!
Atossa, cursed with ev'ry granted pray'r,
Childless with all her children, wants an heir.
To heirs unknown descends th' unguarded store,
Or wanders, heav'n-directed, to the poor.
  Pictures like these, dear Madam, to design,
Asks no firm hand, and no unerring line;
Some wand'ring touch, or some reflected light,
Some flying stroke alone can hit 'em right:
For how should equal colours do the knack?
Chameleons who can paint in white and black?
  'Yet Cloe sure was formed without a spot.'—
Nature in her then erred not, but forgot.
'With every pleasing, every prudent part,
Say, what can Cloe want?'—She wants a heart.
She speaks, behaves, and acts, just as she ought,
But never, never reached one gen'rous thought.
Virtue she finds too painful an endeavour,
Content to dwell in decencies for ever.
So very reasonable, so unmoved,
As never yet to love, or to be loved.
She, while her lover pants upon her breast,
Can mark the figures on an Indian chest;

And when she sees her friend in deep despair,
Observes how much a chintz exceeds mohair.
Forbid it, heav'n, a favour or a debt
She e'er should cancel—but she may forget.
Safe is your secret still in Cloe's ear;
But none of Cloe's shall you ever hear.
Of all her dears she never slandered one,
But cares not if a thousand are undone.
Would Cloe know if you're alive or dead?
She bids her footman put it in her head.
Cloe is prudent—would you too be wise?
Then never break your heart when Cloe dies.
One certain portrait may (I grant) be seen,
Which heav'n has varnished out, and made a Queen:
The same for ever! and described by all
With truth and goodness, as with crown and ball.
Poets heap virtues, painters gems, at will,
And show their zeal, and hide their want of skill.
'Tis well—but artists! who can paint or write,
To draw the naked is your true delight:
That robe of quality so struts and swells,
None see what parts of nature it conceals.
Th' exactest traits of body or of mind,
We owe to models of an humble kind.
If Queensberry to strip there's no compelling,
'Tis from a handmaid we must take a Helen.
From peer or bishop 'tis no easy thing
To draw the man who loves his God or King:
Alas! I copy (or my draught would fail)
From honest Mah'met, or plain Parson Hale.
But grant, in public men sometimes are shown,
A woman's seen in private life alone:
Our bolder talents in full light displayed,
Your virtues open fairest in the shade.
Bred to disguise, in public 'tis you hide;
There, none distinguish 'twixt your shame or pride,
Weakness or delicacy; all so nice,
That each may seem a virtue or a vice.
In men we various ruling passions find,
In women, two almost divide the kind;
Those, only fixed, they first or last obey,
The love of pleasure, and the love of sway.
That, nature gives; and where the lesson taught
Is but to please, can pleasure seem a fault?

mohair] silk fabric in imitation of the material originally made from the hair of the Angora goat

Experience, this; by man's oppression cursed,
They seek the second not to lose the first.
  Men, some to bus'ness, some to pleasure take;
But ev'ry woman is at heart a rake:
Men, some to quiet, some to public strife;
But ev'ry lady would be queen for life.
  Yet mark the fate of a whole sex of queens!
Pow'r all their end, but beauty all the means.
In youth they conquer with so wild a rage,
As leaves them scarce a subject in their age:
For foreign glory, foreign joy, they roam;
No thought of peace or happiness at home.
But wisdom's triumph is well-timed retreat,
As hard a science to the fair as great!
Beauties, like tyrants, old and friendless grown,
Yet hate to rest, and dread to be alone,
Worn out in public, weary ev'ry eye,
Nor leave one sigh behind them when they die.
  Pleasures the sex, as children birds, pursue,
Still out of reach, yet never out of view;
Sure, if they catch, to spoil the toy at most,
To covet flying, and regret when lost:
At last, to follies youth could scarce defend,
'Tis half their age's prudence to pretend;
Ashamed to own they gave delight before,
Reduced to feign it, when they give no more:
As hags hold sabbaths, less for joy than spite,
So these their merry, miserable night;
Still round and round the ghosts of beauty glide,
And haunt the places where their honour died.
  See how the world its veterans rewards!
A youth of frolics, an old age of cards;
Fair to no purpose, artful to no end,
Young without lovers, old without a friend;
A fop their passion, but their prize a sot,
Alive, ridiculous, and dead, forgot!
  Ah, friend! to dazzle let the vain design;
To raise the thought and touch the heart be thine!
That charm shall grow, while what fatigues the Ring
Flaunts and goes down, an unregarded thing.
So when the sun's broad beam has tired the sight,
All mild ascends the moon's more sober light;
Serene in virgin modesty she shines,
And unobserved the glaring orb declines.
  Oh! blessed with temper, whose unclouded ray
Can make tomorrow cheerful as today;

She who can love a sister's charms, or hear
Sighs for a daughter with unwounded ear;
She who ne'er answers till a husband cools,
Or, if she rules him, never shows she rules;
Charms by accepting, by submitting sways,
Yet has her humour most when she obeys;
Lets fops or fortune fly which way they will;
Disdains all loss of tickets, or codille;
Spleen, vapours, or small-pox, above them all,
And mistress of herself, though china fall.
  And yet, believe me, good as well as ill,
Woman's at best a contradiction still.
Heav'n, when it strives to polish all it can
Its last best work, but forms a softer man;
Picks from each sex, to make its fav'rite blest,
Your love of pleasure, our desire of rest,
Blends, in exception to all gen'ral rules,
Your taste of follies, with our scorn of fools,
Reserve with frankness, art with truth allied,
Courage with softness, modesty with pride,
Fixed principles, with fancy ever new;
Shakes all together, and produces—you.
  Be this a woman's fame; with this unblest,
Toasts live a scorn, and queens may die a jest.
This Phoebus promised (I forget the year)
When those blue eyes first opened on the sphere;
Ascendant Phoebus watched that hour with care,
Averted half your parents' simple pray'r,
And gave you beauty, but denied the pelf
Which buys your sex a tyrant o'er itself.
The gen'rous god, who wit and gold refines,
And ripens spirits as he ripens mines,
Kept dross for duchesses, the world shall know it,
To you gave sense, good-humour, and a poet.

(1735)

169 from *One Thousand Seven Hundred and Thirty Eight, Dialogue II*

[*The Defence of Satire*]

  ASK you what provocation I have had?
The strong antipathy of good to bad.
When truth or virtue an affront endures,

168 codille] a term in the card game of ombre

Th' affront is mine, my friend, and should be yours.
Mine, as a foe professed to false pretence,
Who thinks a coxcomb's honour like his sense;
Mine, as a friend to ev'ry worthy mind;
And mine as man, who feel for all mankind.
F. You're strangely proud.
P. So proud, I am no slave:
So impudent, I own myself no knave:
So odd, my country's ruin makes me grave.
Yes, I am proud; I must be proud to see
Men not afraid of God, afraid of me:
Safe from the bar, the pulpit, and the throne,
Yet touched and shamed by Ridicule alone.
O sacred weapon! left for truth's defence,
Sole dread of folly, vice, and insolence!
To all but heav'n-directed hands denied,
The Muse may give thee, but the gods must guide.
Rev'rent I touch thee! but with honest zeal,
To rouse the watchmen of the public weal,
To virtue's work provoke the tardy Hall,
And goad the prelate slumb'ring in his stall.
Ye tinsel insects! whom a court maintains,
That counts your beauties only by your stains,
Spin all your cobwebs o'er the eye of day!
The Muse's wing shall brush you all away:
All his Grace preaches, all his lordship sings,
All that makes saints of queens, and gods of kings,
All, all but truth, drops dead-born from the press,
Like the last Gazette, or the last address.
When black ambition stains a public cause,
A monarch's sword when mad vain-glory draws,
Not Waller's wreath can hide the nation's scar,
Nor Boileau turn the feather to a star.
Not so, when diademed with rays divine,
Touched with the flame that breaks from Virtue's shrine,
Her priestless Muse forbids the good to die,
And opes the temple of eternity . . .
Let Envy howl, while heav'n's whole chorus sings,
And bark at honour not conferred by kings;
Let Flatt'ry sickening see the incense rise,
Sweet to the world, and grateful to the skies:
Truth guards the poet, sanctifies the line,
And makes immortal verse as mean as mine.
Yes, the last pen for Freedom let me draw,
When Truth stands trembling on the edge of law:
Here, last of Britons! let your names be read;

Are none, none living? let me praise the dead,
And for that cause which made your fathers shine,
Fall by the votes of their degen'rate line.
F. Alas! alas! pray end what you began,
And write next winter more *Essays on Man*.

(1738)

170 *Epigram Engraved on the Collar of a Dog which I gave to his Royal Highness*

I AM his Highness' dog at Kew;
Pray tell me, sir, whose dog are you?

(1738)

171 *On the Benefactions in the Late Frost*

YES! 'tis the time! I cried, impose the chain,
Destined and due to wretches self-enslaved!
But when I saw such charity remain,
I half could wish this people might be saved.
Faith lost, and Hope, their Charity begins;
And 'tis a wise design on pitying heav'n,
If this can cover multitudes of sins,
To take the only way to be forgiven.

(1740)

172 from *The Dunciad*, Book IV

(i)

[*A Young Traveller is Presented to the Goddess Dulness*]

IN flowed at once a gay embroidered race,
And titt'ring pushed the pedants off the place:
Some would have spoken, but the voice was drowned
By the French horn, or by the op'ning hound.
The first came forwards, with as easy mien
As if he saw St. James's and the Queen.
When thus th' attendant orator begun,
'Receive, great empress! thy accomplished son:
Thine from the birth, and sacred from the rod,
A dauntless infant! never scared with God.

The sire saw, one by one, his virtues wake:
The mother begged the blessing of a rake.
Thou gav'st that ripeness, which so soon began,
And ceased so soon, he ne'er was boy, nor man.
Through school and college, thy kind cloud o'ercast,
Safe and unseen the young Aeneas passed:
Thence bursting glorious, all at once let down,
Stunned with his giddy larum half the town.
Intrepid then, o'er seas and lands he flew:
Europe he saw, and Europe saw him too.
There all thy gifts and graces we display,
Thou, only thou, directing all our way!
To where the Seine, obsequious as she runs,
Pours at great Bourbon's feet her silken sons;
Or Tiber, now no longer Roman, rolls,
Vain of Italian arts, Italian souls:
To happy convents, bosomed deep in vines,
Where slumber abbots, purple as their wines:
To isles of fragrance, lily-silvered vales,
Diffusing languor in the panting gales:
To lands of singing, or of dancing slaves,
Love-whisp'ring woods, and lute-resounding waves.
But chief her shrine where naked Venus keeps,
And Cupids ride the lion of the deeps;
Where, eased of fleets, the Adriatic main
Wafts the smooth eunuch and enamoured swain.
Led by my hand, he sauntered Europe round,
And gathered ev'ry vice on Christian ground;
Saw ev'ry court, heard ev'ry king declare
His royal sense of op'ras or the fair;
The stews and palace equally explored,
Intrigued with glory, and with spirit whored;
Tried all *hors-d'œuvres*, all *liqueurs* defined,
Judicious drank, and greatly-daring dined;
Dropped the dull lumber of the Latin store,
Spoiled his own language, and acquired no more;
All classic learning lost on classic ground;
And last turned air, the echo of a sound!
See now, half-cured, and perfectly well-bred,
With nothing but a solo in his head;
As much estate, and principle, and wit,
As Jansen, Fleetwood, Cibber shall think fit;
Stol'n from a duel, followed by a nun,
And, if a borough choose him, not undone;
See, to my country happy I restore
This glorious youth, and add one Venus more.

Her too receive (for her my soul adores),
So may the sons of sons of sons of whores
Prop thine, O empress! like each neighbour throne,
And make a long posterity thy own.'
  Pleased, she accepts the hero, and the dame
Wraps in her veil, and frees from sense of shame.

(ii)

[*Carnations and Butterflies*]

  Then thick as locusts black'ning all the ground,
A tribe, with weeds and shells fantastic crowned,
Each with some wond'rous gift approached the pow'r,
A nest, a toad, a fungus, or a flow'r.
But far the foremost, two, with earnest zeal
And aspect ardent to the throne appeal.
  The first thus opened: 'Hear thy suppliant's call,
Great queen, and common mother of us all!
Fair from its humble bed I reared this flow'r,
Suckled, and cheered, with air, and sun, and show'r,
Soft on the paper ruff its leaves I spread,
Bright with the gilded button tipped its head;
Then throned in glass, and named it Caroline:
Each maid cried, "Charming!" and each youth, "Divine!"
Did Nature's pencil ever blend such rays,
Such varied light in one promiscuous blaze?
Now prostrate! dead! behold that Caroline:
No maid cries, "Charming!" and no youth, "Divine!"
And lo, the wretch! whose vile, whose insect lust
Laid this gay daughter of the spring in dust.
Oh, punish him, or to th' Elysian shades
Dismiss my soul, where no carnation fades!'
  He ceased, and wept. With innocence of mien,
Th' accused stood forth, and thus addressed the queen:
  'Of all th' enamelled race, whose silv'ry wing
Waves to the tepid zephyrs of the spring,
Or swims along the fluid atmosphere,
Once brightest shined this child of heat and air.
I saw, and started from its vernal bow'r
The rising game, and chased from flow'r to flow'r.
It fled, I followed; now in hope, now pain;
It stopped, I stopped; it moved, I moved again.
At last it fixed, 'twas on what plant it pleased,
And where it fixed, the beauteous bird I seized:
Rose or carnation was below my care;

I meddle, goddess! only in my sphere.
I tell the naked fact without disguise,
And, to excuse it, need but show the prize;
Whose spoils this paper offers to your eye,
Fair ev'n in death! this peerless butterfly.'
  'My sons!' (she answered) 'both have done your parts:
Live happy both, and long promote our arts.
But hear a mother, when she recommends
To your fraternal care our sleeping friends.
The common soul, of heav'n's more frugal make,
Serves but to keep fools pert, and knaves awake:
A drowsy watchman, that just gives a knock,
And breaks our rest, to tell us what's o'clock.
Yet by some object ev'ry brain is stirred;
The dull may waken to a humming-bird;
The most recluse, discreetly opened, find
Congenial matter in the cockle-kind;
The mind, in metaphysics at a loss,
May wander in a wilderness of moss;
The head that turns at super-lunar things,
Poised with a tail, may steer on Wilkins' wings.
  'O! would the sons of men once think their eyes
And reason giv'n them but to study flies!
See Nature in some partial narrow shape,
And let the Author of the whole escape:
Learn but to trifle; or, who most observe,
To wonder at their Maker, not to serve.'

(iii)

[*The Triumph of Dulness*]

  Then, blessing all, 'Go, children of my care!
To practice now from theory repair.
All my commands are easy, short, and full:
My sons! be proud, be selfish, and be dull.
Guard my prerogative, assert my throne:
This nod confirms each privilege your own.
The cap and switch be sacred to his Grace;
With staff and pumps the marquis lead the race;
From stage to stage the licensed earl may run,
Paired with his fellow-charioteer, the sun;
The learned baron butterflies design,
Or draw to silk Arachne's subtle line;
The judge to dance his brother sergeant call;
The senator at cricket urge the ball;
The bishop stow (pontific luxury!)

An hundred souls of turkeys in a pie;
The sturdy squire to Gallic masters stoop,
And drown his lands and manors in a soup.
Others import yet nobler arts from France,
Teach kings to fiddle, and make senates dance.
Perhaps more high some daring son may soar,
Proud to my list to add one monarch more;
And nobly conscious princes are but things
Born for first ministers, as slaves for kings,
Tyrant supreme! shall three estates command,
And make one mighty Dunciad of the land!'
More she had spoke, but yawned—all Nature nods:
What mortal can resist the yawn of gods?
Churches and chapels instantly it reached
(St. James's first, for leaden Gilbert preached);
Then catched the schools; the Hall scarce kept awake;
The Convocation gaped, but could not speak:
Lost was the nation's sense, nor could be found,
While the long solemn unison went round:
Wide, and more wide, it spread o'er all the realm;
Ev'n Palinurus nodded at the helm:
The vapour mild o'er each committee crept;
Unfinished treaties in each office slept;
And chiefless armies dozed out the campaign;
And navies yawned for orders on the main.
O Muse! relate (for you can tell alone,
Wits have short memories, and dunces none)
Relate, who first, who last resigned to rest;
Whose heads she partly, whose completely blest;
What charms could faction, what ambition lull,
The venal quiet, and entrance the dull;
Till drowned was sense, and shame, and right, and wrong—
O sing, and hush the nations with thy song!

* * * * *

In vain, in vain—the all-composing hour
Resistless falls: the Muse obeys the pow'r.
She comes! she comes! the sable throne behold
Of Night primeval, and of Chaos old!
Before her, Fancy's gilded clouds decay,
And all its varying rainbows die away.
Wit shoots in vain its momentary fires,
The meteor drops, and in a flash expires.
As one by one, at dread Medea's strain,
The sick'ning stars fade off th' ethereal plain;
As Argus' eyes by Hermes' wand oppressed,

Closed one by one to everlasting rest;
Thus at her felt approach, and secret might,
Art after art goes out, and all is night.
See skulking Truth to her old cavern fled,
Mountains of casuistry heaped o'er her head!
Philosophy, that leaned on heav'n before,
Shrinks to her second cause, and is no more.
Physic of Metaphysic begs defence,
And Metaphysic calls for aid on Sense!
See Mystery to Mathematics fly!
In vain! they gaze, turn giddy, rave, and die.
Religion blushing veils her sacred fires,
And unawares Morality expires.
Nor public flame, nor private, dares to shine,
Nor human spark is left, nor glimpse divine!
Lo! thy dread empire, Chaos! is restored;
Light dies before thy uncreating word;
Thy hand, great Anarch! lets the curtain fall,
And universal darkness buries all.

(1742)

ROBERT DODSLEY

1703–1764

173 *An Epistle to My Friend J.B.*

Why, Jack, how now? I hear strange stories
How Molly what-d'ye-call't your whore is—
Hold, blot that word, rhyme forced it in—
Your dear kind mistress, sir, I mean;
And people say, but whisper that,
That she, poor soul! is big with brat.
If this, as I believe, is true,
In what a cursèd case are you!
You must the child maintain and father,
Or hang or marry, which you'd rather:
Confounded choices all, I vow:
But you ne'er dreamed of these till now.
These thoughts, alas! were ne'er in your head,
Th' unlucky feat was done hand o'er head:
Reason was then esteemed a bastard,
True pleasure's foe, a fearful dastard,

And by stiff passion over-mastered.
But don't you think yourself an ass
To vent your spleen upon a lass,
A silly, unexperienced girl,
Who, you might swear, in time would tell?
Besides, you might, better than there,
Have spit your venom you know where,
And then no further harm had come on't;
Now you must reap the fruit of some on't.
O bitter fruit! to those that taste it;
You've cause to pray that heav'n may blast it,
And from the tree abortive cast it.
For should the wicked embryon
(As all ill weeds are apt) come on,
The Lord have mercy on poor John!
Who'll then be cursedly surrounded
With noise and squall; and quite confounded
With highting, dancing, jumping, jowling,
And th' hateful noise of cradle rolling:
Now deafed with mammy's lullaby,
In consort with the peevish cry
Of squeaking, squalling, roaring brat,
Enough to make one tear one's hat.
   Then (to say nothing of the shame
It brings unhappy dad and mam)
Your silver will be ever flying;
Something or other always buying:
Clouts, blankets, barrows, hippins, swaddles,
Fine painted gew-gaws, corals, rattles,
Caps, aprons, bibs, white frocks and mantling,
To clothe the little sh—n bantling.
   On th' other side, when pregnant foetus
Breaks from the womb with strong impetus,
And comes into this world of grief
(O that it ne'er may come with life!),
There's such a hurry! such a pother!
Old wives and midwives one with th' other;
Such eating, drinking and devouring;
Such washing, rinsing, scrubbing, scouring;
Such waiting, running and attending;
Thy purse had need to have no ending.
   But hold, I run on hand o'er head,
And quite forget poor Moll in bed.
'Ah John!', the new-made granny cries,

hippins] baby clothes

'Behold my girl with pitying eyes,
See, see, poor soul! how sick she lies!
How weak, how faint and how decayed;
Some strengthening cordials must be had.'
Then *item* this, and that—and that;
And *item—item*—God knows what;
For mammy some, and some for brat.
And now look back again, and view
The mischiefs thou hast run into,
Led blindly on by sinful passion
(God knows!) and small consideration!
See what a num'rous train of plagues
Attend upon the damned intrigues
Of that part of the female sex!
See, and beware, their future wiles,
Fly, fly their false deluding smiles:
Shun 'em as basilisks, whose eyes
Dart wounds, and he that's wounded dies.
Fly their temptations, fly their charms,
Fly their damned deceitful arms.
Avoid them as the plague or pox,
Shun 'em as precipices, rocks,
Dire rocks! near which whoever came,
Was sure to split, and sink, and damn.

(1732)

GEORGE FAREWELL

fl. 1733

174 *An Adieu to my Landlady*

MAYST thou die desp'rate in some dirty pool,
Catching, conceited, choleric old fool!
Thus prays thy lodger with his heart and pen;
And all who know thee sure will say—Amen.
Patience, ye gods, to write my bill of fare!
Stale bread of bran ill-baked, and dead small beer;
Tripe from the tanner's; bacon dung-hill fed;
Shrove-Tuesday fowls; and flank bull-beef instead
Of young rump-steaks, of fat without a grain,
Stewed with leek-broth for sauce in frying-pan;
Mutton last left upon the market-day,
And then avowed the best in all her way.

Hereof complaint is made in manner meek,
When lo! her pig's-eyes glare, her tawny cheek
Unshrivelling bloateth bluff; then pert, and proud
Of nasty craft, short off does Granny scud.
But since her buttock-bubbies thus she dares
Just at mine elbow boldly to reverse
Pat for the purpose, with sarcastic switch
I can't forbear to flog the wicked witch.

(1733)

175 *Privy-love for my Landlady*

HERE costive many minutes did I strain,
Still squeezing, sweating, swearing, all in vain;
When lo! who should pop by but mother Masters,
At whose bewitching look soon stubborn arse stirs.
No more my wanton wit shall whip thy wife,
Dear, doting Dick, for O! she saved my life.

(1733)

176 from *The Country Man*

(i)

THE crunking crane heard high amongst the clouds
Alarums up the peasant, whilst the cock,
Strutting most stately with a towering comb,
Clapping his wings proclaims th' approach of day.
He rouses up his fellow-labourers;
All at the crowing put together on
Their coarse patched coats upon their shivering backs,
And then their hats, and clumsy thick-soled shoes.
After he's yoked the well-fed steers together,
He whoops, and goads them forth into the field;
There in long furrows wears the ploughshare thin,
And whistling all the while beguiles his pains.
When now the evening-star ariseth bright
From off the eastern sea, and burnishes
With many-coloured rays the earth, whose grass
Between the silver gildings glitters green,
Flutt'ring her little wings the nightingale
Salutes him homeward with melodious note.
Behold! the flower-fetching western gales

Now thaw the hoar-frost on the mountain tops.
The stars, that seem to wander through the sky,
Smile sweetly sparkling in the firmament.
The queen of evening through the clear expanse
Gracefully lashes on her ling'ring team.
The orbit also of the brother-star
Appears more trim; which o'er and o'er again
Wrings sprinklings from his locks like honey sweet,
Which with a fertile dew fill full the field.
The fost'ring earth, seen spruce of countenance,
In fair abundance yielding verdant growth,
Her forehead crowns with buds of every sort.
The snow-white withywind just blows, and dies,
Nor does the lily boast much longer life;
But flower-gentles, clad in holy hue,
Do everlastingly that hue preserve.
Poppy too, darling of the wheaten queen,
And friend to sleep, does here expand its leaves.
The daffodilly does self-smitten gape,
As with self-admiration still possessed.
Under a temp'rate breeze the saffron blows,
Which to the city sends a sweet perfume,
There wafted by a gentle blast of wind.
Here too the marigold with flamy leaf
Stands full unfolded near the melilot.
That corn-field there puts forth a purple blush;
This turf in lively yellow waving lies;
These blades with azure-stones, and those with pearl
Comparing do outvie; the verdant grass
Gay glisters all abroad through hillocks high,
Or shadowy shines along the hill-edged dale,
Or on the silent-sliding river's bank:
In joyful plenty all things brightly smile.

(ii)

Over the meadow bounds the skittish colt,
And dashes in swift course the bord'ring wave,
Or scours the hollow of the lofty mount,
And plashes through the stony stream unshod.
Fierce shines his comely front, his waving mane
Wantons in wind, his ears prick quavering up.
From his round jetty head his ample eye
Out standeth full; from his wide nostril darts
The breath as if on flame; his curving neck

withywind] bindweed   flower-gentles] amaranths

Stands lofty up, such as full forward bears
The bird, whose voice bids lions stand in awe,
Whose watchful note calls up the loit'ring morn.
Round-circling plump does swell his breast abroad,
With courage fraught undaunted; high arise
His even shoulders, ridging slender up.
And now his back the saddle well becomes.
Along his loins does double run the chine;
Thick flanks truss up his belly tight and smooth;
His buttocks in good liking spread themselves;
He cocks his tail rough-frisling full of hair;
The copious locks o'erflow his lusty neck,
Down his right shoulder floating to and fro.
Bold does he turn his nimble shank around
Tied firm within a knee shaped round and long.
Fierce he bears forward with his look aloft,
And prances stately neighing all the way.
His deep horn hollow hoof treads thund'ring down;
Resembling so the stamping dance and noise
Of brazen cymbals loud, wherewith her priests
Did celebrate the rites of Cybele.

(iii)

Let us moreover view the poultry tribe,
And the plumed leaders of the comb-crowned race;
Whose clapping wings the stars do not abide,
Whose watchful crowings summon up the day.
Lo! two prepare to try in furious fight
Which afterwards shall absolute command.
With bills adverse they hostile offers make;
With quick attacks they whet each other's rage;
Their breasts opposed direct meet quashing full;
Their courage kindles high; and swift and strong
Spiteful they clash their heels, rebounding quick.
The conqueror's crow triumphant does avouch
The day his own; and on his vanquished foe
He leaps insulting; with a tread unkind
He spurns him cowering, creeping, hushed in fear
To lurk in some dark corner, where he pines
To bear the victor's domineering pride.
Good reason now the common flock should walk
In close attendance by th' undoubted chief:
Their comely chief, upon whose crown aloft
The comb up-towering reddens purple-hued.
Upon his crest in wandering waves of light

The trembling feathers glitter shadowy.
Adown his golden neck and shoulders run
The glorious beauties; gracefully his gills
Ample wax white from off the upper red,
And like a beard hang on his breast so plump.
Curved at the end his beak stands tapering out;
His tawny eyes shine sparkling fierce in flame;
And wide his ears unfold themselves all pale.
Shaggy with hairs his legs stand stiff and straight,
Meeting above in jointure close and firm.
With sharp and sturdy spurs his heels are armed;
His rough-haired thighs and pinions spread full wide;
In a row twofold upward borne on high
Quiver large, curving plumes upon his tail.
He by himself alone in lechery strong
Fills fruitful the whole family of fowls.
With his sharp claws he now tears up the ground,
And pries in every corner for the grain.
Warily now he views the sky o'ercast,
And so keeps out of danger from the hawk,
That bird of prey; nor does the scaly snake
Craftily creeping bite him by surprise.
  Upon the pond lo! with a slabby foot
The duck with painted collar rows along,
And quacking fond allures her brood to swim;
Erect now stretching; plunging now below.
The thrush sets up his star-bespangled tail
Largely unfurling, proud to court his mate.
Picking on figs, or mill-dust gathering up,
He fattens sleeky; till the fowler false
With wheedling note allures him to his net.
Close by a wall the turtle pampering sits
Hoarse sounding mournful, with her lover by
Piteously breathing out his amorous tale.
  To me, ye powers above, grant such a life,
Such pastimes, such refreshments after work,
Riches so void of care! 'tis all I pray:
Here limited shall stand my wildest wish.

(1733)

slabby] muddy

177

Molly Moor

TULLY, the queen of beauty's boast,
Through all America the toast,
Does, that her face more eyes may catch,
Reform it with a negro-patch.
Venus for ever does delight
In thickest shade, and ebon night.
Does not Tom Serjeant try to make
His person passant dressed in black?
Observe the coal of purest jet
The fiercest flame does still beget.
As the most cloudy mysteries
The mussulmans devoutest prize,
So smartest beaux and wits adore
The gloomy grace of Molly Moor.
The proudest snowy forms at last
Must in a sable pall be dressed:
E'en Dolly Dowglass' self must go
Down to the negro-shades below;
Into the pitchy kingdom, where
This raven lass shall queen appear;
And sit on Proserpina's throne,
When she is up to Ceres gone.

(1733)

178

To the Archdeacon

UNDER the sun is nothing new?
Nothing, if Solomon says true.
Archdeacon, you'll excuse me then
If I today should not be seen
Amidst the goodly row of friends
Which on your reverence attends
To hail you happy this new year,
Wishing it full of health and cheer:
But lo! sir, compliments apart,
My muse shall greet you from her heart.
Through many good old years O! may
Your present temper not decay!
That temper, which denoteth plain
A mind and body free from pain.
And can my wishes not succeed?

They must, if sages have decreed
Aright in their philosophy,
Who thus of nature all agree—
That as by envy's evil eye
The hated wretch may blasted die,
So he, whose riches are bestowed
In constant offices of good;
In giving to the fatherless
And widow food and cheerfulness,
By blessed sympathy shall share
The strength renewed of them and her.
  A wish of wealth for such a man
Would be superfluous and vain;
For fair abundance surely will
By just account his coffers fill,
Who lends so much unto the lord,
To be with int'rest high restored.
  When you must pay the only debt
Was e'er demanded of you yet,
May a good, gentle hundredth year
Commit you softly to the bier;
Whilst your white locks will seem to be
But blossoms of the mystic tree
Of life eternal, which shall spread
Up to the sky its glorious head:
Where none but youthful years attend;
And now farewell, my heavenly friend.

(1733)

179 *Quaerè*

WHETHER at doomsday (tell, ye reverend wise)
My friend Priapus with myself shall rise?

(1733)

180 *There's Life in a Mussel. A Meditation*

COME here, thou proud pretender unto arts,
Most self-amazing sophy, look and learn;
Nor travel more from east to west for food.
Advert thine eye, in contemplation close,

180 sophy] sage

On these thy little betters heaven-fed.
Up to yon luminary raise a thought,
Whose majesty so mild, in all her forms,
The mighty ocean follows faithfully:
View her with wonder leading up the waves
To give unto this mussel due repast.
In full felicity behold it fixed,
Contented waiting the appointed time;
Now sleeping in its cell, wherein anon
'Twill drinking lie at ease, like Romans couched.
  Solomon clothed in all his glory (said
The truth itself) was less than lily fair.
O may I modest, and with reverence
To that great oracle, go on to say
His table, on a festival, could not
Exhibit entertainment suited more
To hunger and to health, nor so superb
As Neptune feasts this less than reptile with.
  O Fate, thou grand disposer of events,
Director of man's metamorphosis,
Grant me at death a change to mussel-life!
Or, if not too presumptuous in the wish,
More nobly bless me in the oyster-bed!
  You furious folk, for fame infatuate,
Who Alexander down your days abrupt
For one long night upon Bellona's pillow,
Because 'tis curtained round with specious ensigns;
I tell you, fighting fools, this mussel-bed
As much of honour has, and more delight.
  Hail, happy shell! from heart-ache ever free!
The basis beautiful of Christendom,
The source of all the potentates on earth,
In its best attitude resembles thee.
Patient, like thee, that prime of nature lies
T' imbibe the quintessence of flowing sweets.

(1733)

SAMUEL BOWDEN

fl. 1726–1771

181 from *The Paper Kite*

THE kite, completed thus, is borne along
By some blest leaders of the shining throng,
Who to the fields elate with joy repair,
And wait the blast that wafts her in the air.
So when some new-built ship is launched for sail,
And only tarries for the prosp'rous gale,
Th' impatient crew each rising breeze explore,
And long to see her sail, and quit the shore.
Now from the central string extends the line,
And for the flight lie harnessed rolls of twine.
This takes the string, remote his partner stands,
And holds the kite, impatient, in his hands.
She tugs to go; he scarce without a prayer
Commits the struggling engine to the air.
But oh! what passions fluctuate in his mind,
To whom th' important office is consigned,
To whom 'tis giv'n to steer the rising kite,
Pilot her motions, and assist her flight!
Soon as she mounts, he flying meets the wind,
Oft chides his mate, and often looks behind.
The trickling twine glides through his glowing hand,
And joy transporting flushes all the band;
Applauding shouts pursue her as she flies,
And raise the wind that bears her to the skies.
So larks on poisèd pinions soar sublime,
In ether lost, still singing as they climb.
The paper yacht high hovers with its train,
While birds affrighted leave th' ethereal plain
All vacant to her sweep, and wond'ring find
Their empire lessened, and their flight confined.
Oft when th' unbalanced kite requires more sail,
Their hats and handkerchiefs assist the tail.
Oh happy boy! who now with pleasure sees
His flying glove mount on the airy breeze.
How does he almost fly with rapt'rous charms,
To meet the bird descending to his arms!
And how transported tell to list'ning crowds,
This is the glove which lately reached the clouds!
Scarce are deluded Papists pleased so much,

When their blest robes retain some idol's touch.
Not seamen more, from Nile, or Ganges' coast,
Or Plata's shores, their far-fetched treasure boast.
  But if the line by some misfortune breaks,
Her lofty seat the prone machine forsakes,
In many a giddy vortex whirled around,
Like Icarus swift rushes to the ground,
All torn; the anxious troop about her throng,
And weeping bear the shattered frame along.
While all to view each gaping breach are grieved,
As if themselves had every wound received,
And as their hands the shipwrecked bird repair,
Some blame the architect, and some the air.
  But if supported by a gentle breeze,
She glides serene, and rises by degrees,
Far as the line permits she still ascends,
Till in the clouds her lofty voyage ends:
Beyond our narrow ken will dare to soar,
Where never vent'rous bird has reached before.
Now swift on wavy wings descending slow,
She's kept from headlong flight by guides below;
Then with a gentle fall salutes the earth,
Caressed by puny bands with shouting mirth.
Their infant accents ring from field to field,
As when glad victors tattered ensigns wield;
While fair their curlèd locks in breezes flow,
And smiling blushes in each aspect glow.
  O happiest state of life! bright spring of youth!
Fair period, fraught with innocence and truth.
Of golden eras and Saturnian times,
Let poets story in romantic rhymes;
This age, if any, is the age of gold,
Ere thrice five winters have their circles rolled.
No flames of love nor wine their breasts annoy,
No cares of business interrupt their joy:
In soft amusements and the sweets of play,
The thoughtless chorus spend the shining day;
To grateful sports as grateful books are joined,
And study's made a plaything to the mind.
Man's life in its first bud still fairest shows,
As orchards in their bloom most sweets disclose.
  Sometimes a scene more wondrous feasts the sight,
When the mechanic bird is raised by night.
For in a paper orb by artists made,
With dext'rous skill a candle is conveyed;
Tied to the tail the pendant lantern glows,

And, mounting, lights its passage as it goes.
The kite remote soars in a path unseen,
While the bright tail far-stretching hangs between.
Thus Jupiter we see in light arrayed,
While his attending moons are hid in shade.
Still comet-like it sweeps, erratic fire,
And crowds beneath the floating blaze admire.
  The country swains, who at a distance gaze,
Survey the painted meteor with amaze,
Quote from old almanacs portentous times,
Spell future ills, and ponder former crimes.
Partridge and mystic Moore are oft turned o'er,
And Bunyan brought to light, ne'er seen before;
Some long ago these wonders could foretell,
When salt prophetic at the table fell;
This sight, blue flame and hares which crossed the road,
This, dreams presaged, and ravens used to bode.
  But high the wavy luminary shines,
Till the spent taper droops, and sick'ning pines;
Through the dark air the gilded phantom flies,
And rustles like a whirlwind down the skies.
So with her lamp the Muse ascends the sphere,
Pleased in her little orb to flutter there,
Till the dim light expiring dies away,
Like the last ruins of declining day;
And thus descending with the paper kite,
With her alike concludes th' advent'rous flight.

(1733)

ANONYMOUS

182 *A Receipt to Cure a Love Fit*

TIE one end of a rope fast over a beam,
And make a slip-noose at the other extreme;
Then just underneath let a cricket be set,
On which let the lover most manfully get;
Then over his head let the snecket be got,
And under one ear be well settled the knot.
The cricket kicked down, let him take a fair swing;
And leave all the rest of the work to the string.

(1733)

182 cricket] stool   snecket] noose

JOHN BANCKS

1709–1751

183

A Fragment

In Cloe's chamber, she and I
Together sat, no creature nigh:
The time and place conspired to move
A longing for the joys of love.
I sighed and kissed, and pressed her hand;
Did all—to make her understand.
She, pretty, tender-hearted creature,
Obeyed the dictates of good-nature,
As far as modesty would let her.
A melting virgin seldom speaks
But with her breasts, and eyes, and cheeks:
Nor was it hard from these to find
That Cloe had—almost a mind.
Thus far 'twas well; but to proceed,
What should I do?—Grow bold.—I did.—
At last she faltered, 'What would'st have?'—
'Your love,' said I, 'or else my grave.'—
'Suppose it were the first,' quoth she,
'Could you forever constant be?'
'Forever? Cloe, by those eyes,
Those bubbies, which so fall and rise,
By all that's soft, and all that's fair,
By your whole sacred self, I swear,
Your fondest wishes ne'er shall crave
So constant, so complete a slave!'
'Damon, you know too well the art,'
She sighing said, 'to reach my heart!
Yet oh! I can't, I won't comply.—
Why will you press? Dear Damon why?'

* * * * * * *

Desunt Caetera

For Cloe coming in one day,
As on my desk the copy lay,
'What means this rhyming fool?' she cries:
'Why some folks may believe these lies!'
So on the fire she threw the sheet.
I burned my hand—to save this bit.

(1733)

184 A Description of London

HOUSES, churches, mixed together,
Streets unpleasant in all weather;
Prisons, palaces contiguous,
Gates, a bridge, the Thames irriguous.

Gaudy things enough to tempt ye,
Showy outsides, insides empty;
Bubbles, trades, mechanic arts,
Coaches, wheelbarrows and carts.

Warrants, bailiffs, bills unpaid,
Lords of laundresses afraid;
Rogues that nightly rob and shoot men,
Hangmen, aldermen and footmen.

Lawyers, poets, priests, physicians,
Noble, simple, all conditions:
Worth beneath a threadbare cover,
Villainy bedaubed all over.

Women black, red, fair and grey,
Prudes and such as never pray,
Handsome, ugly, noisy, still,
Some that will not, some that will.

Many a beau without a shilling,
Many a widow not unwilling;
Many a bargain, if you strike it:
This is London! How d'ye like it?

(1738)

PHILIP DORMER STANHOPE, EARL OF CHESTERFIELD

1694–1773

185 To a Lady on Reading Sherlock Upon Death

MISTAKEN fair, lay *Sherlock* by,
His doctrine is deceiving;
For, whilst he teaches us to die,
He cheats us of our living.

To die's a lesson we shall know
  Too soon, without a master;
Then let us only study now
  How we may live the faster.

To live's to love; to bless, be blessed
  With mutual inclination;
Share then my ardour in your breast,
  And kindly meet my passion.

But if thus blessed I may not live,
  And pity you deny,
To me, at least, your *Sherlock* give,
  'Tis I must learn to die.

(1733)

186 *Advice to a Young Lady*

ASSES' milk, half a pint, take at seven, or before,
Then sleep for an hour or two, and no more.
At nine stretch your arms, and oh! think, when alone,
There's no pleasure in bed.—'Mary, bring me my gown.'
Slip on that ere you rise; let your caution be such,
Keep all cold from your breast, there's already too much.
Your pinners set right, your twitcher tied on,
Your prayers at an end, and your breakfast quite done,
Retire to some author improving and gay,
And with sense like your own, set your mind for the day.
At twelve you may walk, for at this time o' th' year,
The sun, like your wit, is as mild as it's clear:
But mark in the meadows the ruin of time,
Take the hint, and let life be improved in its prime.
Return not in haste, nor of dressing take heed,
For such beauty as yours no assistance can need.
With an appetite, thus, down to dinner you sit,
Where the chief of the feast is the flow of your wit:
Let this be indulged, and let laughter go round;
As it pleases your mind, to your health 'twill redound.
After dinner two glasses at least I approve;
Name the first to the king, and the last to your love:
Thus cheerful with wisdom, with innocence gay,
And calm with your joys, gently glide through the day.
The dews of the ev'ning most carefully shun,
They are tears of the sky for the loss of the sun.

Then in chat, or at play, with a dance or a song,
Let the night, like the day, pass with pleasure along;
All cares, but of love, banish far from your mind,
And those you may end when you please to be kind.

(1736)

187 *On Mr. Nash's Present of his own Picture at Full Length, Fixed between the Bustos of Mr. Pope and Sir Is. Newton, in the Long Room at Bath*

IMMORTAL Newton never spoke
More truth than here you'll find;
Nor Pope himself e'er penned a joke
More cruel on mankind.

This picture, placed the busts between,
Gives Satire all his strength:
Wisdom and Wit are little seen,
But Folly at full length.

(1741)

188 *Song*

WHENEVER, Chloe, I begin
Your heart, like mine, to move,
You tell me of the crying sin
Of unchaste lawless love.

How can that passion be a sin,
Which gave to Chloe birth?
How can those joys but be divine,
Which make a heaven on earth?

To wed, mankind the priests trepanned
By some sly fallacy,
And disobeyed God's great command,
Increase and multiply.

You say that love's a crime; content:
Yet this allow you must,
More joy's in heav'n if one repent,
Than over ninety just.

Sin then, dear girl, for heaven's sake,
Repent and be forgiven;
Bless me, and by repentance make
A holy day in heaven.

(1748)

ROBERT TATERSAL

fl. 1734

189 *The Bricklayer's Labours*

AT length the soft nocturnal minutes fly,
And crimson blushes paint the orient sky;
When, by a kind of drowsy stretch and yawn,
I ope my eyes, and view the scarlet dawn;
But stealing sleep my vitals still surprise,
And with a slumb'ring softness seal my eyes,
Till open light corroborates the day,
And through the casement darts his signal ray;
When up I start, and view the eastern sky,
And by my mark find six o'clock is nigh.
Then hanging on my threadbare coat and hose,
My hat, my cap, my breeches and my shoes,
With sheepskin apron girt about my waist,
Downstairs I go to visit my repast,
Which rarely doth consist of more than these:
A quartern loaf and half a pound of cheese.
Then in a linen bag, on purpose made,
My day's allowance o'er my shoulder's laid:
And first, to keep the fog from coming in,
I whet my whistle with a dram of gin;
So thus equipped, my trowel in my hand,
I haste to work, and join the ragged band.
And now each one his different post assigned,
And three to three in ranks completely joined,
When 'Bricks and mortar' echoes from on high,
'Mortar and bricks' the common, constant cry.
Each sturdy slave their different labours share,
Some brickmen called, and some for mortar are:
With sultry sweat and blow without allay,
Travel the standard up and down all day.
And now the sun, with more exalted ray,
With glowing beams distributes riper day,

When amidst dust and smoke, and sweat and noise,
'A line, a line,' the foreman cries, 'my boys';
When tuck and pat with Flemish bond they run,
Till the whole course is struck complete and done:
Then on again, while two exalt the quoin,
And draw the midmost men another line.
The course laid out when, through the fleeting air,
A solemn sound salutes the willing ear;
When universal *Yo-hos* echo straight,
Our constant signal to the hour of eight.
And now precipitant away we steer
To eat our viands, and to get some beer;
Where midst the clamour, noise and smoky din
Of dust, tobacco, chaws and drinking gin,
The short half-hour we merrily do spin.
When for dessert some, with their sunburnt fists,
Cram in a chaw of half an ounce at least,
And then to sweep the passage clean within,
Wash down their throats a quartern full of gin.
And now again the signal greets our ear,
We're called to book, must at the bar appear:
When the grim host examines what we've done,
And scores sometimes devoutly two for one.
And now refreshed again we mount on high,
While one calls 'Mortar', others 'Bricks' do cry,
And then 'A line, a line' 's the constant sound;
By line and rule our daily labour's crowned,
While to divert the sultry hours along,
One tells a tale, another sings a song.
And now the sun, with full meridian ray,
With scorching beams confirms the perfect day.
Full twelve o'clock, the labourers cry 'Yo-ho',
When some to sleep, and some to dinner go:
Some that have victuals eat; others who've none
Supply the place with drink and gin alone;
Mod'rate in food, but in good beer profuse,
Which for the heat we modestly excuse.
And now the gliding minutes almost gone,
And a loud noise proclaims the hour of one;
Again we reassume the dusty stage,
And mortar chafed again we do engage.
This the most tedious part of all the day,
Full five hours' space to toil without allay:
Now parched with heat, and almost choked with dust,

Flemish bond] method of laying bricks quoin] key- or corner-stone chaws] chewing tobacco

We join our pence to satiate our thirst.
At length the western breezes gently play,
And Sol declining moderates his ray;
Now the approaching welcome hour draws near,
And now again the signal glads our ear;
The happy hour we waited for all day
At length arrives our labours to repay.
And now, the tools reposited with care
Until the morning rays again appear,
Some homewards bend, some to the alehouse steer,
Others more sober feast on better cheer.
But when the days contract and wintry hours rise,
And sable clouds and fogs invest the skies,
When frost and cold congeal the atmosphere,
And trees disrobed and hoary fields appear;
When all the earth in ice and snow is bound,
And naught but desolation all around,
Then hapless me! I wander up and down,
With half an apron wondrous greasy grown!
With anxious looks my countenance is clad,
And all my thoughts are like the winter, sad!
This scene of life corrodes my troubled mind;
I seek for work, but none, alas! can find;
Sometimes, by chance, I have a grate to set,
To hang a copper, or a hole replete;
A day or two to exercise my skill,
But seldom more, reluctant to my will.
And thus I pass the tedious winter on,
Sometimes repast I have, and sometimes none;
Till cheerful Phoebus, with a grateful ray,
Through vernal airs explores his willing way,
Dispels all cares, and gladdens every vein,
And all the joyous scene revolves again.

(1734)

JEAN ADAMS

1710–1765

190 *A Dream, or the Type of the Rising Sun*

LOOSED from its bonds my spirit fled away,
And left behind its moving tent of clay.
Aloft it soars through fields of painted air,
Which Fancy's pencil could not paint too fair.

I looked, and saw the God of Day arise;
With graceful steps he travels up the skies:
By just degrees at length he reached the line.
I saw the utmost limits of him shine:
While moon and stars before his chariot fly,
He in the floating mirror fixed his eye.
'Here fix, my eye, come to the porch, my ear:
Sit still, my thought, that I the sound may hear.'
They all obeyed, when lo, I heard a cry,
'Come out and meet the ruler of the sky.'
Implicit Nature all together ran,
Their numerous voices seemed a single man.
How from my heart the flame leaped to my eye,
While through the clear perspective I descry
Pure Nature's unconsulted harmony.
'I am his bed,' cried out the torrid clime,
'He fixed my periods,' cried revolving Time;
'He is my husband,' cried the quick'ning shower,
'He's my physician,' cried the drooping flower.
I heard the little insect world all cry,
'He gave me life, and force, and wings to fly.'
The vine cried out, 'He nursed me when a plant,
Ev'n to this hour he gives me what I want;
His virtue brought the moisture to my crop,
He formed the blossoms on my trembling top;
He made my clusters ready for the press,
And shall not I express my thankfulness?'
'He cut my channels,' cried exulting flood,
'I owe him all my beauties,' cried the wood.
'He gave me light and heat,' said smiling flame,
'I am his shadow,' cried exalted Fame.
'I am his darling,' cried unfeignèd Truth,
'And so am I,' replied the wingèd youth;
'In all his actions thou may'st see me move.'
'Nay, I have all his soul,' cried divine Love.
Dumb Echo cried, 'He taught me to repeat;
None else could e'er teach me to imitate.'
'I am his cup,' cried pure unmixèd Grief;
Said heavenly Joy, 'I fly to his relief.'
'I am his sword,' cried uncorrupted Hate;
'I quake before him,' cried relentless Fate.
This harmony was noble and divine:
All joyed to see their benefactor shine.
The feathered choir clapped all their wings for joy,
Whose notes made up a perfect harmony.
Now russet garments on the fields are spread,

And now palm branches in his way are laid.
All Nature seemed to wanton in her prime;
Pure pleasure seemed to turn the wheel of Time.
Forward I went, and saw society,
The pleasure-garden of the deity;
In which almighty Jove took such delight,
He walked around her walls both day and night.
At his own cost he built the threefold wall
So high, that thieves could never miss to fall.
The wall of Duty seemèd to my eye
For altitude above the starry sky.
Rich curious carvings were upon the stone;
A fair foundation it was laid upon:
I saw inscribèd conscious Fortitude.
The glorious hedge of Honour next I saw,
One of the fairest rules in Nature's law:
The hedge of Honour was of holy thorn,
Its natural fruit was high heroic scorn.
I thought him mad, who would attempt to climb
Where every thorn must fix its point in him.
The hedge of Int'rest was but very low,
Yet to the eye it had a glaring show;
Its worth was less than anything I saw,
But I observed it keepèd most in awe.

(1734)

ANONYMOUS

191 *On a Female Rope-Dancer*

WHILST in her prime and bloom of years,
Fair Celia trips the rope,
Alternately she moves our fears,
Alternately our hope.

But when she sinks, or rises higher,
Or graceful does advance,
We know not which we most admire,
The dancer, or the dance.

(1734)

THOMAS GILBERT

1713?–1747

192

from *A View of the Town. In an Epistle to a Friend*

[*Against Homosexuality*]

FORLORN Saphira, with reclining head,
Sighs for her absent lord in bridal bed;
He to St. James's Park with rapture flies,
And roams in search of some vile ingle prize;
Courts the foul pathic in the fair one's place,
And with unnatural lust defiles his race.
From whence could such polluted wretches spring,
How learn to propagate so foul a sin?
The sons of Sodom were destroyed by fire,
Gomorrah felt the Lord's destructive fire:
The great metropolis of England's isle
Had like to've been the nation's funeral pile.
Bold race of men! whom nothing can affright,
Not e'en their consciences in dead of night.
Let Jesuits some subtler pains invent,
For hanging is too mild a punishment;
Let them lay groaning on the racking-wheel,
Or feel the tortures of the burning steel,
Whips, poisons, daggers, inquisitions, flames:
This crime the most exalted vengeance claims;
Or else be banished to some desert place,
And perish in each other's foul embrace.

(1735)

ANONYMOUS

193

Laudanum

WHERE Somnus' temple rises from a ground,
Spreading a gloomy, dusky shade around,
The poppy, blushing with its livid red,
Rises, and nodding waves its drowsy head.

Blest flower! whose juice such influence contains,
As quells the body's agonising pains;
And gently lulls into a soothing rest
The swelling sorrows of a troubled breast;
All my attempts, great sov'reign, are too low,
In numbers worthy of thyself, to show
The great acknowledgements to thee we owe.
When, deaf to prayers and tears, th' obdurate fair
Looks on her suppliant with an haughty air;
When with a careless look she hears him trace
The sev'ral beauties of her shape and face;
Hears the dear titles, angel, charmer, queen,
With seemingly an absent air and mien;
Full of despair, to mitigate his grief
To thee he flies, and finds a sure relief;
In one soft hour the supercilious eye,
The toss indignant and the keen reply,
Are all hushed up and lost: the downy balm
Lulls all the boiling passions to a calm.
The evils or the cares of life, t' evade,
Not the rude vulgar only crave thy aid.
Impartially beneficent! e'en he
Who sweats beneath the load of majesty,
Fatigued with honour or the cares of state
(The sad insep'rables of being great),
Delights his regal honours to resign
To thee, and worship humbly at thy shrine.
'Tis not still silence nor a bed of down:
Thou great specific, thou can'st blunt alone
Those thorns, which line the circle of a crown.
But most of all, and most in vain, implores
The guilty wretch thy sov'reign healing powers.
Where'er he moves, a train of plagues display
Their several terrors in a dread array;
'Tis now he sees the injured widow's tears,
And now relenting hears the orphan's pray'rs;
Eternal sorrows being thus begun,
Where shall he go? himself he cannot shun:
'Tis true, by thee the terrors of his breast
Are, for a while, hushed to a soothing rest;
But the relief is short; a while—and then
His baleful company awake again,
And of thy absence dreadfully complain.
Thrice happy, who in virtue's paths delight,
Whose lives, like harmless infants' tears, invite
The gentle slumbers of the peaceful night.

But while thy dosing virtues I rehearse,
I feel thy drowsy influence in my verse;
And lest, great sirs, to you it should extend,
Command your sleepy poet to descend.

(1735)

MATTHEW GREEN

1696–1737

194 *On Barclay's Apology for the Quakers*

These sheets primeval doctrines yield,
Where revelation is revealed:
Soul-phlegm from literal feeding bred,
Systems lethargic to the head,
They purge, and yield a diet thin,
That turns to gospel-chyle within.
Truth sublimate may here be seen
Extracted from the parts terrene.
In these is shown how men obtain
What of Prometheus poets feign:
To scripture-plainness dress is brought,
And speech, apparel to the thought.
They hiss from instinct at red coats,
And war, whose work is cutting throats,
Forbid, and press the law of love,
Breathing the spirit of the dove.
Lucrative doctrines they detest,
As manufactured by the priest:
And throw down turnpikes, where we pay
For stuff which never mends the way;
And tithes, a Jewish tax, reduce,
And frank the gospel for our use.
They sable standing armies break,
But the militia useful make;
Since all unhired may preach and pray,
Taught by these rules as well as they,
Rules, which, when truths themselves reveal,
Bid us but follow what we feel.
The world can't hear the small still voice,
Such is its bustle and its noise;
Reason the proclamation reads,

194 chyle] milky fluid formed in the stomach by the digestive process

But not one riot passion heeds.
Wealth, honour, power the graces are,
Which here below our homage share:
They, if one votary they find
To mistress more divine inclined,
In truth's pursuit to cause delay
Throw golden apples in his way.
  Place me, O heav'n, in some retreat,
There let the serious death-watch beat,
There let me self in silence shun,
To feel thy will, which should be done.
  Then comes the spirit to our hut,
When fast the senses' doors are shut;
For so divine and pure a guest
The emptiest rooms are furnished best.
  O Contemplation! air serene,
From damps of sense, and fogs of spleen!
Pure mount of thought! thrice holy ground,
Where grace, when waited for, is found!
  Here 'tis the soul feels sudden youth,
And meets, exulting, virgin Truth;
Here, like a breeze of gentlest kind,
Impulses rustle through the mind;
Here shines that light with glowing face,
The fuse divine that kindles grace,
Which, if we trim our lamps, will last
Till darkness be by dying past,
And then goes out at end of night,
Extinguished by superior light.
  Ah me! the heats and colds of life,
Pleasure's and Pain's eternal strife,
Breed stormy passions which, confined,
Shake, like th' Aeolian cave, the mind,
And raise despair my lamp can last,
Placed where they drive their furious blast.
  False eloquence, big empty sound,
Like showers that rush upon the ground,
Little beneath the surface goes,
All streams along and muddy flows.
This sinks, and swells the buried grain,
And fructifies like southern rain.
  His art, well hid in mild discourse,
Exerts persuasion's winning force,
And nervates so the good design,
That King Agrippa's case is mine.

nervates] strengthens

Well-natured, happy shade, forgive!
Like you I think, but cannot live.
Thy scheme requires the world's contempt,
That, from dependence life exempt,
And constitution framed so strong,
This world's worst climate cannot wrong.
Not such my lot, not fortune's brat,
I live by pulling off the hat,
Compelled by station every hour
To bow to images of power,
And, in life's busy scenes immersed,
See better things, and do the worst.
Eloquent Want, whose reasons sway,
And make ten thousand truths give way,
While I your scheme with pleasure trace,
Draws near and stares me in the face.
'Consider well your state,' she cries,
'Like others kneel, that you may rise;
Hold doctrines, by no scruples vexed,
To which preferment is annexed,
Nor madly prove, where all depends,
Idolatry upon your friends.
See how you like my rueful face;
Such you must wear, if out of place.
Cracked is your brain to turn recluse
Without one farthing out at use.
They who have lands and safe bank-stock,
With faith so founded on a rock,
May give a rich invention ease,
And construe scripture how they please.
'The honoured prophet, that of old
Used heav'n's high counsels to unfold,
Did, more than courier angels, greet
The crows, that brought him bread and meat.'

(1735)

195 from *The Spleen. An Epistle to Mr. C—— J——*

FIRST know, my friend, I do not mean
To write a treatise on the spleen;
Nor to prescribe when nerves convulse;

Nor mend th' alarum watch, your pulse.
If I am right, your question lay,
What course I take to drive away
The day-mare spleen, by whose false pleas
Men prove mere suicides in ease;
And how I do myself demean
In stormy world to live serene.
  When by its magic lantern spleen
With frightful figures spread life's scene,
And threat'ning prospects urged my fears,
A stranger to the luck of heirs;
Reason, some quiet to restore,
Showed part was substance, shadow more;
With spleen's dead weight though heavy grown,
In life's rough tide I sunk not down,
But swam, till fortune threw a rope,
Buoyant on bladders filled with hope.
  I always choose the plainest food
To mend viscidity of blood.
Hail! water-gruel, healing power,
Of easy access to the poor;
Thy help love's confessors implore,
And doctors secretly adore;
To thee I fly, by thee dilute,
Through veins my blood doth quicker shoot,
And by swift current throws off clean
Prolific particles of spleen.
  I never sick by drinking grow,
Nor keep myself a cup too low;
And seldom Cloe's lodgings haunt,
Thrifty of spirits which I want.
  Hunting I reckon very good
To brace the nerves, and stir the blood,
But after no field-honours itch,
Achieved by leaping hedge and ditch.
While spleen lies soft relaxed in bed,
Or o'er coal-fires inclines the head,
Hygeia's sons with hound and horn,
And jovial cry awake the morn.
These see her from her dusky plight,
Smeared by th' embraces of the night,
With roral wash redeem her face,
And prove herself of Titan's race,
And, mounting in loose robes the skies,

roral] dewy

Shed light and fragrance as she flies.
Then horse and hound fierce joy display,
Exulting at the Hark-away,
And in pursuit o'er tainted ground
From lungs robust field-notes resound.
Then, as St. George the dragon slew,
Spleen pierced, trod down and dying view,
While all their spirits are on wing,
And woods, and hills, and valleys ring.
  To cure the mind's wrong bias, spleen,
Some recommend the bowling-green;
Some, hilly walks; all, exercise;
Fling but a stone, the giant dies.
Laugh and be well; monkeys have been
Extreme good doctors for the spleen;
And kitten, if the humour hit,
Has harlequined away the fit.
  Since mirth is good on this behalf,
At some partic'lars let us laugh:
Witlings, brisk fools cursed with half sense,
That stimulates their impotence,
Who buzz in rhyme, and, like blind flies,
Err with their wings for want of eyes,
Poor authors worshipping a calf,
Deep tragedies that make us laugh,
A strict dissenter saying grace,
A lect'rer preaching for a place,
Folks, things prophetic to dispense,
Making the past the future tense,
The popish dubbing of a priest,
Fine epitaphs on knaves deceased,
Green-aproned Pythonissa's rage,
Great Aesculapius on his stage,
A miser starving to be rich,
The prior of Newgate's dying speech,
A jointured widow's ritual state,
Two Jews disputing tête-à-tête,
New almanacs composed by seers,
Experiments on felons' ears,
Disdainful prudes, who ceaseless ply
The superb muscle of the eye,
A coquet's April-weather face,
A Queenb'rough mayor behind his mace,
And fops in military show,
Are sov'reign for the case in view.
  If spleen-fogs rise at close of day,

I clear my ev'ning with a play,
Or to some concert take my way.
The company, the shine of lights,
The scenes of humour, music's flights,
Adjust and set the soul to rights.
  Life's moving pictures, well-wrought plays,
To others' griefs attention raise:
Here, while the tragic fictions glow,
We borrow joy by pitying woe;
There, gaily comic scenes delight,
And hold true mirrors to our sight.
Virtue, in charming dress arrayed,
Calling the passions to her aid,
When moral scenes just action join,
Takes shape, and shows her face divine.
  Music has charms, we all may find,
Ingratiate deeply with the mind.
When art does sound's high pow'r advance,
To music's pipe the passions dance;
Motions unwilled its pow'r have shown,
Tarantulated by a tune.
Many have held the soul to be
Nearly allied to harmony.
Her have I known indulging grief,
And shunning company's relief,
Unveil her face, and looking round,
Own, by neglecting sorrow's wound,
The consanguinity of sound.

(1737)

MOSES BROWNE

1704–1787

196

A Survey of the Amphitheatre

On, Pegasus! Why, whither turn ye?
What! lag, ere I've begun my journey?
If you so soon your speed diminish,
You'll grow quite crippled ere we finish.
My riddle by degrees unravels:
Good gentlemen, I'm on my travels.
You're journ'ing too, as I presume;
I warrant you, designed for Rome.

Shall we join chat? You'll quickly be-at-her;
I'm going to the Amphitheatre.
  Bless us, what's here? What hodge-podge ruin!
Is this that famous pile we're viewing,
So cracked up in our schools—and taverns?
This heap of stones and awkward caverns?
Vile place! more fit for brutes than men!
Rome? Phaugh! I think 'tis Daniel's den.
  Stop, let's observe. How vast the building!
In troth, I think they've walled a field in.
Look, tow'rd the centre have you seen-a
Rough pavement? That was their Arena,
The stage where combatants, I wist,
Of old went at it hand to fist.
There, in the fencing-science taught,
Their desp'rate gladiators fought,
Or beasts engaged (like cater-cousins)
Let loose to eat 'em up by dozens.
There, out of all those ugly nooks,
They issued: tigers, bears—adzooks!
While senators, on upper benches,
Sat safely cuddling of their wenches;
And ranged plebeian crowds, unmoved,
The horrid spectacle approved,
Heedless what mischief in the show
Befell poor fighting rogues below.
Some wounded, those by monsters fed on,
This a nose off, that ne'er a head on:
The common fate of gladiators.
Fine shows, where monarchs were spectators!
  Here, from these pipes by time decayed,
Observe, their currents were conveyed;
Which served, when former sports were spent,
Their water-fights to represent,
By authors named—(a pesters take ye!
Why what, ye Muses!)—their Naumachia;
Where soldiers armed made dreadful charges
From broadside hulks and leaky barges,
Brought through this arch, and this, and this through,
Holes, now, a dog could scarcely piss through.
Hang this queer, gloomy, dirty station;
I'm weary of the speculation.
  Let me from scenes so dread repair
Back to my country's milder air:
There visit famed bear-garden heroes,
From whose sham fights ne'er cause of fear rose,

Or trip to view some valiant Hibern
At Sutton's, neighb'ring seat to Tyburn,
Where gentle butchers oft resort,
That brotherhood's peculiar sport.
Here may I sit and fear no slaying,
Mid those meek masters of sword-playing;
Lay wagers, laugh at Figg and Stokes,
And all our harmless fighting folks.
Rome's fencing sparks, say what you please,
In wit fell vastly short of these;
Those met to kill, or to be killed,
But ours to have their pockets filled.
Shame of their boasted Roman sense!
To wisdom they've the best pretence,
Who ne'er in those encounters fight
To die—but get their living by't.

(1736)

197 from *The Shrimp*

A SHRIMP! Black thing as widow's crape
In its primeval, vital shape;
Red as a soldier's coat of cloth
When stewed alive in native broth;
Armed with such tusks at sides and jowl
Would choke a dog to swallow whole;
Seeming (good simile, I hope)
Like flea in cloist'ring microscope,
With staring eyes and whiskers long;
Now—contradict me, if I'm wrong.
A shrimp! (theme ample as I'd wish)
Affords the angler bait to fish;
And cooked up by the kitchen lass
Supplies us, when they're dressed, with sauce;
The oyster, juicy from the shell,
Th' anchovy mixed, delight us well,
But this the lymph with higher *goût*
Both relishes and thickens too.
Lo! when in summer, stived to death,
We roam th' inviting fields for breath,
By Sadler's, rows of water-nymphs
To trav'llers sell salacious shrimps;
The fair receive 'em with delight
In handkerchiefs all lily white,

197 stived] stifled

Cheap purchase, and amuse the way
With feeding on this luscious prey;
While, dreary sight! all scattered round,
In heaps their skeletons are found.
  So in Arachne's web we spy
Full many a fresh-embowelled fly;
Or in old beds (coarse trope, I own)
View bugs, all shrunk to skin and bone.
  Some taste, some smell, you'll all agree
Must at one time most pleasing be;
The shrimp both pleasures will dispense:
But if apart each different sense
You in perfection would regale,
Then taste 'em fresh—and smell 'em stale.
  Good writers moral ends propose.
Mark, mothers, mine, with which I close:
Let not your children, meddling brats,
This banquet taste—nor fav'rite cats;
Lest, heedless of their beards, adsdikkins!
You choke the pretty harmless chickens.

(1739)

JOHN ARMSTRONG

1709–1779

198 from *The Oeconomy of Love. A Poetical Essay*

[*Advice to Lovers*]

SUCH ills attend
Th' obscene embrace of harlots. Wiser thou
Find some soft nymph whom tender sympathy
Attracts to thee, while all her captives else,
Awed by majestic beauty, mourn aloof
Her charms to thee, by nuptial vows and choice
More sure, devoted. Sacrifice to her
The precious hours, nor grudge with such a mate
The summer's day to toy or winter's night.
Now with your happy arms her waist surround,
Fond-grasping; on her swelling bosom now
Recline your cheek, with eager kisses press
Her balmy lips, and drinking from her eyes

Resistless love, the tender flame confess,
Ineffable but by the murmuring voice
Of genuine joy; then hug and kiss again,
Stretched on the flow'ry turf, while joyful glows
Thy manly pride, and throbbing with desire
Pants earnest, felt through all the obstacles
That intervene: but love, whose fervid course
Mountains nor seas oppose, can soon remove
Barriers so slight. Then when her lovely limbs,
Oft lovely deemed, far lovelier now beheld,
Through all your trembling joints increase the flame;
Forthwith discover to her dazzled sight
The stately novelty, and to her hand
Usher the new acquaintance. She perhaps
Averse will coldly chide, and half afraid,
Blushing, half pleased, the tumid wonder view
With neck retorted and oblique regard;
Nor quite her curious eye indulging, nor
Refraining quite. Perhaps when you attempt
The sweet admission, toyful she resists
With shy reluctance; nathless you pursue
The soft attack, and push the gentle war,
Fervent, till quite o'erpowered the melting maid
Faintly opposes. On the brink at last
Arrived of giddy rapture, plunge not in
Precipitant, but spare a virgin's pain.
Oh! spare a gentle virgin! spare yourself!
Lest sanguine war love's tender rites profane
With fierce dilaceration, and dire pangs
Reciprocal. Nor droop because the door
Of bliss seems shut and barricaded strong;
But triumph rather in this faithful pledge
Of innocence, and fair virginity
Inviolate.

(1736)

199 from *The Art of Preserving Health*

(i)

[*Urban Pollution*]

YE who amid this feverish world would wear
A body free of pain, of cares a mind,
Fly the rank city, shun its turbid air;
Breathe not the chaos of eternal smoke

And volatile corruption, from the dead,
The dying, sick'ning, and the living world
Exhaled, to sully heaven's transparent dome
With dim mortality. It is not air
That from a thousand lungs reeks back to thine,
Sated with exhalations rank and fell,
The spoil of dunghills, and the putrid thaw
Of nature; when from shape and texture she
Relapses into fighting elements:
It is not air, but floats a nauseous mass
Of all obscene, corrupt, offensive things.
Much moisture hurts; but here a sordid bath,
With oily rancour fraught, relaxes more
The solid frame than simple moisture can.
Besides, immured in many a sullen bay
That never felt the freshness of the breeze,
This slumb'ring deep remains, and ranker grows
With sickly rest: and (though the lungs abhor
To drink the dun fuliginous abyss)
Did not the acid vigour of the mine,
Rolled from so many thund'ring chimneys, tame
The putrid steams that overswarm the sky,
This caustic venom would perhaps corrode
Those tender cells that draw the vital air,
In vain with all their unctuous rills bedewed;
Or by the drunken venous tubes, that yawn
In countless pores o'er all the pervious skin,
Imbibed, would poison the balsamic blood,
And rouse the heart to every fever's rage.
While yet you breathe, away; the rural wilds
Invite; the mountains call you, and the vales;
The woods, the streams and each ambrosial breeze
That fans the ever-undulating sky;
A kindly sky! whose fost'ring pow'r regales
Man, beast and all the vegetable reign.

(ii)

[*Transience*]

What does not fade? The tower that long had stood
The crush of thunder and the warring winds,
Shook by the slow but sure destroyer Time,
Now hangs in doubtful ruins o'er its base.
And flinty pyramids, and walls of brass,
Descend: the Babylonian spires are sunk;
Achaia, Rome and Egypt moulder down.

Time shakes the stable tyranny of thrones,
And tottering empires rush by their own weight.
This huge rotundity we tread grows old;
And all those worlds that roll around the sun,
The sun himself, shall die; and ancient Night
Again involve the desolate abyss:
Till the great Father through the lifeless gloom
Extend his arm to light another world,
And bid new planets roll by other laws.
For through the regions of unbounded space,
Where unconfined Omnipotence has room,
Being, in various systems, fluctuates still
Between creation and abhorred decay:
It ever did; perhaps and ever will.
New worlds are still emerging from the deep;
The old descending, in their turns to rise.

(iii)

[*Madness*]

'Tis the great art of life to manage well
The restless mind. For ever on pursuit
Of knowledge bent, it starves the grosser powers:
Quite unemployed, against its own repose
It turns its fatal edge, and sharper pangs
Than what the body knows embitter life.
Chiefly where Solitude, sad nurse of Care,
To sickly musing gives the pensive mind,
There Madness enters; and the dim-eyed fiend,
Sour Melancholy, night and day provokes
Her own eternal wound. The sun grows pale;
A mournful visionary light o'erspreads
The cheerful face of nature: earth becomes
A dreary desert, and heaven frowns above.
Then various shapes of cursed illusion rise:
Whate'er the wretched fears, creating Fear
Forms out of nothing; and with monsters teems
Unknown in hell. The prostrate soul beneath
A load of huge imagination heaves;
And all the horrors that the guilty feel
With anxious flutterings wake the guiltless breast.

(1744)

HENRY TAYLOR

1711–1785

200 *The Country Curate*

In t' other hundred, o'er yon swarthy moor,
Deep in the mire with tawny rush beset,
Where bleak sea-breezes echo from the shore
And foggy damps infect the noontide heat,
There lies a country curate's dismal seat:
View well those barren heaths with sober eye,
And wonder how a man can live so wretchedly.

See, to the farmer's yard where close allied
A ragged church th' adjacent dykes commands;
One bell the steeple fills (the tinker's pride!),
The beams are wreathed about with hempen bands,
Wove, as the roof decayed, by pious hands.
Drops from the thatch still keep the whitewash wet:
God bless the holy man that dares to preach in it!

The house stands near, this church's foster-brother,
On crutches, both advanced in hoary eld;
A double rail runs from the one to t' other,
And saves the curate from the dirty field,
Where muck of various kind and hue is melled:
O'er this each Sunday to the church he climbs
And, to preserve his ancient cassock, risks his limbs.

Him liveth near, in dirty neighbourhood,
His clerk, a blacksmith, he of sallow hue,
Whose empty cellar long hath open stood,
A certain sign of penury or rue;
Him would the curate fain persuade to brew.
Still happy man, if I should leave untold
The shrew, who of his life shrill government doth hold.

The well-known power of an English wife
Ne day nor night she ceases to explain;
Her wit unreined promotes eternal strife,
Her beauty makes her arrogant and vain,
And both conspire to sharpen her disdain,
While rank ill-nature poisons all his joys,
Confused in endless squabble and unceasing noise.

melled] mixed

Eight years hath heaven plagued 'em with a boy,
  Who hates a sister younger by a year;
Whose hungry, meagre looks, sans life or joy,
  They view, and frown upon the wrangling pair
  (Who like two rav'nous locusts do appear
On one small flower), repent that e'er they sped,
Since Cupid's golden shafts they find are tipped with lead.

Each sun arises in a noisome fog;
  Tired of their beds, they rise as soon as light.
With like disgust their summers on they drag,
  And o'er a few stray chips the winter night:
  Such is the married Essex-curate's plight!
Though seasons change, no sense of change they know,
But look with discontent on all things here below.

When meagre Lent her famished look uprears,
  Her eyes indent with penury and pine,
Forth go the hungry family to prayers
  And pious sermon, while the farmers dine.
  In vain the children for their meals repine:
The blooming fields administer no cheer,
Joyless they view the purple promise of the year.

Summer attends them with fresh troubles plied;
  His breeches hung aloft for winter's wear,
He spies the flocks fly the returning tide,
  And every tenth he wishes to his share:
  Now to the hayfield trudge the hapless pair,
And, if they kindly treat the country folk,
They compliment his rector with the biggest cock.

Now autumn fruitful fills the teeming mead,
  And plenty frees the farmer's heart from care;
Meantime the thought of surplice-fees delayed,
  And th' hollow gulping of the filtered beer,
  Unpaid for yet! distract his mind with fear:
No hopes another vessel to procure,
Unless with learned scraps he funs th' admiring brewer.

When icy bands the stiffened waves enfold,
  At grudging neighbour's is he often seen,
Chafing with borrowed heat the outward cold;

funs] cajoles

But oh! no beer to thaw the cold within;
And then his wife pursues with hideous din:
Thence in the barn he muses what to say
To mend, yet not offend, her on next Sabbath-day.

Still worse and worse her lashing tongue he feels,
The spurns of fortune and the weight of years.
The post-horse thus, an ancient racer, reels:
No longer now a steady course he steers,
His weak knees tremble and he hangs his ears;
He sweats, he totters, covered o'er with gore,
And falls, alas! unpitied, as he lived before.

(1737)

ANONYMOUS

201 from *The Art of Wenching*

BE punctual then to know
Where maids resort, whether at midnight hour
They steal to wakes, where merriment is made
And gambols played, and antic tricks devised
To honour the deceased; or at the fair
Whether they flock and glitter out so fine,
Shaming the pedlar's stall; or at the ball
Where, warmed with dancing and with music charmed,
You lead them out; or on the Sabbath-day,
When between sermons they are much disposed
And softened to the melting tale of love.
And here remember on the Sabbath-day
To treat church-wardens; drams will drown your sins
And wash you white, preventive of the toil
Of a white sheet in church. Fowl, wild or tame,
Must be the parson's due, if you design
To live and sin secure. In trivial things
We must have patience, would our soul arrive
At extreme bliss and taste the sweets of love:
Journeys by day and supper-wanting nights,
And midnight watch when goblins crowd the gloom,
Bruisings of limbs and drainings of the purse,
Rawness of nose and twitchings of the reins,
And legs of straw and eyes all fiery red,
Will whet the appetite, and make us feed,
And give a relish to the joys they bring.

And yet there is one obstacle most dire
To check our progress, by the vulgar called
A mastiff, who with his incessant growl
Blasphemes the moon; by farmers entertained
To guard the daughter and defend the barn.
Him you must lenify and strive to soothe,
And make familiar, lest his evil tongue
Give signal of a foe and, ere you fly,
With his Cerberean jaws indent a wound.
Well I remember an ill-omened hour,
And cross to love, when through the storm and rain
Darkling I travelled, and with tedious toil,
To visit one who wished me nothing ill.
The mastiff I beheld and cautious kept
Between me and the wind, and softly stole
Safe to the door, and flew into the arms
Of my soul's joy; when, through malignant stars,
Scarce were my wearied limbs sunk in repose,
When th' execrable cur began to growl,
At what I know not, but his hellish din
Raised the good man, who, fearful for his sheep,
For thieves were rife and Lent was just expired,
Uprose and struck a light, and sought the room
Where his young daughter lay. But how aghast
Did he behold her folded in these arms:
Just then a dream was rising to my mind,
That sweetly acted our caresses o'er,
When, lo! my shoulders shoot with sudden pain;
I rub my eyes and, yawning from my dreams,
Behold a cudgel brandished o'er my head,
Horrible outrage! Blows on blows descend;
The cruel sire was deaf to human cries,
And strokes repeated; till with sudden rush
I fled before his face, and made the door
All naked as I was, compelled to leave
Whom my soul loved, unmercifully mauled
With grievous stripes, for neither did he spare
Ev'n his own flesh, nor from his daughter cease,
But bruised her tender body. What could I,
Shudd'ring without and feeling for us both?
My clothes were lost: the harsh, relentless wretch
Kept them for damage done unto his child;
And long I toiled, and mainly yet I toil,
To purchase new. But things like these must be;
For who can say 'Misfortunes know not me'?

(1737)

ANONYMOUS

202 from *The Diseases of Bath. A Satire*

IF to the Pump Room in the morn we go
To drink the waters and remove some woe,
Idle the project we too late explore;
And find, to move one plague, we've dared a score.
What tumult, hurry, noise and nonsense blend,
T' annoy the senses, and the soul t' offend!
What sickly, crude, offensive vapours there
The nostrils snuff up with the tainted air!
Whole groups of foppish slovens foully fine
In dirty shirts and tinsel stink and shine,
Midst crowds of dames who, in their nightly trim,
Just reeking from their beds, still stew and steam:
An ill-bred, restless, wild and cackling host,
Noisy as goslings spreading from their roost.
Shocked at the light and sound, I onward rush
To whence th' up-driven streams hot-smoking gush:
Forced to wade through a mob of unwashed beaus
At th' ill expense of elbows and of clothes.
By patient squeezing to the pump I get;
There, roughly thrust next to some clown, I wait,
Who, when he's rudely swilled his potion up,
Leaves me the slobbered favour of his cup.
Glad at all rates t' obtain the healing draught,
I take the glass with all his drivel fraught.
The pumper dips it, fills; and I (convinced,
By the foul fingerprints, the glass is rinsed)
Attempt to drink: when by my next fool pressed,
The slipping beaker pours along my breast.
Urged by despair I plunge into the bath.
But!—here still heavier plagues incense my wrath:
Nameless diseases joined pollute the stream,
And mix their foul infections with its steam.
Here, long ere Lucifer leads in the dawn,
Each greasy cook has seethed away his brawn:
And sweepers from their chimneys, smeared with soot,
Hither have brought, and left behind, their smut.
Jilts, porters, grooms, and guides, and chairmen bring
Their sev'ral ordures to corrupt the spring.
Add to these nuisances the 'wild'ring noise
Of splashing swimmers and of dabbling boys,

Whose bold, loose, rustic gestures move my rage,
Which Celia's presence scarcely can assuage.
Here lepra too, and scabies more unclean,
Divest their scurf t' invest a purer skin,
Whose peeling scales upon the surface swim,
Till what th' unwholesome shed the wholesome skim.
Nor this the greatest grievance in the flood;
The worst I scarcely wish were understood:
All (from the porter to the courtly nymph)
Pay liquid tributes to the swelling lymph.
What benefit such mixtures can impart,
To know—or ev'n to guess—is past my art.
This I affirm: however great it were,
To such a cure I'd ev'ry plague prefer.
Hence mad and poisoned, from the bath I fling
With all the scales and dirt that round me cling:
Then looking back, I curse that jakes obscene,
Whence I come sullied out who entered clean.

(1737)

AARON HILL

1685–1750

203 *Whitehall Stairs*

FROM Whitehall Stairs, whence oft with distant view
I've gazed whole moonshine hours on hours away,
Blest but to see those roofs which covered you,
And watched beneath what star you sleeping lay;

Launched on the smiling stream, which felt my hope,
And danced and quivered round my gliding boat,
I came this day to give my tongue free scope,
And vent the passion which my looks denote.

To tell my dear, my soul-disturbing Muse
(But that's a name can speak but half her charms),
How my full heart does my pen's aid refuse,
And bids my voice describe my soul's alarms.

To tell what transports your last letter gave,
What heav'ns were opened in your soft complaint;
To tell what pride I take to be your slave,
And how triumphant love disdains restraint.

But when I missed you, and took boat again,
The sympathetic sun condoled my woe,
Drew in his beams to mourn my pitied pain,
And bid the shadowed stream benighted flow.

Sudden, the weeping skies unsluiced their store,
And torrents of big tears unceasing shed;
Sad, I drove homeward to a flooded shore,
And, disappointed, hung my dripping head.

Landed at length, I sable coffee drink
And, ill-surrounded by a noisy tribe,
Scornful of what they do, or say, or think,
I, rapt in your dear heav'n, my loss describe.

(1753)

204 *May-Day*

WELCOME, dear dawn of summer's rising sway,
Fair fav'rite of the year! soul-soft'ning May!
Late I have learned, by love's sweet queen inspired,
Why from my youth this day my bosom fired:
'Twas for her birth that blooming nature sprung,
'Twas in her notes the sky's soft rangers sung!
The breeze blew soft to sigh her soul's sweet frame,
And the boughs bent in homage to her name.
Thick shot the meads, to paint her fruitful mind,
And flow'rs, that rolled her breath, enriched the wind.
For her, the sun waked out to bless our isle,
And lighted up half heav'n, to paint her smile:
Oh! we are lovers all! our Celia reigns,
And the warmed world is sick with my sweet pains.

(1753)

205 *Alone in an Inn at Southampton, April the 25th, 1737*

TWENTY lost years have stol'n their hours away
Since in this inn, ev'n in this room, I lay:
How changed! what then was rapture, fire and air,
Seems now sad silence all, and blank despair!
Is it that youth paints every view too bright,
And, life advancing, Fancy fades her light?

Ah! no—nor yet is day so far declined,
Nor can time's creeping coldness reach the mind.
'Tis—that I miss th' inspirer of that youth,
Her, whose soft smile was love, whose soul was truth;
Her, from whose pain I never wished relief,
And for whose pleasure I could smile at grief.
Prospects that, viewed with her, inspired before,
Now, seen without her, can delight no more.
Death snatched my joys by cutting off her share,
But left her griefs to multiply my care.
Pensive and cold, this room in each changed part
I view and, shocked, from ev'ry object start:
There hung the watch that, beating hours from day,
Told its sweet owner's lessening life away.
There her dear diamond taught the sash my name;
'Tis gone! frail image of love, life and fame.
That glass she dressed at keeps her form no more;
Not one dear footstep tunes th' unconscious floor;
There sat she—yet those chairs no sense retain,
And busy recollection smarts in vain.
Sullen and dim, what faded scenes are here!
I wonder, and retract a starting tear,
Gaze in attentive doubt—with anguish swell,
And o'er and o'er on each weighed object dwell.
Then to the window rush: gay views invite,
And tempt idea to permit delight.
But unimpressive, all in sorrow drowned,
One void, forgetful desert glooms around.
Oh life! deceitful lure of lost desires!
How short thy period, yet how fierce thy fires!
Scarce can a passion start (we change so fast),
Ere new lights strike us and the old are past.
Schemes following schemes so long life's taste explore,
That, ere we learn to live, we live no more.
Who then can think—yet sigh to part with breath,
Or shun the healing hand of friendly Death?
Guilt, penitence and wrongs, and pain and strife,
Form thy whole heaped amount, thou flatterer, Life!
Is it for this that, tossed twixt hope and fear,
Peace, by new shipwrecks, numbers each new year?
Oh, take me, Death! indulge desired repose,
And draw thy silent curtain round my woes.
Yet hold—one tender pang revokes that pray'r;
Still there remains one claim to tax my care.
Gone though she is, she left her soul behind
In four dear transcripts of her copied mind.

They chain me down to life, new task supply,
And leave me not at leisure yet to die!
Busied for them, I yet forgo release,
And teach my wearied heart to wait for peace.
But when their day breaks broad, I welcome night,
Smile at discharge from care, and shut out light.

(Wr. 1737; pub. 1753)

WILLIAM SHENSTONE

1714–1763

206 *The School-Mistress. A Poem. In Imitation of Spenser's Style*

In evrich mart that stands on British ground,
In evrich village less y-known to fame,
Dwells there in cot uncouth, afar renowned,
A matron old, whom we school-mistress name,
Who wont unruly brats with birch to tame:
They grieven sore in durance vile y-pent,
Awed by the pow'r of uncontroulèd dame;
And oft-times, on vagaries idly bent,
For task unconned or unkempt hair are sore y-shent.

Nar to this dome is found a patch so green,
On which the tribe their gambols do display:
Als at the door impris'ning board is seen,
Lest weakly wights of smaller size should stray,
Eager, perdie, to bask in sunshine day.
The noises intermixed, which thence resound,
Do learning's little tenement betray,
Where sits the dame, disguised in look profound,
And eyes her fairy throng, and turns her wheel around.

Right well knew she each temper to descry,
To thwart the proud and the submiss to raise,
Some with vile copper prize exalt on high,
And some entice with pittance small of praise:
And other sorts with baleful sprigs affrays.
Eke in her absence she command doth hold,
While with quaint arts the thoughtless crowd she sways;
Forewarned, if little bird their tricks behold,
'Twill whisper in her ear, and all the scene unfold.

Lo! now with state she utters the command.
Eftsoons the urchins to their tasks repair;
Their books of stature small take they in hand,
Which with pellucid horn securèd are,
To save from finger wet the letters fair:
The work so quaint, that on their backs is seen,
St. George's high achievements does declare;
On which thilk wight that has y-gazing been
Kens the forthcoming rod, unpleasing sight, I ween!

But ah! what pen his woeful plight can trace,
Or what device his loud laments explain,
The form uncouth of his disguisèd face,
The pallid hue that dyes his looks amain,
The plenteous show'r that does his cheek distain,
When he in abject wise implores the dame,
Nor hopeth aught of sweet reprieve to gain;
Or when from high she levels well her aim,
And through the thatch his cries each falling stroke proclaim.

The other tribe, aghast, with sore dismay
Attend, and con their tasks with mickle care:
By turns, astonied, evrich twig survey,
And from their fellow's furrowed bum beware,
Knowing, I wist, how each the same may share:
Till fear has taught 'em a performance meet,
And to the well-known chest the dame repair,
Whence oft with sugared cates she doth 'em greet,
And gingerbread y-rare, now, certes, doubly sweet.

Now to their seats they hie with merry glee,
And in beseemly order sitten there,
All but the wight of bum y-gallèd, he
Abhors both bench and stool and form and chair
(This hand in mouth y-fixed, that rends his hair);
And eke with snubs profound, and heaving breast
Convulsions intermitting! does declare
His grievous wrongs, his dame's unjust behest,
And scorns her proffered love, and shuns to be caressed.

Behind some door, in melancholy thought,
Mindless of food, he, dreary caitiff! pines,
Ne for his fellows' joyaunce careth aught,
But to the winds all merriment resigns.

snubs] sobs

His face besprent with liquid crystal shines,
And many a sullen look askaunce is sent,
Which for his dame's annoyance he designs;
Nathless the more to pleasure him she's bent,
The more doth he, perverse, her 'haviour past resent.

Algates the rest from silk misfortune free,
Stir'n but as nature doth abroad them call;
Then squatten down with hand beneath each knee,
Ne seeken out or secret nook or wall,
But cack in open street—no shame doth them appal.
And may no carl their innocence deride,
While they p–ss boldly in the face of all;
Turning unawed their vestments small aside,
Ne covet hedge ne barn their privy parts to hide.

But when the hour of pleasaunce draweth near,
They usher forth all debonair and gay;
And, standing on the green, with jocund leer,
Salute the stranger passing on his way.
Some builden fragile tenements of clay;
Some to the standing lake their courses bend,
With pebbles smooth at duck-and-drake to play;
Thilk to the huxter's sav'ry cot y-tend,
In pastry kings and queens th' allotted mite to spend.

Here, as each season yields a different store,
Each season's stores in order rangèd been;
Apples with cabbage-net y-covered o'er,
Galling full sore th' unmoneyed wight, are seen,
And gooseb'ry clad in liv'ry red or green;
And here of lovely dye the cath'rine pear,
Fine pear! as lovely for thy juice, I ween.
O! may no wight e'er pennyless come there,
Lest led by thee astray, he shameful theft prepare.

See! cherries here, ere cherries yet abound,
With thread so white in luscious bundles tied,
Scatter like blooming maid their glances round,
And draw with pampered look our eyes aside:
These must be bought, though penury betide;
The plum of purple hue, the nut so brown,
Tempting the passing swain; thilk cakes beside,
Whose much-loved names th' inventress city own,
Rend'ring through Britain's isle Salopia's praises known.

(1737)

Salopia] Shrewsbury

207

Elegy XI

He Complains how Soon the Pleasing Novelty of Life Is Over. To Mr. J[ago]

AH me, my friend! it will not, will not last!
  This fairy-scene, that cheats our youthful eyes!
The charm dissolves; th' aerial music's past;
  The banquet ceases, and the vision flies.

Where are the splendid forms, the rich perfumes,
  Where the gay tapers, where the spacious dome?
Vanished the costly pearls, the crimson plumes,
  And we, delightless, left to wander home!

Vain now are books, the sage's wisdom vain!
  What has the world to bribe our steps astray?
Ere reason learns by studied laws to reign,
  The weakened passions, self-subdued, obey.

Scarce has the sun sev'n annual courses rolled,
  Scarce shown the whole that fortune can supply;
Since, not the miser so caressed his gold,
  As I, for what it gave, was heard to sigh.

On the world's stage I wished some sprightly part,
  To deck my native fleece with tawdry lace;
'Twas life, 'twas taste, and—oh my foolish heart!
  Substantial joy was fixed in pow'r and place.

And you, ye works of art! allured mine eye,
  The breathing picture, and the living stone:
'Though gold, though splendour, heav'n and fate deny,
  Yet might I call one Titian stroke my own!'

Smit with the charms of fame, whose lovely spoil,
  The wreath, the garland, fire the poet's pride,
I trimmed my lamp, consumed the midnight oil—
  But soon the paths of health and fame divide!

Oft too I prayed, 'twas nature formed the pray'r,
  To grace my native scenes, my rural home;
To see my trees express their planter's care,
  And gay, on Attic models, raise my dome.

But now 'tis o'er, the dear delusion's o'er!
A stagnant breezeless air becalms my soul:
A fond aspiring candidate no more,
I scorn the palm, before I reach the goal.

O youth! enchanting stage, profusely blessed!
Bliss ev'n obtrusive courts the frolic mind;
Of health neglectful, yet by health caressed,
Careless of favour, yet secure to find.

Then glows the breast, as op'ning roses fair,
More free, more vivid than the linnet's wing;
Honest as light, transparent ev'n as air,
Tender as buds, and lavish as the spring.

Not all the force of manhood's active might,
Not all the craft to subtle age assigned,
Not science shall extort that dear delight,
Which gay delusion gave the tender mind.

Adieu soft raptures! transports void of care!
Parent of raptures, dear Deceit, adieu!
And you, her daughters, pining with despair,
Why, why so soon her fleeting steps pursue!

Tedious again to curse the drizzling day!
Again to trace the wint'ry tracts of snow!
Or, soothed by vernal airs, again survey
The self-same hawthorns bud, and cowslips blow!

O life! how soon of ev'ry bliss forlorn!
We start false joys, and urge the devious race:
A tender prey, that cheers our youthful morn,
Then sinks untimely, and defrauds the chase.

(Wr. by 1747; pub. 1764)

208 *A Solemn Meditation*

WHAT is this life, this active guest,
Which robs our peaceful clay of rest?
This trifle, which while we retain,
Causes inquietude and pain?
This breath, which we no sooner find,
Than in a moment 'tis resigned?

Whose momentary noise, when o'er,
Is never, never heard of more!
And even monarchs, when it ends,
Become offensive to their friends;
Emit a putrid noisome smell,
To those that loved 'em e'er so well!

Pond'ring these things within my heart,
Surely, said I—life is a f—t!

(1764)

209 *Written at an Inn at Henley*

To thee, fair Freedom! I retire
From flattery, cards, and dice, and din:
Nor art thou found in mansions higher
Than the low cot, or humble inn.

'Tis here with boundless pow'r I reign;
And ev'ry health which I begin
Converts dull port to bright champagne;
Such Freedom crowns it, at an inn.

I fly from pomp, I fly from plate!
I fly from falsehood's specious grin!
Freedom I love, and form I hate,
And choose my lodgings at an inn.

Here, waiter! take my sordid ore,
Which lacqueys else might hope to win;
It buys, what courts have not in store;
It buys me Freedom, at an inn.

And now once more I shape my way
Through rain or shine, through thick or thin,
Secure to meet, at close of day,
With kind reception, at an inn.

Whoe'er has travelled life's dull round,
Where'er his stages may have been,
May sigh to think he still has found
The warmest welcome, at an inn.

(Wr. 1751; pub. 1758)

JOHN WESLEY

1703–1791

210 *Hymn*

THOU hidden love of God, whose height,
  Whose depth unfathomed no man knows,
I see from far thy beauteous light,
  Inly I sigh for thy repose;
My heart is pained, nor can it be
At rest, till it finds rest in thee.

Thy secret voice invites me still,
  The sweetness of thy yoke to prove:
And fain I would: but though my will
  Seem fixed, yet wide my passions rove;
Yet hindrances strew all the way;
I aim at thee, yet from thee stray.

'Tis mercy all, that thou hast brought
  My mind to seek her peace in thee;
Yet while I seek, but find thee not,
  No peace my wand'ring soul shall see;
O when shall all my wand'rings end,
And all my steps to thee-ward tend?

Is there a thing beneath the sun
  That strives with thee my heart to share?
Ah! tear it thence, and reign alone,
  The lord of ev'ry motion there;
Then shall my heart from earth be free,
When it hath found repose in thee.

O hide this self from me, that I
  No more, but Christ in me may live;
My vile affections crucify,
  Nor let one darling lust survive;
In all things nothing may I see,
Nothing desire or seek but thee.

O Love, thy sov'reign aid impart,
  To save me from low-thoughted care:
Chase this self-will through all my heart,
  Through all its latent mazes there:
Make me thy duteous child, that I
Ceaseless may Abba, Father, cry!

Ah no! ne'er will I backward turn:
  Thine wholly, thine alone I am!
Thrice happy he who views with scorn
  Earth's toys, for thee his constant flame;
O help that I may never move
From the blest footsteps of thy love!

Each moment draw from earth away
  My heart that lowly waits thy call:
Speak to my inmost soul, and say,
  I am thy love, thy God, thy all!
To feel thy power, to hear thy voice,
To taste thy love, be all my choice.

(1738)

E. DOWER

fl. 1738

211 *The New River Head, a Fragment*

TIRED with books and rolling on the bed,
I walked one evening to the River Head.
There patient anglers do the fishes tease,
And dogs are washed to clean them from the fleas;
From thence you hear the noise of jangling bells,
Or the soft Italian tunes from Sadler's Wells.
There citizens tell each other who is the winner,
And clergy boast of what they had for dinner;
The lovesick maid from death will not refrain—
Plunges in there, and laughs at future pain.
Some walk there to get appetites to their meat,
And others like me, that has no food to eat.
From the verdant fields comes a fragrant smell,
Whilst the gay town looks like the mouth of hell.

—I thought of woods, palaces and springs,
Riches, poverty and the pomp of kings.
Whilst th' royal swans for food did seem to weep,
I leaned upon my staff and fell asleep.

(1738)

SAMUEL JOHNSON

1709–1784

212 from *London. A Poem in Imitation of the Third Satire of Juvenal*

By numbers here from shame or censure free,
All crimes are safe, but hated poverty.
This, only this, the rigid law pursues,
This, only this, provokes the snarling muse.
The sober trader at a tattered cloak,
Wakes from his dream, and labours for a joke;
With brisker air the silken courtiers gaze,
And turn the varied taunt a thousand ways.
Of all the griefs that harrass the distressed,
Sure the most bitter is a scornful jest;
Fate never wounds more deep the gen'rous heart,
Than when a blockhead's insult points the dart.
Has heaven reserved, in pity to the poor,
No pathless waste, or undiscovered shore;
No secret island in the boundless main?
No peaceful desert yet unclaimed by Spain?
Quick let us rise, the happy seats explore,
And bear oppression's insolence no more.
This mournful truth is ev'rywhere confessed,
SLOW RISES WORTH, BY POVERTY DEPRESSED:
But here more slow, where all are slaves to gold,
Where looks are merchandise, and smiles are sold;
Where won by bribes, by flatteries implored,
The groom retails the favours of his lord.

(1738)

213 *An Epitaph on Claudy Phillips, a Musician*

PHILLIPS! whose touch harmonious could remove
The pangs of guilty pow'r and hapless love,
Rest here, distressed by poverty no more,
Here find that calm thou gav'st so oft before;
Sleep undisturbed within this peaceful shrine,
Till angels wake thee with a note like thine.

(1740)

214 *Prologue, Spoken by Mr. Garrick at the Opening of the Theatre Royal, Drury Lane, 1747*

WHEN Learning's triumph o'er her barb'rous foes
First reared the stage, immortal Shakespeare rose;
Each change of many-coloured life he drew,
Exhausted worlds, and then imagined new:
Existence saw him spurn her bounded reign,
And panting Time toiled after him in vain.
His pow'rful strokes presiding truth impressed,
And unresisted passion stormed the breast.
Then Jonson came, instructed from the school,
To please in method, and invent by rule;
His studious patience, and laborious art,
By regular approach essayed the heart:
Cold Approbation gave the ling'ring bays,
For those who durst not censure, scarce could praise.
A mortal born, he met the gen'ral doom,
But left, like Egypt's kings, a lasting tomb.
The wits of Charles found easier ways to fame,
Nor wished for Jonson's art, or Shakespeare's flame;
Themselves they studied, as they felt they writ;
Intrigue was plot, obscenity was wit.
Vice always found a sympathetic friend;
They pleased their age, and did not aim to mend.
Yet bards like these aspired to lasting praise,
And proudly hoped to pimp in future days.
Their cause was gen'ral, their supports were strong,
Their slaves were willing, and their reign was long:
Till shame regained the post that sense betrayed,
And Virtue called Oblivion to her aid.
Then, crushed by rules, and weakened as refined,
For years the pow'r of tragedy declined:
From bard to bard the frigid caution crept,
Till declamation roared, while passion slept.
Yet still did Virtue deign the stage to tread,
Philosophy remained, though Nature fled.
But forced at length her ancient reign to quit,
She saw great Faustus lay the ghost of wit;
Exulting Folly hailed the joyful day,
And pantomime and song confirmed her sway.
But who the coming changes can presage,
And mark the future periods of the stage?
Perhaps, if skill could distant times explore,

New Behns, new D'Urfeys, yet remain in store.
Perhaps, where Lear has raved and Hamlet died,
On flying cars new sorcerers may ride.
Perhaps, for who can guess th' effects of chance?
Here Hunt may box, or Mahomet may dance.
  Hard is his lot that, here by fortune placed,
Must watch the wild vicissitudes of taste;
With ev'ry meteor of caprice must play,
And chase the new-blown bubbles of the day.
Ah! let not censure term our fate our choice,
The stage but echoes back the public voice.
The drama's laws the drama's patrons give,
For we that live to please, must please to live.
  Then prompt no more the follies you decry,
As tyrants doom their tools of guilt to die;
'Tis yours this night to bid the reign commence
Of rescued Nature and reviving Sense;
To chase the charms of sound, the pomp of show,
For useful mirth, and salutary woe;
Bid scenic Virtue form the rising age,
And Truth diffuse her radiance from the stage.

(1747)

215 *The Vanity of Human Wishes. The Tenth Satire of Juvenal Imitated*

LET observation with extensive view
Survey mankind from China to Peru;
Remark each anxious toil, each eager strife,
And watch the busy scenes of crowded life;
Then say how hope and fear, desire and hate,
O'erspread with snares the clouded maze of fate,
Where wav'ring man, betrayed by vent'rous pride
To tread the dreary paths without a guide,
As treach'rous phantoms in the mist delude,
Shuns fancied ills, or chases airy good.
How rarely reason guides the stubborn choice,
Rules the bold hand, or prompts the suppliant voice;
How nations sink, by darling schemes oppressed,
When vengeance listens to the fool's request.
Fate wings with ev'ry wish th' afflictive dart,
Each gift of nature, and each grace of art;
With fatal heat impetuous courage glows,
With fatal sweetness elocution flows,

Impeachment stops the speaker's pow'rful breath,
And restless fire precipitates on death.
  But scarce observed, the knowing and the bold
Fall in the gen'ral massacre of gold;
Wide-wasting pest! that rages unconfined,
And crowds with crimes the records of mankind;
For gold his sword the hireling ruffian draws,
For gold the hireling judge distorts the laws;
Wealth heaped on wealth nor truth nor safety buys,
The dangers gather as the treasures rise.
  Let hist'ry tell where rival kings command,
And dubious title shakes the madded land,
When statutes glean the refuse of the sword,
How much more safe the vassal than the lord;
Low skulks the hind beneath the rage of pow'r,
And leaves the wealthy traitor in the Tow'r,
Untouched his cottage, and his slumbers sound,
Though confiscation's vultures hover round.
  The needy traveller, serene and gay,
Walks the wild heath, and sings his toil away.
Does envy seize thee? crush th' upbraiding joy,
Increase his riches and his peace destroy;
Now fears in dire vicissitude invade,
The rustling brake alarms, and quiv'ring shade,
Nor light nor darkness bring his pain relief,
One shows the plunder, and one hides the thief.
  Yet still one gen'ral cry the skies assails,
And gain and grandeur load the tainted gales;
Few know the toiling statesman's fear or care,
Th' insidious rival and the gaping heir.
  Once more, Democritus, arise on earth,
With cheerful wisdom and instructive mirth,
See motley life in modern trappings dressed,
And feed with varied fools th' eternal jest:
Thou who couldst laugh where want enchained caprice,
Toil crushed conceit, and man was of a piece;
Where wealth unloved without a mourner died;
And scarce a sycophant was fed by pride;
Where ne'er was known the form of mock debate,
Or seen a new-made mayor's unwieldy state;
Where change of fav'rites made no change of laws,
And senates heard before they judged a cause;
How wouldst thou shake at Britain's modish tribe,
Dart the quick taunt, and edge the piercing gibe?
Attentive truth and nature to descry,
And pierce each scene with philosophic eye.

To thee were solemn toys or empty show,
The robes of pleasure and the veils of woe:
All aid the farce, and all thy mirth maintain,
Whose joys are causeless, or whose griefs are vain.
Such was the scorn that filled the sage's mind,
Renewed at ev'ry glance on humankind;
How just that scorn ere yet thy voice declare,
Search every state, and canvass ev'ry pray'r.
Unnumbered suppliants crowd preferment's gate,
Athirst for wealth, and burning to be great;
Delusive Fortune hears th' incessant call,
They mount, they shine, evaporate and fall.
On ev'ry stage the foes of peace attend,
Hate dogs their flight, and insult mocks their end.
Love ends with hope, the sinking statesman's door
Pours in the morning worshipper no more;
For growing names the weekly scribbler lies,
To growing wealth the dedicator flies,
From every room descends the painted face,
That hung the bright Palladium of the place,
And smoked in kitchens, or in auctions sold,
To better features yields the frame of gold;
For now no more we trace in ev'ry line
Heroic worth, benevolence divine:
The form distorted justifies the fall,
And detestation rids th' indignant wall.
But will not Britain hear the last appeal,
Sign her foes' doom, or guard her fav'rites' zeal?
Through Freedom's sons no more remonstrance rings,
Degrading nobles and controlling kings;
Our supple tribes repress their patriot throats,
And ask no questions but the price of votes;
With weekly libels and septennial ale,
Their wish is full to riot and to rail.
In full-blown dignity, see Wolsey stand,
Law in his voice, and fortune in his hand:
To him the church, the realm, their pow'rs consign,
Through him the rays of regal bounty shine,
Turned by his nod the stream of honour flows,
His smile alone security bestows:
Still to new heights his restless wishes tow'r,
Claim leads to claim, and pow'r advances pow'r;
Till conquest unresisted ceased to please,
And rights submitted left him none to seize.
At length his sov'reign frowns—the train of state
Mark the keen glance, and watch the sign to hate.

Where'er he turns he meets a stranger's eye,
His suppliants scorn him, and his followers fly;
At once is lost the pride of awful state,
The golden canopy, the glitt'ring plate,
The regal palace, the luxurious board,
The liv'ried army, and the menial lord.
With age, with cares, with maladies oppressed,
He seeks the refuge of monastic rest.
Grief aids disease, remembered folly stings,
And his last sighs reproach the faith of kings.
  Speak thou, whose thoughts at humble peace repine,
Shall Wolsey's wealth, with Wolsey's end be thine?
Or liv'st thou now, with safer pride content,
The wisest justice on the banks of Trent?
For why did Wolsey, near the steeps of fate,
On weak foundations raise th' enormous weight?
Why but to sink beneath misfortune's blow,
With louder ruin to the gulfs below?
  What gave great Villiers to th' assassin's knife,
And fixed disease on Harley's closing life?
What murdered Wentworth, and what exiled Hyde,
By kings protected and to kings allied?
What but their wish indulged in courts to shine,
And pow'r too great to keep, or to resign?
  When first the college rolls receive his name,
The young enthusiast quits his ease for fame;
Through all his veins the fever of renown
Burns from the strong contagion of the gown;
O'er Bodley's dome his future labours spread,
And Bacon's mansion trembles o'er his head.
Are these thy views? proceed, illustrious youth,
And virtue guard thee to the throne of truth!
Yet should thy soul indulge the gen'rous heat,
Till captive Science yields her last retreat;
Should Reason guide thee with her brightest ray,
And pour on misty doubt resistless day;
Should no false kindness lure to loose delight,
Nor praise relax, nor difficulty fright;
Should tempting Novelty thy cell refrain,
And Sloth effuse her opiate fumes in vain;
Should Beauty blunt on fops her fatal dart,
Nor claim the triumph of a lettered heart;
Should no disease thy torpid veins invade,
Nor Melancholy's phantoms haunt thy shade;
Yet hope not life from grief or danger free,
Nor think the doom of man reversed for thee:

Deign on the passing world to turn thine eyes,
And pause awhile from letters to be wise;
There mark what ills the scholar's life assail,
Toil, envy, want, the patron, and the jail.
See nations slowly wise, and meanly just,
To buried merit raise the tardy bust.
If dreams yet flatter, once again attend,
Hear Lydiat's life, and Galileo's end.
  Nor deem, when Learning her last prize bestows,
The glitt'ring eminence exempt from foes;
See when the vulgar 'scape, despised or awed,
Rebellion's vengeful talons seize on Laud.
From meaner minds though smaller fines content,
The plundered palace or sequestered rent;
Marked out by dangerous parts he meets the shock,
And fatal Learning leads him to the block:
Around his tomb let Art and Genius weep,
But hear his death, ye blockheads, hear and sleep.
  The festal blazes, the triumphal show,
The ravished standard, and the captive foe,
The senate's thanks, the gazette's pompous tale,
With force resistless o'er the brave prevail.
Such bribes the rapid Greek o'er Asia whirled,
For such the steady Romans shook the world;
For such in distant lands the Britons shine,
And stain with blood the Danube or the Rhine;
This pow'r has praise, that virtue scarce can warm,
Till fame supplies the universal charm.
Yet Reason frowns on war's unequal game,
Where wasted nations raise a single name,
And mortgaged states their grandsires' wreaths regret,
From age to age in everlasting debt;
Wreaths which at last the dear-bought right convey
To rust on medals, or on stones decay.
  On what foundation stands the warrior's pride?
How just his hopes let Swedish Charles decide;
A frame of adamant, a soul of fire,
No dangers fright him, and no labours tire;
O'er love, o'er fear, extends his wide domain,
Unconquered lord of pleasure and of pain;
No joys to him pacific sceptres yield,
War sounds the trump, he rushes to the field;
Behold surrounding kings their pow'r combine,
And one capitulate, and one resign;
Peace courts his hand, but spreads her charms in vain;
'Think nothing gained,' he cries, 'till naught remain,

On Moscow's walls till Gothic standards fly,
And all be mine beneath the polar sky.'
The march begins in military state,
And nations on his eye suspended wait;
Stern Famine guards the solitary coast,
And Winter barricades the realms of frost;
He comes, not want and cold his course delay;—
Hide, blushing Glory, hide Pultowa's day:
The vanquished hero leaves his broken bands,
And shows his miseries in distant lands;
Condemned a needy supplicant to wait,
While ladies interpose, and slaves debate.
But did not Chance at length her error mend?
Did no subverted empire mark his end?
Did rival monarchs give the fatal wound?
Or hostile millions press him to the ground?
His fall was destined to a barren strand,
A petty fortress, and a dubious hand;
He left the name, at which the world grew pale,
To point a moral, or adorn a tale.
  All times their scenes of pompous woes afford,
From Persia's tyrant to Bavaria's lord.
In gay hostility, and barbarous pride,
With half mankind embattled at his side,
Great Xerxes comes to seize the certain prey,
And starves exhausted regions in his way;
Attendant Flatt'ry counts his myriads o'er,
Till counted myriads soothe his pride no more;
Fresh praise is tried till madness fires his mind,
The waves he lashes, and enchains the wind;
New pow'rs are claimed, new pow'rs are still bestowed,
Till rude resistance lops the spreading god;
The daring Greeks deride the martial show,
And heap their valleys with the gaudy foe;
Th' insulted sea with humbler thoughts he gains,
A single skiff to speed his flight remains;
Th' incumbered oar scarce leaves the dreaded coast
Through purple billows and a floating host.
  The bold Bavarian, in a luckless hour,
Tries the dread summits of Caesarian power,
With unexpected legions bursts away,
And sees defenceless realms receive his sway;
Short sway! fair Austria spreads her mournful charms,
The queen, the beauty, sets the world in arms;
From hill to hill the beacon's rousing blaze
Spreads wide the hope of plunder and of praise;

The fierce Croatian, and the wild Hussar,
With all the sons of ravage crowd the war;
The baffled prince in honour's flatt'ring bloom
Of hasty greatness finds the fatal doom,
His foes' derision, and his subjects' blame,
And steals to death from anguish and from shame.
'Enlarge my life with multitude of days,
In health, in sickness,' thus the suppliant prays;
Hides from himself his state, and shuns to know
That life protracted is protracted woe.
Time hovers o'er, impatient to destroy,
And shuts up all the passages of joy:
In vain their gifts the bounteous seasons pour,
The fruit autumnal, and the vernal flow'r,
With listless eyes the dotard views the store,
He views, and wonders that they please no more;
Now pall the tasteless meats, and joyless wines,
And Luxury with sighs her slave resigns.
Approach, ye minstrels, try the soothing strain,
Diffuse the tuneful lenitives of pain:
No sounds, alas, would touch th' impervious ear,
Though dancing mountains witnessed Orpheus near;
Nor lute nor lyre his feeble pow'rs attend,
Nor sweeter music of a virtuous friend,
But everlasting dictates crowd his tongue,
Perversely grave, or positively wrong.
The still-returning tale, and ling'ring jest,
Perplex the fawning niece and pampered guest,
While growing hopes scarce awe the gath'ring sneer,
And scarce a legacy can bribe to hear;
The watchful guests still hint the last offence,
The daughter's petulance, the son's expense,
Improve his heady rage with treach'rous skill,
And mould his passions till they make his will.
Unnumbered maladies his joints invade,
Lay siege to life and press the dire blockade;
But unextinguished av'rice still remains,
And dreaded losses aggravate his pains;
He turns, with anxious heart and crippled hands,
His bonds of debt, and mortgages of lands;
Or views his coffers with suspicious eyes,
Unlocks his gold, and counts it till he dies.
But grant, the virtues of a temp'rate prime
Bless with an age exempt from scorn or crime;
An age that melts with unperceived decay,
And glides in modest innocence away;

Whose peaceful day benevolence endears,
Whose night congratulating conscience cheers;
The gen'ral fav'rite as the gen'ral friend:
Such age there is, and who shall wish its end?
  Yet ev'n on this her load Misfortune flings,
To press the weary minutes' flagging wings:
New sorrow rises as the day returns,
A sister sickens, or a daughter mourns.
Now kindred merit fills the sable bier,
Now lacerated friendship claims a tear.
Year chases year, decay pursues decay,
Still drops some joy from with'ring life away;
New forms arise, and diff'rent views engage,
Superfluous lags the vet'ran on the stage,
Till pitying Nature signs the last release,
And bids afflicted worth retire to peace.
  But few there are whom hours like these await,
Who set unclouded in the gulfs of fate.
From Lydia's monarch should the search descend,
By Solon cautioned to regard his end,
In life's last scene what prodigies surprise,
Fears of the brave, and follies of the wise?
From Marlb'rough's eyes the streams of dotage flow,
And Swift expires a driv'ler and a show.
  The teeming mother, anxious for her race,
Begs for each birth the fortune of a face:
Yet Vane could tell what ills from beauty spring,
And Sedley cursed the form that pleased a king.
Ye nymphs of rosy lips and radiant eyes,
Whom pleasure keeps too busy to be wise,
Whom joys with soft varieties invite,
By day the frolic, and the dance by night,
Who frown with vanity, who smile with art,
And ask the latest fashion of the heart,
What care, what rules your heedless charms shall save,
Each nymph your rival, and each youth your slave?
Against your fame with fondness hate combines,
The rival batters, and the lover mines.
With distant voice neglected Virtue calls,
Less heard and less, the faint remonstrance falls;
Tired with contempt, she quits the slipp'ry reign,
And Pride and Prudence take her seat in vain.
In crowd at once, where none the pass defend,
The harmless freedom, and the private friend.
The guardians yield, by force superior plied;
By Int'rest, Prudence; and by Flatt'ry, Pride.

Now Beauty falls betrayed, despised, distressed,
And hissing Infamy proclaims the rest.
  Where then shall hope and fear their objects find?
Must dull suspense corrupt the stagnant mind?
Must helpless man, in ignorance sedate,
Roll darkling down the torrent of his fate?
Must no dislike alarm, no wishes rise,
No cries attempt the mercies of the skies?
Enquirer, cease, petitions yet remain,
Which heav'n may hear, nor deem religion vain.
Still raise for good the supplicating voice,
But leave to heav'n the measure and the choice,
Safe in his pow'r, whose eyes discern afar
The secret ambush of a specious pray'r.
Implore his aid, in his decisions rest,
Secure whate'er he gives, he gives the best.
Yet when the sense of sacred presence fires,
And strong devotion to the skies aspires,
Pour forth thy fervours for a healthful mind,
Obedient passions, and a will resigned;
For love, which scarce collective man can fill;
For patience sov'reign o'er transmuted ill;
For faith, that panting for a happier seat,
Counts death kind Nature's signal of retreat:
These goods for man the laws of heav'n ordain,
These goods he grants, who grants the pow'r to gain;
With these celestial wisdom calms the mind,
And makes the happiness she does not find.

(1749)

216 *A Short Song of Congratulation*

LONG-EXPECTED one and twenty
  Ling'ring year at last is flown;
Pomp and pleasure, pride and plenty,
  Great Sir John, are all your own.

Loosened from the minor's tether,
  Free to mortgage or to sell,
Wild as wind and light as feather,
  Bid the slaves of thrift farewell.

Call the Bettys, Kates and Jennys,
  Ev'ry name that laughs at care;
Lavish of your grandsire's guineas,
  Show the spirit of an heir.

All that prey on vice and folly
  Joy to see their quarry fly:
Here the gamester light and jolly,
  There the lender grave and sly.

Wealth, Sir John, was made to wander,
  Let it wander as it will;
See the jockey, see the pander,
  Bid them come, and take their fill.

When the bonny blade carouses,
  Pockets full, and spirits high,
What are acres? What are houses?
  Only dirt, or wet or dry.

If the guardian or the mother
  Tell the woes of wilful waste,
Scorn their counsel and their pother,
  You can hang or drown at last.

(Wr. 1780; pub. 1794)

217 *On the Death of Dr. Robert Levet*

CONDEMNED to hope's delusive mine,
  As on we toil from day to day,
By sudden blasts, or slow decline,
  Our social comforts drop away.

Well tried through many a varying year,
  See Levet to the grave descend;
Officious, innocent, sincere,
  Of ev'ry friendless name the friend.

Yet still he fills affection's eye,
  Obscurely wise, and coarsely kind;
Nor, lettered arrogance, deny
  Thy praise to merit unrefined.

When fainting nature called for aid,
  And hov'ring death prepared the blow,
His vig'rous remedy displayed
  The power of art without the show.

In misery's darkest caverns known,
  His useful care was ever nigh,
Where hopeless anguish poured his groan,
  And lonely want retired to die.

No summons mocked by chill delay,
  No petty gain disdained by pride,
The modest wants of ev'ry day
  The toil of ev'ry day supplied.

His virtues walked their narrow round,
  Nor made a pause, nor left a void;
And sure th' Eternal Master found
  The single talent well employed.

The busy day, the peaceful night,
  Unfelt, uncounted, glided by;
His frame was firm, his powers were bright,
  Though now his eightieth year was nigh.

Then with no throbbing fiery pain,
  No cold gradations of decay,
Death broke at once the vital chain,
  And freed his soul the nearest way.

(1783)

MARY COLLIER

fl. 1739–1762

218 from *The Woman's Labour. An Epistle to Mr. Stephen Duck*

[*The Washerwoman*]

  WHEN bright Orion glitters in the skies
In winter nights, then early we must rise;
The weather ne'er so bad, wind, rain or snow,
Our work appointed, we must rise and go,
While you on easy beds may lie and sleep,
Till light does through your chamber-windows peep.
When to the house we come where we should go,
How to get in, alas! we do not know:
The maid quite tired with work the day before,
O'ercome with sleep; we standing at the door,
Oppressed with cold, and often call in vain,
Ere to our work we can admittance gain.
But when from wind and weather we get in,
Briskly with courage we our work begin;

Heaps of fine linen we before us view,
Whereon to lay our strength and patience too;
Cambrics and muslins, which our ladies wear,
Laces and edgings, costly, fine and rare,
Which must be washed with utmost skill and care;
With holland shirts, ruffles and fringes too,
Fashions which our forefathers never knew.
For several hours here we work and slave,
Before we can one glimpse of daylight have;
We labour hard before the morning's past,
Because we fear the time runs on too fast.
  At length bright Sol illuminates the skies,
And summons drowsy mortals to arise;
Then comes our mistress to us without fail,
And in her hand, perhaps, a mug of ale
To cheer our hearts, and also to inform
Herself what work is done that very morn;
Lays her commands upon us, that we mind
Her linen well, nor leave the dirt behind.
Not this alone, but also to take care
We don't her cambrics nor her ruffles tear;
And these most strictly does of us require,
To save her soap and sparing be of fire;
Tells us her charge is great, nay furthermore,
Her clothes are fewer than the time before.
Now we drive on, resolved our strength to try,
And what we can we do most willingly;
Until with heat and work, 'tis often known,
Not only sweat but blood runs trickling down
Our wrists and fingers: still our work demands
The constant action of our lab'ring hands.
  Now night comes on, from whence you have relief,
But that, alas! does but increase our grief.
With heavy hearts we often view the sun,
Fearing he'll set before our work is done;
For, either in the morning or at night,
We piece the summer's day with candlelight.
Though we all day with care our work attend,
Such is our fate, we know not when 'twill end.
When evening's come, you homeward take your way;
We, till our work is done, are forced to stay,
And, after all our toil and labour past,
Sixpence or eightpence pays us off at last;
For all our pains, no prospect can we see
Attend us, but old age and poverty.

(1739)

JOHN GAMBOLD

1711–1771

219 *The Mystery of Life*

So many years I've seen the sun,
And called these eyes and hands my own,
A thousand little acts I've done,
And childhood have and manhood known:
O what is life? and this dull round
To tread, why was a spirit bound?

So many airy draughts and lines,
And warm excursions of the mind,
Have filled my soul with great designs,
While practice grovelled far behind:
O what is thought? and where withdraw
The glories which my fancy saw?

So many tender joys and woes
Have on my quivering soul had power;
Plain life with height'ning passions rose,
The boast or burden of their hour:
O what is all we feel? why fled
Those pains and pleasures o'er my head?

So many human souls divine,
So at one interview displayed,
Some oft and freely mixed with mine,
In lasting bonds my heart have laid:
O what is friendship? why impressed
On my weak, wretched, dying breast?

So many wondrous gleams of light,
And gentle ardours from above,
Have made me sit, like seraph bright,
Some moments on a throne of love:
O what is virtue? why had I,
Who am so low, a taste so high?

Ere long, when sovereign Wisdom wills,
My soul an unknown path shall tread,
And strangely leave, who strangely fills
This frame, and waft me to the dead:

O what is death? 'tis life's last shore,
Where vanities are vain no more;
Where all pursuits their goal obtain,
And life is all retouched again;
Where in their bright result shall rise
Thoughts, virtues, friendships, griefs and joys.

(1739)

SIR CHARLES HANBURY WILLIAMS

1708–1759

220 from *Isabella: or, The Morning*

THE monkey, lap-dog, parrot, and her Grace
Had each retired from breakfast to their place,
When, hark, a knock! 'See, Betty, see who's there.'
' 'Tis Mr. Bateman, ma'am, in his new chair.'
'Dicky's new chair! the charming'st thing in town,
Whose poles are lacquered, and whose lining's brown!'
But see, he enters with his shuffling gait:
'Lord,' says her Grace, 'how could you be so late?'
'I'm sorry, madam, I have made you wait,'
Bateman replied; 'I only stayed to bring
The newest, charming'st, most delightful thing!'
'Oh! tell me what's the curiosity!
Oh! show it me this instant, or I die!'
To please the noble dame, the courtly squire
Produced a tea-pot, made in Staffordshire.
With eager eyes the longing Duchess stood,
And o'er and o'er the shining bauble viewed:
Such were the joys touched young Atrides' breast,
Such all the Grecian host at once expressed,
When from beneath his robe, to all their view,
Laertes' son the famed Palladium drew.
So Venus looked, and with such longing eyes,
When Paris first produced the golden prize.
'Such work as this,' she cries, 'can England do?
It equals Dresden, and outdoes St. Cloud:
All modern china now shall hide its head,
And e'en Chantilly must give o'er the trade.
For lace let Flanders bear away the bell,
In finest linen let the Dutch excel;

For prettiest stuffs let Ireland first be named,
And for best-fancied silks let France be famed;
Do thou, thrice happy England! still prepare
This clay, and build thy fame on earthenware.'
More she'd have said, but that again she heard
The knocker—and the General appeared.
  The General, one of those brave old commanders,
Who served through all the glorious wars in Flanders;
Frank and good-natured, of an honest heart,
Loving to act the steady friendly part:
None led through youth a gayer life than he,
Cheerful in converse, smart in repartee.
Sweet was his night, and joyful was his day,
He dined with Walpole, and with Oldfield lay;
But with old age its vices came along,
And in narration he's extremely long;
Exact in circumstance, and nice in dates,
On every subject he his tale relates.
If you name one of Marlbro's ten campaigns,
He tells you its whole history for your pains:
And Blenheim's field becomes, by his reciting,
As long in telling as it was in fighting.
His old desire to please is still expressed;
His hat's well cocked, his periwig's well dressed:
He rolls his stockings still, white gloves he wears,
And in the boxes with the beaux appears;
His eyes through wrinkled corners cast their rays;
Still he bows graceful, still soft things he says:
And still rememb'ring that he once was young,
He strains his crippled knees, and struts along.
The room he entered smiling, which bespoke
Some worn-out compliment, or thread-bare joke.
(For not perceiving loss of parts, he yet
Grasps at the shade of his departed wit.)
'How does your Grace? I hope I see you well!
What a prodigious deal of rain has fell!
Will the sun never let us see his face?
But who can ever want a sun that sees your Grace?'
  'Your servant, Sir—but see what I have got!
Isn't it a prodigious charming pot?
And ar'n't you vastly glad we make them here?
For Dicky got it out of Staffordshire.
See how the charming vine twines all about!
Lord! what a handle! Jesus! what a spout!
And that old pagod, and that charming child!
If Lady Townsend saw them, she'd be wild!'

To this the General: 'Madam, who would not?
Lord! where could Mr. Bateman find this pot?
Dear Dicky, couldn't you get one for me?
I want some useful china mightily;
Two jars, two beakers, and a pot-pourri.'
'Oh, Mr. Churchill, where d'ye think I've been?
At Margus's, and there such fireworks seen,
So very pretty, charming, odd and new;
And, I assure you, they're right Indian too!
I've bought them all, there's not one left in town;
And if you were to see them, you would own
You never saw such fireworks anywhere.'
—'Oh, Madam, I must beg your pardon there,'
The General cried, 'for—'twas in the year ten—
No, let me recollect, it was not then;
'Twas in the year eight, I think, for then we lay
Encamped with all the army, near Cambray—
Yes, yes, I'm sure I'm right by one event,
We supped together in Cadogan's tent,
Palmes, Meredith, Lumley, and poor George Grove,
And merrily the bumpers round we drove;
To Marlbro's health we drank confounded hard,
For he'd just beat the French at Oudenarde;
And Lord Cadogan then had got, by chance,
The best champagne that ever came from France;
And 'twas no wonder that it was so good,
For some dragoons had seized it on the road;
And they had heard from those they took it from,
It was designed a present for Vendôme.
So we—' But see, another Charles's face
Cuts short the General, and relieves her Grace.
So, when one crop-sick parson, in a doze,
Is reading morning-service through his nose,
Another in the pulpit straight appears,
Claiming the tired-out congregation's ears,
And with a duller sermon ends their pray'rs.
For this old Charles is full as dull as t' other,
Baevius to Maevius was not more a brother;
From two defects his talk no joy affords,
From want of matter, and from want of words.
'I hope,' says he, 'your Grace is well today,
And caught no cold by venturing to the play!'
'Oh, Sir, I'm mighty well—won't you sit down?
Pray, Mr. Stanhope, what's the news in town?'
'Madam, I know of none; but I'm just come
From seeing a curiosity at home:

'Twas sent to Martin Folkes as being rare,
And he and Desaguliers brought it there:
It's called a Polypus'—'What's that?'—'A creature,
The wonderful'st of all the works of nature:
Hither it came from Holland, where 'twas caught
(I should not say it came, for it was brought);
Tomorrow we're to have it at Crane-court,
And 'tis a reptile of so strange a sort,
That if 'tis cut in two, it is not dead;
Its head shoots out a tail, its tail a head;
Take out its middle, and observe its ends,
Here a head rises, there a tail descends;
Or cut off any part that you desire,
That part extends, and makes itself entire.
But what it feeds on still remains a doubt,
Or how it generates is not found out:
But at our Board, tomorrow, 'twill appear,
And then 'twill be considered and made clear,
For all the learned body will be there.'
'Lord, I must see it, or I am undone,'
The Duchess cried, 'pray can't you get me one?
I never heard of such a thing before,
I long to cut it and make fifty more;
I'd have a cage made up in taste for mine,
And, Dicky—you shall give me a design.'
But here the General to a yawn gave way,
And Stanhope had not one more word to say,
So stretched on easy chairs in apathy they lay;
And, on each side the goddess they adored,
One Charles sat speechless, and the other snored.
When chaste Susanna's all-subduing charms
Made two old lovers languish for her arms,
Soon as her eyes had thawed the frost of age,
Their passions mounted into lustful rage;
With brutal violence they attacked their prey,
And almost bore the wished-for prize away.
Hail happy Duchess! 'twixt two elders placed
Whose passions brutal lust has ne'er disgraced;
No warm expressions make your blushes rise,
No ravished kiss shoots light'ning from your eyes.
Let them but visit you, they ask no more;
Guiltless they'll gaze, and innocent adore.

(Wr. 1740; pub. 1765)

Polypus] cuttlefish

RICHARD GLOVER

1712–1785

221

Admiral Hosier's Ghost

As, near Porto-Bello lying
  On the gently swelling flood,
At midnight with streamers flying
  Our triumphant navy rode;
There, while Vernon sat all glorious
  From the Spaniards' late defeat,
And his crews with shouts victorious
  Drank success to England's fleet;

On a sudden, shrilly sounding,
  Hideous yells and shrieks were heard;
Then, each heart with fear confounding,
  A sad troop of ghosts appeared,
All in dreary hammocks shrouded,
  Which for winding-sheets they wore,
And, with looks by sorrow clouded,
  Frowning on that hostile shore.

On them gleamed the moon's wan lustre,
  When the shade of Hosier brave
His pale bands was seen to muster,
  Rising from their watry grave;
O'er the glimm'ring wave he hied him,
  Where the Burford reared her sail,
With three thousand ghosts beside him,
  And in groans did Vernon hail.

'Heed, Oh heed our fatal story!
  I am Hosier's injured ghost.
You, who now have purchased glory
  At this place where I was lost,
Though in Porto-Bello's ruin
  You now triumph, free from fears,
When you think on our undoing,
  You will mix your joy with tears!

'See these mournful spectres sweeping
  Ghastly o'er this hated wave,
Whose wan cheeks are stained with weeping:
  These were English captains brave.

Mark those numbers pale and horrid,
  Who were once my sailors bold,
Lo, each hangs his drooping forehead,
  While his dismal fate is told.

'I, by twenty sail attended,
  Did this Spanish town affright;
Nothing then its wealth defended
  But my orders not to fight;
Oh! that in this rolling ocean
  I had cast them with disdain,
And obeyed my heart's warm motion
  To reduce the pride of Spain.

'For resistance I could fear none,
  But with twenty ships had done
What thou, brave and happy Vernon,
  Hast achieved with six alone.
Then the bastimentos never
  Had our foul dishonour seen,
Nor the sea the sad receiver
  Of this gallant train had been.

'Thus, like thee, proud Spain dismaying,
  And her galleons leading home,
Though, condemned for disobeying,
  I had met a traitor's doom;
To have fall'n, my country crying
  "He has played an English part,"
Had been better far than dying
  Of a grieved and broken heart.

'Unrepining at thy glory,
  Thy successful arms we hail;
But remember our sad story,
  And let Hosier's wrongs prevail.
After this proud foe subduing,
  When your patriot friends you see,
Think on vengeance for my ruin,
  And for England shamed in me.'

(1740)

bastimentos] walls

SARAH DIXON

fl. 1716–1745

222 *Lines Occasioned by the Burning of Some Letters*

Not all pale Hecate's direful charms,
When hell's invoked to rise in swarms,
When graves are ransacked, mandrakes torn,
And rue and baleful nightshade torn,
Could give that torturing, racking pain
These magic lines did once obtain;
There's not a letter in the whole,
But what conspired to wound the soul.

But now! the dread enchantment's o'er;
The spell is broke, they plague no more.
'Twas only paper daubed with art:
Could such a trifle gain a heart,
Obstruct the peace of early life,
And set the passions all at strife,
Admit no cure, till time erased
The fond ideas fancy placed?

Combustible I'm sure you are;
Arise, ye flames! assist me, air!
Waft the vain atoms to the wind,
Disperse the fraud, and purge mankind.
The fatal relics thus removed,
Does Celia look like one who loved,
Who durst her future peace repose
On vows, and oaths, and toys like those?

Fallacious deity! to thee
The guilt, and the simplicity,
Who thought such cobweb-arts could bind,
To all eternity, the mind.
When honour's fled, thy flames expire,
And end in smoke like common fire.

Thus the entangled bird, set free,
Finds treble joy in liberty.
Her little heart may throb and beat,
Nor soon the danger past forget,

Dread to forsake the safeguard wood,
And shun awhile the crystal flood;
But with the next returning spring,
Retire to shades—you'll hear her sing.

(1740)

ANONYMOUS

223 *Epitaph on a Child Killed by Procured Abortion*

O THOU, whose eyes were closed in death's pale night,
Ere fate revealed thee to my aching sight;
Ambiguous something, by no standard fixed,
Frail span, of naught and of existence mixed;
Embryo, imperfect as my tort'ring thought,
Sad outcast of existence and of naught;
Thou, who to guilty love first ow'st thy frame,
Whom guilty honour kills to hide its shame;
Dire offspring! formed by love's too pleasing pow'r!
Honour's dire victim in a luckless hour!
Soften the pangs that still revenge thy doom:
Nor, from the dark abyss of nature's womb,
Where back I cast thee, let revolving time
Call up past scenes to aggravate my crime.
Two adverse tyrants ruled thy wayward fate,
Thyself a helpless victim to their hate;
Love, spite of honour's dictates, gave thee breath;
Honour, in spite of love, pronounced thy death.

(1740)

CHARLES WESLEY

1707–1788

224 *Morning Hymn*

CHRIST, whose glory fills the skies,
  Christ, the true, the only light,
Sun of righteousness, arise,
  Triumph o'er the shades of night:
Day-spring from on high, be near:
Day-star in my heart appear.

Dark and cheerless is the morn
  Unaccompanied by thee,
Joyless is the day's return,
  Till thy mercy's beams I see;
Till they inward light impart,
Glad my eyes, and warm my heart.

Visit then this soul of mine,
  Pierce the gloom of sin and grief,
Fill me, radiancy divine,
  Scatter all my unbelief,
More and more thyself display,
Shining to the perfect day.

(1740)

225 *In Temptation*

JESU, lover of my soul,
  Let me to thy bosom fly,
While the nearer waters roll,
  While the tempest still is high.
Hide me, O my Saviour, hide,
  Till the storm of life is past:
Safe into the haven guide;
  O receive my soul at last.

Other refuge have I none,
  Hangs my helpless soul on thee.
Leave, ah leave me not alone,
  Still support and comfort me.
All my trust on thee is stayed,
  All my help from thee I bring;
Cover my defençeless head
  With the shadow of thy wing.

Wilt thou not regard my call?
  Wilt thou not accept my prayer?
Lo, I sink, I faint, I fall!
  Lo, on thee I cast my care.
Reach me out thy gracious hand!
  While I of thy strength receive,
Hoping against hope I stand,
  Dying, and behold I live!

Thou, O Christ, art all I want;
  More than all in thee I find.
Raise the fallen, cheer the faint,
  Heal the sick, and lead the blind.
Just and holy is thy name;
  I am all unrighteousness:
False and full of sin I am,
  Thou art full of truth and grace.

Plenteous grace with thee is found,
  Grace to cover all my sin:
Let the healing streams abound,
  Make and keep me pure within.
Thou of life the fountain art:
  Freely let me take of thee,
Spring thou up within my heart,
  Rise to all eternity!

(1740)

226 *Wrestling Jacob*

COME, O thou Traveller unknown,
  Whom still I hold, but cannot see,
My company before is gone,
  And I am left alone with thee;
With thee all night I mean to stay,
And wrestle till the break of day.

I need not tell thee who I am,
  My misery or sin declare;
Thyself hast called me by my name,
  Look on thy hands, and read it there.
But who, I ask thee, who art thou?
Tell me thy name, and tell me now.

In vain thou strugglest to get free,
  I never will unloose my hold:
Art thou the Man that died for me?
  The secret of thy love unfold.
Wrestling I will not let thee go,
Till I thy name, thy nature know.

Wilt thou not yet to me reveal
   Thy new, unutterable name?
Tell me, I still beseech thee, tell;
   To know it now resolved I am.
Wrestling I will not let thee go,
Till I thy name, thy nature know.

'Tis all in vain to hold thy tongue,
   Or touch the hollow of my thigh:
Though every sinew be unstrung,
   Out of my arms thou shalt not fly.
Wrestling I will not let thee go,
Till I thy name, thy nature know.

What though my shrinking flesh complain,
   And murmur to contend so long,
I rise superior to my pain,
   When I am weak then I am strong;
And when my all of strength shall fail,
I shall with the God-Man prevail.

My strength is gone, my nature dies,
   I sink beneath thy weighty hand,
Faint to revive, and fall to rise;
   I fall, and yet by faith I stand,
I stand, and will not let thee go,
Till I thy name, thy nature know.

Yield to me now—for I am weak,
   But confident in self-despair:
Speak to my heart, in blessings speak,
   Be conquered by my instant prayer,
Speak, or thou never hence shalt move,
And tell me, if thy name is Love.

'Tis Love, 'tis Love! Thou died'st for me,
   I hear thy whisper in my heart.
The morning breaks, the shadows flee:
   Pure Universal Love thou art;
To me, to all, thy bowels move,
Thy nature and thy name is Love.

My prayer hath power with God; the grace
   Unspeakable I now receive,
Through faith I see thee face to face,
   I see thee face to face, and live:
In vain I have not wept and strove,
Thy nature and thy name is Love.

I know thee, Saviour, who thou art,
  Jesus, the feeble sinner's friend;
Nor wilt thou with the night depart,
  But stay, and love me to the end;
Thy mercies never shall remove,
Thy nature and thy name is Love.

The Sun of Righteousness on me
  Hath rose with healing in his wings,
Withered my nature's strength; from thee
  My soul its life and succour brings,
My help is all laid up above;
Thy nature and thy name is Love.

Contented now upon my thigh
  I halt, till life's short journey end;
All helplessness, all weakness I,
  On thee alone for strength depend,
Nor have I power, from thee, to move;
Thy nature and thy name is Love.

Lame as I am, I take the prey,
  Hell, earth, and sin with ease o'ercome;
I leap for joy, pursue my way,
  And as a bounding hart fly home,
Through all eternity to prove
Thy nature and thy name is Love.

(1742)

227 [*Inextinguishable Blaze*]

O THOU who camest from above,
  The pure, celestial fire t' impart,
Kindle a flame of sacred love
  On the mean altar of my heart;
There let it for thy glory burn
  With inextinguishable blaze,
And trembling to its source return,
  In humble prayer, and fervent praise.

Jesus, confirm my heart's desire
  To work, and speak, and think for thee,
Still let me guard the holy fire,
  And still stir up thy gift in me;

Ready for all thy perfect will
  My acts of faith and love repeat,
Till death thy endless mercies seal,
  And make my sacrifice complete.

(1762)

ANONYMOUS

228 from *Bedlam: A Poem on His Majesty's Happy Escape from his German Dominions*

WHAT mean these loud aerial cracks I hear?
Slumps after slumps that shake my trem'lous ear?
Zounds! they're the Tow'r bombardments, that disgorge
Their roaring thunders for returning George;
Through fugient skies they drive the swift-winged sound,
And tell th' important tale to regions round.
  Ye, who bade safety go and guard his way,
All thanks to you, immortal pow'rs! we pay.
With mirthful hearts and most melodious voice,
Revived and cheered, Britannia's sons rejoice,
And scarce the torrent of their transports bear,
Now they've got safe their Royal Master here.
  Halloo! who's there? Haste! quick, you dog! prepare
Pens, ink and tables, papers and a chair:
I'm forming the grand panegyric plan,
And Albion's mighty monarch is my man;
And while of George and George's deeds I sing,
I'll spread the feathers of a fearless wing.
Milton and Dryden I disdain to name,
Nor deem it glory to outburn their flame.
Nor with Dan Pope a tune I'd deign to try,
For with low lyres loud trumpets scorn to vie.
I'll mount with pinions that ne'er soared before,
Stronger than those my brother Pindar bore,
When he, the bold Dircaean Swan, did fly
Tow'ring through loftiest tracts of th' azure sky.
  Hark! how the burning dog-star raves and barks.
Come down, ye bending skies! and bring me larks:
I'll have them roasted on a string by dozens,
And ask to sup—my loving friends and cousins.

228 fugient] fleeing

But stay, rash Muse! nor start thou thus aside:
No more let devious Fancy's fires misguide.
This day great Phoebus in his car of fire
To's western waves reluctant will retire:
For, hark!—he tells me he'd fain stop his flight,
And shine in compliment to George all night,
But that by heav'n's Eternal Lord he's bound
To walk the world with restless circuits round.
Since he's thus destined, let the god be gone;
We'll strive to emulate the flaming sun.
Nay, we'll surpass th' ethereal house of Jove,
And light more fires below than he above.
Help, goddess! help me; one bright line inspire:
'Our fronts of houses shall be walls of fire.'
Come! once again my weary fancy raise:
'The midnight gloom shall turn to noontide blaze.
While rockets mount to tell the stars he's come,
Such light, great Paul! shall pour upon thy dome,
That counties round with stupid eyes shall stare,
To see thy tow'ring temple shine so fair
Through the night-flaming, elemental air.'

(1741)

WILLIAM DUNKIN

1709?–1765

229 from *An Epistle to R[o]b[er]t N[u]g[en]t, Esq. With a Picture of Doctor Swift* [*in Old Age*]

HIBERNIA's Helicon is dry,
Invention, wit and humour die,
And what remains against the storm
Of malice, but an empty form?
The nodding ruins of a pile
That stood the bulwark of this isle;
In which the sisterhood was fixed
Of candid honour, truth unmixed,
Imperial reason, thought profound,
And charity, diffusing round
In cheerful rivulets the flow
Of fortune to the sons of woe.

Such once, my N[u]g[en]t, was thy Swift,
Endued with each exalted gift.
But, lo! the pure ethereal flame
Is darkened by a misty steam:
The balm exhausted breathes no smell,
The rose is withered ere it fell.
That godlike supplement of law,
That held the wicked world in awe,
And could the tide of faction stem,
Is but a shell without the gem.

(Wr. 1742?; pub. 1770)

NICHOLAS JAMES

fl. 1742

230 from *The Complaints of Poverty*

MAY poverty, without offence, approach
The splendid equipage, the gilded coach?
May it with freedom all its wants make known?
And will not wealth and pow'r assume a frown?
Chimeras all! What can the wretched fear,
Hapless confined to a detested *here*?
No lower can we sink, nor higher rise,
Unless you deign to aid our miseries.
We feel its sad effects in early youth,
The mind a stranger to instructive truth;
Hence vagrant lads pursue the mumping trade,
Or justice' limits impiously invade;
Hence silly girls, seduced, their virtue mourn,
And spend an age in infamy and scorn.
But should our tender years such fortune find
That humble education forms the mind,
If reason in our artless bosom sways,
And if we tread direct in virtue's ways,
Incessant labour waits our future days.
At morning's early dawn it bids us rise,
Nor ends our toil till light forsakes the skies;
Ill-clothed, we winter's freezing cold sustain,
And summer's parching heat augments our pain;
While the harsh master and penurious dame
With cruel hand contract the human frame.

230 mumping] begging

Married, the wretch but multiplies his ills,
And others' mis'ry, sympathising, feels;
Still with each infant wretch his woes increase,
And happy if the wife permits him peace;
Too oft the theme of want her tongue employs,
Too oft she bans her inauspicious choice,
While, prudently, he shuns the wordy war,
And hears, retired, her thunder from afar.
When winter's rage upon the cottage falls,
And the wind rushes through the gaping walls,
When ninepence must their daily wants supply,
With hunger pinched and cold, the children cry;
The gathered sticks but little warmth afford,
And half-supplied the platter meets the board.
Returned at night, if wholesome viands fail,
He from the pipe extracts a smoky meal:
And when, to gather strength and still his woes,
He seeks his last redress in soft repose,
The tattered blanket, erst the fleas' retreat,
Denies his shiv'ring limbs sufficient heat;
Teased with the squalling babes' nocturnal cries,
He restless on the dusty pillow lies.
But when pale sickness wounds with direful blow,
Words but imperfectly his mis'ry show;
Unskilful how to treat the fierce disease,
Well-meaning ignorance curtails our days.
In a dark room and miserable bed
Together lie the living and the dead.
Oh shocking scene! Fate sweeps whole tribes away,
And frees the parish of th' reluctant pay!
Where's the physician now, whom heav'n ordains
Fate to arrest, and check corroding pains?
Or he's detained by those of high degree,
Or won't prescribe without a golden fee.
But should old age bring on its rev'rend hoar,
When strength decayed admits his toil no more,
He begs itinerant, with halting pace,
And, mournful, tells his melancholy case,
With meagre cheek and formidable beard,
A tattered dress of various rags prepared.
Base covetise, who wants the soul to give,
Directs the road where richer neighbours live;
And pride, unmindful of its parent dust,
Scares with the dungeon and the whipping-post.

(1742)

bans] curses

EDWARD YOUNG

1683–1765

231 *The Complaint, or Night Thoughts on Life, Death and Immortality*

from *Night I*

TIRED Nature's sweet restorer, balmy Sleep!
He, like the world, his ready visit pays
Where fortune smiles; the wretched he forsakes:
Swift on his downy pinion flies from woe,
And lights on lids unsullied with a tear.
  From short (as usual) and disturbed repose
I wake: how happy they who wake no more!
Yet that were vain, if dreams infest the grave.
I wake, emerging from a sea of dreams
Tumultuous; where my wrecked desponding thought
From wave to wave of fancied misery
At random drove, her helm of reason lost.
Though now restored, 'tis only change of pain,
(A bitter change!) severer for severe:
The day too short for my distress; and night,
Ev'n in the zenith of her dark domain,
Is sunshine to the colour of my fate.
  Night, sable goddess! from her ebon throne,
In rayless majesty, now stretches forth
Her leaden sceptre o'er a slumbering world.
Silence, how dead! and darkness, how profound!
Nor eye nor list'ning ear an object finds:
Creation sleeps. 'Tis as the general pulse
Of life stood still, and Nature made a pause;
An awful pause! prophetic of her end.
And let her prophecy be soon fulfilled:
Fate! drop the curtain; I can lose no more.
  Silence and Darkness! solemn sisters! twins
From ancient Night, who nurse the tender thought
To reason, and on reason build resolve
(That column of true majesty in man),
Assist me: I will thank you in the grave;
The grave, your kingdom. There this frame shall fall
A victim sacred to your dreary shrine.
But what are ye?—

Thou, who didst put to flight
Primeval Silence, when the morning stars,
Exulting, shouted o'er the rising ball;
O Thou, whose word from solid darkness struck
That spark, the sun; strike wisdom from my soul;
My soul, which flies to Thee, her trust, her treasure,
As misers to their gold, while others rest.
Through this opaque of Nature, and of Soul,
This double night, transmit one pitying ray,
To lighten and to cheer. O lead my mind
(A mind that fain would wander from its woe),
Lead it through various scenes of life and death;
And from each scene the noblest truths inspire.
Nor less inspire my conduct than my song:
Teach my best reason reason; my best will
Teach rectitude; and fix my firm resolve,
Wisdom to wed, and pay her long arrear:
Nor let the phial of thy vengeance, poured
On this devoted head be poured in vain.
The bell strikes one. We take no note of time
But from its loss. To give it then a tongue
Is wise in man. As if an angel spoke,
I feel the solemn sound. If heard aright,
It is the knell of my departed hours:
Where are they? With the years beyond the flood.
It is the signal that demands despatch:
How much is to be done! my hopes and fears
Start up alarmed, and o'er life's narrow verge
Look down—on what? A fathomless abyss;
A dread eternity! how surely mine!
And can eternity belong to me,
Poor pensioner on the bounties of an hour?
How poor, how rich, how abject, how august,
How complicate, how wonderful is man!
How passing wonder He who made him such!
Who centred in our make such strange extremes!
From different natures marvellously mixed,
Connection exquisite of distant worlds!
Distinguished link in being's endless chain!
Midway from nothing to the Deity!
A beam ethereal, sullied and absorbed!
Though sullied and dishonoured, still divine!
Dim miniature of greatness absolute!
An heir of glory! a frail child of dust!
Helpless immortal! insect infinite!
A worm! a god! I tremble at myself,

And in myself am lost! At home a stranger,
Thought wanders up and down, surprised, aghast,
And wond'ring at her own: how reason reels!
O what a miracle to man is man,
Triumphantly distressed! what joy, what dread!
Alternately transported, and alarmed!
What can preserve my life? or what destroy?
An angel's arm can't snatch me from the grave;
Legions of angels can't confine me there.
'Tis past conjecture; all things rise in proof.
While o'er my limbs sleep's soft dominion spreads,
What though my soul fantastic measures trod
O'er fairy fields; or mourned along the gloom
Of pathless woods; or, down the craggy steep
Hurled headlong, swam with pain the mantled pool;
Or scaled the cliff; or danced on hollow winds,
With antic shapes, wild natives of the brain?
Her ceaseless flight, though devious, speaks her nature
Of subtler essence than the trodden clod;
Active, aerial, tow'ring, unconfined,
Unfettered with her gross companion's fall.
Ev'n silent night proclaims my soul immortal:
Ev'n silent night proclaims eternal day.
For human weal, heaven husbands all events;
Dull sleep instructs, nor sport vain dreams in vain.

(1742)

from *Night VII. The Infidel Reclaimed*

There's naught (thou say'st) but one eternal flux
Of feeble essences, tumultuous driven
Through time's rough billows into night's abyss.
Say, in this rapid tide of human ruin,
Is there no rock, on which man's tossing thought
Can rest from terror, dare his fate survey,
And boldly think it something to be born?
Amid such hourly wrecks of being fair,
Is there no central, all-sustaining base,
All-realizing, all-connecting Pow'r,
Which, as it called forth all things, can recall,
And force Destruction to refund her spoil?
Command the grave restore her taken prey?
Bid death's dark vale its human harvest yield,
And earth and ocean pay their debt of man,
True to the grand deposit trusted there?

Is there no potentate, whose outstretched arm,
When rip'ning time calls forth th' appointed hour,
Plucked from foul Devastation's famished maw,
Binds present, past and future to his throne?
His throne how glorious, thus divinely graced
By germinating beings clust'ring round!
A garland worthy the divinity!
A throne, by heav'n's omnipotence in smiles,
Built (like a pharos tow'ring in the waves)
Amidst immense effusions of his love!
An ocean of communicated bliss!
An all-prolific, all-preserving God!
This were a God indeed.—And such is man,
As here presumed: he rises from his fall.
Think'st thou omnipotence a naked root,
Each blossom fair of Deity destroyed?
Nothing is dead; nay, nothing sleeps: each soul
That ever animated human clay
Now wakes; is on the wing: and where, O where
Will the swarm settle?—When the trumpet's call,
As sounding brass, collects us round heav'n's throne
Conglobed, we bask in everlasting day,
(Paternal splendour!) and adhere for ever.
Had not the soul this outlet to the skies,
In this vast vessel of the universe,
How should we gasp, as in an empty void!
How in the pangs of famished hope expire!
How bright *my* prospect shines! how gloomy *thine*!
A trembling world! and a devouring god!
Earth but the shambles of omnipotence!
Heav'n's face all stained with causeless massacres
Of countless millions, born to feel the pang
Of being lost. Lorenzo! can it be?
This bids us shudder at the thoughts of life.
Who would be born to such a phantom world,
Where naught substantial but our misery?
Where joy (if joy) but heightens our distress,
So soon to perish, and revive no more?
The greater such a joy, the more it pains.
A world so far from great (and yet how great
It shines to thee!) there's nothing real in it;
Being, a shadow! consciousness, a dream!
A dream, how dreadful! Universal blank
Before it, and behind! Poor man, a spark

pharos] lighthouse

From non-existence, struck by wrath divine,
Glitt'ring a moment, nor that moment sure;
Midst upper, nether and surrounding night,
His sad, sure, sudden and eternal tomb!

(1744)

from *Night IX. The Consolation*

Lorenzo! such the glories of the world!
What is the world itself? thy world?—A grave!
Where is the dust that has not been alive?
The spade, the plough disturb our ancestors;
From human mould we reap our daily bread.
The globe around earth's hollow surface shakes,
And is the ceiling of her sleeping sons.
O'er devastation we blind revels keep;
While buried towns support the dancer's heel.
The moist of human frame the sun exhales:
Winds scatter, through the mighty void, the dry:
Earth repossesses part of what she gave,
And the freed spirit mounts on wings of fire:
Each element partakes our scattered spoils;
As nature wide, our ruins spread: man's death
Inhabits all things but the thought of man.
Nor man alone; his breathing bust expires,
His tomb is mortal; empires die. Where now
The Roman? Greek? They stalk, an empty name!
Yet few regard them in this useful light;
Though half our learning is their epitaph.
When down thy vale, unlocked by midnight thought,
That loves to wander in thy sunless realms,
O Death! I stretch my view; what visions rise!
What triumphs! toils imperial! arts divine!
In withered laurels glide before my sight!
What lengths of far-famed ages, billowed high
With human agitation, roll along
In unsubstantial images of air!
The melancholy ghosts of dead renown,
Whisp'ring faint echoes of the world's applause,
With penitential aspect, as they pass,
All point at earth, and hiss at human pride,
The wisdom of the wise, and prancings of the great.

(1745)

THOMAS GRAY

1716–1771

232

Ode on the Spring

Lo! where the rosy-bosomed Hours,
Fair Venus' train, appear,
Disclose the long-expecting flowers,
And wake the purple year!
The Attic warbler pours her throat,
Responsive to the cuckoo's note,
The untaught harmony of spring:
While whispering pleasure as they fly,
Cool zephyrs through the clear blue sky
Their gathered fragrance fling.

Where'er the oak's thick branches stretch
A broader browner shade;
Where'er the rude and moss-grown beech
O'er-canopies the glade,
Beside some water's rushy brink
With me the Muse shall sit and think
(At ease reclined in rustic state)
How vain the ardour of the crowd,
How low, how little are the proud,
How indigent the great!

Still is the toiling hand of Care;
The panting herds repose.
Yet hark, how through the peopled air
The busy murmur glows!
The insect youth are on the wing,
Eager to taste the honeyed spring,
And float amid the liquid noon:
Some lightly o'er the current skim,
Some show their gaily-gilded trim
Quick-glancing to the sun.

To Contemplation's sober eye
Such is the race of man:
And they that creep, and they that fly,
Shall end where they began.
Alike the busy and the gay
But flutter through life's little day,

In fortune's varying colours dressed:
Brushed by the hand of rough Mischance,
Or chilled by age, their airy dance
They leave, in dust to rest.

Methinks I hear in accents low
The sportive kind reply:
'Poor moralist! and what art thou?
A solitary fly!
Thy joys no glittering female meets,
No hive hast thou of hoarded sweets,
No painted plumage to display:
On hasty wings thy youth is flown;
Thy sun is set, thy spring is gone—
We frolic, while 'tis May.'

(Wr. 1742; pub. 1748)

233 *Ode on a Distant Prospect of Eton College*

Ye distant spires, ye antique towers,
That crown the watry glade,
Where grateful Science still adores
Her Henry's holy shade;
And ye that from the stately brow
Of Windsor's heights th' expanse below
Of grove, of lawn, of mead survey,
Whose turf, whose shade, whose flowers among
Wanders the hoary Thames along
His silver-winding way.

Ah, happy hills, ah, pleasing shade,
Ah, fields beloved in vain,
Where once my careless childhood strayed,
A stranger yet to pain!
I feel the gales, that from ye blow,
A momentary bliss bestow,
As waving fresh their gladsome wing,
My weary soul they seem to soothe,
And, redolent of joy and youth,
To breathe a second spring.

Say, Father Thames, for thou hast seen
Full many a sprightly race
Disporting on thy margent green
The paths of pleasure trace,

Who foremost now delight to cleave
With pliant arm thy glassy wave?
The captive linnet which enthral?
What idle progeny succeed
To chase the rolling circle's speed,
Or urge the flying ball?

While some on earnest business bent
Their murm'ring labours ply
'Gainst graver hours, that bring constraint
To sweeten liberty:
Some bold adventurers disdain
The limits of their little reign,
And unknown regions dare descry:
Still as they run they look behind,
They hear a voice in every wind,
And snatch a fearful joy.

Gay hope is theirs by fancy fed,
Less pleasing when possessed;
The tear forgot as soon as shed,
The sunshine of the breast:
Theirs buxom health of rosy hue,
Wild wit, invention ever-new,
And lively cheer of vigour born;
The thoughtless day, the easy night,
The spirits pure, the slumbers light,
That fly th' approach of morn.

Alas, regardless of their doom,
The little victims play!
No sense have they of ills to come,
Nor care beyond today:
Yet see how all around 'em wait
The ministers of human fate,
And black Misfortune's baleful train!
Ah, show them, where in ambush stand
To seize their prey the murth'rous band!
Ah, tell them, they are men!

These shall the fury Passions tear,
The vultures of the mind,
Disdainful Anger, pallid Fear,
And Shame that skulks behind;
Or pining Love shall waste their youth,
Or Jealousy with rankling tooth,

That inly gnaws the secret heart,
And Envy wan, and faded Care,
Grim-visaged comfortless Despair,
And Sorrow's piercing dart.

Ambition this shall tempt to rise,
Then whirl the wretch from high,
To bitter Scorn a sacrifice,
And grinning Infamy.
The stings of Falsehood those shall try,
And hard Unkindness' altered eye,
That mocks the tear it forced to flow;
And keen Remorse with blood defiled,
And moody Madness laughing wild
Amid severest woe.

Lo, in the vale of years beneath
A grisly troop are seen,
The painful family of Death,
More hideous than their Queen:
This racks the joints, this fires the veins,
That every labouring sinew strains,
Those in the deeper vitals rage:
Lo, Poverty, to fill the band,
That numbs the soul with icy hand,
And slow-consuming Age.

To each his suff'rings: all are men,
Condemned alike to groan;
The tender for another's pain,
Th' unfeeling for his own.
Yet ah! why should they know their fate?
Since sorrow never comes too late,
And happiness too swiftly flies.
Thought would destroy their paradise.
No more; where ignorance is bliss,
'Tis folly to be wise.

(Wr. 1742; pub. 1747)

234 *Sonnet on the Death of Mr. Richard West*

In vain to me the smiling mornings shine,
And red'ning Phoebus lifts his golden fire:
The birds in vain their amorous descant join,
Or cheerful fields resume their green attire:

These ears, alas! for other notes repine,
A different object do these eyes require.
My lonely anguish melts no heart but mine;
And in my breast the imperfect joys expire.
Yet morning smiles the busy race to cheer,
And new-born pleasure brings to happier men:
The fields to all their wonted tribute bear;
To warm their little loves the birds complain.
I fruitless mourn to him that cannot hear,
And weep the more because I weep in vain.

(Wr. 1742; pub. 1775)

235 *Ode on the Death of a Favourite Cat, Drowned in a Tub of Gold Fishes*

'TWAS on a lofty vase's side,
Where China's gayest art had dyed
 The azure flowers, that blow;
Demurest of the tabby kind,
The pensive Selima reclined,
 Gazed on the lake below.

Her conscious tail her joy declared;
The fair round face, the snowy beard,
 The velvet of her paws,
Her coat that with the tortoise vies,
Her ears of jet and emerald eyes,
 She saw; and purred applause.

Still had she gazed; but 'midst the tide
Two angel forms were seen to glide,
 The genii of the stream:
Their scaly armour's Tyrian hue
Through richest purple to the view
 Betrayed a golden gleam.

The hapless nymph with wonder saw:
A whisker first and then a claw,
 With many an ardent wish,
She stretched in vain to reach the prize.
What female heart can gold despise?
 What cat's averse to fish?

Presumptuous maid! with looks intent
Again she stretched, again she bent,
   Nor knew the gulf between.
(Malignant Fate sat by and smiled)
The slipp'ry verge her feet beguiled,
   She tumbled headlong in.

Eight times emerging from the flood
She mewed to every watry god,
   Some speedy aid to send.
No dolphin came, no Nereid stirred:
Nor cruel Tom nor Susan heard.
   A fav'rite has no friend!

From hence, ye beauties, undeceived,
Know, one false step is ne'er retrieved,
   And be with caution bold.
Not all that tempts your wand'ring eyes
And heedless hearts is lawful prize;
   Nor all that glisters gold.

(1748)

236 *Tophet*

SUCH Tophet was; so looked the grinning fiend
Whom many a frighted prelate called his friend;
I saw them bow and, while they wished him dead,
With servile simper nod the mitred head.
Our Mother-Church with half-averted sight
Blushed as she blessed her grisly proselyte:
Hosannahs rung through hell's tremendous borders,
And Satan's self had thoughts of taking orders.

(Wr. 1749?; pub. 1783)

237 *Elegy Written in a Country Churchyard*

THE curfew tolls the knell of parting day,
The lowing herd wind slowly o'er the lea,
The ploughman homeward plods his weary way,
And leaves the world to darkness and to me.

Now fades the glimmering landscape on the sight,
And all the air a solemn stillness holds,
Save where the beetle wheels his droning flight,
And drowsy tinklings lull the distant folds;

Save that from yonder ivy-mantled tow'r
The moping owl does to the moon complain
Of such as, wand'ring near her secret bow'r,
Molest her ancient solitary reign.

Beneath those rugged elms, that yew-tree's shade,
Where heaves the turf in many a mould'ring heap,
Each in his narrow cell for ever laid,
The rude forefathers of the hamlet sleep.

The breezy call of incense-breathing morn,
The swallow twitt'ring from the straw-built shed,
The cock's shrill clarion or the echoing horn,
No more shall rouse them from their lowly bed.

For them no more the blazing hearth shall burn,
Or busy housewife ply her evening care:
No children run to lisp their sire's return,
Or climb his knees the envied kiss to share.

Oft did the harvest to their sickle yield,
Their furrow oft the stubborn glebe has broke;
How jocund did they drive their team afield!
How bowed the woods beneath their sturdy stroke!

Let not Ambition mock their useful toil,
Their homely joys and destiny obscure;
Nor Grandeur hear, with a disdainful smile,
The short and simple annals of the poor.

The boast of heraldry, the pomp of pow'r,
And all that beauty, all that wealth e'er gave,
Awaits alike the inevitable hour.
The paths of glory lead but to the grave.

Nor you, ye Proud, impute to these the fault,
If Mem'ry o'er their tomb no trophies raise,
Where through the long-drawn aisle and fretted vault
The pealing anthem swells the note of praise.

Can storied urn or animated bust
Back to its mansion call the fleeting breath?
Can Honour's voice provoke the silent dust,
Or Flatt'ry soothe the dull cold ear of Death?

Perhaps in this neglected spot is laid
Some heart once pregnant with celestial fire;
Hands that the rod of empire might have swayed,
Or waked to ecstasy the living lyre.

But Knowledge to their eyes her ample page
Rich with the spoils of time did ne'er unroll;
Chill Penury repressed their noble rage,
And froze the genial current of the soul.

Full many a gem of purest ray serene
The dark unfathomed caves of ocean bear:
Full many a flower is born to blush unseen
And waste its sweetness on the desert air.

Some village-Hampden that with dauntless breast
The little tyrant of his fields withstood;
Some mute inglorious Milton here may rest,
Some Cromwell guiltless of his country's blood.

Th' applause of list'ning senates to command,
The threats of pain and ruin to despise,
To scatter plenty o'er a smiling land,
And read their hist'ry in a nation's eyes,

Their lot forbade: nor circumscribed alone
Their growing virtues, but their crimes confined;
Forbade to wade through slaughter to a throne,
And shut the gates of mercy on mankind,

The struggling pangs of conscious truth to hide,
To quench the blushes of ingenuous shame,
Or heap the shrine of Luxury and Pride
With incense kindled at the Muse's flame.

Far from the madding crowd's ignoble strife
Their sober wishes never learned to stray;
Along the cool sequestered vale of life
They kept the noiseless tenor of their way.

Yet ev'n these bones from insult to protect
Some frail memorial still erected nigh,
With uncouth rhymes and shapeless sculpture decked,
Implores the passing tribute of a sigh.

Their name, their years, spelt by th' unlettered muse,
The place of fame and elegy supply:
And many a holy text around she strews,
That teach the rustic moralist to die.

For who to dumb Forgetfulness a prey,
This pleasing anxious being e'er resigned,
Left the warm precincts of the cheerful day,
Nor cast one longing ling'ring look behind?

On some fond breast the parting soul relies,
Some pious drops the closing eye requires;
Ev'n from the tomb the voice of Nature cries,
Ev'n in our ashes live their wonted fires.

For thee who, mindful of th' unhonoured dead,
Dost in these lines their artless tale relate;
If chance, by lonely Contemplation led,
Some kindred spirit shall inquire thy fate,

Haply some hoary-headed swain may say,
'Oft have we seen him at the peep of dawn
Brushing with hasty steps the dews away
To meet the sun upon the upland lawn.

'There at the foot of yonder nodding beech
That wreathes its old fantastic roots so high,
His listless length at noontide would he stretch,
And pore upon the brook that babbles by.

'Hard by yon wood, now smiling as in scorn,
Muttering his wayward fancies he would rove,
Now drooping, woeful wan, like one forlorn,
Or crazed with care, or crossed in hopeless love.

'One morn I missed him on the customed hill,
Along the heath and near his fav'rite tree;
Another came; nor yet beside the rill,
Nor up the lawn, nor at the wood was he;

'The next with dirges due in sad array
Slow through the church-way path we saw him borne.
Approach and read (for thou canst read) the lay,
Graved on the stone beneath yon aged thorn.'

THE EPITAPH

Here rests his head upon the lap of earth
A youth to fortune and to fame unknown.
Fair Science frowned not on his humble birth,
And Melancholy marked him for her own.

Large was his bounty and his soul sincere,
Heaven did a recompense as largely send:
He gave to Mis'ry all he had, a tear,
He gained from heav'n ('twas all he wished) a friend.

No farther seek his merits to disclose,
Or draw his frailties from their dread abode
(There they alike in trembling hope repose),
The bosom of his Father and his God.

(Wr. 1746?–50; pub. 1751)

238 *The Progress of Poesy. A Pindaric Ode*

I. 1

AWAKE, Aeolian lyre, awake,
And give to rapture all thy trembling strings.
From Helicon's harmonious springs
A thousand rills their mazy progress take:
The laughing flowers, that round them blow,
Drink life and fragrance as they flow.
Now the rich stream of music winds along,
Deep, majestic, smooth, and strong,
Through verdant vales and Ceres' golden reign:
Now rolling down the steep amain,
Headlong, impetuous, see it pour:
The rocks and nodding groves rebellow to the roar.

I. 2

Oh! Sovereign of the willing soul,
Parent of sweet and solemn-breathing airs,
Enchanting shell! the sullen Cares
And frantic Passions hear thy soft control.
On Thracia's hills the Lord of War
Has curbed the fury of his car,
And dropped his thirsty lance at thy command.
Perching on the sceptred hand

Of Jove, thy magic lulls the feathered king
With ruffled plumes and flagging wing:
Quenched in dark clouds of slumber lie
The terror of his beak and lightnings of his eye.

I. 3

Thee the voice, the dance, obey,
Tempered to thy warbled lay.
O'er Idalia's velvet-green
The rosy-crownèd Loves are seen
On Cytherea's day
With antic Sports and blue-eyed Pleasures,
Frisking light in frolic measures;
Now pursuing, now retreating,
Now in circling troops they meet:
To brisk notes in cadence beating
Glance their many-twinkling feet.
Slow melting strains their Queen's approach declare:
Where'er she turns the Graces homage pay.
With arms sublime, that float upon the air,
In gliding state she wins her easy way:
O'er her warm cheek and rising bosom move
The bloom of young desire and purple light of love.

II. 1

Man's feeble race what ills await,
Labour, and penury, the racks of pain,
Disease, and sorrow's weeping train,
And death, sad refuge from the storms of fate!
The fond complaint, my song, disprove,
And justify the laws of Jove.
Say, has he giv'n in vain the heav'nly Muse?
Night and all her sickly dews,
Her spectres wan and birds of boding cry,
He gives to range the dreary sky:
Till down the eastern cliffs afar
Hyperion's march they spy and glitt'ring shafts of war.

II. 2

In climes beyond the solar road,
Where shaggy forms o'er ice-built mountains roam,
The Muse has broke the twilight-gloom
To cheer the shiv'ring native's dull abode.
And oft beneath the od'rous shade
Of Chile's boundless forests laid,

She deigns to hear the savage youth repeat
In loose numbers wildly sweet
Their feather-cinctured chiefs and dusky loves.
Her track, where'er the goddess roves,
Glory pursue and generous Shame,
Th' unconquerable Mind, and Freedom's holy flame.

II. 3

Woods that wave o'er Delphi's steep,
Isles that crown th' Aegean deep,
Fields that cool Ilissus laves,
Or where Maeander's amber waves
In lingering lab'rinths creep,
How do your tuneful echoes languish,
Mute but to the voice of anguish?
Where each old poetic mountain
Inspiration breathed around:
Every shade and hallowed fountain
Murmured deep a solemn sound:
Till the sad Nine in Greece's evil hour
Left their Parnassus for the Latian plains.
Alike they scorn the pomp of tyrant-power,
And coward Vice that revels in her chains.
When Latium had her lofty spirit lost,
They sought, oh Albion! next thy sea-encircled coast.

III. I

Far from the sun and summer-gale,
In thy green lap was Nature's darling laid,
What time, where lucid Avon strayed,
To him the mighty Mother did unveil
Her awful face: the dauntless child
Stretched forth his little arms and smiled.
'This pencil take,' (she said) 'whose colours clear
Richly paint the vernal year:
Thine too these golden keys, immortal boy!
This can unlock the gates of joy;
Of horror that and thrilling fears,
Or ope the sacred source of sympathetic tears.'

III. 2

Nor second he, that rode sublime
Upon the seraph-wings of Ecstasy,
The secrets of th' abyss to spy.
He passed the flaming bounds of place and time:

The living throne, the sapphire-blaze,
Where angels tremble while they gaze,
He saw; but, blasted with excess of light,
Closed his eyes in endless night.
Behold, where Dryden's less presumptuous car,
Wide o'er the fields of glory, bear
Two coursers of ethereal race,
With necks in thunder clothed, and long-resounding pace.

III. 3

Hark, his hands the lyre explore!
Bright-eyed Fancy hovering o'er
Scatters from her pictured urn
Thoughts that breathe, and words that burn.
But ah! 'tis heard no more—
Oh! lyre divine, what daring spirit
Wakes thee now? Though he inherit
Nor the pride nor ample pinion,
That the Theban eagle bear
Sailing with supreme dominion
Through the azure deep of air:
Yet oft before his infant eyes would run
Such forms as glitter in the Muse's ray
With orient hues, unborrowed of the sun:
Yet shall he mount, and keep his distant way
Beyond the limits of a vulgar fate,
Beneath the Good how far—but far above the Great.

(Wr. 1751–4; pub. 1757)

239 *The Bard. A Pindaric Ode*

I. 1

'RUIN seize thee, ruthless king!
Confusion on thy banners wait,
Though fanned by Conquest's crimson wing
They mock the air with idle state.
Helm nor hauberk's twisted mail,
Nor even thy virtues, tyrant, shall avail
To save thy secret soul from nightly fears,
From Cambria's curse, from Cambria's tears!'
Such were the sounds, that o'er the crested pride
Of the first Edward scattered wild dismay,

As down the steep of Snowdon's shaggy side
He wound with toilsome march his long array.
Stout Glo'ster stood aghast in speechless trance:
'To arms!', cried Mortimer and couched his quivering lance.

I. 2

On a rock, whose haughty brow
Frowns o'er old Conway's foaming flood,
Robed in the sable garb of woe,
With haggard eyes the poet stood
(Loose his beard and hoary hair
Streamed, like a meteor, to the troubled air);
And, with a master's hand and prophet's fire,
Struck the deep sorrows of his lyre.
'Hark, how each giant-oak and desert cave
Sighs to the torrent's awful voice beneath!
O'er thee, oh king! their hundred arms they wave,
Revenge on thee in hoarser murmurs breathe;
Vocal no more, since Cambria's fatal day,
To high-born Hoel's harp, or soft Llewellyn's lay.

I. 3

'Cold is Cadwallo's tongue,
That hushed the stormy main:
Brave Urien sleeps upon his craggy bed:
Mountains, ye mourn in vain
Modred, whose magic song
Made huge Plinlimmon bow his cloud-topped head.
On dreary Arvon's shore they lie,
Smeared with gore and ghastly pale:
Far, far aloof th' affrighted ravens sail;
The famished eagle screams and passes by.
Dear lost companions of my tuneful art,
Dear as the light that visits these sad eyes,
Dear as the ruddy drops that warm my heart,
Ye died amidst your dying country's cries—
No more I weep. They do not sleep.
On yonder cliffs, a grisly band,
I see them sit, they linger yet,
Avengers of their native land;
With me in dreadful harmony they join,
And weave with bloody hands the tissue of thy line.'

II. 1

"Weave the warp and weave the woof,
The winding-sheet of Edward's race.
Give ample room and verge enough
The characters of hell to trace.
Mark the year and mark the night,
When Severn shall re-echo with affright
The shrieks of death, through Berkeley's roofs that ring,
Shrieks of an agonizing King!
She-wolf of France, with unrelenting fangs,
That tear'st the bowels of thy mangled mate,
From thee be born who o'er thy country hangs
The scourge of heav'n. What terrors round him wait!
Amazement in his van, with Flight combined,
And Sorrow's faded form, and Solitude behind.

II. 2

"Mighty victor, mighty lord,
Low on his funeral couch he lies!
No pitying heart, no eye, afford
A tear to grace his obsequies.
Is the sable warrior fled?
Thy son is gone. He rests among the dead.
The swarm that in thy noon-tide beam were born?
Gone to salute the rising morn.
Fair laughs the morn and soft the zephyr blows,
While proudly riding o'er the azure realm
In gallant trim the gilded vessel goes;
Youth on the prow and Pleasure at the helm,
Regardless of the sweeping whirlwind's sway,
That, hushed in grim repose, expects his evening-prey.

II. 3

"Fill high the sparkling bowl,
The rich repast prepare,
Reft of a crown, he yet may share the feast:
Close by the regal chair
Fell Thirst and Famine scowl
A baleful smile upon their baffled guest.
Heard ye the din of battle bray,
Lance to lance and horse to horse?
Long years of havoc urge their destined course,
And through the kindred squadrons mow their way.

Ye towers of Julius, London's lasting shame,
With many a foul and midnight murther fed,
Revere his consort's faith, his father's fame,
And spare the meek usurper's holy head.
Above, below, the rose of snow,
Twined with her blushing foe, we spread:
The bristled Boar in infant-gore
Wallows beneath the thorny shade.
Now, brothers, bending o'er th' accursed loom,
Stamp we our vengeance deep, and ratify his doom.

III. 1

"Edward, lo! to sudden fate
(Weave we the woof. The thread is spun)
Half of thy heart we consecrate.
(The web is wove. The work is done.)"
'Stay, oh stay! nor thus forlorn
Leave me unblessed, unpitied, here to mourn;
In yon bright track, that fires the western skies,
They melt, they vanish from my eyes.
But oh! what solemn scenes on Snowdon's height
Descending slow their glitt'ring skirts unroll?
Visions of glory, spare my aching sight,
Ye unborn ages, crowd not on my soul!
No more our long-lost Arthur we bewail.
All-hail, ye genuine kings, Britannia's issue, hail!

III. 2

'Girt with many a baron bold
Sublime their starry fronts they rear;
And gorgeous dames, and statesmen old
In bearded majesty, appear.
In the midst a form divine!
Her eye proclaims her of the Briton-line;
Her lion-port, her awe-commanding face,
Attempered sweet to virgin-grace.
What strings symphonious tremble in the air,
What strains of vocal transport round her play!
Hear from the grave, great Taliessin, hear;
They breathe a soul to animate thy clay.
Bright Rapture calls and, soaring as she sings,
Waves in the eye of heav'n her many-coloured wings.

III. 3

'The verse adorn again
Fierce war and faithful love,
And truth severe, by fairy fiction dressed.
In buskined measures move
Pale Grief and pleasing Pain,
With Horror, tyrant of the throbbing breast.
A voice as of the cherub-choir
Gales from blooming Eden bear;
And distant warblings lessen on my ear,
That lost in long futurity expire.
Fond impious man, think'st thou yon sanguine cloud,
Raised by thy breath, has quenched the orb of day?
Tomorrow he repairs the golden flood,
And warms the nations with redoubled ray.
Enough for me: with joy I see
The different doom our fates assign.
Be thine despair and sceptred care;
To triumph, and to die are mine.'
He spoke, and headlong from the mountain's height
Deep in the roaring tide he plunged to endless night.

(1757)

240 from *Ode on the Pleasure Arising from Vicissitude*

Now the golden Morn aloft
Waves her dew-bespangled wing;
With vermeil cheek and whisper soft
She woos the tardy spring,
Till April starts, and calls around
The sleeping fragrance from the ground;
And lightly o'er the living scene
Scatters his freshest, tenderest green.

New-born flocks in rustic dance
Frisking ply their feeble feet.
Forgetful of their wintry trance
The birds his presence greet.
But chief the sky-lark warbles high
His trembling thrilling ecstasy,
And, lessening from the dazzled sight,
Melts into air and liquid light.

Yesterday the sullen year
Saw the snowy whirlwind fly;
Mute was the music of the air,
The herd stood drooping by:
Their raptures now that wildly flow
No yesterday nor morrow know;
'Tis man alone that joy descries
With forward and reverted eyes.

Smiles on past Misfortune's brow
Soft Reflection's hand can trace;
And o'er the cheek of Sorrow throw
A melancholy grace;
While Hope prolongs our happier hour,
Or deepest shades, that dimly lour
And blacken round our weary way,
Gilds with a gleam of distant day.

Still, where rosy Pleasure leads,
See a kindred Grief pursue;
Behind the steps that Misery treads,
Approaching Comfort view:
The hues of bliss more brightly glow,
Chastised by sabler tints of woe;
And blended form, with artful strife,
The strength and harmony of life.

See the wretch, that long has tossed
On the thorny bed of pain,
At length repair his vigour lost,
And breathe and walk again:
The meanest flowret of the vale,
The simplest note that swells the gale,
The common sun, the air and skies,
To him are opening paradise.

(Wr. 1754?; pub. 1775)

241

The Death of Hoel

HAD I but the torrent's might,
With headlong rage and wild affright
Upon Deïra's squadrons hurled,
To rush and sweep them from the world!
  Too, too secure in youthful pride,

By them my friend, my Hoël, died,
Great Cian's son: of Madoc old
He asked no heaps of hoarded gold;
Alone in nature's wealth arrayed,
He asked and had the lovely maid.
  To Cattraeth's vale in glitt'ring row
Twice two hundred warriors go;
Every warrior's manly neck
Chains of regal honour deck,
Wreathed in many a golden link:
From the golden cup they drink
Nectar, that the bees produce,
Or the grape's ecstatic juice.
Flushed with mirth and hope they burn:
But none from Cattraeth's vale return,
Save Aeron brave and Conan strong
(Bursting through the bloody throng),
And I, the meanest of them all,
That live to weep and sing their fall.

(Wr. 1761; pub. 1775)

242 *On L[or]d H[olland']s Seat near M[argat]e, K[en]t*

OLD and abandoned by each venal friend,
  Here H[olland] took the pious resolution
To smuggle some few years and strive to mend
  A broken character and constitution.
On this congenial spot he fixed his choice;
  Earl Godwin trembled for his neighbouring sand;
Here seagulls scream and cormorants rejoice,
  And mariners, though shipwrecked, dread to land.
Here reign the blust'ring North and blighting East,
  No tree is heard to whisper, bird to sing:
Yet nature cannot furnish out the feast,
  Art he invokes new horrors still to bring.
Now mould'ring fanes and battlements arise,
  Arches and turrets nodding to their fall,
Unpeopled palaces delude his eyes,
  And mimic desolation covers all.
'Ah', said the sighing peer, 'had Bute been true
  Nor Shelburne's, Rigby's, Calcraft's friendship vain,
Far other scenes than these had blessed our view
  And realised the ruins that we feign.

Purged by the sword and beautified by fire,
  Then had we seen proud London's hated walls:
Owls might have hooted in St. Peter's choir,
  And foxes stunk and littered in St. Paul's.'

(1769)

ROBERT BLAIR

1699–1746

243 from *The Grave*

  WHILST some affect the sun and some the shade,
Some flee the city, some the hermitage,
Their aims as various as the roads they take
In journeying through life—the task be mine
To paint the gloomy horrors of the tomb,
Th' appointed place of rendezvous, where all
These travellers meet. Thy succours I implore,
Eternal King! whose potent arm sustains
The keys of hell and death. The Grave, dread thing!
Men shiver when thou'rt named; Nature, appalled,
Shakes off her wonted firmness. Ah! how dark
Thy long-extended realms and rueful wastes,
Where naught but silence reigns, and night, dark night,
Dark as was Chaos ere the infant sun
Was rolled together, or had tried his beams
Athwart the gloom profound! The sickly taper
By glimmering through thy low-browed misty vaults
(Furred round with mouldy damps and ropy slime)
Lets fall a supernumerary horror,
And only serves to make thy night more irksome.
Well do I know thee by thy trusty yew,
Cheerless, unsocial plant! that loves to dwell
Midst skulls and coffins, epitaphs and worms;
Where light-heeled ghosts and visionary shades,
Beneath the wan cold moon (as fame reports)
Embodied thick, perform their mystic rounds.
No other merriment, dull tree! is thine.
  See yonder hallowed fane—the pious work
Of names once famed, now dubious or forgot,
And buried midst the wreck of things which were;
There lie interred the more illustrious dead.

The wind is up—hark! how it howls! Methinks
Till now I never heard a sound so dreary.
Doors creak, and windows clap, and night's foul bird,
Rooked in the spire, screams loud. The gloomy aisles,
Black-plastered, and hung round with shreds of 'scutcheons
And tattered coats of arms, send back the sound
Laden with heavier airs, from the low vaults,
The mansions of the dead. Roused from their slumbers,
In grim array the grisly spectres rise,
Grin horrible, and obstinately sullen
Pass and repass, hushed as the foot of night.
Again the screech-owl shrieks—ungracious sound!
I'll hear no more; it makes one's blood run chill.
  Quite round the pile, a row of reverend elms
(Coeval near with that) all ragged show,
Long lashed by the rude winds; some rift half down
Their branchless trunks, others so thin at top
That scarce two crows could lodge in the same tree.
Strange things, the neighbours say, have happened here:
Wild shrieks have issued from the hollow tombs,
Dead men have come again, and walked about,
And the great bell has tolled, unrung, untouched.
(Such tales their cheer, at wake or gossiping,
When it draws near to witching time of night.)
  Oft in the lone churchyard at night I've seen,
By glimpse of moonshine chequering through the trees,
The schoolboy with his satchel in his hand,
Whistling aloud to bear his courage up,
And lightly tripping o'er the long flat stones
(With nettles skirted and with moss o'ergrown),
That tell in homely phrase who lie below.
Sudden he starts, and hears, or thinks he hears,
The sound of something purring at his heels;
Full fast he flies, and dares not look behind him,
Till out of breath he overtakes his fellows;
Who gather round, and wonder at the tale
Of horrid apparition, tall and ghastly,
That walks at dead of night, or takes his stand
O'er some new-opened grave, and (strange to tell!)
Evanishes at crowing of the cock.

(1743)

rooked] huddled

JOSIAH RELPH

1712–1743

244 *Hay-Time; or The Constant Lovers. A Pastoral* [*in the Cumberland Dialect*]

CURSTY and PEGGY

WARM shone the sun, the wind as warmly blew,
No longer cooled by draughts of morning dew;
When in the field a faithful pair appeared,
A faithful pair full happily endeared:
Hasty in rows they raked the meadow's pride,
Then sank amid the softness side by side,
To wait the withering force of wind and sun;
And thus their artless tale of love begun.

Cursty A finer hay-day seer was never seen;
The greenish sops already luik less green;
As weel the greenish sops will suin be dried
As Sawney's bacco spred by th' ingle side.

Peggy And see how finely striped the fields appear,
Striped like the gown 'at I on Sundays wear;
White shows the rye, the big of blaker hue,
The bluimen pezz green ment wi' reed and blue.

Cursty Let other lads to spworts and pastimes run,
And spoil their Sunday clease and clash their shoon;
If Peggy in the field my partner be,
To work at hay is better spwort to me.

Peggy Let other lasses ride to Rosely-fair,
And mazle up and down the market there;
I envy not their happy treats and them,
Happier my sell, if Roger bides at heame.

Cursty It's hard aw day the heavy scy' to swing;
But if my lass a holesome breakfast bring,
Even mowing-time is better far I swear,
Then Cursenmas and aw its dainty chear.

Peggy Far is the Gursin off, top full the kits,
But if my Cursty bears the milk by fits,
For gallopin to wakes I ne'er gang wood,
For ev'ry night's a wake, or full as good.

seer] sure sops] wet grass ingle side] fireside big] barley pezz] peas ment] mixed clease] clothes shoon] shoes mazle] wander aimlessly Cursenmas] Christmas Gursin] pasture kits] pails wood] mad

Cursty Can thou remember, I remember't weel,
Sin call wee things we clavered owr yon steel;
Lang willy-wands for hoops I yust to bay,
To meake my canny lass a leady gay.
Peggy Then dadged we to the bog owr meadows dree,
To plet a sword and seevy cap for thee;
Set off with seevy cap and seevy sword
My Cursty luiked as great as anny lword.
Cursty Beneath a dyke full menny a langsome day,
We sat and beelded houses fine o'clay;
For dishes acorn cups stuid dessed in rows,
And broken pots for dublers mensed the waws.
Peggy O may we better houses get than thar,
Far larger dishes, dublers brighter far;
And ever mair delighted may we be,
I to meake Cursty fine, and Cursty me.
Cursty Right oft at schuil I've speldered owr thy rows,
Faull manny a time I've foughten in thy cause;
And when in winter miry ways let in,
I bear thee on my back through thick and thin.
Peggy As suin as e'er I learned to kest a loup,
Warm mittens wapped thy fingers warmly up;
And when at heels I spied thy stockings out,
I darned them suin, or suin set on a clout.
Cursty O how I liked to see thee on the fleer;
At spworts, if I was trier to be seer,
I reached the fancy ruddily to thee
For nin danced hawf sae weel in Cursty's eye.
Peggy O how I swet when, for the costly prize,
Thou grupped some lusty lad of greater size;
But when I saw him scrawlen on the plain,
My heart aw flackered for't I was sae fain.
Cursty See! owr the field the whurlin sunshine whiews,
The shadow fast the sunshine fair pursues;
From Cursty thus oft Peggy seemed to hast,
As fair she fled, he after her as fast.
Peggy Ay, laddy, seemed indeed for, truth to tell,
Oft wittingly I stummered, oft I fell,
Pretendin some unlucky wramp or strean
For Cursty's kind guid-natured heart to mean.

call] callow(?) clavered] clambered steel] stile willy-wands] willows bay] bend dadged] sauntered dree] long seevy cap] cap made of rushes dessed] laid carefully dublers] platters mensed] decorated waws] walls speldered] spelled kest a loup] knit wapped] wrapped fleer] floor fancy] prize ruddily] readily scrawlen] sprawling flackered] fluttered whiews] flies stummered] stumbled wramp] sprain strean] strain mean] moan

Cursty Sweet is this kiss as smell of dwallowed hay,
Or the fresh prumrose on the furst of May;
Sweet to the teaste as pears or apples moam,
Nay, sweeter than the sweetest honeycomb.
Peggy But let us rise—the sun's owr Carrack fell,
And luik—whae's yon 'at's walking to the well?
Up, Cursty, up; for God's sake let me gang,
For fear the maister put us in a sang.

(Wr. by 1743; pub. 1747)

THOMAS MATHISON

d. 1754

245 from *The Goff. An Heroi-Comical Poem*, Canto III

[*Victory on the Last Green*]

To free the ball the chief now turns his mind,
Flies to the bank where lay the orb confined;
The pond'rous club upon the ball descends,
Involved in dust th' exulting orb ascends;
Their loud applause the pleased spectators raise;
The hollow bank resounds Castalio's praise.
A mighty blow Pygmalion then lets fall;
Straight from th' impulsive engine starts the ball,
Answ'ring its master's just design, it hastes,
And from the hole scarce twice two clubs' length rests.
Ah! what avails thy skill, since Fate decrees
Thy conqu'ring foe to bear away the prize?
Full fifteen clubs' length from the hole he lay,
A wide cart-road before him crossed his way;
The deep-cut tracks th' intrepid chief defies,
High o'er the road the ball triumphing flies,
Lights on the green, and scours into the hole:
Down with it sinks depressed Pygmalion's soul.
Seized with surprise th' affrighted hero stands,
And feebly tips the ball with trembling hands;

dwallowed] withered moam] mellow
245 Goff] golf

The creeping ball its want of force complains,
A grassy tuft the loit'ring orb detains:
Surrounding crowds the victor's praise proclaim,
The echoing shore resounds Castalio's name.

(1743)

PAUL WHITEHEAD

1710–1774

246 from *The Gymnasiad, or Boxing Match,* Book III

As when two monarchs of the brindled breed
Dispute the proud dominion of the mead,
They fight, they foam, then wearied in the fray,
Aloof retreat, and low'ring stand at bay:
So stood the heroes, and indignant glared,
While grim with blood their rueful fronts were smeared,
Till with returning strength new rage returns,
Again their arms are steeled, again each bosom burns.
  Incessant now their hollow sides they pound,
Loud on each breast the bounding bangs resound;
Their flying fists around the temples glow,
And the jaws crackle with the massy blow.
The raging combat ev'ry eye appals,
Strokes following strokes, and falls succeeding falls.
Now drooped the youth yet, urging all his might,
With feeble arm still vindicates the fight:
Till on the part where heaved the panting breath,
A fatal blow impressed the seal of death.
Down dropped the hero, welt'ring in his gore,
And his stretched limbs lay quiv'ring on the floor.
So when a falcon skims the airy way,
Stoops from the clouds and pounces on his prey,
Dashed on the earth the feathered victim lies,
Expands its feeble wings and, flutt'ring, dies.
His faithful friends their dying hero reared,
O'er his broad shoulders dangling hung his head;
Dragging its limbs, they bear the body forth,
Mashed teeth and clotted blood came issuing from his mouth.
  Thus then the victor—'O celestial pow'r!
Who gave this arm to boast one triumph more,

Now grey in glory, let my labours cease,
My blood-stained laurel wed the branch of peace;
Lured by the lustre of the golden prize,
No more in combat this proud crest shall rise;
To future heroes future deeds belong,
Be mine the theme of some immortal song.'
  This said—he seized the prize, while round the ring
High soared applause on acclamation's wing.

(1744)

JAMES DANCE (*later* LOVE)

1722–1774

247 from *Cricket. An Heroic Poem*

WHEN the returning sun begins to smile,
And shed its glories round this sea-girt isle;
When newborn nature, decked in vivid green,
Chases dull winter from the charming scene;
High-panting with delight, the jovial swain
Trips it exulting o'er the flow'r-strewed plain.
Thy pleasures, Cricket! all his heart control;
Thy eager transports dwell upon his soul.
He weighs the well-turned bat's experienced force
And guides the rapid ball's impetuous course;
His supple limbs with nimble labour plies,
Nor bends the grass beneath him as he flies.
The joyous conquests of the late-flown year,
In fancy's paint, with all their charms appear,
And now again he views the long-wished season near.
O thou, sublime inspirer of my song,
What matchless trophies to thy worth belong!
Look round the globe, inclined to mirth, and see
What daring sport can claim the prize from thee!
  Not puny Billiards where, with sluggish pace,
The dull ball trails before the feeble mace;
Where no triumphant shouts, no clamours, dare
Pierce through the vaulted roof and wound the air,
But stiff spectators quite inactive stand,

247 mace] cue

Speechless attending to the striker's hand;
Where nothing can your languid spirits move,
Save where the marker bellows out 'Six-love!',
Or when the ball, close-cushioned, slides askew,
And to the op'ning pocket runs, a *cou*!
Nor yet that happier game, where the smooth Bowl
In circling mazes wanders to the goal;
Where, much divided between fear and glee,
The youth cries 'Rub!—O flee, you ling'rer, flee!'
  Not Tennis' self, thy sister sport, can charm,
Or with thy fierce delights our bosoms warm:
Though full of life, at ease alone dismayed,
She calls each swelling sinew to her aid,
Her echoing courts confess the sprightly sound,
While from the racket the brisk balls rebound.
Yet, to small space confined, ev'n she must yield
To nobler Cricket the disputed field.
  O parent Britain, minion of renown!
Whose far-extended fame all nations own,
Of sloth-promoting sports, forewarned, beware!
Nor think thy pleasures are thy meanest care.
Shun with disdain the squeaking masquerade,
Where fainting Vice calls Folly to her aid;
Leave the dissolving song, the baby dance,
To soothe the slaves of Italy and France.
While the firm limb and strong-braced nerve are thine,
Scorn eunuch sports, to manlier games incline,
Feed on the joys that health and vigour give;
Where Freedom reigns, 'tis worth the while to live.
  Nursed on thy plains, first Cricket learned to please,
And taught thy sons to slight inglorious ease:
And see where busy counties strive for fame,
Each greatly potent at this mighty game!
Fierce Kent, ambitious of the first applause,
Against the world combined asserts her cause;
Gay Sussex sometimes triumphs o'er the field,
And fruitful Surrey cannot brook to yield;
While London, queen of cities! proudly vies,
And often grasps the well-disputed prize.

(1744)

cou] *coup*; pocketing the ball without first striking another

ANONYMOUS

248 *On the Death of Mr. Pope*

SEAL up the book, all vision's at an end,
For who durst now to poetry pretend?
Since Pope is dead, it must be sure confessed
The Muse's sacred inspiration's ceased;
And we may only what is writ rehearse:
His works are the apocalypse of verse.

(1744)

ANONYMOUS

249 *Spoken Extempore on the Death of Mr. Pope*

VICE now may lift aloft her speckled head,
And front the sun undaunted: Pope is dead!

(1744)

WILLIAM COLLINS

1721–1759

250 *A Song from Shakespeare's Cymbeline*

TO fair Fidele's grassy tomb
  Soft maids and village hinds shall bring
Each op'ning sweet of earliest bloom,
  And rifle all the breathing spring.

No wailing ghost shall dare appear
  To vex with shrieks this quiet grove;
But shepherd lads assemble here,
  And melting virgins own their love.

No withered witch shall here be seen,
  No goblins lead their nightly crew;
The female fays shall haunt the green,
  And dress thy grave with pearly dew!

The redbreast oft at ev'ning hours
  Shall kindly lend his little aid:
With hoary moss and gathered flowers
  To deck the ground where thou art laid.

When howling winds and beating rain
  In tempests shake the sylvan cell,
Or midst the chase on ev'ry plain,
  The tender thought on thee shall dwell.

Each lonely scene shall thee restore,
  For thee the tear be duly shed:
Beloved, till life could charm no more,
  And mourned, till Pity's self be dead.

(1744)

251

Ode to Fear

STROPHE

THOU, to whom the world unknown
With all its shadowy shapes is shown;
Who see'st appalled th' unreal scene,
While Fancy lifts the veil between:
  Ah Fear! ah frantic Fear!
  I see, I see thee near!
I know thy hurried step, thy haggard eye!
Like thee I start, like thee disordered fly.
For lo, what monsters in thy train appear!
Danger, whose limbs of giant mould
What mortal eye can fixed behold?
Who stalks his round, an hideous form,
Howling amidst the midnight storm,
Or throws him on the ridgy steep
Of some loose hanging rock to sleep;
And with him thousand phantoms joined,
Who prompt to deeds accursed the mind;
And those, the fiends who, near allied,
O'er nature's wounds and wrecks preside;

Whilst Vengeance, in the lurid air,
Lifts her red arm, exposed and bare:
On whom that rav'ning brood of Fate,
Who lap the blood of sorrow, wait:
Who, Fear, this ghastly train can see,
And look not madly wild, like thee?

EPODE

In earliest Greece, to thee, with partial choice,
  The grief-full Muse addressed her infant tongue;
The maids and matrons on her awful voice,
  Silent and pale, in wild amazement hung.

Yet he, the bard who first invoked thy name,
  Disdained in Marathon its pow'r to feel:
For not alone he nursed the poet's flame,
  But reached from Virtue's hand the patriot's steel.

But who is he whom later garlands grace,
  Who left awhile o'er Hybla's dews to rove,
With trembling eyes thy dreary steps to trace,
  Where thou and Furies shared the baleful grove?

Wrapped in thy cloudy veil th' incestuous queen
  Sighed the sad call her son and husband heard,
When once alone it broke the silent scene,
  And he, the wretch of Thebes, no more appeared.

O Fear, I know thee by my throbbing heart,
  Thy with'ring pow'r inspired each mournful line:
Though gentle Pity claim her mingled part,
  Yet all the thunders of the scene are thine!

ANTISTROPHE

Thou who such weary lengths hast passed,
Where wilt thou rest, mad nymph, at last?
Say, wilt thou shroud in haunted cell,
Where gloomy Rape and Murder dwell?
Or in some hollowed seat,
'Gainst which the big waves beat,
Hear drowning seamen's cries in tempests brought?
Dark pow'r, with shudd'ring, meek, submitted thought,
Be mine to read the visions old
Which thy awak'ning bards have told:

And, lest thou meet my blasted view,
Hold each strange tale devoutly true;
Ne'er be I found, by thee o'erawed,
In that thrice-hallowed eve abroad
When ghosts, as cottage-maids believe,
Their pebbled beds permitted leave,
And goblins haunt, from fire or fen,
Or mine or flood, the walks of men!
O thou whose spirit most possessed
The sacred seat of Shakespeare's breast!
By all that from thy prophet broke,
In thy divine emotions spoke,
Hither again thy fury deal,
Teach me but once like him to feel:
His cypress wreath my meed decree,
And I, O Fear, will dwell with thee!

(1746)

252 *Ode on the Poetical Character*

I

As once, if not with light regard
I read aright that gifted bard
(Him whose school above the rest
His loveliest Elfin Queen has blessed),
One, only one, unrivalled fair
Might hope the magic girdle wear,
At solemn tourney hung on high,
The wish of each love-darting eye;
Lo! to each other nymph in turn applied,
As if, in air unseen, some hov'ring hand,
Some chaste and angel-friend to virgin fame,
With whispered spell had burst the starting band,
It left unblest her loathed, dishonoured side;
Happier, hopeless fair, if never
Her baffled hand with vain endeavour
Had touched that fatal zone to her denied!
Young Fancy thus, to me divinest name,
To whom, prepared and bathed in heav'n,
The cest of amplest pow'r is giv'n,
To few the godlike gift assigns,
To gird their blest prophetic loins,
And gaze her visions wild, and feel unmixed her flame!

252 zone, cest] girdle or belt

2

The band, as fairy legends say,
Was wove on that creating day,
When He, who called with thought to birth
Yon tented sky, this laughing earth,
And dressed with springs and forests tall,
And poured the main engirting all,
Long by the loved Enthusiast wooed,
Himself in some diviner mood,
Retiring, sat with her alone,
And placed her on his sapphire throne;
The whiles, the vaulted shrine around,
Seraphic wires were heard to sound,
Now sublimest triumph swelling,
Now on love and mercy dwelling;
And she, from out the veiling cloud,
Breathed her magic notes aloud:
And thou, thou rich-haired youth of morn,
And all thy subject life was born!
The dang'rous Passions kept aloof,
Far from the sainted growing woof;
But near it sat ecstatic Wonder,
List'ning the deep applauding thunder;
And Truth, in sunny vest arrayed,
By whose the tarsel's eyes were made;
All the shad'wy tribes of Mind,
In braided dance their murmurs joined,
And all the bright uncounted pow'rs
Who feed on heaven's ambrosial flow'rs.
Where is the bard whose soul can now
Its high presuming hopes avow?
Where he who thinks, with rapture blind,
This hallowed work for him designed?

3

High on some cliff, to heav'n up-piled,
Of rude access, of prospect wild,
Where, tangled round the jealous steep,
Strange shades o'erbrow the valleys deep,
And holy genii guard the rock,
Its glooms embrown, its springs unlock,
While on its rich ambitious head,
An Eden, like his own, lies spread;

tarsel] male hawk

I view that oak, the fancied glades among,
  By which as Milton lay, his ev'ning ear,
From many a cloud that dropped ethereal dew,
  Nigh sphered in heav'n, its native strains could hear,
On which that ancient trump he reached was hung:
  Thither oft, his glory greeting,
  From Waller's myrtle shades retreating,
With many a vow from hope's aspiring tongue,
My trembling feet his guiding steps pursue:
  In vain—such bliss to one alone
  Of all the sons of soul was known;
  And Heav'n and Fancy, kindred pow'rs,
Have now o'erturned th' inspiring bow'rs,
Or curtained close such scene from ev'ry future view.

(1746)

253 *Ode Written in the Beginning of the Year 1746*

HOW sleep the brave, who sink to rest,
By all their country's wishes blest!
When Spring, with dewy fingers cold,
Returns to deck their hallowed mould,
She there shall dress a sweeter sod
Than Fancy's feet have ever trod.

By fairy hands their knell is rung,
By forms unseen their dirge is sung;
There Honour comes, a pilgrim grey,
To bless the turf that wraps their clay;
And Freedom shall a while repair,
To dwell a weeping hermit there!

(1746)

254 *Ode to Evening*

IF aught of oaten stop, or pastoral song,
May hope, chaste Eve, to soothe thy modest ear,
  Like thy own solemn springs,
  Thy springs and dying gales,
O nymph reserved, while now the bright-haired sun
Sits in yon western tent, whose cloudy skirts,
  With brede ethereal wove,
  O'erhang his wavy bed;

Now air is hushed, save where the weak-eyed bat
With short shrill shriek flits by on leathern wing,
  Or where the beetle winds
  His small but sullen horn,
As oft he rises midst the twilight path,
Against the pilgrim borne in heedless hum:
  Now teach me, maid composed,
  To breathe some softened strain,
Whose numbers, stealing through thy dark'ning vale,
May not unseemly with its stillness suit,
  As, musing slow, I hail
  Thy genial loved return!
For when thy folding-star arising shows
His paly circlet, at his warning lamp
  The fragrant hours, and elves
  Who slept in flowers the day,
And many a nymph who wreathes her brows with sedge,
And sheds the fresh'ning dew, and, lovelier still,
  The pensive Pleasures sweet,
  Prepare thy shadowy car.
Then lead, calm vot'ress, where some sheety lake
Cheers the lone heath, or some time-hallowed pile,
  Or upland fallows grey,
  Reflect its last cool gleam.
But when chill blust'ring winds, or driving rain,
Forbid my willing feet, be mine the hut,
  That from the mountain's side
  Views wilds, and swelling floods,
And hamlets brown, and dim-discovered spires,
And hears their simple bell, and marks o'er all
  Thy dewy fingers draw
  The gradual dusky veil.
While Spring shall pour his show'rs, as oft he wont,
And bathe thy breathing tresses, meekest Eve!
  While Summer loves to sport
  Beneath thy ling'ring light;
While sallow Autumn fills thy lap with leaves,
Or Winter, yelling through the troublous air,
  Affrights thy shrinking train,
  And rudely rends thy robes;
So long, sure-found beneath the sylvan shed,
Shall Fancy, Friendship, Science, rose-lipped Health
  Thy gentlest influence own,
  And love thy fav'rite name!

(1746)

255 *Ode Occasioned by the Death of Mr. Thomson*

In yonder grave a Druid lies,
  Where slowly winds the stealing wave!
The year's best sweets shall duteous rise
  To deck its poet's sylvan grave!

In yon deep bed of whisp'ring reeds
  His airy harp shall now be laid,
That he, whose heart in sorrow bleeds,
  May love through life the soothing shade.

Then maids and youths shall linger here,
  And, while its sounds at distance swell,
Shall sadly seem in Pity's ear
  To hear the woodland pilgrim's knell.

Remembrance oft shall haunt the shore
  When Thames in summer-wreaths is dressed,
And oft suspend the dashing oar
  To bid his gentle spirit rest!

And oft as Ease and Health retire
  To breezy lawn or forest deep,
The friend shall view yon whit'ning spire,
  And mid the varied landscape weep.

But thou, who own'st that earthy bed,
  Ah! what will ev'ry dirge avail?
Or tears, which Love and Pity shed
  That mourn beneath the gliding sail!

Yet lives there one, whose heedless eye
  Shall scorn thy pale shrine glimm'ring near?
With him, sweet bard, may Fancy die,
  And Joy desert the blooming year.

But thou, lorn stream, whose sullen tide
  No sedge-crowned Sisters now attend,
Now waft me from the green hill's side,
  Whose cold turf hides the buried friend!

And see, the fairy valleys fade,
  Dun Night has veiled the solemn view!
—Yet once again, dear parted shade,
  Meek Nature's child, again adieu!

The genial meads, assigned to bless
  Thy life, shall mourn thy early doom,
Their hinds and shepherd-girls shall dress
  With simple hands thy rural tomb.

Long, long, thy stone and pointed clay
  Shall melt the musing Briton's eyes:
'O! vales and wild woods,' shall he say,
  'In yonder grave your Druid lies!'

(1749)

256 *An Ode on the Popular Superstitions of the Highlands of Scotland, Considered as the Subject of Poetry*

HOME, thou return'st from Thames, whose Naiads long
  Have seen thee ling'ring, with a fond delay,
  Mid those soft friends, whose hearts, some future day,
Shall melt, perhaps, to hear thy tragic song.
Go, not unmindful of that cordial youth,
  Whom, long endeared, thou leav'st by Lavant's side;
Together let us wish him lasting truth,
  And joy untainted with his destined bride.
Go! nor regardless, while these numbers boast
  My short-lived bliss, forget my social name;
But think far off how, on the southern coast,
  I met thy friendship with an equal flame!
Fresh to that soil thou turn'st, whose ev'ry vale
  Shall prompt the poet, and his song demand:
To thee thy copious subjects ne'er shall fail;
  Thou need'st but take the pencil to thy hand,
And paint what all believe who own thy genial land.

There must thou wake perforce thy Doric quill,
  'Tis Fancy's land to which thou sett'st thy feet;
  Where still, 'tis said, the fairy people meet
Beneath each birken shade, on mead or hill.
There each trim lass that skims the milky store
  To the swart tribes their creamy bowl allots;
By night they sip it round the cottage-door,
  While airy minstrels warble jocund notes.
There ev'ry herd, by sad experience, knows
  How, winged with fate, their elf-shot arrows fly,
When the sick ewe her summer food forgoes,

Or, stretched on earth, the heart-smit heifers lie.
Such airy beings awe th' untutored swain:
Nor thou, though learned, his homelier thoughts neglect;
Let thy sweet muse the rural faith sustain:
These are the themes of simple, sure effect,
That add new conquests to her boundless reign,
And fill with double force her heart-commanding strain.

Ev'n yet preserved, how often may'st thou hear,
Where to the pole the Boreal mountains run,
Taught by the father to his list'ning son
Strange lays, whose pow'r had charmed a Spenser's ear.
At ev'ry pause, before thy mind possessed,
Old Runic bards shall seem to rise around,
With uncouth lyres, in many-coloured vest,
Their matted hair with boughs fantastic crowned:
Whether thou bidd'st the well-taught hind repeat
The choral dirge that mourns some chieftain brave,
When ev'ry shrieking maid her bosom beat,
And strewed with choicest herbs his scented grave;
Or whether, sitting in the shepherd's shiel,
Thou hear'st some sounding tale of war's alarms;
When, at the bugle's call, with fire and steel,
The sturdy clans poured forth their bonny swarms,
And hostile brothers met to prove each other's arms.

'Tis thine to sing how, framing hideous spells,
In Skye's lone isle the gifted wizard seer,
Lodged in the wintry cave with [ ]
Or in the depth of Uist's dark forests dwells;
How they, whose sight such dreary dreams engross,
With their own visions oft astonished droop,
When o'er the watry strath or quaggy moss
They see the gliding ghosts unbodied troop.
Or if in sports, or on the festive green,
Their [ ] glance some fated youth descry,
Who, now perhaps in lusty vigour seen
And rosy health, shall soon lamented die.
For them the viewless forms of air obey,
Their bidding heed, and at their beck repair.
They know what spirit brews the stormful day,
And heartless, oft like moody madness stare
To see the phantom train their secret work prepare.

[*Stanza 5 and the first eight lines of stanza 6 missing.*]

shiel] hut

What though far off, from some dark dell espied,
  His glimm'ring mazes cheer th' excursive sight,
Yet turn, ye wand'rers, turn your steps aside,
  Nor trust the guidance of that faithless light!
For watchful, lurking mid th' unrustling reed,
  At those mirk hours the wily monster lies,
And listens oft to hear the passing steed,
  And frequent round him rolls his sullen eyes,
If chance his savage wrath may some weak wretch surprise.

Ah, luckless swain, o'er all unblest indeed!
  Whom late bewildered in the dank, dark fen,
  Far from his flocks and smoking hamlet then!
To that sad spot his [ ]:
On him enraged, the fiend, in angry mood,
  Shall never look with pity's kind concern,
But instant, furious, raise the whelming flood
  O'er its drowned banks, forbidding all return.
Or, if he meditate his wished escape
  To some dim hill that seems uprising near,
To his faint eye the grim and grisly shape,
  In all its terrors clad, shall wild appear.
Meantime, the watry surge shall round him rise,
  Poured sudden forth from ev'ry swelling source.
What now remains but tears and hopeless sighs?
  His fear-shook limbs have lost their youthly force,
And down the waves he floats, a pale and breathless corse.

For him in vain his anxious wife shall wait,
  Or wander forth to meet him on his way;
  For him in vain, at to-fall of the day,
His bairns shall linger at th' unclosing gate.
Ah, ne'er shall he return! Alone, if night
  Her travelled limbs in broken slumbers steep,
With dropping willows dressed, his mournful sprite
  Shall visit sad, perhaps, her silent sleep:
Then he, perhaps, with moist and watry hand,
  Shall fondly seem to press her shudd'ring cheek,
And with his blue swoll'n face before her stand,
  And, shiv'ring cold, these piteous accents speak:
'Pursue, dear wife, thy daily toils pursue
  At dawn or dusk, industrious as before;
Nor e'er of me one hapless thought renew,
  While I lie welt'ring on the osiered shore,
Drowned by the kaelpie's wrath, nor e'er shall aid thee more!'

mirk] dark   to-fall] close   kaelpie] water-spirit

Unbounded is thy range; with varied style
  Thy Muse may, like those feath'ry tribes which spring
  From their rude rocks, extend her skirting wing
Round the moist marge of each cold Hebrid isle,
To that hoar pile which still its ruin shows:
  In whose small vaults a pigmy-folk is found,
Whose bones the delver with his spade upthrows,
  And culls them, wond'ring, from the hallowed ground!
Or thither, where beneath the show'ry west
  The mighty kings of three fair realms are laid;
Once foes, perhaps, together now they rest.
  No slaves revere them, and no wars invade:
Yet frequent now, at midnight's solemn hour,
  The rifted mounds their yawning cells unfold,
And forth the monarchs stalk with sov'reign pow'r
  In pageant robes, and wreathed with sheeny gold,
And on their twilight tombs aerial council hold.

But O! o'er all, forget not Kilda's race,
  On whose bleak rocks, which brave the wasting tides,
  Fair Nature's daughter, Virtue, yet abides!
Go, just as they, their blameless manners trace!
Then to my ear transmit some gentle song
  Of those whose lives are yet sincere and plain,
Their bounded walks the ragged cliffs along,
  And all their prospect but the wintry main.
With sparing temp'rance, at the needful time,
  They drain the sainted spring, or, hunger-pressed,
Along th' Atlantic rock undreading climb,
  And of its eggs despoil the solan's nest.
Thus blest in primal innocence they live,
  Sufficed and happy with that frugal fare
Which tasteful toil and hourly danger give.
  Hard is their shallow soil, [   ] and bare;
Nor ever vernal bee was heard to murmur there!

Nor need'st thou blush, that such false themes engage
  Thy gentle mind, of fairer stores possessed;
  For not alone they touch the village breast,
But filled in elder time th' historic page.
There Shakespeare's self, with ev'ry garland crowned,
In musing hour, his Wayward Sisters found,
  And with their terrors dressed the magic scene.
From them he sung, when mid his bold design,
  Before the Scot afflicted and aghast,

solan] gannet

The shadowy kings of Banquo's fated line
  Through the dark cave in gleamy pageant passed.
Proceed, nor quit the tales which, simply told,
  Could once so well my answ'ring bosom pierce;
Proceed, in forceful sounds and colours bold
  The native legends of thy land rehearse;
To such adapt thy lyre and suit thy pow'rful verse.

In scenes like these, which, daring to depart
  From sober truth, are still to nature true,
  And call forth fresh delights to Fancy's view,
Th' heroic Muse employed her Tasso's art!
How have I trembled when, at Tancred's stroke,
  Its gushing blood the gaping cypress poured;
When each live plant with mortal accents spoke,
  And the wild blast up-heaved the vanished sword!
How have I sat, where piped the pensive wind,
  To hear his harp, by British Fairfax strung,
Prevailing poet, whose undoubting mind
  Believed the magic wonders which he sung!
Hence at each sound imagination glows;
Hence his warm lay with softest sweetness flows;
  Melting it flows, pure, num'rous, strong and clear,
And fills th' impassioned heart, and lulls th' harmonious ear.

All hail, ye scenes that o'er my soul prevail,
  Ye [ ] friths and lakes which, far away,
  Are by smooth Annan filled, or past'ral Tay,
Or Don's romantic springs, at distance, hail!
The time shall come when I, perhaps, may tread
  Your lowly glens, o'erhung with spreading broom,
Or o'er your stretching heaths by Fancy led:
Then will I dress once more the faded bow'r,
  Where Jonson sat in Drummond's [ ] shade;
Or crop from Tiviot's dale each [ ]
  And mourn on Yarrow's banks [.]
Meantime, ye pow'rs, that on the plains which bore
  The cordial youth, on Lothian's plains attend,
Where'er he dwell, on hill or lowly muir,
  To him I lose, your kind protection lend,
And, touched with love like mine, preserve my absent friend.

(Wr. 1750; pub. 1788)

JOSEPH WARTON

1722–1800

257 from *The Enthusiast: or The Lover of Nature*

Ye green-robed Dryads, oft at dusky eve
By wondering shepherds seen, to forests brown,
To unfrequented meads, and pathless wilds,
Lead me from gardens decked with art's vain pomps.
Can gilt alcoves, can marble-mimic gods,
Parterres embroidered, obelisks, and urns,
Of high relief; can the long, spreading lake,
Or vista lessening to the sight; can Stow
With all her Attic fanes, such raptures raise,
As the thrush-haunted copse, where lightly leaps
The fearful fawn the rustling leaves along,
And the brisk squirrel sports from bough to bough,
While from an hollow oak, whose naked roots
O'erhang a pensive rill, the busy bees
Hum drowsy lullabies? The bards of old,
Fair Nature's friends, sought such retreats, to charm
Sweet Echo with their songs; oft too they met
In summer evenings, near sequestered bow'rs,
Or mountain-nymph, or Muse, and eager learned
The moral strains she taught to mend mankind.
As to a secret grot Aegeria stole
With patriot Numa, and in silent night
Whispered him sacred laws, he list'ning sat,
Rapt with her virtuous voice, old Tiber leaned
Attentive on his urn, and hushed his waves.
  Rich in her weeping country's spoils, Versailles
May boast a thousand fountains, that can cast
The tortured waters to the distant heav'ns;
Yet let me choose some pine-topped precipice
Abrupt and shaggy, whence a foamy stream,
Like Anio, tumbling roars; or some bleak heath,
Where straggling stand the mournful juniper,
Or yew-tree scathed; while in clear prospect round,
From the grove's bosom spires emerge, and smoke
In bluish wreaths ascends, ripe harvests wave,
Low, lonely cottages, and ruined tops
Of Gothic battlements appear, and streams
Beneath the sunbeams twinkle.—The shrill lark,
That wakes the woodman to his early task,
Or lovesick Philomel, whose luscious lays

Soothe lone night-wanderers, the moaning dove
Pitied by listening milkmaid, far excel
The deep-mouthed viol, the soul-lulling lute,
And battle-breathing trumpet. Artful sounds!
That please not like the choristers of air,
When first they hail th' approach of laughing May.

. . . .

All-beauteous Nature! by thy boundless charms
Oppressed, O where shall I begin thy praise,
Where turn th' ecstatic eye, how ease my breast
That pants with wild astonishment and love!
Dark forests, and the op'ning lawn, refreshed
With ever-gushing brooks, hill, meadow, dale,
The balmy bean-field, the gay-coloured close,
So sweetly interchanged, the lowing ox,
The playful lamb, the distant water-fall
Now faintly heard, now swelling with the breeze,
The sound of pastoral reed from hazel-bower,
The choral birds, the neighing steed, that snuffs
His dappled mate, stung with intense desire,
The ripened orchard when the ruddy orbs
Betwixt the green leaves blush, the azure skies,
The cheerful sun that through earth's vitals pours
Delight and health and heat; all, all conspire
To raise, to soothe, to harmonise the mind,
To lift on wings of praise, to the great Sire
Of being and of beauty, at whose nod
Creation started from the gloomy vault
Of dreary Chaos, while the grisly king
Murmured to feel his boisterous power confined.
  What are the lays of artful Addison,
Coldly correct, to Shakespeare's warblings wild?
Whom on the winding Avon's willowed banks
Fair Fancy found, and bore the smiling babe
To a close cavern (still the shepherds show
The sacred place, whence with religious awe
They hear, returning from the field at eve,
Strange whisp'rings of sweet music through the air):
Here, as with honey gathered from the rock,
She fed the little prattler, and with songs
Oft soothed his wond'ring ears; with deep delight
On her soft lap he sat, and caught the sounds.

(1744–8)

258 from *Ode to Fancy*

O WARM, enthusiastic maid,
Without thy powerful vital aid,
That breathes an energy divine,
That gives a soul to every line,
Ne'er may I strive with lips profane
To utter an unhallowed strain,
Nor dare to touch the sacred string,
Save when with smiles thou bidd'st me sing.
O hear our prayer, O hither come
From thy lamented Shakespeare's tomb,
On which thou lov'st to sit at eve,
Musing o'er thy darling's grave;
O queen of numbers, once again
Animate some chosen swain,
Who, filled with unexhausted fire,
May boldly smite the sounding lyre,
Who with some new, unequalled song,
May rise above the rhyming throng,
O'er all our list'ning passions reign,
O'erwhelm our souls with joy and pain,
With terror shake and pity move,
Rouse with revenge, or melt with love.
O deign t' attend his evening walk,
With him in groves and grottoes talk;
Teach him to scorn with frigid art
Feebly to touch th' unraptured heart;
Like lightning, let his mighty verse
The bosom's inmost foldings pierce;
With native beauties win applause,
Beyond cold critic's studied laws;
O let each Muse's fame increase,
O bid Britannia rival Greece!

(1746)

259 *The Dying Indian*

THE dart of Izdabel prevails! 'twas dipped
In double poison—I shall soon arrive
At the blest island, where no tigers spring
On heedless hunters; where ananas bloom
Thrice in each moon; where rivers smoothly glide,
Nor thundering torrents whirl the light canoe

Down to the sea: where my forefathers feast
Daily on hearts of Spaniards!—O my son,
I feel the venom busy in my breast.
Approach, and bring my crown, decked with the teeth
Of that bold Christian who first dared deflower
The virgins of the sun; and, dire to tell!
Robbed Vitzipultzi's statue of its gems!
I marked the spot where they interred this traitor,
And once at midnight stole I to his tomb,
And tore his carcass from the earth, and left it
A prey to poisonous flies. Preserve this crown
With sacred secrecy: if e'er returns
Thy much-loved mother from the desert woods
Where, as I hunted late, I hapless lost her,
Cherish her age. Tell her I ne'er have worshipped
With those that eat their God. And when disease
Preys on her languid limbs, then kindly stab her
With thine own hands, nor suffer her to linger,
Like Christian cowards, in a life of pain.
I go! great Copac beckons me! farewell!

(1755)

MARK AKENSIDE

1720–1771

260 from *The Pleasures of Imagination*

(i)

[*The Creative Process*]

SUCH is the secret union, when we feel
A song, a flow'r, a name at once restore
Those long-connected scenes where first they moved
Th' attention; backward through her mazy walks
Guiding the wanton fancy to her scope,
To temples, courts or fields; with all the band
Of painted forms, of passions and designs
Attendant: whence, if pleasing in itself,
The prospect from that sweet accession gains
Redoubled influence o'er the list'ning mind.
 By these mysterious ties the busy pow'r
Of Mem'ry her ideal train preserves

Entire;[1] or when they would elude her watch,
Reclaims their fleeting footsteps from the waste
Of dark oblivion; thus collecting all
The various forms of being to present,
Before the curious aim of mimic art,
Their largest choice: like spring's unfolded blooms
Exhaling sweetness, that the skilful bee
May taste at will, from their selected spoils
To work her dulcet food. For not th' expanse
Of living lakes, in summer's noontide calm,
Reflects the bord'ring shade and sun-bright heav'ns
With fairer semblance; not the sculptured gold
More faithful keeps the graver's lively trace,
Than he whose birth the sister-pow'rs of art
Propitious viewed, and from his genial star
Shed influence to the seeds of fancy kind;
Than his attempered bosom must preserve
The seal of nature. There alone unchanged,
Her form remains. The balmy walks of May
There breathe perennial sweets: the trembling chord
Resounds for ever in th' abstracted ear,
Melodious; and the virgin's radiant eye,
Superior to disease, to grief, and time,
Shines with unbating lustre. Thus at length
Endowed with all that nature can bestow,
The child of fancy oft in silence bends
O'er these mixed treasures of his pregnant breast,
With conscious pride. From them he oft resolves
To frame he knows not what excelling things;
And win he knows not what sublime reward
Of praise and wonder. By degrees the mind
Feels her young nerves dilate: the plastic pow'rs
Labour for action: blind emotions heave
His bosom; and with loveliest frenzy caught,
From earth to heav'n he rolls his daring eye,
From heav'n to earth. Anon ten thousand shapes,
Like spectres trooping to the wizard's call,
Fleet swift before him. From the womb of earth,
From ocean's bed they come: th' eternal heav'ns
Disclose their splendours, and the dark abyss
Pours out her births unknown. With fixed gaze
He marks the rising phantoms. Now compares
Their diff'rent forms; now blends them, now divides;

[1] *By these mysterious ties*, &c.] The act of remembering seems almost wholly to depend on the association of ideas.

Enlarges and extenuates by turns;
Opposes, ranges in fantastic bands,
And infinitely varies. Hither now,
Now thither fluctuates his inconstant aim,
With endless choice perplexed. At length his plan
Begins to open. Lucid order dawns;
And as from Chaos old the jarring seeds
Of nature at the voice divine repaired
Each to its place, till rosy earth unveiled
Her fragrant bosom, and the joyful sun
Sprung up the blue serene; by swift degrees
Thus disentangled, his entire design
Emerges. Colours mingle, features join,
And lines converge: the fainter parts retire;
The fairer eminent in light advance;
And every image on its neighbour smiles.
Awhile he stands, and with a father's joy
Contemplates. Then with Promethean art,
Into its proper vehicle he breathes
The fair conception; which embodied thus,
And permanent, becomes to eyes or ears
An object ascertained: while thus informed,
The various organs of his mimic skill,
The consonance of sounds, the featured rock,
The shadowy picture and impassioned verse,
Beyond their proper pow'rs attract the soul
By that expressive semblance, while in sight
Of nature's great original we scan
The lively child of art; while line by line,
And feature after feature we refer
To that sublime exemplar whence it stole
Those animating charms. Thus beauty's palm
Betwixt 'em wav'ring hangs: applauding love
Doubts where to choose; and mortal man aspires
To tempt creative praise.

(ii)

[*Love of Nature*]

Oh! blest of heav'n, whom not the languid songs
Of Luxury, the siren! not the bribes
Of sordid wealth, nor all the gaudy spoils
Of pageant honour can seduce to leave
Those ever-blooming sweets, which from the store
Of nature fair imagination culls

To charm th' enliven'd soul! What though not all
Of mortal offspring can attain the heights
Of envied life; though only few possess
Patrician treasures or imperial state;
Yet nature's care, to all her children just,
With richer treasures and an ampler state
Endows at large whatever happy man
Will deign to use them. His the city's pomp,
The rural honours his. Whate'er adorns
The princely dome, the column and the arch,
The breathing marbles and the sculptured gold,
Beyond the proud possessor's narrow claim,
His tuneful breast enjoys. For him, the spring
Distils her dews, and from the silken gem
Its lucid leaves unfolds: for him, the hand
Of autumn tinges every fertile branch
With blooming gold and blushes like the morn.
Each passing hour sheds tribute from her wings;
And still new beauties meet his lonely walk;
And loves unfelt attract him. Not a breeze
Flies o'er the meadow, not a cloud imbibes
The setting sun's effulgence, not a strain
From all the tenants of the warbling shade
Ascends, but whence his bosom can partake
Fresh pleasure, unreproved. Nor thence partakes
Fresh pleasure only: for th' attentive mind,
By this harmonious action on her pow'rs,
Becomes herself harmonious: wont so long
In outward things to meditate the charm
Of sacred order, soon she seeks at home
To find a kindred order, to exert
Within herself this elegance of love,
This fair-inspired delight: her tempered pow'rs
Refine at length, and every passion wears
A chaster, milder, more attractive mien.
But if to ampler prospects, if to gaze
On nature's form where, negligent of all
These lesser graces, she assumes the port
Of that eternal majesty that weighed
The world's foundations, if to these the mind
Exalt her daring eye; then mightier far
Will be the change, and nobler. Would the forms
Of servile custom cramp her generous pow'rs?
Would sordid policies, the barb'rous growth
Of ignorance and rapine, bow her down
To tame pursuits, to indolence and fear?

Lo! she appeals to nature, to the winds
And rolling waves, the sun's unwearied course,
The elements and seasons; all declare
For what th' eternal maker has ordained
The pow'rs of man: we feel within ourselves
His energy divine: he tells the heart,
He meant, he made us to behold and love
What he beholds and loves, the general orb
Of life and being; to be great like him,
Beneficent and active. Thus the men
Whom nature's works can charm, with God himself
Hold converse; grow familiar, day by day,
With his conceptions; act upon his plan;
And form to his, the relish of their souls.

(1744)

(iii)

[*Poetic Genius*]

A different task remains; the secret paths
Of early genius to explore: to trace
Those haunts where Fancy her predestined sons,
Like to the demigods of old, doth nurse
Remote from eyes profane. Ye happy souls,
Who now her tender discipline obey,
Where dwell ye? What wild river's brink at eve
Imprint your steps? What solemn groves at noon
Use ye to visit, often breaking forth
In rapture mid your dilatory walk,
Or musing, as in slumber, on the green?
—Would I again were with you!—O ye dales
Of Tyne, and ye most ancient woodlands; where
Oft as the giant flood obliquely strides,
And his banks open, and his lawns extend,
Stops short the pleasèd traveller to view
Presiding o'er the scene some rustic tower
Founded by Norman or by Saxon hands:
O ye Northumbrian shades, which overlook
The rocky pavement and the mossy falls
Of solitary Wensbeck's limpid stream;
How gladly I recall your well-known seats
Beloved of old, and that delightful time
When all alone, for many a summer's day,
I wandered through your calm recesses, led
In silence by some powerful hand unseen.

Nor will I e'er forget you. Nor shall e'er
The graver tasks of manhood, or the advice
Of vulgar wisdom, move me to disclaim
Those studies which possessed me in the dawn
Of life, and fixed the colour of my mind
For every future year: whence even now
From sleep I rescue the clear hours of morn,
And, while the world around lies overwhelmed
In idle darkness, am alive to thoughts
Of honourable fame, of truth divine
Or moral, and of minds to virtue won
By the sweet magic of harmonious verse . . .

(1772)

261 *Inscription for a Grotto*

TO me, whom in their lays the shepherds call
Actaea, daughter of the neighbouring stream,
This cave belongs. The fig-tree and the vine,
Which o'er the rocky entrance downward shoot,
Were placed by Glycon. He with cowslips pale,
Primrose, and purple Lychnis, decked the green
Before my threshold, and my shelving walls
With honeysuckle covered. Here at noon,
Lulled by the murmur of my rising fount,
I slumber: here my clustering fruits I tend;
Or from the humid flowers, at break of day,
Fresh garlands weave, and chase from all my bounds
Each thing impure or noxious. Enter in,
O stranger, undismayed. Nor bat nor toad
Here lurks: and if thy breast of blameless thoughts
Approve thee, not unwelcome shalt thou tread
My quiet mansion: chiefly, if thy name
Wise Pallas and the immortal Muses own.

(1758)

262 *Inscription*

WHOE'ER thou art whose path in summer lies
Through yonder village, turn thee where the grove
Of branching oaks a rural palace old
Embosoms. There dwells Albert, generous lord

Of all the harvest round. And onward thence
A low plain chapel fronts the morning light
Fast by a silent riv'let. Humbly walk,
O stranger, o'er the consecrated ground;
And on that verdant hillock, which thou see'st
Beset with osiers, let thy pious hand
Sprinkle fresh water from the brook and strew
Sweet-smelling flow'rs. For there doth Edmund rest,
The learned shepherd; for each rural art
Famed, and for songs harmonious, and the woes
Of ill-requited love. The faithless pride
Of fair Matilda sank him to the grave
In manhood's prime. But soon did righteous heaven
With tears, with sharp remorse, and pining care,
Avenge her falsehood. Nor could all the gold
And nuptial pomp, which lured her plighted faith
From Edmund to a loftier husband's home,
Relieve her breaking heart, or turn aside
The strokes of death. Go, traveller; relate
The mournful story. Haply some fair maid
May hold it in remembrance, and be taught
That riches cannot pay for truth or love.

(1758)

SNEYD DAVIES

1709–1769

263 from *A Voyage to Tintern Abbey*

THE crooked bank still winds to something new,
Oars, scarcely turned, diversify the view;
Of trees and stone an intermingled scene,
The shady precipice and rocky green.
Nature behold, to please and to surprise,
Swell into bastions, or in columns rise:
Here sinking spaces with dark boughs o'ergrown,
And there the naked quarries look a town.
At length our pilgrimage's home appears,
Tintern her venerable fabric rears,
While the sun, mildly glancing in decline,
With his last gilding beautifies the shrine:
Enter with reverence her hallowed gate,
And trace the glorious relics of her state;

The meeting arches, pillared walks admire,
Or, musing, hearken to the silenced choir.
Encircling groves diffuse a solemn grace,
And dimly fill th' historic window's place;
While pitying shrubs on the bare summit try
To give the roofless pile a canopy.
Here, O my friends, along the mossy dome
In pleasurable sadness let me roam:
Look back upon the world in haven safe,
Weep o'er its ruins, at its follies laugh.

(Wr. 1742; pub. 1745)

264 *A Scene [after Hunting] at Swallowfield in Berkshire*

Dr. Thirlby There's pleasure, sure, in being clad in green,
Which none but huntsmen know. How did my limbs
Exult, to find themselves disrobed of black!
What is the scold of bedmakers to that
Harmonious pack! or what the solemn note
Of beadle Simpson to our huntsman shrill!
I felt unusual courage when the fox,
Wiliest of creatures, stared me in the face
(Through enterprise or fear, I cannot tell);
But sure the beast was hideous. Yet I stood
Undaunted, at the time that Whaley's self
Fled in dismay, and sought the neighbouring copse.
Had not my noblest champion, generous Dodd,
Spurred to my aid, that moment were my last.

Whaley You wrong me, Doctor, by the manes great
Of my all-trading sire: I ne'er was deemed
A coward; no, not when the gander dire,
Furious with poked-out neck and flapping wings,
Assailed me sore perplexed; but soon the gaggling
Monster a victim fell to stone or stick.
Then call it caution; for believe me, sirs,
I took the grinning monster for a wolf.

Mr. Dodd gives Whaley a slap on the face, and says,

Thou art the vilest coward that e'er lived;
I saw thee as thou fled'st, and if my sense
Divined aright, methought I smelt thee too.
In vain the standing corn opposed my speed,

In vain the farmer swore; nor hedge nor oaths
Deterred me; hedge I broke, and oaths returned
With recompense, and came in need extreme
To save my friend, waging unequal war.
But thy o'er-wearied spirits ask recruit.
A cordial for the Doctor!—As for him,
I'll make example dire, and to be rued
By cowards yet unborn; that all may learn
Boldness and enterprise, and fear to fear.
Here, take him hence!

Whaley Ah me! how happy once!
Exit

Dodd O for invention to chastise the crime!
Through all my house, through kitchen, pantry, hall,
To grooms, and cook, and butler, be it known
That 'tis my pleasure Whaley fast this day;
And whoso'er clandestine shall appease
His longing maw, himself shall fast I swear.

Dr. Thirlby Consider, sir, lest indignation, just
In principle, transport you to pronounce
A sentence too severe, and o'er-proportioned
To the transgression (foul, I must confess);
But must not mercy whisper to the thought
A mulct less rigid?

Dodd Doctor, this age,
This dastard and fox-fearing age, demands
Severity and rigour.
Farrel, be thou the bearer of my will!

Whaley in his apartments. To him Farrel.

Farrel Excuse me, sir, if duty bids me speak
What kindness would conceal. Thus said my master:
'Through all my house, through kitchen, pantry, hall,
To grooms, and cook, and butler, be it known
That 'tis my pleasure Whaley fast this day;
And whoso'er clandestine shall appease
His longing maw, himself shall fast I swear.'

Whaley O Mr. Farrel,
Supreme of valets, gently hast thou told
Thy message, which would else in telling wound,
And in performing end me. Some few hours
Pass, and you'll see my hunger-quaking cheeks,
And my loose skin, descending and unnerved,
Apron my nether parts. But I submit,
And will prepare, if possible, to fast. *Exit Farrel.*

Whaley solus Nimrod, I hate thee, premier hunter vile,
Beast of a man! and of all other beasts,
The fox is my aversion. Brute accursed,
Lamb-eating, narrow-snouted, stinking villain!
Author of all my sorrows! but for him
I yet had flourished, unimpeached of fear.
Yet why the fox accused? how could he help
My trembling nature's fault, not his? or how
Contrive not to be taken for a wolf?
'Tis I, I only am to blame. O cowardice!
What ills dost thou create? But chief of thee,
Of thee I most complain, O want of food!
I've often heard, indeed, of that word *fast*,
But never yet the meaning could devise.
Ah! by severe experience now I feel
To fast is to abstain from meat and drink.
Happy the meagre, cloistered man resigned!
He at set periods, by spare diet taught,
Can his commanded appetites renounce,
And pine with voluntary want. But I,
Pampered, and sleek, and jovial, ill can brook
Th' abstemious trial. Flesh and blood can't bear it.
I will not fast. How not? ah! there's the question,
While surly grooms each avenue secure.
For twice twelve livelong hours must I then rue
Hunger and thirst, and my delighted spirits,
So oft in nectar bathed, exhausted flag!
Must I then lose thee, burgundy; nor taste
Delicious morsels, carp, or hare, or quail?
Unfortunate! Ev'n now perhaps the guests
At the thronged board make merry with my woes.
One asks with sneering purport, 'Where is Whaley?'
'Dining with good Duke Humphrey,' cries another.
Pratt smiles malignantly, and Davies grins
At my undoing; nay, perchance he rhymes
(Vile bard!), and on my ruin builds his song.
No more—I'll to the window. Beauteous scene
Of water and of hills, of lawns and trees,
What respite can ye give to lean distress?
And you, plump deer, that scud along the lawn,
Serve but to raise my venison appetite!
Am I deceived, or through the waving boughs
An alehouse sign peeps forth?—I'm not deceived,
For through the boughs an alehouse sign peeps forth;

Dining . . . Humphrey] going dinnerless

Would I were there!—but ah! what gulf's between!
When will tomorrow come?——

Bell rings to dinner. Whaley faints away.

(Wr. by 1745; pub. 1778)

ANONYMOUS

265 *Delia Very Angry*

POH! did ever one see such a troublesome bear?
No, I will not get up from my seat now, I swear.
Lord! what can you mean by this pulling and teasing?
Sure, there's nothing so bad as a man without reason!
Come, prithee be quiet! For God's sake! See there!
Why, you spoil all my work and all tousle my hair.
You know it as well as myself do, or Nanny,
That this gown must be fitted by four.—Christ! how can ye?
It has put me already quite into a flurry.
Shuh! how can you do so, when one's in a hurry?
It came but this morning, you saw it brought in:
Not an hour ago I had scarce stuck a pin.
'Tis for passionate Mary, the minister's maid.
When she gave me the stuff, did you hear what she said?
What wishes she wished, and what oaths too she took,
That she'd roast me to death (and you know she's a cook)
If I was not precisely as good as my word:
For she goes to a burying.—Devil take ye!—O Lord!
Now, aren't you ashamed? Well, observe what I say:
If I speak t' ye again for six months (mark the day!),
May you call me a fool, sir, as long as I live!
Do you think one has nothing to do but *forgive*?

(1745)

ISAAC HAWKINS BROWNE

1705–1760

266 *The Fire Side. A Pastoral Soliloquy*

THRICE happy, who free from ambition and pride,
In a rural retreat, has a quiet *fire side*;
I love my *fire side*, there I long to repair,
And to drink a delightful oblivion of care.
Oh! when shall I 'scape to be truly my own,
From the noise, and the smoke, and the bustle of town?
Then I live, then I triumph, whene'er I retire
From the pomp and parade that the many admire.
Hail, ye woods and ye lawns, shady vales, sunny hills,
And the warble of birds, and the murmur of rills,
Ye flow'rs of all hues that embroider the ground,
Flocks feeding or frisking in gambols around;
Scene of joy to behold! joy, that who would forgo,
For the wealth and the pow'r that a court can bestow?
I have said it at home, I have said it abroad,
That the town is man's world, but that this is of God;
Here my trees cannot flatter, plants nursed by my care
Pay with fruit or with fragrance, and incense the air;
Here contemplative solitude raises the mind
(Least alone, when alone) to ideas refined.
Methinks hid in groves, that no sound can invade,
Save when Philomel strikes up her sweet serenade,
I revolve on the changes and chances of things,
And pity the wretch that depends upon kings.
  Now I pass with old authors an indolent hour,
And reclining at ease turn Demosthenes o'er.
Now facetious and vacant, I urge the gay flask
With a set of old friends—who have nothing to ask;
Thus happy, I reck not of France nor of Spain,
Nor the balance of power what hand shall sustain.
The balance of power? Ah! till that is restored,
What solid delight can retirement afford?
Some must be content to be drudges of state,
That the sage may securely enjoy his retreat.
In weather serene, when the ocean is calm,
It matters not much who presides at the helm;
But soon as clouds gather and tempests arise
Then a pilot there needs, a man dauntless and wise.
If such can be found, sure he ought to come forth

And lend to the public his talents and worth.
Whate'er inclination or ease may suggest,
If the state wants his aid, he has no claim to rest;
But who is the man, a bad game to redeem?
He whom Turin admires, who has Prussia's esteem,
Whom the Spaniard has felt; and whose iron with dread
Haughty Lewis saw forging to fall on his head.
Holland loves him, nor less in the North all the powers
Court, honour, revere, and the Empress adores.
Hark! what was that sound? for it seemed more sublime
Than befits the low genius of pastoral rhyme:
Was it Wisdom I heard? or can fumes of the brain
Cheat my ears with a dream? Ha! repeat me that strain:
Yes, Wisdom, I hear thee; thou deign'st to declare
Me, me, the sole Atlas to prop this whole sphere:
Thy voice says, or seems in sweet accents to say,
'Haste to save sinking Britain';—resigned, I obey;
And O! witness ye powers, that ambition and pride
Have no share in this change—*for I love my fire side.*
Thus the shepherd; then throwing his crook away steals
Direct to St. J[ame]s's and takes up the S[eal]s.

(1746)

JOHN DOBSON

fl. 1746

267 *Robin. A Pastoral Elegy*

DOWN by the brook which glides through yonder vale
His hair all matted, and his cheeks all pale,
Robin, sad swain, by love and sorrow pained,
Of slighted vows, and Susan, thus complained:
'Hear me, ye groves, who saw me blessed so late;
Echo, ye hills, my sad reverse of fate;
Ye winds, that bear my sighs, soft murmurs send;
Come pay me back, ye streams, the drops I lend.
And you, sweet Susan, source of all my smart,
Bestow some pity on a broken heart.
'Happy the times, by painful mem'ry blessed,
When you possessing, Robin all possessed.
Passed by your side, each day brought new delight,
And one sweet slumber shortened ev'ry night.

My play your service, for no toil seemed hard,
When your kind favour was the hoped reward.
I rose to milking, though 'twas ne'er so cool;
I called the cows up; I kept off the bull.
Home on my head I bore the pail upright;
The pail was heavy, but love made it light:
And when you spilt the milk, and 'gan to cry,
I took the blame, and simply said—'twas I.
'When by the haycock's side you sleeping lay,
Sent by good angels, there I chanced to stray,
Just as a loathsome adder reared his crest,
To dart his poison in your lily breast.
Straight with a stone I crushed the monster's head;
You waked, and fainted, though you found him dead.
Then, from the pond, I water brought apace,
My hat brimful and dashed it in your face:
Still, blue as bilberry, your cold lips did quake,
Till my warm kisses called the cherry back.
'When, looking through his worship's garden gate,
Ripe peaches tempted, and you longed to eat;
Though the grim mastiff growled, and sternly stalked,
Though guns were loaded, and old Madam walked,
Nor dogs, nor darkness, guns or ghosts could fright,
When Robin ventured for his Sue's delight.
Joyful of midnight, quick I post away,
Leap the high wall, and fearless pluck the prey;
Down in your lap a plenteous show'r they fall;
Glad you received them, and you ate them all.
'When fair-day came, I donned my Sunday suit,
Brushed the best pillion clean, and saddled Cut.
Then up we got; you clung about my waist;
Pleased to be hugged, I charged you clip me fast:
And when you loosed your hold, and backward slipped,
I held your petticoats, and never peeped.
The posied garters, and the top-knot fine,
The golden ginger-bread, and all was mine:
I paid the puppet-show, the cakes, the sack,
And, fraught with fairings, brought you laughing back.
'Susan but spoke, and each gay flow'r was there,
To dress her bough-pot, or adorn her hair;
For her the choicest of the woods I cull,
Sloes, hips, and strawberries, her belly full;
My hoard of apples I to her confessed:
My heart was hers, well might she have the rest.
'And Susan well approved her Robin's care;
Yes, you was pleased, at least you said you were.

In love's soft fire you seemed like me to burn,
And soothed my fondness with a kind return.
At our long table when we sat to dine,
You stretched your knees, and mingled feet with mine;
With fattest bacon you my trencher plied,
And sliced my pudding from the plumby side;
And well I wot, when our small-beer was stale,
You stole into the barn, and brought me ale.
'But oh, the soldier, blaster of my hopes!
(Curse on pretending kings, and papish popes):
He came from Flanders with the red-coat crew,
To fight with rebels, and he conquered you.
His dowlas ruffles, and his copper lace,
His brickdust stockings, and his brazen face,
These are the charms for which you slight my youth,
Charms much too potent for a maiden's truth!
Soon on the feathered fool you turned your eyes;
Eager you listened to the braggard's lies;
And, scorning me, your heart to him resign,
Your faithless heart, by vows and service mine.
'True, he is gone, by our brave Duke's command,
To humble Britain's foes in foreign land:
Ah, what is that? the spoiler bears away
The only thing for which 'twas worth to stay.
'But sorrow's dry—I'll slake it in the brook;
O well-a-day! how frightful pale I look!
Care's a consumer (so the saying speaks):
The saying's true, I read it in my cheeks.
Fie! I'll be cheerful, 'tis a fancied pain;
A flame so constant cannot meet disdain:
I'll wash my face, and shake off foul despair,
My love is kind; alas! I would she were.
'Well says our parson; and our parson said,
"True love and tithes should ever well be paid."
Susan, from you my heart shall never roam;
If yours be wand'ring, quickly call it home.'

(1746)

TOBIAS SMOLLETT

1721–1771

268 *The Tears of Scotland. Written in the Year 1746*

MOURN, hapless Caledonia, mourn
Thy banished peace, thy laurels torn!
Thy sons, for valour long renowned,
Lie slaughtered on their native ground;
Thy hospitable roofs no more
Invite the stranger to the door;
In smoky ruins sunk they lie,
The monuments of cruelty.

The wretched owner sees afar
His all become the prey of war;
Bethinks him of his babes and wife,
Then smites his breast, and curses life.
Thy swains are famished on the rocks,
Where once they fed their wanton flocks:
Thy ravished virgins shriek in vain;
Thy infants perish on the plain.

What boots it then, in every clime,
Through the wide-spreading waste of time,
Thy martial glory, crowned with praise,
Still shone with undiminished blaze?
Thy tow'ring spirit now is broke,
Thy neck is bended to the yoke.
What foreign arms could never quell,
By civil rage and rancour fell.

The rural pipe and merry lay
No more shall cheer the happy day:
No social scenes of gay delight
Beguile the dreary winter night:
No strains but those of sorrow flow,
And naught be heard but sounds of woe,
While the pale phantoms of the slain
Glide nightly o'er the silent plain.

O baneful cause, oh, fatal morn,
Accursed to ages yet unborn!
The sons against their fathers stood,
The parent shed his children's blood.

Yet, when the rage of battle ceased,
The victor's soul was not appeased;
The naked and forlorn must feel
Devouring flames, and murd'ring steel!

The pious mother doomed to death,
Forsaken, wanders o'er the heath.
The bleak wind whistles round her head,
Her helpless orphans cry for bread;
Bereft of shelter, food, and friend,
She views the shades of night descend,
And, stretched beneath th' inclement skies,
Weeps o'er her tender babes, and dies.

While the warm blood bedews my veins,
And unimpaired remembrance reigns,
Resentment of my country's fate
Within my filial breast shall beat;
And, spite of her insulting foe,
My sympathizing verse shall flow:
'Mourn, hapless Caledonia, mourn
Thy banished peace, thy laurels torn.'

(1746)

MARY LEAPOR

1722–1746

269 *An Essay on Woman*

WOMAN, a pleasing but a short-lived flow'r,
Too soft for business and too weak for pow'r:
A wife in bondage, or neglected maid;
Despised, if ugly; if she's fair, betrayed.
'Tis wealth alone inspires ev'ry grace,
And calls the raptures to her plenteous face.
What numbers for those charming features pine,
If blooming acres round her temples twine!
Her lip the strawberry, and her eyes more bright
Than sparkling Venus in a frosty night;

Pale lilies fade and, when the fair appears,
Snow turns a negro and dissolves in tears,
And, where the charmer treads her magic toe,
On English ground Arabian odours grow;
Till mighty Hymen lifts his sceptred rod,
And sinks her glories with a fatal nod,
Dissolves her triumphs, sweeps her charms away,
And turns the goddess to her native clay.
  But, Artemisia, let your servant sing
What small advantage wealth and beauties bring.
Who would be wise, that knew Pamphilia's fate?
Or who be fair, and joined to Sylvia's mate?
Sylvia, whose cheeks are fresh as early day,
As ev'ning mild, and sweet as spicy May:
And yet that face her partial husband tires,
And those bright eyes, that all the world admires.
Pamphilia's wit who does not strive to shun,
Like death's infection or a dog-day's sun?
The damsels view her with malignant eyes,
The men are vexed to find a nymph so wise:
And wisdom only serves to make her know
The keen sensation of superior woe.
The secret whisper and the list'ning ear,
The scornful eyebrow and the hated sneer,
The giddy censures of her babbling kind,
With thousand ills that grate a gentle mind,
By her are tasted in the first degree,
Though overlooked by Simplicus and me.
Does thirst of gold a virgin's heart inspire,
Instilled by nature or a careful sire?
Then let her quit extravagance and play,
The brisk companion and expensive tea,
To feast with Cordia in her filthy sty
On stewed potatoes or on mouldy pie;
Whose eager eyes stare ghastly at the poor,
And fright the beggars from her hated door;
In greasy clouts she wraps her smoky chin,
And holds that pride's a never-pardoned sin.
  If this be wealth, no matter where it falls;
But save, ye Muses, save your Mira's walls:
Still give me pleasing indolence and ease,
A fire to warm me and a friend to please.
  Since, whether sunk in avarice or pride,
A wanton virgin or a starving bride;
Or wond'ring crowds attend her charming tongue,
Or, deemed an idiot, ever speaks the wrong;

Though nature armed us for the growing ill
With fraudful cunning and a headstrong will;
Yet, with ten thousand follies to her charge,
Unhappy woman's but a slave at large.

(Wr. by 1746; pub. 1751)

270 *Mira's Will*

Imprimis—My departed shade I trust
To heav'n—My body to the silent dust;
My name to public censure I submit,
To be disposed of as the world thinks fit;
My vice and folly let oblivion close,
The world already is o'erstocked with those;
My wit I give, as misers give their store,
To those who think they had enough before.
Bestow my patience to compose the lives
Of slighted virgins and neglected wives;
To modish lovers I resign my truth,
My cool reflection to unthinking youth;
And some good-nature give ('tis my desire)
To surly husbands, as their needs require;
And first discharge my funeral—and then
To the small poets I bequeath my pen.
  Let a small sprig (true emblem of my rhyme)
Of blasted laurel on my hearse recline;
Let some grave wight, that struggles for renown
By chanting dirges through a market-town,
With gentle step precede the solemn train;
A broken flute upon his arm shall lean.
Six comic poets may the corse surround,
And all free-holders, if they can be found:
Then follow next the melancholy throng,
As shrewd instructors, who themselves are wrong.
The virtuoso, rich in sun-dried weeds,
The politician, whom no mortal heeds,
The silent lawyer, chambered all the day,
And the stern soldier that receives no pay.
But stay—the mourners should be first our care:
Let the freed 'prentice lead the miser's heir;
Let the young relict wipe her mournful eye,
And widowed husbands o'er their garlic cry.
  All this let my executors fulfil,

And rest assured that this is Mira's will,
Who was, when she these legacies designed,
In body healthy, and composed in mind.

(Wr. by 1746; pub. 1748)

271 *An Epistle to a Lady*

In vain, dear Madam, yes, in vain you strive,
Alas! to make your luckless Mira thrive,
For Tycho and Copernicus agree,
No golden planet bent its rays on me.
'Tis twenty winters, if it is no more,
To speak the truth it may be twenty-four:
As many springs their 'pointed space have run,
Since Mira's eyes first opened on the sun.
'Twas when the flocks on slabby hillocks lie,
And the cold Fishes rule the watry sky:
But though these eyes the learned page explore,
And turn the pond'rous volumes o'er and o'er,
I find no comfort from their systems flow,
But am dejected more as more I know.
Hope shines a while, but like a vapour flies
(The fate of all the curious and the wise),
For, ah! cold Saturn triumphed on that day,
And frowning Sol denied his golden ray.
You see I'm learned, and I show't the more,
That none may wonder when they find me poor.
Yet Mira dreams, as slumb'ring poets may,
And rolls in treasures till the breaking day,
While books and pictures in bright order rise,
And painted parlours swim before her eyes:
Till the shrill clock impertinently rings,
And the soft visions move their shining wings:
Then Mira wakes—her pictures are no more,
And through her fingers slides the vanished ore.
Convinced too soon, her eye unwilling falls
On the blue curtains and the dusty walls:
She wakes, alas! to business and to woes,
To sweep her kitchen, and to mend her clothes.
But see pale Sickness with her languid eyes,
At whose appearance all delusion flies:
The world recedes, its vanities decline,
Clorinda's features seem as faint as mine;

slabby] damp, muddy

Gay robes no more the aching sight admires,
Wit grates the ear, and melting music tires.
Its wonted pleasures with each sense decay,
Books please no more, and paintings fade away,
The sliding joys in misty vapours end:
Yet let me still, ah! let me grasp a friend:
And when each joy, when each loved object flies,
Be you the last that leaves my closing eyes.
But how will this dismantled soul appear,
When stripped of all it lately held so dear,
Forced from its prison of expiring clay,
Afraid and shiv'ring at the doubtful way?
Yet did these eyes a dying parent see,
Loosed from all cares except a thought for me,
Without a tear resign her short'ning breath,
And dauntless meet the ling'ring stroke of death.
Then at th' Almighty's sentence shall I mourn,
'Of dust thou art, to dust shalt thou return'?
Or shall I wish to stretch the line of fate,
That the dull years may bear a longer date,
To share the follies of succeeding times
With more vexations and with deeper crimes?
Ah no—though heav'n brings near the final day,
For such a life I will not, dare not pray;
But let the tear for future mercy flow,
And fall resigned beneath the mighty blow.
Nor I alone—for through the spacious ball,
With me will numbers of all ages fall:
And the same day that Mira yields her breath,
Thousands may enter through the gates of death.

(Wr. by 1746; pub. 1748)

JOHN ELLIS

1698–1791

272 *Sarah Hazard's Love Letter*

To the Printer of the Chester Courant

December 10, 1747.

The following epistle I met with at a neighbouring seaport, and showed it to our curate, who said that the girl's sentiments were much the same with those of Ovid's heroines, were theirs to be stripped of poetical decorations.

A day or two afterwards he brought it to me, as likewise an attempt to versify it; both which I herewith send you, and am

Your friend and servant,
G.Z.

Lovin Der Charls,

This with my kind lov to yow, is to tel yow, after all owr sport and fon, i am lik to pa fort, for i am with Child, and were of mi Sister Nan knose it, and cals me hore and bech, and is ready to ter mi sol owt, yet Jack Peny kices hur every tim he cums ashor, and the saaci Dog wud a lade with me to, but i wud not let him, for i will be alwas honest to yow, therfore Der Charls, cum ashor, and let us be mared to safe mi vartu, and if yow hav no munni, i wil pawn mi new staies, and sel the smocks yow gav me, and that will pa the Parson, and find us a diner. and pra, Der lovin Charls cum ashor, and, Der Charls, don't be fraad for want of a ring, for i hav stol my sister Nans, and the naaty tode shal never hav it no more, for she tels about, that i am going to hav a basterd, and god bless yowr lovin sol cum sune, for i longs to be mared accordin to yowr promis, and i wil be yowr own der vartus wife tel deth,

SA. HAZARD.

P.S. Pra dont let yowr mesmate Jack se this, for if yow shud, he'l tel owr Nan, and ther wil be the Divil to do.

DEAR object of my love, whose pow'rful charms
With bliss ecstatic filled my clinging arms!
That bliss is past; and nought for me remains,
But foul reproach, and never-pitied pains!
For (nature baffling ev'ry art I tried)
My sister has my waxing waist descried,
And brands me oft with each opprobious name,
Though the crack's conscious she deserves the same:
Her loose associate, sated, from her flies,
And oft, though vainly, to seduce me tries;
True as a wife, I only want the name;
O haste to wed me, and restore my fame.
No lack of coin our union shall defer,
For my pawned stays will well supply my dear;
And those good smocks which once your fondness gave,
Those smocks I'll sell, or any clothes I have:
What these produce will pay the coupling priest,
And furnish dainties for our nuptial feast.
O how I long my loving Charles to see,
Haste then, my life! to happiness and me;
Nor anxious be 'bout that material thing,
For I've just stol'n my saucy sister's ring:

crack] whore

In vain she may expect me to restore;
No! faith, the slut shall never have it more.
Come quick, my love, for far she spreads my shame;
Come, patch my virtue, and defend my fame.
Take me, and make me soon thy lawful spouse,
Then heav'n shall bless thy due regard to vows,
And will reward thee with what lasts for life,
A tender, duteous, fond and faithful wife.

P.S. These earnest dictates of my anxious heart
I beg you would not to your friend impart;
For oft beneath fair friendship's specious show
Lurks the false, trait'rous, undermining foe.

(1747)

ANONYMOUS

273 [*The Poetess's Bouts-Rimés*]

DEAR Phoebus, hear my only vow;
If e'er you loved me, hear me now.
That charming youth—but idle fame
Is ever so inclined to blame—
These men will turn it to a jest;
I'll tell the rhymes and drop the rest:
——— ——— ——— desire,
——— ——— ——— fire,
——— ——— ——— lie,
——— ——— ——— thigh,
——— ——— ——— wide,
——— ——— ——— ride,
——— ——— ——— night,
——— ——— ——— delight.

(1747)

WILLIAM WHITEHEAD

1715–1785

274 *New Night Thoughts on Death. A Parody*

O NIGHT! dark Night! wrapped round with Stygian gloom!
Thy riding-hood opaque, wrought by the hands
Of Clotho and of Atropos:—those hands
Which spin my thread of life!—so near its end.
Ah wherefore, silent goddess, dost thou now
Alarm with terrors?—Silence sounds alarms
To me, and darkness dazzles my weak mind!
Hark, 'tis the death-watch! Posts themselves can speak
His awful language. Stop, insatiate worm!
I feel thy summons:—to my fellow-worms
Thou bidd'st me hasten!—I obey thy call,
For wherefore should I live?—Vain life to me
Is but a tattered garment, a patched rag,
That ill defends me from the cold of age.
Cramped are my faculties! my eyes grow dim;
No music charms my ear—no meats my taste;
The females fly me—and my very wife,
Poor woman! knows me not!——
  Ye fluttering, idle vanities of life,
Where are you flown?—The birds that used to sing
Amidst my spreading branches now forsake
The lifeless trunk, and find no shelter there.
  What's life?—What's death?—thus coveted and feared:
Life is a fleeting shadow:—death no more!
Death's a dark lantern, life a candle's end
Stuck on a save-all, soon to end in stink.
The grave's a privy; life the alley green
Directing there—where 'chance on either side
A sweetbriar hedge, or shrubs of brighter hue,
Amuse us, and their treach'rous sweets dispense.
Death chases life, and stops it ere it reach
The topmost round of Fortune's restless wheel.
Wheel! Life's a wheel, and each man is the ass
That turns it round, receiving in the end
But water or rank thistles for his pains!
And yet, Lorenzo, if considered well,
A life of labour is a life of ease;
Pain gives true joy, and want is luxury.
Pleasure not chaste is like an opera tune,

Makes man not man, and castrates real joy.
Would you be merry? Search the charnel-house,
Where Death inhabits,—give the king of fears
A midnight ball, and lead up Holben's dance.
How weak, yet strong, how easy, yet severe,
Are Laughter's chains! which thrall a willing world.
The noisy idiot shakes her bells at all,
Nor e'en the Bible or the poet spares.
Fools banter heav'n itself, O Young!—and thee!

(1747)

275 *The Sweepers*

I SING of sweepers, frequent in thy streets,
Augusta, as the flowers which grace the spring,
Or branches withering in autumnal shades
To form the brooms they wield. Preserved by them
From dirt, from coach-hire, and th' oppressive rheums
Which clog the springs of life, to them I sing,
And ask no inspiration but their smiles.
  Hail, unowned youths, and virgins unendowed!
Whether on bulk begot, while rattled loud
The passing coaches, or th' officious hand
Of sportive link-boy wide around him dashed
The pitchy-flame, obstructive of the joy.
Or more propitious, to the dark retreat
Of round-house owe your birth, where Nature's reign
Revives, and prompted by untaught desire
The mingling sexes share promiscuous love.
And scarce the pregnant female knows to whom
She owes the precious burthen, scarce the sire
Can claim, confused, the many-featured child.
  Nor blush that hence your origin we trace:
'Twas thus immortal heroes sprung of old
Strong from the stol'n embrace; by such as you,
Unhoused, unclothed, unlettered and unfed,
Were kingdoms modelled, cities taught to rise,
Firm laws enacted, Freedom's rights maintained,
The gods and patriots of an infant world!
  Let others meanly chaunt in tuneful song
The blackshoe race, whose mercenary tribes
Allured by halfpence take their morning stand

Augusta] London

Where streets divide, and to their proffered stools
Solicit wand'ring feet; vain pensioners,
And placemen of the crowd! Not so you pour
Your blessings on mankind; nor traffic vile
Be your employment deemed, ye last remains
Of public spirit, whose laborious hands,
Uncertain of reward, bid kennels know
Their wonted bounds, remove the bord'ring filth,
And give th' obstructed ordure where to glide.
  What though the pitying passenger bestows
His unextorted boon, must they refuse
The well-earned bounty, scorn th' obtruded ore?
Proud were the thought and vain. And shall not we
Repay their kindly labours, men like them,
With gratitude unsought? I too have oft
Seen in our streets the withered hands of age
Toil in th' industrious task; and can we there
Be thrifty niggards? haply they have known
Far better days, and scattered liberal round
The scanty pittance we afford them now.
Soon from this office grant them their discharge,
Ye kind church-wardens! take their meagre limbs
Shiv'ring with cold and age, and wrap them warm
In those blest mansions Charity has raised.
  But you of younger years, while vigour knits
Your lab'ring sinews, urge the generous task.
Nor lose in fruitless brawls the precious hours
Assigned to toil. Be your contentions who
First in the dark'ning streets, when Autumn sheds
Her earliest showers, shall clear th' obstructed pass;
Or last shall quit the field when Spring distils
Her moist'ning dews, prolific there in vain.
So may each lusty scavenger, ye fair,
Fly ardent to your arms; and every maid,
Ye gentle youths, be to your wishes kind.
Whether Ostrea's fishy fumes allure
As Venus' tresses fragrant, or the sweets
More mild and rural from her stall who toils
To feast the sages of the Samian school.
  Nor ever may your hearts elate with pride
Desert this sphere of love; for should ye, youths,
When blood boils high, and some more lucky chance
Has swelled your stores, pursue the tawdry band
That romp from lamp to lamp, for health expect

kennels] gutters

Disease, for fleeting pleasure foul remorse,
And daily, nightly, agonising pains.
In vain you call for Aesculapius' aid
From White-cross alley, or the azure posts
Which beam through Haydon-yard; the god demands
More ample offerings, and rejects your prayer.
  And you, ye fair, O let me warn your breasts
To shun deluding men: for some there are,
Great lords of countries, mighty men of war,
And well-dressed courtiers, who with leering eye
Can in the face begrimed with dirt discern
Strange charms, and pant for Cynthia in a cloud.
  But let Lardella's fate avert your own.
Lardella once was fair, the early boast
Of proud St. Giles's, from its ample pound
To where the column points the seven-fold day.
Happy, thrice happy, had she never known
A street more spacious! but ambition led
Her youthful footsteps, artless, unassured,
To Whitehall's fatal pavement. There she plied
Like you the active broom. At sight of her
The coachman dropped his lash, the porter oft
Forgot his burthen, and with wild amaze
The tall well-booted sentry, armed in vain,
Leaned from his horse to gaze upon her charms.
  But Fate reserved her for more dreadful ills:
A lord beheld her, and with powerful gold
Seduced her to his arms. What can not gold
Effect, when aided by the matron's tongue,
Long tried and practised in the trade of vice,
Against th' unwary innocent! A while
Dazzled with splendour, giddy with the height
Of unexperienced greatness, she looks down
With thoughtless pride, nor sees the gulf beneath.
But soon, too soon, the high-wrought transport sinks
In cold indifference, and a newer face
Alarms her restless lover's fickle heart.
Distressed, abandoned, whither shall she fly?
How urge her former task, and brave the winds
And piercing rains with limbs whose daintier sense
Shrinks from the evening breeze? nor has she now,
Sweet Innocence, thy calmer heart-felt aid
To solace or support the pangs she feels.
  Why should the weeping Muse pursue her steps
Through the dull round of infamy, through haunts
Of public lust, and every painful stage

Of ill-feigned transport, and uneasy joy?
Too sure she tried them all, till her sunk eye
Lost its last languish, and the bloom of health,
Which revelled once on beauty's virgin cheek,
Was pale disease, and meagre penury.
Then loathed, deserted, to her life's last pang
In bitterness of soul she cursed in vain
Her proud betrayer, cursed her fatal charms,
And perished in the streets from whence she sprung.

(1754)

THOMAS WARTON

1728–1790

276 from *The Pleasures of Melancholy*

BENEATH yon ruined abbey's moss-grown piles
Oft let me sit, at twilight hour of eve,
Where through some western window the pale moon
Pours her long-levelled rule of streaming light;
While sullen sacred silence reigns around,
Save the lone screech-owl's note, who builds his bow'r
Amid the mould'ring caverns dark and damp,
Or the calm breeze, that rustles in the leaves
Of flaunting ivy, that with mantle green
Invests some wasted tow'r. Or let me tread
Its neighb'ring walk of pines, where mused of old
The cloistered brothers: through the gloomy void
That far extends beneath their ample arch
As on I pace, religious horror wraps
My soul in dread repose. But when the world
Is clad in Midnight's raven-coloured robe,
Mid hollow charnel let me watch the flame
Of taper dim, shedding a livid glare
O'er the wan heaps; while airy voices talk
Along the glimm'ring walls; or ghostly shape,
At distance seen, invites with beck'ning hand
My lonesome steps, through the far-winding vaults.
Nor undelightful is the solemn noon
Of night, when haply wakeful from my couch
I start: lo, all is motionless around!
Roars not the rushing wind; the sons of men

And every beast in mute oblivion lie;
All nature's hushed in silence and in sleep.
O then how fearful is it to reflect,
That through the still globe's awful solitude,
No being wakes but me! till stealing sleep
My drooping temples bathes in opiate dews.
Nor then let dreams, of wanton folly born,
My senses lead through flowery paths of joy;
But let the sacred Genius of the night
Such mystic visions send, as Spenser saw,
When through bewild'ring Fancy's magic maze,
To the fell house of Busyrane, he led
Th' unshaken Britomart; or Milton knew,
When in abstracted thought he first conceived
All heav'n in tumult, and the Seraphim
Come tow'ring, armed in adamant and gold.

(1747)

277 *Sonnet*

To the River Lodon

AH! what a weary race my feet have run,
  Since first I trod thy banks with alders crowned,
  And thought my way was all through fairy ground,
  Beneath thy azure sky, and golden sun:
Where first my Muse to lisp her notes begun!
  While pensive memory traces back the round,
  Which fills the varied interval between,
  Much pleasure, more of sorrow, marks the scene.
Sweet native stream! those skies and suns so pure
  No more return, to cheer my evening road!
  Yet still one joy remains, that not obscure,
Nor useless, all my vacant days have flowed,
  From youth's gay dawn to manhood's prime mature;
  Nor with the Muse's laurel unbestowed.

(1777)

278 *Verses on Sir Joshua Reynolds's Painted Window at New College, Oxford*

AH, stay thy treacherous hand, forbear to trace
Those faultless forms of elegance and grace!
Ah, cease to spread the bright transparent mass,

With Titian's pencil, o'er the speaking glass!
Nor steal, by strokes of art with truth combined,
The fond illusions of my wayward mind!
For long, enamoured of a barbarous age,
A faithless truant to the classic page,
Long have I loved to catch the simple chime
Of minstrel-harps, and spell the fabling rhyme;
To view the festive rites, the knightly play,
That decked heroic Albion's elder day;
To mark the mouldering halls of barons bold,
And the rough castle, cast in giant mould;
With Gothic manners Gothic arts explore,
And muse on the magnificence of yore.
  But chief, enraptured have I loved to roam,
A lingering votary, the vaulted dome,
Where the tall shafts, that mount in massy pride,
Their mingling branches shoot from side to side;
Where elfin sculptors, with fantastic clew,
O'er the long roof their wild embroidery drew;
Where Superstition, with capricious hand
In many a maze the wreathèd window planned,
With hues romantic tinged the gorgeous pane,
To fill with holy light the wondrous fane;
To aid the builder's model, richly rude,
By no Vitruvian symmetry subdued;
To suit the genius of the mystic pile:
Whilst as around the far-retiring aisle,
And fretted shrines with hoary trophies hung,
Her dark illumination wide she flung,
With new solemnity, the nooks profound,
The caves of death, and the dim arches frowned.
From bliss long felt unwillingly we part:
Ah, spare the weakness of a lover's heart!
Chase not the phantoms of my fairy dream,
Phantoms that shrink at Reason's painful gleam!
That softer touch, insidious artist, stay,
Nor to new joys my struggling breast betray!
  Such was a pensive bard's mistaken strain.—
But, oh, of ravished pleasures why complain?
No more the matchless skill I call unkind
That strives to disenchant my cheated mind.
For when again I view thy chaste design,
The just proportion, and the genuine line;
Those native portraitures of Attic art,
That from the lucid surface seem to start;
Those tints, that steal no glories from the day,

Nor ask the sun to lend his streaming ray;
The doubtful radiance of contending dyes,
That faintly mingle, yet distinctly rise;
Twixt light and shade the transitory strife;
The feature blooming with immortal life:
The stole in casual foldings taught to flow,
Not with ambitious ornaments to glow;
The tread majestic, and the beaming eye
That lifted speaks its commerce with the sky;
Heaven's golden emanation, gleaming mild
O'er the mean cradle of the virgin's child:
Sudden, the sombrous imagery is fled,
Which late my visionary rapture fed:
Thy powerful hand has broke the Gothic chain,
And brought my bosom back to truth again:
To truth, by no peculiar taste confined,
Whose universal pattern strikes mankind;
To truth, whose bold and unresisted aim
Checks frail caprice, and fashion's fickle claim;
To truth, whose charms deception's magic quell,
And bind coy Fancy in a stronger spell.
  Ye brawny prophets, that in robes so rich,
At distance due, possess the crispèd niche;
Ye rows of patriarchs, that sublimely reared
Diffuse a proud primeval length of beard:
Ye saints, who clad in crimson's bright array,
More pride than humble poverty display:
Ye virgins meek, that wear the palmy crown
Of patient faith, and yet so fiercely frown:
Ye angels, that from clouds of gold recline,
But boast no semblance to a race divine:
Ye tragic tales of legendary lore,
That draw devotion's ready tear no more:
Ye martyrdoms of unenlightened days,
Ye miracles, that now no wonder raise:
Shapes, that with one broad glare the gazer strike,
Kings, bishops, nuns, apostles, all alike!
Ye colours, that th' unwary sight amaze,
And only dazzle in the noontide blaze!
No more the sacred window's round disgrace,
But yield to Grecian groups the shining space.
Lo, from the canvas Beauty shifts her throne,
Lo, Picture's powers a new formation own!
Behold she prints upon the crystal plain,
With her own energy, th' expressive stain!
The mighty master spreads his mimic toil

More wide, nor only blends the breathing oil;
But calls the lineaments of life complete
From genial alchemy's creative heat;
Obedient forms to the bright fusion gives,
While in the warm enamel Nature lives.
  Reynolds, 'tis thine, from the broad window's height,
To add new lustre to religious light:
Not of its pomp to strip this ancient shrine,
But bid that pomp with purer radiance shine:
With arts unknown before, to reconcile
The willing Graces to the Gothic pile.

(1782)

ROBERT NUGENT, EARL NUGENT

1702–1788

279 *To Clarissa*

'TWAS when the friendly shade of night
Suspends the busy cares of light,
And on the various world bestows
Or sprightly joy, or calm repose.
With gen'rous wine the glass was crowned,
And mirth, and talk, and toasts went round.
  Clarissa came to bless the feast,
Clarissa, dearly welcome guest.
Not such she looked as when by day
She blazes in the diamond's ray;
And, adding to each gem a grace,
Gives India's wealth the second place:
But soft reclined in careless ease,
More pleasing, less intent to please.
Loose flowed her hair in wanton pride,
Her robe unbound, her zone untied;
Half bare to view her milk-white breast,
A slender veil scarce shades the rest;
Her eye with sparkling lustre glows,
And wit in sweetest accent flows.
  Now soothed the angel's voice I hear,
And drink in love at either ear;
Now stung with wilder rapture gaze,
While our eyes meet with blended rays;

And kindling in th' infectious flame,
I feel what words want pow'r to name.
  Awaking from the silent trance,
Cautious I steal a broken glance;
In clam'rous mirth each pang disguise,
And laughter swell with bursting sighs;
For envy, pallid fiend, was there,
And jealousy with watchful care.
  Now ends the feast, each guest retires,
And with them, all my soul desires,
Clarissa goes—Ah! cruel fate!
She goes with her ill-sorted mate:
Sullen and slow he moves along,
And heavy hums a drowsy song.
O! drowsy may the monster lie,
And instant slumbers seal his eye!
So shalt thou, best beloved, escape
The horrors of a legal rape.
  Or should the brutish instinct goad,
And thou must bear th' unwelcome load;
If struggle, pray'r, pretence be vain,
To shun what tyrant-laws ordain;
Ah! sparing deal out scanty dues,
And keep whate'er thou can'st refuse!
Ah! give no bounding pulse to beat,
No cheek to glow with genial heat!
No breast to heave in am'rous play,
No limbs to twine, no hands to stray;
But sluggish press the joyless bed,
And lie in cold indiff'rence dead:
Nor let the blasting spoiler sip
The fragrance of thy balmy lip!
To share with him the lover's part
Were rank adultery of the heart.
  But if, in chaster love's despite,
Warm nature catch the known delight;
While fierce desires tumultuous rise,
And rapture melts thy closing eyes;
Ah! be those joys for me designed,
And let me rush upon thy mind!
To me the burning kiss impart,
On me impress the humid dart,
For me unlock the nectared store,
Then sigh, and dream the transport o'er!
  Thus with her loved idea fraught,
Delusive fancy charms my thought;

And joining in the flatt'ring cheat,
Willing I hug the dear deceit;
From fiction real bliss receive,
And all I fondly wish believe;
Nor envy to a husband's arms
The dull fruition of her charms.
But when, regardless of my truth,
She smiles on some more favoured youth:
And, while he whispers in her ears,
With more than wonted pleasure hears;
My jealous thought his voice supplies,
And reads perdition in her eyes.
Then torn with envy, love and hate,
I wish her with her wedded mate.

(1748)

280 *Epigrams*

(i)

I LOVED thee beautiful and kind,
And plighted an eternal vow;
So altered are thy face and mind,
'Twere perjury to love thee now.

(ii)

SINCE first you knew my am'rous smart,
Each day augments your proud disdain;
'Twas then enough to break my heart,
And now, thank heav'n! to break my chain.
Cease, thou scorner, cease to shun me!
Now let love and hatred cease!
Half that rigour had undone me,
All that rigour gives me peace.

(iii)

MY heart still hovering round about you,
I thought I could not live without you;
Now we have lived three months asunder,
How I lived with you is the wonder.

(1748)

THOMAS EDWARDS

1699–1757

281 *Sonnet on a Family-Picture*

WHEN pensive on that portraiture I gaze,
  Where my four brothers round about me stand,
  And four fair sisters smile with graces bland,
The goodly monument of happier days;
And think how soon insatiate death, who preys
  On all, has cropped the rest with ruthless hand,
  While only I survive of all that band,
Which one chaste bed did to my father raise;
It seems that, like a column left alone,
  The tott'ring remnant of some splendid fane,
    Scaped from the fury of the barb'rous Gaul
And wasting time, which has the rest o'erthrown,
  Amidst our house's ruins I remain,
    Single, unpropped, and nodding to my fall.

(1748)

ANONYMOUS

282 from *A Collection of Hymns . . . of the Moravian Brethren, Part III*

Hymn 33

CHICKEN blessed and caressed,
Little bee on Jesu's breast,
From the hurry and the flurry
Of this earth thou'rt now at rest:
From our care in lower regions
Thou art taken to the legions
Who 'bove human griefs are raised;
There thou'rt kept, the Lamb be praised!
Chicken blessed, bee caressed,
Thou that sleep'st on Jesu's breast.

(1748)

from *Hymn 110*

What does a bird in Cross's air,
When it flies up to the Lamb near,
When round the Lamb it moves and sings,
And claps the *Ave* with its wings?
Dear hearts! look, look and see,
The little bird finds presently
Its nest in the dear cavity,
From whence the Church was dug.
Within the hole, where blood casts rays,
The bird itself entangled has;
And round the castle of the side
Are wound-swans in the canal wide;
There learns the little piper
In th' hole to be a dipper.

Chorus

My heart with joy, with joy abounds,
I've found the ocean of the wounds;
There I'm a little dove, a fish,
There is my bed, table and dish,
  and all things.

(1748)

CHRISTOPHER SMART

1722–1771

283 *A Morning-Piece, or, An Hymn for the Hay-Makers*

BRISK Chaunticleer his matins had begun,
  And broke the silence of the night,
 And thrice he called aloud the tardy sun,
  And thrice he hailed the dawn's ambiguous light;
Back to their graves the fear-begotten phantoms run.

 Strong Labour got up with his pipe in his mouth,
  And stoutly strode over the dale,
 He lent new perfumes to the breath of the south,
  On his back hung his wallet and flail.
Behind him came Health from her cottage of thatch,
Where never physician had lifted the latch.

First of the village Colin was awake,
And thus he sung, reclining on his rake:
 Now the rural graces three
 Dance beneath yon maple tree;
 First the vestal Virtue, known
 By her adamantine zone;
 Next to her in rosy pride,
 Sweet Society, the bride;
 Last Honesty, full seemly dressed
 In her cleanly home-spun vest.
The abbey bells in wak'ning rounds
 The warning peal have giv'n;
And pious Gratitude resounds
 Her morning hymn to heav'n.

All nature wakes—the birds unlock their throats,
And mock the shepherd's rustic notes.
 All alive o'er the lawn,
 Full glad of the dawn,
 The little lambkins play,
Sylvia and Sol arise,—and all is day—

 Come, my mates, let us work,
 And all hands to the fork,
While the sun shines, our hay-cocks to make,
 So fine is the day,
 And so fragrant the hay,
That the meadow's as blithe as the wake.

 Our voices let's raise
 In Phoebus's praise;
Inspired by so glorious a theme,
 Our musical words
 Shall be joined by the birds,
And we'll dance to the tune of the stream.

(1748)

284 *A Night-Piece, or, Modern Philosophy*

'TWAS when bright Cynthia with her silver car,
 Soft stealing from Endymion's bed,
 Had called forth ev'ry glitt'ring star,
And up th' ascent of heav'n her brilliant host had led.

Night, with all her negro train,
Took possession of the plain;
In an hearse she rode reclined,
Drawn by screech-owls slow and blind:
Close to her, with printless feet,
Crept Stillness, in a winding-sheet.
Next to her deaf Silence was seen,
Treading on tip-toes over the green;
Softly, lightly, gently she trips,
Still holding her fingers sealed to her lips.
You could not see a sight,
You could not hear a sound,
But what confessed the night,
And horror deepened round.

Beneath a myrtle's melancholy shade,
Sophron the wise was laid:
And to the answ'ring wood these sounds conveyed:
'While others toil within the town,
And to Fortune smile or frown,
Fond of trifles, fond of toys,
And married to that woman, Noise;
Sacred Wisdom be my care,
And fairest Virtue, Wisdom's heir.'

His speculations thus the sage begun,
When, lo! the neighbouring bell
In solemn sound struck one:—
He starts—and recollects—he was engaged to Nell.
Then up he sprang nimble and light,
And rapped at fair Ele'nor's door;
He laid aside virtue that night,
And next morn pored in Plato for more.

(1748)

285 from *Hymn to the Supreme Being on Recovery from a Dangerous Fit of Illness*

But, O immortals! What had I to plead
When death stood o'er me with his threat'ning lance,
When reason left me in the time of need,
And sense was lost in terror or in trance?
My sick'ning soul was with my blood inflamed,
And the celestial image sunk, defaced and maimed.

I sent back memory, in heedful guise,
  To search the records of preceding years;
Home, like the raven to the ark, she flies,
  Croaking bad tidings to my trembling ears.
O sun, again that thy retreat was made,
And threw my follies back into the friendly shade!

But who are they, that bid affliction cease?—
  Redemption and forgiveness, heavenly sounds!
Behold the dove that brings the branch of peace,
  Behold the balm that heals the gaping wounds—
Vengeance divine's by penitence suppressed—
She struggles with the angel, conquers, and is blessed.

Yet hold, presumption, nor too fondly climb,
  And thou too hold, O horrible despair!
In man humility's alone sublime,
  Who diffidently hopes he's Christ's own care—
O all-sufficient Lamb! in death's dread hour
Thy merits who shall slight, or who can doubt thy power?

But soul-rejoicing health again returns,
  The blood meanders gently in each vein,
The lamp of life renewed with vigour burns,
  And exiled reason takes her seat again—
Brisk leaps the heart, the mind's at large once more,
To love, to praise, to bless, to wonder and adore.

The virtuous partner of my nuptial bands
  Appeared a widow to my frantic sight;
My little prattlers, lifting up their hands,
  Beckon me back to them, to life, and light;
I come, ye spotless sweets! I come again,
Nor have your tears been shed, nor have ye knelt in vain.

All glory to th' Eternal, to th' Immense,
  All glory to th' Omniscient and Good,
Whose power's uncircumscribed, whose love's intense;
  But yet whose justice ne'er could be withstood,
Except through him—through him, who stands alone,
Of worth, of weight allowed for all mankind t' atone!

He raised the lame, the lepers he made whole,
  He fixed the palsied nerves of weak decay,
He drove out Satan from the tortured soul,
  And to the blind gave or restored the day,—
Nay more,—far more, unequalled pangs sustained,
Till his lost fallen flock his taintless blood regained.

My feeble feet refused my body's weight,
  Nor would my eyes admit the glorious light,
My nerves convulsed shook fearful of their fate,
  My mind lay open to the powers of night.
He pitying did a second birth bestow,
A birth of joy—not like the first of tears and woe.

(1756)

286 from *Jubilate Agno*, Fragment B

(i)

LET Ephah rejoice with Buprestis, the Lord endue us with temperance and humanity, till every cow have her mate!
For I am come home again, but there is nobody to kill the calf or to pay the musick.
Let Sarah rejoice with the Redwing, whose harvest is in the frost and snow.
For the hour of my felicity, like the womb of Sarah, shall come at the latter end.
Let Rebekah rejoice with Iynx, who holds his head on one side to deceive the adversary.
For I shou'd have availed myself of waggery, had not malice been multitudinous.
Let Shuah rejoice with Boa, which is the vocal serpent.
For there are still serpents that can speak—God bless my head, my heart and my heel.
Let Ehud rejoice with Onocrotalus, whose braying is for the glory of God, because he makes the best musick in his power.
For I bless God that I am of the same seed as Ehud, Mutius Scaevola, and Colonel Draper.
Let Shamgar rejoice with Otis, who looks about him for the glory of God, and sees the horizon compleat at once.
For the word of God is a sword on my side—no matter what other weapon a stick or a straw.
Let Bohan rejoice with the Scythian Stag—he is beef and breeches against want and nakedness.
For I have adventured myself in the name of the Lord, and he hath marked me for his own.
Let Achsah rejoice with the Pigeon who is an antidote to malignity and will carry a letter.
For I bless God for the Postmaster general and all conveyancers of letters under his care especially Allen and Shelvock.
Let Tohu rejoice with the Grouse—the Lord further the cultivating of heaths and the peopling of deserts.

For my grounds in New Canaan shall infinitely compensate for the flats and maynes of Staindrop Moor.
Let Hillel rejoice with Ammodytes, whose colour is deceitful and he plots against the pilgrim's feet.
For the praise of God can give to a mute fish the notes of a nightingale.
Let Eli rejoice with Leucon—he is an honest fellow, which is a rarity.
For I have seen the White Raven and Thomas Hall of Willingham and am my self a greater curiosity than both.
Let Jemuel rejoice with Charadrius, who is from the HEIGHT and the sight of him is good for the jaundice.
For I look up to heaven which is my prospect to escape envy by surmounting it.
Let Pharaoh rejoice with Anataria, whom God permits to prey upon the ducks to check their increase.
For if Pharaoh had known Joseph, he woud have blessed God and me for the illumination of the people.
Let Lotan rejoice with Sauterelle. Blessed be the name of the Lord from the Lote-tree to the Palm.
For I pray God to bless improvements in gardening till London be a city of palm-trees.
Let Dishon rejoice with the Landrail, God give his grace to the society for preserving the game.
For I pray to give his grace to the poor of England, that Charity be not offended and that benevolence may increase.
Let Hushim rejoice with the King's Fisher, who is of royal beauty, tho' plebeian size.
For in my nature I quested for beauty, but God, God hath sent me to sea for pearls.

(ii)

Let Shobi rejoice with the Kastrel—blessed be the name JESUS in falconry and in the MALL
For I blessed God in St James's Park till I routed all the company.
Let Elkanah rejoice with Cymindis—the Lord illuminate us against the powers of darkness.
For the officers of the peace are at variance with me, and the watchman smites me with his staff.
Let Ziba rejoice with Glottis whose tongue is wreathed in his throat.
For I am the seed of the WELCH WOMAN and speak the truth from my heart.
Let Micah rejoice with the spotted Spider, who counterfeits death to effect his purposes.
For they lay wagers touching my life.—God be gracious to the winners.
Let Rizpah rejoice with the Eyed Moth who is beautiful in corruption.
For the piety of Rizpah is imitable in the Lord—wherefore I pray for the dead.
Let Naharai, Joab's armour-bearer rejoice with Rock who is a bird of stupendous magnitude.

For the Lord is my ROCK and I am the bearer of his CROSS.
Let Abiezer, the Anethothite, rejoice with Phrynos who is the scaled frog.
For I am like a frog in the brambles, but the Lord hath put his whole armour upon me.
Let Nachon rejoice with Parcas who is a serpent more innocent than others.
For I was a Viper-catcher in my youth and the Lord delivered me from his venom.
Let Lapidoth with Percnos—the Lord is the builder of the wall of CHINA—REJOICE.
For I rejoice that I attribute to God, what others vainly ascribe to feeble man.
Let Ahinoam rejoice with Prester—The seed of the woman hath bruised the serpents head.
For I am ready to die for his sake—who lay down his life for all mankind.
Let Phurah rejoice with Penelopes, the servant of Gideon with the fowl of the brook.
For the son of JOSHUA shall prevail against the servant of Gideon—Good men have their betters.
Let Jether, the son of Gideon, rejoice with Ecchetae which are musical grasshoppers.
For my seed shall worship the Lord JESUS as numerous and musical as the grasshoppers of Paradise.
Let Hushai rejoice with the Ospray who is able to parry the eagle.
For I pray God to turn the council of Ahitophel into foolishness.
Let Eglah rejoice with Phalaris who is a pleasant object upon the water.
For the learning of the Lord increases daily, as the sun is an improving angel.
Let Haggith rejoice with the white Weasel who devoureth the honey and it's maker.
For I pray God for a reformation amongst the women and the restoration of the veil.
Let Abital rejoice with Ptyas who is arrayed in green and gold.
For beauty is better to look upon than to meddle with and tis good for a man not to know a woman.
Let Maacah rejoice with Dryophyte who was blessed of the Lord in the valley.
For the Lord Jesus made him a nosegay and blessed it and he blessed the inhabitants of flowers.
Let Zabud Solomon's friend rejoice with Oryx who is a frolicksome mountaineer.
For a faithful friend is the medicine of life, but a neighbour in the Lord is better than he.
Let Adoniram the receiver general of the excise rejoice with Hypnale the sleepy adder.
For I stood up betimes in behalf of LIBERTY, PROPERTY and NO EXCISE.

Let Pedahel rejoice with Pityocampa who eateth his house in the pine.
For they began with grubbing up my trees and now they have excluded the planter.
Let Ibzan rejoice with the Brandling—the Lord further the building of bridges and making rivers navigable.
For I am the Lord's builder and free and accepted MASON in CHRIST JESUS.
Let Gilead rejoice with the Gentle—the Lord make me a fisher of men.
For I bless God in all gums and balsams and every thing that ministers relief to the sick.
Let Zelophehad rejoice with Ascalabotes who casteth not his coat till a new one is prepared for him.
For the Sun's at work to make me a garment and the Moon is at work for my wife.
Let Mahlah rejoice with Pellos who is a tall bird and stately.
For tall and stately are against me, but humiliation on humiliation is on my side.
Let Tirzah rejoice with Tylus which is the Cheeslip and food for the chicken.
For I have a providential acquaintance with men who bear the names of animals.
Let Hoglah rejoice with Leontophonos who will kill the lion, if he is eaten.
For I bless God to Mr Lion Mr Cock Mr Cat Mr Talbot Mr Hart Mrs Fysh Mr Grub, and Miss Lamb.
Let Milcah rejoice with the Horned Beetle who will strike a man in the face.
For they throw my horns in my face and reptiles make themselves wings against me.
Let Noah rejoice with Hibris who is from a wild boar and a tame sow.
For I bless God for the immortal soul of Mr Pigg of DOWNHAM in NORFOLK.
Let Abdon rejoice with the Glede who is very voracious and may not himself be eaten.
For I fast this day even the 31st of August N.S. to prepare for the SABBATH of the Lord.

(iii)

For the doubling of flowers is the improvement of the gardners talent.
For the flowers are great blessings.
For the Lord made a Nosegay in the meadow with his disciples and preached upon the lily.
For the angels of God took it out of his hand and carried it to the Height.
For a man cannot have publick spirit, who is void of private benevolence.
For there is no Height in which there are not flowers.
For flowers have great virtues for all the senses.

For the flower glorifies God and the root parries the adversary.
For the flowers have their angels even the words of God's Creation.
For the warp and woof of flowers are worked by perpetual moving spirits.
For flowers are good both for the living and the dead.
For there is a language of flowers.
For there is a sound reasoning upon all flowers.
For elegant phrases are nothing but flowers.
For flowers are peculiarly the poetry of Christ.
For flowers are medicinal.
For flowers are musical in ocular harmony.
For the right names of flowers are yet in heaven. God make gard'ners better nomenclators.
For the Poorman's nosegay is an introduction to a Prince.

(iv)

For the spiritual musick is as follows.
For there is the thunder-stop, which is the voice of God direct.
For the rest of the stops are by their rhimes.
For the trumpet rhimes are sound bound, soar more and the like.
For the Shawm rhimes are lawn fawn moon boon and the like.
For the harp rhimes are sing ring string and the like.
For the cymbal rhimes are bell well toll soul and the like.
For the flute rhimes are tooth youth suit mute and the like.
For the dulcimer rhimes are grace place beat heat and the like.
For the Clarinet rhimes are clean seen and the like.
For the Bassoon rhimes are pass, class and the like. God be gracious to Baumgarden.
For the dulcimer are rather van fan and the like and grace place &c are of the bassoon.
For beat heat, weep peep &c are of the pipe.
For every word has its marrow in the English tongue for order and for delight.
For the dissyllables such as able table &c are the fiddle rhimes.
For all dissyllables and some trissyllables are fiddle rhimes.
For the relations of words are in pairs first.
For the relations of words are sometimes in oppositions.
For the relations of words are according to their distances from the pair.

(v)

For I will consider my Cat Jeoffry.
For he is the servant of the Living God duly and daily serving him.
For at the first glance of the glory of God in the East he worships in his way.
For is this done by wreathing his body seven times round with elegant quickness.
For then he leaps up to catch the musk, which is the blessing of God upon his prayer.

For he rolls upon prank to work it in.
For having done duty and received blessing he begins to consider himself.
For this he performs in ten degrees.
For first he looks upon his fore-paws to see if they are clean.
For secondly he kicks up behind to clear away there.
For thirdly he works it upon stretch with the fore paws extended.
For fourthly he sharpens his paws by wood.
For fifthly he washes himself.
For Sixthly he rolls upon wash.
For Seventhly he fleas himself, that he may not be interrupted upon the beat.
For Eighthly he rubs himself against a post.
For Ninthly he looks up for his instructions.
For Tenthly he goes in quest of food.
For having consider'd God and himself he will consider his neighbour.
For if he meets another cat he will kiss her in kindness.
For when he takes his prey he plays with it to give it chance.
For one mouse in seven escapes by his dallying.
For when his day's work is done his business more properly begins.
For he keeps the Lord's watch in the night against the adversary.
For he counteracts the powers of darkness by his electrical skin and glaring eyes.
For he counteracts the Devil, who is death, by brisking about the life.
For in his morning orisons he loves the sun and the sun loves him.
For he is of the tribe of Tiger.
For the Cherub Cat is a term of the Angel Tiger.
For he has the subtlety and hissing of a serpent, which in goodness he suppresses.
For he will not do destruction, if he is well-fed, neither will he spit without provocation.
For he purrs in thankfulness, when God tells him he's a good Cat.
For he is an instrument for the children to learn benevolence upon.
For every house is incompleat without him and a blessing is lacking in the spirit.
For the Lord commanded Moses concerning the cats at the departure of the Children of Israel from Egypt.
For every family had one cat at least in the bag.
For the English Cats are the best in Europe.
For he is the cleanest in the use of his fore-paws of any quadrupede.
For the dexterity of his defence is an instance of the love of God to him exceedingly.
For he is the quickest to his mark of any creature.
For he is tenacious of his point.
For he is a mixture of gravity and waggery.
For he knows that God is his Saviour.
For there is nothing sweeter than his peace when at rest.
For there is nothing brisker than his life when in motion.

For he is of the Lord's poor and so indeed is he called by benevolence perpetually—Poor Jeoffry! poor Jeoffry! the rat has bit thy throat.
For I bless the name of the Lord Jesus that Jeoffry is better.
For the divine spirit comes about his body to sustain it in compleat cat.
For his tongue is exceeding pure so that it has in purity what it wants in musick.
For he is docile and can learn certain things.
For he can set up with gravity which is patience upon approbation.
For he can fetch and carry, which is patience in employment.
For he can jump over a stick which is patience upon proof positive.
For he can spraggle upon waggle at the word of command.
For he can jump from an eminence into his master's bosom.
For he can catch the cork and toss it again.
For he is hated by the hypocrite and miser.
For the former is affraid of detection.
For the latter refuses the charge.
For he camels his back to bear the first notion of business.
For he is good to think on, if a man would express himself neatly.
For he made a great figure in Egypt for his signal services.
For he killed the Ichneumon-rat very pernicious by land.
For his ears are so acute that they sting again.
For from this proceeds the passing quickness of his attention.
For by stroaking of him I have found out electricity.
For I perceived God's light about him both wax and fire.
For the Electrical fire is the spiritual substance, which God sends from heaven to sustain the bodies both of man and beast.
For God has blessed him in the variety of his movements.
For, though he cannot fly, he is an excellent clamberer.
For his motions upon the face of the earth are more than any other quadrupede.
For he can tread to all the measures upon the musick.
For he can swim for life.
For he can creep.

(Wr. *c.* 1759–61; pub. 1939)

287 from *A Song to David*

O DAVID, highest in the list
Of worthies, on God's ways insist,
The genuine word repeat:
Vain are the documents of men,
And vain the flourish of the pen
That keeps the fool's conceit.

Praise above all—for praise prevails;
Heap up the measure, load the scales,
And good to goodness add:
The gen'rous soul her saviour aids,
But peevish obloquy degrades;
The Lord is great and glad.

For Adoration all the ranks
Of angels yield eternal thanks,
And David in the midst;
With God's good poor, which, last and least
In man's esteem, thou to thy feast,
O blessed bridegroom, bidd'st.

For Adoration seasons change,
And order, truth, and beauty range,
Adjust, attract, and fill:
The grass the polyanthus cheques;
And polished porphyry reflects,
By the descending rill.

Rich almonds colour to the prime
For Adoration; tendrils climb,
And fruit-trees pledge their gems;
And Ivis,[1] with her gorgeous vest,
Builds for her eggs her cunning nest,
And bell-flowers bow their stems.

With vinous syrup cedars spout;
From rocks pure honey gushing out,
For Adoration springs:
All scenes of painting crowd the map
Of nature; to the mermaid's pap
The scalèd infant clings.

The spotted ounce and playsome cubs
Run rustling 'mongst the flow'ring shrubs,
And lizards feed the moss;
For Adoration beasts embark,
While waves upholding halcyon's ark
No longer roar and toss.

[1] Humming-bird.

While Israel sits beneath his fig,
With coral root and amber sprig
  The weaned advent'rer sports;
Where to the palm the jasmin cleaves,
For Adoration 'mongst the leaves
  The gale his peace reports.

Increasing days their reign exalt,
Nor in the pink and mottled vault
  Th' opposing spirits tilt;
And, by the coasting reader spied,
The silverlings and crusions glide
  For Adoration gilt.

For Adoration rip'ning canes
And cocoa's purest milk detains
  The western pilgrim's staff;
Where rain in clasping boughs inclosed,
And vines with oranges disposed,
  Embow'r the social laugh.

Now labour his reward receives,
For Adoration counts his sheaves
  To peace, her bounteous prince;
The nectarine his strong tint imbibes,
And apples of ten thousand tribes,
  And quick peculiar quince.

The wealthy crops of whit'ning rice,
'Mongst thyine woods and groves of spice,
  For Adoration grow;
And, marshalled in the fencèd land,
The peaches and pomegranates stand,
  Where wild carnations blow.

The laurels with the winter strive;
The crocus burnishes alive
  Upon the snow-clad earth:
For Adoration myrtles stay
To keep the garden from dismay,
  And bless the sight from dearth.

crusions] carp   thyine] a tree mentioned in *Revelations*

The pheasant shows his pompous neck;
And ermine, jealous of a speck,
  With fear eludes offence:
The sable, with his glossy pride,
For Adoration is descried,
  Where frosts the wave condense.

The cheerful holly, pensive yew,
And holy thorn, their trim renew;
  The squirrel hoards his nuts:
All creatures batten o'er their stores,
And careful nature all her doors
  For Adoration shuts.

For Adoration, David's psalms
Lift up the heart to deeds of alms;
  And he, who kneels and chants,
Prevails his passions to control,
Finds meat and med'cine to the soul,
  Which for translation pants.

For Adoration, beyond match,
The scholar bullfinch aims to catch
  The soft flute's iv'ry touch;
And, careless on the hazel spray,
The daring redbreast keeps at bay
  The damsel's greedy clutch.

For Adoration, in the skies,
The Lord's philosopher espies
  The Dog, the Ram, and Rose;
The planet's ring, Orion's sword;
Nor is his greatness less adored
  In the vile worm that glows.

For Adoration on the strings[1]
The western breezes work their wings,
  The captive ear to soothe.—
Hark! 'tis a voice—how still, and small—
That makes the cataracts to fall,
  Or bids the sea be smooth!

[1] Aeolian harp.

For Adoration, incense comes
From bezoar, and Arabian gums,
  And on the civet's fur:
But as for prayer, or e'er it faints,
Far better is the breath of saints
  Than galbanum and myrrh.

For Adoration from the down
Of damsons to th' anana's crown,
  God sends to tempt the taste;
And while the luscious zest invites,
The sense, that in the scene delights,
  Commands desire be chaste.

For Adoration, all the paths
Of grace are open, all the baths
  Of purity refresh;
And all the rays of glory beam
To deck the man of God's esteem,
  Who triumphs o'er the flesh.

For Adoration, in the dome
Of Christ the sparrows find an home,
  And on his olives perch:
The swallow also dwells with thee,
O man of God's humility,
  Within his Saviour's Church.

Sweet is the dew that falls betimes,
And drops upon the leafy limes;
  Sweet Hermon's fragrant air:
Sweet is the lily's silver bell,
And sweet the wakeful tapers smell
  That watch for early pray'r.

Sweet the young nurse with love intense,
Which smiles o'er sleeping innocence;
  Sweet when the lost arrive:
Sweet the musician's ardour beats,
While his vague mind's in quest of sweets,
  The choicest flow'rs to hive.

bezoar] a medicinal stone, supposedly formed in the stomachs of animals   galbanum] a Persian gum resin   anana] pineapple

Sweeter, in all the strains of love,
The language of thy turtle dove,
  Paired to thy swelling chord;
Sweeter, with ev'ry grace endued,
The glory of thy gratitude,
  Respired unto the Lord.

Strong is the horse upon his speed;
Strong in pursuit the rapid glede,
  Which makes at once his game:
Strong the tall ostrich on the ground;
Strong through the turbulent profound
  Shoots xiphias[1] to his aim.

Strong is the lion—like a coal
His eyeball—like a bastion's mole
  His chest against the foes:
Strong, the gier-eagle on his sail,
Strong against tide, th' enormous whale
  Emerges as he goes.

But stronger still, in earth and air,
And in the sea, the man of prayer,
  And far beneath the tide;
And in the seat to faith assigned,
Where ask is have, where seek is find,
  Where knock is open wide.

Beauteous the fleet before the gale;
Beauteous the multitudes in mail,
  Ranked arms and crested heads:
Beauteous the garden's umbrage mild,
Walk, water, meditated wild,
  And all the bloomy beds.

Beauteous the moon full on the lawn;
And beauteous, when the veil's withdrawn,
  The virgin to her spouse:
Beauteous the temple, decked and filled,
When to the heav'n of heav'ns they build
  Their heart-directed vows.

[1] The sword-fish.

glede] falcon

Beauteous, yea beauteous more than these,
The shepherd king upon his knees,
  For his momentous trust;
With wish of infinite conceit,
For man, beast, mute, the small and great,
  And prostrate dust to dust.

Precious the bounteous widow's mite;
And precious, for extreme delight,
  The largesse from the churl:
Precious the ruby's blushing blaze,
And alba's blest imperial rays,
  And pure cerulean pearl.

Precious the penitential tear;
And precious is the sigh sincere,
  Acceptable to God:
And precious are the winning flow'rs,
In gladsome Israel's feast of bow'rs,
  Bound on the hallowed sod.

More precious that diviner part
Of David, ev'n the Lord's own heart,
  Great, beautiful, and new:
In all things where it was intent,
In all extremes, in each event,
  Proof—answ'ring true to true.

Glorious the sun in mid-career;
Glorious th' assembled fires appear;
  Glorious the comet's train:
Glorious the trumpet and alarm;
Glorious th' almighty stretched-out arm;
  Glorious th' enraptured main:

Glorious the northern lights astream;
Glorious the song, when God's the theme;
  Glorious the thunder's roar:
Glorious hosanna from the den;
Glorious the catholic amen;
  Glorious the martyr's gore:

alba] pearl

Glorious—more glorious is the crown
Of Him, that brought salvation down
  By meekness, called thy Son;
Thou at stupendous truth believed,
And now the matchless deed's achieved,
  Determined, Dared, and Done.

(1763)

288 *On a Bed of Guernsey Lilies*

(Written in September 1763)

YE beauties! O how great the sum
  Of sweetness that ye bring;
On what a charity ye come
  To bless the latter spring!
How kind the visit that ye pay,
Like strangers on a rainy day,
  When heartiness despaired of guests:
No neighbour's praise your pride alarms,
No rival flow'r surveys your charms,
  Or heightens, or contests!

Lo, through her works gay nature grieves
  How brief she is and frail,
As ever o'er the falling leaves
  Autumnal winds prevail.
Yet still the philosophic mind
Consolatory food can find,
  And hope her anchorage maintain:
We never are deserted quite;
'Tis by succession of delight
  That love supports his reign.

(1764)

289 *Hymn. St. Philip and St. James*

NOW the winds are all composure,
  But the breath upon the bloom,
Blowing sweet o'er each inclosure
  Grateful off'rings of perfume.

Tansy, calaminth and daisies
  On the river's margin thrive;
And accompany the mazes
  Of the stream that leaps alive.

Muse, accordant to the season,
  Give the numbers life and air;
When the sounds and objects reason
  In behalf of praise and pray'r.

All the scenes of nature quicken,
  By the genial spirit fanned;
And the painted beauties thicken
  Coloured by the master's hand.

Earth her vigour repossessing
  As the blasts are held in ward;
Blessing heaped and pressed on blessing
  Yield the measure of the Lord.

Beeches, without order seemly,
  Shade the flow'rs of annual birth,
And the lily smiles supremely,
  Mentioned by the Lord on earth.

Cowslips seize upon the fallow,
  And the cardamine in white,
Where the corn-flow'rs join the mallow,
  Joy and health and thrift unite.

Study sits beneath her arbour,
  By the basin's glossy side;
While the boat from out its harbour
  Exercise and pleasure guide.

Pray'r and praise be mine employment,
  Without grudging or regret;
Lasting life and long enjoyment
  Are not here, and are not yet.

Hark! aloud the blackbird whistles,
  With surrounding fragrance blessed,
And the goldfinch in the thistles
  Makes provision for her nest.

Ev'n the hornet hives his honey,
  Bluecap builds his stately dome,
And the rocks supply the coney
  With a fortress and an home.

But the servants of their Saviour,
  Which with gospel-peace are shod,
Have no bed but what the paviour
  Makes them in the porch of God.

O thou house that hold'st the charter
  Of salvation from on high,
Fraught with prophet, saint, and martyr,
  Born to weep, to starve and die!

Great today thy song and rapture
  In the choir of Christ and Wren,
When two prizes were the capture
  Of the hand that fished for men.

To the man of quick compliance
  Jesus called, and Philip came;
And began to make alliance
  For his master's cause and name.

James, of title most illustrious,
  Brother of the Lord allowed;
In the vineyard how industrious,
  Nor by years nor hardship bowed!

Each accepted in his trial,
  One the Cheerful, one the Just;
Both of love and self-denial,
  Both of everlasting trust.

Living they dispensed salvation,
  Heav'n-endowed with grace and pow'r;
And they died in imitation
  Of their Saviour's final hour:

Who, for cruel traitors pleading,
  Triumphed, in his parting breath,
O'er all miracles preceding
  His inestimable death.

(1765)

290 *Hymn. The Nativity of Our Lord and Saviour Jesus Christ*

WHERE is this stupendous stranger,
  Swains of Solyma, advise;
Lead me to my Master's manger,
  Show me where my Saviour lies.

O most Mighty! O most Holy!
  Far beyond the seraph's thought,
Art thou then so mean and lowly
  As unheeded prophets taught?

O the magnitude of meekness!
  Worth from worth immortal sprung;
O the strength of infant weakness,
  If eternal is so young!

If so young and thus eternal,
  Michael tune the shepherd's reed,
Where the scenes are ever vernal,
  And the loves be love indeed!

See the God blasphemed and doubted
  In the schools of Greece and Rome;
See the pow'rs of darkness routed,
  Taken at their utmost gloom.

Nature's decorations glisten
  Far above their usual trim;
Birds on box and laurels listen,
  As so near the cherubs hymn.

Boreas now no longer winters
  On the desolated coast;
Oaks no more are riv'n in splinters
  By the whirlwind and his host.

Spinks and ouzels sing sublimely,
  'We too have a Saviour born';
Whiter blossoms burst untimely
  On the blest Mosaic thorn.

God all-bounteous, all-creative,
  Whom no ills from good dissuade,
Is incarnate, and a native
  Of the very world he made.

(1765)

291 *Gratitude*

I UPON the first creation
  Clapped my wings with loud applause,
Cherub of the highest station,
  Praising, blessing, without pause.

I in Eden's bloomy bowers
  Was the heav'nly gard'ner's pride,
Sweet of sweets, and flow'r of flowers,
  With the scented tinctures dyed.

Hear, ye little children, hear me,
  I am God's delightful voice;
They who sweetly still revere me,
  Still shall make the wisest choice.

Hear me not like Adam trembling,
  When I walked in Eden's grove;
And the host of heav'n assembling,
  From the spot the traitor drove.

Hear me rather as the lover
  Of mankind, restored and free;
By the word ye shall recover
  More than that ye lost by Me.

I'm the Phoenix of the singers
  That in upper Eden dwell;
Hearing me Euphrates lingers,
  As my wondrous tale I tell.

'Tis the story of the Graces,
  Mercies without end or sum;
And the sketches and the traces
  Of ten thousand more to come.

List, my children, list within you,
  Dread not ye the tempter's rod;
Christ our gratitude shall win you,
  Weaned from earth, and led to God.

(1770)

292 *For Saturday*

NOW'S the time for mirth and play,
Saturday's an holiday;
Praise to heav'n unceasing yield,
I've found a lark's nest in the field.

A lark's nest, then your playmate begs
You'd spare herself and speckled eggs;
Soon she shall ascend and sing
Your praises to th' eternal King.

(1770)

293 *Pray Remember the Poor*

I JUST came by the prison door,
I gave a penny to the poor:
Papa did this good act approve,
And poor Mamma cried out for love.

Whene'er the poor comes to my gate,
Relief I will communicate;
And tell my sire his sons shall be
As charitably great as he.

(1770)

HENRY BROOKE

1703?–1783

294 from *Jack the Giant Queller. An Antique History*

(i) *Air*

FOR often my mammy has told,
  And sure she is wond'rous wise,
In cities that all you behold
  Is a fair, but a faithless, disguise:
That the modes of a court education
  Are train-pits and traitors to youth;
And the only fine language in fashion
  A tongue that is foreign to truth.

Where honour is barely an oath,
  Where knaves are with noblemen classed,
Where nature's a stranger to both,
  And love an old tale of times past;
Where laughter no pleasure dispenses,
  Where smiles are the envoys of art,
Where joy lightly swims on the senses,
  But never can enter the heart.

Where hopes and kind hugs are trepanners,
  Where virtue's divorced from success,
Where cringing goes current for manners,
  And worth is no deeper than dress;
Where favour creeps lamely on crutches,
  Where friendship is nothing but face,
And the title of Duke or of Duchess
  Is all that entitles to grace.

(ii) *Air*

  Arise, arise, arise!
  Each shape, and sort, and size
  Of honesty, where ye lie
  Unheeded, on dank or dry,
  From cottages, sheds and steads, to court,
  My brothers of worth and want, resort;
Arise to labour, arise to play,
For Virtue dawns, a newborn day.

  To court, to court repair,
  Though destitute, poor and bare,
  And yet unskilled in aught
  That Euclid or Machiavel taught;
  By naked probity, you acquire
  A garb beyond the silk of Tyre;
And every talent and every art
Is furnished in an upright heart.

  Let Jollity e'en devour
  His interval of an hour,
  Yet pity his transient roar
  For list—and he laughs no more.
  The purest pleasures that Guilt can bring
  Are like the tickling of a sting;
The tickling leaves no sweet behind,
The sting remains and stabs the mind.

But Virtue in the breast
Composes her halcyon nest,
And soothes and smooths each storm
That would the fair seat deform,
Herself most frolic and sweetly free,
To cordial jollity, cordial glee.
The fountain of all that's blessed and bright,
Of orient pleasure, of orient light!

And from this mental dawn,
O'er village, and lake, and lawn,
New radiance shall expand
To lighten a dusky land,
And Truth, from this approving stage,
Shall beam through every act and age;
And Truth, from this approving stage,
Shall beam through every act and age.

(1749)

ANONYMOUS ('C.G.H.')

295 *The Power of Innocence*

A NORTHERN pair, we waive the name,
Rich, young and not unknown to fame,
When first the nuptial state they tried,
With poets' gods in pleasure vied.
New to the mighty charm, they feel
A joy that all their looks reveal.
We love whate'er has pow'r to please,
So Nature's ancient law decrees;
And thus the pair, while each had pow'r
To bless the fond, sequestered hour,
With mutual love enraptured glow,
And love in kind complaisance show.
But when familiar charms no more
Inspire the bliss they gave before,
Each less delighting, less was loved:
Now this, now that was disapproved;
Some trifling fault, which love concealed,
Indiff'rence ev'ry day revealed.

Complaisance flies, neglect succeeds,
Neglect disdain and hatred breeds.
The wish to please forsakes the breast,
The wish to rule has each possessed.
Perpetual war, that wish to gain,
They wage, alas! but wage in vain.
Now hope of conquest swells the heart
No more—at length content to part.
The rural seat, that sylvan shade,
Where first the nuptial vows were paid,
That seat attests the dire intent,
And hears the parting settlement.
This house, these fields my lady's own,
Sir John must ride to town alone.
The chariot waits—they bid adieu;
But still the chariot was in view.
Tom tires with waiting long in doubt,
And lights a pipe—and smokes it out—
Mysterious! wherefore this delay?
The sequel shall the cause display.
One lovely girl the lady bore,
Dear pledge of joys she tastes no more;
The father's, mother's darling, she
Now lisped and prattled at their knee.
Sir John, now rising to depart,
Turned to the darling of his heart,
And cried, with ardour in his eye,
'Come, Betsey, bid mamma goodbye.'
The lady, trembling, answered, 'No—
Go, kiss papa, my Betsey, go.
Sir John, the child shall live with me.'—
'The child herself shall choose,' said he.
Poor Betsey looked at each by turns,
And each the starting tear discerns.
My lady asks, with doubt and fear,
'Will you not live with me, my dear?'
'Yes,' half-resolved, replied the child,
And, half-suppressed her tears, she smiled.
'Come, Betsey,' cried Sir John, 'you'll go
And live with dear papa, I know.'
'Yes,' Betsey cried. The lady then
Addressed the wond'ring child again:
'The time to live with both is o'er;
This day we part to meet no more:
Choose then'—here grief o'erflowed her breast,
And tears broke out, too long suppressed.

The child, who tears and chiding joined,
Supposed papa displeased, unkind;
And tried, with all her little skill,
To soothe his oft-relenting will.
'Do,' cried the lisper, 'Pappy! do
Love dear mamma!—Mamma loves you!'
Subdued the force of manly pride,
No more his looks his heart belied;
The tender transport forced its way,
They both confessed each other's sway;
And prompted by the social smart,
Breast rushed to breast, and heart to heart.
Each clasp their Betsey o'er and o'er,
And Tom drove empty from the door.

Ye that have passions for a tear,
Give nature vent, and drop it here!

(1749)

CATHERINE JEMMAT

fl. 1750–1771

296 *The Rural Lass*

My father and mother (what ails 'em?)
Pretend I'm too young to be wed;
They expect, but in troth I shall fail 'em,
That I finish my chairs and my bed.

Provided our minds are but cheery,
Wooden chairs wonnot argue a glove,
Any bed will hold me and my deary,
The main chance in wedlock is love.

My father, when asked if he'd lend us
An horse to the parson to ride,
In a wheel-barrow offered to send us,
And John for the footman beside.

Would we never had asked him, for, whip it!
To the church though two miles and a half,
Twice as far 'twere a pleasure to trip it;
But then how the people would laugh!

The neighbours are nettled most sadly,
'Was e'er such a forward bold thing!
Sure never girl acted so madly!'
Through the parish these backbitings ring.

Yet I will be married tomorrow,
And charming young Harry's the man;
My brother's blind nag we can borrow,
And he may prevent us that can.

Not waiting for parents' consenting,
My brother took Nell of the Green,
Yet both, far enough from repenting,
Now live like a king and a queen.

Pray when will your gay things of London
Produce such a strapper as Nell's?
There wives by their husbands are undone,
As Saturday's newspaper tells.

Poll Barnley said, over and over,
I soon should be left in the lurch;
For Harry, she knows, was a rover,
And never would venture to church.

And I know the sorrows that wound her;
He courted her once, he confessed:
With another too great when he found her,
He bid her take him she liked best.

But all that are like her, or would be,
May learn from my Harry and me,
If maids would be maids while they should be,
How faithful their sweethearts would be.

My mother says clothing and feeding
Will soon make me sick of a brat:
But though I prove sick in my breeding,
I care not a farthing for that.

For if I'm not hugely mistaken,
We can live by the sweat of our brow,
Stick a hog, once a year, for fat bacon,
And all the year round keep a cow.

I value no dainties a button,
  Coarse food will our stomachs allay;
If we cannot get veal, beef and mutton,
  A chine and a pudding we may.

A fig for your richest brocading;
  In linsey there's nothing that's base;
Your finery soon sets a-fading,
  My dowlas will last beyond lace.

I envy not wealth to the miser,
  Nor would I be plagued with his store:
To eat all and wear all is wiser;
  Enough must be better than more.

So nothing shall tempt me from Harry,
  His heart is as true as the sun:
Eve with Adam was ordered to marry;
  This world it should end as begun.

(1750)

ANONYMOUS

297

A Song

My head on moss reclining,
  Hard by a murm'ring stream,
My sleep, more soft than rhyming,
  Dissolved into a dream.
The willows that surrounded
  Methought began to talk;
And men by love confounded
  Like Hamlet's ghost did stalk.

'Friends,' say the mournful willows,
  'Should you our garlands wear,
And thus forsake your pillows,
  Nor shun the fatal snare,
You soon would be as we are,
  Fast-rooted on the shore;
For we were men as you are,
  But shall be so no more.'

Then ev'ry silent lover
  His drooping head did rear,
Say'ng, 'What we sought to smother,
  To you we will declare;
We each have been a lover,
  And wore love's fatal chain;
With awe each strove to move her,
  Who slew him with disdain.'

'But since such low submission
  Our fair ones could not move,
To hide our sad condition
  From mortals we have strove.'
Then little Cupid, laughing,
  Dropped from an azure cloud,
And while his wings were chaffing,
  He settled in the crowd.

And told them that his mother
  Such lovers would despise:
'Then seek not love to smother,
  But seize each man his prize;
And then caress and press her,
  Nor give her room to fly,
But in soft murmurs tell her,
  'Twere happy so to die.

'And by the lips' injection
  Drive love into her brain,
And then for his protection,
  Go purchase Hymen's chain.'
I started from my pillow
  Of moss most soft and green,
And nothing but the willow
  Remained there to be seen.

(1750)

PHILIP DODDRIDGE

1702–1751

298 *Meditations on the Sepulchre in the Garden*

John 19: 41

THE sepulchres, how thick they stand
Through all the road on either hand!
And burst upon the startling sight
In ev'ry garden of delight!

Thither the winding alleys tend;
There all the flow'ry borders end;
And forms, that charmed the eyes before,
Fragrance and music are no more.

Deep in that damp and silent cell
My fathers and my brethren dwell;
Beneath its broad and gloomy shade
My kindred and my friends are laid.

But, while I tread the solemn way,
My faith that Saviour would survey,
Who deigned to sojourn in the tomb,
And left behind a rich perfume.

My thoughts with ecstasy unknown,
While from his grave they view his throne,
Through mine own sepulchre can see
A paradise reserved for me.

(Wr. by 1751; pub. 1755)

ANONYMOUS

299 *Strip Me Naked, or Royal Gin for Ever. A Picture*

I MUST, I will have gin!—that skillet take,
Pawn it.—No more I'll roast, or boil or bake.
This juice immortal will each want supply;
Starve on, ye brats! so I but bung my eye.

299 bung my eye] drink my dram

Starve? No! This gin ev'n mother's milk excels,
Paints the pale cheeks, and hunger's darts repels.
The skillet's pawned already? Take this cap;
Round my bare head I'll yon brown paper wrap.
Ha! half my petticoat was torn away
By dogs (I fancy) as I maudlin lay.
How the wind whistles through each broken pane!
Through the wide-yawning roof how pours the rain!
My bedstead's cracked; the table goes hip-hop.—
But see! the gin! Come, come, thou cordial drop!
Thou sovereign balsam to my longing heart!
Thou husband, children, all! We must not part!
Drinks Delicious! O! Down the red lane it goes;
Now I'm a queen, and trample on my woes.
Inspired by gin, I'm ready for the road;
Could shoot my man, or fire the King's abode.
Ha! my brain's cracked.—The room turns round and round;
Down drop the platters, pans: I'm on the ground.
My tattered gown slips from me.—What care I?
I was born naked, and I'll naked die.

(1751)

SOAME JENYNS

1704–1787

300 *The Modern Fine Lady*

SKILLED in each art that can adorn the fair,
The sprightly dance, the soft Italian air,
The toss of quality and high-bred fleer,
Now Lady Harriot reached her fifteenth year.
Winged with diversions all her moments flew,
Each, as it passed, presenting something new;
Breakfasts and auctions wear the morn away,
Each evening gives an opera, or a play;
Then brag's eternal joys all night remain,
And kindly usher in the morn again.
For love no time has she, or inclination,
Yet must coquet it for the sake of fashion;
For this she listens to each fop that's near,
Th' embroidered colonel flatters with a sneer,

300 brag] a card game

And the cropped ensign nuzzles in her ear.
But with most warmth her dress and airs inspire
Th' ambitious bosom of the landed squire,
Who fain would quit plump Dolly's softer charms
For withered lean right honourable arms;
He bows with reverence at her sacred shrine,
And treats her as if sprung from race divine,
Which she returns with insolence and scorn,
Nor deigns to smile on a plebeian born.
  Ere long by friends, by cards and lovers crossed,
Her fortune, health and reputation lost;
Her money gone, yet not a tradesman paid,
Her fame, yet she still damned to be a maid,
Her spirits sink, her nerves are so unstrung,
She weeps, if but a handsome thief is hung:
By mercers, lacemen, mantua-makers pressed,
But most for ready cash for play distressed,
Where can she turn?—the squire must all repair,
She condescends to listen to his pray'r,
And marries him at length in mere despair.
  But soon th' endearments of a husband cloy,
Her soul, her frame incapable of joy:
She feels no transports in the bridal bed,
Of which so oft sh' has heard, so much has read;
Then vexed that she should be condemned alone
To seek in vain this philosophic stone,
To abler tutors she resolves t' apply,
A prostitute from curiosity.
Hence men of ev'ry sort and ev'ry size,
Impatient for heav'n's cordial drop, she tries;
The fribbling beau, the rough unwieldy clown,
The ruddy templar newly on the town,
Th' Hibernian captain of gigantic make,
The brimful parson, and th' exhausted rake.
  But still malignant Fate her wish denies,
Cards yield superior joys, to cards she flies;
All night from rout to rout her chairmen run,
Again she plays, and is again undone.
  Behold her now in Ruin's frightful jaws!
Bonds, judgements, executions ope their paws;
Seize jewels, furniture and plate, nor spare
The gilded chariot, or the tasseled chair;
For lonely seat she's forced to quit the town,
And Tubbs conveys the wretched exile down.

rout] an evening assembly

Now rumbling o'er the stones of Tyburn-road,
Ne'er pressed with a more grieved or guilty load,
She bids adieu to all the well-known streets,
And envies ev'ry cinder-wench she meets.
And now the dreaded country first appears:
With sighs unfeigned the dying noise she hears
Of distant coaches fainter by degrees,
Then starts, and trembles at the sight of trees.
Silent and sullen, like some captive queen,
She's drawn along, unwilling to be seen,
Until at length appears the ruined hall,
Within the grass-green moat and ivied wall,
The doleful prison where for ever she,
But not, alas! her griefs, must buried be.
Her coach the curate and the tradesmen meet,
Great-coated tenants her arrival greet,
And boys with stubble bonfires light the street,
While bells her ears with tongues discordant grate,
Types of the nuptial ties they celebrate:
But no rejoicings can unbend her brow,
Nor deigns she to return one awkward bow,
But bounces in, disdaining once to speak,
And wipes the trickling tear from off her cheek.
Now see her in the sad decline of life,
A peevish mistress, and a sulky wife;
Her nerves unbraced, her faded cheek grown pale
With many a real, and many a fancied ail;
Of cards, admirers, equipage bereft,
Her insolence and title only left;
Severely humbled to her one-horse chair,
And the low pastimes of a country fair:
Too wretched to endure one lonely day,
Too proud one friendly visit to repay,
Too indolent to read, too criminal to pray.
At length half-dead, half-mad, and quite confined,
Shunning, and shunned by, all of human kind,
Ev'n robbed of the last comfort of her life,
Insulting the poor curate's callous wife,
Pride, disappointed pride, now stops her breath,
And with true scorpion rage she stings herself to death.

(1751)

301 *The Temple of Venus*

In her own isle's remotest grove
  Stands Venus' lovely shrine,
Sacred to beauty, joy and love,
  And built by hands divine.

The polished structure, fair and bright
  As her own ivory skin,
Without is alabaster white,
  And ruby all within.

Above, a cupola charms the view
  White as unsullied snow;
Two columns of the same fair hue
  Support the dome below.

Its walls a trickling fountain laves,
  In which such virtue reigns
That, bathed in its balsamic waves,
  No lover feels his pains.

Before th' unfolding gates there spreads
  A fragrant spicy grove,
That with its curling branches shades
  The labyrinths of love.

Bright Beauty there her captives holds,
  Who kiss their easy chains,
And in the softest, closest folds,
  Her willing slaves detains.

Would'st thou, who ne'er these seas hast tried,
  Find where this island lies,
Let pilot Love the rudder guide,
  And steer by Chloe's eyes.

(1752)

JOHN BROWN

1715–1766

302 [*A Rhapsody, Written at the Lakes in Westmorland*]

NOW sunk the sun, now twilight sunk, and Night
Rode in her zenith; nor a passing breeze
Sighed to the groves, which in the midnight air
Stood motionless, and in the peaceful floods
Inverted hung. For now the billow slept
Along the shore, nor heaved the deep, but spread
A shining mirror to the moon's pale orb,
Which, dim and waning, o'er the shadowy clifts,
The solemn woods and spiry mountain-tops,
Her glimmering faintness threw. Now every eye,
Oppressed with toil, was drowned in deep repose;
Save that the unseen shepherd in his watch,
Propped on his crook, stood list'ning by the fold,
And gazed the starry vault and pendant moon;
Nor voice nor sound broke on the deep serene,
But the soft murmur of swift-gushing rills,
Forth-issuing from the mountain's distant steep
(Unheard till now, and now scarce heard), proclaimed
All things at rest, and imaged the still voice
Of Quiet whispering to the ear of Night.

(Wr. 1753?; pub. 1776)

ANONYMOUS

303 *Tree-Topped Hill*

ON tree-topped hill, on tufted green
While yet Aurora's vest is seen,
Before the sun has left the sea,
Let the fresh morning breathe on me.

To furze-blown heath, or pasture mead,
Do thou my happy footsteps lead;
Then show me to the pleasing stream,
Of which at night so oft I dream.

At noon the mazy wood I'll tread,
  With autumn leaves and dry moss spread;
And cooling fruits for thee prepare,
  For sure I think thou wilt be there.

Till birds begin their evening song,
  With thee the time seems never long;
O let us speak our love that's past,
  And count how long it has to last.

I'll say eternally, and thou
  Shall only look as kind as now;
I ask no more, for that affords
  What is not in the force of words.

(1753)

ANONYMOUS

304

Juggy's Christening

WHEN Sol had loosed his weary teams,
  And turned his steeds a-grazing,
Ten fathom deep in Neptune's streams
  His Thetis lay embracing;
The stars tripped in the firmament
  Like milkmaids on a May-day,
Or country lasses a-mumming sent,
  Or schoolboys on a play-day.

When apace grew on the grey-eyed morn,
  The herds in fields were lowing,
And 'mongst the poultry in the barn
  The ploughman's cock was crowing;
When Roger, dreaming of golden joys,
  Was waked by a revel rout, sir,
And Cicely told him he needs must rise,
  For his Juggy was crying out, sir.

Not half so merry the cups go round
  At the tapping a good ale-firkin,
As Roger when his hosen and shoon he'd found,
  And buttoned his leathern jerkin;

Grey mare he saddled with wond'rous speed,
  With pillion on buttock right, sir,
And for an old midwife away he rode,
  To bring the young brat to light, sir.

'O good mother, I pray get up,
  The fruit of my labour's now come,
And there lies struggling in Juggy's womb,
  And cannot get out till you come';
'I'll help it,' cries the old hag, 'ne'er doubt
  Thy Juggy shall do well again, boy,
For I'se warrant thee I can get the kid out
  As well as thou got'st in, boy.'

The mare now mounting very soon,
  No whip nor spur was wanting,
And soon as the old wife enters the room,
  'Whew!' cries out the bantling.
A female chit so small was born,
  You might have put it into a flagon,
And it must be christ'ned that very morn,
  For fear it should die a pagan.

There was Roger and Doll, and constant Kate,
  Gossips to this great christ'ning,
And while the good wives did merrily prate,
  Juggy in bed lay list'ning;
Some talked of this, some talked of that,
  Of chat they were not sparing:
Some said it was so small a brat
  'Twas hardly worth the rearing.

But Roger he strutted about the hall,
  As great as the Prince of Condi.
He cried, 'Although her parts are small,
  They may be bigger one day:
What though her thighs and legs be close,
  And as little as any spider,
You need not fear but in sixteen year
  She'll lay them a great deal wider.

'For then she'll be a woman grown,
  I'se hauld five pound in money,
And will have a little one of her own,
  As well as Juggy, my honey;

O these will be joyful days to see,
  And I'll strive for to advance her,
That Juggy may a granny be,
  Then I shall be a grandsire.'

The nappy ale went swiftly round,
  As brown as any berry,
With which the good wives being crowned,
  They all were wond'rous merry;
Then Roger he tipped it over the thumb
  To every honest neighbour,
Saying, 'A twelvemonth hence, pray come
  Once more to my Juggy's labour.'

(1753)

ANONYMOUS

305 *Autumn*

I AT my window sit, and see
Autumn his russet fingers lay
  On ev'ry leaf of ev'ry tree.
I call, but Summer will not stay.

  She flies, the boasting goddess flies,
And, pointing where th' espaliers shoot,
  'Deserve my parting gift,' she cries,
'I take the leaves but not the fruit.'

  Let me the parting gift improve,
And emulate the just reply,
  As life's short seasons swift remove,
Ere fixed in Winter's frost I lie.

  Health, beauty, vigour now decline,
The pride of Summer's splendid day,
  Leaves, which the stem must now resign,
The mournful prelude of decay.

  But let fair Virtue's fruit remain,
Though Summer with my leaves be fled;
  Then, not despised, I'll not complain,
But cherish Autumn in her stead.

(1753)

ANONYMOUS

306 *A Description of the Spring in London*

Now new-vamped silks the mercer's window shows,
And his spruce 'prentice wears his Sunday clothes;
His annual suit with nicest taste renewed,
The reigning cut and colour still pursued.
  The barrow now, with oranges a score,
Driv'n by at once a gamester and a whore,
No longer gulls the stripling of his pence,
Who learns that poverty is nurse to sense.
Much-injured trader whom the law pursues,
The law which winked and beckoned to the Jews,
Why should the beadle drive thee from the street?
To sell is always a pretence to cheat.
  'Large stewing-oysters!', in a deep'ning groan,
No more resounds, nor 'Mussels!' shriller tone;
Sev'n days to labour now is held no crime,
And Moll 'New mack'rel!' screams in sermon-time.
  In ruddy bunches radishes are spread,
And Nan with choice-picked salad loads her head.
  Now, in the suburb window, Christmas green,
The bays and holly are no longer seen,
But sprigs of garden-mint in vials grow,
And gathered laylocks perish as they blow.
  The truant schoolboy now at eve we meet,
Fatigued and sweating through the crowded street,
His shoes embrowned at once with dust and clay,
With whitethorn loaded, which he takes for May:
Round his flapped hat in rings the cowslips twine,
Or in cleft osiers form a golden line.
  On milk-pail reared the borrowed salvers glare,
Topped with a tankard which two porters bear;
Reeking, they slowly toil o'er rugged stones,
And joyless beldams dance with aching bones.
More blithe the powdered, tie-wigged sons of soot
Trip to their shovel with a shoeless foot.
In gay Vauxhall now saunter beaux and belles,
And happier cits resort to Sadler's Wells.

(1754)

laylocks] lilacs

JOHN DALTON

1709–1763

307 from *A Descriptive Poem, Addressed to Two Ladies, at their Return from Viewing the Mines, near Whitehaven*

AGAPE the sooty collier stands,
His axe suspended in his hands,
His Ethiopian teeth the while
'Grin horrible a ghastly smile,'
To see two goddesses so fair
Descend to him from fields of air.
Not greater wonder seized th' abode
Of gloomy Dis, infernal god,
With pity when th' Orphean lyre
Did ev'ry iron heart inspire,
Soothed tortured ghosts with heavenly strains,
And respited eternal pains.
But on you move through ways less steep
To loftier chambers of the deep,
Whose jetty pillars seem to groan
Beneath a ponderous roof of stone.
Then with increasing wonder gaze
The dark inextricable maze,
Where cavern crossing cavern meets
(City of subterraneous streets!),
Where in a triple storey end
Mines that o'er mines by flights ascend.
But who in order can relate
What terrors still your steps await?
How issuing from the sulphurous coal
Thick Acherontic rivers roll?
How in close centre of these mines,
Where orient morning never shines,
Nor the winged zephyrs e'er resort,
Infernal Darkness holds her court?
How, breathless, with faint pace and slow,
Through her grim sultry realm you go,
Till purer rising gales dispense
Their cordials to the sick'ning sense?
Your progress next the wondering muse
Through narrow galleries pursues;

Where earth, the miner's way to close,
Did once the massy rock oppose.
In vain: his daring axe he heaves,
Towards the black vein a passage cleaves:
Dissevered by the nitrous blast,
The stubborn barrier bursts at last.
Thus, urged by Hunger's clamorous call,
Incessant Labour conquers all.
In spacious rooms once more you tread,
Whose roofs with figures quaint o'erspread
Wild nature paints with various dyes,
With such as tinge the evening skies.
A different scene to this succeeds:
The dreary road abruptly leads
Down to the cold and humid caves,
Where hissing fall the turbid waves.
Resounding deep through glimmering shades
The clank of chains your ears invades.
Through pits profound from distant day
Scarce travels down light's languid ray.
High on huge axis heaved above,
See balanced beams unwearied move!
While, pent within the iron womb
Of boiling cauldrons, pants for room
Expanded Steam, and shrinks or swells,
As cold restrains or heat impels;
And, ready for the vacant space,
Incumbent Air resumes his place,
Depressing with stupendous force
Whate'er resists his downward course.
Pumps moved by rods from ponderous beams
Arrest the unsuspecting streams,
Which soon a sluggish pool would lie;
Then spout them foaming to the sky.
Sagacious Savery! Taught by thee
Discordant elements agree,
Fire, water, air, heat, cold unite,
And listed in one service fight;
Pure streams to thirsty cities send,
Or deepest mines from floods defend.
Man's richest gift thy work will shine;
Rome's aqueducts were poor to thine!
At last the long descent is o'er;
Above your heads the billows roar.
High o'er your heads they roar in vain:
Not all the surges of the main

The dark recess can e'er disclose,
Rocks heaped on rocks th' attempt oppose;
Thrice Dover's cliff from you the tides
With interposing roof divides!
  From such abyss restored to light,
Invade no more the realms of night.
For heroines it may well suffice
Once to have left these azure skies.
Heroes themselves, in days of yore,
Bold as they were, achieved no more.
Without a dread descent you may
The mines in their effects survey,
And with an easy eye look down
On that fair port and happy town.
  Where late, along the naked strand,
The fisher's cot did lonely stand,
And his poor bark unsheltered lay,
Of every swelling surge the prey,
Now lofty piers their arms extend,
And with their strong embraces bend
Round crowded fleets, which safe defy
All storms that rend the wintry sky,
And bulwarks beyond bulwarks chain
The fury of the roaring main.
The peopled vale fair dwellings fill,
And lengthening streets ascend the hill;
Where Industry, intent to thrive,
Brings all her honey to the hive,
Religion strikes with reverent awe,
Example works th' effect of law,
And Plenty's flowing cup we see
Untainted yet by Luxury.
  These are the glories of the mine!
Creative Commerce, these are thine!

(1755)

ROBERT LLOYD

1733–1764

308 *The Cit's Country Box*

THE wealthy Cit, grown old in trade,
Now wishes for the rural shade,
And buckles to his one-horse chair
Old Dobbin or the foundered mare;
While, wedged in closely by his side,
Sits Madam, his unwieldy bride,
With Jacky on a stool before 'em,
And out they jog in due decorum.
Scarce past the turnpike half a mile,
How all the country seems to smile!
And as they slowly jog together,
The Cit commends the road and weather;
While Madam dotes upon the trees,
And longs for ev'ry house she sees,
Admires its views, its situation,
And thus she opens her oration:
'What signify the loads of wealth,
Without that richest jewel, health?
Excuse the fondness of a wife,
Who dotes upon your precious life!
Such easeless toil, such constant care,
Is more than human strength can bear.
One may observe it in your face—
Indeed, my dear, you break apace:
And nothing can your health repair,
But exercise and country air.
Sir Traffic has a house, you know,
About a mile from Cheney Row:
He's a *good* man, indeed 'tis true,
But not so *warm*, my dear, as you:
And folks are always apt to sneer—
One would not be out-done, my dear!'
Sir Traffic's name so well applied
Awaked his brother-merchant's pride;
And Thrifty, who had all his life
Paid utmost deference to his wife,
Confessed her arguments had reason,
And by th' approaching summer season,

Cit] citizen, tradesman

Draws a few hundreds from the stocks,
And purchases his country box.
  Some three or four mile out of town
(An hour's ride will bring you down),
He fixes on his choice abode,
Not half a furlong from the road:
And so convenient does it lay,
The stages pass it ev'ry day:
And then so snug, so mighty pretty,
To have an house so near the city!
Take but your places at the Boar,
You're set down at the very door.
  Well then, suppose them fixed at last,
White-washing, painting, scrubbing past,
Hugging themselves in ease and clover,
With all the fuss of moving over;
Lo, a new heap of whims are bred,
And wanton in my lady's head:
  'Well, to be sure, it must be owned
It is a charming spot of ground;
So sweet a distance for a ride,
And all about so *countrified!*
'Twould come to but a trifling price
To make it quite a paradise;
I cannot bear those nasty rails,
Those ugly, broken, mouldy pales:
Suppose, my dear, instead of these,
We build a railing, all Chinese.
Although one hates to be exposed,
'Tis dismal to be thus inclosed;
One hardly any object sees—
I wish you'd fell those odious trees.
Objects continual passing by
Were something to amuse the eye,
But to be pent within the walls—
One might as well be at St. Paul's.
Our house beholders would adore,
Was there a level lawn before,
Nothing its views to incommode,
But quite laid open to the road;
While ev'ry trav'ler in amaze
Should on our little mansion gaze,
And, pointing to the choice retreat,
Cry, "That's Sir Thrifty's country seat."'
  No doubt her arguments prevail,
For Madam's *taste* can never fail.

Blest age! when all men may procure
The title of a connoisseur;
When noble and ignoble herd
Are governed by a single word;
Though, like the royal German dames,
It bears an hundred Christian names,
As Genius, Fancy, Judgement, Goût,
Whim, Caprice, Je-ne-sais-quoi, Virtù:
Which appellations all describe
Taste, and the modern *tasteful* tribe.
Now bricklay'rs, carpenters and joiners,
With Chinese artists and designers,
Produce their schemes of alteration,
To work this wond'rous reformation.
The useful dome, which secret stood
Embosomed in the yew-tree's wood,
The trav'ler with amazement sees
A temple, Gothic, or Chinese,
With many a bell and tawdry rag on,
And crested with a sprawling dragon;
A wooden arch is bent astride
A ditch of water, four foot wide,
With angles, curves and zigzag lines,
From Halfpenny's exact designs.
In front, a level lawn is seen,
Without a shrub upon the green,
Where Taste would want its first great law,
But for the skulking, sly *ha-ha*,
By whose miraculous assistance,
You gain a prospect two fields' distance.
And now from Hyde-Park Corner come
The gods of Athens and of Rome.
Here squabby Cupids take their places,
With Venus and the clumsy Graces:
Apollo there, with aim so clever,
Stretches his leaden bow for ever;
And there, without the pow'r to fly,
Stands fixed a tip-toe Mercury.
The villa thus completely graced,
All own that Thrifty has a Taste;
And Madam's female friends and cousins,
With common-council-men by dozens,
Flock ev'ry Sunday to the seat,
To stare about them, and to eat.

(1756)

common-council-men] London town-councillors

309 from *Shakespeare, an Epistle to David Garrick, Esq.*

[*True Genius*]

SHALL ancient worth, or ancient fame,
Preclude the moderns from their claim?
Must they be blockheads, dolts and fools,
Who write not up to Grecian rules?
Who tread in buskins or in socks,
Must they be damned as heterodox,
Nor merit of good works prevail,
Except within the classic pale?
'Tis stuff that bears the name of knowledge,
Not current half a mile from college;
Where half their lectures yield no more
(Besure I speak of times of yore)
Than just a niggard light, to mark
How much we all are in the dark.
As rushlights, in a spacious room,
Just burn enough to form a gloom.
  When Shakespeare leads the mind a dance
From France to England, hence to France,
Talk not to me of time and place;
I own I'm happy in the chase.
Whether the drama's here or there,
'Tis nature, Shakespeare, everywhere.
The poet's fancy can create,
Contract, enlarge, annihilate,
Bring past and present close together,
In spite of distance, seas, or weather;
And shut up in a single action,
What cost whole years in its transaction.
So, ladies at a play, or rout,
Can flirt the universe about,
Whose geographical account
Is drawn and pictured on the mount.
Yet, when they please, contract the plan,
And shut the world up in a fan.
  True Genius, like Armida's wand,
Can raise the spring from barren land.
While all the art of imitation
Is pilf'ring from the first creation;
Transplanting flowers, with useless toil,
Which wither in a foreign soil.

As conscience often sets us right
By its interior active light,
Without th' assistance of the laws
To combat in the moral cause;
So Genius, of itself discerning,
Without the mystic rules of learning,
Can, from its present intuition,
Strike at the truth of composition.

(1760)

310 from *A Familiar Epistle to J.B. Esq.*

[*Public Schools*]

A PUBLIC school's the place alone
Where talents may be duly known.
It has, no doubt, its imperfections,
But then, such friendships! such connections!
The parent, who has formed his plan,
And in his child considered man,
What is his grand and golden rule?
'Make your connections, child, at school.
Mix with your equals, fly inferiors,
But follow closely your superiors,
On them your ev'ry hope depends.
Be prudent, Tom, get useful friends;
And therefore like a spider wait,
And spin your web about the great.
If my Lord's genius wants supplies,
Why—you must make his exercise.
Let the young Marquis take your place,
And bear a whipping for his Grace.
Suppose (such things may happen once)
The nobles wits, and you the dunce,
Improve the means of education,
And learn commodious adulation.
Your master scarcely holds it sin:
He chucks his Lordship on the chin,
And would not for the world rebuke,
Beyond a pat, the schoolboy Duke.
The pastor there of—what's the place?—
With smiles eternal in his face,
With dimpling cheek and snowy hand,
That shames the whiteness of his band;
Whose mincing dialect abounds

In hums and hahs, and half-formed sounds;
Whose elocution, fine and chaste,
Lays his *commainds* with judgement *vaist*;
And lest the company should hear,
Whispers his nothings in your ear:
Think you 'twas zeal, or virtue's care,
That placed the smirking doctor there?
No—'twas connections formed at school
With some rich wit or noble fool,
Obsequious flattery and attendance,
A wilful, useful, base dependance,
A supple bowing of the knees
To any human god you please.
(For true good-breeding's so polite,
'Twould call the very devil white.)
'Twas watching others' shifting will,
And veering to and fro with skill:
These were the means that made him rise.
Mind your connections, and be wise.'

Methinks I hear son Tom reply,
'I'll be a bishop by and by.'

(1762)

KENRICK PRESCOT

1702–1779

311 *Balsham Bells*

SWEET waft their rounds those tuneful brothers five;
Learn, brothers, hence with harmony to live.
At eve the swains stir up the pleasing sounds,
Themselves repast, with music fill the grounds.
These notes abroad, each other noise is still;
Dusk and clear peals do all the region fill.
The crescent moon just sheds an infant light,
Stars and sweet sounds spread all abroad delight.
The herds in music chew the feasts of day;
Peals strike the ear; the eye, stars bright and gay.
The village-cur intoxicated lies,
He lists to music and his anger dies.
So when the softer tunes began to creep
On Cerberus, he lost his heads in sleep.
The harp of Orpheus could infernals tame,

And music softened those of direst frame.
  On such an eve it is a festival,
And only those come forth whom joy can call.
Like umbered shades, pass nymphs and swains in arms,
Seek balks and woods, and watch the bells' alarms.
For sports agreed, they then are diverse seen
From hedge, through gaps, to fleet along the green.
These a spectator, as aloof he stood,
Fables and vows the fairies of the wood.
In rings they meet, there each their haste reveals,
Rebreathe, and laugh, and list to sweet-mouthed peals.
  Gallops the princely hare to yonder grove,
Where glimmers light in shade, to meet his love.
His eyes are glow-worms, and a kingly face
Denotes a lineage to the lion race.
Not wholly wild or tame; each sloe-tipped ear
Lifts to a point; his hue a brown in fire.
Not level stretched as in the hunting race,
He curves, and alters, and checks in his pace.
Who on this beauteous peer the scut discerns,
But thinks of passing ships with rich-flagged sterns?
Light move the shoulders, strong the limbs behind,
At will to amble or outstrip the wind.
Screened by the hedge, or cross the open lea,
He and his mate to lesser closes flee,
By instinct brought on those sweet herbs to feed,
Which round the molehill lift their flow'ry head.
There at their meal attention pleased they give,
While echo crowds the changing tuneful five.
  The grateful rounds amuse the traveller;
The peals from distance die upon the ear.
Homeward he tends; scarce lodged at ease, he tells
How charmed the ways, with starlight and with bells.
  About to cease, the tuneful brothers five
Swift and more loud to send their sounds they strive.
Some slower turns; the breezes of the air
Impress the music sweeter on the ear.
Brisker they break, they clang, recover, fall;
In time the tenor hastes to cover all;
They mingled speak, alive in part, part mute,
Still hear the sonorous tenor in pursuit.
Few rounds distinct at last in order run,
Expiring notes—they and these lines are done.

April 27th, 1757 (Pub. 1772)

balks] unploughed ridges   scut] tail

ROBERT ANDREWS

d. 1766?

312 *Mercury. On Losing my Pocket Milton at Luss near Ben Lomond, and other Mountains*

LUSS! be for ever sunk beneath
  Ben's horrors piled around:
Sun's livening ray ne'er pierce thy gloom,
  Thy hideous deep be drained!
Fishes be turned t' infernal snakes,
  Boatswain to Cerberus!
Mouth of th' Avernian Gulf be thou,
  Its mortal damp thy air!
All o'er thy plains volcanoes thick
  Their burning sands disgorge!
Birds never trill their swelling chaunt,
  Nor roam the humming bee!
Herds never graze, nor sheep nor goat,
  Nor play the shepherd's lute!
Crags other echo ne'er repeat
  Than dismal Furies' yell!
Swift on a morning-ray then, lo!
  The airy-sandalled god,
Mercury, came, and smiling: 'I
  Thy pillow's treasure stole.
Milton no more be fancy's fount
  Of borrowed ecstasies.
Phoebus ordained: presenting, see,
  The laurel never sere.'

(1757)

313 *Urania*

WHENCE this impatience fluttering in my breast!
This boiling blood as it would burst the veins?
This leaping heart? These glowings? Gushing eyes?
Sight how confused! how lost! or how transformed,
Matter refining into thought! Thus you
Blind Thamyris! and blind Maeonides!

Nor last on fame's interminable course,
Bold Milton thou, Virtue's sweet child sublime!
On Fancy's wing who lately o'er th' immense
Of nature's beauty, rangest now in heaven
On thought intu'tive: thus too you, entranced
In the celestial, lost your mortal sight.
These forms how springing from material things,
As rose from chaos that wide solar sphere!
In thick procession the ideal train
Substantial, fair, divine, eternal, clear,
Fill beatific each distended power.
  So rapt the soul in visionary bliss
Deigned the Aonian Choir; and lower still
Sweeping from south to north a round career
All over glowing fanned me as they flew.
Not the parched, weary pilgrim, faint, alone,
Despairing, if his feeble eye dismayed,
Wand'ring along the vast Arabian sands,
Light on some fount, so cheers the vital draught;
As that cool breeze your sacred wings, ye Nine!
Wafted and sprung aloft. My eye pursued
Ah! your too rapid glory: list'ning ear
Your wondrous harmony: soon fixed in vain:
Ear first, then eye, to grovelling earth confined,
My infirmity upbraided. Pensive long
Sat I lamenting: why so transient glance
Flashed the kind Nine? Down sunk my weary powers.
But soon from sleep's dark troubled chaos waked.
For lo! descending Pindus' queen alights,
And with mild air that stilled my blushing fears:
'Whom virtue and prime nature's forms inspire,
Our smiles desert not. Their aspiring strains,
O'er earth wide-floating through the fragrant air,
To Pluto's realm spread silence, awe, self-hate:
And list'ning we our chorus oft suspend;
Or catch your feebler notes, and swell aloft
Echoing, while central Phoebus smiling views
Glad vigour quick'ning his remotest spheres.
This cordial take.' I drank. Urania flew.

(1757)

ANONYMOUS ('AGRICOLA')

314 *The D[ave]ntry Wonder. Showing how Farmer B—ll's Bees issued out of their Hives as if Swarming, at Midnight, between the 24th and 25th of Dec. 1756, Old Style*

Now Cynthia shone serene, and ev'ry star
Through the clear ether twinkled from afar;
An hoary frost o'erspread the glitt'ring ground,
And ev'ry sprig with white was robed around;
Delightful to behold! scarce flow'ry May
Presents a sight more delicately gay.
'Twas near the midnight hour on Christmas Eve,
When bees will swarm, as good old dames believe.
To see this sight a tribe of females went,
And straight to Farmer B—ll's their course they bent.
The farmer slept secure in Sylvia's arms,
Nor dreamed of bees, much less of winter swarms.
Lo! in his garden sundry hives there stood
(Some on broad stones, and some on planks of wood),
All neatly capped, in just arrangement placed:
Sheltered behind; the southern aspect faced.
They listened here awhile—but nothing stirred;
All still as death—and not a hum was heard.
'We are too soon by half an hour, indeed!'
Cries one; 'Let's take a walk'. They all agreed.
Far as Pope-well in pairs they strolled along,
And sweetly chaunted, as they went, a song:
A good old carol, for the season fit,
Such rhymes as Sternhold and as Hopkins writ.
Now jangling bells from many a steeple near,
The summons to a midnight peal, they hear.
Who knows but bees from hence may take alarm?
For ringing, Maro says, will make 'em swarm.
Attend the muse, the muse who dares not lie,
Nor would the truth conceal, were Aff——k by.
Meanwhile ('tis said) a wag disturbed the bees,
Shook all the hives, then skulked behind the trees.
The frighted insects waked and, pouring out,
Like swarms in May hummed, buzzed and flew about.
Our gentry now return—'twas just midnight
(Precise the time to see this wond'rous sight);

They came—they saw—and at each other gazed,
And silent stood awhile o'erawed, amazed!
Till one at length, more eager than the rest,
Broke silence and her comrades thus addressed:
'Companions dear! now our own eyes behold
This marv'lous sight, reported much of old;
This sight my grand-dame had full often seen,
And often fairies dancing on the green;
And often ghosts across the churchyard glide,
And Welton witches on a broomstick ride.
I shudder still, whene'er I call to mind
The wond'rous stories which she left behind.
When crickets sung and owls fled screaming by,
The sick, she said, were always sure to die.
Such warnings now this impious age disdains,
And infidelity unrivalled reigns.
Happy for her in better days t' have lived,
When faith was more, and learning less, received.
She too had seen the Glastonbury thorn,
Convinced that Christ this very night was born.
This miracle, my friends, confirms it plain;
We cannot doubt our eyes, or think it vain.
Let learned Macclesfield say what he will,
Spite of New Style, we'll keep old Christmas still.'

(1757)

ANONYMOUS ('J.T.')

315 *A Sea-Chaplain's Petition to the Lieutenants in the Ward-room, for the Use of the Quarter-Gallery*

YOU who can grant, or can refuse, the pow'r
Low from the stern to drop the golden show'r,
When nature prompts, oh! patient deign to hear,
If not a parson's, yet a poet's pray'r!
Ere taught the deference to commissions due,
Presumptuous, I aspired to eat with you;
But now, the difference known 'twixt sea and shore,
That mighty happiness I ask no more.
An humbler boon, and of a different kind
(Grant, heav'n, it may a different answer find!),

Attends you now (excuse the rhyme to write):
'Tis, though I eat not with you, let me sh—e!
  When, in old bards, Arion tunes his song,
The ravished dolphins round the vessel throng;
Verse soothed of old the monsters of the sea,
Verse saved Arion, verse may plead for me!
And, if the Muse can aught of truth divine,
The boon the Muse petitions shall be mine;
For, sure, this answer would be wondrous odd:
'Sh—e with the common tars, thou Man of God!'
  Of those more vulgar tubes, which downward peep
Near where the lion awes the raging deep,
The waggish youth (I tell what I am told)
Oft smear the sides with excremental gold;
Say then, when pease, within the belly pent,
Roar at the port and struggle for a vent,
Say, shall I squat on dung remissly down,
And with unseemly ordure stain the gown?
Or shall I—terrible to think!—displode
Against th' unbuttoned plush the smoky load,
The laugh of swabbers?—Heavens avert the jest,
And from th' impending scorn preserve your priest!
  But grant that Cloacina, gracious queen!
Preserves her od'rous shrine forever clean,
Yet frequent must I feel th' offensive spray,
When the tossed vessel ploughs the swelling sea;
Yet, as I sit, incessant must I hear
The language of the nauseous galley near,
Where blockheads, by the list'ning priest unawed,
Though uncommissioned, dare blaspheme their God!
  Happy the man, admitted oft to ride
Within the ward-room, where his tools abide,
The Man of Leather! he, when nature calls,
Can for the needful space repose his awls;
And, while I squeeze o'er some ignobler seat,
There disembogue his vile burgoo in state;
While peeping Nereids smoke the Christian jest,
The honoured cobbler and neglected priest,
And swear by Styx, and all the pow'rs below,
In good old heathen days 'twas never so!
  Ah! what avails it that, in days of yore,
Th' instructive lashes of the birch I bore;
For four long years with logic stuffed my head,
And, feeding thought, went supperless to bed;

burgoo] porridge

That, last, enrolled in Alma's graduate band,
I felt the hallowing load of Hoadly's hand:
Since you, with whom my lot afloat is thrown
(O sense! O elegance! to land unknown!),
Superior rev'rence to the man refuse
Who mends your morals, than who mends your shoes!
  But Crispin saves your purse, you answer. True:
Nor does your priest without his off'ring sue.
Whene'er, compelled, I seek the needful hole,
In some by-nook I'll leave some moral scroll;
The moral scroll who next succeeds may reach,
And to his brains apply it, or his br——.
Thus shall old journals plead a just excuse,
And one sea-chaplain boast his works of use.
  And as yourselves from time to time repair
To drop the relics of digestion there,
Still may your pork an easy exit gain,
Nor cause to form one ugly face in vain;
Still may your flip, refined to amber, flow
In streams salubrious to the brine below,
Nor ever in too hot a current hiss;
But may all holes prove innocent as this!
  Thus grant my suit, as grant unhurt you may,
Your chaplain, and without your groats,[1] shall pray!

(1758)

DAVID GARRICK

1717–1779

316 *Heart of Oak*

COME cheer up my lads, 'tis to glory we steer,
To add something more to this wonderful year.
To honour we call you, not press you like slaves,
For who are so free as we sons of the waves?

Chorus

Heart of oak are our ships, heart of oak are our men;
We always are ready—steady, boys, steady—
We'll fight and we'll conquer again and again.

[1] Every common seaman pays a groat a month out of his pay to the chaplain, but the lieutenants pay nothing.

We ne'er see our foes but we wish 'em to stay.
They never see us but they wish us away.
If they run, why, we follow and run 'em ashore,
For if they won't fight us, we cannot do more.

Heart of oak etc.

They swear they'll invade us, these terrible foes.
They frighten our women, our children and beaux.
But should their flat-bottoms in darkness get o'er,
Still Britons they'll find to receive them on shore.

Heart of oak etc.

We'll still make 'em run and we'll still make 'em sweat,
In spite of the devil and *Brussels Gazette.*
Then cheer up my lads, with one heart let us sing
Our soldiers, our sailors, our statesmen and King.

Heart of oak etc.

(1759)

FRANCES GREVILLE

172–?–1789

317 *A Prayer for Indifference*

OFT I've implored the gods in vain,
  And prayed till I've been weary;
For once I'll try my wish to gain
  Of Oberon, the fairy.

Sweet airy being, wanton sprite,
  That liv'st in woods unseen,
And oft by Cynthia's silver light
  Trip'st gaily o'er the green;

If e'er thy pitying heart was moved,
  As ancient stories tell,
And for th' Athenian maid, who loved,
  Thou sought'st a wondrous spell,

Oh! deign once more t' exert thy power;
  Haply some herb or tree,
Sovereign as juice from western flower,
  Conceals a balm for me.

I ask no kind return in love,
  No tempting charm to please;
Far from the heart such gifts remove,
  That sighs for peace and ease.

Nor ease nor peace that heart can know,
  That, like the needle true,
Turns at the touch of joy or woe,
  But, turning, trembles too.

Far as distress the soul can wound,
  'Tis pain in each degree;
Bliss goes but to a certain bound,
  Beyond is agony.

Take then this treacherous sense of mine,
  Which dooms me still to smart;
Which pleasure can to pain refine,
  To pain new pangs impart.

Oh! haste to shed the sovereign balm
  My shattered nerves new-string;
And for my guest, serenely calm,
  The nymph Indifference bring.

At her approach, see Hope, see Fear,
  See Expectation fly,
With Disappointment in the rear,
  That blasts the promised joy.

The tears, which pity taught to flow,
  My eyes shall then disown;
The heart, that throbbed at others' woe,
  Shall then scarce feel its own.

The wounds, which now each moment bleed,
  Each moment then shall close,
And peaceful days shall still succeed
  To nights of sweet repose.

Oh, fairy elf, but grant me this,
  This one kind comfort send,
And so may never-fading bliss
  Thy flowery paths attend!

So may the glow-worm's glimmering light
  Thy tiny footsteps lead
To some new region of delight,
  Unknown to mortal tread;

And be thy acorn goblets filled
  With heaven's ambrosial dew,
From sweetest, freshest flowers distilled,
  That shed fresh sweets for you.

And what of life remains for me
  I'll pass in sober ease,
Half-pleased, contented will I be,
  Contented, half to please.

(1759)

JOHN MACLAURIN, LORD DREGHORN

1734–1796

318

Elegy

NOR Hammond's love nor Shenstone's was sincere,
  For they, though poor, to high-born maids laid claim.
A handsome housemaid causes my despair,
  And Nelly, not Neaera, is her name.

What though devoid of all coquettish care,
  Bare-footed she, except on Sundays, goes,
To wash her hands forgets, and comb her hair,
  Nor with her fingers scorns to blow her nose?

On ev'ry feature and on ev'ry limb,
  Beauty and strength have lavished all their care;
A food too rich is skim-milk cheese for him
  That would with her the city-flirt compare.

In vain, to win her, proffered oft have I
  The gaudy ribbon and the curious lace,
In vain, displayed to her relentless eye
  The guinea's seldom unsuccessful face.

Repulsed, I often have indignant swore,
  Some freedoms often struggled hard to force,
But soon, too soon, severely checked, forbore,
  She more enraged, and my reception worse.

The brimful milking-pail, the empty can,
  Th' unwieldy besom, big with prickly fate,
The nauseous mop, and hissing frying-pan,
  Have fall'n vindictive on my guardless pate.

Yet I, infatuate, pursue her still,
  Happy to lurk, insidious and unseen,
Among the willows, nurslings of the rill,
  That winds irriguous through the washing-green,

For there, with forcible alternate tread,
  From the soaked linen ev'ry stain to press,
The tub-enclosed and unsuspecting maid,
  Furls unashamed th' impediments of dress.

This scene augments my ardour to succeed:
  Nor from the heart her cruelty to me;
Nay, she acknowledged once it did proceed,
  Not from dislike, but diff'rence of degree.

'Tis true, for though she spurns my fond address,
  Yet to her equals is no coyness shown;
She, unconstrained, will Tom the gard'ner kiss,
  Toy, romp and wanton with the ploughman John.

Heav'n knows, for thee, sole mistress of my heart!
  I to the meanest station would descend,
Drive whistling cheerfully the coal-fraught cart,
  Or buttered milk from unscoured barrels vend.

With scanty wages and with weekly meal,
  A thatch-roofed cottage and turf-kindled fire,
Content and happy, I through life would steal,
  Nor envy once the heiress-married squire.

By thee rejected, me my fields no more,
  No more, my art-created gardens please;
I loathe my greenhouse, so admired before,
  And undelighted wander through my trees.

Since I in grief must pine my youth away,
  If disappointed of this virtuous maid,
How weak, how foolish, is it to delay,
  The low, but lovely villager to wed.

What would my parents, what my kindred say?
  What defamation would I undergo,
At rout, ball, concert, opera and play,
  The jest of ev'ry fortune-hunting beau!

No four-wheel chaise, of nice new-fashioned shape,
  Would ever stop at my dishonoured house;
No well-dressed footman, with tremendous rap,
  Announce a visit to my humble spouse.

Fond youth, t' indulge the mean idea cease,
  A flame disgraceful to extinguish strive,
And bear resigned, when, of the jolly piece,
  A country-wedding shall thy hopes deprive.

(Wr. 1760; pub. 1769)

JAMES MACPHERSON

1736–1796

319 from *Fragments of Ancient Poetry, Collected in the Highlands of Scotland*

I SIT by the mossy fountain; on the top of the hill of winds. One tree is rustling above me. Dark waves roll over the heath. The lake is troubled below. The deer descend from the hill. No hunter at a distance is seen; no whistling cow-herd is nigh. It is mid-day: but all is silent. Sad are my thoughts as I sit alone. Didst thou but appear, O my love, a wanderer on the heath! thy hair floating on the wind behind thee; thy bosom heaving on the sight; thine eyes full of tears for thy friends, whom the mist of the hill had concealed! Thee I would comfort, my love, and bring thee to thy father's house.

But is it she that there appears, like a beam of light on the heath? bright as the moon in autumn, as the sun in a summer-storm?—She speaks: but how weak her voice! like the breeze in the reeds of the pool. Hark!

'Returnest thou safe from the war? Where are thy friends, my love? I heard of thy death on the hill; I heard and mourned thee, Shilric!'

'Yes, my fair, I return; but I alone of my race. Thou shalt see them no more: their graves I raised on the plain. But why art thou on the desert hill? why on the heath, alone?'

'Alone I am, O Shilric! alone in the winter-house. With grief for thee I expired. Shilric, I am pale in the tomb.'

She fleets, she sails away; as grey mist before the wind!—and, wilt thou not stay, my love? Stay and behold my tears? fair thou appearest, my love! fair thou wast, when alive!

By the mossy fountain I will sit; on the top of the hill of winds. When mid-day is silent around, converse, O my love, with me! come on the wings of the gale! on the blast of the mountain, come! Let me hear thy voice, as thou passest, when mid-day is silent around.

(1760)

ANONYMOUS

320 *The Linen Weaver*

ON Saturday with joy Bill dubs his half,
And plaits it most exact, then folds it up
And into wallets puts, then throws it o'er
His shoulder and, with many an eager stride,
He gravely stalks along. At warehouse door
He makes his entrance, takes his wallet down,
And empties the contents. His master's man
With poring eye surveys the piece before him,
And finds no fault. 'Why then,' cries honest Bill,
'A shilling more you'll give for work like this.'
'Nay,' says the servant. 'Then I'll bring my reed,
For this has been a most confounded piece,'
The weaver cries. 'Go call my master, I
Act only by instruction.' Then appears
A man dressed like a squire, or justice-like,
With large white wig and ruffles o'er his hands,
Enough to daunt a bolder man than Bill.

320 dubs his half] trims his cloth   wallets] bags   reed] a weaver's instrument

'Come, what's the matter, weaver?'—'He demands
A shilling more, sir, than the common wage.'
'No, sure! Does any other master give it?'
'I can't say so,' cries Bill.—'Why then should I
Give more than they? Maid, fetch a jug of ale:
Let's drink together, Bill, to thy good health.'
'I thank you, master.'—'Come, here's to'rds your own,
And all your family.' The matter ends.
But should some surly weaver chance to miss
His stripe, or selvedge mar, the game begins:
'Jack, you must bate for this.'—'Bate! What d'ye mean?'
Then by his G— and by his S— he swears
He never will, but, forced at last, he flings
Out of the warehouse door with dreadful curse:
'Must I, like slave in Turkey, hag and work
My heart's blood out to gratify the pride
Of wanton b——s, flounced and furbelowed
In silk and silver, sipping tea and cream,
Or powder check-men's wigs? No, d—n oppression;
I've brought my hogs t'a pretty market sure,
To slave for upstart gentry. I'll go serve,
With willing mind, his majesty King George.'

(1760)

WILLIAM WOTY

1731–1791

321 *White Conduit House*

WISHED Sunday's come: mirth brightens ev'ry face,
And paints the rose upon the housemaid's cheek,
Harriot or Moll, more ruddy. Now the heart
Of prentice, resident in ample street
Or alley kennel-washed, Cheapside, Cornhill,
Or Cranborne, thee for calcuments renowned,
With joy distends. His meal meridian o'er,
With switch in hand, he to White Conduit House
Hies merry-hearted. Human beings here

selvedge] edging of the cloth bate] make a reduction hag] weary (myself)
check-men] inspectors
321 calcuments] shoes

In couples multitudinous assemble,
Forming the drollest group that ever trod
Fair Islingtonian plains: male after male,
Dog after dog succeeding, husbands, wives,
Fathers and mothers, brothers, sisters, friends,
And pretty little boys and girls. Around,
Across, along the garden's shrubby maze,
They walk, they sit, they stand. What crowds press on,
Eager to mount the stairs, eager to catch
First vacant bench or chair in long-room placed!
Here prig with prig holds conference polite,
And indiscriminate the gaudy beau
And sloven mix. Here he, who all the week
Took bearded mortals by the nose, or sat
Weaving dead hairs and whistling wretched strain,
And eke the sturdy youth, whose trade it is
Stout oxen to contund, with gold-bound hat
And silken stocking strut. The red-armed belle
Here shows her tasty gown, proud to be thought
The butterfly of fashion; and, forsooth,
Her haughty mistress deigns for once to tread
The same unhallowed floor. 'Tis hurry all
And rattling cups and saucers. 'Waiter' here,
And 'Waiter' there, and 'Waiter' here *and* there,
At once is called: 'Joe—Joe—Joe—Joe—Joe'—
'Joe' on the right, and 'Joe' upon the left,
For ev'ry vocal pipe re-echoes 'Joe'.
Alas, poor Joe! Like Francis in the play
He stands confounded, anxious how to please
The many-headed throng. But should I paint
The language, humours, custom of the place,
Together with all curtsies, lowly bows,
And compliments extern, 'twould swell my page
Beyond its limits due. Suffice it then
For my prophetic muse to say, 'So long
As fashion rides upon the wing of time,
While tea and cream and buttered rolls can please,
While rival beaux and jealous belles exist,
So long, White Conduit House, shall be thy fame.'

(1760)

prig] fop contund] beat

322 from *A Mock Invocation to Genius*

I NOW solicit not the Muses nine,
Terpsichore jig-dancing, Clio famed
For bold romance in history, or thee,
Goddess land-measuring, Thalia called:
Nor thee, Euterpe! do I supplicate,
Flute-am'rous virgin, or that other maid,
Erato hight, renowned for wanton tale
Risiferous, or lively song jocose.
Urania too I leave, star-gazing fair,
And dear Calliope, who first produced
Harmonious bag-pipe, causing ev'ry child
In Scotland's dreary region to rejoice;
And thee, Melpomene! with blubbered face,
I quit disdainful; neither will I pay,
Hymn-singing methodist, of phiz demure,
Oh Polyhymnia! one salute to thee!
Sooner I'd kneel unto the *modern nine*
Alike perfectioned, though a virgin's name
They cannot boast—to hornpipe-loving Moll,
Nymph of the blackest eyes where all are black,
Born in some visto leading to the street
Expansive of Saint Giles—or unto thee
I'd rather bend, Oh ballad-learned quean,
Amber-haired Susan! thee, whose twanging voice
Hath often stopped the drayman and his dray.
Or sooner would I seek relief from Nell,
Town-tramping, oyster-laden—or from thee,
Soap-lathering Bess, the chief of all thy train,
Great mistress of the washing-tub, well-skilled
In friction ambidextrous. Ye, my fair!
Ye first should have my vows, green-vendent Peg!
(Than whom none sooner decks the verdant stall
With fruit cucumerous) and shrimp-crowned Doll,
In alehouse well-agnized, with brawny Jane,
Who constant plies the market, basket-armed.
Nor less doth deep-mouthed, piscatory Kate
(Whose voice is melody through all the realm
Of Billingsgate, admired for flow of words
And well-timed oratory, far beyond
Whate'er St. Stephen's clamant sons can boast),
Or brick-dust Nan attract my due regard.

fruit cucumerous] cucumbers   -agnized] -recognized

But these I not invoke—for at thy shrine
Alone, Oh GENIUS! do I kneel devout
With galligaskins pure, that never yet
Needed the aid of dust-expelling brush.
  Whate'er in future I presume to write
Adventurous—or grand majestic ode
Of import lofty, or the tender song
Dulci-sonant—or whether on the plain
Of panegyric smooth, with daisies pied,
My lays I frame, or tread the thorny road
That leads to where rough satire lifts her rod
Thrice dipped in brine—be ready to my aid,
Thou great original!—in each attempt
Do thou legitimate each bastard thought!
Teach me the bellows of thy forge to blow
With skill superior, and redoubled force
Super-vulcanian—so the mounting sparks
Of fire-eyed Fancy shall prevent their charms,
And on thine anvil shall I hammer out
The thought chaotic to prefulgid form.

(1770)

323 *Lines Written in the Dog-Days. How Hot It Is!*

THE sun now darts his fervid rays
With most intense and ardent blaze.
The herds all pant for want of rains,
And sadly each to each complains.
They whisk the tail and lick the mouth,
The withered pasture's parched with drouth.
The flies and gnats around them cling,
Their twitching backs denote the sting.
In yonder fields,
Where plenty yields
A harvest—how well got it is!
The farmers yet
God's gift forget.
O bless my heart! how hot it is!

All hands at work—at times they rest,
Quite over-heated and oppressed,
Their tiresome labours then renew,
To their employers ever true.

322 galligaskins] breeches   prefulgid] brightly shining

The little dog, with naught to do
But watch the scrip and bottle too,
On some old vestment panting lies
With lolling tongue and half-shut eyes.
        I pity those,
        Kind heaven knows,
To toil so hard whose lot it is,
        Whose masters grudge
        Each weary drudge,
Considering not how hot it is!

  My head it aches, my pulse is high,
A fever sure is drawing nigh,
My temples burn beneath the glare:
O what a dreadful shoot was there!
I feel a something, void of name,
That renders languid all my frame.
My breath is short and very quick,
I find myself extremely sick.
        In yonder nook,
        I spy a brook
And house—how snug a cot it is!
        I'll baffle there
        The sultry air.
God bless my heart! how hot it is!

  Dame, did you ever feel such heat?
'No truly, sir, it makes me sweat.
My stays, though somewhat worse for wear
And patched all o'er, I scarce can bear;
And, were I sure 'twould not offend,
I'd strip myself from end to end,
And walk barefooted on the floor
Fore every comer-in and goer.'
        Tush—quick, some ale;
        Or mild or stale,
Good, bad, I care not what it is.
        My thirst to slake
        A quart I'll take.
O bless my heart! how hot it is!

  'There, how do y'like it?'—Very good:
It tastes as all brisk, mild ale should.
Are you a widow, wife or maid?
'Good dear! I'm neither, sir', she said;
'I never yet could bear control.

I hate it from my very soul,
So keep unmarried to be free
From any husband's tyranny.'
Pray, what's your sign?
I can't divine.
'The worn-out sack of wool it is.'
Your servant, dame.
'To you the same.'
How charming now, and cool it is!

(1789)

JAMES CAWTHORN

1719–1761

324 from *Of Taste. An Essay*

TIME was, a wealthy Englishman would join
A rich plum-pudding to a fat sirloin;
Or bake a pasty, whose enormous wall
Took up almost the area of his hall:
But now, as art improves, and life refines,
The demon Taste attends him when he dines,
Serves on his board an elegant regale,
Where three stewed mushrooms flank a larded quail;
Where infant turkeys, half a month resigned
To the soft breathings of a southern wind,
And smothered in a rich ragout of snails,
Outstink a lenten supper at Versailles.
Is there a saint that would not laugh to see
The good man piddling with his fricassee;
Forced by the luxury of taste to drain
A flask of poison, which he calls champagne!
While he, poor idiot! though he dare not speak,
Pines all the while for porter and ox-cheek?
Sure 'tis enough to starve for pomp and show,
To drink, and curse the clarets of Bordeaux:
Yet such our humour, such our skill to hit
Excess of folly through excess of wit,
We plant the garden, and we build the seat,
Just as absurdly as we drink and eat.
For is there aught that nature's hand has sown
To bloom and ripen in her hottest zone?

Is there a shrub which, ere its verdures blow,
Asks all the suns that beam upon the Po?
Is there a flowret whose vermilion hue
Can only catch its beauty in Peru?
Is there a portal, colonnade or dome,
The pride of Naples, or the boast of Rome?
We raise it here, in storms of wind and hail,
On the bleak bosom of a sunless vale;
Careless alike of climate, soil and place,
The cast of nature, and the smiles of grace.
  Hence all our stuccoed walls, mosaic floors,
Palladian windows and Venetian doors,
Our Gothic fronts, whose Attic wings unfold
Fluted pilasters tipped with leaves of gold,
Our massy ceilings, graced with gay festoons,
The weeping marbles of our damp salons,
Lawns fringed with citrons, amaranthine bow'rs,
Expiring myrtles, and unop'ning flow'rs.
Hence the good Scotsman bids th' anana blow
In rocks of crystal or in Alps of snow;
On Orcus' steep extends his wide arcade,
And kills his scanty sunshine in a shade.
  One might expect a sanctity of style,
August and manly, in an holy pile,
And think an architect extremely odd
To build a playhouse for the church of God:
Yet half our churches, such the mode that reigns,
Are Roman theatres or Grecian fanes;
Where broad-arched windows to the eye convey
The keen diffusion of too strong a day;
Where, in the luxury of wanton pride,
Corinthian columns languish side by side,
Closed by an altar, exquisitely fine,
Loose and lascivious as a Cyprian shrine.
  Of late, 'tis true, quite sick of Rome and Greece,
We fetch our models from the wise Chinese:
European artists are too cool and chaste,
For Mand'rin only is the man of taste;
Whose bolder genius, fondly wild to see
His grove a forest, and his pond a sea,
Breaks out—and, whimsically great, designs
Without the shackles or of rules or lines:
Formed on his plans, our farms and seats begin
To match the boasted villas of Pekin.
On every hill a spire-crowned temple swells,
Hung round with serpents and a fringe of bells:

Junks and balons along our waters sail,
With each a gilded cockboat at his tail;
Our choice exotics to the breeze exhale,
Within th' inclosure of a zigzag rail;
In Tartar huts our cows and horses lie,
Our hogs are fatted in an Indian sty;
On ev'ry shelf a joss divinely stares,
Nymphs laid on chintzes sprawl upon our chairs;
While o'er our cabinets Confucius nods,
Midst porcelain elephants and china gods.

(Wr. by 1761; pub. 1771)

FRANCIS FAWKES

1720–1777

325 *An Elegy on the Death of Dobbin, the Butterwoman's Horse*

THE death of faithful Dobbin I deplore;
Dame Jolt's brown horse, old Dobbin, is no more.
The cruel Fates have snapped his vital thread,
And Gammer Jolt bewails old Dobbin dead.
From stony Cudham down to watery Cray,
This honest horse brought butter every day,
Fresh butter meet to mix with nicest rolls,
And sometimes eggs, and sometimes geese and fowls;
And though this horse to stand had ne'er a leg,
He never dropped a goose, or broke an egg.
Ye maids of Cray your buttered rolls deplore,
Dame Jolt's brown horse, old Dobbin, is no more.

Oft did the squire, that keeps the great hall-house,
Invite the willing vicar to a goose;
For goose could make his kindred Muse aspire
From earth to air, from water to the fire;
But now, alas! his towering spirit's fled,
His Muse is foundered, for poor Dobbin's dead.
Last Friday was a luckless day, I wot,
For Friday last lean Dobbin went to pot;

324 balons] Siamese state-barges joss] figure of a Chinese deity

No drinks could cherish, no prescriptions save;
In C——n's hounds he found a living grave:
  Weep all, and all (except sad dogs) deplore,
  Dame's Jolt's brown horse, old Dobbin, is no more.

Skulk, Reynard, skulk in the securest grounds,
Now Dobbin hunts thee in the shape of hounds.
Late sure but slow he marched as foot could fall,
Sure to march slow whene'er he marched at all;
Now fleeter than the pinions of the wind,
He leaves the huntsman and the hunt behind,
Pursues thee o'er the hills and down the steep,
Through the rough copse, wide woods and waters deep,
Along th' unbounded plain, along the lea,
But has no pullet and no goose for thee.
  Ye dogs, ye foxes, howl for Dobbin dead,
  Nor thou, O Muse, disdain the tear to shed;
  Ye maids of Cray your buttered rolls deplore,
  Dame Jolt's brown horse, old Dobbin, is no more.

(1761)

JOHN CUNNINGHAM

1729–1773

326

Morning

In the barn the tenant cock,
  Close to partlet perched on high,
Briskly crows (the shepherd's clock!),
  Jocund that the morning's nigh.

Swiftly from the mountain's brow,
  Shadows, nursed by night, retire:
And the peeping sunbeam now
  Paints with gold the village spire.

Philomel forsakes the thorn,
  Plaintive where she prates at night;
And the lark, to meet the morn,
  Soars beyond the shepherd's sight.

From the low-roofed cottage ridge,
  See the chatt'ring swallow spring;
Darting through the one-arched bridge,
  Quick she dips her dappled wing.

Now the pine-tree's waving top
  Gently greets the morning gale:
Kidlings now begin to crop
  Daisies on the dewy dale.

From the balmy sweets, uncloyed
  (Restless till her task be done),
Now the busy bee's employed
  Sipping dew before the sun.

Trickling through the creviced rock,
  Where the limpid stream distils,
Sweet refreshment waits the flock
  When 'tis sun-drove from the hills.

Colin's for the promised corn
  (Ere the harvest hopes are ripe)
Anxious;—whilst the huntsman's horn,
  Boldly sounding, drowns his pipe.

Sweet, O sweet, the warbling throng
  On the white emblossomed spray!
Nature's universal song
  Echoes to the rising day.

(1761)

THOMAS MORRIS

1732–1806?

327 [*Sapphics: At the Mohawk-Castle, Canada. To Lieutenant Montgomery*]

EASE is the pray'r of him who, in a whaleboat
Crossing Lake Champlain, by a storm's o'ertaken;
Not struck his blanket,[1] not a friendly island
        Near to receive him.

[1] The soldier's blanket, used by the army as a sail.

Ease is the wish too of the sly Canadian;
Ease the delight of bloody Caghnawagas;
Ease, Richard, ease, not to be bought with wampum,
Nor paper money.

Not colonel's pay, nor yet a dapper sergeant,
Orderly waiting with recovered halberd,
Can chase the crowd of troubles still surrounding
Laced regimentals.

That sub lives best who, with a sash in tatters
Worn by his grandsire at the fight of Blenheim,
To fear a stranger, and to wild ambition,
Snores on a bearskin.

Why like fine-fellows are we ever scheming,
We short-lived mortals? Why so fond of climates
Warmed by new suns? O who, that runs from home, can
Run from himself too?

Care climbs radeaux[1] with four-and-twenty pounders,
Not quits our light troops, or our Indian warriors,
Swifter than moose-deer, or the fleeter east wind,
Pushing the clouds on.

He, whose good humour can enjoy the present,
Scorns to look forward; with a smile of patience
Temp'ring the bitter. Bliss uninterrupted
None can inherit.

Death instantaneous hurried off Achilles;
Age far-extended wore away Tithonus:
Who will live longer, thou or I, Montgom'ry?
Dicky or Tommy?

Thee twenty messmates, full of noise and laughter,
Cheer with their sallies; thee the merry damsels
Please with their titt'ring; whilst thou sitt'st adorned with
Boots, sash and gorget.

[1] Floating batteries, used on Lake Champlain.

sub] subaltern

Me to Fort Hendrick, midst a savage nation,
Dull Connajohry, cruel fate has driven.
O think on Morris, in a lonely chamber,
Dabbling in Sapphic.

(Wr. 1761; pub. 1796)

EMANUEL COLLINS

b. 1712?

328 *The Fatal Dream: or, The Unhappy Favourite. An Elegy*

WEEPING Melpomene assist my lays,
Whilst I unhappy Tysey mourn and praise!
Denied thy aid, what bard presumes to tell
How loved he lived, or how lamented fell!
Come then, thou mournful Sister of the Nine,
Come, aid this plaintive, elegiac strain!
So shall my verse to future times deplore
The beauteous, breathless Tysey, now no more.

Ye little happy brutes on whom the fair
Bestow their morning and their evening care;
That rob the injured lover of his bliss,
And lick those lips he scarce presumes to kiss;
Whose shaggy limbs too often do supply
The place where hapless Damon ought to lie:
Hear Tysey's fate! O shun the tempting snare!
And by his ills forewarned your own beware.

Betty just now had washed my little Tyse,
And dried him on a cloth, so clean, so nice!
Had dandled him an hour upon her knee,
And from his little noddle picked each flea,
Had combed, and kissed, and danced this finest spark
That e'er did wag a tail or ever bark.

Cocked was this tail of his, his skin was snow,
Conscious he strutted like a very beau,
And Betty, to adorn his shaggy neck,
With crimson velvet did the spark bedeck;
Then brought him to her sleepy madam's bed,
And on her milk-white bosom laid his head.

So innocently decked the lambkin lies,
Till breathless on the altar stretched he dies.
For lo! poor Tysey, in a hapless time,
By wand'ring southward to some warmer clime,
Unluckily had left those hills of snow,
And died a martyr in the vale below.
For Morpheus, god of dreams, who now possessed
With warmest images her virgin breast,
Presented Nimrod[1] to the burning dame,
Nimrod, that mighty hunter of the game.

Charmed with the form, the unreservèd maid
Her every ripened beauty open laid,
Freely admits him to her glowing breast,
Till the unrivalled youth had all possessed.
Fully she's bent to quench her am'rous flame;
But, maidens, this was only in a dream!

'Pour in the balm of love, oh heal my smart,
Still nearer yet and nearer to my heart,'
The panting virgin cried; then strongly thrice
Within her lovely thighs embraced poor Tyse.
The little brute, unable to sustain
Such strong convulsions and such mighty pain,
On the dear spot expired.—Here Chloe woke,
And, finding the delusion, weeping spoke:
'Hear, Delia, hear, oh Dian, give thy aid,
And help, in pity help, thy mournful maid.

'When the swift antelope shall lose his speed;
When rural squires shall Locke and Milton read;
When doctors shall look great in little wigs;
When our grave bishops hornpipes dance and jigs;
When Horwood[2] on his fiddle plays one tune;
When skating shall divert us here in June;
Then, only then, shall my dear Tysey be
Forgotten by his fond Penelope[3].'

(1762)

[1] A country squire that courted her.

[2] The vile crowdero [fiddler] of that neighbourhood, whose noise was the very reverse of harmony.

[3] The lady who so fondly wept the dog.

THOMAS MOZEEN

d. 1768

329

The Bedlamite

'TIS not on the face displayed,
  What I suffer, cruel maid!
A burning poison lurks unseen:
  O ease me; ease my sad chagrin!
See through yon fiery lake, yon flaming flood,
Fierce dragons come to drink my blood.
        Why, Jove, dost thou thus set them on?
          O what have I done,
          My dear, dear, dazzling sun,
            That no wind from the sea
            Blows tidings to me,
          Whilst the tyrant frowns on my throne?

Shall we to the meadows go,
  Where the butter-flowers blow,
And the dainty daisies grow?
              I say No, no, no, no, no, no.
For lend me a while your ear;
        How can I be merry,
        Whilst you guzzle sherry,
And I must sip small beer?——

        Give me the reward,
        Give me the reward;
    And fill the goblet high:
    I now the traitor spy;——
            Tread soft and fair,
            All light as air,
            'Tis my belief,
            Yon plantain leaf
    Conceals him from your eye.

    'Tis a Spaniard on my life!——
    Tawny face——bloody knife!——
But let the bells merrily ring;
  We have store of great guns,
  And fine Chelsea buns,
  And the burgundy runs;
And we love and we honour the King.

Nay, be not so harsh with your smiles;
  Your frowns are more pleasant to me.
Hark! hearken to puss on the tiles!——
  She's just such a lady as thee.

Ah Fanny! Why dost thou so sadly complain?
Thou canst not sure envy my temperate brain.
        Off, off the course,
        That damned trotting horse:
        I'll hold six to four
        You hear on't no more;
For Prussia has beat them again.——

  Of reason I held a lease,
But long, very long 't has been out:
  O landlord, renew, if you please!
Help, counsellor——bring it about.
  What!——Nothing without your fees?——
Ah, tickle me not for a trout.———

      How now, saucy Jack;
      Why appear'st thou in black?——
A packet to me, say'st, directed;
          Ha! ha! ha! ha!
       Bow, enemies, bow!
       Or I'll harass you now:
'Tis the comet so long we've expected.——

Nay, soothe me not; for well I know,
To cure my tortured heart of woe
  Is not to mortal given:
She only can my sense restore
Who robbed me of it once before;
  An angel, now in heaven.

(1762)

ANONYMOUS

330 *Corydon's Farewell, on Sailing in the Late Expedition Fleet*

FAREWELL, the bell upon a ram's neck hung,
Farewell, the rustic song by shepherd sung;
Farewell, the hungry falcon's cat-like note,
As down the glade he stoops for mouse or stoat;
Farewell, the fearful lapwing's chiding quest,
When Rover ranges near, too near, her nest;
Farewell, the jetty raven's scornful scoff,
Who, proud, to prouder man cries out 'off, off',
So fancy forms his ill-betiding croak;
And thou, farewell, that from the hollow oak,
The bird of wisdom cleped, does send around
Thy man-like halloos hunters to confound.
Embowered in birchen groves, thou wooing dove,
Emblem of spotless innocence and love,
Farewell: O say! with thy companion sat,
How oft thou'st seen me with as fair a mate.
Farewell, the busy hum of bees that bring
Extracted honey from the pride of spring;
No more your toil shall Corydon molest
When buzzing near my Cloe's tender breast,
Whether to sting her was your sad intent,
Or whether sweets to steal was all ye meant.
Farewell, each hill, each dale, each conscious grove,
Adieu, each witness of my constant love.
Farewell, of distant bells the liquid sound,
That, while I lay stretched careless on the ground,
Would softly undulate along the glade,
And bring such news as pleasing fancy made:
Haply a wedding, or an heir, maybe,
Or glorious vict'ry gained by land and sea;
For joy the very fairies dance and sing,
And leave their footsteps in a verdant ring.
The bells, in triple cadence other times,
At matins please the ear in softer chimes:
When good old dowager, oppressed with cares,
Or maiden aunt with Jacky steals to pray'rs.
The evening knell reminds us of our folly,
And substitutes a pleasing melancholy.

Farewell, the lonely cot in neatness dressed,
Which neighb'ring squire does annually invest
With decent livery of purest white,
A pleasing object to allure the sight;
Fixed near a spacious wood of aged oak,
Which shows the chimney's noonday azure smoke,
Near it a limpid stream for ever flows,
Where linen-suited Sal for water goes,
To boil her cates or wash her cotton hose;
A neatcut hedge that can with tulips vie,
Where Sally hangs her favours out to dry.
Farewell, the woodman's 'hem' at ev'ry stroke,
Who hems, and inter-whistles *Hearts of Oak*.
The sawyers working in the inmost wood
Attentive hear the tune and think it good:
They make their motions with the measure chime,
All arms now rise and fall in perfect time.
Their boys around, blest pledges! play their pranks,
Some houses build with chips, some swing on planks.
The tender, watchful mother sits hard by,
Knitting, awhile the girls raise up dirt-pie.
O happy presage of their future lives,
Useful in arts the boys, the girls domestic wives.
Farewell, each thing, each place I fondly know:
To distant climes poor Corydon must go;
The homefelt joys, beyond expression dear,
Deserve an elegy, a parting tear.

(1762)

JAMES EYRE WEEKS

b. 1719?

331 *On the Great Fog in London, December 1762*

LOST and bewildered in the thickening mist,
We stray amid th' irrefragable gloom,
Nor can the penetrating lance of day
Bleed the thick vein; behind a sizy cloud
The rays of light, his orient messengers,
Are intercepted, nor can steer their course,

331 sizy] thick

Wrecked on a coast of jet—even beauty's eye,
Composed of azure, here is impotent,
And, all-subduing, is itself subdued.
  We jostle each, by vision unapprised
Of meeting, till, like vessels, we run foul,
And board each other in the sullen waste.
This mockery of night, like vanity,
Conceals us from ourselves; our shadows too,
Lately our dear associates and compeers,
Have, like false lovers, left us in the fog
To seek our own identity in vain.
Nature herself seems in the vapours now;
Dim is the prospect—shall we call it so?
A purblind view, next to invisible?
Or rather darkness visible to sight.
'Tis a black curtain drawn across the sky
Disgustful, and shuts out the scenes of day.
Or if a sun-beam glimmer—lo! the trees,
As we approach 'em, seem like hanging webs
Spun by the spider—even the great St. Paul,
With his huge dome and cupola, appears
A craggy precipice, rude, uninformed;
Or, like the ruins of an ancient fort
Upon a hill, when twilight shuts the day.
The morning, like a widow, all in weeds,
Stalks forth incog, unwilling to be known,
Veiled and disguised behind the mask of night.
  Or, if meridian Phoebus show his face,
He seems a ball of molten copper-ore,
Like a red beacon on a foggy coast.
  Absolute shade maintains despotic sway,
Palpable darkness, for we see by touch;
If hearing not apprise us of approach,
The coach or wagon by its rumbling warns
To shun the danger; from our ears we see
The threatening wheels; while often touch informs,
When unawares we strike against a post,
Like ships against a bank or sunken rock,
For sight is useless in so drear a blank.
The beams of day, refracted in the cloud,
Like birds in storms, are dubious where to fly,
And waste their radiance on the tawny air.
When sable night appears in ebon car,
The lamps are feeble like the socket-snuffs
Of tapers just expiring, rush-lights dim
Like dying wicks within a dreary vault.

'Tis general mourning, every colour fades;
Even the fine roseate on the virgin's cheek
Turns to a livid blue, and charms no more.
The soldiers in the Park seem undertakers,
While every coach or carriage, like a hearse,
Displays the pageant of a funeral pomp.
Long streets of houses look like black perspectives
Of charcoal prospects, the design of boys;
While by no marks directed oft we miss
Our well-known passage, boats upon the Thames
Appear but as the buoys of distant ships,
Or corks afloat upon the sullen flood.

(1762)

GEORGE ALEXANDER STEVENS

1710–1784

332 *Bartleme Fair*

WHILE gentlefolks strut in their silver and satins,
We poor folks are tramping in straw hats and pattens,
As merrily Old English ballads can sing-o,
As they at their opperores outlandish ling-o
Calling out, bravo, encoro, and caro,
Tho'f I will sing nothing but Bartleme Fair-o.

Here first of all, crowds against other crowds driving,
Like wind and tide meeting, each contrary striving;
Here's fiddling and fluting, and shouting and shrieking,
Fifes, trumpets, drums, bagpipes, and barrow-girls squeaking.
My ware round and sound, here's choice of fine ware-o,
Though all is not sound sold at Bartleme Fair-o.

Here are drolls, hornpipe dancing, and showing of postures;
Plum-porridge, black-puddings, and op'ning of oysters;
The taphouse guests swearing, and gall'ry folks squalling,
With salt-boxes, solos, and mouth-pieces bawling;
Pimps, pick-pockets, strollers, fat landladies, sailors,
Bawds, baileys, jilts, jockeys, thieves, tumblers and tailors.

332 pattens] clogs

Here's Punch's whole play of the gunpowder-plot, sir,
Wild beasts all alive, and pease-porridge hot, sir:
Fine sausages fried, and the Black on the wire;
The whole court of France, and nice pig at the fire.
The ups-and-downs, who'll take a seat in the chair-o?
There are more ups and downs than at Bartleme Fair-o.

Here's Whittington's cat, and the tall dromedary,
The chaise without horses, and Queen of Hungary;
The merry-go-rounds, come who rides? come who rides?
Wine, beer, ale and cakes, fire-eating besides;
The famed learned dog that can tell all his letters,
And some men, as scholars, are not much his betters.

This world's a wide fair, where we ramble 'mong gay things;
Our passions, like children, are tempted by play-things;
By sound and by show, by trash and by trumpery,
The fal-lals of fashion, and Frenchified frumpery.
Life is but a droll, rather wretched than rare-o,
And thus ends the ballad of Bartleme Fair-o.

(1762)

333 *Repentance*

'THE dictates of nature prove school-knowledge weak;
Does not instinct beyond all the orators speak?
From their parts of speech we'll not borrow one part;
Our lips, without words, find the way to the heart.'

Thus as last night I sung, with my lass on my knee,
Methought one below hoarse enquired for me;
We listened and heard him, his breathing seemed scant,
And upstairs he stepped with asthmatical pant.

The door op'ning wide, solus entered the sprite,
Black and all black his dress, sable emblem of night.
His livid lips quivered, pronouncing my name,
And, head and staff shaking, declared me to blame.

'Repentance,' quoth he, 'won't admit of delays;
I insist, from this moment, you alter your ways.'
As I stared at him, slyly my bottle I hid,
Then punct'ally promised to do as he bid.

With unkerchiefed neck, sparkling eyes and loose hair,
Her gown single-pinned, burst from closet my fair;
There she fled when the fright appeared in the room,
Then fell at his feet in the health of Love's bloom.

So graceful she knelt, and so tender her tone,
Then she sent such a look, Silverbeard was her own.
I saw his eyes twinkle, blood flattered his face,
He fondly, though feebly, essayed an embrace.

I left them and, just as I fancied, the churl
Made a strengthless attempt to be rude with my girl.
She shrieked, I rushed in as he strove to escape,
And the watch took Repentance away for a rape.

Ever since, when we wanton in rapt'rous embrace,
The reproach-bearing wretch dares not show us his face.
May each fond of each thus enjoyment improve;
Be henceforth Repentance a stranger to Love.

(1772)

334 *A Simple Pastoral*

AURORA, lady grey,
  Hides her face in blushes;
Budding, blanching May
  Whitens hawthorn bushes.

See the clouds transparent,
  See the sunshine rising;
London rakes, I warrant,
  Would think this surprising.

See the sturdy swains
  Trenching-ploughs are holding;
Some on pebbly plains
  Last night's pens unfolding.

How the swineyards woo!
  How the herds are lowing!
While the pigeons coo,
  Barndoor fowls are crowing.

Here are Flora's dressings,
  Air-filled perfume here is,
Here Pomona's blessings,
  Here the gifts of Ceres.

Hark! the tinkling rills,
  And the bubbling fountains,
Cascade o'er the hills,
  Tumble down the mountains.

See! at welcome wakes,
  Show-folks fire-eating;
While, with ale and cakes,
  Jack his Gill is treating.

Hark! the distant drum,
  Lasses all look frighted;
But, when soldiers come,
  Girls, how you're delighted.

Night her shutters closing,
  All the village still is,
Save where, unreposing,
  Captain calls on Phillis.

While she lets her spark in,
  Shooting-stars are sailing,
Farmer's dogs are barking,
  Comets dreadful trailing.

For, to scholars thinking,
  Omens must be telling
Whether worlds are sinking,
  Or if waists are swelling.

But, my lads and lasses,
  Mind a friend's advisings;
Let us fill our glasses
  To our falls and risings.

(1772)

JOHN COLLIER

1708–1786

335 *The Pluralist and Old Soldier*

A SOLDIER maimed and in the beggars' list
Did thus address a well-fed pluralist:
Sol. At Guadeloupe my leg and thigh I lost,
    No pension have I, though its right I boast;
    Your reverence, please some charity bestow,
    Heav'n will pay double—when you're there, you know.
Plu. Heav'n pay me double! Vagrant—know that I
    Ne'er give to strollers, they're so apt to lie:
    Your parish and some work would you become,
    So haste away—or constable's your doom.
Sol. May't please your reverence, hear my case, and then
    You'll say I'm poorer than the most of men:
    When Marlbro siegèd Lisle, I first drew breath,
    And there my father met untimely death;
    My mother followed, of a broken heart,
    So I've no friend or parish, for my part.
Plu. I say, begone.
                        —With that, he loudly knocks,
And Timber-toe begins to smell the stocks.
Away he stumps—but, in a rood or two,
He cleared his weasand and his thoughts broke through:
Sol. This 'tis to beg of those who sometimes preach
    Calm charity, and ev'ry virtue teach;
    But their disguise to common sense is thin:
    A pocket buttoned—hypocrite within.
    Send me, kind heav'n, the well-tanned captain's face,
    Who gives me twelvepence and a curse, with grace;
    But let me not, in house or lane or street,
    These treble-pensioned parsons ever meet;
    And when I die, may I still numbered be
    With the rough soldier, to eternity.

(1763)

weasand] throat

ANONYMOUS

336 *To a Gentleman, Who Desired Proper Materials for a Monody*

FLOWRETS—wreaths—thy banks along—
Silent eve—th'accustomed song—
Silver-slippered—whilom—lore—
Druid—Paynim—mountain hoar—
Dulcet—eremite—what time—
('Excuse me—here I want a rhyme.')
Black-browed night—Hark! screech-owls sing!
Ebon car—and raven wing—
Charnel-houses—lonely dells—
Glimmering tapers—dismal cells—
Hallowed haunts—and horrid piles—
Roseate hues—and ghastly smiles—
Solemn fanes—and cypress bowers—
Thunder-storms—and tumbling towers—
  Let these be well together blended—
Dodsley's your man—the poem's ended.

(1763)

CHARLES CHURCHILL

1731–1764

337 from *The Rosciad*

[*Character of a Critic*]

  WITH that low cunning, which in fools supplies,
And amply too, the place of being wise,
Which nature, kind indulgent parent, gave
To qualify the blockhead for a knave;
With that smooth falsehood, whose appearance charms,
And reason of each wholesome doubt disarms,
Which to the lowest depths of guile descends,
By vilest means pursues the vilest ends,

Wears friendship's mask for purposes of spite,
Fawns in the day, and butchers in the night;
With that malignant envy, which turns pale
And sickens, even if a friend prevail,
Which merit and success pursues with hate,
And damns the worth it cannot imitate;
With the cold caution of a coward's spleen,
Which fears not guilt, but always seeks a screen,
Which keeps this maxim ever in her view—
What's basely done, should be done safely too;
With that dull, rooted, callous impudence,
Which, dead to shame and ev'ry nicer sense,
Ne'er blushed, unless, in spreading vice's snares,
She blundered on some virtue unawares;
With all these blessings, which we seldom find
Lavished by nature on one happy mind,
A motley figure, of the Fribble tribe,
Which heart can scarce conceive, or pen describe,
Came simp'ring on; to ascertain whose sex
Twelve sage impannelled matrons would perplex.
Nor male, nor female; neither, and yet both;
Of neuter gender, though of Irish growth;
A six-foot suckling, mincing in his gait,
Affected, peevish, prim and delicate;
Fearful it seemed, though of athletic make,
Lest brutal breezes should too roughly shake
Its tender form, and savage motion spread
O'er its pale cheeks the horrid manly red.
Much did it talk in its own pretty phrase,
Of genius and of taste, of play'rs and plays;
Much too of writings, which itself had wrote,
Of special merit, though of little note,
For fate, in a strange humour, had decreed
That what it wrote, none but itself should read;
Much too it chattered of dramatic laws,
Misjudging critics, and misplaced applause,
Then, with a self-complacent jutting air,
It smiled, it smirked, it wriggled to the chair;
And with an awkward briskness not his own,
Looking around, and perking on the throne,
Triumphant seemed; when that strange savage dame,
Known but to few, or only known by name,
Plain Common Sense appeared, by nature there
Appointed, with plain truth, to guard the chair.
The pageant saw and, blasted with her frown,
To its first state of nothing melted down.

Nor shall the Muse (for even there the pride
Of this vain nothing shall be mortified)
Nor shall the Muse (should fate ordain her rhymes,
Fond pleasing thought! to live in aftertimes)
With such a trifler's name her pages blot;
Known be the character, the thing forgot;
Let it, to disappoint each future aim,
Live without sex, and die without a name!

(1763)

338 from *The Prophecy of Famine*

[*On his own Poetry*]

For bards, like these, who neither sing nor say,
Grave without thought, and without feeling gay,
Whose numbers in one even tenor flow,
Attuned to pleasure, and attuned to woe,
Who, if plain Common Sense her visit pays,
And mars one couplet in their happy lays,
As at some ghost affrighted, start and stare,
And ask the meaning of her coming there;
For bards like these a wreath shall Mason bring,
Lined with the softest down of Folly's wing;
In Love's pagoda shall they ever doze,
And Gisbal kindly rock them to repose;
My Lord—to letters as to faith most true—
At once their patron and example too—
Shall quaintly fashion his love-laboured dreams,
Sigh with sad winds, and weep with weeping streams,
Curious in grief (for real grief, we know,
Is curious to dress up the tale of woe),
From the green umbrage of some druid's seat,
Shall his own works in his own way repeat.
Me, whom no muse of heav'nly birth inspires,
No judgement tempers when rash genius fires,
Who boast no merit but mere knack of rhyme,
Short gleams of sense, and satire out of time,
Who cannot follow where trim fancy leads
By prattling streams o'er flow'r-empurpled meads;
Who often, but without success, have prayed
For apt Alliteration's artful aid,
Who would, but cannot, with a master's skill
Coin fine new epithets, which mean no ill;
Me, thus uncouth, thus ev'ry way unfit

For pacing poesy, and ambling wit,
Taste with contempt beholds, nor deigns to place
Amongst the lowest of her favoured race.
Thou, Nature, art my goddess—to thy law
Myself I dedicate—hence, slavish awe
Which bends to fashion, and obeys the rules,
Imposed at first, and since observed by fools.

(1763)

339 from *Gotham*, Book I

(i)

[*European Crimes*]

HAPPY the savage of those early times,
Ere Europe's sons were known, and Europe's crimes!
Gold, cursed gold! slept in the womb of earth,
Unfelt its mischiefs, as unknown its worth;
In full content he found the truest wealth;
In toil he found diversion, food and health;
Strange to the ease and luxury of courts,
His sports were labours, and his labours sports;
His youth was hardy, and his old age green;
Life's morn was vig'rous, and her eve serene;
No rules he held, but what were made for use;
No arts he learned, nor ills which arts produce;
False lights he followed, but believed them true;
He knew not much, but lived to what he knew.
Happy, thrice happy now, the savage race,
Since Europe took their gold, and gave them grace!
Pastors she sends to help them in their need,
Some who can't write, with others who can't read,
And, on sure grounds the gospel-pile to rear,
Sends missionary felons ev'ry year;
Our vices, with more zeal than holy pray'rs,
She teaches them, and in return takes theirs;
Her rank oppressions give them cause to rise,
Her want of prudence means and arms supplies,
Whilst her brave rage, not satisfied with life,
Rising in blood, adopts the scalping-knife;
Knowledge she gives, enough to make them know
How abject is their state, how deep their woe;
The worth of freedom strongly she explains,
Whilst she bows down and loads their necks with chains;

Faith too she plants, for her own ends impressed,
To make them bear the worst, and hope the best;
And whilst she teaches on vile int'rest's plan,
As laws of God, the wild decrees of man,
Like Pharisees, of whom the Scriptures tell,
She makes them ten times more the sons of hell.

(ii)

[*The Poet as King of Gotham*]

THE Snowdrop, who, in habit white and plain,
Comes on the herald of fair Flora's train;
The coxcomb Crocus, flow'r of simple note,
Who by her side struts in a herald's coat;
The Tulip, idly glaring to the view,
Who, though no clown, his birth from Holland drew,
Who, once full-dressed, fears from his place to stir,
The fop of flow'rs, the More of a parterre;
The Woodbine, who her Elm in marriage meets,
And brings her dowry in surrounding sweets;
The Lily, silver mistress of the vale,
The Rose of Sharon which perfumes the gale;
The Jessamine, with which the queen of flow'rs
To charm her god adorns his fav'rite bow'rs,
Which brides, by the plain hand of neatness dressed,
Unenvied rival, wear upon their breast,
Sweet as the incense of the morn, and chaste
As the pure zone, which circles Dian's waist;
All flow'rs, of various names and various forms,
Which the sun into strength and beauty warms,
From the dwarf Daisy, which, like infants, clings,
And fears to leave the earth from whence it springs,
To the proud giant of the garden race,
Who, madly rushing to the sun's embrace,
O'ertops her fellows with aspiring aim,
Demands his wedded love, and bears his name;
All, one and all, shall in this chorus join,
And, dumb to others' praise, be loud in mine:

Rejoice, ye happy Gothamites, rejoice;
Lift up your voice on high, a mighty voice,
The voice of gladness, and on ev'ry tongue,
In strains of gratitude, be praises hung,
The praises of so great and good a King;
Shall Churchill reign, and shall not Gotham sing?

Forming a gloom, through which to spleen-struck minds
Religion, horror-stamped, a passage finds,
The Ivy crawling o'er the hallowed cell,
Where some old hermit's wont his beads to tell
By day, by night; the Myrtle ever-green,
Beneath whose shade Love holds his rites unseen;
The Willow weeping o'er the fatal wave,
Where many a lover finds a wat'ry grave;
The Cypress sacred held, when lovers mourn
Their true love snatched away; the Laurel worn
By poets in old time, but destined now
In grief to wither on a Whitehead's brow;
The Fig, which, large as what in India grows,
Itself a grove, gave our first parents clothes;
The Vine, which, like a blushing new-made bride,
Clust'ring, empurples all the mountain's side;
The Yew, which, in the place of sculptured stone,
Marks out the resting-place of men unknown;
The hedgerow Elm, the Pine of mountain race;
The Fir, the Scotch Fir, never out of place;
The Cedar, whose top mates the highest cloud,
Whilst his old father Lebanon grows proud
Of such a child, and his vast body laid
Out many a mile, enjoys the filial shade;
The Oak, when living, monarch of the wood;
The English Oak, which, dead, commands the flood;
All, one and all, shall in this chorus join,
And, dumb to others' praise, be loud in mine:

Rejoice, ye happy Gothamites, rejoice;
Lift up your voice on high, a mighty voice,
The voice of gladness, and on ev'ry tongue,
In strains of gratitude, be praises hung,
The praises of so great and good a King;
Shall Churchill reign, and shall not Gotham sing?

The Show'rs, which make the young hills, like young lambs,
Bound and rebound, the old hills, like old rams,
Unwieldy, jump for joy; the Streams, which glide,
Whilst Plenty marches smiling by their side,
And from their bosom rising Commerce springs;
The Winds, which rise with healing on their wings,
Before whose cleansing breath contagion flies;
The Sun who, travelling in eastern skies,
Fresh, full of strength, just risen from his bed,
Though in Jove's pastures they were born and bred,

With voice and whip, can scarce make his steeds stir,
Step by step, up the perpendicular;
Who, at the hour of eve, panting for rest,
Rolls on amain, and gallops down the west,
As fast as Jehu, oiled for Ahab's sin,
Drove for a crown, or post-boys for an inn;
The Moon, who holds o'er night her silver reign,
Regent of tides, and mistress of the brain,
Who to her sons, those sons who own her pow'r,
And do her homage at the midnight hour,
Gives madness as a blessing, but dispenses
Wisdom to fools, and damns them with their senses;
The Stars who, by I know not what strange right,
Preside o'er mortals in their own despite,
Who without reason govern those, who most
(How truly, judge from hence!) of reason boast,
And, by some mighty magic yet unknown,
Our actions guide, yet cannot guide their own;
All, one and all, shall in this chorus join,
And, dumb to others' praise, be loud in mine:

Rejoice, ye happy Gothamites, rejoice;
Lift up your voice on high, a mighty voice,
The voice of gladness, and on ev'ry tongue,
In strains of gratitude, be praises hung,
The praises of so great and good a King;
Shall Churchill reign, and shall not Gotham sing?

The Moment, Minute, Hour, Day, Week, Month, Year,
Morning and Eve, as they in turn appear;
Moments and Minutes which, without a crime,
Can't be omitted in accounts of time,
Or, if omitted (proof we might afford),
Worthy by parliaments to be restored;
The Hours which, dressed by turns in black and white,
Ordained as handmaids, wait on Day and Night;
The Day, those hours I mean, when light presides,
And Business in a cart with Prudence rides;
The Night, those hours I mean with darkness hung,
When Sense speaks free, and Folly holds her tongue;
The Morn, when Nature, rousing from her strife
With death-like sleep, awakes to second life;
The Eve, when, as unequal to the task,
She mercy from her foe descends to ask;
The Week, in which six days are kindly given
To think of earth, and one to think of heaven;

The Months, twelve sisters, all of diff'rent hue,
Though there appears in all a likeness too,
Not such a likeness, as, through Hayman's works,
Dull mannerist, in Christians, Jews and Turks,
Cloys with a sameness in each female face,
But a strange something, born of Art and Grace,
Which speaks them all, to vary and adorn,
At diff'rent times of the same parents born;
All, one and all, shall in this chorus join,
And, dumb to others' praise, be loud in mine:

Rejoice, ye happy Gothamites, rejoice;
Lift up your voice on high, a mighty voice,
The voice of gladness, and on ev'ry tongue,
In strains of gratitude, be praises hung,
The praises of so great and good a King;
Shall Churchill reign, and shall not Gotham sing?

(1764)

JAMES GRAINGER

1721–1766

340 from *The Sugar Cane*

(i)

[*Compost*]

OF composts shall the Muse descend to sing,
Nor soil her heavenly plumes? The sacred Muse
Naught sordid deems, but what is base; naught fair
Unless true Virtue stamp it with her seal.
Then, planter, wouldst thou double thine estate,
Never, ah never, be ashamed to tread
Thy dung-heaps, where the refuse of thy mills,
With all the ashes, all thy coppers yield,
With weeds, mould, dung and stale, a compost form,
Of force to fertilize the poorest soil.
But, planter, if thy lands lie far remote
And of access are difficult; on these,
Leave the cane's sapless foliage; and with pens
Wattled (like those the Muse hath oft-times seen
When frolic fancy led her youthful steps,
In green Dorchestria's plains), the whole inclose:

There well thy stock with provender supply;
The well-fed stock will soon that food repay. . . .
  Whether the fattening compost in each hole
'Tis best to throw, or on the surface spread,
Is undetermined: trials must decide.
Unless kind rains and fostering dews descend,
To melt the compost's fertilizing salts,
A stinted plant, deceitful of thy hopes,
Will from those beds slow spring where hot dung lies:
But, if 'tis scattered generously o'er all,
The cane will better bear the solar blaze;
Less rain demand; and, by repeated crops,
Thy land improved its gratitude will show.
  Enough of composts, Muse. . . .

(ii)

[*Slaves*]

  YET, planter, let humanity prevail.—
Perhaps thy negro, in his native land,
Possessed large fertile plains, and slaves, and herds:
Perhaps, whene'er he deigned to walk abroad,
The richest silks, from where the Indus rolls,
His limbs invested in their gorgeous pleats:
Perhaps he wails his wife, his children, left
To struggle with adversity: perhaps
Fortune, in battle for his country fought,
Gave him a captive to his deadliest foe:
Perhaps, incautious, in his native fields
(On pleasurable scenes his mind intent)
All as he wandered, from the neighbouring grove,
Fell ambush dragged him to the hated main.—
Were they even sold for crimes; ye polished say!
Ye to whom Learning opes her amplest page!
Ye, whom the knowledge of a living God
Should lead to virtue! are ye free from crimes?
Ah pity, then, these uninstructed swains;
And still let mercy soften the decrees
Of rigid justice, with her lenient hand.
  Oh, did the tender Muse possess the power,
Which monarchs have, and monarchs oft abuse:
'Twould be the fond ambition of her soul
To quell tyrannic sway; knock off the chains
Of heart-debasing slavery; give to man,
Of every colour and of every clime,

Freedom, which stamps him image of his God.
Then laws, Oppression's scourge, fair Virtue's prop,
Offspring of Wisdom! should impartial reign,
To knit the whole in well-accorded strife:
Servants, not slaves; of choice, and not compelled;
The blacks should cultivate the Cane-land isles.

(1764)

OLIVER GOLDSMITH

1730?–1774

341 from *The Traveller, or A Prospect of Society*

[*Britain*]

CREATION'S mildest charms are there combined,
Extremes are only in the master's mind.
Stern o'er each bosom reason holds her state,
With daring aims irregularly great;
Pride in their port, defiance in their eye,
I see the lords of human kind pass by,
Intent on high designs, a thoughtful band,
By forms unfashioned, fresh from nature's hand;
Fierce in their native hardiness of soul,
True to imagined right, above control,
While even the peasant boasts these rights to scan,
And learns to venerate himself as man.
  Thine, Freedom, thine the blessings pictured here,
Thine are those charms that dazzle and endear;
Too blest, indeed, were such without alloy,
But fostered even by Freedom, ills annoy:
That independence Britons prize too high,
Keeps man from man and breaks the social tie;
The self-dependent lordlings stand alone,
All claims that bind and sweeten life unknown;
Here by the bonds of nature feebly held,
Minds combat minds, repelling and repelled.
Ferments arise, imprisoned factions roar,
Repressed ambition struggles round her shore,
Till over-wrought, the general system feels
Its motions stopped, or frenzy fire the wheels.
  Nor this the worst. As nature's ties decay,
As duty, love and honour fail to sway,

Fictitious bonds, the bonds of wealth and law,
Still gather strength and force unwilling awe.
Hence all obedience bows to these alone,
And talent sinks and merit weeps unknown;
Till time may come when, stripped of all her charms,
The land of scholars and the nurse of arms,
Where noble stems transmit the patriot flame,
Where kings have toiled and poets wrote for fame,
One sink of level avarice shall lie,
And scholars, soldiers, kings unhonoured die.

(1764)

342 *An Elegy on the Death of a Mad Dog*

GOOD people all, of every sort,
  Give ear unto my song;
And if you find it wond'rous short,
  It cannot hold you long.

In Islington there was a man,
  Of whom the world might say
That still a godly race he ran,
  Whene'er he went to pray.

A kind and gentle heart he had,
  To comfort friends and foes;
The naked every day he clad,
  When he put on his clothes.

And in that town a dog was found,
  As many dogs there be,
Both mongrel, puppy, whelp and hound,
  And curs of low degree.

This dog and man at first were friends;
  But when a pique began,
The dog, to gain some private ends,
  Went mad and bit the man.

Around from all the neighbouring streets
  The wondering neighbours ran,
And swore the dog had lost his wits,
  To bite so good a man.

The wound it seemed both sore and sad
  To every Christian eye;
And while they swore the dog was mad,
  They swore the man would die.

But soon a wonder came to light,
  That showed the rogues they lied:
The man recovered of the bite,
  The dog it was that died.

(1766)

343 [*Song*]

WHEN lovely woman stoops to folly,
  And finds too late that men betray,
What charm can soothe her melancholy,
  What art can wash her guilt away?

The only art her guilt to cover,
  To hide her shame from every eye,
To give repentance to her lover,
  And wring his bosom—is to die.

(1766)

344 *The Deserted Village*

SWEET Auburn, loveliest village of the plain,
Where health and plenty cheered the labouring swain,
Where smiling spring its earliest visit paid,
And parting summer's lingering blooms delayed:
Dear lovely bowers of innocence and ease,
Seats of my youth, when every sport could please,
How often have I loitered o'er thy green,
Where humble happiness endeared each scene;
How often have I paused on every charm,
The sheltered cot, the cultivated farm,
The never-failing brook, the busy mill,
The decent church that topped the neighbouring hill,
The hawthorn bush, with seats beneath the shade,
For talking age and whispering lovers made.
How often have I blessed the coming day,
When toil remitting lent its turn to play,

And all the village train, from labour free,
Led up their sports beneath the spreading tree,
While many a pastime circled in the shade,
The young contending as the old surveyed;
And many a gambol frolicked o'er the ground,
And sleights of art and feats of strength went round.
And still as each repeated pleasure tired,
Succeeding sports the mirthful band inspired;
The dancing pair that simply sought renown,
By holding out to tire each other down;
The swain mistrustless of his smutted face,
While secret laughter tittered round the place;
The bashful virgin's sidelong looks of love,
The matron's glance that would those looks reprove.
These were thy charms, sweet village; sports like these,
With sweet succession, taught even toil to please;
These round thy bowers their cheerful influence shed,
These were thy charms—but all these charms are fled.
  Sweet smiling village, loveliest of the lawn,
Thy sports are fled and all thy charms withdrawn;
Amidst thy bowers the tyrant's hand is seen,
And desolation saddens all thy green:
One only master grasps the whole domain,
And half a tillage stints thy smiling plain:
No more thy glassy brook reflects the day,
But, choked with sedges, works its weedy way.
Along thy glades, a solitary guest,
The hollow-sounding bittern guards its nest;
Amidst thy desert walks the lapwing flies,
And tires their echoes with unvaried cries.
Sunk are thy bowers in shapeless ruin all,
And the long grass o'ertops the mouldering wall;
And trembling, shrinking from the spoiler's hand,
Far, far away, thy children leave the land.
  Ill fares the land, to hastening ills a prey,
Where wealth accumulates and men decay:
Princes and lords may flourish or may fade;
A breath can make them, as a breath has made;
But a bold peasantry, their country's pride,
When once destroyed, can never be supplied.
  A time there was, ere England's griefs began,
When every rood of ground maintained its man;
For him light labour spread her wholesome store,
Just gave what life required, but gave no more:
His best companions, innocence and health;
And his best riches, ignorance of wealth.

But times are altered; trade's unfeeling train
Usurp the land and dispossess the swain;
Along the lawn, where scattered hamlets rose,
Unwieldy wealth and cumbrous pomp repose;
And every want to opulence allied,
And every pang that folly pays to pride.
These gentle hours that plenty bade to bloom,
Those calm desires that asked but little room,
Those healthful sports that graced the peaceful scene,
Lived in each look and brightened all the green;
These, far departing, seek a kinder shore,
And rural mirth and manners are no more.
Sweet Auburn! parent of the blissful hour,
Thy glades forlorn confess the tyrant's power.
Here as I take my solitary rounds,
Amidst thy tangling walks and ruined grounds,
And, many a year elapsed, return to view
Where once the cottage stood, the hawthorn grew,
Remembrance wakes with all her busy train,
Swells at my breast and turns the past to pain.
In all my wanderings round this world of care,
In all my griefs—and God has given my share—
I still had hopes my latest hours to crown,
Amidst these humble bowers to lay me down;
To husband out life's taper at the close
And keep the flame from wasting by repose.
I still had hopes, for pride attends us still,
Amidst the swains to show my book-learned skill,
Around my fire an evening group to draw,
And tell of all I felt and all I saw;
And, as a hare, whom hounds and horns pursue,
Pants to the place from whence at first she flew,
I still had hopes, my long vexations past,
Here to return—and die at home at last.
O blest retirement, friend to life's decline,
Retreats from care that never must be mine,
How happy he who crowns in shades like these
A youth of labour with an age of ease;
Who quits a world where strong temptations try,
And, since 'tis hard to combat, learns to fly.
For him no wretches, born to work and weep,
Explore the mine or tempt the dangerous deep;
No surly porter stands in guilty state
To spurn imploring famine from the gate;
But on he moves to meet his latter end,
Angels around befriending virtue's friend;

Bends to the grave with unperceived decay,
While resignation gently slopes the way;
And, all his prospects brightening to the last,
His heaven commences ere the world be past!
Sweet was the sound, when oft at evening's close
Up yonder hill the village murmur rose;
There, as I passed with careless steps and slow,
The mingling notes came softened from below;
The swain responsive as the milkmaid sung,
The sober herd that lowed to meet their young;
The noisy geese that gabbled o'er the pool,
The playful children just let loose from school;
The watchdog's voice that bayed the whispering wind,
And the loud laugh that spoke the vacant mind;
These all in sweet confusion sought the shade,
And filled each pause the nightingale had made.
But now the sounds of population fail,
No cheerful murmurs fluctuate in the gale,
No busy steps the grassgrown foot-way tread,
For all the bloomy flush of life is fled.
All but yon widowed, solitary thing
That feebly bends beside the plashy spring;
She, wretched matron, forced, in age, for bread,
To strip the brook with mantling cresses spread,
To pick her wintry faggot from the thorn,
To seek her nightly shed and weep till morn;
She only left of all the harmless train,
The sad historian of the pensive plain.
Near yonder copse, where once the garden smiled,
And still where many a garden flower grows wild;
There, where a few torn shrubs the place disclose,
The village preacher's modest mansion rose.
A man he was to all the country dear,
And passing rich with forty pounds a year;
Remote from towns he ran his godly race,
Nor e'er had changed, nor wished to change, his place;
Unpractised he to fawn, or seek for power,
By doctrines fashioned to the varying hour;
Far other aims his heart had learned to prize,
More skilled to raise the wretched than to rise.
His house was known to all the vagrant train,
He chid their wanderings, but relieved their pain;
The long-remembered beggar was his guest,
Whose beard descending swept his aged breast;
The ruined spendthrift, now no longer proud,
Claimed kindred there and had his claims allowed;

The broken soldier, kindly bade to stay,
Sat by his fire and talked the night away;
Wept o'er his wounds or tales of sorrow done,
Shouldered his crutch and showed how fields were won.
Pleased with his guests, the good man learned to glow,
And quite forgot their vices in their woe;
Careless their merits or their faults to scan,
His pity gave ere charity began.
  Thus to relieve the wretched was his pride,
And even his failings leaned to virtue's side;
But in his duty prompt at every call,
He watched and wept, he prayed and felt, for all.
And, as a bird each fond endearment tries
To tempt its new-fledged offspring to the skies,
He tried each art, reproved each dull delay,
Allured to brighter worlds, and led the way.
  Beside the bed where parting life was laid,
And sorrow, guilt, and pain by turns dismayed,
The reverend champion stood. At his control,
Despair and anguish fled the struggling soul;
Comfort came down the trembling wretch to raise,
And his last faltering accents whispered praise.
  At church, with meek and unaffected grace,
His looks adorned the venerable place;
Truth from his lips prevailed with double sway,
And fools, who came to scoff, remained to pray.
The service past, around the pious man,
With steady zeal each honest rustic ran;
Even children followed with endearing wile,
And plucked his gown, to share the good man's smile.
His ready smile a parent's warmth expressed,
Their welfare pleased him and their cares distressed;
To them his heart, his love, his griefs were given,
But all his serious thoughts had rest in heaven.
As some tall cliff, that lifts its awful form,
Swells from the vale and midway leaves the storm,
Though round its breast the rolling clouds are spread,
Eternal sunshine settles on its head.
  Beside yon straggling fence that skirts the way,
With blossomed furze unprofitably gay,
There, in his noisy mansion, skilled to rule,
The village master taught his little school;
A man severe he was and stern to view;
I knew him well, and every truant knew;
Well had the boding tremblers learned to trace
The day's disasters in his morning face;

Full well they laughed, with counterfeited glee,
At all his jokes, for many a joke had he;
Full well the busy whisper, circling round,
Conveyed the dismal tidings when he frowned;
Yet he was kind, or, if severe in aught,
The love he bore to learning was in fault;
The village all declared how much he knew;
'Twas certain he could write and cipher too;
Lands he could measure, terms and tides presage,
And even the story ran that he could gauge.
In arguing too, the parson owned his skill,
For even though vanquished, he could argue still;
While words of learned length and thundering sound
Amazed the gazing rustics ranged around,
And still they gazed, and still the wonder grew,
That one small head could carry all he knew.
  But past is all his fame. The very spot,
Where many a time he triumphed, is forgot.
Near yonder thorn, that lifts its head on high,
Where once the signpost caught the passing eye,
Low lies that house where nutbrown draughts inspired,
Where greybeard mirth and smiling toil retired,
Where village statesmen talked with looks profound,
And news much older than their ale went round.
Imagination fondly stoops to trace
The parlour splendours of that festive place;
The white-washed wall, the nicely sanded floor,
The varnished clock that clicked behind the door;
The chest contrived a double debt to pay,
A bed by night, a chest of drawers by day;
The pictures placed for ornament and use,
The twelve good rules, the royal game of goose;
The hearth, except when winter chilled the day,
With aspen boughs and flowers and fennel gay;
While broken teacups, wisely kept for show,
Ranged o'er the chimney, glistened in a row.
  Vain, transitory splendours! Could not all
Reprieve the tottering mansion from its fall!
Obscure it sinks, nor shall it more impart
An hour's importance to the poor man's heart;
Thither no more the peasant shall repair
To sweet oblivion of his daily care;
No more the farmer's news, the barber's tale,
No more the woodman's ballad shall prevail;

cipher] practise arithmetic   gauge] calculate capacity of vessels

No more the smith his dusky brow shall clear,
Relax his ponderous strength and lean to hear;
The host himself no longer shall be found
Careful to see the mantling bliss go round;
Nor the coy maid, half willing to be pressed,
Shall kiss the cup to pass it to the rest.
  Yes! let the rich deride, the proud disdain,
These simple blessings of the lowly train;
To me more dear, congenial to my heart,
One native charm than all the gloss of art;
Spontaneous joys, where nature has its play,
The soul adopts and owns their firstborn sway;
Lightly they frolic o'er the vacant mind,
Unenvied, unmolested, unconfined:
But the long pomp, the midnight masquerade,
With all the freaks of wanton wealth arrayed,
In these, ere triflers half their wish obtain,
The toiling pleasure sickens into pain;
And, even while fashion's brightest arts decoy,
The heart distrusting asks, if this be joy.
  Ye friends to truth, ye statesmen, who survey
The rich man's joys increase, the poor's decay,
'Tis yours to judge how wide the limits stand
Between a splendid and an happy land.
Proud swells the tide with loads of freighted ore,
And shouting Folly hails them from her shore;
Hoards, even beyond the miser's wish, abound,
And rich men flock from all the world around.
Yet count our gains. This wealth is but a name
That leaves our useful products still the same.
Not so the loss. The man of wealth and pride
Takes up a space that many poor supplied;
Space for his lake, his park's extended bounds,
Space for his horses, equipage and hounds;
The robe that wraps his limbs in silken sloth
Has robbed the neighbouring fields of half their growth;
His seat, where solitary sports are seen,
Indignant spurns the cottage from the green;
Around the world each needful product flies,
For all the luxuries the world supplies:
While thus the land, adorned for pleasure all,
In barren splendour feebly waits the fall.
  As some fair female unadorned and plain,
Secure to please while youth confirms her reign,
Slights every borrowed charm that dress supplies,
Nor shares with art the triumph of her eyes;

But when those charms are passed, for charms are frail,
When time advances and when lovers fail,
She then shines forth, solicitous to bless,
In all the glaring impotence of dress:
Thus fares the land, by luxury betrayed,
In nature's simplest charms at first arrayed;
But verging to decline, its splendours rise,
Its vistas strike, its palaces surprise;
While scourged by famine from the smiling land,
The mournful peasant leads his humble band;
And while he sinks, without one arm to save,
The country blooms—a garden and a grave.
  Where then, ah where, shall poverty reside,
To 'scape the pressure of contiguous pride?
If to some common's fenceless limits strayed,
He drives his flock to pick the scanty blade,
Those fenceless fields the sons of wealth divide,
And even the bare-worn common is denied.
  If to the city sped—what waits him there?
To see profusion that he must not share;
To see ten thousand baneful arts combined
To pamper luxury and thin mankind;
To see those joys the sons of pleasure know
Extorted from his fellow-creature's woe.
Here, while the courtier glitters in brocade,
There the pale artist plies the sickly trade;
Here, while the proud their long-drawn pomps display,
There the black gibbet glooms beside the way.
The dome where Pleasure holds her midnight reign
Here, richly decked, admits the gorgeous train;
Tumultuous grandeur crowds the blazing square,
The rattling chariots clash, the torches glare.
Sure scenes like these no troubles e'er annoy!
Sure these denote one universal joy!
Are these thy serious thoughts?—Ah, turn thine eyes
Where the poor, houseless, shivering female lies.
She once, perhaps, in village plenty blessed,
Has wept at tales of innocence distressed;
Her modest looks the cottage might adorn,
Sweet as the primrose peeps beneath the thorn;
Now lost to all; her friends, her virtue fled,
Near her betrayer's door she lays her head,
And, pinched with cold and shrinking from the shower,
With heavy heart deplores that luckless hour,

artist] workman

When idly first, ambitious of the town,
She left her wheel and robes of country brown.
  Do thine, sweet Auburn, thine, the loveliest train,
Do thy fair tribes participate her pain?
Even now, perhaps, by cold and hunger led,
At proud men's doors they ask a little bread!
  Ah, no. To distant climes, a dreary scene,
Where half the convex world intrudes between,
Through torrid tracts with fainting steps they go,
Where wild Altama murmurs to their woe.
Far different there from all that charmed before
The various terrors of that horrid shore:
Those blazing suns that dart a downward ray,
And fiercely shed intolerable day;
Those matted woods where birds forget to sing,
But silent bats in drowsy clusters cling;
Those poisonous fields with rank luxuriance crowned,
Where the dark scorpion gathers death around;
Where at each step the stranger fears to wake
The rattling terrors of the vengeful snake;
Where crouching tigers wait their hapless prey,
And savage men more murderous still than they;
While oft in whirls the mad tornado flies,
Mingling the ravaged landscape with the skies.
Far different these from every former scene,
The cooling brook, the grassy-vested green,
The breezy covert of the warbling grove,
That only sheltered thefts of harmless love.
  Good heaven! what sorrows gloomed that parting day,
That called them from their native walks away;
When the poor exiles, every pleasure past,
Hung round their bowers and fondly looked their last,
And took a long farewell, and wished in vain
For seats like these beyond the western main;
And shuddering still to face the distant deep,
Returned and wept, and still returned to weep.
The good old sire the first prepared to go
To new-found worlds, and wept for others' woe;
But for himself, in conscious virtue brave,
He only wished for worlds beyond the grave.
His lovely daughter, lovelier in her tears,
The fond companion of his helpless years,
Silent went next, neglectful of her charms,
And left a lover's for a father's arms.
With louder plaints the mother spoke her woes,
And blessed the cot where every pleasure rose;

And kissed her thoughtless babes with many a tear,
And clasped them close, in sorrow doubly dear;
Whilst her fond husband strove to lend relief
In all the silent manliness of grief.
  O luxury! thou cursed by heaven's decree,
How ill exchanged are things like these for thee!
How do thy potions with insidious joy
Diffuse their pleasures only to destroy!
Kingdoms, by thee to sickly greatness grown,
Boast of a florid vigour not their own.
At every draught more large and large they grow,
A bloated mass of rank unwieldy woe;
Till sapped their strength and every part unsound,
Down, down they sink and spread a ruin round.
  Even now the devastation is begun,
And half the business of destruction done;
Even now, methinks, as pondering here I stand,
I see the rural virtues leave the land.
Down where yon anchoring vessel spreads the sail,
That idly waiting flaps with every gale,
Downward they move, a melancholy band,
Pass from the shore and darken all the strand.
Contented toil and hospitable care,
And kind connubial tenderness are there;
And piety, with wishes placed above,
And steady loyalty and faithful love.
And thou, sweet Poetry, thou loveliest maid,
Still first to fly where sensual joys invade;
Unfit, in these degenerate times of shame,
To catch the heart or strike for honest fame;
Dear charming nymph, neglected and decried,
My shame in crowds, my solitary pride;
Thou source of all my bliss and all my woe,
That found'st me poor at first and keep'st me so;
Thou guide by which the nobler arts excel,
Thou nurse of every virtue, fare thee well!
Farewell, and oh, where'er thy voice be tried,
On Torno's cliffs or Pambamarca's side,
Whether where equinoctial fervours glow,
Or winter wraps the polar world in snow,
Still let thy voice, prevailing over time,
Redress the rigours of the inclement clime;
Aid slighted truth; with thy persuasive strain
Teach erring man to spurn the rage of gain;
Teach him that states of native strength possessed,
Though very poor, may still be very blest;

That trade's proud empire hastes to swift decay,
As ocean sweeps the laboured mole away;
While self-dependent power can time defy,
As rocks resist the billows and the sky.

(1770)

345 from *Retaliation*

(i)

[*Edmund Burke*]

HERE lies our good Edmund, whose genius was such,
We scarcely can praise it or blame it too much;
Who, born for the universe, narrowed his mind,
And to party gave up what was meant for mankind;
Though fraught with all learning, kept straining his throat
To persuade Tommy Townshend to lend him a vote;
Who, too deep for his hearers, still went on refining,
And thought of convincing, while they thought of dining;
Though equal to all things, for all things unfit;
Too nice for a statesman, too proud for a wit;
For a patriot, too cool; for a drudge, disobedient;
And too fond of the *right* to pursue the *expedient*.
In short, 'twas his fate, unemployed or in place, sir,
To eat mutton cold and cut blocks with a razor.

(ii)

[*David Garrick*]

HERE lies David Garrick, describe me who can,
An abridgement of all that was pleasant in man;
As an actor, confessed without rival to shine,
As a wit, if not first, in the very first line;
Yet with talents like these and an excellent heart,
The man had his failings, a dupe to his art.
Like an ill-judging beauty his colours he spread,
And beplastered with rouge his own natural red.
On the stage he was natural, simple, affecting:
'Twas only that, when he was off, he was acting.
With no reason on earth to go out of his way,
He turned and he varied full ten times a day.
Though secure of our hearts, yet confoundedly sick,
If they were not his own by finessing and trick,

He cast off his friends, as a huntsman his pack,
For he knew when he pleased he could whistle them back.
Of praise a mere glutton, he swallowed what came,
And the puff of a dunce, he mistook it for fame;
Till his relish grown callous, almost to disease,
Who peppered the highest was surest to please.
But let us be candid and speak out our mind:
If dunces applauded, he paid them in kind.
Ye Kenricks, ye Kellys and Woodfalls so grave,
What a commerce was yours, while you got and you gave!
How did Grub-street re-echo the shouts that you raised,
While he was be-Rosciused and you were be-praised!
But peace to his spirit, wherever it flies,
To act as an angel and mix with the skies:
Those poets, who owe their best fame to his skill,
Shall still be his flatterers, go where he will.
Old Shakespeare receive him with praise and with love,
And Beaumonts and Bens be his Kellys above.

(iii)

[*Sir Joshua Reynolds*]

HERE Reynolds is laid and, to tell you my mind,
He has not left a better or wiser behind:
His pencil was striking, resistless and grand;
His manners were gentle, complying and bland;
Still born to improve us in every part,
His pencil our faces, his manners our heart;
To coxcombs averse, yet most civilly steering,
When they judged without skill he was still hard of hearing;
When they talked of their Raphaels, Correggios and stuff,
He shifted his trumpet and only took snuff.

(1774)

LEONARD HOWARD

1699?–1767

346 *The Humours of the King's Bench Prison, a Ballad*

NOW we're met, my brethren Benchers,
  In this mean unhappy place,
Though so deep our foes entrench us,
  We can show a cheerful face.

Though our worldly schemes miscarry,
  And our persons are in thrall,
We have still facetious Harry
  To keep up the jovial ball.

We have parsons quite lighthearted,
  Though by patrons left in lurch:
Who can say that we're deserted,
  When with us we've got the Church?

We have merchants, lawyers, sages,
  Those who never thought think here;
We have captains, prince's pages;
  To our College all repair.

We have Jack, who no disaster
  Can his careless temper seize;
We have little Driver's master,
  Who always strives his friends to please.

The young Cantab. from chopping logic,
  Just commenced *magister art.*,
Takes his Covent Garden frolic,
  Then comes here to feel the smart.

Mamma with chiding tips a guinea,
  Grieves to see her sprig confined:
'The De—l sure,' she says, 'was in you';
  'O no, 'twas love, and love is blind.'

Here are men of all conditions;
  Flashy wits and stupid fools;
Quacks and regular physicians
  Sit on our repentance stools.

Bloods and bucks undone by wenches
  To Dog and Duck with pains repair;
Their youthful fires that Lethe quenches;
  No cure is like St. George's air.

Our creditors we've oft petitioned,
  For us our weeping friends have met;
'Discharge them and be good-conditioned',
  But Shylock will have flesh or debt.

When committed first we whimper,
  Wring our hands at fortune's stroke;
But a bumper makes us simper,
  Fill it up, the gall is broke.

The Marshal, if by our behaviour
  In his graces we can get,
Loves to show his prisoners favour,
  And by being good is great.

Though we've squandered our possessions,
  Marson's[1] pity here extends,
Scorns to load us with oppressions,
  Treats us all like men and friends.

Tapsters here are only surly,
  And if chalked behind the door,
O what noise and hurly-burly,
  Pay we must, or call no more.

This is Falstaff's field of battle,
  Want of cash may strifes create;
Morris[2] will regard no prattle,
  No scoring's here but on the pate.

What joy to see a pot of porter,
  With nick and froth the humming beer;
Beyond a girl, in thirst we court her,
  O what cloth and colour's here!

Angry fathers, envious brothers,
  Nature's duties here neglect;
Scraping misers make their pothers,
  On our conduct all reflect.

But ev'ry man has got his failing,
  Ev'ry class produces fools;
Vice is through the world prevailing,
  Benchers only live by *rules*.[3]

(1765)

[1] The Marshal's Deputy of the Prison.
[2] The man who keeps the tap.
[3] The Liberties of the King's Bench are called the Rules.

THOMAS PERCY

1729–1811

347 *The Friar of Orders Gray*

Dispersed through Shakespeare's plays are innumerable little fragments of ancient ballads, the entire copies of which could not be recovered. Many of these being of the most beautiful and pathetic simplicity, the Editor was tempted to select some of them and, with a few supplemental stanzas, to connect them together and form them into a little Tale, which is here submitted to the Reader's candour. One small fragment was taken from Beaumont and Fletcher.

It was a friar of orders gray,
  Walkt forth to tell his beades;
And he met with a lady faire,
  Clad in a pilgrime's weedes.

Now Christ thee save, thou reverend friar,
  I pray thee tell to me,
If ever at yon holy shrine
  My true love thou didst see.

And how should I know your true love,
  From many another one?
O by his cockle hat, and staff,
  And by his sandal shoone[1].

But chiefly by his face and mien,
  That were so fair to view;
His flaxen locks that sweetly curled,
  And eyne of lovely blue.

O lady, he is dead and gone!
  Lady, he's dead and gone!
And at his head a green grass turfe,
  And at his heels a stone.

Within these holy cloysters long
  He languisht, and he dyed,
Lamenting of a ladyes love,
  And 'playning of her pride.

[1] These are the distinguishing marks of a pilgrim. The chief places of devotion being beyond sea, the pilgrims were wont to put cockle shells in their hats to denote the intention or performance of their pilgrimage. Warburton, *Shakespear.* Vol. 8. p. 224.

Here bore him barefaced on his bier
  Six proper youths and tall,
And many a tear bedewed his grave
  Within yon kirk-yard wall.

And art thou dead, thou gentle youth!
  And art thou dead and gone!
And didst thou dye for love of me!
  Break, cruel heart of stone!

O weep not, lady, weep not soe;
  Some ghostly comfort seek:
Let not vain sorrow rive thy heart
  Ne teares bedew thy cheek.

O do not, do not, holy friar,
  My sorrow now reprove;
For I have lost the sweetest youth,
  That e'er wan ladyes love.

And nowe, alas! for thy sad losse,
  I'll evermore weep and sigh;
For thee I only wisht to live,
  For thee I wish to dye.

Weep no more, lady, weep no more,
  Thy sorrowe is in vaine:
For, violets pluckt the sweetest showers
  Will ne'er make grow againe.

Our joys as wingèd dreams doe flye,
  Why then should sorrow last?
Since grief but aggravates thy losse,
  Grieve not for what is past.

O say not soe, thou holy friar;
  I pray thee, say not soe:
For since my true-love dyed for mee,
  'Tis meet my tears should flow.

And will he ne'er come again!
  Will he ne'er come again?
Ah! no, he is dead and laid in his grave,
  For ever to remain.

His cheek was redder than the rose,
  The comliest youth was he:—
But he is dead and laid in his grave:
  Alas, and woe is me!

Sigh no more, lady, sigh no more,
  Men were deceivers ever:
One foot on sea and one on land,
  To one thing constant never.

Hadst thou been fond, he had been false,
  And left thee sad and heavy;
For young men ever were fickle found,
  Since summer trees were leafy.

Now say not so, thou holy friar,
  I pray thee say not soe:
My love he had the truest heart:
  O he was ever true!

And art thou dead, thou much-loved youth,
  And didst thou dye for mee?
Then farewell home; for, ever-more
  A pilgrim I will bee.

But first upon my true-love's grave
  My weary limbs I'll lay,
And thrice I'll kiss the green-grass turf,
  That wraps his breathless clay.

Yet stay, fair lady; rest awhile
  Beneath this cloyster wall:
See through the hawthorn blows the cold wind,
  And drizzly rain doth fall.

O stay me not, thou holy friar;
  O stay me not I pray:
No drizzly rain that falls on me,
  Can wash my fault away.

Yet stay, fair lady, turn again,
  And dry those pearly tears;
For see beneath this gown of gray
  Thy owne true-love appears.

Here forced by grief, and hopeless love,
These holy weeds I sought;
And here amid these lonely walls
To end my days I thought.

But haply for my year of grace[1]
Is not yet past away,
Might I still hope to win thy love,
No longer would I stay.

Now farewell grief, and welcome joy
Once more unto my heart:
For since I have found thee, lovely youth,
We never more will part.

(1765)

CHRISTOPHER ANSTEY

1724–1805

348 from *The New Bath Guide*

Letter XIV. In which Miss Prudence B[lunde]r[hea]d Informs Lady Betty that she has been Elected to Methodism by a Vision

HEARKEN, Lady Betty, hearken
To the dismal news I tell;
How your friends are all embarking
For the fiery gulf of hell.

Brother Simkin's grown a rakehell,
Cards and dances ev'ry day.
Jenny laughs at tabernacle,
Tabby Runt is gone astray.

Blessed I, though once rejected,
Like a little wand'ring sheep,
Who this morning was elected,
By a vision in my sleep:

For I dreamed an apparition
Came, like Roger, from above;
Saying, 'By divine commission
I must fill you full of love.'

[1] The year of probation, or noviciate.

Just with Roger's head of hair on,
  Roger's mouth and pious smile;
Sweet, methinks, as beard of Aaron
  Dropping down with holy oil.

I began to fall a-kicking,
  Panted, struggled, strove in vain;
When the spirit whipped so quick in,
  I was cured of all my pain.

First I thought it was the nightmare
  Lay so heavy on my breast;
But I found new joy and light there,
  When with heav'nly love possessed.

Come again then, apparition,
  Finish what thou hast begun;
Roger, stay, thou soul's physician,
  I with thee my race will run.

Faith her chariot has appointed,
  Now we're stretching for the goal;
All the wheels with grace anointed,
  Up to heav'n to drive my soul.

(1766)

EVAN LLOYD

1734–1776

349 from *The Methodist*

[*Religion and the Lower Classes*]

THE bricklay'r throws his trowel by,
And now builds mansions in the sky;
The cobbler, touched with holy pride,
Flings his old shoes and last aside,
And now devoutly sets about
Cobbling of souls that ne'er wear out;
The baker, now a preacher grown,
Finds man lives not by bread alone,

And now his customers he feeds
With pray'rs, with sermons, groans and creeds;
The tinman, moved by warmth within,
Hammers the Gospel just like tin;
Weavers inspired their shuttles leave,
Sermons and flimsy hymns to weave;
Barbers unreaped will leave the chin,
To trim and shave the man within;
The waterman forgets his wherry,
And opens a celestial ferry;
The brewer, bit by frenzy's grub,
The mashing- for the preaching-tub
Resigns, those waters to explore
Which, if you drink, you thirst no more;
The gard'ner, weary of his trade,
Tired of the mattock and the spade,
Changed to Apollo's in a trice,
Waters the plants of Paradise;
The fishermen no longer set
For fish the meshes of their net,
But catch, like Peter, men of sin,
For catching is to take them in.

(1766)

FREDERICK FORREST

fl. 1766

350 *St. Anthony and his Pig. A Cantata*

Recitative

Let clownish Cymon, in fond rustic strains,
To lovely Iphigene declare his pains;
Let tink'ring Tom for dustcart Sylvia pine,
I sing St. Anthony and his fav'rite swine:
Who, strange to tell, like you and I could speak,
When other grov'ling pigs could only squeak.
But when, or how, this wonder came to pass,
Remains unnoticed by the scribbling class:
Let it suffice, as oft he did caress her,
Thus, like a lovesick swain, he would address her.

Air

O my pretty piggy-wiggy,
More sweet than is the figgy,
That grows on yonder twiggy,
          Or sugar candy;
My love for thee surpasses
All that which pretty lasses
Have for their looking-glasses,
          Or *Tristram Shandy*.

Recitative

With little doting eyes, and ears upright,
To all he says she listens with delight:
Then, like the sluggish ass in scripture told,
In grunting accent did her mind unfold.

Air

How shall I my thanks declare, sir,
In a learned genteel air, sir?
I the court have never seen,
Or at boarding-school have been;

Nor a singer am, you know, sir,
To delight like Beard and Lowe, sir;
But since I must play my part,
Thank you, sir, with all my heart.

Recitative

The hoary dotard gazes on her charms,
And fondly clasps her in his withered arms;
Then gently stroking first her bristled hide,
Smacked her soft balmy snout, and thus replied.

Air

Let sordid mortals toil all day,
   For gold and silver search and dig;
A greater treasure I enjoy
   In this, my charming talking pig.

Though mighty monarchs on their thrones
  In pride and state look fierce and big,
They are not so content and blessed
  As is old Tony with his pig.

I neither care who's in or out,
  Whether Tory, whether Whig,
I love my country, King and Queen,
  But best of all I love my pig.

(1766)

ANONYMOUS

351 *Sir Dilberry Diddle, Captain of Militia. An Excellent New Song*

Of all the brave captains that ever were seen,
Appointed to fight by a king or a queen,
By a queen or a king appointed to fight,
Sure never a captain was like this brave knight.

He pulled off his slippers and wrapper of silk,
And foaming as furious—as whisk-pared milk—
Says he to his lady, 'My lady, I'll go.
My company calls me; you must not say no.'

With eyes all in tears, says my lady, says she,
'O cruel Sir Dilberry, do not kill me!
For I never will leave thee, but cling round thy middle,
And die in the arms of Sir Dilberry Diddle.'

Says Diddle again to his lady, 'My dear!'
(And with a white handkerchief wiped off a tear)
'The hottest of actions will only be farce,
For sure thou art Venus!' Says she, 'Thou art Mars!'

Awhile they stood simp'ring, like master and miss,
And Cupid thought he would have given one kiss;
'Twas what she expected, admits no dispute,
But he touched his own finger, and blew a salute.

By a place I can't mention, not knowing its name,
At the head of his company Dilberry came,
And the drums to the window call every eye,
To see the defence of the nation pass by.

Old bible-faced women, through spectacles dim,
With hemming and coughing, cried, 'Lord! it is him!'
While boys and the girls, who more clearly could see,
Cried, 'Yonder's Sir Dilberry Diddle, that's he.'

Of all the fair ladies that came to the show,
Sir Diddle's fair lady stood first in the row;
'O charming,' says she, 'how he looks, all in red;
How he turns out his toes! how he holds up his head!

'Do but see his cockade, and behold his dear gun,
Which shines like a looking-glass held in the sun;
O! see thyself now, thou'rt so martially smart,
And look as you looked when you conquered my heart!'

The sweet-sounding notes of Sir Dilberry Diddle
More ravished his ears than the sound of a fiddle,
And as it grew faint, that he heard it no more,
He softened the word of command to—*encore.*

The battle now over without any blows,
The heroes unarm and strip off their clothes;
The captain, refreshed with a sip of rosewater,
Hands his dear to the coach, bows, and then steps in after.

John's orders were special, to drive very slow,
For fevers oft follow fatigue, we all know;
But prudently cautious, in Venus's lap,
His head under her apron, brave Mars took a nap.

He dreamed, Fame reports, that he cut all the throats
Of the French, as they landed in flat-bottomed boats:
In his sleep if such dreadful destruction he makes,
What havoc, ye gods, shall we have when he wakes?

(1766)

RICHARD JAGO

1715–1781

352 from *Edge-Hill, or The Rural Prospect Delineated and Moralised*, Book III

[*The Iron Industry in Birmingham*]

HERE, in huge cauldrons, the rough mass they stow,
Till, by the potent heat, the purer ore
Is liquefied, and leaves the dross afloat.
Then, cautious, from the glowing pond they lead
The fiery stream along the channelled floor;
Where, in the mazy moulds of figured sand,
Anon it hardens and, in ingots rude,
Is to the forge conveyed; whose weighty strokes,
Incessant aided by the rapid stream,
Spread out the ductile ore, now tapering
In lengthened masses, ready to obey
The workman's will, and take its destined form.
  Soon o'er thy furrowed pavement, Bremicham!
Ride the loose bars obstrep'rous; to the sons
Of languid sense and frame too delicate,
Harsh noise perchance, but harmony to thine.
  Instant innumerable hands prepare
To shape and mould the malleable ore.
Their heavy sides th' inflated bellows heave,
Tugged by the pulleyed line, and, with their blast
Continuous, the sleeping embers rouse
And kindle into life. Straight the rough mass,
Plunged in the blazing hearth, its heat contracts,
And glows transparent. Now, Cyclopean chief!
Quick on the anvil lay the burning bar,
And, with thy lusty fellows, on its sides
Impress the weighty stroke. See, how they strain
The swelling nerve, and lift the sinewy arm
In measured time; while, with their clatt'ring blows,
From street to street the propagated sound
Increasing echoes, and, on ev'ry side,
The tortured metal spreads a radiant show'r.
  'Tis noise and hurry all! The throngèd street,
The close-piled warehouse, and the busy shop!
With nimble stroke the tinkling hammers move;
While slow and weighty the vast sledge descends,

In solemn bass responsive, or apart,
Or socially conjoined in tuneful peal.
The rough file grates; yet useful is its touch,
As sharp corrosives to the scirrhous flesh,
Or, to the stubborn temper, keen rebuke.
  How the coarse metal brightens into fame,
Shaped by their plastic hands! what ornament!
What various use! See there the glitt'ring knife
Of tempered edge! The scissors' double shaft,
Useless apart, in social union joined,
Each aiding each! Emblem how beautiful
Of happy nuptial leagues! The button round,
Plain, or embossed, or bright with steely rays!
Or oblong buckle, on the laquered shoe,
With polished lustre, bending elegant
Its shapely rim. But how shall I recount
The thronging merchandise? From gaudy signs,
The littered counter, and the show-glass trim,
Seals, rings, twees, bodkins, crowd into my verse,
Too scanty to contain their num'rous tribes.
  Nor this alone thy praise! With secret art,
Thy sons a compound form of various grains,
And to the fire's dissolvent pow'r commit
The precious mixture; oft, with sleepless eye,
Watching the doubtful process, if perchance
A purer ore may bless their midnight toil;
Or wished enamel clear, or sleek japan
Meet their impatient sight. Nor skilful stroke
Is wanting of the graver's pointed steel;
Nor artful pencil, o'er the polished plate
Swift stealing, and with glowing tints well-fraught.
Thine too, of graceful form, the lettered type!
The friend of learning, and the poet's pride!
Without thee what avail his splendid aims,
And midnight labours? Painful drudgery!
And pow'rless effort! But that thought of thee
Imprints fresh vigour on his panting breast,
As thou ere long shalt on his work impress;
And, with immortal fame, his praise repay.

(1767)

scirrhous] hardened   twees] etuis, cases of small instruments   japan] *see* poem 103

MICHAEL BRUCE

1746–1767

353

Ode: To the Cuckoo

HAIL, beauteous stranger of the wood,
  Attendant on the spring!
Now heav'n repairs thy rural seat,
  And woods thy welcome sing.

Soon as the daisy decks the green,
  Thy certain voice we hear:
Hast thou a star to guide thy path,
  Or mark the rolling year?

Delightful visitant! with thee
  I hail the time of flow'rs,
When heav'n is filled with music sweet
  Of birds among the bow'rs.

The schoolboy, wand'ring in the wood
  To pull the flow'rs so gay,
Starts, thy curious voice to hear,
  And imitates thy lay.

Soon as the pea puts on the bloom,
  Thou fly'st thy vocal vale,
An annual guest in other lands,
  Another spring to hail.

Sweet bird! thy bow'r is ever green,
  Thy sky is ever clear;
Thou hast no sorrow in thy song,
  No winter in thy year!

O could I fly, I'd fly with thee:
  We'd make, with social wing,
Our annual visit o'er the globe,
  Companions of the spring.

(Wr. by 1767; pub. 1770)

354 from *Elegy: To Spring*

FAREWELL, ye blooming fields! ye cheerful plains!
Enough for me the churchyard's lonely mound,
Where Melancholy with still Silence reigns,
And the rank grass waves o'er the cheerless ground.

There let me wander at the shut of eve,
When sleep sits dewy on the labourer's eyes,
The world and all its busy follies leave,
And talk with wisdom where my Daphnis lies.

There let me sleep forgotten in the clay,
When death shall shut these weary aching eyes,
Rest in the hopes of an eternal day,
Till the long night's gone, and the last morn arise,

(Wr. by 1767; pub. 1770)

ANONYMOUS ('WORCESTER')

355 *A Pastoral. In the Modern Style. Pastora and Galatea*

BENEATH the umbrageous shadow of a shade,
Where glowing foliage on the surface played,
And golden roses fanned the silver breeze,
In many a maze light-echoing through the trees,
Pastora tuned the sweetly-panting string,
And ruddy notes thus waked the flattering spring,
While from th' alternate margin of an oak,
A woodland Naiad thus meand'ring spoke.
Past. The reed disports upon the sounding thorn,
And Philomel salutes the noontide morn.
The buzzing bees, poetic from their hive,
In smooth alliteration seem alive:
But ah! my virgin swain is chaster far
Than Cupid's painted shafts or sparrows are,
Sparrows that perch, like Sappho's, on my lay,
Or hop in concert with the dancing day.
Gal. What sound was that, which dawned a bleating hue,
And blushed a sigh? Pastora, was it you?
Your notes, sweet maid, this proverb still shall foil:
'The pot that's watched was never known to boil'.

Past. Ah, no! whate'er thou art, or sigh or word,
Or golden water famed, or talking bird;
Source of my joy, or genius of my notes,
Or ocean's landscape stamped with lyric boats,
Ah, no! far hence thy aromatic strains
Recoil, and beautify our vaulted plains.
Gal. Thy dazzling harmony affects me so,
In azure symmetry I sigh—ah, no!
'Ah, no! ah, no!', the woods irradiate sing,
'Ah, no! ah, no!', for joy the grottoes ring;
Ev'n Heraclitus' vocal tears would flow
To hear thee murmur thy melodious 'No'!
Thy voice, 'tis true, Pastora, gilds the sky,
But woods and grottoes flutter in my eye.
Past. When night pellucid warbles into day,
And morn sonorous floats upon the May,
With well-blown bugle through the wilds of air
I roam accordant, while the bounding hare
In covert claps her wings, to see me pass
Ethereal meadows of transparent grass.
Gal. Magnetic thunders now illume the air,
And fragrant music variegates the year.
Light trips the dolphin through cerulean woods,
And spotless tigers harmonise the floods.
Ev'n Thetis smooths her brow and laughs to see
Kind nature weep in symphony with me.
Past. This young conundrum let me first propose;
It puzzles half our dainty belles and beaux.
What makes my lays in blue-eyed order shine
So far superior, when compared with thine?
Gal. Expound me this, and I'll disclaim the prize,
Whose lustre blushes with Peruvian dyes.
When crowing foxes whistle in their dens,
Or radiant hornpipes dance to cocks and hens,
What makes sly Reynard and his cackling mate,
That saved the capitol, resign to fate?
Past. But see, Aquarius fills his ample vase,
And Taurus warbles to Vitruvian laws:
So, crab-like Cancer all her speed assumes,
And Virgo, still a maid, elastic blooms.
My rose-lipped ewes in mystic wonder stand
To hear me sing, and court my conscious hand.
Adieu, my goats; for ne'er shall rural muse
Your philosophic beards to stroke refuse.

(1767)

WILLIAM JULIUS MICKLE

1735–1788

356 *There's nae Luck about the House*

AND are ye sure the news is true?
  And are ye sure he's weel?
Is this a time to think o' wark?
  Mak haste, lay by your wheel;
Is this the time to spin a thread
  When Colin's at the door?
Reach me my cloak, I'll to the quay
  And see him come ashore.
For there's nae luck about the house,
  There's nae luck at a',
There's little pleasure in the house
  When our gudeman's awa.

And gie to me my bigonet,
  My bishop's satin gown;
For I maun tell the bailie's wife
  That Colin's come to town.
My Turkey slippers maun gae on,
  My stockings pearly blue;
It's a' to pleasure my gudeman,
  For he's baith leel and true.
      For there's nae luck, &c.

Rise, lass, and mak a clean fireside,
  Put on the muckle pot,
Gie little Kate her button gown,
  And Jock his Sunday coat;
And mak their shoon as black as slaes,
  Their hose as white as snaw,
It's a' to please my ain gudeman,
  For he's been lang awa.
      For there's nae, &c.

There's twa fat hens upo' the bauk
  Been fed this month and mair,
Mak haste and thraw their necks about,
  That Colin weel may fare;

bigonet] bonnet   bauk] cross-beam

And mak the table neat and clean,
  Let everything look braw,
For wha can tell how Colin fared
  When he was far awa?
    Ah, there's nae, &c.

Sae true his heart, sae smooth his speech,
  His breath like cauler air,
His very foot has music in't
  As he comes up the stair!
And shall I see his face again,
  And shall I hear him speak?
I'm downright dizzy wi' the thought,
  In troth I'm like to greet.
    For there's nae, &c.

If Colin's weel, and weel content,
  I hae nae mair to crave—
And gin I live to keep him sae,
  I'm blest aboon the lave.
And shall I see his face again,
  And shall I hear him speak?
I'm downright dizzy wi' the thought,
  In troth I'm like to greet.
    For there's nae, &c.

(1769)

THOMAS MOSS

1740?–1808

357 *The Beggar*

PITY the sorrows of a poor old man!
Whose trembling limbs have borne him to your door,
Whose days are dwindled to the shortest span.
Oh! give relief—and heaven will bless your store.

These tattered clothes my poverty bespeak,
These hoary locks proclaim my lengthened years,
And many a furrow in my grief-worn cheek
Has been a channel to a stream of tears.

356 cauler] fresh   lave] remainder

Yon house, erected on the rising ground,
With tempting aspect drew me from my road,
For Plenty there a residence has found,
And Grandeur a magnificent abode.

Hard is the fate of the infirm and poor!
Here craving for a morsel of their bread,
A pampered menial forced me from the door
To seek a shelter in a humbler shed.

Oh! take me to your hospitable dome,
Keen blows the wind and piercing is the cold!
Short is my passage to the friendly tomb,
For I am poor—and miserably old.

Should I reveal the source of every grief,
If soft humanity e'er touched your breast,
Your hands would not withhold the kind relief,
And tears of pity could not be repressed.

Heaven sends misfortunes—why should we repine?
'Tis heaven has brought me to that state you see:
And your condition may be soon like mine,
The child of sorrow and of misery.

A little farm was my paternal lot,
Then like the lark I sprightly hailed the morn;
But ah! oppression forced me from my cot,
My cattle died and blighted was my corn.

My daughter—once the comfort of my age!
Lured by a villain from her native home,
Is cast abandoned on the world's wide stage,
And doomed in scanty poverty to roam.

My tender wife—sweet soother of my care!
Struck with sad anguish at the stern decree,
Fell, lingering fell, a victim to despair,
And left the world to wretchedness and me.

Pity the sorrows of a poor old man!
Whose trembling limbs have borne him to your door,
Whose days are dwindled to the shortest span.
Oh! give relief—and heaven will bless your store.

(1769)

JOHN GERRARD

fl. 1769

358 *A Remonstrance*

WHAT'S he that, in yon gilded coach elate,
Lolls at his ease and swells with empty state;
Whose ruffled brow and supercilious eye
Loured with disdain to see me trudging by,
In homely weeds, with heat and labour faint,
A drudge by birth and pilgrim by restraint;
What's he whom station common grace denies,
Too fine for earth, too haughty for the skies?
Speak, recollection, from what goddess-dame
This great contractor of his eyelids came.
Where yonder valley, flushed with pastures green,
Displays its worth, as suing to be seen;
Where lofty turrets for mementoes rise
And boast their infamy to blushing skies;
There dwelt a clown some sixty years ago,
An honest wight, as churls and niggards go.
An humble villa then the mansion stood,
Hid in an old, inhospitable wood,
Beneath whose roof a small partition rose
To screen the cattle's from their lord's repose.
A surly mastiff welcomed from the door
The smooth town-visitor and crying poor.
Free to collect, yet frugal to disburse,
He knew each virtue of a close-mouthed purse;
At fairs and markets versed as well as any
To stand three hours contending for a penny;
Would pay his rates, and but a little mumble
At the necessitous, and swear and grumble;
When sure to win would risk some trifling bet,
And, threatened with the law, discharge a debt.
His parish church would constantly frequent,
To dun his tenants in the yard for rent,
And often in the porch, by dint of thought,
Calves, bullocks, sheep and pigs full cheap hath bought;
For well he knew, when men were preached awake,
Their conscience at the tend'rest time to take.
Some other virtues had—to follow gain
By each shrewd purpose of a fertile brain;
To treat no friend within his sober hall,

And shut the door of pity upon all;
His griping heart each solace to deny,
And in his bargains thought it meet to lie.
Such pious tenets formed his saving creed,
And other faith was heresy indeed.
  A perfect proselyte his wife—she knew
How much the farthing as the pound was due.
Corn, butter, bacon, eggs, each coming day,
Were cash to workmen, to the poor were pay.
Great wit she had beyond each sage of old,
And every moveable could turn to gold.
She, much unlike your modern wives, would scorn
To keep within-doors, save at night and morn;
Her ready hand could sow the yearly field,
Could reap, could mow and well the flail could wield;
At morn the dairy was her soft pursuit,
Then to lade dung with Ralph and keep him to't;
No costly clothes she wore, no marks of pride,
No printed gown or mantle Tyrrhene-dyed,
But a firm jacket of her own-spun grey
And leathern bodice were her trim array.
Full many a year she earned in sweat of brow
Great wealth, by dairy, dung-cart, poor and plough;
While he at market and at fair would vend
Her num'rous wares, and none to better end.
  At length, oppressed with zeal too great to tell,
At Mammon's shrine the greedy matron fell!
One harvest day, with griping thoughts o'erborne,
As from the poor she raked the straggled corn,
Three weighty ears escaped, which when she spied
In want's pale hand, she sickened, dropped and died!
  Her loss, for future hoards, her goodman rues,
And full two thousand lower sunk his views.
No thought of past acquirements gave relief;
At last he sold her clothes, and stopped his grief.
  Still Fortune smiled upon his growing pelf,
And to fourscore she lent him to himself;
Then the green hillock closely wrapped him o'er,
And to dirt gave him—dirt so loved before.
  His want of issue soon the law repairs,
Skilful as footmen at creating heirs.
A wealthy brother of their rightful tribe
Produced his claim—and sealed it with a bribe;
A potent bribe, not such as barely draws
A needy juryman from obvious laws,
But such as in the senate once inclined

Old patriot Turbulo to change his mind.
  And now the mansion soars, of costly stone;
The hedges fall, the woods of ages grown;
The spacious park its naked visage shows,
And all Arabia in the garden blows;
Walks, fountains, statues from each point are seen,
And heroes, puppies, peacocks shaped in green.
But low ambition will in grandeur thrive,
And thirst for more an affluent change survive.
Patriot and senator at once he's grown,
To raise his country's fortune in his own.
'Gainst secret influence in the House he roars,
And cries down pensions in the gross by scores.
He knows 'promotion comes not west nor south',
And gapes for *Northern* dust to stop his mouth.
Place, title, pension now his tongue forsake,
He kindly on himself these loads will take;
Will ease his country of each root of evil,
And dare to vault like Curtius to the devil.
  So great a favour by the parent done
Ensured the same reward for this his son.
This his great son! decked with dishonour's plumes,
Who in one infamy his life consumes,
Who crowds his shield with arms unknown to fame,
And, copying others' greatness, boasts his shame.
Know, traitor, that I prize, with thanks to fate,
Rough honesty before thy painted state,
Plain virtue, which shall one day vice outshine,
And truth in rags a diamond from the mine.

(1769)

ANONYMOUS

359 *A Song*

WHILE a thousand fine projects are planned ev'ry day,
Old England to whitewash, and make her look gay,
The exorbitant price of provisions forgot,
And starving, I fear, is the poor people's lot.

Though the markets are stored with good mutton and beef,
To the tradesman no help, to the poor no relief;
By cursèd forestallers the rates are so high,
That none but a Jew or a Dutchman can buy.

Whilst the streets to enlarge our good citizens scheme,
And on pulling down houses continually dream;
These clever projectors, their wisdom so great,
Forget, while they labour, poor wretches must eat.

While the purse-proud directors, with riches o'ergrown,
Are raising up mountains of timber and stone,
The poor scarce a bit of belly-timber can find,
To patch up their bodies and keep out the wind.

While our eastern bashaws are amassing great treasure,
And making and unmaking nabobs at their pleasure;
While these wealthy engrossers their millions tell o'er,
The want of a dinner ten thousand deplore.

As the right of their conquests are now in debate,
By the money obtained, and the blood of the state,
If the nation is wronged, and no recompense made,
Demolish their charter and give a free trade.

While the epicure alderman's cramming his belly,
And feasting on pheasants, on ven'son and jelly;
While turtles and turbots his tables bespread,
A poor family dines on a morsel of bread.

While guttling committees and companies meet,
To eat and to drink, and to drink and to eat;
Full bellies regard not the poor man's distress;
Then what hopes of relief? And what means of redress?

Ye lords of the court, and great dons of the city,
On the poor people's wants and distresses take pity;
And when for the good of the nation you treat,
Contrive that the poor may have something to eat.

(1769)

forestallers] i.e. of the market

THOMAS CHATTERTON

1752–1770

360 from *Aella: A Tragycal Enterlude*

Mynstrelles Songe

O! SYNGE untoe mie roundelaie,
O! droppe the brynie teare wythe mee,
Daunce ne moe atte hallie daie,
Lycke a reynynge[1] ryver bee;
Mie love ys dedde,
Gon to hys death-bedde,
Al under the wyllowe tree.

Blacke hys cryne[2] as the wyntere nyghte,
Whyte hys rode[3] as the sommer snowe,
Rodde hys face as the mornynge lyghte,
Cale he lyes ynne the grave belowe;
Mie love ys dedde,
Gon to hys deathe-bedde,
Al under the wyllowe tree.

Swote hys tyngue as the throstles note,
Quycke ynn daunce as thoughte canne bee,
Defte hys taboure, codgelle stote,
O! hee lyes bie the wyllowe tree:
Mie love ys dedde,
Gonne to hys deathe-bedde,
Alle underre the wyllowe tree.

Harke! the ravenne flappes hys wynge,
In the briered delle belowe;
Harke! the dethe-owle loude dothe synge,
To the nyghte-mares as heie goe;
Mie love ys dedde,
Gone to hys deathe-bedde,
Al under the wyllowe tree.

[1] running. [2] hair. [3] complexion.

cale] cold heie] they

See! the whyte moone sheenes onne hie;
Whyterre ys mie true loves shroude;
Whyterre yanne the mornynge skie,
Whyterre yanne the evenynge cloude;
        Mie love ys dedde,
        Gon to hys deathe-bedde,
        Al under the wyllowe tree.

Heere, uponne mie true loves grave,
Schalle the baren fleurs be layde,
Nee one hallie Seyncte to save
Al the celness of a mayde.
        Mie love ys dedde,
        Gonne to hys death-bedde,
        Alle under the wyllowe tree.

Wythe mie hondes I'lle dente the brieres
Rounde his hallie corse to gre,
Ouphante fairie, lyghte youre fyres,
Heere mie boddie stylle schalle bee.
        Mie love ys dedde,
        Gon to hys death-bedde,
        Al under the wyllowe tree.

Comme, wythe acorne-coppe and thorne,
Drayne mie hartys blodde awaie;
Lyfe and all yttes goode I scorne,
Daunce bie nete, or feaste by daie.
        Mie love ys dedde,
        Gon to hys death-bedde,
        Al under the wyllowe tree.

Waterre wytches, crownede wythe reytes,[1]
Bere mee to yer leathalle tyde.
I die; I comme; mie true love waytes.
Thos the damselle spake, and dyed.

(Wr. 1768–9; pub. 1777)

[1] water-flags.

celness] coldness   Ouphante] elfin

361 *An Excelente Balade of Charitie*

In Virgyne the sweltrie sun gan sheene,
And hotte upon the mees[1] did caste his raie;
The apple rodded[2] from its palie greene,
And the mole[3] peare did bende the leafy spraie;
The peede chelandri[4] sunge the livelong daie;
'Twas nowe the pride, the manhode of the yeare,
And eke the grounde was dighte[5] in its mose defte[6] aumere[7].

The sun was glemeing in the midde of daie,
Deadde still the aire, and eke the welken[8] blue,
When from the sea arist[9] in drear arraie
A hepe of cloudes of sable sullen hue,
The which full fast unto the woodlande drewe,
Hiltring[10] attenes[11] the sunnis fetive[12] face,
And the blacke tempeste swolne and gatherd up apace.

Beneathe an holme, faste by a pathwaie side,
Which dide unto Seyncte Godwine's covent[13] lede,
A hapless pilgrim moneynge did abide,
Pore in his viewe, ungentle[14] in his weede,
Longe bretful[16] of the miseries of neede,
Where from the hail-stone coulde the almer[16] flie?
He had no housen theere, ne anie covent nie.

Look in his glommed[17] face, his sprighte there scanne;
Howe woe-be-gone, how withered, forwynd[18], deade!
Haste to thie church-glebe-house[19], asshrewed[20] manne!
Haste to thie kiste[21], thie onlie dortoure[22] bedde.
Cale, as the claie whiche will gre on thie hedde,
Is Charitie and Love aminge highe elves;
Knightis and Barons live for pleasure and themselves.

[1] meads. [2] reddened, ripened. [3] soft. [4] pied goldfinch. [5] drest, arrayed. [6] neat, ornamental. [7] a loose robe or mantle. [8] the sky, the atmosphere. [9] arose. [10] hiding, shrouding. [11] at once. [12] beauteous. [13] It would have been *charitable*, if the author had not pointed at personal characters in this Ballad of Charity. The Abbot of St. Godwin's at the time of the writing of this was Ralph de Bellomont, a great stickler for the Lancastrian family. Rowley was a Yorkist. [14] beggarly. [15] filled with. [16] beggar. [17] clouded, dejected. A person of some note in the literary world is of opinion, that *glum* and *glom* are modern cant words; and from this circumstance doubts the authenticity of Rowley's Manuscripts. Glum-mong in the Saxon signifies twilight, a dark or dubious light; and the modern word *gloomy* is derived from the Saxon *glum*. [18] dry, sapless. [19] the grave. [20] accursed, unfortunate. [21] coffin. [22] a sleeping room.

The gatherd storme is rype; the bigge drops falle;
The forswat[1] meadowes smethe,[2] and drenche[3] the raine;
The comyng ghastness do the cattle pall,[4]
And the full flockes are drivynge ore the plaine;
Dashde from the cloudes the waters flott[5] againe;
The welkin opes; the yellow levynne[6] flies;
And the hot fierie smothe[7] in the wide lowings[8] dies.

Liste! now the thunder's rattling clymmynge[9] sound
Cheves[10] slowlie on, and then embollen[11] clangs,
Shakes the hie spyre, and losst, dispended, drown'd,
Still on the gallard[12] eare of terroure hanges;
The windes are up; the lofty elmen swanges;
Again the levynne and the thunder poures,
And the full cloudes are braste[13] attenes in stonen showers.

Spurreynge his palfrie oere the watrie plaine,
The Abbote of Seyncte Godwynes convente came;
His chapournette[14] was drented with the reine,
And his pencte[15] gyrdle met with mickle shame;
He aynewarde tolde his bederoll[16] at the same;
The storme encreasen, and he drew aside,
With the mist[17] almes craver neere to the holme to bide.

His cope[18] was all of Lyncolne clothe so fyne,
With a gold button fasten'd neere his chynne;
His autremete[19] was edged with golden twynne,
And his shoone pyke a loverds[20] mighte have binne;
Full well it shewn he thoughten coste no sinne:
The trammels of the palfrye pleasde his sighte,
For the horse-millanare[21] his head with roses dighte.

An almes, sir prieste! the droppynge pilgrim saide,
O! let me waite within your convente dore,
Till the sunne sheneth hie above our heade,
And the loude tempeste of the aire is oer;
Helpless and ould am I alas! and poor;
No house, ne friend, ne moneie in my pouche;
All yatte I call my owne is this my silver crouche.

[1] sun-burnt. [2] smoke. [3] drink. [4] *pall*, a contraction from *appall*, to fright. [5] fly. [6] lightning. [7] steam, or vapours. [8] flames. [9] noisy. [10] moves. [11] swelled, strengthened. [12] frighted. [13] burst. [14] a small round hat, not unlike the shapournette in heraldry, formerly worn by Ecclesiastics and Lawyers. [15] painted. [16] He told his beads backwards; a figurative expression to signify cursing. [17] poor, needy. [18] a cloke. [19] a loose white robe, worn by Priests. [20] a lord's. [21] I believe this trade is still in being, though but seldom employed.

Varlet, replyd the Abbatte, cease your dinne;
This is no season almes and prayers to give;
Mie porter never lets a faitour[1] in;
None touch mie rynge who not in honour live.
And now the sonne with the blacke cloudes did stryve,
And shettynge on the grounde his glairie raie,
The Abbatte spurrde his steede, and eftsoones roadde awaie.

Once moe the skie was blacke, the thounder rolde;
Faste reyneynge oer the plaine a prieste was seen;
Ne dighte full proude, ne buttoned up in golde;
His cope and jape[2] were graie, and eke were clene;
A Limitoure he was of order seene;
And from the pathwaie side then turned hee,
Where the pore almer laie binethe the holmen tree.

An almes, sir priest! the droppynge pilgrim sayde,
For sweete Seyncte Marie and your order sake.
The Limitoure then loosen'd his pouche threade,
And did thereoute a groate of silver take;
The mister pilgrim dyd for halline[3] shake.
Here take this silver, it maie eathe[4] thie care;
We are Goddes stewards all, nete[5] of oure owne we bare.

But ah! unhailie[6] pilgrim, lerne of me,
Scathe anie give a rentrolle to their Lorde.
Here take my semecope[7], thou arte bare I see;
Tis thyne; the Seynctes will give me mie rewarde.
He left the pilgrim, and his waie aborde.
Virgynne and hallie Seyncte, who sitte yn gloure[8],
Or give the mittee[9] will, or give the gode man power.

(Wr. 1770; pub. 1777)

362 *Sentiment*

SINCE we can die but once, what matters it
If rope or garter, poison, pistol, sword,
Slow-wasting sickness, or the sudden burst
Of valve arterial in the noble parts,

[1] a beggar, or vagabond. [2] a short surplice, worn by Friars of an inferior class, and secular priests. [3] joy. [4] ease. [5] nought. [6] unhappy. [7] a short under-cloke. [8] glory. [9] mighty, rich.

Curtail the miseries of human life?
Though varied is the cause, the effect's the same:
All to one common dissolution tends.

(Wr. 1770?; pub. 1784)

GILBERT WHITE

1720–1793

363 *The Naturalist's Summer-Evening Walk*

To Thomas Pennant, Esq.

WHEN day declining sheds a milder gleam,
What time the may-fly haunts the pool or stream;
When the still owl skims round the grassy mead,
What time the timorous hare limps forth to feed;
Then be the time to steal adown the vale,
And listen to the vagrant cuckoo's tale;
To hear the clamorous curlew call his mate,
Or the soft quail his tender pain relate;
To see the swallow sweep the dark'ning plain
Belated, to support her infant train;
To mark the swift in rapid giddy ring
Dash round the steeple, unsubdued of wing:
Amusive birds!—say where your hid retreat
When the frost rages and the tempests beat;
Whence your return, by such nice instinct led,
When spring, soft season, lifts her bloomy head?
Such baffled searches mock man's prying pride,
The God of Nature is your secret guide!
  While deep'ning shades obscure the face of day,
To yonder bench leaf-sheltered let us stray,
Till blended objects fail the swimming sight,
And all the fading landscape sinks in night;
To hear the drowsy dor come brushing by
With buzzing wing, or the shrill cricket cry;
To see the feeding bat glance through the wood;
To catch the distant falling of the flood;
While o'er the cliff th' awakened churn-owl hung
Through the still gloom protracts his chattering song;

363 dor] beetle

While high in air, and poised upon his wings,
Unseen, the soft, enamoured woodlark sings:
These, Nature's works, the curious mind employ,
Inspire a soothing melancholy joy:
As fancy warms, a pleasing kind of pain
Steals o'er the cheek, and thrills the creeping vein!
  Each rural sight, each sound, each smell, combine;
The tinkling sheep-bell, or the breath of kine;
The new-mown hay that scents the swelling breeze,
Or cottage-chimney smoking through the trees.
  The chilling night-dews fall:—away, retire;
For see, the glow-worm lights her amorous fire!
Thus, ere night's veil had half obscured the sky,
Th' impatient damsel hung her lamp on high:
True to the signal, by love's meteor led,
Leander hastened to his Hero's bed.

(Wr. 1769?; pub. 1789)

364 *On the Dark, Still, Dry, Warm Weather Occasionally Happening in the Winter Months*

  TH' imprisoned winds slumber within their caves
Fast-bound: the fickle vane, emblem of change,
Wavers no more, long-settling to a point.
  All nature nodding seems composed: thick steams
From land, from flood up-drawn, dimming the day,
'Like a dark ceiling stand'; slow through the air
Gossamer floats, or stretched from blade to blade
The wavy network whitens all the field.
  Pushed by the weightier atmosphere, up springs
The ponderous mercury, from scale to scale
Mounting, amidst the Torricellian tube[1].
  While high in air, and poised upon his wings
Unseen, the soft, enamoured wood-lark runs
Through all his maze of melody;—the brake
Loud with the blackbird's bolder note resounds.
  Soothed by the genial warmth, the cawing rook
Anticipates the spring, selects her mate,
Haunts her tall nest-trees, and with sedulous care
Repairs her wicker eyrie, tempest-torn.
  The ploughman inly smiles to see up turn
His mellow glebe, best pledge of future crop:

[1] The Barometer.

With glee the gardener eyes his smoking beds:
E'en pining sickness feels a short relief.
  The happy schoolboy brings transported forth
His long-forgotten scourge, and giddy gig:
O'er the white paths he whirls the rolling hoop,
Or triumphs in the dusty fields of taw.
  Not so the museful sage:—abroad he walks
Contemplative, if haply he may find
What cause controls the tempest's rage, or whence
Amidst the savage season winter smiles.
  For days, for weeks prevails the placid calm.
At length some drops prelude a change: the sun
With ray refracted bursts the parting gloom;
When all the chequered sky is one bright glare.
  Mutters the wind at eve: th' horizon round
With angry aspect scowls: down rush the showers,
And float the deluged paths and miry fields.

(1784)

GEORGE SMITH

1713–1776

365 *The Country Lovers; or, Isaac and Marget Going to Town, on a Summer's Morning*

Scene, a farmer's yard at sun-rising

Isaac COME! Marget, come!—the team is at the gate!
Not ready yet!—you always make me wait!
Marget It is not later than the time you set;
For see the hour-glass!—see, 'tis running yet.
It took me up more time to feed thy jay
Than you for Marget willingly would stay.
But when he learns to talk, his head I'll fill
With words to make thee mannerly!—I will!
Isaac I called indeed, and seemed to chide thy stay,
For fear my love should lose the prime of day;
When lab'ring bees to flow'ry fields repair,
To gather sweets that scent the morning air.
Already o'er yon hill the sun appears,
And through the fruit-trees gilds the yoking steers.
See on the kitchen wall, with ballads gay,
The early sunbeams quiver through the spray.

Now Rosamond they leave, and sink apace,
To tremble on the lines of Chevy Chase.
'Tis five exactly when they gild the tack
That holds this corner of the Almanac.

Marget I've nothing now to do but fetch my hood;
For thick will fall the dewdrops in the wood.
But soon, I fear, we shall complain of heat,
When up the ferny hill our cattle sweat.
There, with the sun, the ground is russet dry,
And dust in clouds will round the waggon fly.
No friendly trees are there, no bush, no briar,
To whose kind shade the trav'ler might retire.

Isaac But then we reach the cooling hollow way,
Where silver rills through shady channels play;
Where mossy shrubs are dressed in all their pride,
And hanging maples deck the sloping side;
There thy delight, the wrens, steal out and sing,
Making the little ivied caverns ring.
Above the spreading oaks thick branches meet,
Whose lofty bow'r excludes the sultry heat.
There my delight, the waving rook'ry, rings,
While the young nestlings learn to use their wings.

Marget Well, now I'm ready, long I have not stayed.

Isaac One kiss before we go, my pretty maid.

Marget Go!—don't be foolish, Isaac—get away!
Who loiters now?—I thought you could not stay!
There—that's enough! why, Isaac, sure you're mad!

Isaac One more, my dearest girl——

Marget Be quiet, lad.
See both my cap and hair are rumpled o'er!
The tying of my beads is got before!

Isaac There let it stay, thy brighter blush to show,
Which shames the cherry-coloured silken bow.
Thy lips, which seem the scarlet's hue to steal,
Are sweeter than the candied lemon peel.

Marget Pray take these chickens for me to the cart;
Dear little creatures, how it grieves my heart
To see them tied, that never knew a crime,
And formed so fine a flock at feeding time!

Isaac See, I have made thee up a flow'ry seat
With full-blown clover, cut at noon-tide heat.
Here's weather for thee, love, to go to town!
How many larks are warbling o'er the down!
The sportive robins too, along the way,
Billing each other, rise in wanton play.
While all along the vale, on either side,

Within the hedges dressed in flow'ry pride,
The coupled finches make the coverts ring
With love's fond notes, which they in transport sing;
Or to their nests the mossy spoils convey,
While in the glossy rills their shadows play.
It makes me think of marriage—don't it you,
To see them fly and settle two and two?

Marget Why dost thou wear that dirty frock to town?
The folk will jeer me, and my friends will frown.
Well! thou shalt by and by be cleaner seen!

Isaac When we are married, Marget, don't you mean?
If you desired that happy day like me,
Thy kindred soon a whiter frock would see.
My anxious thoughts would soon be lulled to rest,
And gentle quiet lodge within my breast.
Then come, my fair one, bless my kind retreat;
My tufted daisies long to kiss thy feet.
My oaks in whisp'ring sighs lament thy stay,
And chiding riv'lets mourn thy long delay.
My bees forsake their hives, to thee they fly,
Or in thy absence on the roses die.
Come then, thou richest rosebud nature yields,
And charm my vagrants to their native fields.
Gay to thy wish, my shrub-dressed cottage glows,
With lilacs, woodbines and the blushing rose.
The soft-fringed pinks before my threshold bloom,
And cooling breezes waft a rich perfume.
In knots of box, and figured beds of bone,
A thousand tulips now are finely blown.
Let then thy hand its flow'ry skill display,
To deck my hearth, and make my windows gay.
Ah! come and hear the music of the rills,
Their tuneful murmurs down the stony hills.
These soft transparent waters sweet and cool
O'er shining pebbles hasten to my pool,
Whose crystal bosom, undisturbed with foam,
Reflects the shadow of my peaceful home.
There, pleased with thee, my ducks in idle freaks
Will deck the dancing shades with silver streaks.
My cattle there from pasture come to drink;
There wait the milker's hand beside the brink.
Ah! when wilt thou on my delightful green,
At early morn and ev'ning's close, be seen
To drain the swelling udders of my kine,
And join thy dear, thy pleasing tasks with mine?

Marget Before the green-dressed hazel changes pale,

And nimble squirrels nut along the dale:
Before thy apples with red speckles shine,
Or purple clusters ripen on the vine:
Before thy fav'rite lime begins to fade,
Or sweating reapers seek the cooling shade;
Isaac shall see me coming to his bow'r,
Not to return again at ev'ning hour.

Isaac Oh! happy time!—how pleasing will it be,
To gather in the ripened grain with thee!
When noontide heats the reapers' strength invade,
With thee to seek the cool refreshing shade;
When breezes learn to whisper Marget's vows,
And bear them gladly through the waving boughs;
'Twill make me truly happy, truly blest,
With thee to labour, and with thee to rest.

Marget But when the labours of that month are o'er,
My lap I'll spread to catch thy orchard's store;
A pleasing task!—when days, nor hot nor cold,
Adorn the juicy pippin's rind with gold.
When from the chimney-tops, at op'ning day,
The playful swallows sing a parting lay;
Gath'ring in flocks to cross the wat'ry main,
Till flow'ry April brings them back again.

Isaac For thee the press with apple-juice shall foam!
For thee the bees shall quit their honeycomb!
For thee the elder's purple fruit shall grow!
For thee the pails with cream shall overflow!
But see yon teams, returning from the town,
Wind in the chalky wheel-ruts o'er the down:
We now must haste; for if we longer stay,
They'll meet us ere we leave the narrow way.

(1770)

ISAAC BICKERSTAFFE

1733–1808?

366 from *The Recruiting Serjeant. A Musical Entertainment*

Air

WHAT a charming thing's a battle!
Trumpets sounding, drums a-beating;
Crack, crick, crack, the cannons rattle,

Every heart with joy elating.
With what pleasure are we spying,
From the front and from the rear,
Round us in the smoky air,
Heads and limbs and bullets flying!
Then the groans of soldiers dying,
Just like sparrows as it were:
At each pop,
Hundreds drop,
While the muskets prittle prattle.
Killed and wounded
Lie confounded:
What a charming thing's a battle!
But the pleasant joke of all
Is when to close attack we fall,
Like mad bulls each other butting,
Shooting, stabbing, maiming, cutting;
Horse and foot
All go to't,
Kill's the word, both men and cattle,
Then to plunder:
Blood and thunder,
What a charming thing's a battle!

(1770)

WILLIAM MASON

1724–1797

367 from *The English Garden*, Book III

[*Thomas Gray's View of Nature*]

CLOSED is that curious ear by Death's cold hand
That marked each error of my careless strain
With kind severity; to whom my Muse
Still loved to whisper what she meant to sing
In louder accent; to whose taste supreme
She first and last appealed, nor wished for praise,
Save when his smile was herald to her fame.
Yes, thou art gone; yet Friendship's falt'ring tongue
Invokes thee still; and still, by Fancy soothed,
Fain would she hope her Gray attends the call.
Why then, alas! in this my fav'rite haunt

Place I the urn, the bust, the sculptured lyre,
Or fix this votive tablet, fair inscribed
With numbers worthy thee, for they are thine?
Why, if thou hear'st me still, these symbols sad
Of fond memorial? Ah! my pensive soul!
He hears me not, nor ever more shall hear
The theme his candour, not his taste, approved.
  Oft, 'smiling as in scorn,' oft would he cry,
'Why waste thy numbers on a trivial art,
That ill can mimic ev'n the humblest charms
Of all-majestic Nature?' At the word
His eye would glisten, and his accents glow
With all the poet's frenzy: 'Sov'reign queen!
Behold and tremble, while thou view'st her state
Throned on the heights of Skiddaw: call thy art
To build her such a throne; that art will feel
How vain her best pretensions. Trace her march
Amid the purple crags of Borrowdale;
And try like those to pile thy range of rock
In rude tumultuous chaos. See! she mounts
Her Naiad car, and down Lodore's dread cliff
Falls many a fathom, like the headlong Bard
My fabling fancy plunged in Conway's flood;
Yet not like him to sink in endless night:
For, on its boiling bosom, still she guides
Her buoyant shell, and leads the wave along;
Or spreads it broad, a river or a lake,
As suits her pleasure; will thy boldest song
E'er brace the sinews of enervate art
To such dread daring? Will it ev'n direct
Her hand to emulate those softer charms
That deck the banks of Dove, or call to birth
The bare romantic crags and copses green
That sidelong grace her circuit, whence the rills,
Bright in their crystal purity, descend
To meet their sparkling queen? around each fount
The hawthorns crowd, and knit their blossomed sprays
To keep their sources sacred. Here, ev'n here,
Thy art, each active sinew stretched in vain,
Would perish in its pride. Far rather thou
Confess her scanty power, correct, control,
Tell her how far, nor farther, she may go;
And rein with Reason's curb fantastic Taste.'

(Wr. 1771; pub. 1779)

JAMES BEATTIE

1735–1803

368 from *The Minstrel; or, The Progress of Genius*, Book I

[*The Youth of a Poet*]

Lo! where the stripling, wrapt in wonder, roves
Beneath the precipice o'erhung with pine;
And sees, on high, amidst th' encircling groves,
From cliff to cliff the foaming torrents shine:
While waters, woods and winds in concert join,
And Echo swells the chorus to the skies.
Would Edwin this majestic scene resign
For aught the huntsman's puny craft supplies?
Ah! no: he better knows great Nature's charms to prize.

And oft he traced the uplands, to survey,
When o'er the sky advanced the kindling dawn,
The crimson cloud, blue main and mountain grey,
And lake, dim-gleaming on the smoky lawn;
Far to the west the long long vale withdrawn,
Where twilight loves to linger for a while;
And now he faintly kens the bounding fawn,
And villager abroad at early toil.—
But, lo! the sun appears! and heaven, earth, ocean smile.

And oft the craggy cliff he loved to climb,
When all in mist the world below was lost.
What dreadful pleasure! there to stand sublime,
Like shipwrecked mariner on desert coast,
And view th' enormous waste of vapour, tossed
In billows, lengthening to th' horizon round,
Now scooped in gulfs, with mountains now embossed!
And hear the voice of mirth and song rebound,
Flocks, herds and waterfalls, along the hoar profound!

In truth he was a strange and wayward wight,
Fond of each gentle and each dreadful scene.
In darkness and in storm he found delight:
Nor less, than when on ocean-wave serene
The southern sun diffused his dazzling sheen.

Even sad vicissitude amused his soul:
And if a sigh would sometimes intervene,
And down his cheek a tear of pity roll,
A sigh, a tear so sweet, he wished not to control.

. . . .

Oft when the winter-storm had ceased to rave,
He roamed the snowy waste at even, to view
The cloud stupendous, from th' Atlantic wave
High-towering, sail along th' horizon blue:
Where midst the changeful scenery ever new
Fancy a thousand wondrous forms descries
More wildly great than ever pencil drew,
Rocks, torrents, gulfs and shapes of giant size,
And glittering cliffs on cliffs, and fiery ramparts rise.

Thence musing onward to the sounding shore,
The lone enthusiast oft would take his way,
Listening with pleasing dread to the deep roar
Of the wide-weltering waves. In black array
When sulphurous clouds rolled on the vernal day,
Even then he hastened from the haunt of man,
Along the darkening wilderness to stray,
What time the lightning's fierce career began,
And o'er heaven's rending arch the rattling thunder ran.

Responsive to the sprightly pipe when all
In sprightly dance the village-youth were joined,
Edwin, of melody aye held in thrall,
From the rude gambol far remote reclined,
Soothed with the soft notes warbling in the wind.
Ah then, all jollity seemed noise and folly.
To the pure soul by Fancy's fire refined
Ah, what is mirth, but turbulence unholy,
When with the charm compared of heavenly melancholy!

(1771)

LADY ANNE LINDSAY (*later* BARNARD)

1750–1825

369

Auld Robin Gray

WHEN the sheep are in the fauld, when the cows come hame,
When a' the weary world to quiet rest are gane,
The woes of my heart fa' in showers frae my ee,
Unken'd by my gudeman, who soundly sleeps by me.

Young Jamie loo'd me weel, and sought me for his bride;
But saving ae crown-piece, he'd naething else beside.
To make the crown a pound, my Jamie gaed to sea;
And the crown and the pound, oh! they were baith for me!

Before he had been gane a twelvemonth and a day,
My father brak his arm, our cow was stown away;
My mither she fell sick—my Jamie was at sea—
And auld Robin Gray, oh! he came a-courting me.

My father cou'dna work, my mother cou'dna spin;
I toil'd day and night, but their bread I cou'dna win;
And Rob maintain'd them baith, and, wi' tears in his ee,
Said, 'Jenny, oh! for their sakes, will you marry me?'

My heart it said na, and I look'd for Jamie back;
But hard blew the winds, and his ship was a wrack:
His ship it was a wrack! Why didna Jenny dee?
Or, wherefore am I spared to cry out, Woe is me!

My father argued sair—my mother didna speak,
But she look'd in my face till my heart was like to break:
They gied him my hand, but my heart was in the sea;
And so auld Robin Gray, he was gudeman to me.

I hadna been his wife, a week but only four,
When mournfu' as I sat on the stane at my door,
I saw my Jamie's ghaist—I cou'dna think it he,
Till he said, 'I'm come hame, my love, to marry thee!'

O sair, sair did we greet, and mickle say of a';
Ae kiss we took, nae mair—I bad him gang awa.
I wish that I were dead, but I'm no like to dee;
For O, I am but young to cry out, Woe is me!

I gang like a ghaist, and I carena much to spin;
I darena think o' Jamie, for that wad be a sin.
But I will do my best a gude wife aye to be,
For auld Robin Gray, oh! he is sae kind to me.

(Wr. 1771; pub. 1776)

GEORGE KEATE

1729–1797

370 from *A Burlesque Ode, On the Author's Clearing a New House of Some Workmen*

MIDST the fair range of buildings which, new-reared,
The Bloomsbury and St. Giles gang divide,
A crew of workmen, who no mortal feared,
Sat idling by th' unfinished chimney's side.
A dusky smoke the smould'ring shavings pour,
Bruised empty porter-pots bestrew the floor,
And while their tools lie useless on the ground,
In wonted chorus thus the song goes round:
'Let confusion mark our toil,
What we cannot mend we'll spoil;
Let our worthy masters gain,
Do,—and then undo again.
Fling about the iron crow,
Give this finished part a blow,
Glue a little, saw a bit,
Plane this panel, t' other split,
Making, marring is our duty,
Ne'er for line or plummet care,
Damn the compass, damn the square,
Crooked is the Line of Beauty.'

A pickled dog then rose, and told
What house best purl and spirits sold,
Of many an alehouse-gambol played,
Of matches fought and wagers laid,
Nay, more, and which worst is,
How oft he scaped justice,

370 purl] an infusion of herbs in beer

How he'd blast a man's eyes with a jerk,
How down two pair of stairs
He once kicked two surveyors,
Who dared to examine his work.
How he damned Sir John Fielding, and gave him the lie,
  How for Wilkes he got drunk
  Till his cash was all sunk,
  And went to gaol for—Liberty.
Each roared applause, and all the caitiff throng,
Renewing first their quids, renewed their song:
    'Let confusion mark our toil,' [*etc.*]

What toils await the trifling race of man!
Who multiply their cares the most they can;
Still sighing after something more,
They want a shelf, they want a door,
   Heav'ns! what a fuss about it!
'Tis done—In joiners who'd confide?
The shelf's awry, the door's too wide;
   They'd better been without it!—

While unheeded fly the moments,
   Giv'n to pleasure, lost in prate,
Others feel them linger tedious,
   Weighed with anguish, black with fate.
My giddy pen forgot to say
It chanced 'twas Execution Day,
    The hanging hour was past;
A half-scared mason rushing in,
Exclaimed, 'To idle thus is sin,
     I saw him breathe his last.—
Poor Jack upon the three-legged tree!
A pretty carpenter was he!
      Good lack!—
      Poor Jack!—
      Gone in a crack!—
There's more of us will follow thee.

  'Though 'tis my belief
  That the dog was a thief
     And both given to drinking and raking,
  Yet he knew well his trade,
  All advantages made,
     But mistook for house-building, house-breaking.'

quids] i.e. of chewing-tobacco

Fixed terror glared in ev'ry workman's face,
Each knowing Jack's was nearly his own case;
All rose, and searched their tools in sullen mood,
While the grim mason thus his tale pursued:

'Through St. Giles moving slowly
(All the gaping crowd intent),
Jack, with looks that pictured sorrow,
Sucked an orange as he went.
High and low,
Above, below,
From garret tops
Down to the shops
'Twas all one staring face to view the mournful show.

'Ye chips of the block,
What had been your shock
Had you seen when to Tyburn he came?
How he changed colour often
As he looked at his coffin,
And his coat that reproached him with shame,
For his coat and his coffin were both ready made,
Being stolen or borrowed in Jack's way of trade.
As he stood in the cart
It quite pierced my heart
To see him so tremble and snivel;
Soon the slip-knot was tied,
So he prayed, sang and cried;
And I hope he's not gone to the devil.'

As when a macaroni of high note
Trips through the streets in a short-skirted coat,
With self-applause humming an op'ra air,
If chance some chimney-sweeper unaware
Should turn short on him, and his dollship brush,
Or some rude porter's load his nosegay crush,
Ah, what can hide, what heal the shame!
His coat, his nosegay gave him fame!
No more his looks their wonted ease confess,
But on his altered brow is pictured pale distress:
So changed the features of this miscreant crew,
Who, by the story warned, their several tasks renew.

macaroni] dandy

Labour now resumes his reign,
All are busy once again;
Hurry, hurry,
Bustle, bustle,
Workmen against workmen justle.

Hear you not the iron crow?
See you not the glue-pot flare?
Sharper far the echoes grow,
Dust and shavings choke the air!
With sounds that split the ear they nail and wedge,
And jagged saws set all one's teeth on edge!

Come and aid me, meek-eyed Patience,
Teach me to support delay;
Thou, O Time, at length relieve me,
Drive these wretches far away.
And lo! good heaven! their loit'ring course is run,
All's puzzled out at last, their destined labour's done.

Off, behold the vile troop pack,
Each his budget at his back,
Error stamping all their notions,
Error guiding all their motions;—
Nay,—move quick, ye idle train,
Ne'er, oh ne'er return again!—
They close the door—but parting go
To cause some other person woe.
Ah, luckless mortal! for thy heart I grieve,
Which with unnumbered cares this caitiff crew shall rive.

(Wr. 1772; pub. 1781)

CHARLES JENNER

1736–1774

371 from *Eclogue IV. The Poet*

[*A Soliloquy in the Suburbs*]

THRICE happy authors, who with little skill
In two short weeks can two short volumes fill!
Who take some Miss, of Christian-name inviting,
And plunge her deep in love, and letter-writing;

Perplex her well with jealous parents' cares,
Expose her virtue to a lover's snares;
Give her false friends and perjured swains by dozens,
With all the episodes of aunts and cousins;
Make parents thwart her, and her lover scorn her,
And some mishap spring up at ev'ry corner;
Make her lament her fate, with *ahs* and *ohs*,
And tell some dear Miss Willis all her woes,
Whilst now with love and now with grief she rages;
Till, having brought her through two hundred pages,
Finding, at length, her father's heart obdurate,
Will make her take the Squire, and leave the Curate;
She scales the garden wall, or fords a river,
Elopes, gets married, and her friends forgive her.
How easy flows a chit-chat tale like this!
In modern novels nothing comes amiss.
Fielding, they say, and Richardson had learning;
But, surely, readers then were more discerning:
Our modern writers please the town as well,
Who know no grammar, and but learn to spell.
Critics indeed may maul their flimsy ware,
But where's the work that monthly critics spare?
What though my labours in the Magazine
Lie all secure, below their dreaded spleen,
To kind and humble readers only known,
Who think bought wit must needs surpass their own,
Better to do, as other authors use,
And brave the thunder of the two *Reviews*,
Than thus to waste my patience and my time
In all the pangs of uncomplying rhyme:
Such labours ill with hungry men agree;
Why will ye, Misses, study poetry?
In vain, alas, shall city bards resort,
For past'ral images, to Tottenham-court;
Fat droves of sheep, consigned from Lincoln fens,
That swearing drovers beat to Smithfield pens,
Give faint ideas of Arcadian plains,
With bleating lambkins and with piping swains.
I've heard of Pope, of Philips and of Gay,
They wrote not past'rals in the king's highway:
On Thames' smooth banks, they framed the rural song,
And wandered free, the tufted groves among;
Culled ev'ry flow'r the fragrant mead affords,
And wrote in solitude, and dined with lords.
Alas for me! what prospects can I find
To raise poetic ardour in my mind?

Where'er around I cast my wand'ring eyes,
Long burning rows of fetid bricks arise,
And nauseous dunghills swell in mould'ring heaps,
Whilst the fat sow beneath their covert sleeps.
I spy no verdant glade, no gushing rill,
No fountain bubbling from the rocky hill,
But stagnant pools adorn our dusty plains,
Where half-starved cows wash down their meal of grains.
No traces here of sweet simplicity,
No lowing herd winds gently o'er the lea,
No tuneful nymph, with cheerful roundelay,
Attends to milk her kine, at close of day,
But droves of oxen through yon clouds appear,
With noisy dogs and butchers in their rear,
To give poetic fancy small relief,
And tempt the hungry bard with thoughts of beef.
From helps like these, how very small my hopes!
My past'rals, sure, will never equal Pope's.
Since then no images adorn the plain,
But what are found as well in Gray's-Inn-Lane,
Since dust and noise inspire no thought serene,
And three-horse stages little mend the scene,
I'll stray no more to seek the vagrant muse,
But ev'n go write at home, and save my shoes.

(1772)

JAMES GRAEME

1749–1772

372

The Mortified Genius

WHAT now avails to gain a woman's heart
The sage's wisdom or the poet's art?
Pox on the times! the genius of old
Would whip you off a girl in spite of gold,
In spite of liv'ries, equipage and lace,
And all the Gothic grandeur of a race.
But now the mill'ner's 'prentice with a sneer,
Blessing herself, cries, 'Heav'ns! what have we here?
A man of rhyme, worth—fifty lines a year.'
  Our wit still pleases; but 'tis dev'lish hard
What saves the elegy should damn the bard;

That gains access to dressing-, drawing-rooms,
A wished-for, welcome guest where'er it comes;
But *me*, the luckless author, scorned and poor,
Each surly porter drives from ev'ry door.
  Conscious of secret worth, I hurry home,
And now the master damn and now the dome;
Firmly resolved, whatever shall betide,
No more to ask what has been once denied;
Resolved, indeed! but ev'ry pow'r above
Laughs at our weak resolves, and chiefly Love:
'Brush the brown hat, and darn the breeches' knee;
The wealthy pride may suit, but suits not thee:
Papa, I own, looked mighty sour and grim,
But, if the daughter smile, a fig for him!
Marked you the secret motions of her eye?
How kind yon glance had been, had none been by!
Yon proud reserve, yon shyness, I could swear
Is prudènce all, and pure pretence with her:
'Tis right—old fellows, that can thousands give,
May claim at least some rev'rence while they live:
A few, few years lays Fuscus in his grave,
And Mira's yours perhaps, and all he gave!'
  Intent on future harm, thus said the god,
Who bends the stubborn purpose with a nod,
Constrains the stiffest gladly to obey,
Makes the gay gloomy and the gloomy gay.
Resist who will, I knew too well his pow'r,
In vain resisted, to resist it more!
My hands instinctive, at the forceful call,
At once seize gloves, and hat, and staff, and all;
Then forth I walk and ever, as I go,
Con o'er my manners and practise a bow;
Spread, careful spread, the cravat on my breast,
As prim and formal as a parish priest.
  The knocker clacks.—'Who's there?'—'Is Miss within?'
'Confound the booby, what a monstrous din!
She has no time, she says, to speak with you;
For Mr Florimel came here just now.'
My heart beat thick, and ev'ry word he said
Distained my hollow cheeks with foreign red;
O brutish times! and is that thing of silk,
That sapless sipper of an ass's milk,
That tea-nursed grinner, whose consumptive cough,
Should he but mint a laugh, would cut him off,
Preferred to me! in whose athletic grasp
Ten thousand buzzing beaux were but a wasp.

Sure, wit and learning greater honour claim;
No wit, no learning, ever smiled on him:
I'll lay my lexicon, for all his airs,
That fellow cannot read the arms he bears;
Nor, kneeling, Mira! on his trembling knee,
Explain one half of all he says to thee.
'No matter, he has gold, whose precious hue
Is beauty, virtue, wit and learning too:
O blind to worth! what lovelier than a chaise,
Two bowing footmen and a pair of bays?
What virtue like an handsome country-seat,
A good *per annum*, and a course of plate?
And then for wit—a clever library;
He cannot read a book, but he can buy.
A fig for learning! Learning does he lack,
Whose factor both can write and sign—a tack?
Besides, you know, for ten or less *per ann.*
Even you, or any scholar, is his man.'
  Bear me, ye gods! O bear me where you please!
To unknown regions, over unknown seas;
Place me where dews refreshing never drop,
On Niger's banks, a swarthy Aethiop;
Or melt me to the fashionable size,
Below the scorching heat of Indian skies:
No, there, ev'n there, the lust of gold prevails,
Each river groans with ships, each breeze with sails:
The land abounds, nay ocean's farthest creeks,
With dirt that's sought for, or with dirt that seeks.
Fix me an icen statue at the pole,
Where winds can't carry and where waves can't roll;
To man, to greedy man, your bard prefers
White foxes, sables, ermines, cats and bears,
And all the furry monsters Greenland can call hers.
  Or is the boon too great for gods to give?
Recall the mighty word that bade me live:
So in the dust forever shall I shun
That worst of evils that affronts the sun,
A fool, whose crimes, or father's, have made great,
Spurning true genius prostrate at his feet.

(Wr. by 1772; pub. 1773)

tack] tenure of land

ROBERT FERGUSSON

1750–1774

373

The Daft-Days

Now mirk December's dowie face
Glours owr the rigs wi' sour grimace,
While, thro' his minimum of space,
The bleer-eyed sun,
Wi' blinkin light and stealing pace,
His race doth run.

From naked groves nae birdie sings,
To shepherd's pipe nae hillock rings,
The breeze nae od'rous flavour brings
From Borean cave,
And dwyning nature droops her wings,
Wi' visage grave.

Mankind but scanty pleasure glean
Frae snawy hill or barren plain,
Whan Winter, midst his nipping train,
Wi' frozen spear,
Sends drift owr a' his bleak domain,
And guides the weir.

Auld Reikie! thou'rt the canty hole,
A bield for mony caldrife soul,
Wha snugly at thine ingle loll,
Baith warm and couth;
While round they gar the bicker roll
To weet their mouth.

When merry Yule-day comes, I trow
You'll scantlins find a hungry mou';
Sma' are our cares, our stamacks fou
O' gusty gear,
And kickshaws, strangers to our view,
Sin fairn-year.

dowie] dismal rigs] ridges dwyning] declining Auld Reikie] Edinburgh canty] pleasant bield] shelter caldrife] chilly ingle] fire couth] sociable bicker] wooden cup scantlins] scarcely gusty gear] tasty liquor kickshaws] novelties fairn-year] last year

Ye browster wives, now busk ye bra,
And fling your sorrows far awa';
Then come and gie's the tither blaw
Of reaming ale,
Mair precious than the well of Spa,
Our hearts to heal.

Then, tho' at odds wi' a' the warl',
Amang oursells we'll never quarrel;
Tho' Discord gie a cankered snarl
To spoil our glee,
As lang's there's pith into the barrel
We'll drink and 'gree.

Fidlers, your pins in temper fix,
And roset weel your fiddle-sticks,
And banish vile Italian tricks
From out your quorum,
Nor *fortes* wi' *pianos* mix,
Gie's *Tulloch Gorum*.

For nought can cheer the heart sae weil
As can a canty Highland reel,
It even vivifies the heel
To skip and dance:
Lifeless is he wha canna feel
Its influence.

Let mirth abound, let social cheer
Invest the dawning of the year;
Let blithesome innocence appear
To crown our joy,
Nor envy wi' sarcastic sneer
Our bliss destroy.

And thou, great god of Aqua Vitae!
Wha sways the empire of this city,
When fou we're sometimes capernoity,
Be thou prepared
To hedge us frae that black banditti,
The City-Guard.

(1772)

browster] brewer busk] dress reaming] foaming roset] rub with resin quorum] select company fou] drunk capernoity] bad-tempered

374

Braid Claith

YE wha are fain to hae your name
Wrote in the bonny book of fame,
Let merit nae pretension claim
To laurelled wreath,
But hap ye weel, baith back and wame,
In gude Braid Claith.

He that some ells o' this may fa',
An' slae-black hat on pow like snaw,
Bids bauld to bear the gree awa',
Wi' a' this graith,
Whan bienly clad wi' shell fu' braw
O' gude Braid Claith.

Waesuck for him wha has na fek o't!
For he's a gowk they're sure to geck at,
A chiel that ne'er will be respekit
While he draws breath,
Till his four quarters are bedeckit
Wi' gude Braid Claith.

On Sabbath-days the barber spark,
Whan he has done wi' scrapin wark,
Wi' siller broachie in his sark,
Gangs trigly, faith!
Or to the Meadow, or the Park,
In gude Braid Claith.

Weel might ye trow, to see them there,
That they to shave your haffits bare,
Or curl an' sleek a pickle hair,
Would be right laith,
Whan pacing wi' a gawsy air
In gude Braid Claith.

If ony mettled stirrah green
For favour frae a lady's ein,
He maunna care for being seen
Before he sheath
His body in a scabbard clean
O' gude Braid Claith.

hap] wrap wame] belly fa'] obtain pow] head gree] prize graith] dress bienly] comfortably waesuck for] woe betide fek] plenty gowk] fool geck] scoff sark] shirt trigly] trimly haffits] cheeks pickle] small amount of gawsy] fine stirrah] young fellow green] yearn

For, gin he come wi' coat thread-bare,
A feg for him she winna care,
But crook her bonny mou' fu' sair,
And scald him baith.
Wooers should ay their travel spare
Without Braid Claith.

Braid Claith lends fock an unco heese,
Makes mony kail-worms butterflies,
Gies mony a doctor his degrees
For little skaith:
In short, you may be what you please
Wi' gude Braid Claith.

For thof ye had as wise a snout on
As Shakespeare or Sir Isaac Newton,
Your judgement fouk would hae a doubt on,
I'll tak my aith,
Till they could see ye wi' a suit on
O' gude Braid Claith.

(1772)

375 *The Sow of Feeling*

MALIGNANT planets! do ye still combine
Against this wayward, dreary life of mine!
Has pitiless oppression—cruel case!
Gained sole possession of the human race?
By cruel hands has ev'ry virtue bled,
And innocence from men to vultures fled!
Thrice happy, had I lived in Jewish time,
When swallowing pork or pig was doomed a crime;
My husband long had blest my longing arms,
Long, long had known love's sympathetic charms!
My children too—a little suckling race,
With all their father growing in their face,
From their prolific dam had ne'er been torn,
Nor to the bloody stalls of butchers borne.
Ah! luxury! to you my being owes
Its load of misery—its load of woes!
With heavy heart, I saunter all the day,
Gruntle and murmur all my hours away!

374 fock] folk unco] great heese] lift skaith] pains aith] oath

In vain I try to summon old desire,
For favourite sports—for wallowing in the mire:
Thoughts of my husband—of my children slain,
Turn all my wonted pleasure into pain!
How oft did we, in Phoebus' warming ray,
Bask on the humid softness of the clay?
Oft did his lusty head defend my tail
From the rude whispers of the angry gale;
While nose-refreshing puddles streamed around,
And floating odours hailed the dung-clad ground.
Near by a rustic mill's enchanting clack,
Where plenteous bushels load the peasant's back,
In straw-crowned hovel, there to life we came,
One boar our father and one sow our dam:
While tender infants on the mother's breast,
A flame divine on either shone confessed;
In riper hours love's more than ardent blaze
Enkindled all his passion, all his praise!
No deadly, sinful passion fired his soul,
Virtue o'er all his actions gained control!
That cherub which attracts the female heart,
And makes them soonest with their beauty part,
Attracted mine:—I gave him all my love,
In the recesses of a verdant grove:
'Twas there I list'ned to his warmest vows,
Amidst the pendant melancholy boughs;
'Twas there my trusty lover shook for me
A show'r of acorns from the oaken tree;
And from the teeming earth, with joy, ploughed out
The roots salubrious with his hardy snout.
But Happiness, a floating meteor thou,
That still inconstant art to man and sow,
Left us in gloomiest horrors to reside,
Near by the deep-dyed sanguinary tide,
Where whetting steel prepares the butch'ring knives,
With greater ease to take the harmless lives
Of cows, and calves, and sheep, and hog, who fear
The bite of bull-dogs, that incessant tear
Their flesh, and keenly suck the blood-distilling ear!
At length the day, th' eventful day drew near,
Detested cause of many a briny tear!
I'll weep till sorrow shall my eyelids drain,
A tender husband, and a brother slain!
Alas! the lovely languor of his eye,
When the base murd'rers bore him captive by!
His mournful voice! the music of his groans,

Had melted any hearts—but hearts of stones!
O! had some angel at that instant come,
Giv'n me four nimble fingers and a thumb,
The blood-stained blade I'd turned upon his foe,
And sudden sent him to the shades below—
Where, or Pythagoras' opinion jests,
Beasts are made butchers—butchers changed to beasts.
  In early times the law had wise decreed,
For human food but reptiles few should bleed;
But monstrous man, still erring from the laws,
The curse of heaven on his banquet draws!
Already has he drained the marshes dry
For frogs, new emblems of his luxury;
And soon the toad and lizard will come home,
Pure victims to the hungry glutton's womb:
Cats, rats and mice their destiny may mourn,
In time their carcases on spits must turn;
They may rejoice today—while I resign
Life, to be numbered 'mongst the *feeling swine*.

(1773)

HORACE WALPOLE, EARL OF ORFORD

1717–1797

376 *To Lady* [*Anne Fitzpatrick*], *When about Five Years Old, with a Present of Shells*

O NYMPH, compared with whose young bloom
  Hebe's herself an ancient fright;
May these gay shells find grace and room
  Both in your baby-house and sight!
'Shells! What are shells?' you ask, admiring
  With stare half pleasure half surprise;
And fly with nature's art, enquiring
  In dear mamma's all-speaking eyes.
Shells, fairest Anne, are playthings, made
  By a brave god called Father Ocean,
Whose frown from pole to pole's obeyed,
  Commands the waves, and stills their motion.

376 baby-house] doll's-house

From that old sire a daughter came,
As like mamma as blue to blue;
And, like mamma, the sea-born dame
An urchin bore, not unlike you.
For him fond grand-papa compels
The floods to furnish such a state
Of corals and of cockleshells,
Would turn a little lady's pate.
The chit has tons of baubles more;
His nurs'ry's stuffed with doves and sparrows;
And littered is its azure floor
With painted quivers, bows and arrows.
Spread, spread your frock; you must be friends;
His toys shall fill your lap and breast:
Today the boy this sample sends,
—And some years hence he'll send the rest.

(Wr. 1772; pub. 1798)

377 *Epitaph on Two Piping-Bullfinches of Lady Ossory's, Buried under a Rose-Bush in her Garden*

ALL flesh is grass, and so are feathers too:
Finches must die, as well as I and you.
Beneath a damask rose, in good old age,
Here lies the tenant of a noble cage.
For forty moons he charmed his lady's ear,
And piped obedient oft as she drew near,
Though now stretched out upon a clay-cold bier.
But when the last shrill flageolet shall sound,
And raise all dickybirds from holy ground,
His little corpse again its wings shall plume,
And sing eternally the self-same tune,
From everlasting night to everlasting noon.

On the Other Bullfinch, Buried in the Same Place

Beneath the same bush rests his brother—
What serves for one will serve for t' other.

(Wr. 1783; pub. 1798)

WILLIAM COWPER

1731–1800

378

Walking with God

OH! for a closer walk with God,
  A calm and heav'nly frame;
A light to shine upon the road
  That leads me to the Lamb!

Where is the blessedness I knew
  When first I saw the Lord?
Where is the soul-refreshing view
  Of Jesus, and his word?

What peaceful hours I once enjoyed!
  How sweet their mem'ry still!
But they have left an aching void
  The world can never fill.

Return, O holy Dove, return,
  Sweet messenger of rest;
I hate the sins that made thee mourn,
  And drove thee from my breast.

The dearest idol I have known,
  Whate'er that idol be,
Help me to tear it from thy throne,
  And worship only thee.

So shall my walk be close with God,
  Calm and serene my frame;
So purer light shall mark the road
  That leads me to the Lamb.

(Wr. 1767; pub. 1772)

379

Light Shining out of Darkness

GOD moves in a mysterious way,
  His wonders to perform;
He plants his footsteps in the sea,
  And rides upon the storm.

Deep in unfathomable mines
 Of never-failing skill,
He treasures up his bright designs,
 And works his sovereign will.

Ye fearful saints fresh courage take,
 The clouds ye so much dread
Are big with mercy, and shall break
 In blessings on your head.

Judge not the Lord by feeble sense,
 But trust him for his grace;
Behind a frowning providence,
 He hides a smiling face.

His purposes will ripen fast,
 Unfolding ev'ry hour;
The bud may have a bitter taste,
 But sweet will be the flow'r.

Blind unbelief is sure to err,
 And scan his work in vain;
God is his own interpreter,
 And he will make it plain.

(1774)

380 *'Hatred and Vengeance, my Eternal Portion'*

HATRED and vengeance, my eternal portion,
Scarce can endure delay of execution,
Wait, with impatient readiness, to seize my
 Soul in a moment.

Damned below Judas: more abhorred than he was,
Who for a few pence sold his holy master.
Twice betrayed, Jesus me, the last delinquent,
 Deems the profanest.

Man disavows, and Deity disowns me:
Hell might afford my miseries a shelter;
Therefore hell keeps her ever-hungry mouths all
 Bolted against me.

Hard lot! encompassed with a thousand dangers,
Weary, faint, trembling with a thousand terrors,
I'm called, if vanquished, to receive a sentence
 Worse than Abiram's.

Him the vindictive rod of angry justice
Sent quick and howling to the centre headlong;
I, fed with judgement, in a fleshly tomb, am
Buried above ground.

(Wr. 1774?; pub. 1816)

381 *To Mr. Newton on his Return from Ramsgate*

THAT ocean you of late surveyed,
Those rocks I too have seen,
But I, afflicted and dismayed,
You, tranquil and serene.

You from the flood-controlling steep
Saw stretched before your view,
With conscious joy, the threat'ning deep,
No longer such to you.

To me, the waves that ceaseless broke
Upon the dang'rous coast,
Hoarsely and ominously spoke
Of all my treasure lost.

Your sea of troubles you have passed,
And found the peaceful shore;
I, tempest-tossed, and wrecked at last,
Come home to port no more.

(Wr. 1780; pub. 1803)

382 *Verses, Supposed to be Written by Alexander Selkirk, During his Solitary Abode in the Island of Juan Fernandez*

I AM monarch of all I survey,
My right there is none to dispute;
From the centre all round to the sea,
I am lord of the fowl and the brute.
Oh, solitude! where are the charms
That sages have seen in thy face?
Better dwell in the midst of alarms,
Than reign in this horrible place.

I am out of humanity's reach,
  I must finish my journey alone,
Never hear the sweet music of speech;
  I start at the sound of my own.
The beasts, that roam over the plain,
  My form with indifference see;
They are so unacquainted with man,
  Their tameness is shocking to me.

Society, friendship, and love,
  Divinely bestowed upon man,
Oh, had I the wings of a dove,
  How soon would I taste you again!
My sorrows I then might assuage
  In the ways of religion and truth,
Might learn from the wisdom of age,
  And be cheered by the sallies of youth.

Religion! what treasure untold
  Resides in that heavenly word!
More precious than silver and gold,
  Or all that this earth can afford.
But the sound of the church-going bell
  These valleys and rocks never heard,
Ne'er sighed at the sound of a knell,
  Or smiled when a sabbath appeared.

Ye winds, that have made me your sport,
  Convey to this desolate shore
Some cordial endearing report
  Of a land I shall visit no more.
My friends, do they now and then send
  A wish or a thought after me?
O tell me I yet have a friend,
  Though a friend I am never to see.

How fleet is a glance of the mind!
  Compared with the speed of its flight,
The tempest itself lags behind,
  And the swift-winged arrows of light.
When I think of my own native land,
  In a moment I seem to be there;
But alas! recollection at hand
  Soon hurries me back to despair.

But the sea-fowl is gone to her nest,
  The beast is laid down in his lair,
Ev'n here is a season of rest,
  And I to my cabin repair.
There is mercy in every place;
  And mercy, encouraging thought!
Gives even affliction a grace,
  And reconciles man to his lot.

(1782)

383 *Epitaph on a Hare*

HERE lies, whom hound did ne'er pursue,
  Nor swifter greyhound follow,
Whose foot ne'er tainted morning dew,
  Nor ear heard huntsman's 'hallo',

Old Tiney, surliest of his kind,
  Who, nursed with tender care,
And to domestic bounds confined,
  Was still a wild jack-hare.

Though duly from my hand he took
  His pittance ev'ry night,
He did it with a jealous look,
  And, when he could, would bite.

His diet was of wheaten bread,
  And milk, and oats, and straw,
Thistles, or lettuces instead,
  With sand to scour his maw.

On twigs of hawthorn he regaled,
  On pippins' russet peel;
And, when his juicy salads failed,
  Sliced carrot pleased him well.

A Turkey carpet was his lawn,
  Whereon he loved to bound,
To skip and gambol like a fawn,
  And swing his rump around.

His frisking was at evening hours,
  For then he lost his fear;
But most before approaching show'rs,
  Or when a storm drew near.

Eight years and five round-rolling moons
  He thus saw steal away,
Dozing out all his idle noons,
  And ev'ry night at play.

I kept him for his humour's sake,
  For he would oft beguile
My heart of thoughts that made it ache,
  And force me to a smile.

But now, beneath this walnut-shade
  He finds his long, last home,
And waits in snug concealment laid,
  Till gentler Puss shall come.

He, still more agèd, feels the shocks
  From which no care can save,
And, partner once of Tiney's box,
  Must soon partake his grave.

(1784)

384 *The Poplar-Field*

THE poplars are felled, farewell to the shade
And the whispering sound of the cool colonnade,
The winds play no longer, and sing in the leaves,
Nor Ouse on his bosom their image receives.

Twelve years have elapsed since I last took a view
Of my favourite field and the bank where they grew,
And now in the grass behold they are laid,
And the tree is my seat that once lent me a shade.

The blackbird has fled to another retreat
Where the hazels afford him a screen from the heat,
And the scene where his melody charmed me before,
Resounds with his sweet-flowing ditty no more.

My fugitive years are all hasting away,
And I must ere long lie as lowly as they,
With a turf on my breast, and a stone at my head,
Ere another such grove shall arise in its stead.

'Tis a sight to engage me, if any thing can,
To muse on the perishing pleasures of man;
Though his life be a dream, his enjoyments, I see,
Have a being less durable even than he.

(1785)

385 from *The Task*

(i)

[*Rural Sights and Sounds*]

FOR I have loved the rural walk through lanes
Of grassy swarth, close cropped by nibbling sheep,
And skirted thick with intertexture firm
Of thorny boughs; have loved the rural walk
O'er hills, through valleys, and by rivers' brink,
E'er since a truant boy I passed my bounds
T' enjoy a ramble on the banks of Thames;
And still remember, nor without regret
Of hours that sorrow since has much endeared,
How oft, my slice of pocket-store consumed,
Still hung'ring, penniless and far from home,
I fed on scarlet hips and stony haws,
Or blushing crabs, or berries that emboss
The bramble, black as jet, or sloes austere.
Hard fare! but such as boyish appetite
Disdains not; nor the palate, undepraved
By culinary arts, unsav'ry deems.
No sofa then awaited my return;
Nor sofa then I needed. Youth repairs
His wasted spirits quickly, by long toil
Incurring short fatigue; and though our years
As life declines speed rapidly away,
And not a year but pilfers as he goes
Some youthful grace that age would gladly keep;
A tooth or auburn lock, and by degrees
Their length and colour from the locks they spare;
Th' elastic spring of an unwearied foot
That mounts the stile with ease, or leaps the fence,

That play of lungs, inhaling and again
Respiring freely the fresh air, that makes
Swift pace or steep ascent no toil to me,
Mine have not pilfered yet; nor yet impaired
My relish of fair prospect; scenes that soothed
Or charmed me young, no longer young, I find
Still soothing and of pow'r to charm me still.
And witness, dear companion of my walks,
Whose arm this twentieth winter I perceive
Fast locked in mine, with pleasure such as love,
Confirmed by long experience of thy worth
And well-tried virtues, could alone inspire—
Witness a joy that thou hast doubled long.
Thou know'st my praise of nature most sincere,
And that my raptures are not conjured up
To serve occasions of poetic pomp,
But genuine, and art partner of them all.
How oft upon yon eminence our pace
Has slackened to a pause, and we have borne
The ruffling wind, scarce conscious that it blew,
While admiration, feeding at the eye,
And still unsated, dwelt upon the scene.
Thence with what pleasure have we just discerned
The distant plough slow moving, and beside
His lab'ring team, that swerved not from the track,
The sturdy swain diminished to a boy!
Here Ouse, slow winding through a level plain
Of spacious meads with cattle sprinkled o'er,
Conducts the eye along its sinuous course
Delighted. There, fast rooted in his bank,
Stand, never overlooked, our fav'rite elms,
That screen the herdsman's solitary hut;
While far beyond, and overthwart the stream
That, as with molten glass, inlays the vale,
The sloping land recedes into the clouds;
Displaying on its varied side the grace
Of hedgerow beauties numberless, square tow'r,
Tall spire, from which the sound of cheerful bells
Just undulates upon the list'ning ear,
Groves, heaths, and smoking villages, remote.
Scenes must be beautiful, which, daily viewed,
Please daily, and whose novelty survives
Long knowledge and the scrutiny of years.
Praise justly due to those that I describe.
   Nor rural sights alone, but rural sounds,
Exhilarate the spirit, and restore

The tone of languid nature. Mighty winds,
That sweep the skirt of some far-spreading wood
Of ancient growth, make music not unlike
The dash of ocean on his winding shore,
And lull the spirit while they fill the mind;
Unnumbered branches waving in the blast,
And all their leaves fast flutt'ring, all at once.
Nor less composure waits upon the roar
Of distant floods, or on the softer voice
Of neighb'ring fountain, or of rills that slip
Through the cleft rock, and, chiming as they fall
Upon loose pebbles, lose themselves at length
In matted grass, that with a livelier green
Betrays the secret of their silent course.
Nature inanimate employs sweet sounds,
But animated nature sweeter still,
To soothe and satisfy the human ear.
Ten thousand warblers cheer the day, and one
The livelong night: nor these alone, whose notes
Nice-fingered art must emulate in vain,
But cawing rooks, and kites that swim sublime
In still repeated circles, screaming loud,
The jay, the pie, and ev'n the boding owl
That hails the rising moon, have charms for me.
Sounds inharmonious in themselves and harsh,
Yet heard in scenes where peace for ever reigns,
And only there, please highly for their sake.

(ii)

[*Against Slavery*]

OH for a lodge in some vast wilderness,
Some boundless contiguity of shade,
Where rumour of oppression and deceit,
Of unsuccessful or successful war,
Might never reach me more. My ear is pained,
My soul is sick, with ev'ry day's report
Of wrong and outrage with which earth is filled.
There is no flesh in man's obdurate heart,
It does not feel for man; the nat'ral bond
Of brotherhood is severed as the flax
That falls asunder at the touch of fire.
He finds his fellow guilty of a skin
Not coloured like his own; and, having pow'r
T' enforce the wrong, for such a worthy cause

Dooms and devotes him as his lawful prey.
Lands intersected by a narrow frith
Abhor each other. Mountains interposed
Make enemies of nations, who had else,
Like kindred drops, been mingled into one.
Thus man devotes his brother, and destroys;
And, worse than all, and most to be deplored,
As human nature's broadest, foulest blot,
Chains him, and tasks him, and exacts his sweat
With stripes, that mercy, with a bleeding heart,
Weeps when she sees inflicted on a beast.
Then what is man? And what man, seeing this,
And having human feelings, does not blush,
And hang his head, to think himself a man?
I would not have a slave to till my ground,
To carry me, to fan me while I sleep,
And tremble when I wake, for all the wealth
That sinews bought and sold have ever earned.
No: dear as freedom is, and in my heart's
Just estimation prized above all price,
I had much rather be myself the slave,
And wear the bonds, than fasten them on him.
We have no slaves at home.—Then why abroad?
And they themselves, once ferried o'er the wave
That parts us, are emancipate and loosed.
Slaves cannot breathe in England; if their lungs
Receive our air, that moment they are free;
They touch our country, and their shackles fall.
That's noble, and bespeaks a nation proud
And jealous of the blessing. Spread it then,
And let it circulate through ev'ry vein
Of all your empire; that where Britain's pow'r
Is felt, mankind may feel her mercy too.

(iii)

[*Winter Evening*]

JUST when our drawing-rooms begin to blaze
With lights, by clear reflection multiplied
From many a mirror, in which he of Gath,
Goliath, might have seen his giant bulk
Whole, without stooping, tow'ring crest and all,
My pleasures, too, begin. But me, perhaps,
The glowing hearth may satisfy awhile
With faint illumination, that uplifts

The shadow to the ceiling, there by fits
Dancing uncouthly to the quiv'ring flame.
Not undelightful is an hour to me
So spent in parlour twilight: such a gloom
Suits well the thoughtful or unthinking mind,
The mind contemplative, with some new theme
Pregnant, or indisposed alike to all.
Laugh ye, who boast your more mercurial pow'rs,
That never feel a stupor, know no pause,
Nor need one; I am conscious, and confess,
Fearless, a soul that does not always think.
Me oft has fancy, ludicrous and wild,
Soothed with a waking dream of houses, tow'rs,
Trees, churches, and strange visages, expressed
In the red cinders, while with poring eye
I gazed, myself creating what I saw.
Nor less amused have I quiescent watched
The sooty films that play upon the bars,
Pendulous, and foreboding, in the view
Of superstition, prophesying still,
Though still deceived, some stranger's near approach.
'Tis thus the understanding takes repose
In indolent vacuity of thought,
And sleeps and is refreshed. Meanwhile the face
Conceals the mood lethargic with a mask
Of deep deliberation, as the man
Were tasked to his full strength, absorbed and lost.
Thus oft, reclined at ease, I lose an hour
At ev'ning, till at length the freezing blast,
That sweeps the bolted shutter, summons home
The recollected pow'rs; and, snapping short
The glassy threads with which the fancy weaves
Her brittle toys, restores me to myself.
How calm is my recess; and how the frost,
Raging abroad, and the rough wind, endear
The silence and the warmth enjoyed within!
I saw the woods and fields, at close of day,
A variegated show; the meadows green,
Though faded; and the lands, where lately waved
The golden harvest, of a mellow brown,
Upturned so lately by the forceful share.
I saw far off the weedy fallows smile
With verdure not unprofitable, grazed
By flocks, fast feeding, and selecting each
His fav'rite herb; while all the leafless groves,
That skirt th' horizon, wore a sable hue,

Scarce noticed in the kindred dusk of eve.
Tomorrow brings a change, a total change!
Which even now, though silently performed,
And slowly, and by most unfelt, the face
Of universal nature undergoes.
Fast falls a fleecy show'r: the downy flakes,
Descending, and with never-ceasing lapse,
Softly alighting upon all below,
Assimilate all objects. Earth receives
Gladly the thick'ning mantle; and the green
And tender blade, that feared the chilling blast,
Escapes unhurt beneath so warm a veil.

(iv)

[*A Frosty Morning*]

'TIS morning; and the sun, with ruddy orb
Ascending, fires th' horizon: while the clouds,
That crowd away before the driving wind,
More ardent as the disc emerges more,
Resemble most some city in a blaze,
Seen through the leafless wood. His slanting ray
Slides ineffectual down the snowy vale,
And, tingeing all with his own rosy hue,
From ev'ry herb and ev'ry spiry blade
Stretches a length of shadow o'er the field.
Mine, spindling into longitude immense,
In spite of gravity, and sage remark
That I myself am but a fleeting shade,
Provokes me to a smile. With eye askance
I view the muscular proportioned limb
Transformed to a lean shank. The shapeless pair,
As they designed to mock me, at my side
Take step for step; and, as I near approach
The cottage, walk along the plastered wall,
Prepost'rous sight! the legs without the man.
The verdure of the plain lies buried deep
Beneath the dazzling deluge; and the bents,
And coarser grass, upspearing o'er the rest,
Of late unsightly and unseen, now shine
Conspicuous, and, in bright apparel clad
And fledged with icy feathers, nod superb.
The cattle mourn in corners where the fence
Screens them, and seem half petrified to sleep
In unrecumbent sadness. There they wait

Their wonted fodder; not like hung'ring man,
Fretful if unsupplied; but silent, meek,
And patient of the slow-paced swain's delay.
He from the stack carves out th' accustomed load,
Deep-plunging, and again deep-plunging oft,
His broad keen knife into the solid mass:
Smooth as a wall the upright remnant stands,
With such undeviating and even force
He severs it away: no needless care,
Lest storms should overset the leaning pile
Deciduous, or its own unbalanced weight.
Forth goes the woodman, leaving unconcerned
The cheerful haunts of man; to wield the axe
And drive the wedge, in yonder forest drear,
From morn to eve his solitary task.
Shaggy, and lean, and shrewd, with pointed ears
And tail cropped short, half lurcher and half cur—
His dog attends him. Close behind his heel
Now creeps he slow; and now, with many a frisk
Wide-scamp'ring, snatches up the drifted snow
With iv'ry teeth, or ploughs it with his snout;
Then shakes his powdered coat, and barks for joy.
Heedless of all his pranks, the sturdy churl
Moves right toward the mark; nor stops for aught,
But now and then with pressure of his thumb
T' adjust the fragrant charge of a short tube
That fumes beneath his nose: the trailing cloud
Streams far behind him, scenting all the air.

. . . .

The streams are lost amid the splendid blank,
O'erwhelming all distinction. On the flood,
Indurated and fixed, the snowy weight
Lies undissolved; while silently beneath,
And unperceived, the current steals away.
Not so where, scornful of a check, it leaps
The mill-dam, dashes on the restless wheel,
And wantons in the pebbly gulf below:
No frost can bind it there; its utmost force
Can but arrest the light and smoky mist
That in its fall the liquid sheet throws wide.
And see where it has hung th' embroidered banks
With forms so various, that no pow'rs of art,
The pencil or the pen, may trace the scene!
Here glitt'ring turrets rise, upbearing high
(Fantastic misarrangement!) on the roof

Large growth of what may seem the sparkling trees
And shrubs of fairy land. The crystal drops
That trickle down the branches, fast congealed,
Shoot into pillars of pellucid length,
And prop the pile they but adorned before.
Here grotto within grotto safe defies
The sunbeam; there, embossed and fretted wild,
The growing wonder takes a thousand shapes
Capricious, in which fancy seeks in vain
The likeness of some object seen before.
Thus nature works as if to mock at art,
And in defiance of her rival pow'rs;
By these fortuitous and random strokes
Performing such inimitable feats
As she with all her rules can never reach.

(1785)

386 *Sweet Meat has Sour Sauce or, The Slave-Trader in the Dumps*

A TRADER I am to the African shore,
But since that my trading is like to be o'er,
I'll sing you a song that you ne'er heard before,
Which nobody can deny, deny,
Which nobody can deny.

When I first heard the news it gave me a shock,
Much like what they call an electrical knock,
And now I am going to sell off my stock,
Which nobody, &c.

'Tis a curious assortment of dainty regales,
To tickle the negroes with when the ship sails,
Fine chains for the neck, and a cat with nine tails,
Which nobody, &c.

Here's supple-jack plenty, and store of rattan,
That will wind itself round the sides of a man,
As close as a hoop round a bucket or can,
Which nobody, &c.

386 supple-jack/rattan] kinds of cane

Here's padlocks and bolts, and screws for the thumbs,
That squeeze them so lovingly till the blood comes,
They sweeten the temper like comfits or plums,
Which nobody, &c.

When a negro his head from his victuals withdraws,
And clenches his teeth and thrusts out his paws,
Here's a notable engine to open his jaws,
Which nobody, &c.

Thus going to market, we kindly prepare
A pretty black cargo of African ware,
For what they must meet with when they get there,
Which nobody, &c.

'Twould do your heart good to see 'em below
Lie flat on their backs all the way as we go,
Like sprats on a gridiron, scores in a row,
Which nobody, &c.

But ah! if in vain I have studied an art
So gainful to me, all boasting apart,
I think it will break my compassionate heart,
Which nobody, &c.

For oh! how it enters my soul like an awl!
This pity, which some people self-pity call,
Is sure the most heart-piercing pity of all,
Which nobody, &c.

So this is my song, as I told you before;
Come buy off my stock, for I must no more
Carry Caesars and Pompeys to Sugar-cane shore,
Which nobody can deny, deny,
Which nobody can deny.

(Wr. 1788; pub. 1836)

387 *On the Death of Mrs. Throckmorton's Bullfinch*

Ye nymphs! if e'er your eyes were red
With tears o'er hapless fav'rites shed,
O share Maria's grief!
Her fav'rite, even in his cage
(What will not hunger's cruel rage?),
Assassined by a thief.

Where Rhenus strays his vines among,
The egg was laid from which he sprung,
    And though by nature mute,
Or only with a whistle blessed,
Well-taught, he all the sounds expressed
    Of flageolet or flute.

The honours of his ebon poll
Were brighter than the sleekest mole;
    His bosom of the hue
With which Aurora decks the skies,
When piping winds shall soon arise
    To sweep up all the dew.

Above, below, in all the house,
Dire foe alike to bird and mouse,
    No cat had leave to dwell;
And Bully's cage supported stood
On props of smoothest-shaven wood,
    Large-built and latticed well.

Well-latticed—but the grate, alas!
Not rough with wire of steel or brass,
    For Bully's plumage sake,
But smooth with wands from Ouse's side,
With which, when neatly peeled and dried,
    The swains their baskets make.

Night veiled the pole—all seemed secure—
When led by instinct sharp and sure,
    Subsistence to provide,
A beast forth-sallied on the scout,
Long-backed, long-tailed, with whiskered snout,
    And badger-coloured hide.

He, ent'ring at the study-door,
Its ample area 'gan explore;
    And something in the wind
Conjectured, sniffing round and round,
Better than all the books he found,
    Food, chiefly, for the mind.

Just then, by adverse fate impressed,
A dream disturbed poor Bully's rest;
In sleep he seemed to view
A rat, fast-clinging to the cage,
And, screaming at the sad presage,
Awoke and found it true.

For, aided both by ear and scent,
Right to his mark the monster went—
Ah, Muse! forbear to speak
Minute the horrors that ensued;
His teeth were strong, the cage was wood—
He left poor Bully's beak.

He left it—but he should have ta'en
That beak, whence issued many a strain
Of such mellifluous tone,
Might have repaid him well, I wote,
For silencing so sweet a throat,
Fast set within his own.

Maria weeps—The Muses mourn—
So when, by Bacchanalians torn,
On Thracian Hebrus' side
The tree-enchanter Orpheus fell,
His head alone remained to tell
The cruel death he died.

(1789)

388 *On the Receipt of My Mother's Picture out of Norfolk, the Gift of my Cousin Ann Bodham*

Oh that those lips had language! Life has passed
With me but roughly since I heard thee last.
Those lips are thine—thy own sweet smiles I see,
The same that oft in childhood solaced me;
Voice only fails, else how distinct they say,
'Grieve not, my child, chase all thy fears away!'
The meek intelligence of those dear eyes
(Blessed be the art that can immortalize,
The art that baffles time's tyrannic claim
To quench it) here shines on me still the same.

Faithful remembrancer of one so dear,
Oh welcome guest, though unexpected, here!
Who bidd'st me honour with an artless song,
Affectionate, a mother lost so long,
I will obey, not willingly alone,
But gladly, as the precept were her own;
And, while that face renews my filial grief,
Fancy shall weave a charm for my relief—
Shall steep me in Elysian reverie,
A momentary dream that thou art she.
My mother! when I learned that thou wast dead,
Say, wast thou conscious of the tears I shed?
Hovered thy spirit o'er thy sorrowing son,
Wretch even then, life's journey just begun?
Perhaps thou gav'st me, though unseen, a kiss;
Perhaps a tear, if souls can weep in bliss—
Ah that maternal smile! it answers—Yes.
I heard the bell tolled on thy burial day,
I saw the hearse that bore thee slow away,
And, turning from my nurs'ry window, drew
A long, long sigh, and wept a last adieu!
But was it such?—It was.—Where thou art gone
Adieus and farewells are a sound unknown.
May I but meet thee on that peaceful shore,
The parting sound shall pass my lips no more!
Thy maidens grieved themselves at my concern,
Oft gave me promise of a quick return.
What ardently I wished I long believed,
And, disappointed still, was still deceived;
By disappointment every day beguiled,
Dupe of *tomorrow* even from a child.
Thus many a sad tomorrow came and went,
Till, all my stock of infant sorrow spent,
I learned at last submission to my lot;
But, though I less deplored thee, ne'er forgot.
Where once we dwelt our name is heard no more,
Children not thine have trod my nurs'ry floor;
And where the gard'ner Robin, day by day,
Drew me to school along the public way,
Delighted with my bauble coach, and wrapped
In scarlet mantle warm, and velvet-capped,
'Tis now become a history little known,
That once we called the past'ral house our own.
Short-lived possession! but the record fair
That mem'ry keeps of all thy kindness there,
Still outlives many a storm that has effaced

A thousand other themes less deeply traced.
Thy nightly visits to my chamber made,
That thou might'st know me safe and warmly laid;
Thy morning bounties ere I left my home,
The biscuit, or confectionary plum;
The fragrant waters on my cheeks bestowed
By thy own hand, till fresh they shone and glowed;
All this, and more endearing still than all,
Thy constant flow of love, that knew no fall,
Ne'er roughened by those cataracts and brakes
That humour interposed too often makes;
All this still legible in mem'ry's page,
And still to be so, to my latest age,
Adds joy to duty, makes me glad to pay
Such honours to thee as my numbers may;
Perhaps a frail memorial, but sincere,
Not scorned in heav'n, though little noticed here.
  Could time, his flight reversed, restore the hours,
When, playing with thy vesture's tissued flow'rs,
The violet, the pink and jessamine,
I pricked them into paper with a pin
(And thou wast happier than myself the while,
Would'st softly speak, and stroke my head and smile),
Could those few pleasant hours again appear,
Might one wish bring them, would I wish them here?
I would not trust my heart—the dear delight
Seems so to be desired, perhaps I might.—
But no—what here we call our life is such,
So little to be loved, and thou so much,
That I should ill requite thee to constrain
Thy unbound spirit into bonds again.
  Thou, as a gallant bark from Albion's coast
(The storms all weathered and the ocean crossed)
Shoots into port at some well-havened isle,
Where spices breathe and brighter seasons smile,
There sits quiescent on the floods that show
Her beauteous form reflected clear below,
While airs impregnated with incense play
Around her, fanning light her streamers gay;
So thou, with sails how swift! hast reached the shore
'Where tempests never beat nor billows roar,'
And thy loved consort on the dang'rous tide
Of life, long since, has anchored at thy side.
But me, scarce hoping to attain that rest,

humour] mood, temper

Always from port withheld, always distressed—
Me howling winds drive devious, tempest-tossed,
Sails ripped, seams op'ning wide, and compass lost,
And day by day some current's thwarting force
Sets me more distant from a prosp'rous course.
But oh the thought, that thou art safe, and he!
That thought is joy, arrive what may to me.
My boast is not that I deduce my birth
From loins enthroned, and rulers of the earth;
But higher far my proud pretensions rise—
The son of parents passed into the skies.
And now, farewell—time, unrevoked, has run
His wonted course, yet what I wished is done.
By contemplation's help, not sought in vain,
I seem t' have lived my childhood o'er again;
To have renewed the joys that once were mine,
Without the sin of violating thine:
And, while the wings of fancy still are free,
And I can view this mimic show of thee,
Time has but half succeeded in his theft—
Thyself removed, thy power to soothe me left.

(Wr. 1790; pub. 1798)

389 *Yardley Oak*

SURVIVOR sole, and hardly such, of all
That once lived here thy brethren, at my birth
(Since which I number threescore winters past)
A shattered veteran, hollow-trunked perhaps
As now, and with excoriate forks deform,
Relicts of ages! could a mind, imbued
With truth from heav'n, created thing adore,
I might with rev'rence kneel and worship thee.
It seems idolatry with some excuse
When our forefather Druids in their oaks
Imagined sanctity. The conscience yet
Unpurified by an authentic act
Of amnesty, the meed of blood divine,
Loved not the light, but gloomy into gloom
Of thickest shades, like Adam after taste
Of fruit proscribed, as to a refuge, fled.
Thou wast a bauble once; a cup and ball,
Which babes might play with; and the thievish jay
Seeking her food, with ease might have purloined
The auburn nut that held thee, swallowing down

Thy yet close-folded latitude of boughs
And all thine embryo vastness, at a gulp.
But Fate thy growth decreed: autumnal rains
Beneath thy parent tree mellowed the soil
Designed thy cradle, and a skipping deer,
With pointed hoof dibbling the glebe, prepared
The soft receptacle in which secure
Thy rudiments should sleep the winter through.
  So Fancy dreams—Disprove it, if ye can,
Ye reas'ners broad awake, whose busy searce
Of argument, employed too oft amiss,
Sifts half the pleasures of short life away.
  Thou fell'st mature, and in the loamy clod
Swelling, with vegetative force instinct
Didst burst thine egg, as theirs the fabled Twins
Now stars; two lobes, protruding, paired exact;
A leaf succeeded, and another leaf,
And all the elements thy puny growth
Fost'ring propitious, thou becam'st a twig.
  Who lived when thou wast such? Oh couldst thou speak,
As in Dodona once thy kindred trees
Oracular, I would not curious ask
The future, best unknown, but at thy mouth
Inquisitive, the less ambiguous past.
  By thee I might correct, erroneous oft,
The clock of history, facts and events
Timing more punctual, unrecorded facts
Recov'ring, and misstated setting right—
Desp'rate attempt, till trees shall speak again!
  Time made thee what thou wast—King of the woods;
And time hath made thee what thou art—a cave
For owls to roost in. Once thy spreading boughs
O'erhung the champain; and the numerous flock
That grazed it stood beneath that ample cope
Uncrowded, yet safe-sheltered from the storm.
No flock frequents thee now. Thou hast outlived
Thy popularity and art become
(Unless verse rescue thee awhile) a thing
Forgotten, as the foliage of thy youth.
  While thus through all the stages thou hast pushed
Of treeship, first a seedling hid in grass,
Then twig, then sapling, and, as century rolled
Slow after century, a giant bulk
Of girth enormous, with moss-cushioned root
Upheaved above the soil, and sides embossed

searce] sieve

With prominent wens globose, till at the last
The rottenness, which time is charged t' inflict
On other mighty ones, found also thee—
What exhibitions various hath the world
Witnessed of mutability in all
That we account most durable below!
Change is the diet on which all subsist,
Created changeable, and change at last
Destroys them.—Skies uncertain now the heat
Transmitting cloudless, and the solar beam
Now quenching in a boundless sea of clouds,—
Calm and alternate storm, moisture and drought,
Invigorate by turns the springs of life
In all that live, plant, animal and man,
And in conclusion mar them. Nature's threads,
Fine passing thought, ev'n in her coarsest works,
Delight in agitation, yet sustain
The force that agitates not unimpaired,
But, worn by frequent impulse, to the cause
Of their best tone their dissolution owe.
  Thought cannot spend itself, comparing still
The great and little of thy lot, thy growth
From almost nullity into a state
Of matchless grandeur, and declension thence
Slow into such magnificent decay.
Time was when, settling on thy leaf, a fly
Could shake thee to the root—and time has been
When tempests could not. At thy firmest age
Thou hadst within thy bole solid contents
That might have ribbed the sides or planked the deck
Of some flagged admiral; and tortuous arms,
The shipwright's darling treasure, didst present
To the four-quartered winds, robust and bold,
Warped into tough knee-timber, many a load.
But the axe spared thee; in those thriftier days
Oaks fell not, hewn by thousands, to supply
The bottomless demands of contest waged
For senatorial honours. Thus to Time
The task was left to whittle thee away
With his sly scythe, whose ever-nibbling edge
Noiseless, an atom and an atom more
Disjoining from the rest, has, unobserved,
Achieved a labour, which had far and wide
(By man performed) made all the forest ring.

admiral] flagship   knee-timber] naturally bent timber

Embowelled now, and of thy ancient self
Possessing naught but the scooped rind, that seems
An huge throat calling to the clouds for drink,
Which it would give in riv'lets to thy root,
Thou temptest none, but rather much forbid'st
The feller's toil, which thou couldst ill requite.
Yet is thy root sincere, sound as the rock,
A quarry of stout spurs and knotted fangs,
Which, crooked into a thousand whimsies, clasp
The stubborn soil, and hold thee still erect.
So stands a kingdom, whose foundations yet
Fail not, in virtue and in wisdom laid,
Though all the superstructure, by the tooth
Pulverized of venality, a shell
Stands now, and semblance only of itself.
Thine arms have left thee. Winds have rent them off
Long since, and rovers of the forest wild
With bow and shaft have burnt them. Some have left
A splintered stump bleached to a snowy white;
And some memorial none where once they grew.
Yet life still lingers in thee, and puts forth
Proof not contemptible of what she can,
Even where death predominates. The spring
Thee finds not less alive to her sweet force
Than yonder upstarts of the neighbour wood,
So much thy juniors, who their birth received
Half a millennium since the date of thine.
But since, although well qualified by age
To teach, no spirit dwells in thee, nor voice
May be expected from thee, seated here
On thy distorted root, with hearers none
Or prompter save the scene, I will perform
Myself the oracle, and will discourse
In my own ear such matter as I may.
Thou, like myself, hast stage by stage attained
Life's wintry bourn; thou, after many years,
I after few; but few or many prove
A span in retrospect; for I can touch
With my least finger's end my own decease
And with extended thumb my natal hour,
And hadst thou also skill in measurement
As I, the past would seem as short to thee.
Evil and few—said Jacob—at an age
Thrice mine, and few and evil, I may think
The Prediluvian race, whose buxom youth
Endured two centuries, accounted theirs.

'Shortlived as foliage is the race of man.
The wind shakes down the leaves, the budding grove
Soon teems with others, and in spring they grow.
So pass mankind. One generation meets
Its destined period, and a new succeeds.'
Such was the tender but undue complaint
Of the Maeonian in old time; for who
Would drawl out centuries in tedious strife
Severe with mental and corporeal ill,
And would not rather choose a shorter race
To glory, a few decades here below?
  One man alone, the Father of us all,
Drew not his life from woman; never gazed,
With mute unconsciousness of what he saw,
On all around him; learned not by degrees,
Nor owed articulation to his ear;
But, moulded by his Maker into Man,
At once upstood intelligent, surveyed
All creatures, with precision understood
Their purport, uses, properties, assigned
To each his name significant, and, filled
With love and wisdom, rendered back to heav'n
In praise harmonious the first air he drew.
He was excused the penalties of dull
Minority. No tutor charged his hand
With the thought-tracing quill, or tasked his mind
With problems. History, not wanted yet,
Leaned on her elbow, watching Time, whose course,
Eventful, should supply her with a theme;

* * * * *

(Wr. 1791; pub. 1804, 1900)

390 *To Mary*

THE twentieth year is well-nigh past,
Since first our sky was overcast;
Ah would that this might be the last!
        My Mary!

Thy spirits have a fainter flow,
I see thee daily weaker grow—
'Twas my distress that brought thee low,
        My Mary!

Thy needles, once a shining store,
For my sake restless heretofore,
Now rust disused, and shine no more,
My Mary!

For though thou gladly wouldst fulfil
The same kind office for me still,
Thy sight now seconds not thy will,
My Mary!

But well thou played'st the housewife's part,
And all thy threads with magic art
Have wound themselves about this heart,
My Mary!

Thy indistinct expressions seem
Like language uttered in a dream;
Yet me they charm, whate'er the theme,
My Mary!

Thy silver locks, once auburn bright,
Are still more lovely in my sight
Than golden beams of orient light,
My Mary!

For could I view nor them nor thee,
What sight worth seeing could I see?
The sun would rise in vain for me.
My Mary!

Partakers of the sad decline,
Thy hands their little force resign;
Yet, gently pressed, press gently mine,
My Mary!

And then I feel that still I hold
A richer store ten thousandfold
Than misers fancy in their gold,
My Mary!

Such feebleness of limbs thou prov'st,
That now at every step thou mov'st
Upheld by two; yet still thou lov'st,
My Mary!

And still to love, though pressed with ill,
In wintry age to feel no chill,
With me is to be lovely still,
My Mary!

But ah! by constant heed I know
How oft the sadness that I show
Transforms thy smiles to looks of woe,
My Mary!

And should my future lot be cast
With much resemblance of the past,
Thy worn-out heart will break at last,
My Mary!

(Wr. 1793; pub. 1803)

391 *Lines Written upon a Window-Shutter at Weston*

FAREWELL, dear scenes, for ever closed to me,
Oh, for what sorrows must I now exchange ye!
July 22 1795

Me miserable! how could I escape
Infinite wrath and infinite despair!
Whom Death, Earth, Heaven, and Hell consigned to ruin,
Whose friend was God, but God swore not to aid me!
July 27 '95

(Pub. 1800, 1836)

392 *The Castaway*

OBSCUREST night involved the sky,
Th' Atlantic billows roared,
When such a destined wretch as I,
Washed headlong from on board,
Of friends, of hope, of all bereft,
His floating home for ever left.

No braver chief could Albion boast
Than he with whom he went,
Nor ever ship left Albion's coast
With warmer wishes sent.

He loved them both, but both in vain,
Nor him beheld nor her again.

Not long beneath the whelming brine,
  Expert to swim, he lay;
Nor soon he felt his strength decline,
  Or courage die away,
But waged with death a lasting strife,
Supported by despair of life.

He shouted: nor his friends had failed
  To check the vessel's course,
But so the furious blast prevailed,
  That, pitiless perforce,
They left their outcast mate behind,
And scudded still before the wind.

Some succour yet they could afford;
  And, such as storms allow,
The cask, the coop, the floated cord,
  Delayed not to bestow.
But he (they knew) nor ship nor shore,
Whate'er they gave, should visit more.

Nor, cruel as it seemed, could he
  Their haste himself condemn,
Aware that flight, in such a sea,
  Alone could rescue them;
Yet bitter felt it still to die
Deserted, and his friends so nigh.

He long survives, who lives an hour
  In ocean, self-upheld;
And so long he, with unspent pow'r,
  His destiny repelled;
And ever, as the minutes flew,
Entreated help, or cried—'Adieu!'

At length, his transient respite past,
  His comrades, who before
Had heard his voice in ev'ry blast,
  Could catch the sound no more.
For then, by toil subdued, he drank
The stifling wave, and then he sank.

No poet wept him: but the page
Of narrative sincere,
That tells his name, his worth, his age,
Is wet with Anson's tear.
And tears by bards or heroes shed
Alike immortalize the dead.

I therefore purpose not or dream,
Descanting on his fate,
To give the melancholy theme
A more enduring date:
But misery still delights to trace
Its semblance in another's case.

No voice divine the storm allayed,
No light propitious shone,
When, snatched from all effectual aid,
We perished, each alone:
But I beneath a rougher sea,
And whelmed in deeper gulfs than he.

(Wr. 1799; pub. 1803)

PHILLIS WHEATLEY
1753?–1784

393 *On Being Brought from Africa to America*

'Twas mercy brought me from my pagan land,
Taught my benighted soul to understand
That there's a God, that there's a Saviour too:
Once I redemption neither sought nor knew.
Some view our sable race with scornful eye:
'Their colour is a diabolic dye.'
Remember, Christians, negroes black as Cain
May be refined and join th' angelic train.

(1773)

ANONYMOUS

394 *Morning*

OFFSPRING of modern poetry, attend,
  Nymph with thy sunburnt cheek and ostrich eye!
Ah, heed my call, thy footsteps hither bend,
  Still thoughtless, prattling still, Simplicity.

Thou that delightest o'er the level lawn
  To pace along with never-varying feet,
Till dusky evening from the peep of dawn,
  Nor wish one flower thy vacant eye to greet.

Come, with thy pleasing robe of heathy brown,
  Of woollen manufacture trimly dight,
Which flows indeed, and scarcely flows, adown,
  And not a fold misleads the steady sight.

I call thee, Nymph; for o'er the British plains
  Wide and more wide thou spread'st thy sovereign sway;
Inspire my ready pen with such sweet strains
  As modern poets neither sing nor say.

Bright morning be the theme, domestic morn;
  Then will the poem like the subject shine,
If thou, Simplicity, my verse adorn,
  And shed thy soothing self o'er every line.

Lo! the gay sun, high-raised, his livelier gleams
  Warm through my window now begins to pour,
Where waving woodbines interrupt his beams
  With chequered shadows trembling on the floor.

Scene of calm breakfasting and wedded peace,
  Smiling I view thee, where no cares intrude;
Where dwell Love, Harmony and placid Ease,
  Sworn foes to sullen frowns and jarrings rude.

And what sweet voice allures my list'ning ears?
  Methought I heard my lovely Jessy's call:
Saw'st thou thy mistress, Hannah, come downstairs?
  'Yes, sir, she just now passed along the hall.'

Did she? Bid John then hither bring my shoes,
  And, Hannah, get the breakfast ready soon;
Say, are the letters brought, or is the news?
  That tedious postman seldom comes till noon.

But soft ye now—here comes my gentle dame.
  My love—behold the things in order stand;
Dear partner of my life and of my name,
  The glossy teacups wait thy ready hand.

She smiles obliging and we sit serene;
  Whatever can, to sight or smell or taste
(Like, raptured Milton, thy sweet garden scene),
  Be thought or found adorns the calm repast.

Gratefully mild, the fragrant hyson tea
  Best pleases me, exotic teas among;
With strong distaste I shun the harsh bohea,
  Whose grating roughness much offends the tongue.

How cool these tea-rolls in the summer hours!
  The smoking muffin now averse we fly;
Cold bread and well-washed butter now be ours,
  'But no hot rolls and butter in July.'

Thus while my humble board kind heav'n shall bless,
  Is there aught else, my love, that I can wish?
Is there?—You doubt: what would that look express?
  She smiles, and smiling cries, 'Another dish.'

True, my arch-monitress—all thanks are poor—
  Crown then my wishes in this dear repast,
Crown them, my Jessy, yet with one dish more,
  And let this dish be sweeter than the last.

But hark! methought I heard the clarion blow,
  With swelling cheeks which tardy postmen use:
Well, John, what brings he? Any letters?—'No,
  He brings you nothing, sir, except the news.'

Well then—the *Chronicle* of high St. James—
  We'll read this history of weeks and days,
Of kings and queens and squires and wedded dames,
  Wars, burials, births, Pantheons, books, highways.

hyson tea] green tea from China   bohea] black tea

Their Majesties to Richmond are retired,
  In peaceful solitude to pass their hours.
Thrice happy pair! your virtues are admired;
  Be love, be harmony, for ever yours!

The King (God bless him!) is an honest man;
  To the Queen's virtues Envy's self is just:
I'll praise him sometimes—as I sometimes can—
  And praise her always—as I always must.

Look, Jessy, what a busy bustling world!
  What India-scenes of plunder and debate!
What realms and states in dire confusion hurled,
  Impelled by savage pride and more than savage hate!

Here the stern Russian raves with horrid speed;
  See there the Turk advancing half the way:
Grim Death applauds the scene and takes his meed
  By thousands and ten thousands in a day.

Was it for this, vain man, that God designed
  His fair creation with such wond'rous art?
Was it for this he gave th' immortal mind,
  And stamped the heavenly form and feeling heart?

Oh, if war's horrid storm its rage must pour,
  Far may it howl from this our humble shed;
At distance may we hear the savage roar
  Of human tigers that with blood are fed!

Tired of the scene, with pleasure I return,
  Dear peaceful home! to rest my mind on thee:
For thee with gratitude to heaven I burn,
  Which gave me all—for thou art all to me.

Blest be that gracious Pow'r who kindly laid,
  From the world's sea, my little bark ashore;
Gave me content in still retirement's shade,
  And bade my heart be happy and be poor;

That gave me thee, my Jessy—thee, my wife;
  Well-pleased I dwell upon that tender name,
Which speaks th' endearing ties of social life
  In titles nobler than the rolls of fame.

You smile, my Jessy, at my full fond heart;
  'Love forms these smiles—but business of the day
Demands my care': then kiss me ere we part.
  Here, Hannah, take these breakfast things away.

(1773)

JOHN LANGHORNE

1735–1779

395 from *The Country Justice*

(i)

[*Gypsies*]

  THE gypsy-race my pity rarely move,
Yet their strong thirst of liberty I love:
Not Wilkes, our freedom's holy martyr, more,
Nor his firm phalanx of the common shore.
  For this in Norwood's patrimonial groves
The tawny father with his offspring roves;
When summer suns lead slow the sultry day,
In mossy caves where welling waters play,
Fanned by each gale that cools the fervid sky,
With this in ragged luxury they lie.
Oft at the sun the dusky elfins strain
The sable eye, then, snugging, sleep again:
Oft, as the dews of cooler evening fall,
For their prophetic mother's mantle call.
  Far other cares that wand'ring mother wait,
The mouth, and oft the minister, of fate!
From her to hear, in ev'ning's friendly shade,
Of future fortune, flies the village-maid,
Draws her long-hoarded copper from its hold;
And rusty halfpence purchase hopes of gold.
  But ah! ye maids, beware the gypsy's lures!
She opens not the womb of time, but yours.
Oft has her hands the hapless Marian wrung,
Marian, whom Gay in sweetest strains has sung!
The parson's maid—sore cause had she to rue
The gypsy's tongue; the parson's daughter too.
Long had that anxious daughter sighed to know
What Vellum's sprucy clerk, the valley's beau,

Meant by those glances which at church he stole,
Her father nodding to the psalm's slow drawl;
Long had she sighed, at length a prophet came,
By many a sure prediction known to fame,
To Marian known, and all she told, for true:
She knew the future, for the past she knew.
Where, in the darkling shed, the moon's dim rays
Beamed on the ruins of a one-horse chaise,
Villaria sat, while faithful Marian brought
The wayward prophet of the woe she sought.
Twice did her hands, the income of the week,
On either side the crooked sixpence seek;
Twice were those hands withdrawn from either side,
To stop the titt'ring laugh, the blush to hide.
The wayward prophet made no long delay,
No novice she in fortune's devious way!
'Ere yet,' she cried, 'ten rolling months are o'er,
Must ye be mothers; maids, at least, no more.
With you shall soon, O lady fair, prevail
A gentle youth, the flower of this fair vale.
To Marian, once of Colin Clout the scorn,
Shall Bumkin come, and Bumkinets be born.'
Smote to the heart, the maidens marvelled sore
That ten short months had such events in store;
But holding firm what village-maids believe,
'That strife with fate is milking in a sieve',
To prove their prophet true, though to their cost,
They justly thought no time was to be lost.
These foes to youth that seek, with dang'rous art,
To aid the native weakness of the heart,
These miscreants from thy harmless village drive,
As wasps felonious from the lab'ring hive.

(1774)

(ii)

[*The Poor*]

LET Age no longer toil with feeble strife,
Worn by long service in the war of life;
Nor leave the head, that time hath whitened, bare
To the rude insults of the searching air;
Nor bid the knee, by labour hardened, bend,
O thou, the poor man's hope, the poor man's friend!
If, when from heav'n severer seasons fall,
Fled from the frozen roof and mouldering wall,

Each face the picture of a winter day,
More strong than Teniers' pencil could portray;
If then to thee resort the shivering train,
Of cruel days and cruel man complain,
Say to thy heart (remembering Him who said)
'These people come from far, and have no bread.'
  Nor leave thy venal clerk empowered to hear;
The voice of Want is sacred to *thy* ear.
He, where no fees his sordid pen invite,
Sports with their tears, too indolent to write;
Like the fed monkey in the fable, vain
To hear more helpless animals complain.
  But chief thy notice shall one monster claim,
A monster furnished with a human frame,
The Parish-Officer! Though Verse disdain
Terms that deform the splendour of the strain,
It stoops to bid thee bend the brow severe
On the sly, pilfering, cruel overseer;
The shuffling farmer, faithful to no trust,
Ruthless as rocks, insatiate as the dust!
  When the poor hind, with length of years decayed,
Leans feebly on his once subduing spade,
Forgot the service of his abler days,
His profitable toil and honest praise,
Shall this low wretch abridge his scanty bread,
This slave, whose board his former labours spread?
  When harvest's burning suns and sickening air
From labour's unbraced hand the grasped hook tear,
Where shall the helpless family be fed,
That vainly languish for a father's bread?
See the pale mother, sunk with grief and care,
To the proud farmer fearfully repair;
Soon to be sent with insolence away,
Referred to vestries, and a distant day!
Referred—to perish! Is my verse severe?
Unfriendly to the human character?
Ah! to this sigh of sad experience trust:
The truth is rigid, but the tale is just.
  If in thy courts this caitiff wretch appear,
Think not that patience were a virtue here.
His low-born pride with honest rage control,
Smite his hard heart, and shake his reptile soul.
  But, hapless! oft through fear of future woe,
And certain vengeance of th' insulting foe,

farmer] not agricultural: one who has contracted to 'farm' the poor

Oft, ere to thee the poor prefer their pray'r,
The last extremes of penury they bear. . . .
  Unnumbered objects ask thy honest care,
Beside the orphan's tear, the widow's prayer.
Far as thy power can save, thy bounty bless,
Unnumbered evils call for thy redress.
  Seest thou afar yon solitary thorn,
Whose aged limbs the heath's wild winds have torn?
While yet to cheer the homeward shepherd's eye,
A few seem straggling in the evening sky!
Not many suns have hastened down the day,
Or blushing moons immersed in clouds their way,
Since there a scene, that stained their sacred light,
With horror stopped a felon in his flight:
A babe just born, that signs of life expressed,
Lay naked o'er the mother's lifeless breast.
The pitying robber, conscious that, pursued,
He had no time to waste, yet stood and viewed:
To the next cot the trembling infant bore,
And gave a part of what he stole before;
Nor known to him the wretches were, nor dear,
He felt as man, and dropped a human tear.
  Far other treatment she who breathless lay
Found from a viler animal of prey.
  Worn with long toil on many a painful road,
That toil increased by nature's growing load,
When evening brought the friendly hour of rest,
And all the mother thronged about her breast,
The ruffian officer opposed her stay,
And, cruel, bore her in her pangs away;
So far beyond the town's last limits drove,
That to return were hopeless, had she strove.
Abandoned there, with famine, pain, and cold,
And anguish, she expired—the rest I've told.
  'Now let me swear—for, by my soul's last sigh,
That thief shall live, that overseer shall die.'
  Too late!—His life the generous robber paid,
Lost by that pity which his steps delayed. . . .
  The living object of thy honest rage,
Old in parochial crimes and steeled with age,
The grave churchwarden!—unabashed he bears
Weekly to church his book of wicked prayers;
And pours, with all the blasphemy of praise,
His creeping soul in Sternhold's creeping lays!

(1775)

CHARLES DIBDIN

1745–1814

396 *[The Jolly Young Waterman]*

AND did you not hear of a jolly young waterman,
  Who at Blackfriars Bridge used for to ply?
And he feathered his oars with such skill and dexterity,
  Winning each heart, and delighting each eye;
He looked so neat, and rowed so steadily,
The maidens all flocked in his boat so readily,
And he eyed the young rogues with so charming an air,
That this waterman ne'er was in want of a fare.

What sights of fine folks he oft rowed in his wherry,
  'Twas cleaned out so nice, and so painted withal;
He was always first oars when the fine city ladies
  In a party to Ranelagh went or Vauxhall.
And oftentimes would they be giggling and leering,
But 'twas all one to Tom, their gibing and jeering,
For loving or liking he little did care,
For this waterman ne'er was in want of a fare.

And yet but to see how strangely things happen,
  As he rowed along, thinking of nothing at all,
He was plied by a damsel so lovely and charming,
  That she smiled and so straightway in love he did fall;
And would this young damsel but banish his sorrow,
He'd wed her tonight before tomorrow:
And how should this waterman ever know care,
When he's married and never in want of a fare?

(1774)

397 *[A Popular Functionary]*

DID but the law appoint us one,
  Tired couples to release again,
What shoals of all degrees would run,
  To break their matrimonial chain!
    The widow old,
    Herself and gold

Who to the healthy spendthrift gave;
        And the rich churl,
        Who took a girl,
Poor wretch! with one foot in the grave.

Prudes, who at men would never look,
    Yet slyly tasted Hymen's joy;
And wild coquets, who husbands took,
    When they could get no other toy:
        Millions would try
        The knot to untie:
Towards the goal of liberty,
        Lord! what a throng
        Would crowd along,
And in the midst my wife and me!

(1774)

398 *Poor Tom*

HERE, a sheer hulk, lies poor Tom Bowling,
    The darling of our crew,
No more he'll hear the tempest howling,
    For death has broached him to.
His form was of the manliest beauty,
    His heart was kind and soft,
Faithful below he did his duty,
    But now he's gone aloft.

Tom never from his word departed,
    His virtues were so rare,
His friends were many, and true-hearted,
    His Poll was kind and fair:
And then he'd sing so blithe and jolly,
    Ah many's the time and oft!
But mirth is turned to melancholy,
    For Tom is gone aloft.

Yet shall poor Tom find pleasant weather,
    When he, who all commands,
Shall give, to call life's crew together,
    The word to pipe all hands.
Thus death, who kings and tars despatches,
    In vain Tom's life has doffed,
For though his body's under hatches,
    His soul is gone aloft.

(1790)

399 *The Lady's Diary*

LECTURED by Pa and Ma o'er night,
Monday at ten quite vexed and jealous,
Resolved in future to be right,
And never listen to the fellows:
Stitched half a wristband, read the text,
Received a note from Mrs Racket:
I hate that woman, she sat next
All church-time to sweet Captain Clackit.

Tuesday got scolded, did not care,
The toast was cold, 'twas past eleven;
I dreamed the Captain through the air
On Cupid's wings bore me to heaven:
Pouted and dined, dressed, looked divine,
Made an excuse, got Ma to back it;
Went to the play, what joy was mine!
Talked loud and laughed with Captain Clackit.

Wednesday came down no lark so gay,
'The girl's quite altered,' said my mother;
Cried Dad, 'I recollect the day
When, dearee, thou wert such another':
Danced, drew a landscape, skimmed a play,
In the paper read that widow Flackit
To Gretna Green had run away,
The forward minx, with Captain Clackit.

Thursday fell sick: 'poor soul she'll die';
Five doctors came with lengthened faces;
Each felt my pulse; 'ah me,' cried I,
'Are these my promised loves and graces?'
Friday grew worse; cried Ma, in pain,
'Our day was fair, heaven do not black it;
Where's your complaint, love?'—'In my brain.'
'What shall I give you?'—'Captain Clackit.'

Early next morn a nostrum came
Worth all their cordials, balms and spices;
A letter, I had been to blame;
The Captain's truth brought on a crisis.
Sunday, for fear of more delays,
Of a few clothes I made a packet,
And Monday morn stepped in a chaise
And ran away with Captain Clackit.

(1798)

400 *The Anchorsmiths*

LIKE Etna's dread volcano see the ample forge
Large heaps upon large heaps of jetty fuel gorge,
While, salamander-like, the ponderous anchor lies
Glutted with vivid fire through all its pores that flies;
The dingy anchorsmiths, to renovate their strength,
Stretched out in deathlike sleep are snoring at their length,
Waiting the master's signal when the tackle's force
Shall, like split rocks, the anchor from the fire divorce;
While, as old Vulcan's Cyclops did the anvil bang,
In deafening concert shall their ponderous hammers clang,
And into symmetry the mass incongruous beat,
To save from adverse winds and waves the gallant British Fleet.

Now, as more vivid and intense each splinter flies,
The temper of the fire the skilful master tries;
And, as the dingy hue assumes a brilliant red,
The heated anchor feeds that fire on which it fed.
The huge sledgehammers round in order they arrange,
And waking anchorsmiths await the looked-for change,
Longing with all their force the ardent mass to smite,
When issuing from the fire arrayed in dazzling white;
And, as old Vulcan's Cyclops did the anvil bang,
To make in concert rude their ponderous hammers clang,
So the misshapen lump to symmetry they beat,
To save from adverse winds and waves the gallant British Fleet.

The preparations thicken; with forks the fire they goad,
And now twelve anchorsmiths the heaving bellows load,
While, armed from every danger and in grim array,
Anxious as howling demons waiting for their prey;
The forge the anchor yields from out its fiery maw,
Which, on the anvil prone, the cavern shouts 'hurraw!'
And now the scorched beholders want the power to gaze,
Faint with its heat, and dazzled with its powerful rays;
While, as old Vulcan's Cyclops did the anvil bang,
To forge Jove's thunderbolts, their ponderous hammers clang:
And, till its fire's extinct, the monstrous mass they beat
To save from adverse winds and waves the gallant British Fleet.

(1798)

THOMAS PENROSE

1742–1779

401 *The Helmets, a Fragment*

The scene of the following event is laid in the neighbourhood of Donnington Castle, in a house built after the Gothic taste upon a spot famous for a bloody encounter between the armies of Charles and the Parliament.

The prognostication alludes to civil dissension, which some have foretold would arise in England, in consequence of the disputes with America.

'TWAS midnight—every mortal eye was closed
Through the whole mansion, save an antique crone's,
That o'er the dying embers faintly watched
The broken sleep (fell harbinger of Death)
Of a sick boteler. Above indeed
In a drear gallery (lighted by one lamp
Whose wick the poor departing seneschal
Did closely imitate) paced slow and sad
The village curate, waiting late to shrive
The penitent when 'wake. Scarce showed the ray
To fancy's eye the portrayed characters
That graced the wall. On this and t' other side
Suspended, nodded o'er the sleepy stair,
In many a trophy formed, the knightly group
Of helms and targets, gauntlets, maces strong,
And horses' furniture, brave monuments
Of ancient chivalry. Through the stained pane
Low gleamed the moon—not bright, but of such power
As marked the clouds, black, threat'ning overhead,
Full mischief-fraught; from these in many a peal
Growled the near thunder, flashed the frequent blaze
Of lightning blue. While round the fretted dome
The wind sung surly, with unusual clank
The armour shook tremendous. On a couch
Placed in the oriel sunk the churchman down:
For who, alone at that dread hour of night,
Could bear portentous prodigy?—
'I hear it,' cries the proudly gilded Casque
(Filled by the soul of one, who erst took joy
In slaught'rous deeds), 'I hear amidst the gale
The hostile spirit shouting—once, once more

boteler/seneschal] head-servant, steward

In the thick harvest of the spears we'll shine—
There will be work anon.'
                    'I'm wakened too,'
Replied the sable Helmet (tenanted
By a like inmate); 'hark! I hear the voice
Of the impatient ghosts, who straggling range
Yon summit (crowned with ruined battlements,
The fruits of civil discord); to the din
The spirits, wand'ring round this Gothic pile,
All join their yell—the song is war and death—
There will be work anon.'
                    'Call armourers, ho!
Furbish my vizor—close my rivets up—
I brook no dallying.'
                    'Soft, my hasty friend,'
Said the black Beaver, 'neither of us twain
Shall share the bloody toil. War-worn am I;
Bored by a happier mace, I let in fate
To my once master: since unsought, unused,
Pensile I'm fixed. Yet too your gaudy pride
Has naught to boast: the fashion of the fight
Has thrown your gilt and shady plumes aside
For modern foppery; still do not frown,
Nor lour indignantly your steely brows;
We've comfort left enough. The bookman's lore
Shall trace our sometime merit; in the eye
Of antiquary taste we long shall shine:
And as the scholar marks our rugged front,
He'll say, this Cressy saw, this Agincourt:
Thus dwelling on the prowess of his fathers,
He'll venerate their shell. Yet more than this,
From our inactive station we shall hear
The groans of butchered brothers, shrieking plaints
Of ravished maids, and matrons' frantic howls;
Already hov'ring o'er the threatened lands,
The famished raven snuffs the promised feast,
And hoarslier croaks for blood—'twill flow.'
                    'Forbid it, heaven!
O shield my suffering country!—shield it!', prayed
The agonising priest.

(1775)

ANONYMOUS

402 *Between an Unemployed Artist and his Wife*

[Alone

She HARD is my fate, thus to want bread;
Curse on the day that I did wed!
While single I had food to eat,
My labour still procured me meat;
In a good place I lived at ease,
No careful thoughts my mind to tease;
In peace enjoyed a plenteous board,
With even delicacies stored;
Till simple love, and mounting pride,
First drew my foolish thoughts aside;
Soothed my fond ears with flatt'ry's sound,
And whispered pleasures should abound;
Service I learned thus to detest,
A place was irksome to my breast,
Thoughts of dependence broke my rest.
A master soon became my dread—
I cried, 'I'll work no more for bread;
I'll mistress of my actions move,
United to the man I love'.
I longed to taste a marriage life,
So plunged into a sea of strife;
And thinking to become more free,
Gave up at once my liberty,
To thraldom and necessity;
Consented to accept a chain,
And let two tyrants o'er me reign—
Want and a husband, who still rule,
Confining me now passion's cool;
Distresses will affection damp,
Gold is the oil that feeds love's lamp.
Here horrors darken all the place,
There famine stares me in the face;
For bread my children loudly cry,
Which I am forced—forced to deny.

[Enter Husband.

You're come—What, have you met success?
With aught will heav'n our wishes bless,
To mitigate our sharp distress?

Artist] artisan, craftsman

He No; there's no diff'rence in our fate—
Famine does but procrastinate
That death which quickly must attend,
And in the grave my mis'ries end:
I come home empty as I went,
Only more tired, and less content.
She Is there no work then to be got?
He Not the least job—indeed there's not:
The masters say their shops are full,
And business either dead or dull;
'They've goods enough' is all their cry,
And yet no customers to buy;
Their correspondents daily break—
Their all's continually at stake;
Scarce any money circulates,
But paper due at distant dates;
Their debts are large, and they must stay,
For all are tardy now in pay:
Respecting debts, both great and small,
Happy to get them in at all;
Many as desp'rate are confessed,
And dubious e'en the very best.
She Ah! I believe my heart will break.
He You must these ills with patience take.
She Preach the sea calm, when the winds rage;
Can patience hungry mouths assuage?
Will patience gives your babes a meal,
Who all the pangs of famine feel?
For bread to me all day they cry,
While I cannot their wants supply,
Till through fatigue they fall asleep,
Then wake again to call and weep.
Will patience make your children still,
Or their poor empty bellies fill?
Our landlord, ask if he's content
Your patience to receive for rent;
The baker's bill will patience pay,
Or send the butcher pleased away?
While you are out in seeking work,
They join to use me like a Turk;
With threats and menaces pursue,
Of what they say they're bent to do;
In vain to them were patience thrown,
For frequently I lose my own.
He Alas! what would you have me do?
She Can't you some other trade pursue?

Perhaps you might some work obtain,
T' enable us to live again.
He 'Tis all the same—all trades are dead;
Through town a gen'ral murmur's spread:
Besides, to take a trade in hand
I do not clearly understand—
Masters would call me stupid sot,
And say they've better workmen got;
'Think you,' they'd say, 'that we'll employ
A man our business to destroy?
Trade of itself is very lame;
You'd bring our shop at once to shame,
And hurt our credit and our name.
No, while good hands can be procured,
Bunglers ought not to be endured.'
Such, such would be the master's song,
While thus the men would use their tongue:
'Business is not already bad,
Though there's scarce any to be had,
But you an interloper come
Where all is full, and there's no room.
Too indolent you seem to be,
For such still love variety;
And like a lounging lazy drone,
You steal our trade and quit your own.'
Thus neither good success nor gains
Would recompense my honest pains.
She What can we do?—Have you no friends
For fortune's frowns to make amends?
None that, in this our scene of woe,
A little succour would bestow?
He I've tried them all a thousand ways;
All those who, in more prosp'rous days,
The firmest friendship to me swore,
And learned their bounty to implore;
But all in vain, their *words* were wind,
And, oh! their *deeds*—unkind, unkind.
It pains, it tortures me to speak
The cruelty I've met this week;
While I had money, I had friends,
Who meant to serve their private ends;
The friendship of these grov'ling men
Was to my circumstances then;
Now in the world no friendship reigns;
'Tis marred with interested stains;
And those who think this passion true,

An airy phantom but pursue;
Which when they vainly think they've caught,
Will 'scape them quick as nimble thought.
Of friendship judge by my success
In this our imminent distress:
The first whose heart I thought to touch
Was one who often promised much;
But he cried out with careless air,
'You're idle, that's the whole affair;
Do not on my good nature press;
I can't encourage idleness.'
Another, fond of hoarded pelf,
Replied, 'Indeed I'm poor myself.'
One said, 'You joke—you don't speak true,
I'm sure there's work enough to do;
Then learn to turn yourself about,
And seek some snug employment out;
Fortune will kindly for you carve:
While you have hands you cannot starve.'
Another cried, 'Why, go to sea,
You'll make yourself and family;
The sea you know will not refuse;
A better thing you cannot choose.'
This asks me if I thought him mad,
To lend where matters were so bad;
And that was quite amazed to find
That he should come across my mind.
Thus all in diff'rent ways denied,
And bid me for myself provide;
And tried to hide ingratitude,
Beneath advice or sayings shrewd.
She Then at the last, what hope remains,
To end or mitigate our pains?
He There's one dull light to cheer our gloom;
A workhouse is our certain doom.
Thither we all, alas! must go,
Where death will quickly end my woe.

(1775)

403 *Between a Contractor and his Wife*

He A GOOD day's work, two contracts made,
A very pretty swinging trade;
If these, with management and skill,
Won't buy a coach, then nothing will;

I've got another in my eye,
That I shall talk of by and by;
And if I come upon it souse,
Why that will yield a country house.
She Husband, why don't you come to bed?
He I've other matters in my head.
She Yes, you have more than what are good,
And more by half than what you should;
You're all but what you ought to be,
You think of ev'ry thing but me.
He You jade, I think of you too much.
Hussy, I shall two contracts touch;
You shall in a gilt chariot ride,
There's eatables to feed your pride.
She Your pardon, husband, I'll entreat,
Indeed, my dear, my words I'll eat:
I did not think you'd been so kind,
You're a good deary now I find.
He Give me a kiss, ye coaxing jade,
I tell you that our fortune's made.
She My dear, your meaning pray explain.
What are the contracts? I'm in pain;
My spirits all are in a flutter,
I scarce know how a word to utter;
I do believe I shall not speak
Another syllable this week.
He But I believe, before you're dumb,
I shall be worth a double plumb;
But now the contracts.——
She ——Now my dear.
He Well, hussy, hold your tongue and hear.
Why, I'm to farm the parish poor,
And there's, you know, above eight score.
She Why, husband, sure you've lost your eyes.
D'ye look on that as such a prize?
I fear you'll plough a barren field,
The poor but poor allowance yield.
He Indeed the thing you quite mistake,
I'll pretty picking of them make.
I'll briskly put 'em all to work,
Like a taskmaster to a Turk;
Their labour shall their living clear,
The pay shall all be saved, my dear.
Somewhat perhaps in labour too
May to our private purse accrue;

souse] directly, rapidly plumb] £100,000

They need not, ev'ry day they eat,
To be indulged, you know, with meat;
Because you know that living well,
As we can by experience tell,
Makes people fat, and fat, they say,
To disobedience leads the way;
Then idleness o'er all descends,
And impudence besure attends:
So that I think that little food
Becalms the spirits and the blood:
Keeps down each thought to rant and riot,
And makes the half-starved creatures quiet.
She Why, what you say, my dear, persuades.
I've tried the maxim with my maids;
The worse they live, I needs must say,
By much the better they obey;
I think poor people ought to starve,
And that's e'en more than they deserve:
The punishment's too good by far,
They should be hanged or burnt, my dear.
He Aye, they may talk of liberty,
They shan't grow saucy under me;
For in the workhouse close confined,
I'll make them all their business mind;
A good taskmaster shall attend,
With arguments at a rope's end.
She The sick will at your profits strike.
He The sick and well shall fare alike;
Let them recover if they choose it,
Or die content if they refuse it;
The thing is all the same to me,
Let them and death alone agree.
She Aye, they howe'er sometimes must eat;
Love, with what butcher shall you treat?
He Tom Touzer is to find the meat,
Not over good you may suppose,
But I'll hear no appeals from *nose*:
I'll say it's good, and if they doubt it,
Why, they may freely go without it;
Tasting will clarify the brain,
And take out ev'ry stupid stain.
She But if they chance to die, my soul?
He Why, they'll be buried, that's the whole.
She I'm glad your conscience is not queasy,
And that you'll manage matters easy.
He No, no, I've laid a solid plan,

To act with prudence like a man:
Why, can the wretches think it cruel,
If they're oft fed with water-gruel?
Should I indulge a workhouse breed,
Why, it would be absurd indeed.
No, through the business I'll go stitch,
The poor I mean shall make me rich;
I'll bend the mongrels to my will,
And make their hands my pockets fill.
So of the vagrants there's an end,
On them no farther thoughts I'll spend.
To t' other contract we'll draw near:
It is to light the lamps, my dear;
The lamps themselves I must provide,
And find the oil and men beside.
She Oh! that will be a charming thing,
And you may live like any king.
He Finely the parish I'll beguile,
And cheat them both in men and oil;
For thus the business I'll pursue:
One man shall do the work of two.
Yet I shall still the sum enlarge,
And for a double number charge;
With oil I mean the lamps to stock,
To burn till only twelve o'clock.
She Suppose the people should complain?
He Whate'er they say will be in vain;
I'll swear there's num'rous rogues abroad,
That do the lamps of oil defraud;
That my men rob I will declare,
And make a tale of how I fare,
Yet say I must these ills endure,
Since I can't honester procure.
The vestry thus I shall amuse,
And they th' omissions will excuse.
For the parishioners, I say,
Should be at home ere close of day;
If not, why let them grope their way;
Or, if it chances, break their shins,
And let him slyly laugh that wins.
She You'll certainly a fortune raise;
How I admire your cunning ways!
He Aye, deary, you'll admire much more,
When I have run the thing quite o'er.
She Then let me hear—Come tell your wife,
Cheating's the pleasure of my life.

He Why, if the lamps are stol'n away,
The parish must the cost defray.
She Yes, but admitting that is true,
What will the profit be to you?
He The profit!—why, you silly elf,
I mean to steal the lamps myself.
She But will no danger come to you,
If, as you say, you chance to do?
He No, love, I shall contrive it so,
Old Nick himself shall hardly know;
I'll either steal the lamps or break 'em,
And they in *statu quo* must make 'em.
The glass-man is a Trojan brother,
And slyly will the matter smother;
Sell me again the lamps I steal,
Which he will for a while conceal;
Thus I shall gain a double prize,
And cheat the most discerning eyes.
She But I suppose for this concealing,
The glass-man has a fellow-feeling.
He Oh! that's but right and just you know,
From honour's rules I would not go;
There's honour among thieves 'tis clear;
Then with contractors be it dear.
She Contracting is a charming trade,
Since fortunes are so easy made;
I'll think of what must soon approach,
And fit myself to fit a coach.

(1775)

RICHARD BRINSLEY SHERIDAN

1751–1816

404 from *The Duenna*

Air

I NE'ER could any lustre see
In eyes that would not look on me:
I ne'er saw nectar on a lip,
But where my own did hope to sip.

Has the maid who seeks my heart
Cheeks of rose untouched by art?
I will own the colour true,
When yielding blushes aid their hue.
Is her hand so soft and pure?
I must press it to be sure:
Nor can I be certain then
Till it grateful press again.
Must I with attentive eye
Watch her heaving bosom sigh?
I will do so when I see
That heaving bosom sigh for me.

(1775)

405 from *The School for Scandal*

Song

HERE'S to the maiden of bashful fifteen;
  Here's to the widow of fifty;
Here's to the flaunting, extravagant quean,
  And here's to the housewife that's thrifty.
Chorus.
    Let the toast pass,—
    Drink to the lass,
I'll warrant she'll prove an excuse for the glass.

Here's to the charmer whose dimples we prize;
  Now to the maid who has none, sir:
Here's to the girl with a pair of blue eyes,
  And here's to the nymph with but *one*, sir.
    Chorus. Let the toast pass, &c.

Here's to the maid with a bosom of snow,
  Now to her that's as brown as a berry:
Here's to the wife with a face full of woe,
  And now for the damsel that's merry.
    Chorus. Let the toast pass, &c.

For let 'em be clumsy, or let 'em be slim,
  Young or ancient, I care not a feather;
So fill a pint-bumper quite up to the brim,
  And let us e'en toast 'em together.
    Chorus. Let the toast pass, &c.

(1777)

AUGUSTUS MONTAGU TOPLADY

1740–1778

406 *A Living and Dying Prayer for the Holiest Believer in the World*

ROCK of ages, cleft for me,
Let me hide myself in thee!
Let the water and the blood,
From thy riven side which flowed,
Be of sin the double cure;
Cleanse me from its guilt and pow'r.

Not the labours of my hands
Can fulfil thy law's demands:
Could my zeal no respite know,
Could my tears for ever flow,
All for sin could not atone:
Thou must save, and thou alone!

Nothing in my hand I bring;
Simply to thy Cross I cling;
Naked, come to thee for dress;
Helpless, look to thee for grace;
Foul, I to the fountain fly:
Wash me, Saviour, or I die!

While I draw this fleeting breath—
When my eye-strings break in death—
When I soar through tracts unknown—
See thee on thy judgement-throne—
Rock of ages, cleft for me,
Let me hide myself in thee.

(1776)

ANONYMOUS

407

Boston in Distress

WHILE pleasure reigns unrivalled on this shore,
The streets of Boston stream with British gore;
While like fall'n Romans for new joys we sigh,
Our friends drop breathless, or for mercy cry.
Perhaps the soldier, lost to pity's charms,
Now stabs the infant in the mother's arms;
Perhaps the husband sees his better part
Welt'ring in gore and bleeding from the heart;
Perhaps the lover, plunged in bitter woe,
Is torn from her whom most he loves below,
And sees the life he values as his own
Yielded in pangs, or hears the dying groan;
Perhaps the son, O agony of pain!
Sees, fatal sight! his aged parent slain;
Perhaps whole families, together hurled,
Seek the dread confines of another world.
O! scene of slaughter fiends alone enjoy,
Fiends who love death and wait but to destroy.
Are widows' tears that never cease to roll,
Are mothers' pangs that penetrate the soul,
Are shrieks of infants sacrificed to rage,
The horrid trophies of the present age?
Eternal Father! in thy mercy quell
The flames of faction that arise from hell;
Pour into British hearts the balm of peace,
And bid, O bid, this cruel carnage cease;
Like Isaac's sons let Britons meet again,
Nor be one brother by the other slain.

(1776)

ANONYMOUS ('M.')

408

On the Frequent Review of the Troops

REVIEWS are gaudy shows—allowed,
And gay folks crowd about 'em,
Yet England ought not to be proud,
For she does best without 'em.

Ten thousand paltry fighting beaus
May chance to gain a battle;
But England buys the bloody clothes,
And all the guns that rattle.

But, when completed all the plan,
And all the people murdered,
Let casuists tell us, if they can,
Is England's welfare furthered?

(1776)

ANONYMOUS

409 *Hob upon a Holiday*

HOB yawned three times and rubbed his eyes,
Dreaming 'twas near his hour to rise;
By instinct knew that day was broke,
And up he got, and then he woke;
Bethought him well 'twas holiday,
And reached him down his best array.
His frock from the same piece was ta'en
That is the tilt upon his wain;
His doublet underneath must be,
So we'll suppose what we can't see.
A leathern thong each knee did grace,
Two more were shoe-strings by their place;
The shoes themselves those shoe-strings tie
With Dobbin's might, or Whitefoot's, vie;
Of iron they wore an equal load,
Not Grecian chiefs went better shod.
Happy 't had been for Thetis' son,
Had in those days Hob's shoes been known.
Lank locks of black, at t' other end,
Beneath a beaver white depend:
The ribbon on't, true blue, some say
Had bound Doll's hose her wedding-day.
Kind Nature, and the sun as kind,
To fit him well with gloves had joined.
He wore no band of point, indeed,
But a stiff collar was instead.
His belt was buff; the same of old

At the Nemean fair were sold:
Hob won him at the wake hard by,
Owned chief in feats of chivalry.
His person did his garb so fit,
It seemed to have been made for it:
His legs were massy and well freight,
And the ground witnessed to the weight:
His head walked foremost as the best,
But they soon followed with the rest.
Brown as his bread a face he wore,
Summers long ceased to bake it more.
Smut was his joke, loud laugh his smile,
And box the teeth he showed the while.
Fat, though most days to god of heat
He sacrificed a pound in sweat:
Hence sav'ry fumes disperse in air,
Hence Towzer scents his lord so far.
Such Hob; and, without help of glass,
He scoured his fist upon his face;
New-combed him, and then scratched his head
To know which way his luck would lead.
A crab-tree in his hand he took,
And issued out in his best look.
Beware, ye lasses every one,
Bridget and Nancy, Nell and Joan!
The god of love's abroad this day,
And ev'ry girl he finds is prey:
Trust not your hearts, your ears, your eyes,
He means to take you by surprise,
For Hob is Cupid in disguise.

(1776)

ANONYMOUS

410 *Little Britain*

IN ancient times, no matter where,
A nation lived of wise men,
Who lawyers fed with special care,
Bum-bailiffs and excisemen;

409 box] yellow

Who made good laws to guard a hare,
  A partridge or a pheasant,
But left the poor to nature's care:
  Say, was not this right pleasant?

Who shut up men within brick walls,
  Because they were indebted;
Then let them out when hunger's calls
  Had them to shadows fretted;

Who paid ten thousand fools and knaves,
  And twenty thousand villains,
To make their fellow-subjects slaves,
  And steal their pence and shillings;

Who cut each others' throats for fun,
  On land and on the water,
While half the world looked weeping on,
  And half was burst with laughter.

Who to this country would not run,
  Where only freedom's got at?
Where birds escape the fatal gun,
  And men alone are shot at.

(1776)

SUSANNA BLAMIRE

1747–1794

411 from *Stoklewath; or, The Cumbrian Village*

FROM where dark clouds of curling smoke arise,
And the tall column mounts into the skies;
Where the grim arches of the forge appear,
Whose fluted pillars prop the thickening air;
Where domes of peers and humble roofs are found
Alike to spread their mingled vapours round;
From denser air and busy towns I run,
To catch a glimpse of the unclouded sun;
Foe to the toils which wealth and pomp create,
And all the hard-wrought tinsel of the great.

. . . .

Adown the stream where woods begin to throw
Their verdant arms around the rocks below,
A rustic bridge across the tide is thrown,
Where briars and woodbine hide the hoary stone;
A simple arch salutes th' admiring eye,
And the mill's clack the tumbling waves supply.
But lest society some loss should share,
And nearest neighbours lack their neighbour's fare,
The tottering step-stones cross the stream are laid,
O'er which trips lightly many a busy maid,
And many a matron; when one failing cow
Bids no big cheese within the cheese-vat grow,
Their wealthier neighbour then, her bowls to swell,
Will gladly take what they as gladly sell.
The morning toils are now completely o'er,
The bowls well scalded, and well swept the floor.
The daughter at the needle plies the seam,
While the good mother hastens to the stream:
There the long webs, that wintry moons began,
Lie stretched and beaming in the summer's sun;
And lest he scorch them in his fervid hours,
She scoops along the nice conducted showers;
Till like the snow, that tips the mountain's height,
The brown's dull shade gives place to purest white;
While her sweet child knee-deep is wading seen,
Picking bright stones, or tumbling on the green.
But now the sun's bright whirling wheels appear
On the broad front of noon, in full career.
A sign more welcome hangs not in the air,
For now the sister's call the brothers hear;
Dinner's the word, and every cave around
Devours the voice, and feasts upon the sound.
''Tis dinner, father!' all the brothers cry,
Throw down the spade, and heave the pickaxe by;
''Tis dinner, father!' Home they panting go,
While the tired parent still pants on more slow.
Now the fried rasher meets them on the way,
And savoury pancakes welcome steams convey.
Their pace they mend, till at the pump they stand,
Deluge the face and purify the hand,
And then to dinner. There the women wait,
And the tired father fills his chair of state;
Smoking potatoes meet their thankful eyes,
And Hunger wafts the grateful sacrifice;
To her libations of sweet milk are poured,
And Peace and Plenty watch around the board.

Now, till the sun has somewhat sunk in height,
Yet long before he dips his wheels in night,
The nut-brown labourers their senses steep
In the soft dews of renovating sleep;
The worthy sire to the soft bed repairs,
The sons beneath the shade forget their cares.
The clock strikes two, it beats upon the ear,
And soon the parent's anxious voice they hear:
'Come, come, my lads, you must not sleep all day!'
They rub their eyes, start up, then stalk away.

. . . .

From noon till morn rests female toil; save come
The evening hours when lowing cows draw home.
Now the good neighbour walks her friend to see,
And knit an hour, and drink a dish of tea.
She comes unlooked for—wheat-bread is to seek,
The baker has none, got no yeast last week;
And little Peggy thinks herself ill sped,
Though she has got a great piece gingerbread.
Home she returns, but disappointment's trace
Darkens her eye, and lengthens all her face;
She whispers lowly in her sister's ear,
Scarce can restrain the glistening, swelling tear.
The mother marks, and to the milk-house goes,
Blithe Peggy smiles, she well the errand knows;
There from the bowl, where cream so coolly swims,
The future butter generously skims,
And, flour commixing, forms a rural bread
That for the wheaten loaf oft stands in stead;
Cup after cup sends steaming circles round,
And oft the weak tea's in the full pot drowned;
It matters not, for while their news they tell
The mind's content, and all things move on well.
The sun has now his saffron robe put on,
Stepped from his chariot that with rubies shone;
The glittering monarch gains the western gate,
And for a moment shines in regal state;
His streaming mantle floats along the sky,
While he glides softly from the gazing eye;
From saffron tinge to yellow soon it flew,
Sea-green the next, and then to darkest blue.
Now different cares employ the village train,
The rich in cattle press the milky vein;
When, lo! a voice sends direful notes around,
And sharp vexation mingles in the sound;

'Tis little Peggy, she the pail would fill,
And on old Hawky try her early skill.
She stroked and clapped her, but she'd not allow;
The well-known hand best pleased the knowing cow;
Though cabbage leaves before her band was cast,
Hawky refused the coaxing rich repast;
And when the little hand unapt she found,
She kicked, and whelmed her on the slippery ground.
Along yon hedge now mouldering and decayed,
In gathered heaps you see the fragments laid;
Piled up with care to swell the nightly blaze,
And in the widow's hut a fire to raise.
See where she comes with her blue apron full,
Crowned with some scattered locks of dingy wool.
In years she seems, and on her well-patched clothes
Want much has added to her other woes.
There is a poor-house; but some little pride
Forbids her there her humbled head to hide;
O'er former scenes of better days she runs,
And everything like degradation shuns!
Now hooded Eve slow-gliding comes in view,
Busied in threading pearls of diamond dew;
Waking the flowers that early close the eye,
And giving drops to those that else would die.
And what is man but such a tender flower,
That buds, blooms, fades and dies within the hour?
Where round yon cottage the rosemary grows,
And turncap lilies flaunt beside the rose,
Two aged females turn the weary wheel,
And, as they turn, their slumbering thoughts reveal:
'How long is't, think ye, since th' old style was lost?
Poor England may remember't to her cost!
E'er since that time the weather has grown cold'
(For Jane forgets that she is now grown old).
'I knew when I lived servant at Woodmile,
So scorching hot the weather was in April,
The cows would startle, and by ten o'clock
My master used his horses to unyoke;
'Tis not so now; the sun has lost its power;
The very apples now-a-days are sour!
Could not the Parson tell the reason why
There are such changes both in earth and sky?'
' 'Tis not these only,' Margaret replied,
'For many a change besides have I espied.
Look at the girls!—they all dress now-a-days
Like them fine folk who act them nonsense plays!

No more the decent mob surrounds the face,
Bordered with edging, or bit good bone-lace;
Gauze flappets soon—that will not last a day—
We'll see them flaunting whilst they're making hay!
All things are changed, the world's turned upside down,
And every servant wears a cotton gown,
Bit flimsy things, that have no strength to wear,
And will like any blotting-paper tear!
I made my Nelly a half-worsted gown,
She slighting told me 't would not do in town!
This pride! this pride! it sure must have a fall,
And bring some heavy judgement on us all!
They're grown so bold too, and their lads allow,
When courting them, to skulk behind a cow,
Till all's in bed. My John, when courting me,
Used after supper to come manfully;
For oft he used to say he knew no place
Where honesty need fear to show its face.
No more it need! My master used to cry,
He feared but two things—to turn thief, and lie.'

(Wr. *c.*1776?; pub. 1842)

JOHN CODRINGTON BAMPFYLDE

1754–1796

412 *Sonnet*

As when, to one who long hath watched, the morn
  Advancing slow forewarns th' approach of day
  (What time the young and flowery-kirtled May
  Decks the green hedge and dewy grass unshorn
With cowslips pale and many a whitening thorn);
  And now the sun comes forth with level ray,
  Gilding the high-wood top and mountain grey,
  And, as he climbs, the meadows 'gins adorn;
The rivers glisten to the dancing beam,
  Th' awakened birds begin their amorous strain,
  And hill and vale with joy and fragrance teem;
Such is the sight of thee, thy wished return,
  To eyes like mine, that long have waked to mourn,
  That long have watched for light, and wept in vain.

(1778)

413 *On a Frightful Dream*

THIS morn, ere yet had rung the matin peal,
The cursèd Merlin with his potent spell
Aggrieved me sore, and from his wizard cell
(First fixing on mine eyes a magic seal)
Millions of ghosts and shadowy shapes let steal,
Who, swarming round my couch, with horrid yell
Chattered and mowed, as though from deepest hell
They had escaped.—I oft, with fervent zeal
Essayed, and prayer, to mar th' Enchanter's pow'r.
In vain; for thicker still the crew came on,
And now had weighed me down, but that the day
Appeared, and Phoebus, from his eastern tow'r,
With new-tricked beam like Truth immortal shone,
And chased the visionary forms away.

(1778)

414 *To the Evening*

WHAT numerous votaries 'neath thy shadowy wing,
O mild and modest Evening, find delight!
First, to the grove his lingering fair to bring,
The warm and youthful lover, hating light,
Sighs oft for thee.—And next the boisterous string
Of school-imps, freed from Dame's all-dreaded sight,
Round village cross in many a wanton ring
Wishes thy stay.—Then too, with vasty might
From steeple's side to urge the bounding ball,
The lusty hinds await thy fragrant call.
I, friend to all by turns, am joined with all,
Lover, and elfin gay, and harmless hind;
Nor heed the proud, to real wisdom blind,
So as my heart be pure and free my mind.

(1778)

415 *On a Wet Summer*

ALL ye who, far from town, in rural hall,
Like me were wont to dwell near pleasant field,
Enjoying all the sunny day did yield,
With me the change lament, in irksome thrall

By rains incessant held; for now no call
From early swain invites my hand to wield
The scythe; in parlour dim I sit concealed,
And mark the lessening sand from hourglass fall,
Or 'neath my window view the wistful train
Of dripping poultry, whom the vine's broad leaves
Shelter no more.—Mute is the mournful plain,
Silent the swallow sits beneath the thatch,
And vacant hind hangs pensive o'er his hatch,
Counting the frequent drop from reeded eaves.

(1778)

JOHN NEWTON

1725–1807

416

The Name of Jesus

How sweet the name of Jesus sounds
In a believer's ear!
It soothes his sorrows, heals his wounds,
And drives away his fear.

It makes the wounded spirit whole,
And calms the troubled breast;
'Tis manna to the hungry soul,
And to the weary rest.

Dear name! the rock on which I build,
My shield and hiding-place;
My never-failing treas'ry filled
With boundless stores of grace.

By thee my pray'rs acceptance gain,
Although with sin defiled;
Satan accuses me in vain,
And I am owned a child.

Jesus! my shepherd, husband, friend,
My prophet, priest, and king;
My lord, my life, my way, my end,
Accept the praise I bring.

Weak is the effort of my heart,
  And cold my warmest thought,
But when I see thee as thou art,
  I'll praise thee as I ought.

Till then I would thy love proclaim
  With ev'ry fleeting breath;
And may the music of thy name
  Refresh my soul in death.

(1779)

417 *Zion, or the City of God*

GLORIOUS things of thee are spoken,
  Zion, city of our God!
He, whose word cannot be broken,
  Formed thee for his own abode.
On the rock of ages founded,
  What can shake thy sure repose?
With salvation's walls surrounded,
  Thou may'st smile at all thy foes.

See! the streams of living waters,
  Springing from eternal love,
Well supply thy sons and daughters,
  And all fear of want remove.
Who can faint while such a river
  Ever flows their thirst t' assuage:
Grace which, like the Lord the giver,
  Never fails from age to age?

Round each habitation hov'ring,
  See the cloud and fire appear!
For a glory and a cov'ring,
  Showing that the Lord is near:
Thus deriving from their banner
  Light by night and shade by day,
Safe they feed upon the manna
  Which he gives them when they pray.

Blest inhabitants of Zion,
  Washed in the Redeemer's blood!
Jesus, whom their souls rely on,
  Makes them kings and priests to God:

'Tis his love his people raises
  Over self to reign as kings,
And as priests, his solemn praises
  Each for a thank-off'ring brings.

Saviour, if of Zion's city
  I through grace a member am,
Let the world deride or pity,
  I will glory in thy name:
Fading is the worldling's pleasure,
  All his boasted pomp and show;
Solid joys and lasting treasure
  None but Zion's children know.

(1779)

J. WILDE

fl. 1779

418 *Verses to Miss ——*

FROM six o'clock I traversed to and fro,
Oft stopped confounded, knew not where to go,
Then gazed around; the evening was quite mild,
But had you seen me you'd have thought me wild.
I envied then the slow hound his fine scent,
Which had I got, I'd smelt the way you went:
But greyhound-like I only run by sight,
And you like lightning sure had ta'en your flight.
I never could behold one trace you made,
And sure you did not go there as you said.

But don't you think it was a dang'rous way
For me to walk with disappointment, pray?
Thanks to the brook, it covered but the ground,
Or I, perhaps, might have leaped in and drowned:
And this, indeed, might be the thing you meant;
But, if 'twas yours, it was not my intent.
So home I came, went quietly to bed,
Got a sound sleep, indeed, indeed I did,
Though all this stuff laid somewhere in my head.

(1779)

ANONYMOUS ('BRIAN BENDO')

419 *The Dream*

'TWAS when Tacita hushed the noisy world,
And wrangling clamour into silence hurled,
I lay involved in sleep close by the side
Of her I wish had never been my bride!
Methought into my cottage Morpheus came,
And me compelled to leave my wayward dame;
Straight unto Bridewell hurried me away,
Where I was doomed for just twelve months to stay.
There all the day I laboured like a Turk,
And in the ev'ning, when I left my work,
Upon the floor I instantly was chained,
And all the night beneath these bands remained:
But when the morning streaked the eastern skies
With red—I to my drudgery did rise.
Whene'er my master called, I did obey,
His precepts harsh I never did delay;
It was my duty, and my interest too,
For to complete whate'er he bade me do.
My meals, though small, with them I was content,
I took with gladness what my mistress sent.
Then hied to work as soon as I was done,
And finishèd what I'd before begun.
The time I spent with pleasure and delight,
Yet drudged all day, and bore my chains at night.
Methought, when in this pleasing dream I lay,
I could for ever in the prison stay:
I was content to stay there all my life,
As I was far from wedlock and my wife;
The farther I was from the wanton shrew,
The less of grief and wickedness I knew.
The year was with great satisfaction spent,
For with my slav'ry I was well content.
But oh! the time! the time too soon arrived,
When I of peace and prison was deprived.
Bridewell's restraint I with much pleasure bore;
But wedlock's damned confinement I abhor.
While there I stayed, I was from marriage free,
I had no freakish wife to trouble me;
No wrath to shun, no fury to avoid,
No woes to feel, but always peace enjoyed;

No wiles to cheat, no strife for to appease;
No trull to plague, no termagant to please;
No jilt to soothe, no harlot me to mock,
No prude to please, nor cradle for to rock.
No whore to clothe, no lechery to heed,
No wench to chide, no lawless brats to feed;
No threats to awe, no cries to stun my ear;
No frowns to dread, nor bludgeons for to fear.
No lust to quench, no vicious deeds to vex;
No bawd to scold, no strumpet to perplex;
No harm to hurt, no mischief for to flee;
No jade to scorn, nor wife to cuckold me!
Methought when I was forced to leave Bridewell,
I was harrassed beyond what tongue can tell;
For well I knew that home I must return,
To her alas! that gave me cause to mourn:
The thought of which did banish sleep away,
And lo! the cuckold with the strumpet lay.

(1779)

JOHN HAWTHORN

fl. 1779

420 *On his Writing Verses*

WELL may they write, that sit in parlours fine,
To raise their spirits can quaff luscious wine;
To keep out noise, the parlour door is shut;
The servants scarce dare speak, or budge a foot;
Under no fear, no terror, or no task,
But coolly can sit at a writing-desk.
How different with me the time is spent,
Enclosed with dragoons in a little tent;
Some darning stockings, others blacking shoes;
Some singing, others telling jests and news:
Their different sounds do ill confound my writing;
One should be solitary, when inditing;
Yet I must be a bard, naught less will do me,
And so [I] write as nature dictates to me.

(1779)

421 from *The Journey and Observations of a Countryman*

[*A Deathbed*]

A LITTLE house there stood within a glen,
But rather seemed a hole or fox's den;
Instead of straw, the cot was thatched with furze;
Around the door grew nettles, docks and burs,
Where neither was seen corn, oats or hay,
But a few rags that on the bushes lay;
And from the door, I heard a woman crying,
'Alas! alas! my husband's just a-dying':
Thinks I, awhile into this house I'll go,
It's good to visit all such scenes of woe;
So in I steps.—Now if I could relate
How poverty here sat, on her throne of state,
How smoke did choke me, and the soot did drop,
And in the floor stood many a crooked prop;
No windows, but a few old shattered panes,
And walls all crumbling with the oozing rains:
These things I pass, and only this I'll say,
That on a wisp the owner dying lay;
Naught did him cover but a dirty sheet,
And on the floor lay his bare naked feet;
Strongly he gasped, and stared, and strove for breath,
And struggled in the agonies of death:
I stood appalled, the tears rushed in my eyes,
To see my fellow creature's agonies;
Sweat dewed my face, my heart it fell a-beating,
To think of soul and body separating;
His poor, disconsolate wife sat on the bed,
And strove for to support his sinking head;
Whilst his two daughters sat by the bed side;
Sorely they wept, but yet in silence cried.
Says I, 'This man cannot live long, it's plain;
Has he no son for to keep up his name?'
'Oh yes,' the woman cries, 'I have a son,
A graceless wretch, that's to the cock-fight gone;
He broke my box, and took the cash away,
That was to lay his father in the clay;
But oh! alas! I now may hold my tongue,
I should have kept him down when he was young.'
Says I, 'It's strange he thinks it not a sin.'
Just as I said the word, the son came in;

A boorish clown with a rough tawdry head,
That was between a yellow and a red;
His clothes were flying, and all torn in rags,
No shoes on's feet, or stockings on his legs;
A great large rope was tied round his middle,
His shins were burnt blacker than a griddle;
So drunk that he could scarcely keep a leg,
And smelled of liquor like a brandy keg;
He really had a bad look in his eye,
And yet the rogue was near to six feet high;
Had a great staff that would have killed a bull,
Or dashed in pieces a ram's horny skull.
When he came in, he wildly at me stared;
Tobacco spittle hung upon his beard:
He passed his father quite unnoticed by,
Nor once unto the bed did turn his eye;
And though the phlegm did rattle in his throat,
He heeded him no more than an old goat;
He to the corner went, and down did sit,
And muttered out, 'Is he no better yet?'
And though the sun's fierce heat would roasted eggs,
He drew the fire still between his legs.
I grew enraged:—says I, 'You clumsy fool,
Raise up your heavy buttocks off that stool;
The man's no better, nor will ever be,
Till he does launch into eternity.'
He glimmered up, through his long sandy hair,
And like a tiger he did at me stare:
'Down on your knees,' says I, 'and make petition,
To ease your father out of this condition.'
'Well, I'll begin,' says he; 'curse on the day
That e'er the ginger cock did run away;
But though on him I lost my good half-crown,
I knocked great Armstrong, the hander, down;
'Twas that good staff that staggered cocker Ned';
With that he wheeled his cudgel round his head.
'Your coin,' says I, 'was better than your knockings,
It would have bought a pair of shoes and stockings,
Or laid your father underneath a stone;
But that is not my business, I must own.'
If that I durst, I fainly would deride him,
But, faith, I feared the staff that stood beside him:
I said no more, the mother shook her head,
And in a few minutes more the man was dead.

hander] handler **cocker] gamecock breeder**

Oh! then I thought their shouts would rend the skies,
And even the ragged son set up his cries;
He leaped up with a most hideous squeak,
And cries, 'I thought he would not die this week';
The woman's grief was great, I ne'er saw stronger;
So out I came, I could not stand it longer.
No sight to me was ever half so hateful,
As children to their parents being ungrateful;
I would excuse a man that blood did spill,
Before a wretch that used his parents ill. . . .

(1779)

JOHN FREETH

1731?–1808

422 *Bunker's Hill, or the Soldier's Lamentation*

I AM a jolly soldier,
Enlisted years ago,
To serve my king and country,
Against the common foe.
But when across th' Atlantic
My orders were to go,
I grieved to think that English hearts
Should draw their swords on those
Who fought and conquered by their side,
When Frenchmen were their foes.

In drubbing French and Spaniards
A soldier takes delight,
But troops cooped up in Boston,
Are in so sad a plight,
That many think their stomachs more
Inclined to eat than fight,
And like us would be loth to stir;
For ev'ry vet'ran knows,
We fought and conquered side by side,
When Frenchmen were our foes.

'Twas on the seventeenth of June,
I can't forget the day,
The flower of our army
For Charles-Town sailed away.

The town was soon in ashes laid,
When bombs began to play:
But oh! the cruel scene to paint,
It makes my blood run chill;
Pray heaven grant I never more
May climb up Bunker's Hill.

America to frighten
The tools of power strove,
But ministers are cheated,
Their schemes abortive prove.
The men they told us would not fight
Are to the combat drove,
And to our gallant officers,
It proved a bitter pill,
For numbers dropped before they reached
The top of Bunker's Hill.

I should not be amazed to hear
Wolfe's ghost had left the shades,
To check that shameful bloody work,
Which England's crown degrades.
The lads, who scorn to turn their backs
On Gallia's best brigades,
Undaunted stood, but frankly own
They better had lain still,
Than such a dear-bought victory gain,
As that of Bunker's Hill.

Did they, who bloody measures crave,
Our toil and danger share,
Not one to face the rifle-men
A second time would dare.
Ye Britons who your country love,
Be this your ardent pray'r:
To Britain and her colonies,
May peace be soon restored,
And knaves of high and low degree
Be *destined to the cord.*

(1780?)

423 *The Cottager's Complaint, on the Intended Bill for Enclosing Sutton-Coldfield*

How sweetly did the moments glide,
How happy were the days!
When no sad fear my breast annoyed,
Or e'er disturbed my ease;
Hard fate! that I should be compelled
My fond abode to lose,
Where threescore years in peace I've dwelled,
And wish my life to close.

Chorus

Oh the time! the happy, happy time,
Which in my cot I've spent;
I wish the church-yard was his doom,
Who murders my content.

My ewes are few, my stock is small,
Yet from my little store
I find enough for nature's call,
Nor would I ask for more!
That word, ENCLOSURE! to my heart
Such evil doth bespeak,
I fear I with my all must part,
And fresh employment seek.
Chorus—Oh the time, &c.

What little of the spacious plain
Should power to me consign,
For want of means, I can't obtain,
Would not long time be mine:
The stout may combat fortune's frowns,
Nor dread the rich and great;
The young may fly to market-towns,
But where can I retreat?
Chorus—Oh the time, &c.

What kind of feelings must that man
Within his mind possess,
Who, from an avaricious plan,
His neighbours would distress?
Then soon, in pity to my case,
To Reason's ear incline;
For on his heart it stamps disgrace,
Who formed the base design.

Chorus

Oh the time! the happy, happy time,
  Which in my cot I've spent;
I wish the church-yard was his doom,
  Who murders my content.

(1782)

424 *Botany Bay*

AWAY with all whimsical bubbles of air,
Which only excite a momentary stare;
Attention to plans of utility pay,
Weigh anchor and steer towards Botany Bay.

Let no one think much of a trifling expense,
Who knows what may happen a hundred years hence;
The loss of America what can repay?
New colonies seek for at Botany Bay.

O'er Neptune's domain how extensive the scope!
Of quickly returning how distant the hope!
The Cape must be doubled, and then bear away
Two thousand good leagues to reach Botany Bay.

Of those *precious* souls which for nobody care,
It seems a large cargo the kingdom can spare;
To ship a few hundreds off make no delay,
They cannot too soon go to Botany Bay.

They go of an island to take special charge,
Much warmer than Britain, and ten times as large;
No Custom-house duty, no freightage to pay,
And tax-free they'll live when at Botany Bay.

This garden of Eden, this new promised land,
The time to set sail for is almost at hand;
Ye worst of land-lubbers, make ready for sea,
There's room for you all about Botany Bay.

As scores of each sex to this place must proceed,
In twenty years time—only think of the breed;
Major Semple, should Fortune much kindness display,
May live to be king over Botany Bay.

For a general good, make a general sweep,
The beauty of life is good order to keep;
With night-prowling hateful disturbers away,
And send the whole tribe into Botany Bay.

Ye chiefs who go out on this naval exploit,
The work to accomplish, and set matters right;
To Ireland be kind, call at Cork on your way,
And take a few White Boys to Botany Bay.

Commercial arrangements give prospect of joy,
Fair and firm may be kept ev'ry national tie;
And mutual confidence those who betray,
Be sent to the bottom of Botany Bay.

(1786)

ANONYMOUS

425 *A Translation of the Cywdd to Morvydd, an Elegiac Ode, written about four hundred years ago by David ap Gwilim who has been called the Ovid of Wales*

FOR seven long years I had declared my passion
To the slender and gentle maid: but in vain.
My tongue was eloquent in the expression of my love:
But till last night sorrow was the sole fruit of my cares.
Then I obtained the reward of all my disappointments
From her whose complexion is the image of the wave.
Then, favourably receiving my addresses,
She admitted me to all the happy mysteries of love—
To converse without restraint,
To kiss the dear fair-one with the jetty eyebrows,
And with my arm support her head;
Bright maid, with the snowy hue:
How charming the lovely burden!
While I was thus enjoying, with my inestimable jewel,
The most perfect felicity that love can bestow,
I prudently mentioned (it was an angry reflection!)
That the appointed day was approaching
When her jealous husband would return:
And thus the snowy maid replied:

Morvith My accomplished love, gentle and amiable,
We shall hear, ere it dawns, the song of the chanting bird,
The loud clear voice of the stately cock.
David What if the jealous churl
Should come in before the dawn appears?
M. David, speak of a more agreeable subject;
Faint, alas! and gloomy are thy hopes.
D. My charmer, bright as the fields that glitter with the gossamer,
I perceive daylight through the crevice of the door.
M. It is the new moon, and the twinkling stars,
And the reflection of their beams upon the pillar.
D. No, my charmer, bright as the sun,
By all that's sacred, it has been day this hour.
M. Then, if thou art so inconstant,
Follow thy inclinations and depart.

I arose, and fled from all search,
With my garments in my hand, and fear in my breast:
I ran through wood and brake,
From the face of day into the green thickets of the dale.
Looking forward, I beheld an absence longer than ages;
Behind me, the folly of my flight.

(1781)

JOHN SCOTT

1730–1783

426 *Ode*

I HATE that drum's discordant sound,
Parading round, and round, and round:
To thoughtless youth it pleasure yields,
And lures from cities and from fields,
To sell their liberty for charms
Of tawdry lace, and glittering arms;
And when Ambition's voice commands,
To march and fight, and fall, in foreign lands.

I hate that drum's discordant sound,
Parading round, and round, and round:
To me it talks of ravaged plains,
And burning towns, and ruined swains,
And mangled limbs, and dying groans,
And widows' tears, and orphans' moans;
And all that Misery's hand bestows
To fill the catalogue of human woes.

(1782)

SAMUEL HENLEY

1740–1815

427 *Verses Addressed to a Friend, Just Leaving a Favourite Retirement, Previous to Settling Abroad. Written in the Close of Winter*

ERE yet your footsteps quit the place
Your presence long hath deigned to grace,
With softening eye and heart deplore
The conscious scenes, your own no more.
When vernal clouds their influence shower,
Disclose the bud and rear the flower,
Who to yon leafing grove will come
Where the rathe primrose loves to bloom,
And fondly seek, with heedful tread,
The forward floret's downy head:
Or, when the violet leaves the ground,
Scent the perfume pure-breathing round?
The garden tribes that gladlier grew,
While cherished by your fostering view,
No more resume their wonted hues,
No more their wonted scents diffuse!
Who first will spy the swallow's wing,
Or hear the cuckoo greet the spring?
Unmarked shall then th' assiduous dove,
With ruffling plumage, urge his love!
Unnoted, though in lengthened strain,
The bashful nightingale complain!
The bleating group of new-born lambs,
That frisk around their pasturing dams,
No more allure the passing eye,

Or, shorn, invite your sympathy!
Who listless now will sauntering stay
Where buxom rustics ted their hay,
And o'er the field survey askance
The wavy vapour quivering dance?
Or, sunk supine with musing eyes,
Enjoy the hum of noonday flies;
Or watch the bee from bell to bell,
Where fleckered foxgloves edge the dell?
Or, mid the sultry heat, reclined
Beneath the poplar, woo the wind,
While, to the lightest air that strays,
Each leaf its hoary side displays?
Who, drawn by nature's varying face,
O'er heav'n the spreading tempest trace?
Or, in the rear of sunny rain,
Admire the bright bow's gorgeous train,
Till all its glowing tints decay,
And the dimmed vision melts away?
Who now surmount the upland's height,
When morning beams her blushing light,
To view the goss'mer pearled with dew,
That tremulous shoots each mingling hue?
Or mark the clouds in liveries gay,
Precede the radiant orb of day?
Who, when his amplest course is run,
Wistful pursue the sinking sun?
To common eyes he vainly shines,
Unheeded rises or declines!
Aslant their brows, the golden ray
In vain th' empurpled hills display.
Steep sidelong woods, with farms between;
Dark hedgerow elms, with meadows green;
The white church, peeping half through trees;
Slopes waving corn, as wills the breeze;
The podding beanfield, striped with balks;
The hurdled sheep-cote; hoof-trod walks;
The road that winds athwart the down;
The skirting furze-brake; fallow brown;
The windmill's scarcely-circling vane;
The villager's returning wain;
The western window's crimson blaze,
That flares obtrusive on the gaze;
The eager heifer's echoing low,
Far from her calf compelled to go;
The throstle's wild melodious lay,

That bids farewell to parting day;
The cottage smoke that straight ascends;
The labourer blithe that homeward bends;
The gathering fumes that lightly skim
O'er the clear brook's undimpled brim;
The plank and rail that bridge the stream;
The rising full-moon's ampler gleam—
No more the onward foot beguile,
Where pollards rude protect the stile.
Whose look now scans the dusky sphere
To note each kindling star appear?
Who now the flushing dawn describes,
That upward streams o'er northern skies?
Or the wan meteor's lurid light,
That, headlong glancing, mocks the sight?
In the dank lane who now require
The glow-worm's ineffectual fire?
Or catch the bells from distant vale,
That load by fits the freshening gale,
Till, startled from the rustling spray,
The moping owl re-wings her way?
When autumn sere the copse invades,
No more you haunt the woodland glades
To eye the change on ev'ry bough;
Or eddying leaf descending slow;
Or peering squirrel nimbly glean
Each nut that hung before unseen;
Or flitting down from thistle borne;
Or glossy haw that crowds the thorn,
Whence oft in saws observers old
Portend the length of winter's cold.
Waked by the flail's redoubling sound,
When spangling hoar-frost crisps the ground,
No more forgo bewildering sleep
To climb with health yon airy steep.
When deepening snows oppress the plain,
The birds no more their boon obtain;
The redbreast hovering round your doors,
No more his stated meal implores.
Where all that needed found relief,
No tearful eye laments their grief;
No lenient hand dispels their pain;
Fainting they sue, yet sue in vain.
But though the scenes you now deplore,
With heart and eye, be yours no more,
Though ev'ry long-known object seem

Unreal as the morning's dream,
You still with retrospective glance,
Or rapt in some poetic trance,
At will may ev'ry charm renew,
Each smiling prospect still review;
Through memory's power and fancy's aid,
The pictured phantoms ne'er shall fade.
And, oh! where'er your footsteps roam,
Where'er you fix your future home,
May joys attending crown the past,
And heaven's blest mansion be your last!

(1782)

—— O'BRIEN

fl. 1782

428 *The Ghost*

I IS the ghost of Stevey Fizzlegig,
If you'll believe me,
Who died for love of Sukey Swizzleswig,
It did so grieve me:
For nobody did never see,
In my life's time, that day when she
Did say, 'For Stevey Fizzlegig
I keres a single ha'penny'.
Chorus. Oh! Oh! Oh!

To Fag-lane, near the sign o' th' Morniment,
If you'll believe me,
To tell my love, oft'times, forlorn I went,
Which much did grieve me:
For there this Sukey Swizzleswig
Baked faggots, maws and hogs-feet sells,
Jest oppersite Bess Frowzy's shed,
Who in it cat's and dog's meat sells.
Chorus. Oh! Oh! Oh!

I could not work at all, through loving so,
If you'll believe me,
Yet she prefarred one they calls cussing Joe,
Which much did grieve me,

'Cause he duz treat her oftentimes,
  And her out on a Sunday take;
And (though he'd better mind his work)
  With her oft does St. Monday make.
                Chorus. Oh! Oh! Oh!

Says I, 'Through Joe your scorn you throws at me',
  If you'll believe me;
At them words she turns up her nose at me;
  How that did grieve me!
But, when I sed 'I doubts he in
  A sartin place oft stops a gap',
She calls me sniv'ling cull, and then
  Gave each of these here chops a slap.
                Chorus. Oh! Oh! Oh!

Through this, when to my room up stairs I goes,
  If you'll believe me,
Says I, 'How full of thoughts and cares I grows,
  Which much does grieve me.'
And then, as I'd no chair, I fetched
  My master's little darter's stool,
And cried cause Suk had sarved me so,
  While I did off my garters pull.
                Chorus. Oh! Oh! Oh!

First, that they wouldn't eas'ly break I tries,
  If you'll believe me;
Next, one end of 'em round my neck I ties,
  And that did grieve me:
The stool I then did mount, and to
  A joist tied t'other end of 'em,
Then kicked the stool away, and swung
  Like our cuckoo-clock pendulum.
                Chorus. Oh! Oh! Oh!

E'en when intarred she called me snotty fool,
  If you'll believe me,
Because my love was fur too hot to cool,
  And which did grieve me:
But, as I knows they're in the dark
  In Suk's back room, I'll whiz through air,
And in revenge I'll frighten 'em
  Until they sweat, nay, p——, through fear.
                Chorus. Oh! Oh! Oh!

(1782)

St. Monday make] take Monday as a holiday

EDWARD THOMPSON

1739?–1786

429 from *An Humble Wish. Off Porto-Sancto, March 29, 1779*

I'VE served my country nine and twenty years,
A mere light chip, the sport of all the spheres:
To India I was early sent in youth;
Then bandied to the north, the west, and south;
France, Holland, Prussia, Portugal, and Spain,
America, and all the western main.
Now I'm for Guinea, in an infant war,
Chief of a gallant ship, where ev'ry tar,
Ragged and lousy, hungry is and poor,
Well fitted a rich Frenchman to devour.
As for sea hardships, they create my smiles—
We'll bury them in the Canary Isles,
In the soft lap of beauteous Portuguese,
The olive Sirens of those summer seas.
Now for my wish—and Venus hear the strain!
When I've this bark conducted o'er the main,
And I return with golden laurels bound,
Parcel me out a little fertile ground,
And build thereon a house, by some thick wood,
And at the mountain's foot a rapid flood:
The river stored with trout, the wood with game,
And lovely Emma my propitious dame!
Retired from war, the bustle of the seas,
Let me repose with her in health and ease;
I seek no star or honours of the land;
I'd rather have a kiss of her white hand
Than all the salutations of St. James,
Where nobles truck their characters for names.
I only bend my knee to her and heaven,
Nor pray for aught, but thank for what is given.
If ye who rule the clouds, and guide the sun,
Will perfect this before my sand is run,
I bow—if not, your mighty wills be done.

(1783)

430 *To Emma, Extempore. Hyaena, off Gambia, June 4, 1779*

THOUGH love's my daily and my nightly theme,
Yet of his softer joys I seldom dream;
And though I press my pillow with a pray'r
That ev'ry god makes Emma all his care,
Yet still I ne'er recount her beauteous charms,
Nor in idea clasp her in my arms.
This is both adverse, cruel and unkind,
When all my body, all my soul and mind,
Are bound, devoted, to her vital sway,
The empress of my heart, whom I obey.
But what kind impulse touched on Cupid's breast
Last night, I cannot tell—but when at rest,
And rolling, tumbling, on this scorching wave,
A mere sea-drudge, a very Guinea slave—
Methought I met you, tidy, gay and neat,
White with pink ribbons, in St. James's-street:
You smiled, you looked most fair, and smartly said,
'Come home to tea, and bless thy Emma, Ned.'
Whether this pleasing assignation proved
Too great a transport to the mind that loved—
I waked—with horror cursed my cruel state,
That you was fled, and Africa my fate.
But be this coast my curse—make love my theme,
And beauteous Emma ev'ry night my dream!

(1783)

431 *The Indian Maid. Demararie, Oct. 27, 1781*

THE Indian maid who lightly trips,
  The Dryad of the Guava grove,
The zone of Venus round her hips,
  And graced with youth, and blessed in love!
Gold rings adorn her nose and arms,
And leaves of beads veil naked charms.

Or if she quits the golden wood,
  Pierced by the scorching solar beam,
She plunges in the cooler flood,
  And swims the Naiad of the stream:
Adores the god in ev'ry air,
And smiles the maid without a care.

Or if more distant creeks invite
  To fish, to fowl, or seek her love,
She paddles the canoe upright,
  Where Christian maids would fear to move;
On some fair tree her hammock swings,
Nor envies she the beds of kings.

Like other belles of other shores,
  She daubs her limbs, her face, her hair:
Raucoo and launa[1] stop the pores
  Against mosquitoes and the air.
But these, I trust, nor spoil her skin,
They're to defend—not lure to sin.

A beauteous bronze she stands confessed,
  Venus nor Hebe more complete;
With various feathers tricked and dressed,
  Perfumed with Tonkay[2] flow'rs most sweet!
And when she moves, her mien and grace
Prove her the goddess of the place!

(1783)

GEORGE CRABBE

1754–1832

432 *The Village*, Book I

THE village life, and every care that reigns
O'er youthful peasants and declining swains;
What labour yields, and what, that labour past,
Age, in its hour of languor, finds at last;
What forms the real picture of the poor,
Demands a song—the Muse can give no more.
Fled are those times, if e'er such times were seen,
When rustic poets praised their native green;
No shepherds now, in smooth alternate verse,
Their country's beauty or their nymphs' rehearse;
Yet still for these we frame the tender strain,
Still in our lays fond Corydons complain,

[1] Paints used by the Indians; the first red, the latter black.

[2] The Tonkay tree, one of the largest of the creation. It bears a sweet flower, which sets in a bean, and smells like new hay.

And shepherds' boys their amorous pains reveal,
The only pains, alas! they never feel.
  On Mincio's banks, in Caesar's bounteous reign,
If Tityrus found the Golden Age again,
Must sleepy bards the flattering dream prolong,
Mechanic echoes of the Mantuan song?
From truth and nature shall we widely stray,
Where Virgil, not where Fancy, leads the way?
  Yes, thus the Muses sing of happy swains,
Because the Muses never knew their pains.
They boast their peasants' pipes, but peasants now
Resign their pipes and plod behind the plough;
And few amid the rural tribe have time
To number syllables and play with rhyme;
Save honest Duck, what son of verse could share
The poet's rapture and the peasant's care?
Or the great labours of the field degrade
With the new peril of a poorer trade?
  From one chief cause these idle praises spring,
That themes so easy few forbear to sing;
They ask no thought, require no deep design,
But swell the song and liquefy the line;
The gentle lover takes the rural strain,
A nymph his mistress and himself a swain;
With no sad scenes he clouds his tuneful prayer,
But all, to look like her, is painted fair.
I grant indeed that fields and flocks have charms
For him that gazes or for him that farms;
But when amid such pleasing scenes I trace
The poor laborious natives of the place,
And see the mid-day sun, with fervid ray,
On their bare heads and dewy temples play;
While some, with feebler hands and fainter hearts,
Deplore their fortune, yet sustain their parts:
Then shall I dare these real ills to hide
In tinsel trappings of poetic pride?
  No, cast by Fortune on a frowning coast,
Which can no groves nor happy valleys boast;
Where other cares than those the Muse relates,
And other shepherds dwell with other mates;
By such examples taught, I paint the cot,
As truth will paint it, and as bards will not:
Nor you, ye poor, of lettered scorn complain,
To you the smoothest song is smooth in vain;
O'ercome by labour and bowed down by time,
Feel you the barren flattery of a rhyme?

Can poets soothe you, when you pine for bread,
By winding myrtles round your ruined shed?
Can their light tales your weighty griefs o'erpower,
Or glad with airy mirth the toilsome hour?
  Lo! where the heath, with withering brake grown o'er,
Lends the light turf that warms the neighbouring poor;
From thence a length of burning sand appears,
Where the thin harvest waves its withered ears;
Rank weeds, that every art and care defy,
Reign o'er the land and rob the blighted rye:
There thistles stretch their prickly arms afar,
And to the ragged infant threaten war;
There poppies, nodding, mock the hope of toil,
There the blue bugloss paints the sterile soil;
Hardy and high, above the slender sheaf,
The slimy mallow waves her silky leaf;
O'er the young shoot the charlock throws a shade,
And the wild tare clings round the sickly blade;
With mingled tints the rocky coasts abound,
And a sad splendour vainly shines around.
  So looks the nymph whom wretched arts adorn,
Betrayed by man, then left for man to scorn;
Whose cheek in vain assumes the mimic rose,
While her sad eyes the troubled breast disclose;
Whose outward splendour is but folly's dress,
Exposing most, when most it gilds distress.
  Here joyless roam a wild amphibious race,
With sullen woe displayed in every face;
Who far from civil arts and social fly,
And scowl at strangers with suspicious eye.
  Here too the lawless merchant of the main
Draws from his plough th' intoxicated swain;
Want only claimed the labour of the day,
But vice now steals his nightly rest away.
  Where are the swains, who, daily labour done,
With rural games played down the setting sun;
Who struck with matchless force the bounding ball,
Or made the pond'rous quoit obliquely fall;
While some huge Ajax, terrible and strong,
Engaged some artful stripling of the throng,
And, foiled, beneath the young Ulysses fell,
When peals of praise the merry mischief tell?
Where now are these?—Beneath yon cliff they stand,
To show the freighted pinnace where to land;
To load the ready steed with guilty haste;
To fly in terror o'er the pathless waste,

Or, when detected in their straggling course,
To foil their foes by cunning or by force;
Or, yielding part (when equal knaves contest),
To gain a lawless passport for the rest.
  Here, wand'ring long amid these frowning fields,
I sought the simple life that Nature yields;
Rapine and Wrong and Fear usurped her place,
And a bold, artful, surly, savage race;
Who, only skilled to take the finny tribe,
The yearly dinner, or septennial bribe,
Wait on the shore and, as the waves run high,
On the tossed vessel bend their eager eye,
Which to their coast directs its vent'rous way,
Theirs, or the ocean's, miserable prey.
  As on their neighbouring beach yon swallows stand,
And wait for favouring winds to leave the land,
While still for flight the ready wing is spread:
So waited I the favouring hour, and fled;
Fled from these shores where guilt and famine reign,
And cried, Ah! hapless they who still remain;
Who still remain to hear the ocean roar,
Whose greedy waves devour the lessening shore;
Till some fierce tide, with more imperious sway,
Sweeps the low hut and all it holds away;
When the sad tenant weeps from door to door,
And begs a poor protection from the poor!
  But these are scenes where Nature's niggard hand
Gave a spare portion to the famished land;
Hers is the fault, if here mankind complain
Of fruitless toil and labour spent in vain;
But yet in other scenes, more fair in view,
Where Plenty smiles—alas! she smiles for few,
And those who taste not, yet behold her store,
Are as the slaves that dig the golden ore,
The wealth around them makes them doubly poor.
Or will you deem them amply paid in health,
Labour's fair child, that languishes with wealth?
Go, then! and see them rising with the sun,
Through a long course of daily toil to run;
Like him to make the plenteous harvest grow,
And yet not share the plenty they bestow;
See them beneath the dog-star's raging heat,
When the knees tremble and the temples beat;
Behold them, leaning on their scythes, look o'er
The labour past, and toils to come explore;
See them alternate suns and showers engage,

And hoard up aches and anguish for their age;
Through fens and marshy moors their steps pursue,
When their warm pores imbibe the evening dew;
Then own that labour may as fatal be
To these thy slaves, as luxury to thee.
  Amid this tribe too oft a manly pride
Strives in strong toil the fainting heart to hide;
There may you see the youth of slender frame
Contend with weakness, weariness, and shame;
Yet urged along, and proudly loth to yield,
He strives to join his fellows of the field;
Till long-contending nature droops at last,
Declining health rejects his poor repast,
His cheerless spouse the coming danger sees,
And mutual murmurs urge the slow disease.
Yet grant them health, 'tis not for us to tell,
Though the head droops not, that the heart is well;
Or will you urge their homely, plenteous fare,
Healthy and plain and still the poor man's share?
Oh! trifle not with wants you cannot feel,
Nor mock the misery of a stinted meal;
Homely not wholesome, plain not plenteous, such
As you who envy would disdain to touch.
  Ye gentle souls, who dream of rural ease,
Whom the smooth stream and smoother sonnet please;
Go! if the peaceful cot your praises share,
Go, look within, and ask if peace be there:
If peace be his—that drooping weary sire,
Or theirs, that offspring round their feeble fire,
Or hers, that matron pale, whose trembling hand
Turns on the wretched hearth th' expiring brand.
Nor yet can time itself obtain for these
Life's latest comforts, due respect and ease;
For yonder see that hoary swain, whose age
Can with no cares except its own engage;
Who, propped on that rude staff, looks up to see
The bare arms broken from the withering tree,
On which, a boy, he climbed the loftiest bough,
Then his first joy, but his sad emblem now.
  He once was chief in all the rustic trade,
His steady hand the straightest furrow made;
Full many a prize he won, and still is proud
To find the triumphs of his youth allowed.
A transient pleasure sparkles in his eyes,
He hears and smiles, then thinks again and sighs:
For now he journeys to his grave in pain;

The rich disdain him, nay, the poor disdain;
Alternate masters now their slave command,
And urge the efforts of his feeble hand;
Who, when his age attempts its task in vain,
With ruthless taunts of lazy poor complain.
  Oft may you see him, when he tends the sheep,
His winter-charge, beneath the hillock weep;
Oft hear him murmur to the winds that blow
O'er his white locks and bury them in snow;
When, roused by rage and muttering in the morn,
He mends the broken hedge with icy thorn:
  'Why do I live, when I desire to be
At once from life and life's long labour free?
Like leaves in spring, the young are blown away,
Without the sorrows of a slow decay;
I, like yon withered leaf, remain behind,
Nipped by the frost, and shivering in the wind;
There it abides till younger buds come on,
As I, now all my fellow-swains are gone;
Then, from the rising generation thrust,
It falls, like me, unnoticed to the dust.
  'These fruitful fields, these numerous flocks I see,
Are others' gain, but killing cares to me;
To me the children of my youth are lords,
Slow in their gifts but hasty in their words:
Wants of their own demand their care, and who
Feels his own want and succours others too?
A lonely, wretched man, in pain I go,
None need my help and none relieve my woe;
Then let my bones beneath the turf be laid,
And men forget the wretch they would not aid.'
  Thus groan the old, till, by disease oppressed,
They taste a final woe, and then they rest.
Theirs is yon house that holds the parish poor,
Whose walls of mud scarce bear the broken door;
There, where the putrid vapours, flagging, play,
And the dull wheel hums doleful through the day;
There children dwell, who know no parents' care,
Parents, who know no children's love, dwell there;
Heart-broken matrons on their joyless bed,
Forsaken wives, and mothers never wed;
Dejected widows with unheeded tears,
And crippled age with more than childhood-fears;
The lame, the blind, and, far the happiest they!
The moping idiot and the madman gay.
  Here too the sick their final doom receive,

Here brought, amid the scenes of grief, to grieve,
Where the loud groans from some sad chamber flow,
Mixed with the clamours of the crowd below;
Here, sorrowing, they each kindred sorrow scan,
And the cold charities of man to man:
Whose laws indeed for ruined age provide,
And strong compulsion plucks the scrap from pride;
But still that scrap is bought with many a sigh,
And pride embitters what it can't deny.
Say ye, oppressed by some fantastic woes,
Some jarring nerve that baffles your repose;
Who press the downy couch, while slaves advance
With timid eye to read the distant glance;
Who with sad prayers the weary doctor tease
To name the nameless ever-new disease;
Who with mock patience dire complaints endure,
Which real pain, and that alone, can cure;
How would ye bear in real pain to lie,
Despised, neglected, left alone to die?
How would ye bear to draw your latest breath,
Where all that's wretched paves the way for death?
Such is that room which one rude beam divides,
And naked rafters form the sloping sides;
Where the vile bands that bind the thatch are seen,
And lath and mud is all that lie between,
Save one dull pane, that, coarsely patched, gives way
To the rude tempest, yet excludes the day.
Here, on a matted flock, with dust o'erspread,
The drooping wretch reclines his languid head;
For him no hand the cordial cup applies,
Nor wipes the tear that stagnates in his eyes;
No friends with soft discourse his pain beguile,
Nor promise hope till sickness wears a smile.
But soon a loud and hasty summons calls,
Shakes the thin roof, and echoes round the walls.
Anon, a figure enters, quaintly neat,
All pride and business, bustle and conceit;
With looks unaltered by these scenes of woe,
With speed that, entering, speaks his haste to go,
He bids the gazing throng around him fly,
And carries fate and physic in his eye;
A potent quack, long versed in human ills,
Who first insults the victim whom he kills;
Whose murd'rous hand a drowsy bench protect,
And whose most tender mercy is neglect.
Paid by the parish for attendance here,

He wears contempt upon his sapient sneer;
In haste he seeks the bed where misery lies,
Impatience marked in his averted eyes;
And, some habitual queries hurried o'er,
Without reply, he rushes on the door;
His drooping patient, long inured to pain,
And long unheeded, knows remonstrance vain;
He ceases now the feeble help to crave
Of man, and mutely hastens to the grave.
  But ere his death some pious doubts arise,
Some simple fears, which 'bold bad' men despise;
Fain would he ask the parish priest to prove
His title certain to the joys above;
For this he sends the murmuring nurse, who calls
The holy stranger to these dismal walls;
And doth not he, the pious man, appear,
He, 'passing rich with forty pounds a year'?
Ah! no; a shepherd of a different stock,
And far unlike him, feeds this little flock;
A jovial youth, who thinks his Sunday's task
As much as God or man can fairly ask;
The rest he gives to loves and labours light,
To fields the morning and to feasts the night;
None better skilled the noisy pack to guide,
To urge their chase, to cheer them or to chide;
Sure in his shot, his game he seldom missed,
And seldom failed to win his game at whist;
Then, while such honours bloom around his head,
Shall he sit sadly by the sick man's bed
To raise the hope he feels not, or with zeal
To combat fears that ev'n the pious feel?
  Now once again the gloomy scene explore,
Less gloomy now; the bitter hour is o'er,
The man of many sorrows sighs no more.
  Up yonder hill, behold how sadly slow
The bier moves winding from the vale below;
There lie the happy dead, from trouble free,
And the glad parish pays the frugal fee.
No more, oh Death! thy victim starts to hear
Churchwarden stern, or kingly overseer;
No more the farmer gets his humble bow,
Thou art his lord, the best of tyrants thou!
  Now to the church behold the mourners come,
Sedately torpid and devoutly dumb;
The village children now their games suspend,
To see the bier that bears their ancient friend:

For he was one in all their idle sport,
And like a monarch ruled their little court;
The pliant bow he formed, the flying ball,
The bat, the wicket, were his labours all;
Him now they follow to his grave, and stand
Silent and sad, and gazing, hand in hand;
While bending low, their eager eyes explore
The mingled relics of the parish poor.
The bell tolls late, the moping owl flies round,
Fear marks the flight and magnifies the sound;
The busy priest, detained by weightier care,
Defers his duty till the day of prayer;
And, waiting long, the crowd retire distressed,
To think a poor man's bones should lie unblessed.

(1783)

ANONYMOUS ('W.J')

433 *A City Eclogue*

'TWAS Sunday morning, quite serene the air,
And city beaux began to dress their hair,
Prepared in buggies or in gigs to ride,
With some fair nymph close wedged in by their side,
To smell a dunghill, view a farm or plain,
Then dine, get drunk, and drive to town again!
Smart 'prentice youths and clerks their boots drew on,
Intent on mounting horses had on loan,
And male and female, in promiscuous throng,
To quit the city hurried all along;
When Mrs. Cask her surly spouse addressed
And, smiling softly, thus her wish expressed:
Mrs. C. How sweet the morning air! how vastly fine!
I'd like immensely out of town to dine,
In some gay village near the public road:
You know, my dear, we seldom go abroad;
Confined the week, dear Mr. Cask, as we,
We should on Sunday breathe some air that's free.
Our neighbour Potion says as how 'tis good,
Both for the spirits and to cleanse the blood.
Come, have a coach, and drive somewhere from town;
You make the tea, while I put on my gown.

Mr. C. I hate all jaunts expensive such as these;
I'll dine at home; but after, if you please,
We'll take a walk, as sober folks should do,
To Islington or Bagnigge, I and you.
I'll smoke my pipe and you shall drink your tea,
Poll can go with us—wife, do you agree?
Mrs. C. You still will talk in your old vulgar style.
Pray, do you think that I can walk a mile?
We'll have a coach, as folks of taste should have:
Since you've enough, why 'should I be a slave'?
I cannot walk—I can't, upon my life!
We'll have a coach; say 'yes', and end our strife.
Mr. C. You cannot walk! why not as well as I?
You'd find it easy, if you'd only try.
Mrs. C. Fie! Mr. Cask, how foolishly you talk!
Do you expect that I should meanly walk?
Don't all my neighbours every Sunday ride,
And justly would not they me then deride?
To walk is vulgar; with a cheerful face,
Say 'yes' at once—come, do it with a grace.
Mr. C. Expense for ever! Ay, this is the way,
I slave behind the counter every day;
Scarce stir one moment, weekly, from my shop,
Save just sometimes in at the Sun to pop,
To smoke my pipe and see what's going on,
The price of stocks, the lottery and loan;
Yet this and that and t' other thing you buy,
And every way to ruin me you try.
A thousand things I've got to cause vexation,
Bad debts, sad failures, children's education,
Two sons, a daughter, all at boarding school!
Some folks have told me I'm an arrant fool
To bring up children as great people do,
And this expense is owing all to you.
The half-year's bills I saw the other day,
And very soon I'll have them too to pay:
There's 'dancing, drawing, music, coats, cap, hat,
Clothes mended, ushers'—and the devil knows what!
Again, for Poll—you need not fume nor fret:
You'll see me soon exposed in the *Gazette*.
Mrs. C. Don't many neighbours send their sons to college,
To learn old Greek and get all kinds of knowledge,
At more expense? and yet you trifles grudge.
Why, Mr. Cask, our Jack may be a judge.
Poor wretched woman, that I e'er should be
Fast tied for life unto a bear like thee!

Don't all around me in their satins flaunt,
And of their liveries and attendants vaunt,
See balls and plays in the genteelest style,
Whilst I at home sit moping all the while?
A gown or cap you scarce will e'er bestow,
And what you do is at a price so low
That I'm not fit in public to appear;
And yet you gain a thousand neat a year,
Besides ten thousand out on mortgage lent,
That brings you in a pretty sum per cent.

Mr. C. I'll stop my ears—pray hold your cursèd tongue—
You'll drive me mad—I'm always in the wrong—
O lud!—O lud! my life is wretched sure!
Continual din and noise do I endure.
One time I'm teased to buy a satin gown;
Next day to drive perhaps ten miles from town.
Sometimes, however busy be the day,
I'm dragged by force to coach it to the play.
Each day you find some little pretty things
That I must purchase—china, plate or rings.
I'm scarce allowed a single moment's ease,
Nor must I do but what you, madam, please.
My hat and wig are sometimes ungenteel:
I'm often forced to strip from head to heel;
My old drab coat I long on Sundays wore,
Though whole, is now become a sad eyesore;
My woollen nightcap too offends your sight;
I scarce dare go to smoke my pipe at night,
''Tis low, 'tis mean, 'tis vulgar', still you bawl,
And then poor me you somewhere strive to haul;
And in your mouth you've always this reproach,
That I refuse to treat you with a coach.

Mrs. C. A hackney coach!—had I but proper spirit,
I'd have a carriage, I'd no longer bear it.

Miss C. Indeed, papa, I think you're vastly wrong:
Mama and I have gone on foot too long.

Mr. C. Be quiet, hussy—don't I always pay
Enough for you?—demands come every day;
Trade is low and taxes fast advancing,
So, Miss Pest, I'll pay for no more dancing.

Mrs. C. O cruel man, how can you serve one so?
More rude and bearish every day you grow:
Such treatment surely would provoke a saint!
My smelling bottle! Oh! I faint!—I faint!

Mr. C. Here, Betty! Betty!—salts!—the bottle—run!
Oh! foolish man! what have I, have I done!

My child in tears—my wife in fainting fits!
Oh! neighbours, help!—I'll lose, I'll lose my wits!
Mrs. C. Ah! barb'rous man! and will you not relent?
Must I untimely to my grave be sent?
Mr. C. Dry up your tears—the comfort this of marriage!
Once more, wife, I'll treat you with a carriage.
Run, Betty, quickly, run into the street,
And hire the first neat hackney coach you meet.
These women still somehow have got the art
To overcome us, and to melt the heart;
Let us poor cits do whatsoe'er we may,
Our headstrong spouses still will have their way!

(1783)

THOMAS HOLCROFT

1745–1809

434 *On Shakespeare and Voltaire*

CLAD in the wealthy robes his genius wrought,
  In happy dreams was gentle Shakespeare laid;
His pleased soul wandering through the realms of thought,
  While all his elves and fairies round him played.

Voltaire approached: straight fled the quaint-eyed band,
  For envious breath such sprites may not endure;
He pilfered many a gem with trembling hand,
  Then stabbed and stabbed, to make the theft secure.

Ungrateful man! But vain thy black design,
  Th' attempt, and not the deed, thy hand defiled;
Preserved by his own charms and spells divine,
  Safely the gentle Shakespeare slept and smiled.

(1783)

435 *The Seasons*

ERE the beard of thistle sails,
Ere the tadpoles wag their tails;
When the maids with milking-pails
Doff their mits and blow their nails;

When the cottage chimney smokes,
And wanton greybeards crack their jokes
By the glowing ember's light,
And scare the girls with tale of sprite;
Then will we, o'er ale and cakes,
Brag of feats at autumn wakes.

When the swallows twittering sing
Of the lovely birth of spring;
When bridegrooms make our three bells ring,
Ding dong ding—ding dong ding;
When the valley's face is seen
Veiled in many a shade of green;
When girls of husbands nightly dream,
And jolly swains get clouted cream;
Then we, upon sweet primrose beds,
Will troll our glees and rest our heads.

When the young frog fears the rook,
When the kine stand in the brook;
When sleepy louts lose many a crook,
And codlings drop when trees are shook;
When salt mushrooms nightly spring,
And martins dip the dappled wing;
When the sun with straight-down beam
Lathers well the lusty team;
Then beneath new hay-ricks we
Will sing with might and merry glee.

When the sickle and the scythe
Make the ruddy farmer blithe;
When Hodge the bulky sheaf doth writhe,
And our fat Vicar claims his tithe;
When autumn yields her golden store,
Till well-filled barns can hold no more;
When ripe fruits press the plenteous board,
And old wives cull their wintry hoard;
Then will we, when labour's o'er,
At harvest-home our catches roar.

(1784)

writhe] bind

436

Fool's Song

WHEN swallows lay their eggs in snow,
And geese in wheat-ears build their nests;
When roasted crabs a-hunting go,
And cats can laugh at gossips' jests;
When law and conscience are akin,
And pigs are learnt by note to squeak;
Your worship then shall stroke your chin,
And teach an owl to whistle Greek.

Till when let your wisdom be dumb;
For say, man of Gotham,
What is this world?
A tetotum,
By the finger of Folly twirled;
With a hey-go-up, and about we come;
While the sun a good post-horse is found,
So merrily we'll run round.

When frost, and snow, and hail, and rain,
Are guided by the Almanack;
When Lapland wizards can explain
How many stars will fill a sack;
When courtiers hate to be preferred,
And pearls are made of whitings' eyes;
Instructed by your worship's beard,
The world shall merry be and wise.

Till when let your wisdom be dumb, *etc.*

(1784)

437

Song

When o'er the wold the heedless lamb
Hath, till the dusky twilight, strayed,
His simple plaints cry 'Here I am,
Of night and solitude afraid.'
But if, far off, his dam he hears,
Echoing oft the mournful bleat,
He runs, and stops, and hopes, and fears,
And bounds with pleasure when they meet!

(1784)

436 tetotum] small top

438 *The Dying Prostitute, An Elegy*

WEEP o'er the mis'ries of a wretched maid,
  Who sacrificed to man her health and fame;
Whose love, and truth, and trust were all repaid
  By want and woe, disease and endless shame.

Curse not the poor lost wretch, who ev'ry ill
  That proud unfeeling man can heap sustains;
Sure she enough is cursed o'er whom his will,
  Enflamed by brutal passion, boundless reigns.

Spurn not my fainting body from your door,
  Here let me rest my weary weeping head;
No greater mercy would my wants implore,
  My sorrows soon shall lay me with the dead.

Who now beholds, but loathes my faded face,
  So wan and sallow, changed with sin and care?
Or who can any former beauty trace
  In eyes so sunk with famine and despair?

That I was virtuous once, and beauteous too,
  And free from envious tongues my spotless fame:
These but torment, these but my tears renew,
  These aggravate my present guilt and shame.

Expelled by all, enforced by pining want,
  I've wept and wandered many a midnight hour;
Implored a pittance Lust would seldom grant,
  Or sought a shelter from the driving show'r.

Oft as I roved, while beat the wintry storm,
  Unknowing what to seek, or where to stray,
To gain relief, enticed each hideous form;
  Each hideous form contemptuous turned away.

Where were my virgin honours, virgin charms?
  Oh! whither fled the pride I once maintained?
Or where the youths that wooed me to their arms?
  Or where the triumphs which my beauty gained?

Ah! say, insidious Damon! Monster! where?
  What glory hast thou gained by my defeat?
Art thou more happy for that I'm less fair?
  Or bloom thy laurels o'er my winding-sheet?

(1785)

439 *Gaffer Gray*

Ho! Why dost thou shiver and shake,
  Gaffer Gray?
And why doth thy nose look so blue?
  ''Tis the weather that's cold;
  'Tis I'm grown very old,
And my doublet is not very new,
  Well-a-day!'

Then line thy worn doublet with ale,
  Gaffer Gray;
And warm thy old heart with a glass.
  'Nay but credit I've none;
  And my money's all gone;
Then say how may that come to pass?
  Well-a-day!'

Hie away to the house on the brow,
  Gaffer Gray;
And knock at the jolly priest's door.
  'The priest often preaches
  Against worldly riches;
But ne'er gives a mite to the poor,
  Well-a-day!'

The lawyer lives under the hill,
  Gaffer Gray;
Warmly fenced both in back and in front.
  'He will fasten his locks,
  And will threaten the stocks,
Should he ever more find me in want,
  Well-a-day!'

The squire has fat beeves and brown ale,
  Gaffer Gray;
And the season will welcome you there.
  'His fat beeves and his beer,
  And his merry new year,
Are all for the flush and the fair,
  Well-a-day!'

My keg is but low I confess,
  Gaffer Gray;
What then? While it lasts, man, we'll live.
  The poor man alone,
  When he hears the poor moan,
Of his morsel a morsel will give,
  Well-a-day!

(1794)

440

To Haydn

WHO is the mighty master that can trace
Th' eternal lineaments of Nature's face?
Mid endless dissonance, what mortal ear
Could e'er her peal of perfect concord hear?
Answer, oh, Haydn! strike the magic chord!
And, as thou strik'st, reply and proof afford.
  Whene'er thy genius, flashing native fire,
Bids the soul tremble with the trembling lyre,
The hunter's clatt'ring hoof, the peasant-shout,
The warrior-onset, or the battle's rout,
Din, clamour, uproar, murder's midnight knell,
Hyena-shrieks, the war-whoop, scream and yell—
All sounds, however mingled, strange, uncouth,
Resolve to fitness, system, sense and truth!
To others, noise and jangling; but to thee
'Tis one grand solemn swell of endless harmony.
  When dark and unknown terrors intervene,
And men aghast survey the horrid scene;
Then, when rejoicing fiends flit, gleam and scowl,
And bid the huge tormented tempest howl;
When fire-fraught thunders roll, and whirlwinds rise,
And earthquakes bellow to the frantic skies,
Till the distracted ear, in racking gloom,
Suspects the wreck of worlds, and gen'ral doom:
Then Haydn stands, collecting Nature's tears,
And consonance sublime amid confusion hears.

(1794)

WILLIAM BLAKE

1757–1827

441

To Spring

O THOU with dewy locks, who lookest down
Through the clear windows of the morning, turn
Thine angel eyes upon our western isle,
Which in full choir hails thy approach, O Spring!

The hills tell each other, and the list'ning
Valleys hear; all our longing eyes are turned
Up to thy bright pavilions: issue forth,
And let thy holy feet visit our clime.

Come o'er the eastern hills, and let our winds
Kiss thy perfumèd garments; let us taste
Thy morn and evening breath; scatter thy pearls
Upon our love-sick land that mourns for thee.

O deck her forth with thy fair fingers; pour
Thy soft kisses on her bosom; and put
Thy golden crown upon her languished head,
Whose modest tresses were bound up for thee.

(1783)

442

To the Evening Star

THOU fair-haired angel of the evening,
Now, whilst the sun rests on the mountains, light
Thy bright torch of love; thy radiant crown
Put on, and smile upon our evening bed!
Smile on our loves; and, while thou drawest the
Blue curtains of the sky, scatter thy silver dew
On every flower that shuts its sweet eyes
In timely sleep. Let thy west wind sleep on
The lake; speak silence with thy glimmering eyes,
And wash the dusk with silver. Soon, full soon,
Dost thou withdraw; then the wolf rages wide,
And the lion glares through the dun forest.
The fleeces of our flocks are covered with
Thy sacred dew: protect them with thine influence.

(1783)

443

Song

HOW sweet I roamed from field to field
And tasted all the summer's pride,
Till I the prince of love beheld,
Who in the sunny beams did glide!

He showed me lilies for my hair,
And blushing roses for my brow;
He led me through his gardens fair,
Where all his golden pleasures grow.

With sweet May dews my wings were wet,
And Phoebus fired my vocal rage;
He caught me in his silken net,
And shut me in his golden cage.

He loves to sit and hear me sing,
Then, laughing, sports and plays with me;
Then stretches out my golden wing,
And mocks my loss of liberty.

(1783)

444

Mad Song

THE wild winds weep,
And the night is a-cold;
Come hither, Sleep,
And my griefs enfold:
But lo! the morning peeps
Over the eastern steeps,
And the rustling birds of dawn
The earth do scorn.

Lo! to the vault
Of pavèd heaven,
With sorrow fraught
My notes are driven;
They strike the ear of night,
Make weep the eyes of day;
They make mad the roaring winds,
And with tempests play.

Like a fiend in a cloud
  With howling woe,
After night I do crowd,
  And with night will go;
I turn my back to the east,
  From whence comforts have increased;
For light doth seize my brain
With frantic pain.

(1783)

445 *To the Muses*

WHETHER on Ida's shady brow,
  Or in the chambers of the east,
The chambers of the sun, that now
  From ancient melody have ceased;

Whether in heav'n ye wander fair,
  Or the green corners of the earth,
Or the blue regions of the air,
  Where the melodious winds have birth;

Whether on crystal rocks ye rove,
  Beneath the bosom of the sea
Wand'ring in many a coral grove,
  Fair Nine, forsaking poetry!

How have you left the ancient love
  That bards of old enjoyed in you!
The languid strings do scarcely move!
  The sound is forced, the notes are few!

(1783)

from *SONGS OF INNOCENCE* (1789)

446 *Introduction*

PIPING down the valleys wild,
Piping songs of pleasant glee,
On a cloud I saw a child,
And he laughing said to me:

'Pipe a song about a lamb.'
So I piped with merry cheer;
'Piper, pipe that song again.'
So I piped; he wept to hear.

'Drop thy pipe, thy happy pipe;
Sing thy songs of happy cheer.'
So I sung the same again,
While he wept with joy to hear.

'Piper, sit thee down and write
In a book that all may read.'
So he vanished from my sight:
And I plucked a hollow reed,

And I made a rural pen,
And I stained the water clear,
And I wrote my happy songs
Every child may joy to hear.

447 *The Little Black Boy*

My mother bore me in the southern wild,
And I am black, but O! my soul is white.
White as an angel is the English child,
But I am black as if bereaved of light.

My mother taught me underneath a tree,
And sitting down before the heat of day
She took me on her lap and kissèd me,
And pointing to the east began to say:

'Look on the rising sun! there God does live
And gives his light and gives his heat away;
And flowers and trees and beasts and men receive
Comfort in morning, joy in the noon day.

'And we are put on earth a little space,
That we may learn to bear the beams of love,
And these black bodies and this sun-burnt face
Is but a cloud, and like a shady grove.

'For when our souls have learned the heat to bear
The cloud will vanish, we shall hear his voice,
Saying: "Come out from the grove, my love and care,
And round my golden tent like lambs rejoice."'

Thus did my mother say, and kissèd me;
And thus I say to little English boy:
When I from black and he from white cloud free
And round the tent of God like lambs we joy,

I'll shade him from the heat till he can bear
To lean in joy upon our Father's knee;
And then I'll stand and stroke his silver hair,
And be like him and he will then love me.

448 *Holy Thursday*

'TWAS on a Holy Thursday, their innocent faces clean,
The children walking two and two in red and blue and green;
Grey-headed beadles walked before with wands as white as snow,
Till into the high dome of Paul's they like Thames' waters flow.

Oh, what a multitude they seemed, these flowers of London town!
Seated in companies they sit, with radiance all their own.
The hum of multitudes was there, but multitudes of lambs,
Thousands of little boys and girls raising their innocent hands.

Now like a mighty wind they raise to heaven the voice of song,
Or like harmonious thunderings the seats of heaven among.
Beneath them sit the aged men, wise guardians of the poor:
Then cherish pity, lest you drive an angel from your door.

449 *The Lamb*

LITTLE lamb, who made thee?
Dost thou know who made thee,
Gave thee life and bid thee feed
By the stream and o'er the mead;
Gave thee clothing of delight,
Softest clothing, woolly bright;
Gave thee such a tender voice,
Making all the vales rejoice?
Little lamb, who made thee?
Dost thou know who made thee?

Little lamb, I'll tell thee,
Little lamb, I'll tell thee:
He is called by thy name,
For he calls himself a Lamb;
He is meek and he is mild,
He became a little child:
I a child, and thou a lamb,
We are called by his name.
Little lamb, God bless thee.
Little lamb, God bless thee.

450 *The Chimney-Sweeper*

WHEN my mother died I was very young,
And my father sold me while yet my tongue
Could scarcely cry '*weep* '*weep*, '*weep* '*weep*!
So your chimneys I sweep, and in soot I sleep.

There's little Tom Dacre, who cried when his head,
That curled like a lamb's back, was shaved; so I said,
'Hush Tom, never mind it, for when your head's bare,
You know that the soot cannot spoil your white hair.'

And so he was quiet, and that very night,
As Tom was a-sleeping he had such a sight,
That thousands of sweepers, Dick, Joe, Ned, and Jack,
Were all of them locked up in coffins of black;

And by came an angel, who had a bright key,
And he opened the coffins and set them all free;
Then down a green plain leaping, laughing they run,
And wash in a river and shine in the sun.

Then naked and white, all their bags left behind,
They rise upon clouds and sport in the wind.
And the angel told Tom, if he'd be a good boy,
He'd have God for his father and never want joy.

And so Tom awoke, and we rose in the dark,
And got with our bags and our brushes to work.
Though the morning was cold, Tom was happy and warm;
So if all do their duty, they need not fear harm.

451

The Divine Image

To mercy, pity, peace and love
All pray in their distress;
And to these virtues of delight
Return their thankfulness.

For mercy, pity, peace and love
Is God our father dear;
And mercy, pity, peace and love
Is man, his child and care.

For mercy has a human heart,
Pity, a human face;
And love, the human form divine,
And peace, the human dress.

Then every man of every clime
That prays in his distress,
Prays to the human form divine—
Love, mercy, pity, peace.

And all must love the human form
In heathen, Turk or Jew.
Where mercy, love and pity dwell
There God is dwelling too.

from *SONGS OF EXPERIENCE* (1794)

452

Introduction

Hear the voice of the bard,
Who present, past, and future sees;
Whose ears have heard
The Holy Word,
That walked among the ancient trees,

Calling the lapsèd soul
And weeping in the evening dew:
That might control
The starry pole,
And fallen, fallen light renew!

'O Earth, O Earth, return!
Arise from out the dewy grass;
Night is worn,
And the morn
Rises from the slumberous mass.

'Turn away no more:
Why wilt thou turn away?
The starry floor,
The wat'ry shore
Is given thee till the break of day.'

453 *Earth's Answer*

EARTH raised up her head
From the darkness dread and drear.
Her light fled:
Stony dread!
And her locks covered with grey despair.

'Prisoned on wat'ry shore,
Starry jealousy does keep my den;
Cold and hoar,
Weeping o'er,
I hear the Father of the ancient men.

'Selfish Father of men!
Cruel jealous selfish fear!
Can delight
Chained in night
The virgins of youth and morning bear?

'Does spring hide its joy
When buds and blossoms grow?
Does the sower
Sow by night,
Or the ploughman in darkness plough?

'Break this heavy chain
That does freeze my bones around.
Selfish, vain,
Eternal bane!
That free love with bondage bound.'

454

London

I WANDER through each chartered street
Near where the chartered Thames does flow,
And mark in every face I meet
Marks of weakness, marks of woe.

In every cry of every man,
In every infant's cry of fear,
In every voice, in every ban,
The mind-forged manacles I hear.

How the chimney-sweeper's cry
Every blackening church appalls,
And the hapless soldier's sigh
Runs in blood down palace walls;

But most through midnight streets I hear
How the youthful harlot's curse
Blasts the new-born infant's tear
And blights with plagues the marriage hearse.

455

The Tiger

TIGER, tiger, burning bright
In the forests of the night,
What immortal hand or eye
Could frame thy fearful symmetry?

In what distant deeps or skies
Burnt the fire of thine eyes?
On what wings dare he aspire?
What the hand dare seize the fire?

And what shoulder and what art
Could twist the sinews of thy heart?
And when thy heart began to beat,
What dread hand? And what dread feet?

What the hammer? What the chain?
In what furnace was thy brain?
What the anvil? What dread grasp
Dare its deadly terrors clasp?

When the stars threw down their spears
And watered heaven with their tears,
Did he smile his work to see?
Did he who made the Lamb make thee?

Tiger, tiger, burning bright
In the forests of the night,
What immortal hand or eye
Dare frame thy fearful symmetry?

456

The Human Abstract

PITY would be no more,
If we did not make somebody poor;
And mercy no more could be,
If all were as happy as we;

And mutual fear brings peace,
Till the selfish loves increase.
Then Cruelty knits a snare
And spreads his baits with care.

He sits down with holy fears
And waters the ground with tears;
Then humility takes its root
Underneath his foot.

Soon spreads the dismal shade
Of mystery over his head;
And the caterpillar and fly
Feed on the mystery;

And it bears the fruit of deceit,
Ruddy and sweet to eat,
And the raven his nest has made
In its thickest shade.

The gods of the earth and sea
Sought through nature to find this tree.
But their search was all in vain:
There grows one in the human brain.

457

The Sick Rose

O ROSE, thou art sick:
The invisible worm
That flies in the night,
In the howling storm,

Has found out thy bed
Of crimson joy;
And his dark secret love
Does thy life destroy.

458

The Chimney-Sweeper

A LITTLE black thing among the snow,
Crying *'weep*, *'weep*, in notes of woe!
Where are thy father and mother, say?
'They are both gone up to the church to pray.

'Because I was happy upon the heath
And smiled among the winter's snow,
They clothed me in the clothes of death
And taught me to sing the notes of woe.

'And because I am happy and dance and sing,
They think they have done me no injury:
And are gone to praise God and his priest and king,
Who make up a heaven of our misery.'

459

Holy Thursday

Is this a holy thing to see
In a rich and fruitful land,
Babes reduced to misery,
Fed with cold and usurous hand?

Is that trembling cry a song?
Can it be a song of joy?
And so many children poor?
It is a land of poverty!

And their sun does never shine,
And their fields are bleak and bare,
And their ways are filled with thorns:
It is eternal winter there.

For where'er the sun does shine,
And where'er the rain does fall,
Babe can never hunger there,
Nor poverty the mind appal.

460 *Ah, Sunflower*

AH, sunflower! weary of time,
Who countest the steps of the sun,
Seeking after that sweet golden clime
Where the traveller's journey is done;

Where the youth pined away with desire,
And the pale virgin shrouded in snow,
Arise from their graves and aspire
Where my sunflower wishes to go.

THOMAS MAURICE

1754–1824

461 from *An Epistle to the Right Hon. Charles James Fox*

HOW cursed that country, how severe its doom,
Whose mines of treasure are its children's tomb!
How ought the sires to execrate that gold
By which their progeny for slaves are sold!
But, oh! can Britons, virtuous, brave and free,
For Indians forge the chains of tyranny?
Yes!—the stern victor who from Persia came,
And wrapped their valleys in devouring flame,
Round Delhi when his dark'ning legions poured,
And gave her gasping nobles to the sword—
Not cruel Nadir half such havoc made
As Britons, India, through thy plains have spread.

Reflection shudders, while before my eyes
Such scenes of aggravated horror rise.—
I see thy slaughtered sons in heaps expire,
Thy temples blaze in sacrilegious fire—
I see the venerable Bramin train
Dragged from their shrines, and at their altars slain—
I see thy violated virgins led,
Ere yet mature, to the proud victor's bed—
All rights confounded—property o'erthrown,
And sacred Faith extinct, and guardian Virtue flown.
When will the day of awful vengeance come?
I see it burst from Time's disclosing womb—
When stern-browed Justice shall ascend her throne,
And suffering Hindus shall no longer groan;
When, by their victors taught the art of fight,
The natives shall in arms assert their right,
And, while their souls with indignation burn,
On their proud lords their thirsty weapons turn;
One great revenge for all their woes obtain,
For provinces laid waste and millions slain;
With tides of British blood expunge their stains,
And show mankind a righteous ruler reigns.

(1784)

SIR GEORGE DALLAS

1758–1833

462 from *The India Guide; or, Journal of a Voyage to the East Indies in 1780*

[*Miss Emily Brittle Sails for India*]

O! HOW shall I picture, in *delicate* strain,
The scene which ensued when I first crossed the main;
Or, how shall my muse in *clean* numbers bewail,
My early hard lot, when, reclined o'er a pail,
I was racked by sea-sickness and pains in my head,
Which gave me such torture I wished myself dead!
Forgive the chaste nymph should she wish to conceal
All the risings and swimmings too often I feel;
For whenever it happens the weather's not mild,
I'm as sick and as squeamish as Jenny with child.

You have seen bales of goods and mercantile wares
Raised by pulleys to windows up two pair of stairs;
So stuck in a chair, made on purpose for this,
Sailors hoist upon deck every India-bound miss:
When poised in the air, I happened to show
Too much of my legs to the boat's crew below,
Who, laughing, occasioned the blush of distress.
Indeed, dear Mama, I am obliged to confess,
That indecency so much on ship-board prevailed,
I scarce heard aught else from the moment I sailed.
  The noise in the ship, from every quarter,
Almost split the brain of your poor little daughter:
Twice a week 'twas the custom the drums loud to rattle,
As a signal below to prepare for a battle.
The sailors on deck were for ever a-brawling,
The ladies below in piano were squalling;
The bulkheads of cabins were constantly creaking,
In concert with pigs, who as often were squeaking;
Such a clatter above from the chick to the goose,
I thought the livestock on the poop had broke loose;
Dogs, puppies and monkeys of ev'ry degree,
Howled peals of loud discord in harsh symphony,
Whilst near to my cabin a sad noisy brute
Most cruelly tortured a poor German flute.
Another, a sprightly amusement to find,
A broken bad fiddle with three strings would grind;
And to add to discordance, our third mate Tarpawl
Some vulgar low tune would be certain to bawl.
But to picture the whole I am really unable,
'Twas worse than the noise at the building of Babel;
I declare my poor ears were so sadly distressed
That for many a week I ne'er got any rest. . . .
  It was often the case on a rough squally day,
At dinner our ship on her beam-ends would lay;
Then tables and chairs on the floor all would jumble,
Knives, dishes and bottles upon us would tumble:
As late, when a roll brought us all to the floor,
Whilst the ladies were screaming, the gentlemen swore,
Our Purser, as big as a bullock at least,
Lay on poor little me, like an over-fed beast.
Not many weeks since, I had only to scoop
From my lap the contents of a tureen of soup;
And when with clean clothes I again had sat down,
A vile leg of mutton fell right on my gown.
Sometimes I was soiled from my head to my toe
With nasty pork chops, or a greasy pilau.

Full many a glass of good wine, I may say,
By a violent toss was thrown down the wrong way;
And, as on board ship we have no one to scrub,
As for three months at least there's no thumping the tub,
So I think it but proper that *delicate* women
Should lay in a plentiful stock of clean linen.
  Whenever I walk on the deck, I am sure
To be shocked by such language as none can endure:
Such scolding! such roaring! such blasting of eyes!
You'd think that the crew in rebellion would rise!

. . . .

  Scarce the cloth is removed but the gentlemen go
To discuss a few bottles of Stainforth and Co.
And from dinner sometimes to the hour of nine,
They get drunk and roar catches to pass away time.
And often, in order to show their politeness,
With vile shocking songs will be certain to fright'n us;
Such songs! as to you I can never explain,
For the lowest of women would blush at their strain:
The rude Bachanalians 'twould greatly amuse
My virgin young innocence oft to confuse;
For whenever to tipple below they thought fit,
Loud obscenity passed round their table for wit.
At first with fine cotton I stopped up each ear
That I might not their impudent ribaldry hear;
But I found 'twas in vain, as the words would get in
Through those parts where the cotton would chance to be thin:
And as in the cabin which lay next to mine,
In the passage they drank out twelve chests of red wine,
So of that kind of knowledge I've got a great store,
Of which I had scarce any notion before.
  Another diversion the young men would prize,
'Twas in seeing us all from our pigeon-holes rise;
With them 'tis a proof of politeness, they think,
The ladies' perfections in bumpers to drink;
For often they boast they have had a full view
Of Prim and Flirtetta, myself and Miss Prue.
But what man of good breeding will offer to peep
At a group of fine girls as they lay all asleep?
Since deeming her charms are from all eyes debarred,
The most delicate maid is at times off her guard;
And they who presume this advantage to take
All pretension to manners must surely forsake.
In our ship 'twas one scene, on my word, I may say,

Of boring and stopping on both sides all day:
If we filled up one hole, 'twas the same as before,
With their gimlets another they'd presently bore.
The ship's carpenter swore he was worn of his legs
By constantly running to fill them with pegs:
And when to repel them we found 'twas in vain,
We politely entreated they'd ne'er peep again;
But the vandals still forced us at night to lie down
With a petticoat on, and a morning bed-gown;
If we failed to wear these, they were sure to look through
To see if our shapes they uncovered could view.
Such, such are the scenes which arise to torment her,
Who ploughs foaming billows in search of adventure!

(1785)

ROBERT BURNS

1759–1796

463 *Holy Willie's Prayer*

And send the Godly in a pet to pray—
POPE.

O THOU that in the heavens does dwell!
Wha, as it pleases best thysel,
Sends ane to heaven and ten to hell,
A' for thy glory!
And no for ony gude or ill
They've done before thee.

I bless and praise thy matchless might,
When thousands thou has left in night,
That I am here before thy sight,
For gifts and grace,
A burning and a shining light
To a' this place.

What was I, or my generation,
That I should get such exaltation?
I, wha deserved most just damnation,
For broken laws
Sax thousand years ere my creation,
Through Adam's cause!

When from my mother's womb I fell,
Thou might hae plunged me deep in hell,
To gnash my gooms, and weep, and wail,
In burning lakes,
Where damned devils roar and yell
Chained to their stakes.

Yet I am here, a chosen sample,
To show thy grace is great and ample:
I'm here, a pillar o' thy temple
Strong as a rock,
A guide, a ruler and example
To a' thy flock.

O L—d thou kens what zeal I bear,
When drinkers drink, and swearers swear,
And singin' there, and dancin' here,
Wi' great an' sma';
For I am keepet by thy fear,
Free frae them a'.

But yet—O L—d—confess I must—
At times I'm fashed wi' fleshly lust;
And sometimes too, in warldly trust
Vile Self gets in;
But thou remembers we are dust,
Defiled wi' sin.

O L—d—yestreen—thou kens—wi' Meg—
Thy pardon I sincerely beg!
O may 't ne'er be a living plague,
To my dishonour!
And I'll ne'er lift a lawless leg
Again upon her.

Besides, I farther maun avow,
Wi' Leezie's lass, three times—I trow—
But L—d, that Friday I was fou
When I cam near her;
Or else, thou kens, thy servant true
Wad never steer her.

fashed] troubled   yestreen] yesterday evening   maun] must   fou] drunk

Maybe thou lets this fleshly thorn
Buffet thy servant e'en and morn,
Lest he o'er proud and high should turn,
That he's sae gifted;
If sae, thy hand maun e'en be borne
Until thou lift it.

L—d bless thy Chosen in this place,
For here thou has a chosen race:
But G–d, confound their stubborn face,
And blast their name,
Wha bring thy rulers to disgrace
And open shame.

L—d mind Gaun Hamilton's deserts!
He drinks, and swears, and plays at cartes,
Yet has sae mony taking arts
Wi' great and sma',
Frae G–d's ain priest the people's hearts
He steals awa.

And when we chastened him therefore,
Thou kens how he bred sic a splore,
And set the warld in a roar
O' laughin at us:
Curse thou his basket and his store,
Kail and potatoes.

L—d hear my earnest cry and prayer
Against that Presbytry of Ayr!
Thy strong right hand, L—d, make it bare
Upon their heads!
L—d visit them, and dinna spare,
For their misdeeds!

O L—d my G–d, that glib-tongued Aiken!
My very heart and flesh are quaking
To think how I sat, sweating, shaking,
And p–ssed wi' dread,
While Auld wi' hingin lip gaed sneaking
And hid his head!

splore] uproar

L—d, in thy day o' vengeance try him!
L—d, visit him that did employ him!
And pass not in thy mercy by them,
Nor hear their prayer;
But for thy people's sake destroy them,
And dinna spare!

But L—d, remember me and mine
Wi' mercies temporal and divine!
That I for grace and gear may shine,
Excelled by nane!
And a' the glory shall be thine!
AMEN! AMEN!

(Wr. 1785; pub. 1789)

464 *A Poet's Welcome to his love-begotten Daughter; the first instance that entitled him to the venerable appellation of Father*

THOU's welcome, wean! Mischanter fa' me,
If thoughts o' thee, or yet thy Mamie,
Shall ever daunton me or awe me,
My bonie lady;
Or if I blush when thou shalt ca' me
Tyta, or Daddie.

Though now they ca' me fornicator,
And tease my name in kintra clatter,
The mair they talk, I'm kend the better;
E'en let them clash!
An auld wife's tongue's a feckless matter
To gie ane fash.

Welcome! My bonie, sweet, wee dochter!
Though ye come here a wee unsought for;
And though your comin I hae fought for,
Baith Kirk and Queir;
Yet by my faith, ye're no unwrought for,
That I shall swear!

gear] property

464 wean] child Mischanter] mishap daunton] subdue Tyta] pet-name for father kintra clatter] country gossip feckless] worthless

Wee image o' my bonie Betty,
As fatherly I kiss and daut thee,
As dear and near my heart I set thee,
Wi' as gude will,
As a' the Priests had seen me get thee
That's out o' h——.

Sweet fruit o' monie a merry dint,
My funny toil is no a' tint;
Though ye come to the warld asklent,
Which fools may scoff at,
In my last plack your part's be in't,
The better half o't.

Though I should be the waur bestead,
Thou 's be as braw and bienly clad,
And thy young years as nicely bred
Wi' education,
As any brat o' Wedlock's bed,
In a' thy station.

Lord grant that thou may ay inherit
Thy Mither's looks an' gracefu' merit;
An' thy poor, worthless Daddie's spirit,
Without his failins!
'Twad please me mair to see thee heir it
Than stocked mailins!

For if thou be, what I wad hae thee,
And tak the counsel I shall gie thee,
I'll never rue my trouble wi' thee,
The cost nor shame o't,
But be a loving Father to thee,
And brag the name o't.

(Wr. 1785; pub. 1799)

daut] fondle tint] lost asklent] on the side plack] coin waur bestead] worse placed bienly] warmly mailins] small-holdings

465 *To a Mouse, On turning her up in her Nest, with the Plough, November, 1785*

WEE, sleeket, cowran, tim'rous beastie,
O, what a panic's in thy breastie!
Thou need na start awa sae hasty,
Wi' bickering brattle!
I wad be laith to rin an' chase thee,
Wi' murd'ring pattle!

I'm truly sorry man's dominion
Has broken Nature's social union,
An' justifies that ill opinion,
Which makes thee startle,
At me, thy poor, earth-born companion,
An' fellow-mortal!

I doubt na, whyles, but thou may thieve;
What then? poor beastie, thou maun live!
A daimen-icker in a thrave
'S a sma' request:
I'll get a blessin wi' the lave,
An' never miss 't!

Thy wee-bit housie, too, in ruin!
It's silly wa's the win's are strewin!
An' naething, now, to big a new ane,
O' foggage green!
An' bleak December's winds ensuin,
Baith snell an' keen!

Thou saw the fields laid bare an' wast,
An' weary winter comin fast,
An' cozie here, beneath the blast,
Thou thought to dwell,
Till crash! the cruel coulter past
Out through thy cell.

That wee-bit heap o' leaves an' stibble,
Has cost thee monie a weary nibble!
Now thou's turned out, for a' thy trouble,
But house or hald,
To thole the winter's sleety dribble,
An' cranreuch cauld!

sleeket] glossy bickering brattle] scurrying haste pattle] spade whyles] at times daimen-icker] odd ear of corn thrave] two stooks lave] remainder big] build foggage] coarse grass snell] bitter But] without hald] refuge thole] endure cranreuch] frost

But mousie, thou art no thy-lane,
In proving foresight may be vain:
The best laid schemes o' mice an' men
Gang aft agley,
An' lea'e us nought but grief an' pain,
For promised joy!

Still, thou art blest, compared wi' me!
The present only toucheth thee:
But Och! I backward cast my e'e
On prospects drear!
An' forward, though I canna see,
I guess an' fear!

(1786)

466 *Address to the Deil*

O Prince, O chief of many throned pow'rs,
That led th' embattled Seraphim to war—
MILTON.

O THOU, whatever title suit thee!
Auld Hornie, Satan, Nick, or Clootie,
Wha in yon cavern grim an' sooty
Closed under hatches,
Spairges about the brunstane cootie,
To scaud poor wretches!

Hear me, auld Hangie, for a wee,
An' let poor, damnèd bodies bee;
I'm sure sma' pleasure it can gie,
Ev'n to a deil,
To skelp an' scaud poor dogs like me,
An' hear us squeel!

Great is thy pow'r, an' great thy fame;
Far kenned an' noted is thy name;
An' though yon lowan heugh's thy hame,
Thou travels far;
An' faith! thou 's neither lag nor lame,
Nor blate nor scaur.

no thy-lane] not alone Gang aft agley] go oft awry

466 Spairges] spatters brunstane cootie] brimstone tub scaud] scald lowan heugh] flaming pit blate] shy scaur] scared

Whyles, ranging like a roaring lion,
For prey a' holes an' corners tryin;
Whyles, on the strong-winged tempest flyin,
Tirlan the kirks;
Whyles, in the human bosom pryin,
Unseen thou lurks.

I've heard my rev'rend Graunie say,
In lanely glens ye like to stray;
Or where auld, ruined castles, gray,
Nod to the moon,
Ye fright the nightly wand'rer's way,
Wi' eldritch croon.

When twilight did my Graunie summon
To say her pray'rs, douse, honest woman,
Aft 'yont the dyke she's heard you bumman,
Wi' eerie drone;
Or, rustling, through the boortries coman,
Wi' heavy groan.

Ae dreary, windy, winter night,
The stars shot down wi' sklentan light,
Wi' you, mysel, I gat a fright
Ayont the lough;
Ye, like a rash-buss, stood in sight,
Wi' waving sugh:

The cudgel in my nieve did shake,
Each bristled hair stood like a stake,
When wi' an eldritch, stoor *quaick, quaick,*
Amang the springs,
Awa ye squattered like a drake,
On whistling wings.

Let warlocks grim, an' withered hags,
Tell, how wi' you, on ragweed nags,
They skim the muirs an' dizzy crags,
Wi' wicked speed;
And in kirk-yards renew their leagues,
Owre howcket dead.

Tirlan] rattling eldritch] unearthly douse] decent bumman] humming boortries] elder-trees sklentan] slanting Ayont] byond rash-buss] clump of rushes sugh] rushing sound of wind nieve] fist stoor] harsh squattered] fluttered howcket] dug up

Thence, countra wives, wi' toil an' pain,
May plunge an' plunge the kirn in vain;
For Och! the yellow treasure's taen,
By witching skill;
An' dawtit, twal-pint Hawkie's gane
As yell's the bill.

Thence, mystic knots mak great abuse,
On young guidmen, fond, keen an' croose;
When the best warklum i' the house,
By cantraip wit,
Is instant made no worth a louse,
Just at the bit.

When thowes dissolve the snawy hoord,
An' float the jinglan icy boord,
Then, water-kelpies haunt the foord,
By your direction,
An' nighted trav'llers are allured
To their destruction.

An' aft your moss-traversing spunkies
Decoy the wight that late an' drunk is;
The bleezan, curst, mischievous monkies
Delude his eyes,
Till in some miry slough he sunk is,
Ne'er mair to rise.

When Masons' mystic word an' grip
In storms an' tempests raise you up,
Some cock, or cat, your rage maun stop,
Or, strange to tell!
The youngest brother ye wad whip
Aff straught to h–ll.

Lang syne in Eden's bonie yard,
When youthfu' lovers first were paired,
An' all the soul of love they shared
The raptured hour,
Sweet on the fragrant, flow'ry swaird,
In shady bow'r:

kirn] churn dawtit] petted twal-pint] twelve-pint (at a milking) Hawkie] pet-name for cow yell] dry bill] bull guidmen] husbands croose] cocksure warklum] tool cantraip] witching bit] crisis water-kelpies] water-spirits spunkies] will-o'-the-wisps bleezan] blazing

Then you, ye auld, snick-drawing dog!
Ye cam to Paradise incog,
An' played on a man a cursed brogue,
(Black be your fa'!)
An' gied the infant warld a shog,
'Maist ruined a'.

D'ye mind that day, when in a bizz,
Wi' reekit duds, an' reestet gizz,
Ye did present your smoutie phiz
'Mang better folk,
An' sklented on the man of Uz
Your spitefu' joke?

An' how ye gat him i' your thrall,
An' brak him out o' house an' hal',
While scabs an' botches did him gall,
Wi' bitter claw,
An' lowsed his ill-tongued, wicked scawl
Was warst ava?

But a' your doings to rehearse,
Your wily snares an' fechtin fierce,
Sin' that day Michael[1] did you pierce,
Down to this time,
Wad ding a' Lallan tongue, or Erse,
In prose or rhyme.

An' now, auld Cloots, I ken ye're thinkan,
A certain bardie's rantin, drinkin,
Some luckless hour will send him linkan,
To your black pit;
But faith! he'll turn a corner jinkan,
An' cheat you yet.

But fare you weel, auld Nickie-ben!
O wad ye tak a thought an' men'!
Ye aiblins might—I dinna ken—
Still hae a stake—
I'm wae to think upo' yon den,
Ev'n for your sake.

(1786)

[1] *Vide* Milton, 6th Book.

snick-drawing] crafty brogue] trick shog] shock bizz] flurry reekit duds] smoky clothes reestet gizz] smoke-dried wig sklented] directed maliciously scawl] scold ava] of all fechtin] fighting ding] defeat Lallan] lowland linkan] tripping aiblins] perhaps

467 *To a Louse, On Seeing one on a Lady's Bonnet at Church*

HA! whare ye gaun, ye crowlin' ferlie!
Your impudence protects you sairly:
I canna say but ye strunt rarely,
        Owre gawze and lace;
Though faith, I fear ye dine but sparely,
        On sic a place.

Ye ugly, creepin' blastet wonner,
Detested, shunned, by saunt an' sinner,
How daur ye set your fit upon her,
        Sae fine a lady!
Gae somewhere else and seek your dinner
        On some poor body.

Swith, in some beggar's haffet squattle;
There ye may creep, and sprawl, and sprattle,
Wi' ither kindred, jumping cattle,
        In shoals and nations;
Whare horn nor bane ne'er daur unsettle
        Your thick plantations.

Now haud you there, ye're out o' sight,
Below the fatt'rels, snug and tight,
Na faith ye yet! ye'll no be right,
        Till ye've got on it,
The vera tapmost, towrin height
        O' Miss's bonnet.

My sooth! right bauld ye set your nose out,
As plump an' gray as onie grozet:
O for some rank, mercurial rozet,
        Or fell, red smeddum,
I'd gie you sic a hearty dose o't,
        Wad dress your droddum!

I wad na been surprized to spy
You on an auld wife's flainen toy;
Or aiblins some bit duddie boy,
        On 's wylecoat;
But Miss's fine Lunardi, fie!
        How daur ye do 't?

crowlin' ferlie] creeping marvel   strunt] strut   wonner] wonder   fit] foot   Swith] Quick   haffet] lock of hair   sprattle] scramble   fatt'rels] ribbons   grozet] gooseberry   rozet] resin   smeddum] powder   droddum] backside   flainen toy] flannel cap   duddie] ragged   wylecoat] vest   Lunardi] bonnet

O Jenny, dinna toss your head,
An' set your beauties a' abread!
Ye little ken what cursed speed
The blastie's makin!
Thae winks and finger-ends, I dread,
Are notice takin!

O wad some pow'r the giftie gie us
To see oursels as others see us!
It wad frae monie a blunder free us
An' foolish notion:
What airs in dress an' gait wad lea'e us,
And ev'n devotion!

(1786)

468 from *Love and Liberty. A Cantata*

Recitativo

WHEN lyart leaves bestrow the yird,
Or wavering like the Bauckie-bird[1],
Bedim cauld Boreas' blast;
When hailstanes drive wi' bitter skyte,
And infant frosts begin to bite,
In hoary cranreuch drest;
Ae night at e'en a merry core
O' randie, gangrel bodies,
In Poosie-Nansie's[2] held the splore,
To drink their orra dudies:
Wi' quaffing, and laughing,
They ranted an' they sang;
Wi' jumping, an' thumping,
The vera girdle rang.

First, niest the fire, in auld, red rags,
Ane sat; weel braced wi' mealy bags,
And knapsack a' in order;
His doxy lay within his arm;
Wi' usqebae an' blankets warm,

[1] The old Scotch name for the Bat.

[2] The Hostess of a noted Caravansary in M——, well known to and much frequented by the lowest orders of Travellers and Pilgrims.

blastie] cursed creature

468 lyart] streaked skyte] blow cranreuch] frost core] band gangrel] vagrant splore] carousal orra dudies] spare clothes girdle] griddle

She blinket on her sodger:
An' ay he gies the tozie drab
The tither skelpan kiss,
While she held up her greedy gab,
Just like an aumous dish:
Ilk smack still, did crack still,
Just like a cadger's whip;
Then staggering, an' swaggering,
He roared this ditty up—

Air

I am a son of Mars who have been in many wars,
And show my cuts and scars wherever I come;
This here was for a wench, and that other in a trench,
When welcoming the French at the sound of the drum.
Lal de daudle &c.

My 'prenticeship I past where my leader breathed his last,
When the bloody die was cast on the heights of Abram;
And I served out my trade when the gallant game was played,
And the Moro low was laid at the sound of the drum.

I lastly was with Curtis among the floating batt'ries,
And there I left for witness an arm and a limb;
Yet let my country need me, with Eliott to head me,
I'd clatter on my stumps at the sound of a drum.

And now though I must beg, with a wooden arm and leg,
And many a tattered rag hanging over my bum,
I'm as happy with my wallet, my bottle and my callet,
As when I used in scarlet to follow a drum.

What though, with hoary locks, I must stand the winter shocks,
Beneath the woods and rocks oftentimes for a home,
When the tother bag I sell and the tother bottle tell,
I could meet a troop of hell at the sound of a drum.

Recitativo

He ended; and the kebars sheuk,
Aboon the chorus roar;
While frighted rattons backward leuk,
An' seek the benmost bore:

tozie] tipsy skelpan] smacking gab] mouth aumous dish] alms-dish cadger] hawker callet] wench kebars] rafters rattons] rats benmost bore] inmost crevice

A fairy fiddler frae the neuk,
He skirled out, encore.
But up arose the martial chuck,
An' laid the loud uproar—

Air

I once was a maid, though I cannot tell when,
And still my delight is in proper young men:
Some one of a troop of dragoons was my daddie,
No wonder I'm fond of a sodger laddie.
Sing lal de dal &c.

The first of my loves was a swaggering blade,
To rattle the thundering drum was his trade;
His leg was so tight and his cheek was so ruddy,
Transported I was with my sodger laddie.

But the godly old chaplain left him in the lurch,
The sword I forsook for the sake of the church;
He ventured the soul, and I risked the body,
'Twas then I proved false to my sodger laddie.

Full soon I grew sick of my sanctified sot,
The regiment at large for a husband I got;
From the gilded spontoon to the fife I was ready;
I asked no more but a sodger laddie.

But the peace it reduced me to beg in despair,
Till I met my old boy in a Cunningham fair;
His rags regimental they fluttered so gaudy,
My heart it rejoiced at a sodger laddie.

And now I have lived—I know not how long,
And still I can join in a cup and a song;
But whilst with both hands I can hold the glass steady,
Here's to thee, my hero, my sodger laddie.

. . . .

[*Beggars' Chorus*]

See the smoking bowl before us,
Mark our jovial, ragged ring!
Round and round take up the chorus,
And in raptures let us sing.

neuk] nook skirled] yelled chuck] sweetheart spontoon] half-pike

Chorus

A fig for those by law protected!
  Liberty's a glorious feast!
Courts for cowards were erected,
  Churches built to please the priest.

What is title, what is treasure,
  What is reputation's care?
If we lead a life of pleasure,
  'Tis no matter how or where.
      A fig, &c.

With the ready trick and fable
  Round we wander all the day;
And at night, in barn or stable,
  Hug our doxies on the hay.
      A fig, &c.

Does the train-attended carriage
  Through the country lighter rove?
Does the sober bed of marriage
  Witness brighter scenes of love?
      A fig, &c.

Life is all a variorum,
  We regard not how it goes;
Let them cant about decorum,
  Who have character to lose.
      A fig, &c.

Here's to budgets, bags and wallets!
  Here's to all the wandering train!
Here's our ragged brats and callets!
  One and all cry out, Amen!
    A fig for those by law protected,
      Liberty's a glorious feast!
    Courts for cowards were erected,
      Churches built to please the priest.

(Wr. 1786; pub. 1799)

469 *Ay Waukin O*

SIMMER's a pleasant time,
  Flowers of every colour;
The water rins o'er the heugh,
  And I long for my true lover!

Chorus

  Ay waukin, Oh,
    Waukin still and weary:
    Sleep I can get nane,
    For thinking on my dearie.—

When I sleep I dream,
  When I wauk I'm irie;
Sleep I can get nane,
  For thinking on my dearie.—
        Ay waukin &c.

Lanely night comes on,
  A' the lave are sleepin:
I think on my bonie lad,
  And I bleer my een wi' greetin.—
        Ay waukin &c.

(1790)

470 *John Anderson my Jo*

JOHN Anderson my jo, John,
  When we were first acquent,
Your locks were like the raven,
  Your bony brow was brent;
But now your brow is beld, John,
  Your locks are like the snaw;
But blessings on your frosty pow,
  John Anderson my jo.

John Anderson my jo, John,
  We clamb the hill the gither;
And mony a canty day, John,
  We've had wi' ane anither:

Waukin] waking heugh] crag irie] sad greetin] weeping

470 Jo] sweetheart brent] smooth beld] bald

Now we maun totter down, John,
And hand in hand we'll go;
And sleep the gither at the foot,
John Anderson my jo.

(1790)

471

The Banks o' Doon

Ye banks and braes o' bonie Doon,
How can ye bloom sae fresh and fair;
How can ye chant, ye little birds,
And I sae weary, fu' o' care!
Thou'll break my heart, thou warbling bird,
That wantons through the flowering thorn:
Thou minds me o' departed joys,
Departed, never to return.

Oft hae I roved by bonie Doon,
To see the rose and woodbine twine;
And ilka bird sang o' its luve,
And fondly sae did I o' mine.
Wi' lightsome heart I pu'd a rose,
Fu' sweet upon its thorny tree;
And my fause luver staw my rose,
But, ah! he left the thorn wi' me.

(1792)

472

Song

Ae fond kiss, and then we sever;
Ae fareweel, and then for ever!
Deep in heart-wrung tears I'll pledge thee,
Warring sighs and groans I'll wage thee.

Who shall say that Fortune grieves him,
While the star of hope she leaves him?
Me, nae cheerful twinkle lights me;
Dark despair around benights me.

I'll ne'er blame my partial fancy,
Naething could resist my Nancy:
But to see her was to love her;
Love but her, and love for ever.

Had we never loved sae kindly,
Had we never loved sae blindly!
Never met—or never parted,
We had ne'er been broken-hearted.

Fare-thee-weel, thou first and fairest!
Fare-thee-weel, thou best and dearest!
Thine be ilka joy and treasure,
Peace, enjoyment, love and pleasure!

Ae fond kiss, and then we sever!
Ae fareweel, alas, for ever!
Deep in heart-wrung tears I'll pledge thee,
Warring sighs and groans I'll wage thee.

(1792)

473 *A Red, Red Rose*

O MY luve's like a red, red rose,
That's newly sprung in June;
O my luve's like the melodie
That's sweetly played in tune.

As fair art thou, my bonie lass,
So deep in luve am I;
And I will love thee still, my dear,
Till a' the seas gang dry.

Till a' the seas gang dry, my dear,
And the rocks melt wi' the sun:
I will love thee still, my dear,
While the sands o' life shall run.

And fare thee weel, my only luve!
And fare thee weel, a while!
And I will come again, my luve,
Though it were ten thousand mile!

(Wr. 1794; pub. 1796)

474 *Song: For a' that and a' that*

Is there, for honest poverty
That hings his head, and a' that;
The coward-slave, we pass him by,
We dare be poor for a' that!

For a' that, and a' that,
Our toils obscure, and a' that,
The rank is but the guinea's stamp,
The man's the gowd for a' that.

What though on hamely fare we dine,
Wear hoddin grey, and a' that.
Gie fools their silks, and knaves their wine,
A man's a man for a' that.
For a' that, and a' that,
Their tinsel show, and a' that;
The honest man, though e'er sae poor,
Is king o' men for a' that.

Ye see yon birkie ca'd a lord,
Wha struts, and stares, and a' that,
Though hundreds worship at his word,
He's but a coof for a' that.
For a' that, and a' that,
His ribband, star and a' that,
The man of independent mind,
He looks and laughs at a' that.

A prince can mak a belted knight,
A marquis, duke, and a' that;
But an honest man's aboon his might,
Gude faith he mauna fa' that!
For a' that, and a' that,
Their dignities, and a' that,
The pith o' sense, and pride o' worth
Are higher rank than a' that.

Then let us pray that come it may,
As come it will for a' that,
That sense and worth, o'er a' the earth
Shall bear the gree, and a' that.
For a' that, and a' that,
It's comin yet for a' that,
That man to man the warld o'er,
Shall brothers be for a' that.

(1795)

gowd] gold hoddin] homespun cloth birkie] dandy coof] fool
fa'] obtain bear the gree] come off best

ROBERT MERRY

1755–1798

475 *Sir Roland; a Fragment*

——The knight with starry shield
Chased the gigantic spoiler from the field:
But soon each sorrow of his soul returns,
With jealous rage and fierce revenge he burns;
Spurs his fleet courser on in wild despair,
And calls aloud his violated fair.
  Now midnight reigned, and through the troublous skies
The sharp hail drives, and yelling blasts arise;
Yet brave Sir Roland with unslackened force
O'er the lone heath pursues his eager course;
With curses rends the air, and draws to war
The potent wizard of the shadowy car.
Far off he viewed a solitary light,
Whose paly lustre pierced the gloom of night;
Thither the lovelorn hero bends his speed,
While mountains answer to the neighing steed.
Soon as arrived, his wond'ring eyes behold
A pensive damsel, decked in robes of gold,
While mingling diamonds their effulgence shed,
With the pearl's modest white and ruby's red.
Beneath an aged cypress she reclined;
A pendant lamp was waving in the wind,
That scattered far a melancholy gleam,
And tinged the wat'ry waste with feeble beam.
For near, an ocean roared and dashed around
Its foamy billows with terrific sound;
And ever and anon was heard the cry
Of shipwrecked men in dying agony.
At his approach she starts, then lifts her veil,
And shows a sunken visage ghastly pale;
On the intrepid knight her languid gaze
Intently fixes, and at length she says:
'The wished-for hour is come, by fate's decree,
And thou shalt traverse yonder deep with me.
The bark attends; and lo! the wanton gale
Swells the soft bosom of th' impatient sail.
Then linger not, but all-enraptured share
The promised bliss, nor mourn thy ravished fair:

I love thy manly form, thy youthful face,
Admire thy valour and adore thy grace.'
  The knight observed her with astonished eye,
And much he wished, but more he scorned, to fly:
For, as the breeze assailed her gorgeous vest,
The opening folds disclosed a putrid breast.
Nearer he comes and marks, deprived of skin,
Her haggard jaws display a direful grin.
Onward she goes; by incantation's laws
Th' amazed Sir Roland unresisting draws.
'Here leave thy steed,' she cries, 'and never more
Shalt thou behold him on this hated shore.
But gentlest joys th' approaching hours await,
And Beauty spreads for thee her couch of state.'
Then beck'ning mounts the bark; the knight obeys,
Nor quits her guiding lamp's unhallowed rays.
  Soon as the vessel cuts the foamy tide,
Around strange spectres and fell monsters glide:
One bathed in tears rose from the liquid bed,
With the soft semblance of a virgin's head,
Thrice waved her hand and shook her sedgy hair,
And heaved a piteous sigh, and cried—'Beware!'
Next came an aged seer, whose feeble breath
Could scarcely utter—'Knight, beware of death!'
Then plunging downward in a serpent's form,
They curled the surges like an angry storm.
Now thousand other grisly shapes were seen,
Rolling their fiery eyes the waves between:
Here shrieking maidens felt the forced embrace,
There Murder laughed, and showed his guilty face.
A moment after, all was hushed and o'er,
And such portentous phantoms threat no more.
  But now the female at Sir Roland's side,
Who silent long the dauntless youth had eyed
With foul grimaces, on a sudden pressed
The knight abhorrent to her mangled breast;
Strove with the winning voice of love to speak,
And laid her bare skull on his lily cheek;
Imprints the bony kiss and fain would win
The chaste Sir Roland to the deadly sin.
But when she finds not magic art inspires
The wild commotion of unholy fires,
Observes him shrink beneath her love's excess,
And turn in anguish from the loathed caress,
Starting she left him, and in fury cried,
'O knight accursed! thou soon shalt rue thy pride':

Then seized her lamp and, scowling with disdain,
Sought the calm bottom of the roaring main.
  Dark was the night, and o'er the pathless way
With rapid force the ship appeared to stray.
In vain the youth with eye attentive seeks
The first faint dawning of the eastern streaks;
But all was hopeless, and no glimm'ring light
Gave the wished earnest of departing night.
Now to a shore the bark quick-striking came,
And, as the shock sent forth a sudden flame,
The hero leaps upon th' uncertain strand,
And lifts his unsheathed sword with desperate hand.
While slow he trod this desolated coast,
From the cracked ground uprose a warning ghost,
Whose figure all-confused was dire to view,
And loose his mantle flowed of shifting hue.
He shed a lustre round, and sadly pressed
What seemed his hand upon what seemed his breast;
Then raised his doleful voice, like wolves that roar
In famished troops on Orcus' sleepy shore:
'Approach yon antiquated tow'r,' he cried,
'There bold Rinaldo, fierce Mambrino died:
Thou too, perchance, shalt tread the selfsame road;
Approach (so fate commands) the dark abode.'
The knight advancing struck the fatal door,
And hollow chambers send a sullen roar.
As slow it opens, there appears a page,
With limbs of pliant youth and face of age:
'Welcome,' he cried, 'from dangers thou hast shared;
The banquet's ready and thy bed prepared.'
Through winding passages the knight he leads,
And often sighs, and often tells his beads;
Stops at an entrance stained with blood, and said,
'Accept, brave youth, the banquet and the bed.'
Then screaming loud he vanished from the sight,
And the bell tolled amid the silent night.
Sir Roland enters where, throughout the room,
One taper shows the melancholy gloom;
And rudely hanging by her twisted hair,
A slaughtered female's starting eyeballs glare;
While, from the curtained bed, such groans arose
As spoke the anguish of severest woes,
And smote his heart——

(1786)

JOHN CARR

1732–1807

476

from *Derwent: An Ode*

[*Memories of Childhood*]

LOVED stream, that meanders along
  Where the steps of my infancy strayed,
When first I attuned the rude song,
  That nature all artless essayed;

Though thy borders be stripped of each tree,
  Where trees were indulged to decay,
Their image still pictures to me
  Thy villagers gambolling gay.

Nor by Fancy shall aught be unseen
  Where thy fountains flow murmuring by,
Where I mixed in the sports on the green,
  Where I wept with the woe-begone eye.

'Man born unto trouble' and strife
  Is but little inclined to discern
That, amidst the hard lessons of life,
  He has still many harder to learn.

Hope calls; he no longer delays,
  Nor sees how his way is beset,
Till at length on his happier days
  Out of breath he looks back with regret.

Double *ff*, I remember you well,
  Double *ſſ*, I alone was to blame,
When your persons, in learning to spell,
  To me seemed exactly the same.

The dawning of folly or sense,
  Revolutions in Latin or taw,
The pedagogue armed in defence
  Of Lilly, the fountain of law;

taw] the game of marbles

Keen enmities lasting an hour,
  Much prose and much verse out of joint,
All revive; and I triumph in power
  To decide between comma and point.

Past rapine arises anew,
  Not a bird can be safe in her nest;
That orchard again is in view,
  Those apples were always the best.

The boy quits, enamoured of ease,
  For thy cool embraces, his book;
Thy minnows, that play when they please,
  O Derwent! how happy they look!

How oft, by no pity controlled,
  An impaler of brandlings[1] I've been!
How oft returned hungry and cold,
  Unburthened with booty, I ween!

When thy Hyads impetuously poured
  A deluge from every hill,
The dams by thy torrents devoured
  The miller aghast in his mill;

Thy rage did but temper the air;
  Far distant the mildew of Health,
Where Guilt vainly decorates Care,
  Disdaining the gewgaws of wealth.

Fine houses, fine coaches, fine wives,
  Genealogies bought by the yard!
Why forfeit the peace of your lives,
  Ye wretches, for such a reward?

Far better to perish obscure,
  With ignorance binding your eyes,
Than to riot on spoils of the poor,
  Than be learned without being wise.

Simplicity heard in her cot
  Long tales of hard winters and wars,
And still hoped to better her lot
  By the change of the moon and the stars.

[1] The brandling is a small worm, which is cleansed in moss, and used as a bait in fishing for trouts.

What feats were performed in the snow,
When the track of the hare was descried!
What joys did old Jowler bestow,
What grief, when the veteran died!

How Derwent for liberty fought,
Regardless of riches and ease!
Now liberty's not worth a groat,
And money corrupts all degrees!

Thus the sages of Derwent find out,
As the sages of Greece did before,
That Truth may be elbowed about,
And Honesty kicked out of door.

As the trout still prefers the clear stream,
As the eel still will bask in the mud,
So this is for ever the theme,
All is over and gone that was good.

For a story they stir up the fire,
Till vanquished and silenced by sleep;
No vale like their own they admire,
Not a lake in the land like the Sneep[1].

(1787)

HENRY JAMES PYE

1745–1813

477 from *Aerophorion*

[*The Air Balloon*]

HAIL then ye daring few! who proudly soar
Through paths by mortal eye unviewed before!
From earth and all her humble scenes who rise
To search the extended mansions of the skies.
If firm his breast who first undaunted gave
His fragile vessel to the stormy wave,
How much superior he! whose buoyant car
Borne through the strife of elemental war,

[1] A pool in the river near Muggleswick.

Driven by the veering wind's uncertain tide,
No helm to steer him, and no oar to guide,
Sees earth's stupendous regions spread below,
To hillocks shrunk the mountains' loftiest brow;
Who now his head sublime, astonished, shrouds
In the dull gloom of rain-distended clouds,
And sits enthroned 'mid solitude and shade
Which human eyesight never can pervade,
Or rides amidst the howling tempest's force
Tracing the volleyed lightning to its source;
Or proudly rising o'er the lagging wind
Leaves all the jarring atmosphere behind,
And at his feet, while spreading clouds extend,
While thunders bellow and while storms descend,
Feels on his head the enlivening sunbeams play,
And drinks in skies serene the unsullied stream of day.

(1787)

JOHN FREDERICK BRYANT

1753–1791

478 *On a Piece of Unwrought Pipeclay*

RUDE mass of earth, from which with moilèd hands
  (Compulsive taught) the brittle tubes I form,
  Oft listless, while my vagrant fancy warm
Roves (heedless of necessity's demands)
Amid Parnassian bowers, or wishful eyes
  The flight of Genius, while sublime she soars
  Of moral truth in search, or earth explores,
Or sails with Science through the starry skies:
Yet must I own (unsightly clod) thy claim
  To my attention, for thou art my stead.
  When grows importunate the voice of need,
  And in the furnace thy last change I speed,
Ah! then how eager do I urge the flame,
How anxious watch thee mid that glowing fire,
That threats my eyeballs with extinction dire!

(1787)

ANN YEARSLEY

1756–1806

479 *To Mr. ****, an Unlettered Poet, on Genius Unimproved*

FLORUS, canst thou define that innate spark
Which blazes but for glory? Canst thou paint
The trembling rapture in its infant dawn,
Ere young ideas spring; to local thought
Arrange the busy phantoms of the mind,
And drag the distant timid shadows forth,
Which, still retiring, glide unformed away,
Nor rush into expression? No; the pen,
Though dipped in awful Wisdom's deepest tint,
Can *never* paint the wild ecstatic mood.
Yet, when the bolder image strikes thine eye,
And uninvited grasps thy strongest thought,
Resolved to shoot into this world of things,
Wide fly the gates of Fancy; all alarmed,
The thin ideal troop in haste advance,
To usher in the substance-seeking shade.
And what's the shade which rushes on the world
With pow'rful glare, but emblem of the soul?
Ne'er hail the fabled Nine, or snatch rapt thought
From the Castalian spring; 'tis not for *thee*,
From embers where the pagan's light expires,
To catch a flame divine. From one bright spark
Of never-erring faith more rapture beams
Than wild mythology could ever boast.
Pursue the Eastern Magi through their groves,
Where Zoroaster holds the mystic clue,
Which leads to great Ormazes; there thou'lt find
His god thy own; or bid thy fancy chase
Restless Pythag'ras through his varied forms,
And she shall see him sitting on a heap
Of poor absurdity; where cheerful faith
Shall never rest, nor great omniscience claim.
What are the Muses or Apollo's strains,
But harmony of soul? Like thee, estranged
From Science and old Wisdom's classic lore,
I've patient trod the wild entangled path
Of unimproved idea. Dauntless thought

I eager seized, no formal rule e'er awed;
No precedent controlled; no custom fixed
My independent spirit: on the wing
She still shall guideless soar, nor shall the fool,
Wounding her pow'rs, e'er bring her to the ground.
  Yet Florus, list! to thee I loudly call;
Dare thee, by all the transport mind can reach,
Yea, by the boasted privilege of Man,
To stretch with me the spirit-raising wing
Of artless rapture! Seek earth's farthest bound,
Till Fancy, panting, drops from endless space.
  Deep in the soul live ever-tuneful springs,
Waiting the touch of ecstasy, which strikes
Most pow'rful on defenceless, untaught minds;
Then, in soft unison, the trembling strings
All move in one direction. Then the soul
Sails on idea, and would eager dart
Through yon ethereal way; restless awhile,
Again she sinks to sublunary joy.
  Florus, rove on! pluck from the pathless vale
Of Fancy all her loveliest, wildest sweets,
These best can please; but ah! beware, my friend:
Timid Idea shrinks, when coldly thou
Would'st hail the tender shade; then strongly clasp
The coy, reluctant fugitive, or seize
The rover as she flies; that breast alone
Is hers, all glowing with immortal flame;
And that be thine.

(1787)

L. KER

fl. 1787

480 *The Death of the Gods: An Ode Written in Imitation of Pindar*

I MADE the Muses sick
By a new song,
Not invoking their aid,
And their hearts were afraid!
They are dead, they are gone,
And I'll follow my blow;
The gods all anon,

From Jupiter down to his godship below,
Your poetical gods
Shall no longer survive;
At least it is odds
That they presently die,
If I am alive.
From the combat victorious returned,
The hero is Ker,
Who *alone* made the war;
See, their names and their titles are burned.

Two made their escape,
I wonder they could;
So a party I raised,
They lay hid in a wood.
I was not so stupid
As not to know Cupid,
And Venus the fair,
Who lay lurking there:
They are dying, 'tis a pity,
But no more they see the city.
To finish the battle, I gave a command,
Not once to come in with a wish in their cause,
To the ladies of England: permission obtained,
The victory bloodless I easily gained:
But too late a petition has come to my hand,
To stop and to spare them in spite of the laws.
Sweet ladies of England, go, conquer without
Any charms but your own—there can scarce be a doubt
You will always be conquerors, conquest is sure:
Use but your own charms, and proceed by my rules,
Or your own better sense never taught in the schools.
The wounds you give now, since Apollo is dead,
Will certainly never admit of a cure.
O the nonsense of thinking Apollo could heal
By wisdom or art—No, your charms must prevail.
He none can assist even in writing a line,
I deny he's alive—and the poetry's mine.

The Conclusion

Thus end all the fabulous gods of all times,
And let who will deny—there is truth in my rhymes;
For, fool Superstition, thy charms are all broken:
Their power is gone, and my life is the token.

(1787)

JOHN O'KEEFFE

1747–1833

481 *Air*

A FLAXEN-HEADED cow-boy, as simple as may be,
And next a merry plough-boy, I whistled o'er the lea;
But now a saucy footman, I strut in worsted lace,
And soon I'll be a butler, and wag my jolly face;
When steward I'm promoted, I'll snip a tradesman's bill,
My master's coffers empty, my pockets for to fill;
When lolling in my chariot, so great a man I'll be,
You'll forget the little plough-boy that whistled o'er the lea.

I'll buy votes at elections but, when I've made the pelf,
I'll stand poll for the Parliament, and then vote in myself;
Whatever's good for me, sir, I never will oppose:
When all my Ayes are sold off, why, then I'll sell my Noes.
I'll bawl, harangue and paragraph, with speeches charm the
ear,
And when I'm tired on my legs, then I'll sit down a peer.
In court or city honour, so great a man I'll be,
You'll forget the little plough-boy that whistled o'er the lea.

(1787)

482 *I want a Tenant: A Satire*

(i)

HIS speculation he regretted,
And thus Bob Sowden fumed and fretted:

'I was bewitched to build a house!
Better in Thames my cash to souse:
Up to my knees in brick and mortar,
And work myself like any porter!
My builder charge at such a rate
Above his given estimate!
'Twas first, "Good sir, I'll never dun ye";
And now 'tis—"Zounds, I'll have my money!"

'Without a tenant while it stands,
My house is thrown upon my hands;
'Tis true, 'tis not completely finished,
My cash must not be more diminished:
I can't sell out till stocks are rising,
Then so much spent in advertising!

'From breakfast, dinner, called to show it,
I shall go crazy! yes, I know it:
Obliged to keep an open door,
For folks I never saw before.
And then I'm forced to tell such lies,
In time I shall myself despise;
For those I do not care a damn,
I smile and cringe with "Sir" and "Ma'am."'

Some strangers call by fours and pairs,
Bob leads them up and down the stairs.

'Look, sir! the prospect is so fine,
The Surrey hills—they're quite divine!
Then, ma'am, to make your garden gay,
Some laurestinas here, and bay.'—

'But who's to find this bay and laurel?'—
'For that, dear sir, we shall not quarrel.
Although the yard may yet want pitching—
Pray, ma'am, admire this pretty kitchen.
Here, sir, I mean to sink a well,
And at the gate I'll hang a bell;
Your larder here, so sweet and cool,
And five yards square is by my rule.

'A handsome dining-parlour, sir;
Nice shade from those two rows of fir:
Round here I mean to plant some box;—
See, ma'am, the doors have all brass locks.
A smartish marble I'll put round
This chimney-piece, that I'll be bound.
And then the chimneys do not smoke:
I bought some pots—but they were broke;
Though, should they smoke, I'll take no rent,
My wish is but to give content.
Just point out any alteration,
And all shall suit your inclination.

'Our taxes here are wond'rous light;
Although the attics now are white,
I mean to paper them,—ma'am, you
May choose your pattern, red or blue;
For naked walls keep seldom clean,
And look so beggarly and mean.

'As for the rent, 'tis but a song;
To lose this house, ma'am, you'll be wrong.
For applications I have twenty;
In choice of tenants I am dainty,
But, sir, to you I give the preference,
Your countenance is perfect reference.—

'Just say the word—down comes the bill,
And take possession when you will;
And as for warning, not a whit,
Just when it suits you, you may quit;
It won't stand empty, not a minute,
You'll be quite comfortable in it!
Send in your goods, and take no care,
I'll order fires the rooms to air.'

(ii)

I Have a Tenant!

'My house is let, my heart be gay,
And only look to Quarter Day!
I've nothing now my hopes to damp,
I take my rent, and sign the stamp.
Who that shall furnish, they or I,
Next Michaelmas, aye, that we'll try.

'What do they say? the chimneys smoke!
Pho, pho, my dear, that's all a joke!'

'They say this nuisance must be cured,
So horrid, cannot be endured.
They cannot light the parlour fire,
Unless you raise the chimney higher,
And put a cow upon the top:
They think this may the grievance stop,
But now they are or froze or smothered.'

'Tell them, at once, I'll not be bothered.'

cow] cowl

'My dear, they heavily complain
The house lets in both wind and rain!
With chinks in wall, and cracks in roof,
'Tis neither wind nor water-proof;
They say the walls will never dry.'

'Tell them I say that's all my eye.'

'They wish you'd go and see the state
They're in, before it is too late:
And then you'll see it wants a spout.'

'Tell them, my dear, I've got the gout.'

'They want a knocker and a scraper;
They want the attics hung with paper;
So many gaps, too, in the border,
The garden, too, is all disorder.
Yourself will be the proper judge.'

'Tell them, from me, all this is fudge.'

'Your promise keep—to stay they're willing.'

'I'll not lay out another shilling;
I've no objection, if they please,
That in repairs *they* sport the fees.
Of bricklayers and such cursed stuff,
And carpenters I've had enough!
The bargain clenched, I've saved my bacon,
For seven good years my house is taken;
And half-year's warning after that,
So farther talk is empty chat.'

'They say the fastenings are so slight,
The robbers may break in at night.'

'Well, 'tis their own security,
If folks are robbed, what's that to me?
Must I employ a smith and farrier?
For guard, they'd better keep a terrier.'

'You promised that you'd crop the garden.'

'I'll not lay out another *farden*;
Were I to herb, and plant, and fruit it,
Then they'd buy chickens up to root it;
Must I forsooth their garden dig?
Why, wife, you take me for a pig!'

'The mortar is already crumbling.'

'I'll hear no more their cursed grumbling;
My house is let, and I'm content,
We've only now to take our rent;
So foam the jug, the table wipe,
And silence, whilst I light my pipe.'

Live like wild Arab in a tent,
Before Bob Sowden's house you rent!

(Wr. 1791; pub. 1834)

CHARLES MORRIS

1745–1838

483 *Addressed to Lady ****, Who Asked What the Passion of Love was?*

YOU ask me, *What's love?*—Why, that virtue-fed vapour,
Which poets spread over our longings like gauze,
May do for a swain who can feed upon paper;
But flesh is my diet, and blood is the cause.

A delicate *tendre*, spun into Platonic,
Suits the feminine fop,—whom no beauties provoke;
But the blood of a Welshman is hot and laconic,
And he loves as he fights, with a word and a stroke.

Yet, I grant you, there is a sweet madness of passion,
A raptured delirium of mental delight;
Though, alas! my dear Madam, not five in the nation
Whose souls have an optic to view the blest light.

But we speak not of minds of distinguished selection,
But love, common love, in its earthly attire,
Which, believe me, when dressed in this high-flown affection,
Wears the threadbare disguise of a bankrupt desire.

For the bosom's deceit, like the spendthrift's profusion,
  As the substance declines rich appearances tries;
More gay as more weak, till this splendid delusion
  In a pang of bright vanity dazzles and dies.

Ah! if, in a strain of pure sentiment showing,
  No animal warmth checks the eloquent tongue,
'Tis the trick of a coxcomb to boast your undoing,
  And pride, taste, or impotence prompts the foul wrong!

For love, in a tumult of soft agitation,
  O'ercome with its ardour, bids language retire;
And, lost in emotions of troubled sensation,
  Still breathes the soft accent of silent desire.

Yes, the god's on the wing when a delicate Damon
  In sickly composure sits down to refine;
For love, like a hectic, when weakly the stamen,
  Still brightens the skin as the solids decline.

If such be the love you propose in the question,
  No doubt it's a phantom, dressed up by the mind;
And, believe me, it is not a substance to rest on,
  But the fraud of cold bosoms and vanities blind.

But for me, my dear Madam, a poor carnal sinner,
  Whose love keeps no Lent, or on rhapsody starves,
With the sharp sauce of hunger I fall to my dinner,
  And take, without scruple, what appetite carves.

So, my good Lady ****, all beauty and merit,
  You see, though I dote on your face and your mind,
The devil a grain should I feel of love's spirit,
  If looks didn't warrant your shape and your kind.

With this taste you, perhaps, will upbraid my vile nature:
  But thus stands the case, and in truth to my theme,
Were my mistress the first both in mind and in feature,
  Unsex her, and passion would fade like a dream.

As a poet, indeed, I've a licence for fiction,
  To dress in heroics the treacherous heart;
But take the sad truth, and excuse the plain diction,
  For love moves with me in an honester part.

stamen] essential element

But, perhaps, you may know something more of the matter;
  Then deign to inform the dull soul of a brute—
A hint of your mind would most pleasingly flatter,
  And to hear it I'd always be willing and mute.

(Pub. by 1787)

484 *Country and Town*

In London I never know what to be at,
Enraptured with this and enchanted with that!
I'm wild with the sweets of variety's plan,
And life seems a blessing too happy for man.

But the country, Lord help us, sets all matters right,
So calm and composing from morning till night;
O, it settles the spirits when nothing is seen
But an ass on a common or goose on a green.

In town if it rains, why it damps not our hope,
The eye has its range and the fancy her scope;
Still the same, though it pour all night and all day,
It spoils not our prospects, it stops not our way.

In the country how blessed, when it rains in the fields,
To feast upon transports that shuttlecock yields,
Or go crawling from window to window to see
A hog on a dunghill or crow on a tree.

In London how easy we visit and meet,
Gay pleasure the theme and sweet smiles are our treat;
Our morning's a round of good-humoured delight,
And we rattle in comfort and pleasure all night.

In the country how charming our visits to make
Through ten miles of mud for formality's sake,
With the coachman in drink and the moon in a fog,
And no thought in our head but a ditch and a bog.

In London if folks ill together are put,
A bore may be dropped or a quiz may be cut;
We change without end and, if happy or ill,
Our wants are at hand and our wishes at will.

484 rattle] chatter   quiz] eccentric

In the country you're nailed, like a pale in your park,
To some stick of a neighbour, crammed into the ark;
Or if you are sick or in fits tumble down,
You reach death ere the doctor can reach you from town.

I have heard how that love in a cottage is sweet,
When two hearts in one link of soft sympathy meet;
I know nothing of that, for alas! I'm a swain
Who requires, I own it, more links to my chain.

You jays and your magpies may chatter on trees,
And whisper soft nonsense in groves if they please;
But a house is much more to my mind than a tree,
And for groves, O! a fine grove of chimneys for me.

Then in town let me live and in town let me die,
For in truth I can't relish the country, not I.
If one must have a villa in summer to dwell,
O give me the sweet shady side of Pall Mall.

(Pub. by 1797)

JOHN WOLCOT

1738–1819

485 from *Instructions to a Celebrated Laureat*

[*George III Visits Whitbread's Brewery*]

MUSE, sing the stir that happy Whitbread made;
Poor gentleman! most terribly afraid
He should not charm enough his guests divine:
He gave his maids new aprons, gowns, and smocks;
And lo! two hundred pounds were spent in frocks,
To make th' apprentices and draymen fine:

Busy as horses in a field of clover,
Dogs, cats, and chairs, and stools were tumbled over,
Amidst the Whitbread rout of preparation,
To treat the lofty Ruler of the nation.

Now moved King, Queen, and Princesses so grand,
To visit the first Brewer in the land;
Who sometimes swills his beer and grinds his meat
In a snug corner christened Chiswell-street;
But oft'ner, charmed with fashionable air,
Amidst the gaudy Great of Portman-square.

Lord Aylesbury, and Denbigh's Lord *also*,
  His Grace the Duke of Montague *likewise*,
With Lady Harcourt, joined the raree-show,
  And fixed all Smithfield's marv'ling eyes:
For lo! a greater show ne'er graced those quarters,
Since Mary roasted, just like crabs, the martyrs.

Arrived, the King broad grinned, and gave a nod
To smiling Whitbread, who, had God
  Come with his angels to behold his beer,
With more respect he never could have met—
Indeed the man was in a sweat,
  So much the Brewer did the King revere.

Her Majesty contrived to make a dip:
Light as a feather then the King did skip,
And asked a thousand questions, with a laugh,
Before poor Whitbread comprehended half.

Reader! my Ode should have a simile—
Well! in Jamaica, on a tam'rind tree,
  Five hundred parrots, gabbling just like Jews,
I've seen—such noise the feathered imps did make,
As made my very *pericranium* ache—
  Asking and telling parrot news:

Thus was the brewhouse filled with gabbling noise,
Whilst draymen, and the Brewer's boys,
  Devoured the questions that the King did ask:
In diff'rent parties were they staring seen,
Wond'ring to think they saw a King and Queen!
  Behind a tub were some, and some behind a cask.

Some draymen forced themselves (a pretty luncheon)
Into the mouth of many a gaping puncheon;

puncheon] cask

And through the bung-hole winked with curious eye,
  To view, and be assured what sort of things
  Were Princesses, and Queens, and Kings,
For whose most lofty station thousands sigh!
And lo! of all the gaping puncheon clan,
Few were the mouths that had not got a man!

Now Majesty into a pump so deep
Did with an opera-glass so curious peep;
Examining with care each wondrous matter
          That brought up water!

Thus have I seen a magpie in the street,
A chatt'ring bird we often meet,
A bird for curiosity well known,
          With head awry,
          And cunning eye,
Peep knowingly into a marrow-bone.

And now his curious M[ajest]y did stoop
To count the nails on ev'ry hoop;
And lo! no single thing came in his way,
That, full of deep research, he did not say,
'What's this? hae, hae? what's that? what's this? what's that?'
So quick the words too, when he deigned to speak,
As if each syllable would break its neck.

Thus, to the world of *great* whilst others crawl,
Our Sov'reign peeps into the world of *small*:
Thus microscopic geniuses explore
  Things that too oft provoke the public scorn;
Yet swell of useful knowledges the store,
  By finding systems in a peppercorn.

Now boasting Whitbread serious did declare,
To make the Majesty of England stare,
That he had butts enough, he knew,
Placed side by side, to reach along to Kew:
On which the King with wonder swiftly cried,
'What, if they reach to Kew then, side by side,
  What would they do, what, what, placed end to end?'
To whom, with knitted, calculating brow,
The Man of Beer most solemnly did vow
  Almost to Windsor that they would extend;
On which the King, with wond'ring mien,
Repeated it unto the wond'ring Queen:

On which, quick turning round his haltered head,
The Brewer's horse, with face astonished, neighed;
The Brewer's dog too poured a note of thunder,
Rattled his chain, and wagged his tail for wonder.

(1787)

486 *Ode*

THAT I have often been in love, deep love,
A hundred doleful ditties plainly prove.
By marriage never have I been disjointed,
For matrimony deals prodigious blows:
And yet for this same stormy state, God knows,
I've groaned—and, thank my stars, been disappointed.

With Love's dear passion will I never war:
Let ev'ry man for ever be in love,
E'en if he beats, in age, old Parr:
'Tis for his chilly veins a good warm glove;
It bids the blood with brisker motion start,
Thawing Time's icicles around his heart.

Wedlock's a saucy, sad, familiar state,
Where folks are very apt to scold and hate:
Love keeps a modest distance, is divine,
Obliging, and says ev'rything that's fine.

Love writes sweet sonnets, deals in tender matter:
Marriage, in epigram so keen and satire:
Love seeketh always to oblige the fair,
Full of kind wishes and exalted hope:
Marriage desires to see her in the air,
Suspended at the bottom of a rope.

Love wishes, in the vale or on the down,
To give his dear, dear idol a green gown:
Marriage, the brute, so snappish and ill-bred,
Can kick his sighing turtle out of bed;
Turns bluffly from the charms that taste adores,
Then pulls his night-cap o'er his eyes, and snores.

Wedlock at first, indeed, is vastly pleasant,
A very showy bird, a fine cock-pheasant:
By time, it changeth to a diff'rent fowl,
Sometimes a cuckoo, oft'ner a horn-owl.

give . . . a green gown] make love

Wedlock's a lock, however large and thick,
Which ev'ry rascal has a key to pick.

O Love! for heav'n's sake, never leave my heart:
No! thou and I will never, never part:
Go, Wedlock, to the men of leaden brains,
Who hate variety, and sigh for chains.

(1790)

487 from *Resignation: an Ode to the Journeymen Shoemakers*

Who lately refused to work, except their Wages were raised.

SONS of Saint Crispin, 'tis in vain!
Indeed 'tis fruitless to complain.
  I know ye wish good beef or veal to carve:
But first the hungry Great must all be fed;
Meantime, ye all must chew hard, musty bread,
  Or, what is commonly unpleasant, starve.

Your Masters, like yourselves, oppression feel—
It is not they would wish to stint your meal:
  Then suck your paws like bears, and be resigned.
Perhaps your sins are many; and if so,
Heav'n gives us very frequently, we know,
  The Great as scourges for mankind.
Your Masters soon may follow you, so lank—
Undone by simple confidence in Rank.

The royal Richmond builds his state on coals;
Sal'sb'ry and Hawksb'ry, lofty souls,
  With their fair dames must have the ball and rout;
Kings must our millions have, to make a glare,
Whose sycophants must also have a share;
  But pout not—'tis a libel, sirs, to pout.

Closed be your mouths, or dread the jail or thong:
Ye must not for your money have a song.
Cease, cease your riots, pray, my friends:
It answereth (believe me) no good ends—
  And yet the time will come, I hope to God,
When black-faced, damned Oppression to his den
Shall howling fly before the curse of men,
  And feel of angered Justice the sharp rod.

Go home, I beg of ye, my friends, and eat
Your sour, your mouldy bread, and offal meat;
Till Freedom comes—I see her on her way—
Then shall a smile break forth upon each mien,
The front of banished Happiness be seen,
And, sons of Crispin, you once more be gay.

Now go, and learn submission from your Bible:
Complaint is now-a-day a flagrant libel.
Yes, go and try to chew your mouldy bread—
Justice is sick, I own, but is not dead.
Let Grandeur roll her chariot on our necks,
Submission sweet humility bespeaks:
Let Grandeur's plumes be lifted by our sighs—
Let dice, and chariots, and the stately thrones
Be formed of poor men's hard-worked bones—
We must contribute; or, lo, Grandeur dies.
We are the parish that supports her show;
A truth that Grandeur wishes not to know.

(1792)

488 *To a Fly, Taken out of a Bowl of Punch*

Ah! poor intoxicated little knave,
Now senseless, floating on the fragrant wave;
Why not content the cakes alone to munch?
Dearly thou pay'st for buzzing round the bowl;
Lost to the world, thou busy sweet-lipped soul—
Thus Death, as well as Pleasure, dwells with Punch.

Now let me take thee out, and moralise.—
Thus 'tis with mortals, as it is with flies,
For ever hankering after Pleasure's cup:
Though Fate, with all his legions, be at hand,
The beasts the draught of Circe can't withstand,
But in goes every nose—they *must, will* sup.

Mad are the Passions, as a colt untamed!
When Prudence mounts their backs, to ride them mild,
They fling, they snort, they foam, they rise inflamed,
Insisting on their own sole will so wild.

Gadsbud! my buzzing friend, thou art not dead;
The Fates, so kind, have not yet snipped thy thread—
By heav'ns, thou mov'st a leg, and now its brother,
And kicking, lo, again thou mov'st another!

And now thy little drunken eyes unclose;
And now thou feelest for thy little nose,
  And, finding it, thou rubbest thy two hands,
Much as to say, 'I'm glad I'm here again.'
And well mayst thou rejoice—'tis very plain,
  That near wert thou to Death's unsocial lands.

And now thou rollest on thy back about,
Happy to find thyself alive, no doubt—
  Now turnest—on the table making rings;
Now crawling, forming a wet track,
Now shaking the rich liquor from thy back,
  Now flutt'ring nectar from thy silken wings:

Now standing on thy head, thy strength to find,
And poking out thy small, long legs behind;
And now thy pinions dost thou briskly ply;
Preparing now to leave me—farewell, Fly!

Go, join thy brothers on yon sunny board,
And rapture to thy family afford—
  There wilt thou meet a mistress, or a wife,
That saw thee, drunk, drop senseless in the stream;
Who gave, perhaps, the wide-resounding scream,
  And now sits groaning for thy precious life.
Yes, go and carry comfort to thy friends,
And wisely tell them thy imprudence ends.

Let buns and sugar for the future charm;
These will delight, and feed, and work no harm—
  Whilst Punch, the grinning merry imp of sin,
Invites th' unwary wand'rer to a kiss,
Smiles in his face, as though he meant him bliss,
  Then, like an alligator, drags him in.

(1792)

489 *Ode to a Country Hoyden*

DEAR Dolly, stay thy scampering joints one minute,
  And let me ask thee, mad-cap girl, a question—
Somewhat of consequence there may be in it,
  That, probably, may'nt suit thine high digestion.

Pray what's the meaning of the present glee?
  To ride a nannygoat, or ass, or pig?
Or mount an ox, or ride an apple-tree,
  And on the dancing limb enjoy a jig?

Perhaps thou art infected with an itch
To plague a poor old crone, baptised a witch;
  To smoke her in her hovel—kill her cats,
Or lock her in and rob her garden's peas,
Kick down the lame old granny's hive of bees,
  And break her windows in, with stones and bats.

Perchance, to rob an orchard thou may'st long,
Or neighbour's hen's-nest of its eggs, or young;
  Nay, steal the mother-hen to boot;
Perchance thou hasten'st, fond of vulgar joys,
To tumble on the haycocks with the boys,
  And let them take, at will, the sweet salute.

Thou makest a long face, and answer'st thus—
'Lord, then about a trifle what a fuss!
  As though a body might not ride a pig,
Or nannygoat indeed, or ox, good me!
Or our old Neddy, or an apple-tree,
  Just for one's health to have a little jig!

'Or where's the mighty harm, upon my word,
  In taking a few eggs, or chicks, or hen?
The farmers can't be ruined by't, good Lord!
  Papa says that they're all substantial men.

'Or where's the harm to ride upon a gate?
To snub one so, indeed, at such a rate!
I've tumbled from the trees upon the stones,
And never broke, in all my life, my bones:
See, sir, I have not one black spot about me!
'Tis cruel, then, for nothing, thus to flout me.

'Or where's the mighty crime, I wonder, pray,
With Cousin Dick to tumble on the hay?
Just like a baby with her doll you treat one!
Marry come up! why, Cousin Dick won't eat one!
And then, forsooth, what mighty harm would come
In having bits of fun with Cousin Tom?'

Dolly, thy artless answers force my smile—
I readily believe thee void of guile;
My lovely girl, I think thou mean'st no harm:
But had I daughters just like thee, let loose,
I verily should think myself a goose,
To mark each colt-like lass without alarm.

Doll, get thee home, and tell Mama, so mild,
So fearful that a frown would kill her child,
That not ev'n birch to kill that child is able;
And tell thy Father, a fond fool, from me,
To look a little sharper after thee,
Clip thy wild tongue, and tie thee to the table.

(1794)

490 from *The Royal Tour, and Weymouth Amusements*

[*George III and the Sailor*]

A SAILOR pops upon the Royal Pair,
On crutches borne—an object of despair:
His squalid beard, pale cheek, and haggard eye,
Though silent, pour for help a piercing cry.

'Who, who are you? what, what? hae, what are you?'
'A man, my liege, whom kindness never knew.'

'A sailor! sailor, hae? you've lost a leg.'
'I know it, sir—which forces me to beg.
I've nine poor children, sir, besides a wife—
God bless them! the sole comforts of my life.'

'Wife and nine children, hae?—all, all alive?
No, no, no wonder that you cannot thrive.
Shame, shame, to fill your hut with such a train!
Shame to get brats for others to maintain!

Get, get a wooden leg, or one of cork:
Wood's cheapest—yes, get wood, and go to work.
But mind, mind, Sailor—hae, hae, hae—hear, hear—
Don't go to Windsor, mind, and cut one there:
That's dangerous, dangerous—there I place my traps—
Fine things, fine things, for legs of thieving chaps:
Best traps, my traps—take care—they bite, they bite,
And sometimes catch a dozen legs a night.'

'Oh! had I money, sir, to buy a leg!'

'No money, hae? nor I—go beg—go beg.'—

How sweetly kind to bid the cripple mump,
And cut from other people's trees a stump!
How vastly like our kind Archbishop M[oo]re,
Who loves not beggar tribes at Lambeth door;
Of meaner parsons bids them ask relief—
There, carry their coarse jugs for broth and beef!

'Mine Gote! your Mashesty!—don't hear sush stuff:
De workhouse always geefs de poor enough.
Why make bout dirty leg sush wond'rous fuss?—
And den, what impudence for beg of Us!
In Strelitz, O mine Gote! de beggars skip:
Dere, for a sharity, we geefs a *whip*.
Money make subjects impudent, I'm sure—
Respect be always where de peepel's *poor*.'

'How, Sailor, did you lose your leg?—hae, hae?'

'I lost it, please your Majesty, at sea,
Hard fighting for my country and my King.'

'Hae, what?—that's common, very common thing.
Hae! lucky fellow, that you were not drilled:
Some lose their heads, and many men are killed.
Your parish? where's your parish? hae—where, where?'

'I served my 'prenticeship in Manchester.'

'Fine town, fine town—full, full of trade and riches—
Hae, sailor, hae, can you make leather breeches?
These come from Manchester—there, there I got 'em!'
On which Great Caesar claps his buckskin bottom.

mump] beg

'Must not encourage vagrants—no, no, no—
Must not make laws, my lad, and break 'em too.
Where, where's your parish, hae? and where's your pass?
Well, make haste home—I've got, I've got no brass.'

(1795)

491 from *The Sorrows of Sunday: An Elegy*

The intended annihilation of Sunday's harmless amusements, by three or four most outrageously zealous Members of Parliament, gave birth to the following Elegy.

SUSAN, the constant slave to mop and broom,
And Marian, to the spit's and kettle's art;
Ah! shall not *they* desert the house's gloom,
Breathe the fresh air one moment, and look smart?

Meet, in some rural scene, a Colin's smile,
With love's soft stories wing the happy hour;
Drop in his dear embraces from the stile,
And share his kisses in the shady bow'r?

'No!' roars the Huntingdonian Priest—'No, no!
Lovers are liars—Love's a damnèd trade;
Kissing is damnable—to hell they go—
The Devil's claws await the rogue and jade.

'My chapel is the purifying place:
There let them go to wash their sins away:
There, from my hand, to pick the crumbs of grace,
Smite their poor sinful craws, and howl, and pray.'—

How hard, the lab'ring hands no rest should know,
But toil six days beneath the galling load,
Poor souls! and then, the seventh be forced to go
And box the Devil, in Blackfriars Road![1]

Heav'n glorieth not in phizzes of dismay,
Heav'n takes no pleasure in perpetual sobbing,
Consenting freely that my fav'rite day
May have her tea and rolls, and hob and nobbing.

[1] The place of Mr Rowland Hill's Chapel.

491 craws] stomachs hob and nobbing] drinking together

In sooth, the Lord is pleased when man is blest,
And wisheth not his blisses to blockade:
'Gainst tea and coffee ne'er did he protest,
Enjoyed, in gardens, by the men of trade.

Sweet is White Conduit House, and Bagnigge-Wells,
Chalk Farm, where Primrose Hill puts forth her smile;
And Don Saltero's, where much wonder dwells,
Expelling work-day's matrimonial bile.

Life with the down of cygnets may be clad!
Ah! why not make her path a pleasant track?
'No!' cries the Pulpit Terrorist (how mad!),
'No! let the world be one huge hedgehog's back.'

Vice (did his rigid mummery succeed)
Too soon would smile amid the sacred walls;
Venus in tabernacles make her bed,
And Paphos find herself amid Saint Paul's.

Avaunt Hypocrisy, the solemn jade,
Who, wilful, into ditches leads the blind:
Makes, of her canting art, a thriving trade,
And fattens on the follies of mankind!

Look at Archbishops, Bishops, on a Fast,
Denying hackney-coachmen e'en their beer;
Yet, lo! their butchers knock, with flesh repast;
With turbots, lo! the fishmongers appear!

The potboys howl with porter for their bellies;
The bakers knock, with custards, tarts and pies;
Confectioners, with rare ice-creams and jellies;
The fruiterer, lo! with richest pine supplies!

In secret, thus, they eat, and booze, and nod;
In public, call indulgence a d–mned evil;
Order their simple flocks to walk with God,
And ride themselves an airing with the Devil.

(1795)

WILLIAM CROWE

1745–1829

492 from *Lewesdon Hill*

Up to thy summit, Lewesdon, to the brow
Of yon proud rising, where the lonely thorn
Bends from the rude South-east, with top cut sheer
By his keen breath, along the narrow track
By which the scanty-pastured sheep ascend
Up to thy furze-clad summit, let me climb,
My morning exercise; and thence look round
Upon the variegated scene of hills,
And woods, and fruitful vales, and villages
Half-hid in tufted orchards, and the sea
Boundless, and studded thick with many a sail.
  Ye dew-fed vapours, nightly balm, exhaled
From earth, young herbs and flowers, that in the morn
Ascend as incense to the Lord of day,
I come to breathe your odours; while they float
Yet near this surface, let me walk embathed
In your invisible perfumes, to health
So friendly, nor less grateful to the mind,
Administ'ring sweet peace and cheerfulness.
  How changed is thy appearance, beauteous hill!
Thou hast put off thy wintry garb, brown heath
And russet fern, thy seemly-coloured cloak,
To bide the hoary frosts and dripping rains
Of chill December, and art gaily robed
In livery of the spring: upon thy brow
A cap of flowery hawthorn, and thy neck
Mantled with new-sprung furze and spangles thick
Of golden bloom: nor lack thee tufted woods
Adown thy sides. Tall oaks of lusty green,
The darker fir, light ash, and the nesh tops
Of the young hazel join, to form thy skirts
In many a wavy fold of verdant wreath.
So gorgeously hath Nature dressed thee up
Against the birth of May; and, vested so,
Thou dost appear more gracefully arrayed
Than Fashion's worshippers; whose gaudy shows,
Fantastical as are a sick man's dreams,

nesh] delicate

From vanity to costly vanity
Change ofter than the moon. Thy comely dress,
From sad to gay returning with the year,
Shall grace thee still till Nature's self shall change.
  These are the beauties of thy woodland scene
At each return of spring: yet some delight
Rather to view the change; and fondly gaze
On fading colours, and the thousand tints
Which autumn lays upon the varying leaf.
I like them not; for all their boasted hues
Are kin to sickliness: mortal decay
Is drinking up their vital juice; that gone,
They turn to sere and yellow. Should I praise
Such false complexions, and for beauty take
A look consumption-bred? As soon, if grey
Were mixed in young Louisa's tresses brown,
I'd call it beautiful variety,
And therefore dote on her. Yet I can spy
A beauty in that fruitful change, when comes
The yellow autumn and the hopes o'the year
Brings on to golden ripeness; nor dispraise
The pure and spotless form of that sharp time,
When January spreads a pall of snow
O'er the dead face of th' undistinguished earth.
Then stand I in the hollow combe beneath
And bless this friendly mount, that weather-fends
My reed-roofed cottage, while the wintry blast
From the thick north comes howling: till the spring
Return, who leads my devious steps abroad,
To climb, as now, to Lewesdon's airy top.

(1788)

THOMAS RUSSELL

1762–1788

493 *Sonnet Supposed to be Written at Lemnos*

ON this lone isle, whose rugged rocks affright
  The cautious pilot, ten revolving years
  Great Paean's son, unwonted erst to tears,
Wept o'er his wound: alike each rolling light
Of heaven he watched, and blamed its lingering flight;

By day the sea-mew screaming round his cave
Drove slumber from his eyes; the chiding wave
And savage howlings chased his dreams by night.
Hope still was his: in each low breeze that sighed
Through his rude grot, he heard a coming oar;
In each white cloud a coming sail he spied;
Nor seldom listened to the fancied roar
Of Oeta's torrents, or the hoarser tide
That parts famed Trachis from th' Euboic shore.

(Wr. by 1788; pub. 1789)

ANONYMOUS

494 *The Soldier that has Seen Service. A Sketch from Nature*

FROM Calpe's rock, with loss of leg,
Reduced from port to port to beg,
See the conquering hero comes:
An ass's panniers bear his all,
Two sickly brats that fret and bawl,
And suck, for want of food, their thumbs.

The drooping mother follows near,
Now heaves a sigh, now drops a tear,
And casts the fond, maternal gaze;
Mars bluntly strives to cheat his dame,
Reminds her of his stock of fame,
And bids her hope for better days.

'Alas,' she cries, 'and what is fame?
An empty sound, not worth a name.
Doth fame the needful loaf supply?
I'd give up all the fame you boast
For one fair joint of boiled or roast,
Or griskin fat or mutton-pie.

'Was it for this we left our home
About the troubled world to roam,
To conquer Spain and want a meal?
Ah! had we never bled for those
Who see our still increasing woes,
And comfort's cup refuse to deal!'

griskin] bacon

Mars owns 'tis true, and cries, 'Too late
'Tis now for us to carp at fate,
Or call the moment back that's flown.
Let shame at length the state o'erwhelm,
That knows he fought to save the realm,
And lets the wounded soldier moan.'

'Amen,' she cries; Mars wipes her tear,
Prepares some better theme to cheer,
Of battles, songs or pleasures gone;
From knapsack takes his little store,
Hoping that time will make it more;
Then parts his crust and hobbles on.

(1788)

ANNA SEWARD

1742–1809

495 from *Eyam*

In scenes paternal, not beheld through years,
Nor viewed till now but by a father's side,
Well might the tender tributary tears
From keen regrets of duteous fondness glide.
Its pastor to this human flock no more
Shall the long flight of future days restore;
Distant he droops—and that once gladdening eye
Now languid gleams, e'en when his friends are nigh.

Through this known walk, where weedy gravel lies
Rough and unsightly, by the long coarse grass
Of the once smooth and vivid green, with sighs
To the deserted rectory I pass;
Stray through the darkened chamber's naked bound,
Where childhood's earliest, liveliest bliss I found.
How changed since erst, the lightsome walls beneath,
The social joys did their warm comforts breathe!

Ere yet I go, who may return no more,
That sacred pile, mid yonder shadowy trees,
Let me revisit.—Ancient massy door,
Thou gratest hoarse! My vital spirits freeze,

Passing the vacant pulpit to the space
Where humble rails the decent altar grace;
And where my infant sister's ashes sleep,
Whose loss I left the childish sport to weep.

Now the low beams, with paper garlands[1] hung
In memory of some village youth or maid,
Draw the soft tear from thrilled remembrance sprung;
How oft my childhood marked that tribute paid;
The gloves suspended by the garland's side,
White as its snowy flowers, with ribbands tied:
Dear village! long these wreaths funereal spread,
Simple memorials of thy early dead!

But O! thou blank and silent pulpit! thou
That with a father's precepts, just and bland,
Didst win my ear, as reason's strengthening glow
Showed their full value, now thou seem'st to stand
Before my sad, suffused and trembling gaze,
The dreariest relic of departed days;
Of eloquence paternal, nervous, clear,
Dim apparition thou!—and bitter is my tear.

(Wr. 1788; pub. 1792)

496 *Sonnet*

INGRATITUDE, how deadly is the smart
Thou giv'st, inhabiting the form we love!
How light compared all other sorrows prove!
Thou shed'st a night of woe—from whence depart
The gentle beams of patience, that the heart
Midst lesser ills illume. Thy victims rove,
Unquiet as the ghost that haunts the grove
Where murder spilt the life-blood. O! thy dart
Kills more than life—ev'n all that makes it dear;
Till we 'the sensible of pain' would change
For frenzy, that defies the bitter tear;
Or wish in kindred callousness to range
Where moon-eyed Idiocy, with fallen lip,
Drags the loose knee and intermitting step.

(1789)

[1] The ancient custom of hanging a garland of white roses made of writing-paper, and a pair of white gloves over the pew of the unmarried Villagers, who die in the flower of their age. . . .

497 from *Colebrook Dale*

WHILE neighbouring cities waste the fleeting hours,
Careless of art and knowledge and the smile
Of every Muse, expanding Birmingham,
Illumed by intellect, as gay in wealth,
Commands her aye-accumulating walls
From month to month to climb the adjacent hills;
Creep on the circling plains, now here, now there,
Divergent—change the hedges, thickets, trees,
Upturned, disrooted, into mortared piles,
The streets elongate and the statelier square. . . .
  Warned by the Muse, if Birmingham should draw,
In future years, from more congenial climes
Her massy ore, her labouring sons recall,
And sylvan Colebrook's winding vales restore
To beauty and to song, content to draw
From unpoetic scenes her rattling stores,
Massy and dun; if, thence supplied, she fail,
Britain, to glut thy rage commercial, see
Grim Wolverhampton lights her smouldering fires,
And Sheffield smoke-involved; dim where she stands
Circled by lofty mountains, which condense
Her dark and spiral wreaths to drizzling rains,
Frequent and sullied, as the neighbouring hills
Ope their deep veins and feed her caverned flames;
While to her dusky sister[1] Ketley yields,
From her long-desolate and livid breast,
The ponderous metal. No aerial forms
On Sheffield's arid moor[2] or Ketley's heath
E'er wove the floral crowns, or smiling stretched
The shelly sceptre;—there no poet roved
To catch bright inspirations. Blush, ah, blush,
Thou venal Genius of these outraged groves,
And thy apostate head with thy soiled wings
Veil!—who hast thus thy beauteous charge resigned
To habitants ill-suited; hast allowed
Their rattling forges and their hammers' din,
And hoarse, rude throats, to fright the gentle train,
Dryads and fair-haired Naiades;—the song,

[1] Wolverhampton has the greatest part of her iron from Ketley, a dreary and barren wold in her vicinity.

[2] The East-moor, near Sheffield, which is dreary, though the rest of the country surrounding that town is very fine.

Once loud as sweet, of the wild woodland choir
To silence;—disenchant the poet's spell,
And to a gloomy Erebus transform
The destined rival of Tempean vales.

(Wr. 1790; pub. 1810)

498 *An Old Cat's Dying Soliloquy*

YEARS saw me still Acasto's mansion grace,
The gentlest, fondest of the tabby race;
Before him frisking through the garden glade,
Or at his feet in quiet slumber laid;
Praised for my glossy back of zebra streak,
And wreaths of jet encircling round my neck;
Soft paws that ne'er extend the clawing nail,
The snowy whisker and the sinuous tail;
Now feeble age each glazing eyeball dims,
And pain has stiffened these once supple limbs;
Fate of eight lives the forfeit gasp obtains,
And e'en the ninth creeps languid through my veins.
Much sure of good the future has in store,
When on my master's hearth I bask no more,
In those blest climes, where fishes oft forsake
The winding river and the glassy lake;
There, as our silent-footed race behold
The crimson spots and fins of lucid gold,
Venturing without the shielding waves to play,
They gasp on shelving banks, our easy prey:
While birds unwinged hop careless o'er the ground,
And the plump mouse incessant trots around,
Near wells of cream that mortals never skim,
Warm marum creeping round their shallow brim;
Where green valerian tufts, luxuriant spread,
Cleanse the sleek hide and form the fragrant bed.[1]
Yet, stern dispenser of the final blow,
Before thou lay'st an aged grimalkin low,
Bend to her last request a gracious ear,
Some days, some few short days, to linger here;
So to the guardian of his tabby's weal
Shall softest purrs these tender truths reveal:
'Ne'er shall thy now expiring puss forget
To thy kind care her long-enduring debt,

[1] The affection of cats for marum and valerian is well known. They will beat the stems down, mat them with their feet, and then roll upon them.

Nor shall the joys that painless realms decree
Efface the comforts once bestowed by thee;
To countless mice thy chicken-bones preferred,
Thy toast to golden fish and wingless bird;
O'er marum borders and valerian bed
Thy Selima shall bend her moping head,
Sigh that no more she climbs, with grateful glee,
Thy downy sofa and thy cradling knee;
Nay, e'en at founts of cream shall sullen swear,
Since thou, her more loved master, art not there.'

(1792)

CHARLOTTE SMITH

1749–1806

499 *Sonnet Written in the Church Yard at Middleton in Sussex*

PRESSED by the moon, mute arbitress of tides,
  While the loud equinox its power combines,
  The sea no more its swelling surge confines,
But o'er the shrinking land sublimely rides.
The wild blast, rising from the western cave,
  Drives the huge billows from their heaving bed,
  Tears from their grassy tombs the village dead,
And breaks the silent sabbath of the grave!
With shells and sea-weed mingled, on the shore
  Lo! their bones whiten in the frequent wave;
  But vain to them the winds and waters rave;
They hear the warring elements no more:
While I am doomed—by life's long storm oppressed,
To gaze with envy on their gloomy rest.

(1789)

JOHN WILLIAMS

1761–1818

500 *Matrimony*

In answer to a young lady, who asked the author for his ideas on the subject

'TIS an act of the priest to give patience a test;
'Tis a desperate hope, and a serious jest;
'Tis catching a dolt, when his wit is suspended;
'Tis a toil, where the labour can never be ended;
'Tis a leap in the dark, which both parties agree
To perform hand in hand, though they neither can see;
'Tis walking through mines filled with sulphurous vapour,
Where to find out a path, you must brandish a taper;
'Tis like Tantalus' feast, where the good does but seem,
And both ope their eyes, though they're both in a dream;
'Tis going to sea, in a black stormy night,
Which reason calls madness, but custom delight:
For Wedlock's a minx who deceives by her sleekness,
As Craft wove a cloak to envelop her weakness.
'Tis a comical, tragical, fiery ordeal,
Where the ploughshares are hot, and your faith is not real.

(1789)

SIR SAMUEL EGERTON BRYDGES

1762–1837

501 *Lines Written Immediately after Parting from a Lady*

SHE is gone! The occasion for ever is past!
How each step, as it brought me too near to the last,
  Still gave a new rend to my heart!
'Three moments to fly,' to my bosom I said,
'Three moments, and then the occasion is fled,
  The concern of thy life to impart!'

Woe is me! She is gone! My too fluttering breast,
That scarce knew what 'twas doing, the words half expressed,
And 'Be mine' on my tongue died away!
'Be mine!': at the thought the tear stood in my eye;
And confused as I was, she perchance knew not why,
Came the time she no longer might stay!

She is gone, and she knows not the pangs that I feel!
Perhaps, if she did, the dear angel might heal
The wounds that her beauties have made!
She might smile!—By the gods, how I'd bless her dear smile;
She might say, 'As your words seem devoid of all guile,
I will trust I shall not be betrayed!'

'By the Father of Heav'n,' from my heart I'd reply,
'If all that I speak, that I write, look, or sigh,
Is as warm as the love in my breast,
May my right hand its office forget, and my truth
Ne'er again be believed, but the bud of my youth
With infamy wither oppressed!'

She is gone! Had she heard me thus utter the vow,
Perchance she had deigned a kind look to bestow,
And a tear had returned to mine!
Her kind heart with pity had viewed my distress,
And, like angels, enjoying the pleasure to bless,
Perchance she had said, 'I'll be thine!'

'I'll be thine!' O what rapturous accents to me!
Tears had gushed from mine eyes, and I'd fall'n on my knee,
And blessed her a thousand times o'er!
Perdition revenge me, if ever my voice,
Or my heart, for the kindness to me in her choice,
Forgot the dear maid to adore!

But she's gone! Where, O where am I straying? I dream!
O fancy, with what airy plans dost thou teem!
She is gone, and has heard not my woes!
She is gone, and it was not my angel that smiled;
'Twas her shade my idolatrous fancy beguiled!
On delusion my raptures arose!

(1789)

ANONYMOUS

502 *To a Lady, with a Present of a Fan*

SMILING, sweet girl, this proffered toy approve,
Cool though its use, the gift of warmest love.
  Pressed by thy genial hand, behold it spread,
In pride expansive, its elastic head
(For thy dear fingers' sensitive caress
Instant can raise it, instantly depress);
Then, betwixt polished shafts of equal size,
From the round-swelling centre stately rise;
Till in full lustre all its beauties play,
Like rosebuds opening to the vernal ray:
For to the circulating orb below,
Solely its captivating powers we owe;
Powers, which to pleasure every joint constrain,
Till to its shape relax it shrinks again.
  Its winning graces and seducing air,
Engage the wise, and prepossess the fair;
Ev'n virgin modesty, exempt from harms,
May oft employ its inoffensive charms;
For of its use no mark it leaves, no stain
Can from so pure an effluence remain.
For where's that lynx's piercing eye can trace
The track of eagles through th' ethereal space?
The serpent's devious maze along the plain?
Ship's paths—or winds that ventilate the main?
  The brunette widow too may find relief
From this, to mitigate her ardent grief,
May to her wish this pliant engine frame,
To cool her passions, or to fan their flame.

(1789)

WILLIAM LISLE BOWLES
1762–1850

503 *Sonnet*

EVENING, as slow thy placid shades descend,
Veiling with gentlest hush the landscape still,
The lonely battlement, and farthest hill
And wood, I think of those that have no friend,
Who now, perhaps, by melancholy led,
From the broad blaze of day, where pleasure flaunts,
Retiring, wander 'mid thy lonely haunts
Unseen. They watch the tints that o'er thy bed
Hang lovely, to their pensive fancy's eye
Presenting fairy vales, where the tired mind
Might rest, beyond the murmurs of mankind,
Nor hear the hourly moans of misery!
Ah! beauteous views, that Hope's fair gleams the while
Should smile like you, and perish as they smile!

(1789)

504 *Sonnet. At Ostend, July 22, 1787*

HOW sweet the tuneful bells' responsive peal!
As when, at opening morn, the fragrant breeze
Breathes on the trembling sense of wan disease,
So piercing to my heart their force I feel!
And hark! with lessening cadence now they fall,
And now, along the white and level tide,
They fling their melancholy music wide;
Bidding me many a tender thought recall
Of summer-days, and those delightful years
When by my native streams, in life's fair prime,
The mournful magic of their mingling chime
First waked my wond'ring childhood into tears!
But seeming now, when all those days are o'er,
The sounds of joy once heard, and heard no more.

(1789)

ERASMUS DARWIN

1731–1802

505 *Visit of Hope to Sydney Cove, near Botany-Bay*

WHERE Sydney Cove her lucid bosom swells,
Courts her young navies, and the storm repels,
High on a rock amid the troubled air
Hope stood sublime, and waved her golden hair;
Calmed with her rosy smile the tossing deep,
And with sweet accents charmed the winds to sleep;
To each wild plain she stretched her snowy hand,
High-waving wood and sea-encircled strand.
'Hear me,' she cried, 'ye rising realms! record
Time's opening scenes, and Truth's unerring word.
There shall broad streets their stately walls extend,
The circus widen, and the crescent bend;
There, rayed from cities o'er the cultured land,
Shall bright canals and solid roads expand;
There the proud arch colossus-like bestride
Yon glitt'ring streams, and bound the chasing tide;
Embellished villas crown the landscape scene,
Farms wave with gold, and orchards blush between:—
There shall tall spires and dome-capped towers ascend,
And piers and quays their massy structures blend;
While with each breeze approaching vessels glide,
And northern treasures dance on every tide!'
Then ceased the nymph—tumultuous echoes roar,
And Joy's loud voice was heard from shore to shore—
Her graceful steps descending pressed the plain,
And Peace, and Art, and Labour joined her train.

(1789)

506 from *The Botanic Garden*

(i)

[*Nightmare*]

SO on his Nightmare through the evening fog
Flits the squab Fiend o'er fen, and lake, and bog;
Seeks some love-wildered maid with sleep oppressed,
Alights, and grinning sits upon her breast.

—Such as of late amid the murky sky
Was marked by Fuseli's poetic eye,
Whose daring tints, with Shakespeare's happiest grace,
Gave to the airy phantom form and place.—
Back o'er her pillow sinks her blushing head,
Her snow-white limbs hang helpless from the bed,
While with quick sighs, and suffocative breath,
Her interrupted heart-pulse swims in death.
—Then shrieks of captured towns, and widows' tears,
Pale lovers stretched upon their blood-stained biers,
The headlong precipice that thwarts her flight,
The trackless desert, the cold starless night,
And stern-eyed murderer with his knife behind,
In dread succession agonize her mind.
O'er her fair limbs convulsive tremors fleet,
Start in her hands, and struggle in her feet;
In vain to scream with quivering lips she tries,
And strains in palsied lids her tremulous eyes;
In vain she *wills* to run, fly, swim, walk, creep;
The will presides not in the bower of Sleep.
—On her fair bosom sits the Demon-Ape
Erect, and balances his bloated shape;
Rolls in their marble orbs his Gorgon-eyes,
And drinks with leathern ears her tender cries.

(1789)

(ii)

[*Steam Power*]

THE Giant-Power from earth's remotest caves
Lifts with strong arm her dark reluctant waves,
Each caverned rock and hidden den explores,
Drags her dark coals, and digs her shining ores.—
Next, in close cells of ribbèd oak confined,
Gale after gale, he crowds the struggling wind;
The imprisoned storms through brazen nostrils roar,
Fan the white flame, and fuse the sparkling ore.
Here high in air the rising stream he pours
To clay-built cisterns or to lead-lined towers;
Fresh through a thousand pipes the wave distils,
And thirsty cities drink the exuberant rills.—
There the vast millstone with inebriate whirl
On trembling floors his forceful fingers twirl,
Whose flinty teeth the golden harvests grind,
Feast without blood! and nourish human-kind.

Now his hard hands on Mona's rifted crest,
Bosomed in rock, her azure ores arrest;
With iron lips his rapid rollers seize
The lengthening bars, in thin expansion squeeze;
Descending screws with ponderous fly-wheels wound
The tawny plates, the new medallions round;
Hard dyes of steel the cupreous circles cramp,
And with quick fall his massy hammers stamp.
The Harp, the Lily and the Lion join,
And George and Britain guard the sterling coin.
Soon shall thy arm, unconquered Steam! afar
Drag the slow barge, or drive the rapid car;
Or on wide-waving wings expanded bear
The flying-chariot through the fields of air.
—Fair crews triumphant, leaning from above,
Shall wave their fluttering kerchiefs as they move;
Or warrior-bands alarm the gaping crowd,
And armies shrink beneath the shadowy cloud.

(1791)

ANDREW MACDONALD

1755?–1790

507 *The Lover's Leap. A Tale*

Sir Bumper was a baron bold
As e'er romantic writ enrolled;
For feats of chivalry renowned,
And oft Olympic victor crowned.
In a deep-winding woody vale
His castle stood, antique and grey,
Where winter's storm, nor summer gale,
E'er chased the hov'ring fogs away.
The dull moat all around
Lies in eternal sleep,
Its mould'ring oaks are all half drowned,
Its bending willows ever weep.

See from the gate Sir Bumper stride
With fair round paunch and ruddy face;
And, hark! the horn resounding wide
Proclaims aloud the jocund chase.

For now the sun has left the main,
And gilds the hoary mountains high,
Where young Squire Ringwood and his train
With clamour seem to rend the sky.

His lazy groom Sir Bumper chides—
He mounts—and up the hill he rides;
Just as Squire Ringwood, brisk and gay,
Had giv'n the watch-word—'stole away'.
'Tis a grim, old, malicious fox,
Heav'n save you, sir, from fatal knocks!
For deafened with your whoop and hollow,
My mare denies your course to follow.
She backward casts her rolling eye,
And views Sir Bumper's castle high.

What nymph is that of tempting bloom,
With all her charms profuse displayed?

'Tis Lucy in her dressing-room,
In nature's robes alone arrayed.

Miss Lucy is Sir Bumper's daughter,
And lately had Squire Ringwood taught her
To think herself not quite so well,
And wish for what she could not tell.
Shut, shut, dear girl, oh shut the casement,
And do not kill us with amazement!
To the window see her creep,
Hanging o'er the moat so deep,
There leaning on her arms of snow
She listless eyes the pool below,
Surrounded by the frogs
That sputter through the muddy bogs.

And now the genial season warm
Deep flushes every ripened charm.
Her bosom heaves with wild desire,
Her eyeballs dance in lambent fire.
A subtle trembling, sweet yet strong,
Glides rapid every nerve along.
'Ah! what a sultry, stifling morn!'
She cried, 'and heat's not to be borne;
Straight will I seek the secret cave,
And in the lake my body lave.'
Then in a robe of slight attire

She wraps her lovely bosom bare,
And, swift descending, all unseen,
She like an arrow skims the green,
The cowslip and the daisy sweet
Scarce bending to her feathered feet.

To the west there grew a grove,
Deep in whose sequestered glades
Many a wood-nymph wont to rove,
And shield from blights the favoured shades.
Close-sheltered in its bosom green
A broad extended lake is seen;
And there a rock, abrupt and riv'n,
Heaves its tow'ring head to heav'n:
Stooped within its oozy side
Is a cavern deep and wide,
Deemed of old the ghastly haunt
Of elves and water-goblins gaunt:
But now 'tis reckoned a proper place
For maidens of sweet and bashful face
To come and strip off their tatters,
And take the ben'fit of the waters,
Without fear of shepherds or satyrs,
Or any such matters.

To this green cave fair Lucy came,
And, on the velvet moss reclined,
The robe that wrapped her tempting frame
She, conscious, blushing, slow resigned.
Oh, powers of bliss! what charms she showed!
Charms which no eloquence can tell:
Her cheeks with heav'n's own tincture glowed;
No bursting rose e'er bloomed so well.

See her raven ringlets flowing,
New contrasted power bestowing
On her white and downy skin;
On her swelling bosom lying,
Round her charming shoulders flying,
As an airy mantle thin!

With one quick glance around the wood,
Another to the rock's high head,
She fearless rushes to the flood,
And hides her in a liquid bed.

Secure she spreads her shining limbs,
Paddles, tumbles, dives and swims;
Each various posture wanton she employs,
And all the humid luxury enjoys.

Meanwhile o'er rough ridges, and torrents, and rocks,
Sir Bumper and Ringwood had followed the fox.
'Twas an old fox, I said, and he knew ev'ry trick
That was ever practised, I think, by Old Nick.
But hard run at last, he ascends a wild steep,
And over an old wall he makes a nice leap;
There clings in a bush, which bush you must know
Hung o'er a high crag, with deep waters below.
Soon followed the pack, and ev'ry bold hound
Sprung sheer o'er the verge—plumped down—and was drowned.
This precipice Sir Bumper knew,
And with strong arms his bridle drew.
His gallant steed, the truth to say,
Was pleased this signal to obey,
After scouring such a tract,
With such a woolsack on his back.
Squire Ringwood then had made a round,
To gain th' advantage of the ground;
And, like a jav'lin newly thrown,
He from the heights came headlong down.
Right t'ward the wall he pushes on,
O'er which the fox and hounds had gone.
In vain Sir Bumper raised a roar,
And cracked his whip, and bawled, and swore.
Then in the chase Squire Ringwood's gen'rous mare
With fatal vigour took her leap so fair,
That from the cliff abrupt she launched in empty air.
Astounded,
Confounded,
And stiff as a stake,
Squire Ringwood convulsively clung to her back,
Till he softly came dash
With a horrid flash
Among reeds, and docks, and other aquatic trash.

But the water was deep, which saved his bones;
And the poor mare, after a few snuffles and groans,
Began to swim like a duck,
And by excellent luck
The Squire turned her to that hand
Which was nighest the land.

Round the promontory's base
He wond'rous horsemanship displays:
—'There, my Princess;—forward, hoy;
Tallyho—and—here, my boy':—
Till, as beneath the rock so grey
Slow he worked his wat'ry way,
A sudden turn, which close he took,
Brought him to a woody nook,
Where Lucy, sheltered in the shade,
Sports on the waves herself had made.
With a shriek and a spring the brisk girl in a fright
Fled fast from the sight of this terrible wight,
That on the soft element sailed bolt upright;
With locks heavy-streaming and wild rolling eyes,
To the cavern as fleet as Camilla she flies,
There thrust in an arm in a sleeve of her gown,
Behind a dark willow she scuttles her down.

Ringwood at first was sore amazed,
When from the azure flood she flew;
But soon as on her charms he gazed
This goddess of the lake he knew.

Now 'Tallyho' resounds again,
Impatiently he works the rein,
Whipping, spurring, wriggling, firking,
And fast unbuttoning his jerkin.

Soon as to the cave he got,
He turned his mare into the wood;
And nimbly whipping off his coat,
Before his charming Lucy stood.

Onward, stripping, he proceeds,
Till all his dark and dropping weeds
Reeking in the sun were laid,
Then—'Your servant, Ma'am'—he said.

Sir Bumper, in the meantime, all forlorn,
Lamenting his companion dashed and torn,
With all his hounds for ever lost and gone,
Around the hill came lonely ambling on.

firking] urging forward

Awful in grief to heav'n he raved,
Crying, if he might haply find
From death a single puppy saved,
What ease it would afford his mind;
Or some fragment of Ringwood driv'n to land,
A piece of his skull, or the palm of his hand.

By and by he meets the mare.—
—'Ah! wild devil, art thou there?
Where is Ringwood? tell me, where?
Sleeps he in the caverns deep,
Where the crabs around him creep?
Or along the swelling tide,
Pecked by gor-mews, floats he wide?
O thou most disastrous mare!
Where is Ringwood?—tell me, where?'
Thus mourning wild, he pierced the gloomy wood,
And soon upon the lake's green margin stood.

I really can't say what happened when
He found the Squire and Lucy's den;
But this I know, to make amends,
That, by advice of prudent friends,
Miss Lucy to Ringwood, the very next day,
Was given in a matrimonial way.

(Wr. by 1790; pub. 1791)

WILLIAM SOTHEBY
1757–1833

508 *Netley Abbey. Midnight*

SOFT on the wave the oars at distance sound,
The night-breeze sighing through the leafy spray
With gentle whisper murmurs all around,
Breathes on the placid sea, and dies away.
As sleeps the moon upon her cloudless height,
And the swol'n spring-tide heaves beneath the light,

507 gor-mews] cormorants

Slow lingering on the solitary shore
Along the dewy path my steps I bend,
Lonely to yon forsaken fane descend,
To muse on youth's wild dreams amid the ruins hoar.

Within the sheltered centre of the aisle,
Beneath the ash whose growth romantic spreads
Its foliage trembling o'er the funeral pile,
And all around a deeper darkness sheds;
While through yon arch, where the thick ivy twines,
Bright on the silvered tower the moonbeam shines,
And the grey cloister's roofless length illumes,
Upon the mossy stone I lie reclined,
And to a visionary world resigned
Call the pale spectres forth from the forgotten tombs.

Spirits! the desolated wreck that haunt,
Who frequent by the village maiden seen
When sudden shouts at eve the wanderer daunt,
And shapeless shadows sweep along the green;
And ye, in midnight horrors heard to yell
Round the destroyer of the holy cell,
With interdictions dread of boding sound;
Who, when he prowled the rifled walls among,
Prone on his brow[1] the massy fragment flung;—
Come from your viewless caves, and tread this hallowed
ground!

How oft, when homeward forced at day's dim close,
In youth, as bending back I mournful stood,
Fixed on the favourite spot where first arose
The pointed ruin peeping o'er the wood;
Methought I heard upon the passing wind
Melodious sounds in solemn chorus joined
Echoing the chaunted vesper's peaceful note:
Oft through the veil of night's descending cloud,
Saw gleaming far the visionary crowd
Down the deep vaulted aisle in long procession float.

But now no more the gleaming forms appear,
Within their graves at rest the fathers sleep;
And not a sound comes to the wistful ear,
Save the low murmur of the tranquil deep,

[1] This alludes to a circumstance recorded in Grose's Antiquities, and still believed in the neighbourhood.

Or from the grass that in luxuriant pride
Waves o'er yon eastern window's sculptured side,
  The dewdrops bursting on the fretted stone:
While faintly from the distant coppice heard
The music of the melancholy bird
  Trills to the silent heaven a sweetly-plaintive moan.

Farewell, delightful dreams, that charmed my youth!
  Farewell, the aerial note, the shadowy train!
Now while this shrine inspires sublimer truth,
  While cloistered echo breathes a solemn strain,
In the deep stillness of the midnight hour
Wisdom shall curb wild fancy's magic power,
  And as with life's gay dawn the illusions cease,
Though from the heart steal forth a sigh profound,
Here resignation o'er its secret wound
  Shall pour the lenient balm that soothes the soul to peace.

(1790)

JOANNA BAILLIE

1762–1851

509 *A Disappointment*

On village green, whose smooth and well-worn sod,
Cross-pathed, with every gossip's foot is trod;
By cottage door where playful children run,
And cats and curs sit basking in the sun:
Where o'er the earthen seat the thorn is bent,
Cross-armed, and back to wall, poor William leant.
His bonnet broad drawn o'er his gathered brow,
His hanging lip and lengthened visage show
A mind but ill at ease. With motions strange,
His listless limbs their wayward postures change;
Whilst many a crooked line and curious maze,
With clouted shoon, he on the sand portrays.
The half-chewed straw fell slowly from his mouth,
And to himself low mutt'ring spoke the youth.
  'How simple is the lad, and reft of skill,
Who thinks with love to fix a woman's will:
Who ev'ry Sunday morn, to please her sight,
Knots up his neck-cloth gay and hosen white:

Who for her pleasure keeps his pockets bare,
And half his wages spends on pedlar's ware;
When every niggard clown or dotard old,
Who hides in secret nooks his oft-told gold,
Whose field or orchard tempts with all her pride,
At little cost may win her for his bride;
Whilst all the meed her silly lover gains
Is but the neighbours' jeering for his pains.
On Sunday last when Susan's banns were read,
And I astonished sat with hanging head,
Cold grew my shrinking limbs and loose my knee,
Whilst every neighbour's eye was fixed on me.
Ah, Sue! when last we worked at Hodge's hay,
And still at me you jeered in wanton play;
When last at fair, well pleased by showman's stand,
You took the new-bought fairing from my hand;
When at old Hobb's you sung that song so gay,
'Sweet William' still the burthen of the lay,
I little thought, alas! the lots were cast,
That thou should'st be another's bride at last:
And had, when last we tripped it on the green
And laughed at stiff-backed Rob, small thought, I ween,
Ere yet another scanty month was flown,
To see thee wedded to the hateful clown.
Ay, lucky swain, more gold thy pockets line;
But did these shapely limbs resemble thine,
I'd stay at home and tend the household gear,
Nor on the green with other lads appear.
Ay, lucky swain, no store thy cottage lacks,
And round thy barn thick stand the sheltered stacks;
But did such features hard my visage grace,
I'd never budge the bonnet from my face.
Yet let it be: it shall not break my ease;
He best deserves who doth the maiden please.
Such silly cause no more shall give me pain,
Nor ever maiden cross my rest again.
Such grizzly suitors with their taste agree,
And the black fiend may take them all for me!'
Now through the village rise confusèd sounds,
Hoarse lads, and children shrill, and yelping hounds.
Straight ev'ry matron at the door is seen,
And pausing hedgers on their mattocks lean.
At every narrow lane and alley mouth,
Loud laughing lasses stand, and joking youth.
A near approaching band in colours gay,
With minstrels blithe before to cheer the way,

From clouds of curling dust which onward fly,
In rural splendour break upon the eye.
As in their way they hold so gaily on,
Caps, beads and buttons glancing in the sun,
Each village wag, with eye of roguish cast,
Some maiden jogs and vents the ready jest;
Whilst village toasts the passing belles deride,
And sober matrons marvel at their pride.
But William, head erect, with settled brow,
In sullen silence viewed the passing show;
And oft he scratched his pate with manful grace,
And scorned to pull the bonnet o'er his face;
But did with steady look unmovèd wait,
Till hindmost man had turned the church-yard gate;
Then turned him to his cot with visage flat,
Where honest Tray upon the threshold sat.
Up jumped the kindly beast his hand to lick,
And, for his pains, received an angry kick.
Loud shuts the flapping door with thund'ring din;
The echoes round their circling course begin,
From cot to cot in wide progressive swell;
Deep groans the church-yard wall and neighb'ring dell,
And Tray responsive joins with long and piteous yell.

(1790)

510 *A Mother to her Waking Infant*

NOW in thy dazzling half-oped eye,
Thy curlèd nose and lip awry,
Thy up-hoist arms and noddling head,
And little chin with crystal spread,
Poor helpless thing! what do I see,
That I should sing of thee?

From thy poor tongue no accents come,
Which can but rub thy toothless gum;
Small understanding boasts thy face,
Thy shapeless limbs nor step nor grace;
A few short words thy feats may tell,
And yet I love thee well.

510 dazzling] dazed noddling] nodding

When sudden wakes the bitter shriek,
And redder swells thy little cheek;
When rattled keys thy woes beguile,
And through the wet eye gleams the smile,
Still for thy weakly self is spent
  Thy little silly plaint.

But when thy friends are in distress,
Thou'lt laugh and chuckle ne'er the less;
Nor e'en with sympathy be smitten,
Though all are sad but thee and kitten;
Yet little varlet that thou art,
  Thou twitchest at the heart.

Thy rosy cheek so soft and warm;
Thy pinky hand and dimpled arm;
Thy silken locks that scantly peep,
With gold-tipped ends, where circles deep
Around thy neck in harmless grace
So soft and sleekly hold their place,
Might harder hearts with kindness fill,
  And gain our right good will.

Each passing clown bestows his blessing,
Thy mouth is worn with old wives' kissing:
E'en lighter looks the gloomy eye
Of surly sense, when thou art by;
And yet I think whoe'er they be,
  They love thee not like me.

Perhaps when time shall add a few
Short years to thee, thou'lt love me too.
Then wilt thou through life's weary way
Become my sure and cheering stay:
Wilt care for me, and be my hold,
  When I am weak and old.

Thou'lt listen to my lengthened tale,
And pity me when I am frail—
But see, the sweepy spinning fly
Upon the window takes thine eye.
Go to thy little senseless play—
  Thou dost not heed my lay.

(1790)

511 *A Child to his Sick Grandfather*

GRAND-DAD, they say you're old and frail,
Your stockèd legs begin to fail:
Your knobbèd stick (that was my horse)
Can scarce support your bended corse;
While back to wall you lean so sad,
I'm vexed to see you, dad.

You used to smile and stroke my head,
And tell me how good children did;
But now, I wot not how it be,
You take me seldom on your knee;
Yet ne'ertheless I am right glad
To sit beside you, dad.

How lank and thin your beard hangs down!
Scant are the white hairs on your crown;
How wan and hollow are your cheeks!
Your brow is rough with crossing breaks;
But yet, for all his strength is fled,
I love my own old dad.

The housewives round their potions brew,
And gossips come to ask for you:
And for your weal each neighbour cares,
And good men kneel, and say their pray'rs:
And ev'rybody looks so sad,
When you are ailing, dad.

You will not die, and leave us then?
Rouse up and be our dad again.
When you are quiet and laid in bed,
We'll doff our shoes and softly tread:
And when you wake we'll aye be near,
To fill old dad his cheer.

When through the house you shift your stand,
I'll lead you kindly by the hand;
When dinner's set, I'll with you bide,
And aye be serving by your side;
And when the weary fire burns blue,
I'll sit and talk with you.

I have a tale both long and good,
About a partlet and her brood;
And cunning greedy fox that stole,
By dead of midnight, through a hole,
Which slyly to the hen-roost led—
  You love a story, dad?

And then I have a wond'rous tale
Of men all clad in coats of mail,
With glitt'ring swords—you nod, I think?
Your fixèd eyes begin to wink;
Down on your bosom sinks your head;
  You do not hear me, dad.

(1790)

512 *The Horse and his Rider*

BRACED in the sinewy vigour of thy breed,
In pride of gen'rous strength, thou stately steed,
Thy broad chest to the battle's front is given,
Thy mane fair floating to the winds of heaven.
Thy champing hoofs the flinty pebbles break;
Graceful the rising of thine archèd neck.
White-churning foam thy chafèd bits enlock;
And from thy nostril bursts the curling smoke.
Thy kindling eyeballs brave the glaring south,
And dreadful is the thunder of thy mouth;
Whilst low to earth thy curving haunches bend,
Thy sweepy tail involved in clouds of sand;
Erect in air thou wear'st thy front of pride,
And ring'st the plated harness on thy side.
But, lo! what creature, goodly to the sight,
Dares thus bestride thee, chafing in thy might,
Of portly stature and determined mien,
Whose dark eye dwells beneath a brow serene,
And forward looks unmoved to fields of death,
And, smiling, gently strokes thee in thy wrath,
Whose brandished falchion dreaded gleams afar?
It is a British soldier, armed for war!

(1790)

SAMUEL BISHOP

1731–1795

513 *Epigrams*

(i)

NEED from excess—excess from folly growing,
Keeps Christie's hammer daily, going, going!
Ill-omened prelude! whose dire knell brings on
Profusion's last sad dying speech—'Gone! gone!'

(ii)

''TWAS not so in *my* time,' surly Grumio exclaims,
When our fancies, and fashions, and follies he blames:
But your times, and our times, and all times, old Bluff!
Can show fancies, and fashions, and follies enough!
Your taste was the formal, as ours is the flimsy:
You made wisdom grimace; we make elegance whimsy.
'Tis all the same foppery, dressed different ways!
Yours was yesterday's nonsense; and ours is today's!

(Wr. *c.* 1790; pub. 1796)

JOHN AIKIN

1747–1822

514 *Picturesque; A Fragment*

NEW follies spring; and now we must be taught
To judge of prospects by an artist's rules,
And Picturesque's the word. Whatever scene,
Gay, rich, sublime, stupendous, wide or wild,
Disdains the bounds of canvas, nor supplies
Foreground and background, keeping, lights and shades
To aid the pencil's power, contracts the brow
And curls the nose of Taste's great arbiter,
Too learned far to feel a vulgar joy.
'That station shows too much—the boundless length

Of dazzling distance mars the near effect.
Yon village spire, embosomed in the trees,
Takes from the scene its savage character,
And makes it smack of man; and those sleek kine
And well-fed steeds might grace a country fair,
But tame their outlines, and a heavy mass
Of glaring light gleams from their polished sides.
How stiff that conic hill! Those chalky cliffs
Rush forward on the sight and harshly break
All harmony of keeping! 'tis as bad
As country parson's white-beplastered front!'
   Such the grave doctrines of the modern sage,
The Prospect-Critic, when, with half-shut eye
And hand-formed tube, he squints at Nature's works
And takes them piece by piece; with six-inch square
Metes out the vast horizon; culls, rejects,
Lights up, obscures and blots the blessed sun.
And is it thus the handmaid Art presumes
To rule her mistress? thus would she confine
The Maker's hand to suit the copyist's skill?
   In Nature all is fair—or, if ungraced
With flowing form and harmony of hues,
Yet by the force of some associate charm,
Some touch sublime or contrast's magic power,
It awes, expands, delights or melts the soul.
   I love to see the lonely mountain start
Bold from the plain, whose huge though shapeless bulk
Shrinks Egypt's pyramids to pigmy toys;
I love the piny forest, many a mile
Blackening th' horizon, though a dreary moor
Fill up the space between; I joy to stand
On the bare ridge's utmost verge, air-propped,
And with an eagle's ken the vale below,
With all its fields, groves, farms and winding rills,
At once drink in; still more my transport swells,
If sudden on my easy-turning eye
Bursts the wide ocean, though the dazzling blaze
Of noontide sun reflected from his waves
Confound all space in undistinguished light.
Celestial glory, hail! my ravished soul
Imbibes the bright effulgence, feels how weak
Art's feeble hand to imitate thy fires
And clothe her colours in thy radiant vest.
But O, that once my longing eyes might view
The sky-topped Alps their spiry pinnacles
Build in mid-air; or Norway's ragged cliffs

With fir befringed!—what though their forms grotesque,
With lines abrupt and perpendicular, pain
Those tender optics that demand repose
On beauty's waving line; yet rather far
I'd fill my fancy from those mighty stores
Of vast ideas, graving on my brain
The forms gigantic of those sons of earth,
Than own whatever Claude and Poussin drew.
  Meanwhile my eye not undelighted roams
O'er flower-embroidered meads, whose level length
The lessening alders, dimly-gliding sails,
And sprinkled groups of cattle, faintly mark.
For all that painting gives I would not change
The heart-expanding view, when Autumn's hand
Wide o'er the champaign pours a billowy sea
Of yellow corn, o'erspreading hill and dale,
While, from its isles of verdure scattered round,
Emerging hamlets lapped in plenty smile.
Nor does my sight disdain the rural box
Of ruddy brick or plaster, neat and snug,
With palisades before and walls behind,
And sheer-trimmed hedges for the garden's bound.
The lines, indeed, are stiff, and glaring tints
Refuse to blend, and not a tattered roof
Or mouldering stone affords one single touch
Of *picturesque*; but *happy man* dwells here,
With peace and competence and sweet repose,
And bliss domestic; these the mental eye
Suffice to charm, and all *it* sees is good.

(1791)

RICHARD POLWHELE
1760–1838

515 from *The Influence of Local Attachment*

[*A Visit to the Author's Paternal Seat*]

EACH object by a few short years how changed!
  The hall, where once we hailed the cheerful blaze;
The chairs in social order once arranged;
  Those mouldering panels where we used to gaze
  On the light shadework that in many a maze

Danced to the foliage of yon falling elm,
  While evening tinged its boughs with saffron rays;
Those portraits, where the golden-pictured helm,
The hauberk's mimic steel, dark webs and dust o'erwhelm.

And, as the parlour-hinges harshly grate,
  The torn prints flutter but the type of me,—
Where once so warm each crimson-gleaming seat,
  And once so rich appeared the soft settee;
  Where, the flowered carpet as I trod with glee,
The mirror would reflect my frolic smile,
  Where from yon screen, once wrought in filigree
By some old aunt with ill-requited toil,
I oft the spangles picked and looked askance the while.

There too, above the round-arched portal, hung
  The branching antlers of a forest-deer,
For whom with hounds and horn the deep dales rung.
  But, as enamoured of the wild-wood cheer,
  Full many a moon o'er valleys far and near
He ran, and seemed to scorn the murderous crew;
  Till, where the tops of yon oaks scarce appear,
The gunner bade his blood the copse imbrue—
Yet e'en that relic pale is vanished from the view!

Drear is the sun-clad wall, where erst at noon
  I basked beneath the yet unblushing fruit,
Oft as the gardener's skill was wont to prune
  From the rich nectarine each luxuriant shoot,
  Or net to every trained morella suit.
And lo! where light its twinkling florets played,
  The dark-green jasmine shrivelled to its root!
And the grass-walk, where sighs the poplar-shade,
Sinks deep at every step with leaves and moss o'erlaid.

And see, beyond the garden's northern bound,
  The ruined cottage to the blasts of heav'n
Unroofed, and crumbled to a naked mound!
  There, ere its walls by cruel time were riv'n,
  The rays of sweet domestic peace were giv'n
To bless the cot! The wicket, where it hung,
  Yet to and fro I view, in fancy, driv'n;
And swinging careless there, as erst I swung,
Again the good old hind attack with flippant tongue.

morella] morello, type of cherry

Alas! the chestnut on yon slaty steep
 Which the wild eddies of the west wind braved,
Displays no more its vesture shadowy-deep,
 Nor, late dismantled as the tempest raved,
 Waves the fair blossoms which it whilom waved!
And lo! its withered roots no longer gleam
 Through the clear riv'let that its fibres laved—
There where the pigeon-cote, that met the beam
Of morn, now prostrate lies amid the brawling stream.

Lorn is the landscape since the blissful prime,
 When on the daisy-darting sod I played,
Caught the quick radiance quiv'ring through the lime,
 Breathed the fresh odours of its evening shade,
 And on its bark the rude impression made—
E'en now, half-crusted o'er, the name appears!
 And, where my school-companions crossed the glade,
Lo! other sweet memorials, wakening tears,
Wear, like the joys they speak of, the pale cold damp of years!

(Wr. 1791; pub. 1798)

LAURENCE HYNES HALLORAN

1766–1831

516 *Animal Magnetism. The Pseudo-Philosopher Baffled or, The Biter Bit. A Comic Morning Adventure*

TH' INVITED guests in silent order sat,
 The destined victim in the midst was seen;
Hard by, the mystic Doctor grave as fate,
 While scarce a breath disturbed the solemn scene,
Save now and then the rattling china's sound,
Or buttered toast by greasy grinders ground.

Here sat a Quaker, young, demure and fair,
 A Jew, a pedagogue, a parson there;
A justice (half-ashamed) was placed behind,
 'With fair round belly with fat capon lined';
Here sat an adept with importance big,
And there a doctor with full-bottomed wig.

Curiosity in every part was seen,
With outstretched neck, wild eye and restless mien,
While Expectation, light as wind
On tiptoe nimbly tripped behind.
The fragments were removed, the breakfast o'er,
And Common Sense retiring closed the door.

And now the solemn farce began.
Slow from his seat arose the wonder-working man;
And thrice three steps, mysterious number, took;
  And thrice viewed his devoted fingers' ends;
And thrice the honours of his head he shook,
  And downward thrice his sable brows he bends.

Now he approached the 'subject to be tested'
(Each wond'ring wight with apprehension sweated);
The 'dauntless fair' alone unmoved appeared,
  And boldly dared the awful test;
And now his dexter hand the Doctor reared,
  Now darts it down like lightning at her breast.

And now the left alternate rises,
  And now it falls; but falls alas! in vain.
  Now with impatient haste he strives again:
In vain! not yet appears the 'stubborn crisis'.

  At length enraged, his basilisk-like eyes
He rivets fast upon her orbs of sight:
  With greater vehemence he tries,
And pegs her stomach with augmented might.
Th' intrenching whalebone to his strokes resounds,
And oft th' involuntary 'ah!' rebounds.

  Th' abashed assistants haste to his relief,
And gnash their teeth and wave their hands in air;
  But still in vain: the disappointed chief
With greater force assails th' impenetrable fair.
Till tired at length, her eyes she seemed to close,
And sunk back in her chair; and dozed, or feigned to doze.

  Who but the Doctor now exults?
Th' unbelieving lady conquered by his fluid.
  O'er his fall'n foe th' arch-hypocrite insults:
'Did I not tell you, friends, that I would do it?
  Her want of faith shall not unpunished go,
Two hours a victim to my power she lies!'
  And now he views more near his artful foe,
His hand soft-wandering o'er her mouth and eyes.

When oh! disgraceful to relate—
Would I could veil the dismal thing, or
Conceal the fatal truth beneath—
While with successful pride elate,
She snapped the Doctor's too officious finger,
And held it fast between her teeth.

Loud roared the sufferer. At his sudden roar
The audience turned by instinct towards the door,
And, terrified, downstairs together tumbled.
Th' impostor and his patient left alone,
She loosed his finger. With an hideous groan
He from her presence sneaked, completely humbled!

(1791)

JOHN TAYLOR

1750–1826

517 *The Trumpet of Liberty*

THE trumpet of Liberty sounds through the world,
And the universe starts at the sound;
Her standard Philosophy's hand has unfurled,
And the nations are thronging around.
Chorus.—Fall, tyrants, fall! fall! fall!
These are the days of liberty!
Fall, tyrants, fall!

How noble the ardour that seizes the soul!
How it bursts from the yoke and the chain!
What power can the fervour of Freedom control,
Or its terrible vengeance restrain?
Fall tyrants, fall!

Proud castles of despotism, dungeons and cells,
The tempest shall sweep you away;
From the east to the west the dread hurricane swells,
And the tyrants are chilled with dismay.
Fall, tyrants, fall!

The slave on whose neck the proud despot has trod
  Now feels that himself is a man,
While the lordly usurper who ruled with a nod
  Hides his head 'midst his servile divan.
    Fall, tyrants, fall!

Poor vassals who crawl by the Vistula's stream,
  Hear! hear the glad call, and obey!
Rise, nations who worship the sun's sacred beam,
  And drive your Pizarros away.
    Fall, tyrants, fall!

The cruel dominion of priestcraft is o'er,
  Its thunders, its faggots and chains!
Mankind will endure the vile bondage no more,
  While religion our freedom maintains.
    Fall, tyrants, fall!

Shall Britons the chorus of liberty hear
  With a cold and insensible mind?
No,—the triumphs of freedom each Briton shall share,
  And contend for the rights of mankind.
    Fall, tyrants, fall! etc.

(1791)

JOHN LEARMONT

fl. 1791

518 from *An Address to the Plebeians*

POOR crawlin' bodies, sair neglectit,
Trampled on an' disrespeckit,
Seem born for greater fock to geck at,
    To toil an' slave,
An' rest o' body hae nae feck o't
    Till i' the grave.

518 fock] folk   geck] scoff   feck] benefit

Your raggit claies an' ghastly features
Mak ye be lookit on by betters
As some outlandish half'lin creatures
Nae o' God's mak;
An' born to thole their buffs an' blatters
Upo' your back.

Though Liberty may shaw her face
An' a' ye're betters roun' embrace,
Ye still maun bend wi' hum'le face
Beneath her wand;
An' scarcely get an hour's solace
In ony land.

There maun subordination be;
But O! it maks ane wae to see
The grit fock jamph an' jeer at ye,
Wha bake their bread;
An' scarce'll lat ye taste their brie
Whan ye're i' need.

They gang by ye wi' sic a huff,
An' pridfu' caper, snirt an' snuff,
As gif Death ne'er meant them a cuff
Upo' the head,
To let them ken they're the same stuff
O' which ye're made.

Ye're sair the wyte, ye stupit bodies!
Ye have nae mair sense i' your nodies
Than serves to work amang the clodies,
An' do na see
Man's dignity, whilk his ain God has
Him buskit wi'.

Ye still micht delve i' kailyards green,
Or maw down grass upo' the fen,
Yet mak your reason shaw ye men
Ful bauld an' slee;
An' lat them see ye brawlie ken
Man's dignity. . . .

claies] clothes half'lin] halfling, immature thole] bear buffs] beating blatters] abuse jamph] mock brie] whisky snirt an' snuff] snigger and sniff sair the wyte] sorely to blame buskit] dressed kailyards] kitchen-gardens slee] wise brawlie] admirably

A king cries war! but for what end
Ye never speer, but to it stend,
An' at the cannon's mou' ye bend
    I' mony a thrave,
Syne laurels dipped wi' bluid do send
    Ye to the grave.

Yet ye're the sceptre o' the land,
Wha put kings, lairds, unto a stand;
Gif ye but gather on the strand
    Unto a head,
Ye'll either hae yeu're boon i' hand,
    Or ding them dead.

An' some o' you are nae that ill,
An' hae enough o' ruth at will
For ony ane wham Fortune's wheel
    Has crushed wi' wae;
An' will gie pity, or him fill
    Wi' what ye hae.

Arouse ye up then ane an' a',
An' busk yoursels wi' wisdom braw;
An' though ye wade owr hills o' snaw,
    Or plew the field,
Mak ay true honesty your law
    An' safest shield.

(1791)

ANONYMOUS

519 *The Volunteer*

Dulce est pro patria mori

WHEN fivepence a solid meal cannot supply
To a jolly young man five feet ten inches high,
Who has jogged with his knapsack twelve leagues through the rain,
While his wench and three brats had each ankle to strain,
The poor volunteer to the halberts is tied,
For stealing two chick-eggs and getting them fried:

518 speer] ask   thrave] crowd   ding] beat

What carters and jockeys should suffer he feels,
And the blood gushes down from his nape to his heels.
The Commander-in-Chief, who is almost fifteen,
And a tailor's apprentice by right should have been,
Now struts round the circle, then turns on his heel
To belabour the drummers 'who don't make him feel'—
Swears England could ne'er have produced such a rogue,
And discerns in his howling the true Irish brogue.
The surgeon, whose sympathy swells in each vein,
When a swoon interrupts the convulsions of pain,
Makes them flog till he start to his senses again.
Nay, doctor and drum for attendance are paid,
And his pockets are fleeced while his shoulders are flayed.
He's packed in a transport on every state quarrel,
More tightly than biscuit and beef in a barrel;
In torrents each summer-shower streams through his tent,
In barracks more dismal December is spent;
In damp rotten bedding the moment he's laid,
To the rage of whole armies his rear is betrayed;
In health he infallibly more than half-starves,
In a fever he's used as a rascal deserves.
His Chloe, by hunger compelled to sad pranks,
Is chased as a swindler in form through the ranks;
His children, when some baggage-cart is o'erthrown,
In a ditch, like blind puppies, are suffered to drown.
And when for his King thirty years he has toiled,
In Canada frost-bit, in Africa broiled;
Has been thrice a week handcuffed for drinking his pay,
Got nine thousand lashes for running away;
Has oft like a hero been wounded *before*,
And cleared with a cudgel each concubine's score;
At last, with the Dons point to point he engages,
For more than one-fourth of a scavenger's wages;
Some merciful volley then shatters a leg,
And his crutches procure him permission to beg.

(1791)

Dons] Spaniards

WILLIAM SHEPHERD

1768–1847

520 *Ode on Lord Macartney's Embassy to China*

SWIFT shot the curlew 'thwart the rising blast,
As eve's dun shades enwrapped the billowy main;
Hoarse broke the waves against the sandy waste,
And dim and cheerless swept the drizzling rain:
When bending o'er the briny spray
Stood thy genius, old Cathay,
Her vestments floating on the gale;
With angry glare her eyeballs roll,
Horror shakes her inmost soul,
As thus along the strand swells her portentous wail:

'Athirst for prey, what ruffian band
Dares approach this happy land?
Glimmering through the glooms of eve,
What canvas flutters o'er the wave?
Plunging through the swelling tide,
What prows the whit'ning brine divide?
'Tis Albion's bloody cross that flouts the air,
'Tis Albion's sons that skirt this peaceful shore;
Her cross, oppression's badge, the sign of war;
Her sons that range the world, and peace is seen no more.

'Insatiate spoilers! that, with treach'rous smiles,
In wreaths of olive hide the murderous sword:
Ill fare the tribes, unconscious of your wiles,
Whose honest candour trusts your plighted word.
Hence! ye harbingers of woe—
Too well your deeds of blood I know:
For mid the thickening gloom of night
Oft, as I speed my watchful flight,
A monitory voice I hear—
Keen Sorrow's thrilling cry awakes my list'ning ear.

'A cry resounds from Ganges' flood;
There Oppression's giant brood
Wide the scythe of ruin sweep,
And desolated districts weep.
Terror waves the scourge on high,
Patient Misery heaves the sigh;

Lo! meagre Famine drains the vital springs,
   And points from far where yawns the darksome grave;
Her gifts in vain profusive Plenty flings;
   Stern Avarice guards the store, nor owns the wish to save.

'From Niger's banks resounds the shriek of woe.
   There, inly pining, mourns the hapless slave;
Fraud proudly braves the light with shameless brow,
   And floating charnels plough the restless wave.
      Behold, in desolate array,
      The captives wind their silent way:
      Amid the ranks does Pity find
      A pair by fond affection joined?
      Fell Rapine, reckless of their pain,
      Blasts Misery's final hope—denies a common chain.
      'Hear, O my sons, the warning cry,
      And while you breathe the pitying sigh,
      Deep on Memory's tablet trace
      These triumphs of Britannia's race.
      From age to age, from sire to son,
      Let the eternal record run;
And when, with hollow hearts and honeyed tongues,
   These slaves of gold advance their blood-stained hand,
Shrink from the touch—Remember India's wrongs—
   Remember Afric's woes—and save your destined land.'

(Wr. 1792?; pub. 1797)

JOSEPH MATHER

1737–1804

521 *The File-Hewer's Lamentation*

ORDAINED I was a beggar,
And have no cause to swagger;
It pierces like a dagger,
   To think I'm thus forlorn.
My trade or occupation
Was ground for lamentation,
Which makes me curse my station,
   And wish I'd ne'er been born.

Of slaving I am weary,
From June to January;
To nature it's contrary,
   This, I presume, is fact.
Although, without a stammer,
Our Nell exclaims I clam her,
I've wield my six-pound hammer
   Till I am grown round-backed.

I'm debtor to a many,
But cannot pay one penny;
Sure I've worse luck than any,
   My sticks are marked for sale.
My creditors may sue me,
And curse the day they knew me;
The bailiffs may pursue me,
   And lock me up in jail.

As negroes in Virginia,
In Maryland or Guinea,
Like them I must continue
   To be both bought and sold.
While negro-ships are filling
I ne'er can save one shilling,
And must, which is more killing,
   A pauper die when old.

My troubles never ceased,
While Nell's bairn-time increased;
While hundreds I've rehearsed,
   Ten thousand more remain;
My income for me, Nelly,
Bob, Tom, Poll, Bet and Sally,
Could hardly fill each belly,
   Should we eat salt and grains.

At every week's conclusion
New wants bring fresh confusion,
It is but mere delusion
   To hope for better days;
While knaves with power invested,
Until by death arrested,
Oppress us unmolested
   By their infernal ways.

clam] starve

An hanging day is wanted;
Was it by justice granted,
Poor men distressed and daunted
Would then have cause to sing:
To see in active motion
Rich knaves in full proportion,
For their unjust extortion
And vile offences, swing.

(1792?)

522 *God Save Great Thomas Paine*

GOD save great Thomas Paine,
His 'Rights of Man' explain
To every soul.
He makes the blind to see
What dupes and slaves they be,
And points out liberty,
From pole to pole.

Thousands cry 'Church and King'
That well deserve to swing,
All must allow:
Birmingham blush for shame,
Manchester do the same,
Infamous is your name,
Patriots vow.

Pull proud oppressors down,
Knock off each tyrant's crown,
And break his sword;
Down aristocracy,
Set up democracy,
And from hyprocrisy
Save us good Lord.

Why should despotic pride
Usurp on every side?
Let us be free:
Grant Freedom's arms success,
And all her efforts bless,
Plant through the universe
Liberty's Tree.

Facts are seditious things
When they touch courts and kings,
Armies are raised,
Barracks and bastilles built,
Innocence charged with guilt,
Blood most unjustly spilt,
Gods stand amazed.

Despots may howl and yell,
Though they're in league with hell
They'll not reign long;
Satan may lead the van,
And do the worst he can,
Paine and his 'Rights of Man'
Shall be my song.

(1792?)

RICHARD GRAVES

1715–1804

523 *Maternal Despotism; or, The Rights of Infants*[1]

UNHAND me nurse! thou saucy quean!
What does this female tyrant mean?
Thus, head and foot, in swathes to bind,
'Spite of the 'Rights of human kind';
And lay me stretched upon my back
(Like a poor culprit on the rack);
An infant, like thyself born free,
And independent, slut! on thee.
Have I not right to kick and sprawl,
To laugh or cry, to squeak or squall!
Has ever, by my act and deed,
Thy *right* to rule me been decreed?
How dar'st thou, despot! then control
Th' exertions of a free-born soul?
Though now an infant, when I can,
I'll rise and seize 'The Rights of Man';

[1] In allusion to Paine's *Rights of Man*: and Mrs Wollstonecraft's *Rights of Woman*.

Nor make my haughty nurse alone,
But monarchs tremble, on their throne;
And boys and kings thenceforth you'll see
Enjoy complete *Equality*.

(Wr. 1792?; pub. 1801)

EDWARD RUSHTON

1756–1814

524 *Human Debasement. A Fragment*

In early days
If kings were made by men, and that they were
The light of Nature clearly shows,
How comes it then that earth is filled with slaves?
How comes it then that man, this reasoning thing,
This being with such faculties endowed,
This being formed to trace the great First Cause
Through many a wond'rous path,—how comes it then
That he, in every clime, should cringe, should crouch,
Should bend th' imploring eye and trembling knee
To mere self-raised oppressors? Heav'ns! to think
That not a tithe of all the sons of men
E'er kissed thy sacred cup, O Liberty!
To find, where'er imagination roves,
Millions on millions prostrate in the dust,
Whilst o'er their necks, with proud contemptuous mien,
Kings, emperors, sultans, sophies, what you will,
With all their pampered minions, sorely press,
Grinding God's creatures to the very bone.
Yet man submits to all! He tamely licks
The foot upraised to trample on his rights:
He shakes his chains, and in their horrid clank
Finds melody; else why not throw 'em off?
Seven hundred millions of the human kind
Are held in base subjection, and by whom?
Why, strange to tell, and what futurity,
As children at the tales of witch or spirit,
Will bless themselves to hear, by a small troop
Of weak capricious despots, fiends accursed,
Who drench the earth with tides of human gore

And call the havoc glory! Britons, yes!
Seven hundred millions of your fellow men,
All formed like you the blessing to enjoy,
Now drag the servile chain. Oh fie upon't!
'Twere better far within the clay-cold cell
To waste away, than be at such a price!
Poor whip-galled slaves! Oh! 'tis debasement all!
'Tis filthy cowardice, and shows that man
Merits too oft, by his degenerate deeds,
The yoke which bends him down. Power's limpid stream
Must have its source within a people's heart:
What flows not thence is turbid tyranny.
Rank are the despots' weeds which now o'er-run
This ample world, and choke each goodly growth;
But that supine loud vaunting thing, called man,
Might soon eradicate so foul a pest,
Would he exert those powers which God has given
To be the means of good; and what more good,
More rational, nay, more approaching heav'n,
Than the strong joys which flow from Freedom's fount?
Yon radiant orb, vast emblem of the Pow'r
Who formed him, beams alike on all mankind;
The air which, like a mantle, girts the world
Is too a common good; and even so,
With amplest bounty, Liberty is given
To man, whate'er his tint, swart, brown, or fair;
Whate'er his clime, hot, cold, or temperate;
Whate'er his mode of faith, whate'er his state,
Or rich, or poor, great Nature cries 'Be free'.
How comes it then that man neglects the call?
Nay, like the callous felon, chuckles loud
Amidst corroding chains? Can that Great Cause
Who made man free, both mind and body free,
And gave him reason as a sentinel
To guard the glorious gift, can he be pleased
To see his rich donation cast away,
Or passed with inattention, as not worth
Th' acceptance of his creatures? No, my friends:
Whate'er God gives he gives to be enjoyed,
But not abused; and the mean wretch, who 'neath
A tyrant's feet this precious jewel throws,
Spurns the vast Power who placed it in his hands.
How comes it then that minds are thus abased?
That man, though Nature loudly calls 'Be free,'
Has closed his ears against her, and become
A mean, a grov'lling wretch! Why thus it is,

O Superstition! thou who point'st to man
And call'st the fragile piece a demi-god;
Yes, thou who wand'rest o'er the world, arrayed
In pure Religion's mantle; thou whose breath
Conveys those potent opiates to the brain
Which bring on reason's sleep; O! dark-browed fiend,
All, all these works are thine!

(1793)

JOHN PARRISH

fl. 1793

525 *The Democratic Barber; or, Country Gentleman's Surprise*

GOOD Gad! who's this? What's this, my son?
What a strange figure, 'faith—of fun!
I see the folks can make in town
The clown a fop—the fop a clown;
The last time you to London went,
Remember then you home was sent
With tail which reached all down your back!
And now you've nothing left—but *neck*.
'Ah! wonder not, sir, for, egad,
The London people all are mad;
There rages now a sad disorder
(Amongst the low plebeian order),
A strange chimera of the brain,
Occasioned by the works of Paine;
A disappointed man—quite crazy,
Best pleased when others are uneasy—
And as I wished for information
About this strange infatuation,
I went into a barber's near
The inn—and bade him cut my hair.
He placed a chair—I sat me down—
Then asked what news they had in town.
With that he came direct before me,
As if prepared to tell a story—
And thus began:
'"I trust you've read that glorious plan
That's wrote by Paine—*The Rights of Man*—

By which we're shown that crowns and kings
Are paltry baubles—useless things—
How like to wretched slaves we're loaded,
And how we're with oppression goaded.
Just for a moment cast your eyes
Upon our neighbours great and wise;
Only bestow one single glance
On the wise policy—of France.
Oh! glorious deed—at one bold stroke
They their despotic fetters broke—
At once threw off the tyrant's yoke;
Let us by them example take—
Like them our slavish fetters break—
Blot out the test, cry toleration,
Destroy each title in the nation;
Distinction's pride—and pride's the devil;
A man's a man—and we'll be level.
E'en now they feel their power shaken,
'Tis clearly proved by proclamation;
We know a fabric built on sand
Against a storm can never stand,
And soon we'll put in execution
Our glorious aim—a revolution.
Our great presiders seem quite fractious,
Call us base—low—seditious—factious;
Yet we'll convince them tyrant laws
Shall not pervert our glorious cause;
For soon we will complete our wishes,
Delightful thought—the loaves and fishes."
'His maddened looks did so alarm me,
I really feared the fool might harm me;
He stared, and looked like any fury.
"Come, come," said I, "I'm in a hurry;
Dismiss me, friend."—No more he spoke,
But stepped behind—and at one stroke
(Even before I was aware)
[He] left me as you see me—*bare*.
I felt, jumped up—I stamped and swore—
And like a madman raved and tore.
He sternly cried—"Why this damned passion?
You're just in democratic fashion;
I thought you one of us, and hearty
In the design of our new party.
Our zealous leaders did adopt
The law to have our party *cropped*.
To show our zeal this rule was made,

And I'm resolved, with loss of trade
(Which is my all), to serve the cause,
And starving I'll support their laws.
And if you'd wish our cut to see,"
He, turning, cried—"here—look at me."
'"Scoundrel!" said I, for, on my soul,
He'd scarce a hair to hide his poll.
I strove to strike—he from me flew—
And squared just like the fighting Jew.
'"Sirrah!" said he, "if you dare speak
That word again—I break your cheek.
Scoundrel! What do you mean by that?
Know, sir—I am a Demo-crat;
And I'll convince you that I can,
And will, support *the Rights of Man*."
'My anger now to madness grown,
I raised my arm and knocked him down;
Then seized his scissors (large as shears)
And in my passion lopped his ears.
"There go", said I, "to tutor Paine,
To him who thus inflamed thy brain,
And bid him tack them on again."'
Well done, my boy—'twas e'er thy father's rule
To mark with shame th' insulting knave or fool;
Such lesser pains may rising vice prevent,
When fear of death may fail of its intent.
But yet, methinks, 'twas rather too severe:
It were enough t' have taken either ear;
But as it seems to me an act of fame,
Unto the world I will the deed proclaim.

(1793)

THOMAS COLE

1727?–1796

526 from *The Life of Hubert*, Book I

[*Memories of a Dorset childhood in the 1730s*]

(i)

THE blue expanse of hyacinthine bloom,
Midst whose sweet pendant bells, on crowding stalks,
The wild anemone can scarce find room

To rear in white array its mingled flow'rs,
Attracts our gaze. More still are we amused
To see the frequent nimble rabbit scud
Across our path; and mark the mingled signs
Of caution and of courage in the hare,
Who, popping from the thicket just before us,
Halts as we halt;—and stroking first her face
With dewy paws, upraised on hinder legs
Awhile she stands, one list'ning ear erect,
As singly best to catch the slightest sound.
Then dropping prone, she stamps, with doubtful heels,
Repeatedly and loud against the ground:
And as of perfect safety hence assured,
Calmly begins to crop the way-side grass.
But the least crackling from dry brittle sprigs,
That lightly strew the ground where'er we tread,
Her nibbling checks, and scares her quick from sight.
We linger still to list the various sounds,
Which, wakened by the love-inspiring warmth
Of ether's genial breath, diffusive spread
Through ev'ry quarter of the breeding woods.
And, hark! we hear the slow-repeated note
Of cuckoo, never failing to recall
Delightful thoughts, since first, on May-day eve,
Wafted by vernal breeze, it caught our ear;
And made us loiter long at ev'ry stile
That crossed our meadow pathway; whilst around,
In freshest bloom and youthful verdure clad,
All nature smiled. And now, from diff'rent points,
Ring out at once, of loud magpie and jay
The chatt'ring courtship, and more clam'rous love
Of woodpecker, that knocks with hamm'ring bill
The timber tree; detecting, by the sound,
Where latent grubs their caverned passage eat.
In search of these on sharp tenacious claws,
Suspended sure as fly that rambles light
O'er casement pane, he nimbly roves around
The smooth-barked glossy trunk of spreading beech.
Nor heedless do we hear the crowing voice
Of mated pheasant; the protracted moan,
From ivy-mantled lodge with berries fraught,
Of wild wood-pigeon, faithful as the tame;
And tender cooings of the turtle dove,
Emblem of all that's sacred, pure and true.

(ii)

The time allowed for sleep at length elapsed,
We, quite refreshed, awake at usual hour,
Greeted with usual sounds. The swallow's wing
In chimney tunnel flutt'ring up and down,
And frequent twitt'rings sweet, as bit by bit
She plasters busily, with trowel bill,
The rough-cast layers of her mud-wall cell.
The close-grouped pigeons on the sunny tiles,
Scrambling in languid luxury to bask,
Or roving to and fro on flapping plumes,
In restless ardour to complete their loves;
Whilst, aided by our fancy's eye, we see
Each strutting Tom, with noddling head erect,
Inflated crop, and glossy neck that darts,
At ev'ry turn, a change of rainbow dyes,
Oft as we hear him cooing to his mate.
The early mower of the dewy lawn,
With sandy stone of grating texture rough,
Whetting his scythe in shrill alternate twangs.
The lulling stroke, at true-timed intervals,
Of thresher's flail, now sounding dead on straw,
And now sharp echoed from elastic floor
Of planchèd barn: a tell-tale task, most sure,
If long remitted, to his master's ear
The idle day-work lab'rer to betray.
The rumbling roll of heavy waggon-wheels
O'er the rough pitching of the flinty yard;
With jingling bells from the head-tossing team,
And frequent crack resounding from the lash
Of carter's whip. Just risen from her nest,
The joyous cackling hen, from burden free
Of fresh-delivered egg. The bellowing cow
For calf pent up; bemoaning, in return,
Her cruel lot, at once of freedom robbed
And nat'ral bev'rage of a mother's milk.
The jostling herd of greedy grunting sows
And eager squeaking pigs, when dairy-maid,
Her cheese-curd pressed, from loaded bucket pours
A copious tide of whey into their trough;
To their impure, voracious appetites
Most sav'ry still, though snouts with mud begrimed
And dung-clad feet plunge in at once to taint,

planchèd] made of planks

With compound filth, the sweetness of their mess.
The turkey-cock's loud hoggle-goggling throat,
When midst his mates he rears his fan-tail plumes,
Drops low his archèd wings in stately sweep,
To flirt their pinion quills against the ground.
The hissings fierce, the hoarse defying screams
Of gander, trusting in his potent wing,
When hogs, or dogs, or men approach too near
His fav'rite goose, and yellow gosling train:
And then the earnest gabbling, twattling bills
Of old and young close met, with out-stretched necks,
To greet each other on their safe escape.
At greater distance, though not far remote,
The softened ceaseless lapse of rough cascade
O'er the shut sluices of the deep canal,
Well stored with carp and tench: while near its banks,
From nests close-clust'ring on the topmost boughs
Of ancient grove, or scattered wide on wing,
The long-established colony of rooks
Their num'rous, ceaseless, varied cawings blend.

(1795)

JAMES WOODHOUSE

1735–1820

527 from *The Life and Lucubrations of Crispinus Scriblerus*

(i)

[*Birmingham and Wolverhampton*]

In parts, through prospects scattered far and near,
Pale-glowing gleams and flickering flames appear,
Like new volcanoes mid deep darkness nursed,
From cooking coals in ruddy brilliance burst;
While smoky curls in thickening columns rise,
Obscure the landscapes and involve the skies.
Still, as the sanguine blaze, beneath, ascends,
And deepening blushes with heav'n's vapours blends,
Diffusing all around red, lurid light,
And paint in part the negro-cheeks of Night,

526 twattling] chattering

Deep, sullen sounds through all the region roll,
Shocking with groans and sighs each shuddering soul!
  Here clanking engines vomit scalding streams,
And belch vast volumes of attendant steams—
There thundering forges, with pulsations loud
Alternate striking, pierce the pendant cloud;
While to these distant hills, respiring slow,
Furnaces' iron lungs loud-breathing blow,
Breaking abrupt on Superstition's ear,
And shrink the shuddering frame with shivering fear:
Obtruding on the heart, each heaving breath,
Some vengeful fiend, grim delegate of Death!

(ii)

[*The Tribulations of an Uneducated Poet in the 1760s*]

  'Twas wond'rous, then, a bardling should be found
To twang the lyre on aught but classic ground—
Who dared presume to print poetic page
In such a lettered, such enlightened, age,
Except some critical, some courtly, cook
Formed bill of fare, or dished the dainty book.
Some read with rapture and some drawled with doubt:
'Twas long since Duck had threshed his harvest out—
And since his day no rustic had been seen
Who sung so deftly on the daisied green!
  'Twas then supposed no clown could thrum a verse
So soft, smooth, simple, solid, strong and terse,
Fit for sheer fools in male or female shape—
Much less learned critic's keen remarks to 'scape.
None could bind couplets, stanzas twist, and bend
Figures and tropes at tongue's and finger's end,
But those that folios learned would frequent thumb,
Whose titles strike rude English readers dumb.
None without Latin stilts could stalk sublime
In bold blank verse—or more elaborate rhyme.
None chaunt choice strains but Horace' *Art* must prune,
Confined by modern scale to time and tune;
Or clearly comprehend rhyme's perfect scope
By keen Roscommon or mellifluous Pope—
None gain Parnassus' height with poet's gait,
But Virgil construe and could well translate;
Or Pegasus with whip and rowels ride,
Except old Homer's epics poised each side—

rowels] part of a spur

Ne'er sit secure and prance in rapid ode,
Till often trained in rough Pindaric road;
Nor Bacchanalian song or sonnet boast,
Unless Anacreon learn to sing and toast—
In amorous lays ne'er love's clear language claim,
Till fired with Sappho's fond consuming flame;
Nor in her slippery sandals learn to dance,
Till taught her stagg'ring step and glowing glance. . . .
  When on dull wild such prodigy appears,
Like comets once within long course of years—
Strange! to behold such versifying clown,
Remote from every city, court and town!
A rude, unlettered and unburnished boor,
With court-distinctions at his cottage door!
To see a peer's precursor with dispatch
Ride ambling up and lug his leathern latch!
Note learned lords, in coroneted coach,
His humble hut with complaisance approach,
His lowly lays and virtuous views commend,
And each profess to prove a constant friend—
While numbers more, of different rank and name,
Some led by fancy, some allured by fame,
Some smit by sympathetic pity, some
By bruit of Daphne's beauty, curious come—
Some through mere wanton whim, some chance, some
  choice,
Some to give guineas, some their sage advice,
For specie is expensive, counsel cheap;
Both wise men wish—but neither blockheads keep! . . .
  As tutored bears are led from place to place,
Displaying biped gait and burlesque grace,
Their action clumsy and their shape uncouth,
While grunting bagpipe greets the gaping youth,
And, with most solemn phiz and upright air,
Make witlings titter, whilst the ignorant stare—
As dancing dogs make oafs and children swarm,
Dress, mien, demeanour all in human form—
As monkeys, reared erect on paws or breech,
Well mimic man in all but laugh and speech—
Or as from street to street queer camel's shown,
From other beasts by pipe and tabor known,
Though seldom eye perceives a bungling brute
Whose make and motion less with music suit;
So was he sent the twofold city through,

specie] coinage

For cits, like swains, are pleased with something new,
That each subscriber's eyes might freely range
O'er clown so clever! spectacle so strange!

(Wr. 1795?–1800?; pub. 1896)

JAMES KENNEDY

fl. 1795

528 from *The Exile's Reveries*

The following verses were composed in a melancholy mood, while the hue and cry was raised against the author, his person described in the newspapers, and a reward offered for his apprehension.

June, 1794

TO THE READER

Chased from my calling to this hackneyed trade,
By persecution a poor poet made—
Yet favour court not—scribble not for fame;
To blast oppressors is my only aim.
With pain I started from a private life;
In sorrow left my children and my wife!
But though fair Freedom's foes have turned me out,
At every resting-place I'll wheel about,
And charge the villains!—

PENSIVE, while I stray the shore,
  Trace the wood or climb the glen,
Nature's volume turning o'er,
  Shunning sanguinary men;

Striving to beguile my care,
  Soothe my grief, improve my time,
And disarm the fiend Despair;
  Let me weave a web of rhyme.

Random feelings of the heart,
  Ravings of a lone exile,
Stranger to the rules of art,
  Let me robe in homely style.

Sweet the birds around me sing,
  Fair the flow'rs around me blow;
Conscience wears no guilty sting—
  Why, then, droop, the child of woe?

Here no rotten-hearted spy,
  Spider-like, the snare extends;
Though on grassy couch I lie,
  I am guarded by my friends.

Wand'ring tribes betray me not;
  Even gypsies laugh at kings:
While the tenants of the cot
  Deem them costly, useless things!

Thus they reason—'Do the bees
  Lazy glutton drones expel?
And are we less wise than these
  Tiny guardians of the cell?

'Do we toil while others reap?
  Do we starve while others feast?
Are we sold and shorn like sheep
  By the despot and the priest?

'Are we born for them alone?
  If by Right Divine they rule,
Yonder idiot on a throne
  Reigns by Right Divine a fool.

'Masters of the puppet-show,
  Long they've made us dance at will;
Should we down the curtain throw,
  Farewell to their magic skill.

'Have the jugglers nerves more strong?
  Are their numbers more than ours?
Nay, they could not triumph long,
  If deprived of borrowed pow'rs.

'Should the *sansculottes* come here,
  We may gain, but cannot lose;
Freedom's friends we do not fear;
  Tyrants only are our foes.'

While I wander here unseen,
  Fancy, with her magic wand,
Conjures up the direful scene
  Passing in a sister land.

sansculottes] French revolutionaries

Gallia starts to mental view
  (Ah! her laurels reek with blood)
Trampling on a reptile crew,
  Blasters of the public good.

Truth and Reason, robed in charms,
  Cheering like the morn, advance;
Freedom's trumpet sounds to arms!
  Slav'ry shrinks abashed from France.

Quaking, see the German Lords,
  Scourges of the human race,
Pour on Gaul their savage hordes!
  Ruin marks the backward chase.

Vaunted Mistress of the Deep!
  Freedom—Liberty—thy boast;
Is thy Genius fast asleep?
  Is thy ancient spirit lost?

Swelling with infuriate rage,
  Hast thou joined the mad crusade?
What could tempt thee war to wage?
  Were thy reptiles, too, afraid?

Yes! with guilt thy scourges stung,
  Seem to court a sim'lar fate;
Loud the false alarm is rung,
  Crimps and spies pervade the state.

Justice flies the judge's seat;
  Innocence no shield affords;
Should we dare our wrongs repeat,
  Truth is beaten down with swords.

Commerce droops and trade declines,
  Mis'ry howls along the plain;
Vice wild riots, Virtue pines;
  Patriots drag the felon's chain.

(1795)

Crimps] agents for procuring soldiers and sailors

GEORGE GALLOWAY

b. 1755

529 *To the Memory of Gavin Wilson (Boot, Leg and Arm Maker)*

Auld Reikie, Jan. 21. 1794

THANK heav'n! I'm safely landed frae Ostend,
My broken ribs and shattered arms to mend
By famous Wilson in the Canongate;
These wings of my poor trunk he'll reinstate.
Besides for him ambassador I'm sent,
To post direct to Tournay or to Ghent
Wi' twa three thousand o' his leather skulls,
Legs, thighs an' arms, to equip our battered hulls;
Toes, fingers, noses he must bring in bushels
T' adorn our wounded swads who pine in Brussels.
This news will raise his honest heart wi' joy,
When there for night and day he'll get employ.
But first I'll ca' on Johnny Block. See there!
Speak o' the de'il, gude troth he'll soon appear.
How does my auld acquaintance Johnny Block?
'Just like yoursel', a fair forfoughten cock;
For I've been pressed away and stood below,
Drubbing the French wi' famed Sir Edward Pellew.
But O! ye see I've got an unco fleg,
My thigh is broke and lopped off is my leg;
And now alas! I canna get remede,
For famous Wilson's numbered with the dead.'[1]
Dead! say ye, John? Support me, or I'll faint:
The best o' men to mortals ever lent
By gracious heav'n!—Britannia, hang your head,
Since our far-famed man-mender's numbered wi' the dead.
Mourn wi' us, soldiers, sailors and commanders,
And a' the pride o' Germany and Flanders;
For doctors, surgeons, put them a' together,
They cu'dna' match our mighty God of Leather.
Lord help us, Johnny! this war how it stings;

[1] He died November 1790

swads] soldiers   forfoughten] worn out with fighting   cock] fellow   unco fleg] severe blow

Half-butchered thus, we cripple, lacking wings.
But hush, we'll house in Embro' time to pass,
Humming his elegy out o'er a flowing glass.

(1795)

JOSEPH FAWCETT

1758?–1804

530 from *The Art of War*

[*The Feast of Blood*]

WHAT mean these showy and these sounding signs
Of general joy, my senses that salute?
That bid my brow be smooth, and bosom bound,
And all my heart be holiday?—What means
The cannon's roar that rends the shattered sky?
The stunning peal the merry steeples pour?
At dead of night, along the starry street,
This flaring luxury of festive light,
From every window flung?—Wherefore thus laughs
The hour of gloom?—Now that 'the midnight bell
Doth with his iron tongue and brazen mouth
Strike one,'—why walks abroad the undrowsy world?
Night's ghosts and goblins, groans and shadows dire,
All shone away, that e'en unshudd'ring walks
Bold Superstition forth? why is 'proud Night,
Attended with the pleasures of the world,
Thus all so wanton and so full of gauds?'
What fair event, to polished bosoms dear,
In polished life inspires this pomp of joy?—
Say, hath the African fair freedom found?
Spite of his shade at length confessed a man,
Nor longer whipped because he is not white?—
That were a jubilee for heav'n to join;
To extort the gelid hermit from his cell,
Inflame his brook-fed blood, and force him bring
His sober foot to swell the city rout,
With virtuous riot reeling, and with joy
Gloriously giddy!—But 'tis not for this,
'Tis not for this, the midnight vies with noon.
Sing Io Paean, Io Paean sing!—
Thousands of pulses high with health that leaped,

Whose sprightly spring, to Time's oppression left
Or to Disease's weight, had played perhaps
A length of years, by speedier fates laid still,
Ne'er to go on again or stir, have stopped.—
On yon blest sun, all as a bridegroom gay,
Whom to behold it is a pleasant thing
For every eye; who gives the painted globe
This pomp of colour and this beauteous bloom;
A multitude (th' ecstatic tidings tell)
A multitude of eyes, at which the heart
Looked laughing out upon the day, are closed.—
On his delicious light (transporting thought!)
They never more shall look!—Illume, illume
The glowing street! nor let one window rob
The general rapture of a ray it owes!
Religion joins the joy:—of those fair works,
Which He, whose wondrous wisdom all things made,
Made in his image, or defacement foul
Or fatal rent (more lights, more lights emit!)
A myriad has received.—This is th' event,
The fair event to polished bosoms dear,
In polished life that lights this pomp of joy.
For this the cannon's thunder thumps the ear;
For this their merry peal the steeples pour;
For this dun Night her raven hue resigns,
And, in this galaxy of tapers pranked,
Mimics meridian day!—hence the high joy
That calls the city's swarms from out their cells,
Laughs in each eye and dances in each heart,
Prolongs their vigils, and shakes off the dews
That hovering Sleep from off her wings lets fall
On their light lids, that will not let lie on 'em
The poppy drops, the high excitement such!
All to the feast, the feast of blood! repair.
The high, the low, old men and prattling babes,
Young men and maidens, all to grace the feast,
Light-footed trip,—the feast, the feast of blood!

(1795)

HANNAH MORE

1745–1833

531 *The Riot; or, Half a Loaf is Better than No Bread. In a Dialogue between Jack Anvil and Tom Hod*

'Come, neighbours, no longer be patient and quiet,
Come let us go kick up a bit of a riot;
I am hungry, my lads, but I've little to eat,
So we'll pull down the mills and seize all the meat:
I'll give you good sport, boys, as ever you saw,
So a fig for the justice, a fig for the law.'

Then his pitchfork Tom seized—'Hold a moment,' says Jack,
'I'll show thee thy blunder, brave boy, in a crack.
And if I don't prove we had better be still,
I'll assist thee straightway to pull down every mill;
I'll show thee how passion thy reason does cheat,
Or I'll join thee in plunder for bread and for meat.

'What a whimsy to think thus our bellies to fill,
For we stop all the grinding by breaking the mill!
What a whimsy to think we shall get more to eat
By abusing the butchers who get us the meat!
What a whimsy to think we shall mend our spare diet
By breeding disturbance, by murder and riot!

'Because I am dry, 'twould be foolish, I think,
To pull out my tap and to spill all my drink;
Because I am hungry and want to be fed,
That is sure no wise reason for wasting my bread;
And just such wise reasons for mending their diet
Are used by those blockheads who rush into riot.

'I would not take comfort from others' distresses,
But still I would mark how God our land blesses;
For though in Old England the times are but sad,
Abroad I am told they are ten times as bad;
In the land of the Pope there is scarce any grain,
And 'tis still worse, they say, both in Holland and Spain.

'Let us look to the harvest our wants to beguile,
See the lands with rich crops how they everywhere smile!
Meantime to assist us, by each western breeze,
Some corn is brought daily across the salt seas.
We'll drink little tea, no whisky at all,
But patiently wait and the prices will fall.

'But if we're not quiet, then let us not wonder
If things grow much worse by our riot and plunder;
And let us remember, whenever we meet,
The more ale we drink, boys, the less we shall eat.
On those days spent in riot, *no* bread you brought home:
Had you spent them in labour, you must have had *some.*

'A dinner of herbs, says the wise man, with quiet
Is better than beef amid discord and riot.
If the thing can't be helped, I'm a foe to all strife,
And pray for a peace every night of my life;
But in matters of state not an inch will I budge,
Because I conceive I'm no very good judge.

'But though poor, I can work, my brave boy, with the best,
Let the King and the Parliament manage the rest;
I lament both the war and the taxes together,
Though I verily think they don't alter the weather.
The King, as I take it with very good reason,
May prevent a bad law but can't help a bad season.

'The Parliament-men, although great is their power,
Yet they cannot contrive us a bit of a shower;
And I never yet heard, though our rulers are wise,
That they know very well how to manage the skies;
For the best of them all, as they found to their cost,
Were not able to hinder last winter's hard frost.

'Besides, I must share in the wants of the times,
Because I have had my full share in its crimes;
And I'm apt to believe the distress which is sent
Is to punish and cure us of all discontent.
But harvest is coming—potatoes will come!
Our prospect clears up. Ye complainers be dumb!

'And though I've no money and though I've no lands,
I've a head on my shoulders and a pair of good hands;

So I'll work the whole day and on Sundays I'll seek
At church how to bear all the wants of the week.
The gentlefolks too will afford us supplies;
They'll subscribe—and they'll give up their puddings and pies.

'Then before I'm induced to take part in a riot,
I'll ask this short question—What shall I get by it?
So I'll e'en wait a little till cheaper the bread,
For a mittimus hangs o'er each rioter's head;
And when of two evils I'm asked which is best,
I'd rather be hungry than hanged, I protest.'

Quoth Tom, 'Thou art right; if I rise, I'm a Turk',
So he threw down his pitchfork and went to his work.

(1795)

WILLIAM PARSONS

1758?–1828

532 *To a Friend in Love during the Riots*

In times like these, when widows, orphans weep,
  When Gallia's helpless sons in exile roam,
Wide spreads the civil flame with threatening sweep,
  And every Briton trembles for his home;
While fury kindles in plebeian minds,
  With frenzy stung to gnaw and rend their chain,
While tyrant power that chain still faster binds,
  Slow to concede and stubborn to retain;
In times like these, when fierce contentions rise,
  And dreadful Anarchy his standard rears,
Can love's soft tumults agitate the wise?
  Away such trivial hopes, such trivial fears!
Mark how the blazing flames to heav'n aspire,
  For bread and peace what throngs exclaim aloud,
How plundered dwellings feed the raging fire,
  How armèd horsemen trample on the crowd!
Of ills severe what dire prognostics these!
  And canst thou such tremendous hours employ
In flattering schemes of luxury and ease,
  In airy visions of domestic joy?

Yet truth's cold maxims faintly we pursue,
  And vainly *I* affect the sage's part,
For now, e'en now, might Beauty's power renew
  In *me* the throbbings of a feeling heart!
Each state convulsed, and every monarch hurled
  From his proud throne in dust unpitied down,
Yet would this bosom, heedless of the world,
  Glow at a smile and sicken at a frown!

(Wr. 1795; pub. 1942)

WILLIAM TAYLOR

1765–1836

533

The Vision

We met, a hundred of us met,
  At curfew in the field;
We talked of heav'n and Jesus Christ,
  And all devoutly kneeled.
When lo! we saw, all of us saw,
  The starlight sky unclose,
And heard the far-high thunders roll
  Like seas where storm-wind blows.
We listened, in amazement lost,
  As still as stones for dread,
And heard the war proclaimed above,
  And sins of nations read.
The sound was like a solemn psalm
  That holy Christians sing,
And by and by the noise was ceased
  Of all the angelic ring.
Yet still beyond the cloven sky
  We saw the sheet of fire;
Then came a voice, as from a throne,
  To all the heav'nly choir
Which spake—'Though many men must fall,
  I will that these prevail;
To me the poor man's cause is dear.'—
  Then slowly sank a scale:

The hand that poised was lost in clouds;
One shell did weighty seem,
But sceptres, scutcheons, mitres gold
Flew up and kicked the beam.

(1795)

ANNABELLA PLUMPTRE

d. 1812

534 from *Ode to Moderation*

TO thee, whose cautious step and specious air
Deceive the world; who, simulating *good*,
Drop'st from thine oily tongue the pitying pray'r
T' avert the ills of man and spare his blood:
'To thee I call, but with no friendly voice',
I am no dupe to thine insidious art,
The vaunted mercy of thy traitor heart,
Nor in thy promises can I rejoice.
For well I know thee, hypocrite!—I know
Thou art the fatal source of human woe;
Thine is the shield that bloodiest tyrants bear,
Foul harbinger of death, black herald of despair.

Why groans yon hapless, violated land,
With such continued suff'rance and long care?
'Tis that, deceiver! there thou giv'st command,
That mod'rate justice, mod'rate truth are there.
The poor not quite destroyed, though doomed to toil
From day to day unceasing, yet must hide
Their soul's deep anguish from the gaze of pride,
And greet with smiles the plund'rers of the soil.
The sad seditious thoughts that fire the brain
Must be subdued;—'tis treason to complain;
For order, peace, tranquillity require
They suffer all *unmoved*,—then silently expire.

O rather bear me fury, vengeance wild!
To the red scene of slaughter and dismay,
Where the bold multitude, no more beguiled,
The deathful banners of their rage display.

Ah! let *their* gen'rous ardours burn for me;
  Their fiercest energies my bosom steel,
  Who learn to vindicate, when taught to feel,
And dare th' extreme of all things to be free.
Better by far at once the conflict end,
The gen'ral *foe* prevail or gen'ral *friend*,
Than that faint hope should languish with the throng,
Who love the right but half, but half detest the wrong.

Mark, how the desolating tempest flies,
  And rends the groaning forest from its base;
Its bursting thunders wreck the pow'rless skies,
  Its lightnings nature's loveliest scenes deface.
Anon, behold its transient fury sped,
  More fresh the flowers their vivid tints disclose,
  With richer pride the yellow harvest glows,
More soft the air, more sweet the odours spread.
Thus, from the storms of intellectual strife
The moral system wakes to purer life,
The passions harmonize which late were hurled,
And reason's fairer beams illume a happier world.

'Tis true, seductive is thy mild discourse,
  With dainty terms of soft benevolence,
And honeyed phrases filled, abjuring force,
  Trusting to time, and to progressive sense.
Thus the wild jargons of submissive peace,
  Of calm endurance, petrify the heart,
  Check the bold tear of manhood ere it start,
And bid the holy animation cease.
By due and slow degrees, by sober zeal,
Profess to rectify the public weal,
Which, by confusing parts, confound the whole,
Disorganise the will, and dislocate the soul.

'Tis thine to boast of long-existing laws,
Blame the *effect* of ill, but not the *cause*;
'Tis thine to call it mad erroneous rage,
  When Indignation's spirit nobly glows,
  When, smarting with the sense of bitt'rest woes,
The mass of man the war of nature wage;
'Tis thine with horror then to paint the scene,
As barb'rous tyranny had never been,
Of ruthless anarchy alone complain:
Then if thy victims pause, prepare th' eternal chain.

(1795)

JOHN THELWALL

1764–1834

535

Sonnet. The Cell

WITHIN the dungeon's noxious gloom
 The Patriot still, with dauntless breast,
The cheerful aspect can assume,
 And smile, in conscious virtue blest!

The damp foul floor, the ragged wall,
 And shattered window, grated high,
The trembling ruffian may appal,
 Whose thoughts no sweet resource supply.

But he, unawed by guilty fears
 (To freedom and his country true),
Who o'er a race of well-spent years
 Can cast the retrospective view,
Looks inward to his heart and sees
 The objects that must ever please.

Newgate, 24th. Oct. [1794]

(1795)

536

from *Lines Written at Bridgwater, 27 July 1797*

[*To S. T. Coleridge*]

 DAY of my double birth, if such the year
Thou usherest in, most welcome!—for my soul
Is sick of public turmoil—ah, most sick
Of the vain effort to redeem a race
Enslaved, because degenerate; lost to hope
Because to virtue lost—wrapped up in self,
In sordid avarice, luxurious pomp,
And profligate intemperance—a race
Fierce without courage, abject and yet proud,
And most licentious, though most far from free.
 Ah! let me then, far from the strifeful scenes
Of public life (where Reason's warning voice
Is heard no longer, and the trump of Truth

Who blows, but wakes the ruffian crew of Power
To deeds of maddest anarchy and blood),
Ah! let me, far in some sequestered dell,
Build my low cot; most happy might it prove,
My Samuel! near to thine, that I might oft
Share thy sweet converse, best-beloved of friends!
Long-loved ere known: for kindred sympathies
Linked, though far distant, our congenial souls.
  Ah! 'twould be sweet, beneath the neighb'ring thatch
In philosophic amity to dwell,
Inditing moral verse or tale or theme,
Gay or instructive; and it would be sweet,
With kindly interchange of mutual aid,
To delve our little garden plots, the while
Sweet converse flowed, suspending oft the arm
And half-driven spade, while, eager, one propounds,
And listens one, weighing each pregnant word
And pondering fit reply, that may untwist
The knotty point—perchance of import high—
Of moral truth, of causes infinite,
Creating power, or uncreated worlds
Eternal and uncaused! or whatso'er
Of metaphysic or of ethic lore
The mind with curious subtlety pursues—
Agreeing or dissenting—sweet alike,
When wisdom, and not victory, the end.
And 'twould be sweet, my Samuel, ah! most sweet
To see our little infants stretch their limbs
In gambols unrestrained, and early learn
Practical love and, wisdom's noblest lore,
Fraternal kindliness, while rosiest health
Bloomed on their sunburnt cheeks. And 'twould be sweet,
When what to toil was due, to study what,
And literary effort, had been paid,
Alternate in each other's bower to sit
In summer's genial season; or when, bleak,
The wintry blast had stripped the leafy shade,
Around the blazing hearth, social and gay,
To share our frugal viands and the bowl
Sparkling with home-brewed beverage:—by our sides
Thy Sara and my Susan and, perchance,
Alfoxden's musing tenant and the maid
Of ardent eye, who, with fraternal love,
Sweetens his solitude.

(Wr. 1797; pub. 1801)

ANNA LAETITIA BARBAULD

1743–1825

537 *The Rights of Woman*

YES, injured Woman! rise, assert thy right!
Woman! too long degraded, scorned, oppressed;
O born to rule in partial Law's despite,
Resume thy native empire o'er the breast!

Go forth arrayed in panoply divine,
That angel pureness which admits no stain;
Go, bid proud Man his boasted rule resign
And kiss the golden sceptre of thy reign.

Go, gird thyself with grace, collect thy store
Of bright artillery glancing from afar;
Soft melting tones thy thundering cannon's roar,
Blushes and fears thy magazine of war.

Thy rights are empire: urge no meaner claim,—
Felt, not defined, and if debated, lost;
Like sacred mysteries, which withheld from fame,
Shunning discussion, are revered the most.

Try all that wit and art suggest to bend
Of thy imperial foe the stubborn knee;
Make treacherous Man thy subject, not thy friend;
Thou mayst command, but never canst be free.

Awe the licentious and restrain the rude;
Soften the sullen, clear the cloudy brow:
Be, more than princes' gifts, thy favours sued;—
She hazards all, who will the least allow.

But hope not, courted idol of mankind,
On this proud eminence secure to stay;
Subduing and subdued, thou soon shalt find
Thy coldness soften, and thy pride give way.

Then, then, abandon each ambitious thought;
Conquest or rule thy heart shall feebly move,
In Nature's school, by her soft maxims taught
That separate rights are lost in mutual love.

(Wr. 1795?; pub. 1825)

538 *To Mr. [S. T.] C[olerid]ge*

MIDWAY the hill of science, after steep
And rugged paths that tire the unpractised feet,
A grove extends; in tangled mazes wrought,
And filled with strange enchantment:—dubious shapes
Flit through dim glades, and lure the eager foot
Of youthful ardour to eternal chase.
Dreams hang on every leaf: unearthly forms
Glide through the gloom; and mystic visions swim
Before the cheated sense. Athwart the mists,
Far into vacant space, huge shadows stretch
And seem realities; while things of life,
Obvious to sight and touch, all glowing round,
Fade to the hue of shadows.—Scruples here,
With filmy net, most like the autumnal webs
Of floating gossamer, arrest the foot
Of generous enterprise; and palsy hope
And fair ambition with the chilling touch
Of sickly hesitation and blank fear.
Nor seldom Indolence these lawns among
Fixes her turf-built seat; and wears the garb
Of deep philosophy, and museful sits
In dreamy twilight of the vacant mind,
Soothed by the whispering shade; for soothing soft
The shades; and vistas lengthening into air,
With moonbeam rainbows tinted.—Here each mind
Of finer mould, acute and delicate,
In its high progress to eternal truth
Rests for a space, in fairy bowers entranced;
And loves the softened light and tender gloom;
And, pampered with most unsubstantial food,
Looks down indignant on the grosser world,
And matter's cumbrous shapings. Youth beloved
Of Science—of the Muse beloved,—not here,
Not in the maze of metaphysic lore,
Build thou thy place of resting! lightly tread
The dangerous ground, on noble aims intent;

And be this Circe of the studious cell
Enjoyed, but still subservient. Active scenes
Shall soon with healthful spirit brace thy mind;
And fair exertion, for bright fame sustained,
For friends, for country, chase each spleen-fed fog
That blots the wide creation.—
Now heaven conduct thee with a parent's love!

(Wr. 1797; pub. 1799)

ANONYMOUS ('ORESTES')

539 *A Sonnet to Opium; Celebrating its Virtues. Written at the Side of Julia, when the Author was Inspired with a Dose of Laudanum, more than Sufficient for two moderate Turks*

SOUL-SOOTHING drug! your virtues let me laud,
  Which can with sov'reign sway
Force lawless passion into harmless play!
  Oft have I owned your pow'r
  In many a moody hour,
When grief with viper-tooth my heart hath gnawed.
  Still friendly to the plaintive muse,
  You can a balm infuse.
  If, sick with hopeless love,
  Too tenderly I mourn,
You can the shaft of anguish quick remove;
Or make desire's destructive flame less fiercely burn:
Guardian you are of Julia's innocence,
When madd'ning rapture goads to vice my throbbing sense.

(1796)

EDMUND GARDNER

1752?–1798

540 *Sonnet Written in Tintern Abbey, Monmouthshire*

STRANGER, whoe'er thou art, whose ling'ring feet,
  Enchained by wonder, press this verdant green,
Where thy enraptured sight the dark woods meet,
  Ah pause awhile, and contemplate the scene!
These hoary pillars clasped by ivy round,
  This hallowed floor by holy footsteps trod,
The mould'ring choir by spreading thorns embrowned,
  Where fasting saints devoutly hymned their God.
But ruthless Time, by slow but certain sweep,
  Has laid, alas! their ancient splendour low:
Yet if Reflection sinks its lesson deep,
  The soul's improvement from these walls may flow.
Like them how soon may be thy tottering state!
Man's but a temple of a shorter date.

(1796)

GEORGE COLMAN THE YOUNGER

1762–1836

541 from *The Maid of the Moor, or the Water-Fiends*

COLD blows the blast—the night's obscure;
The mansion's crazy wainscots crack;
The sun had sunk—and all the Moor,
Like ev'ry other Moor—was black.

Alone, pale, trembling, near the fire,
The lovely Molly Dumpling sat;
Much did she fear, and much admire,
What Thomas Gard'ner could be at.

Listening, her hand supports her chin,
But, ah! no foot is heard to stir:
He comes not from the garden in,
Nor he, nor little Bobtail cur.

They cannot come, sweet maid, to thee!
Flesh, both of cur and man, is grass!
And what's impossible can't be,
And never, never, comes to pass!

She paces through the hall antique,
To call her Thomas from his toil;
Opes the huge door—the hinges creak—
Because the hinges wanted oil.

Thrice, on the threshold of the hall,
She 'Thomas' cried, with many a sob;
And thrice on Bobtail did she call,
Exclaiming sweetly—'Bob! Bob! Bob!'

Vain maid! a gard'ner's corpse, 'tis said,
In answers can but ill succeed;
And dogs that hear when they are dead
Are very cunning dogs, indeed!

Back through the hall she bent her way;
All, all was solitude around!
The candle shed a feeble ray—
Though a large mould of four to th' pound.

Full closely to the fire she drew;
Adown her cheek a salt tear stole;
When, lo! a coffin out there flew,
And in her apron burnt a hole!

Spiders their busy death-watch ticked,
A certain sign that fate will frown;
The clumsy kitchen clock, too, clicked,
A certain sign it was not down.

More strong and strong her terrors rose—
Her shadow did the maid appal;
She trembled at her lovely nose—
It looked so long against the wall.

Up to her chamber, damp and cold,
She climbed Lord Hoppergollop's stair;—
Three stories high, long, dull and old—
As great Lords' stories often are.

coffin] oblong piece of coal exploding from the fire, regarded as a prognostic of death

All nature now appeared to pause,
And 'o'er the one half world seemed dead';
No 'curtained sleep' had she—because
She had no curtains to her bed.

Listening she lay—with iron din,
The clock struck *twelve*; the door flew wide;
When Thomas grimly glided in,
With little Bobtail by his side.

Tall, like the poplar, was his size,
Green, green his waistcoat was, as leeks;
Red, red as beetroot, were his eyes,
And pale as turnips were his cheeks!

Soon as the spectre she espied,
The fear-struck damsel faintly said,
'What would my Thomas?'—he replied,
'O! Molly Dumpling! I am dead.

'All in the flower of youth I fell,
Cut off with health's full blossom crowned;
I was not ill—but in a well
I tumbled backwards, and was drowned.

'Four fathom deep thy love doth lie;
His faithful dog his fate doth share;
We're Fiends—this is not he and I;
We are not *here*—for we are *there*.

'Yes—two foul Water-Fiends are we;
Maid of the Moor! attend us now!
Thy hour's at hand—we come for thee!'
The little Fiend-Cur said 'bow wow!'

'To wind her in her cold, cold grave,
A Holland sheet a maiden likes;
A sheet of water thou shalt have;
Such sheets there are in Holland dykes.'

The Fiends approach; the Maid did shrink;
Swift through the night's foul air they spin;
They took her to the green well's brink,
And, with a souse, they plumped her in.

So true the fair, so true the youth,
Maids to this day their story tell:
And hence the proverb rose that Truth
Lies in the bottom of a well.

(1797)

CHARLES NEWTON

b. 1776?

542 from *Stanzas*

[*Wild Nature*]

FRESH were the breathings of the nightborn gale,
Bright was the dew on fern and blade and thorn,
Gay was the lark that did the morning hail,
And glorious thou, O sun, that mad'st it morn;
The herds, indeed, moped with a heavier eye,
But they were happy still—and therefore so was I.

And so I yet may be, let but the Muse
Her loved, inspiring influence bestow,
Let me but Nature's open pages use,
And all but man and man's distresses know;
Here wander, free as the controlless wind,
And leave a warring world and all its cares behind!

Thou sweep of russet heath, ye winding vales,
Ye wavy hillocks, you your poet loves!
And thee, sweet stream, and you ye woodland dales,
And holy aisles of dimly-lighted groves,
Whose towerlike trunks tuft-ivy wrappeth round,
Whose outstretched giant arms sweep wide the grassy ground.

The man that dwells amid such scenes as these,
Sees sunny fields and breathes Creation's air,
Can aught that's low or aught that's little please?
Can Sorrow catch him or can Vice ensnare?
What can he know of wars and murderous strife,
Who whileth thus away his golden hours of life?

O all things wild and shapen by the hand
Of real rude Nature in her roughest mood,
Such as the Lord of Nature did command
That ye should be, and then pronounced you good,
Though rich, yet plain as is your simple show
Let my loose-warbled strains and artless numbers flow!

O all things rustically unrefined,
Honest and bare, accept my meed of praise!
This country coarseness winneth all my mind
And I am wedded to its humble ways,
And I were pleased amid these bowers to stay
More than an evening's hour, or a long summer's day.

(1797)

ROBERT SOUTHEY

1774–1843

543 *The Widow*

Sapphics

COLD was the night wind, drifting fast the snows fell,
Wide were the downs and shelterless and naked,
When a poor wanderer struggled on her journey
Weary and way-sore.

Drear were the downs, more dreary her reflections;
Cold was the night wind, colder was her bosom!
She had no home, the world was all before her,
She had no shelter.

Fast o'er the bleak heath rattling drove a chariot,
'Pity me!' feebly cried the poor night-wanderer.
'Pity me, strangers! lest with cold and hunger
Here I should perish.

'Once I had friends,—but they have all forsook me!
Once I had parents,—they are now in heaven!
I had a home once—I had once a husband—
Pity me, strangers!

'I had a home once—I had once a husband—
I am a widow poor and broken-hearted!'
Loud blew the wind, unheard was her complaining,
On drove the chariot.

On the cold snows she laid her down to rest her;
She heard a horseman, 'pity me!' she groaned out;
Loud blew the wind, unheard was her complaining,
On went the horseman.

Worn out with anguish, toil and cold and hunger,
Down sunk the wanderer, sleep had seized her senses;
There did the traveller find her in the morning,
God had released her.

(1797)

GEORGE CANNING

1770–1827

(with John Hookham Frere 1769–1846)

544 *Sapphics. The Friend of Humanity and the Knife-grinder*

Friend of Humanity

'NEEDY knife-grinder! whither are you going?
Rough is the road, your wheel is out of order—
Bleak blows the blast;—your hat has got a hole in't,
So have your breeches!

'Weary knife-grinder! little think the proud ones,
Who in their coaches roll along the turnpike-
-road, what hard work 'tis crying all day, "Knives and
Scissors to grind O!"

'Tell me, knife-grinder, how came you to grind knives?
Did some rich man tyrannically use you?
Was it the squire? or parson of the parish?
Or the attorney?

'Was it the squire, for killing of his game? or
Covetous parson, for his tithes distraining?
Or roguish lawyer made you lose your little
All in a lawsuit?

'(Have you not read the Rights of Man, by Tom Paine?)
Drops of compassion tremble on my eyelids,
Ready to fall as soon as you have told your
Pitiful story.'

Knife-grinder

'Story! God bless you! I have none to tell, sir,
Only last night a-drinking at the Chequers,
This poor old hat and breeches, as you see, were
Torn in a scuffle.

'Constables came up for to take me into
Custody; they took me before the justice;
Justice Oldmixon put me in the parish-
-Stocks for a vagrant.

'I should be glad to drink your Honour's health in
A pot of beer, if you will give me sixpence;
But for my part, I never love to meddle
With politics, sir.'

Friend of Humanity

'*I* give thee sixpence! I will see thee damned first—
Wretch! whom no sense of wrongs can rouse to vengeance—
Sordid, unfeeling, reprobate, degraded,
Spiritless outcast!'

[*Kicks the knife-grinder, overturns his wheel, and exit in a transport of republican enthusiasm and universal philanthropy.*]

(1797)

(with George Ellis 1753–1815)

545 *Rogero's Song* from *The Rovers; or, The Double Arrangement*

WHENE'ER with haggard eyes I view
  This dungeon that I'm rotting in,
I think of those companions true
  Who studied with me at the U—
          —niversity of Gottingen,—
          —niversity of Gottingen.

[*Weeps, and pulls out a blue kerchief, with which he wipes his eyes; gazing tenderly at it, he proceeds—*

Sweet kerchief, checked with heavenly blue,
  Which once my love sat knotting in !—
Alas! Matilda *then* was true!
  At least I thought so at the U—
          —niversity of Gottingen—
          —niversity of Gottingen.

[*At the repetition of this line, Rogero clanks his chains in cadence.*

Barbs! barbs! alas! how swift you flew,
  Her neat post-waggon trotting in!
Ye bore Matilda from my view;
  Forlorn I languished at the U—
          —niversity of Gottingen—
          —niversity of Gottingen.

This faded form! this pallid hue!
  This blood my veins is clotting in;
My years are many—they were few
  When first I entered at the U—
          —niversity of Gottingen—
          —niversity of Gottingen.

There first for thee my passion grew,
  Sweet! sweet Matilda Pottingen!
Thou wast the daughter of my tu—
  —tor, Law Professor at the U—
          —niversity of Gottingen—
          —niversity of Gottingen.

Barbs] (Barbary) horses

Sun, moon, and thou vain world, adieu,
  That kings and priests are plotting in:
Here doomed to starve on water-gru—
  —el, never shall I see the U—
              —niversity of Gottingen
              —niversity of Gottingen.—

[*During the last stanza, Rogero dashes his head repeatedly against the walls of his prison; and, finally, so hard as to produce a visible contusion. He then throws himself on the floor in an agony. The curtain drops—the music still continuing to play, till it is wholly fallen.*

(1798)

(with John Hookham Frere)

546 from *New Morality*

FROM mental mists to purge a nation's eyes;
To animate the weak, unite the wise;
To trace the deep infection, that pervades
The crowded town, and taints the rural shades;
To mark how wide extends the mighty waste
O'er the fair realms of Science, Learning, Taste;
To drive and scatter all the brood of lies,
And chase the varying falsehood as it flies;
The long arrears of ridicule to pay,
To drag reluctant Dullness back to day;
Much yet remains.—To you these themes belong,
Ye favoured sons of virtue and of song!

. . . .

  If Vice appal thee,—if thou view with awe
Insults that brave, and crimes that 'scape the law;—
Yet may the specious bastard brood, which claim
A spurious homage under Virtue's name,
Sprung from that parent of ten thousand crimes,
The *New Philosophy* of modern times,—
Yet, these may rouse thee!—with unsparing hand,
Oh, lash the vile impostures from the land!
  —First, stern Philanthropy:—not she who dries
The orphan's tears, and wipes the widow's eyes;
Not she, who, sainted Charity her guide,
Of British bounty pours the annual tide:—

But *French* Philanthropy;—whose boundless mind
Glows with the general love of all mankind;
Philanthropy,—beneath whose baneful sway
Each patriot passion sinks and dies away.
  Taught in her school to imbibe thy mawkish strain,
Condorcet, filtered through the dregs of Paine,
Each pert adept disowns a Briton's part,
And plucks the name of England from his heart.
  What, shall a name, a word, a sound control
The aspiring thought, and cramp the expansive soul?
Shall one half-peopled island's rocky round
A love, that glows for all Creation, bound?
And social charities contract the plan
Framed for thy freedom, Universal Man?
—No—through the extended globe his feelings run
As broad and general as the unbounded sun!
No narrow bigot *he*;—*his* reasoned view
Thy interests, England, ranks with thine, Peru!
France at our doors, *he* sees no danger nigh,
But heaves for Turkey's woes the impartial sigh;
A steady Patriot of the World alone,
The friend of every country—but his own.
  Next comes a gentler Virtue.—Ah! beware
Lest the harsh verse her shrinking softness scare.
Visit her not too roughly;—the warm sigh
Breathes on her lips;—the tear-drop gems her eye.
Sweet Sensibility, who dwells enshrined
In the fine foldings of the feeling mind;—
With delicate Mimosa's sense endued,
Who shrinks instinctive from a hand too rude;
Or, like the *anagallis*, prescient flower,
Shuts her soft petals at the approaching shower.
  Sweet child of sickly Fancy!—her of yore
From her loved France Rousseau to exile bore;
And, while midst lakes and mountains wild he ran,
Full of himself, and shunned the haunts of man,
Taught her o'er each lone vale and Alpine steep
To lisp the story of his wrongs, and weep;
Taught her to cherish still, in either eye,
Of tender tears a plentiful supply,
And pour them in the brooks that babbled by;—
—Taught by nice scale to mete her feelings strong,
False by degrees, and exquisitely wrong;—
—For the crushed beetle first,—the widowed dove,
And all the warbled sorrows of the grove;—
Next for poor suff'ring guilt;—and last of all,

For parents, friends, a king and country's fall.
  Mark her fair votaries, prodigal of grief,
With cureless pangs, and woes that mock relief,
Droop in soft sorrow o'er a faded flower;
O'er a dead jack-ass pour the pearly shower;—
But hear, unmoved, of Loire's ensanguined flood,
Choked up with slain;—of Lyons drenched in blood;
Of crimes that blot the age, the world with shame,
Foul crimes, but sicklied o'er with Freedom's name;
Altars and thrones subverted, social life
Trampled to earth,—the husband from the wife,
Parent from child, with ruthless fury torn,—
Of talents, honour, virtue, wit forlorn,
In friendless exile,—of the wise and good
Staining the daily scaffold with their blood,—
Of savage cruelties that scare the mind,
The rage of madness with hell's lusts combined—
Of hearts torn reeking from the mangled breast,—
They hear—and hope, that ALL IS FOR THE BEST.
  Fond hope!—but Justice sanctifies the pray'r—
Justice!—here, Satire, strike! 'twere sin to spare!
Not she in British Courts that takes her stand,
The dawdling balance dangling in her hand,
Adjusting punishments to fraud and vice,
With scrupulous quirks, and disquisition nice:—
But firm, erect, with keen reverted glance,
The avenging angel of regenerate France,
Who visits ancient sins on modern times,
And punishes the Pope for Caesar's crimes.
  Such is the liberal Justice which presides
In these our days, and modern patriots guides;—
Justice, whose blood-stained book one sole decree,
One statute fills—'the People shall be Free.'
Free by what means?—by folly, madness, guilt,
By boundless rapines, blood in oceans spilt;
By confiscation, in whose sweeping toils
The poor man's pittance with the rich man's spoils,
Mixed in one common mass, are swept away,
To glut the short-lived tyrant of the day:—
By laws, religion, morals, all o'erthrown:—
—'Rouse then, ye sovereign people, claim your own:—
The licence that enthrals, the truth that blinds,
The wealth that starves you, and the power that grinds.'
—So Justice bids.—'Twas her enlightened doom,
Louis, thy holy head devoted to the tomb!
'Twas Justice claimed in that accursed hour

The fatal forfeit of too lenient pow'r.
—Mourn for the man we may;—but for the King,—
Freedom, oh! Freedom's such a charming thing!
'Much may be said on both sides.'—Hark! I hear
A well-known voice that murmurs in my ear,—
The voice of Candour.—Hail! most solemn sage,
Thou drivelling virtue of this moral age,
Candour, which softens party's headlong rage.
Candour,—which spares its foes;—nor e'er descends
With bigot zeal to combat for its friends.
Candour,—which loves in see-saw strain to tell
Of *acting foolishly,* but *meaning well*;
Too nice to praise by wholesale, or to blame,
Convinced that *all* men's *motives* are the same;—
And finds, with keen discriminating sight,
Black's not *so* black;—nor white *so very* white.
'Fox, to be sure, was vehement and wrong:—
But then Pitt's words, you'll own, were *rather* strong.
Both must be blamed, both pardoned;—'twas just so
With Fox and Pitt full forty years ago!
So Walpole, Pulteney;—factions in all times,
Have had their follies, ministers their crimes.'
Give me the avowed, the erect, the manly foe,
Bold I can meet—perhaps may turn his blow;
But of all plagues, good heaven, thy wrath can send,
Save, save, oh! save me from the *Candid Friend*!

(1798)

MARY ALCOCK

1742?–1798

547 *The Chimney-Sweeper's Complaint*

A CHIMNEY-SWEEPER'S boy am I;
  Pity my wretched fate!
Ah, turn your eyes; 'twould draw a tear,
  Knew you my helpless state.

Far from my home, no parents I
  Am ever doomed to see;
My master, should I sue to him,
  He'd flog the skin from me.

Ah, dearest madam, dearest sir,
  Have pity on my youth;
Though black, and covered o'er with rags,
  I tell you naught but truth.

My feeble limbs, benumbed with cold,
  Totter beneath the sack,
Which ere the morning dawn appears
  Is loaded on my back.

My legs you see are burnt and bruised,
  My feet are galled by stones,
My flesh for lack of food is gone,
  I'm little else but bones.

Yet still my master makes me work,
  Nor spares me day or night;
His 'prentice boy he says I am,
  And he will have his right.

'Up to the highest top,' he cries,
  'There call out *chimney-sweep*!'
With panting heart and weeping eyes,
  Trembling I upwards creep.

But stop! no more—I see him come;
  Kind sir, remember me!
Oh, could I hide me under ground,
  How thankful should I be!

(Wr. by 1798; pub. 1799)

548

Written in Ireland

How blest would be Iërne's isle,
Were bigotry and all its guile
  Chased as a cloud away;
Then would Religion rear her head,
And sweet Contentment round her spread,
  Like a new dawn of day.

Come then, oh come, thou Truth divine!
With double radiance deign to shine,
  Thy heavenly light expand;
'Tis thine to chase these clouds of night,
Which darken and confound the sight
  In this divided land.

Attendant on thy prosp'rous train
I see sweet Peace with honest gain
  Spread wide her liberal hand,
While Discord, masked in deep disguise,
Abashed from forth her presence flies,
  Struck by her magic wand.

Around, where now in ruins lie
Thy sacred altars, I espy
  Fair Order rear each pile,
Whilst o'er thy wilds forlorn and waste,
Lo, Industry with nimble haste
  Makes hill and valley smile.

No more thy sons in fell despite,
A murderous band *arrayed in white*,
  Shall deal destruction round;
Each man beneath his vine shall rest,
No more by bigotry oppressed,
  But Truth by Peace be crowned.

Then shall Iërne tune her lyre,
And with united voice conspire
  To hail her happy state;
All hail, Iërne, Nature's pride,
No more shall wars thy land divide,
  Wert thou as good as great.

(Wr. by 1798; pub. 1799)

JOSEPH COTTLE

1770–1853

549 from *Malvern Hills*

[*Industrial Evils*]

CITIES and towns, ye haunts of wretchedness!
Where Commerce with a grin of ecstasy
Sits counting o'er her votaries' tears and sighs;
Urged by your splendid poisons, what a host
Of inexperienced sons have left their homes,
The cot's calm comforts and the quiet shades,

To taste your bitter dregs, and be immured
From morn's first dawn till evening far is spent,
In dust and stench and pestilence! remote
From friends, assailed by vice in every shape
That chains to dust the soul, and doomed at length
To linger out their blasted lives in scorn—
Their peace destroyed—their innocence gone by.
  Yet sadder still to mark the infant throng,
Foredoomed by Mammon's ironhearted sons
To deaths untimely, ere the simple lisp
Of infancy be past; to see them toil
And waste their tender strength, perchance to please
Some strict and pious master, who enjoys
Self-satisfaction in the cheering thought
Of giving such unnumbered suppliants bread.
Cease, thoughtless men, your horrible deceits,
And, if to piety your heart incline,
Question it well! for never pious heart
Dwelt with such deeds. Can heaven applauding view
The helpless orphan seized by avarice,
And forced to sacrifice at Lucre's shrine
Its hopes in childhood and its joys in age?
No! if to please thy Maker ever struck
Thy passing thought, when interest was away,
Learn with more certainty than ever man
Foretold tomorrow's sun, it is by deeds
Of tenderness, by viewing all mankind
As offspring of one Sire, who never made
The wondrous human frame to be consumed,
Ere yet the leaves of childhood half expand,
By man's fierce lust of perishable gold.
  Poor children! on the hard world are ye cast,
A world which loves you not (save here and there
One good Samaritan), which strives to check
All that is noble, all that lifts the heart
To heaven and conscious dignity. Like beasts
Ye are compelled to toil, like beasts to live,
Like beasts to die—unwept, uncomforted!
Not knowing what you are, nor whither bound
When doomed to sail, as unstarred mariners,
On that vast ocean death conducts us to.

(1798)

JAMES PLUMPTRE

1770–1832

550 from *Prologue* to *The Lakers: A Comic Opera*

WHERE Cumbria's mountains in the north arise,
Where cloud-capped Skiddaw seeks the azure skies,
Nature hath showered from forth her lavish hand
Her choicest beauties o'er the favoured land.
There verdant hills the fertile vales divide,
And at their base pellucid rivers glide;
Or the broad lake, outstretched in wide expanse,
Discovers to the trav'ller's wond'ring glance
Enchanting scenes, which captivate the soul,
And make therein delightful visions roll.
There the bleak crags their barren bosoms bare,
Stupendous cataracts hideous chasms wear;
From rock to rock they force their headlong way,
Stun with their noise and fill the air with spray;
The hanging cliff its dreadful safety yields,
Where Jove's proud bird its annual eyrie builds.
  Thither, attracted from their peaceful home,
The Poet and the Painter love to roam,
Feed fancy full till, fraught with fire divine,
Their beauties on the page and canvas shine;
There Cumberland enriched his moral muse,
And Farington produced his matchless views.
There too the botanist, with prying eyes,
Culls the fair flowers in all their thousand dyes;
The teeming waters yield the scaly race,
And the keen sportsman joins the noisy chase;
Health, rosy goddess, there unharmed resides,
And Liberty, the mountain nymph, presides.
Each season there delighted myriads throng
To pass their time these charming scenes among:
For pleasure, knowledge, many thither hie,
For fashion some, and some—they know not why.
And these same visitors, e'en one and all,
The natives by the name of Lakers call.

(1798)

ANONYMOUS ('S.')

551 *Ode to the German Drama*

DAUGHTER of Night, chaotic Queen!
  Thou fruitful source of modern lays,
Whose subtle plot and tedious scene
  The monarch spurn, the robber raise—
Bound in thy necromantic spell,
The audience taste the joys of hell;
And Britain's sons indignant groan
With pangs unfelt before at crimes before unknown.

When first, to make the nation stare,
  Folly her painted mask displayed,
Schiller sublimely mad was there,
  And Kotz'bue lent his mighty aid—
Gigantic pair! their lofty soul,
Disdaining reason's weak control,
On changeful Britain sped the blow,
Who, thoughtless of her own, embraced fictitious woe.

Awed by thy scowl tremendous, fly
  Fair Comedy's theatric brood,
Light satire, wit and harmless joy,
  And leave us dungeons, chains and blood;
Swift they disperse, and with them go
Mild Otway, sentimental Rowe;
Congreve averts th' indignant eye,
And Shakespeare mourns to view th' exotic prodigy.

Ruffians in regal mantle dight,
  Maidens immersed in thought profound,
Spectres that haunt the shade of night,
  And spread a waste of ruin round:
These form thy never-varying theme,
While, buried in thy Stygian stream,
Religion mourns her wasted fires,
And Hymen's sacred torch low hisses and expires.

O mildly o'er the British stage,
  Great Anarch, spread thy sable wings;
Not fired with all the frantic rage
  With which thou hurl'st thy darts at kings,

(As thou in native garb art seen)
With scattered tresses, haggard mien,
Sepulchral chains and hideous cry,
By despot arts immured in ghastly poverty.

In specious form, dread Queen, appear,
  Let falsehood fill the dreary waste;
Thy democratic rant be here
  To fire the brain, corrupt the taste.
The fair, by vicious love misled,
Teach me to cherish and to wed,
To low-born arrogance to bend,
Established order spurn, and call each outcast friend.

(1799)

JAMES BISSET

1762?–1832

552 from *Ramble of the Gods through Birmingham*

Next day they rambled round the town, and swore,
'That such a place they never saw before':
They visited our Wharfs, and, wond'ring, found
Some thousand tons of coal piled on the ground,
And scores of boats, in length full sixty feet,
With loads of mineral fuel quite replete;
Whilst carts and country waggons filled each space,
And loaded teams stood ranged around the place.
  The Gods beheld the whole with great surprise,
And asked, 'from whence we gained such large supplies?'
For, though well versed in all empyreal scenes,
They here were posed, to find our 'Ways and Means.'—
  When satisfied—then told some hundred ton
Would be consumed that day, ere setting sun,
In Birmingham alone,—amazed they stood,
And ev'ry pile with admiration viewed.
  They next, attracted by the vivid gleams,
Saw marcasites dissolve in liquid streams,
And stubborn ores expand, and, smelting, flow
By strength of calefaction from below.

552 marcasites] crystallized iron pyrites used for ornamentation

To see the Pin-works then the Gods repair,
Nor wondered less at what they met with there,
To find it was in any mortal's pow'r
To point and cut twelve thousand pins an hour;
And fifty thousand heads their shapes acquire
In half that time, spun round elastic wire.
The different Button-works they next review,
And seemed well pleased with sights so rare and new:
The various ores they saw rich hues impart,
Assuming different shapes, by skilful art;
And beauteous metals polished charms display,
In radiant colours ranged in fair array;
The process of the gilding looked well o'er,
Yet scarce could tell rich-gilt from semilore;
Each stamp, each lathe and press they careful scanned,
Then went to see the paper trays japanned;
Examined nicely ev'ry curious part,
And much admired th' improvements of the art. . .
Next, at the Gun-works, they surprised beheld
The lusty Cyclops musket-barrels weld;
Whilst peals like rattling thunder shook the roof,
When nit'rous powers proclaimed them Standard Proof.
The dread explosions, winged by echoes round,
Made Gods themselves to startle at the sound.
To see the Buckle-works they next repaired;
'Twas ere that fancy trade was so impaired,
When all the makers had a full employ,
Which made some thousand hearts to dance for joy;
For buckles then by high and low were wore,
Nor were by Sprigs of Fashion deemed 'a Bore.'
A fatal epithet, however glossed,
For thousands by that word their bread have lost.
Ingenious engines proved mechanic pow'rs,
And happy passed the months, weeks, days and hours;
'The Toy-Shop of the World' then reared its crest,
Whilst hope and joy alternate filled each breast.
Inventions curious, various kinds of toys,
Then occupied the time of men and boys,
And blooming girls at work were often seen,
That twice their ages joined was scarce fifteen,
Sent by their parents out their bread to seek,
Who'd earn, perhaps, some shillings in a week;
And many women, too, you then might see,
With children on the lap, or round the knee,

semilore] similor, yellow brass used in imitation of gold in cheap jewellery

An honest livelihood intent to gain,
And their sweet infant race help to maintain.
Charmed with the sight, the Gods the whole reviewed,
And seemed with admiration quite subdued.
  To see each warlike weapon they resort,
And viewed the polished blade of various sort,
The scimitar, the sword, the faulchion bright,
Formed for the dreadful horrors of the fight;
Sharp pointed poniards and the sabre keen,
Spikes, spears and lances were in thousands seen.
  From thence they went well satisfied away,
To see the whip ingenious engines play;
Then Lloyd's famed mill for slitting iron rods,
Was honoured by the presence of the Gods.
  To Whitmore's then, intent on earth to scan
The wond'rous works of still more wond'rous man,
They next resorted; and hydraulics new,
Machines and rolling-mills with pleasure view;
Whilst sturdy Cyclops, anvils ranged around,
With thund'ring hammers made the air resound.

(1800)

NOTES AND REFERENCES

THE following references indicate the first publication of each poem and, when this differs, the source of the preferred text. Such information is not included, however, for poets whose works have appeared in the modern scholarly editions cited. The other exception is of poems which were separately published under the title and at the date already given with the text. The notes contain concise explanations of literary and historical allusions, and biographical information about some of the more obscure writers has been included when available, if it has some bearing on the content of their poetry.

1. John Pomfret. Text from *Miscellany Poems on Several Occasions* (1702).

2. Thomas D'Urfey. *The Bath: or, The Western Lass* (1701).

3–4. John Philips. **3.** *A Collection of Poems* (1701); text from *The Splendid Shilling. An Imitation of Milton. Now First Correctly Published* (1705). **4.** Marlborough had defeated the French at Blenheim in August 1704.

5–14. Jonathan Swift. Texts from *Poetical Works*, ed. Herbert Davis (Oxford, 1967). **9.** Dr John Arbuthnot (9), friend of Swift and Pope, had been the late Queen's physician. **10.** Swift's lifelong friendship with Esther Johnson (Stella) had begun in the 1690s when he had been secretary to Sir William Temple. **11.** Thomas Sheridan and Patrick Delany (11 and 12), members of Swift's circle in Dublin, were both versifiers. **14.** There are many references to the literary and political friends with whom Swift had been most intimate before his departure for Ireland, including John Gay, Alexander Pope, John Arbuthnot and Henry St. John, Lord Bolingbroke, who, with William Pulteney, had later become prominent in the opposition to Sir Robert Walpole's government through *The Craftsman*. Elsewhere Swift refers to Henrietta Howard, Countess of Suffolk, mistress of George I (179); Francis Chartres, a notoriously wealthy criminal (189); the booksellers Edmund Curll and Bernard Lintot (197, 253); and such writers as Lewis Theobald, James Moore Smythe, Colley Cibber, the Poet Laureate (200), the 'uneducated' poet Stephen Duck (see poem 156), the eccentric preacher John 'Orator' Henley, and the freethinker, Thomas Woolston (271–98). In the later retrospect of his career, Swift emphasizes his years of political influence before the collapse of the government led by Robert Harley, Earl of Oxford, in 1714; and the spectacular success in 1724–5 of his political pamphlets, published under the pseudonym of 'M. B., Drapier', in resisting the attempt by the English government to impose a debased coinage on Ireland.

15. Daniel Defoe. Text from *A True Collection of the Writings* (1703). The massacre by Dutch settlers of English interlopers at Amboyna (45) in modern Indonesia in 1623 was often recalled during later hostilities with Holland.

17. Lady Mary Chudleigh. *Poems on Several Occasions* (1703).

18. Sarah Fyge Egerton. *Poems on Several Occasions* [1703].

19–22. William Congreve. **19–21.** *Poetical Miscellanies*, vol. v (1704). **22.** *Works* (1710), vol. iii.

23–5. Joseph Addison. **23.** *Poetical Miscellanies*, vol. v (1704). Charles Montagu, Earl of Halifax, was Addison's early patron. **24.** *Spectator*, no. 465 (23 Aug. 1712).

25. *Guardian*, no. 124 (3 Aug. 1713). Addison offered the song ironically to admirers of translations of Italian operas.

26–38. Matthew Prior. Texts from *Literary Works*, ed. H. B. Wright and M. K. Spears (2nd edn., 2 vols., Oxford, 1971). **31.** John Asgill (102) had published *An Argument* (1700), proving that man could enter eternal life without dying. It was burned by order of the House of Commons in 1703. **32.** John Partridge (16) was a well-known astrologer and almanac-maker, satirized by Swift. Syphacio (22) was Giovanni Siface, Italian castrato singer. Bavius (93) was a poetaster ridiculed by Virgil. **34.** Line 26 refers to Horace, *Odes*, III. ix. **37.** Peter Heylyn (1) was the author of *Microcosmus, A Little Description of the Great World* (1629); William Dampier (81) published *A New Voyage Round the World* in 1697.

39. Anonymous. *The Diverting Post* (30 June 1705).

40–2. Edward Ward. **40.** Text from *Works*, vol. iii (1706). **41.** *Nuptial Dialogues* (1710), vol. i. **42.** *The Poetical Entertainer*, no. 4 (1713). The attribution to Ward is not certain. Achilles' battle with the River Xanthus (9) in *Iliad*, bk. xxi, ended when the God of Fire 'drank up' the river.

43–52. Isaac Watts. **43.** *Horae Lyricae* (1706). **44.** *Horae Lyricae* (1706); text from 2nd edn., 1709. **45.** *Hymns* (1707). **46.** *Horae Lyricae* (2nd edn., 1709). Urania (1) was the Muse of Astronomy, later of celestial poetry. René Rapin (6) was an influential French neo-classical critic. **47.** From 'Thoughts and Meditations in a long Sickness, 1712, and 1713', in *Reliquiae Juveniles* (1734). **48–51.** *Divine Songs for . . . the Use of Children* (1715). **52.** *The Psalms of David Imitated* (1719).

53. Andrew Michael Ramsay. *Some Few Poems* (Edinburgh, 1728). John Catanach, the printer, stated that poems were written before Ramsay's departure for the Continent in 1706.

54. Anonymous. *Oxford and Cambridge Miscellany Poems* [1708], ed. Elijah Fenton.

55. William King. *Miscellanies in Prose and Verse* [1709].

56. John Reynolds. *Death's Vision Represented in a Philosophical, Sacred Poem* (Shrewsbury, 1709). This text is preferred to the extensive revision as *A View of Death* (1725), except for an emendation to the first line.

57–8. William Diaper. **57.** Printed posthumously in an adapted form as *Lincolnshire* (Bury St. Edmunds, 1720) and in *Miscellanea*, vol. i (1727); text from Bodleian MS. Rawl. poet. 157.

59–60. Ambrose Philips. **59.** *Tatler*, no. 12 (7 May 1709); text from 1st collected edn. (1710), vol. i. **60.** *Poems* (Dublin, 1725); dated 1 May 1724 in *Pastorals, Epistles, Odes* (1748).

61–9. Alexander Pope. Texts from *The Twickenham Edition of the Poems* (7 vols., 1939–61, revised 1953–63). **61.** James Johnston (50) was a neighbour of Pope at Twickenham; the dog and bitch decorated his garden wall. **62.** Fungoso (92) is a character in Ben Jonson's *Every Man Out of his Humour* (1600). **63.** The poem is dedicated to George Granville, Lord Lansdowne, poet and statesman. Secretary of War since 1710, he was a member of the ministry which had negotiated the Peace of Utrecht celebrated in this poem. **64.** Like Arabella Fermor ('Belinda') and Lord Petre ('the Baron'), John Caryll (canto i, l. 3) was a member of a prominent Catholic landowning family. Caryll suggested that Pope write the poem to put the quarrel over the lock in a humorous perspective. **68.** Wortley (6) is Lady Mary Wortley Montagu (see poems 103–4). Pope's feelings towards her were to sour dramatically (see note to poem 168). **69.** The lady is Henrietta Howard, later Countess of Suffolk.

70. Bernard Mandeville. *Female Tatler*, no. 78 (4 Jan. 1710); text from *Wishes to a Godson, with Other Miscellany Poems* (1712).

71. John Smith. *Poems upon Several Occasions* (1713).

72–3. Anne Finch, Countess of Winchilsea. **72.** *Miscellany Poems, On Several Occasions* (1713). **73.** British Library, MS. Lansdowne 852; first printed by Norman Ault, *A Treasury of Unfamiliar Lyrics* (1938). The poem refers to the South Sea Bubble of 1720.

74–6. Samuel Jones. *Poetical Miscellanies on Several Occasions* (1714).

77. Richardson Pack. *Miscellanies in Verse and Prose* (1719), where it is dated 'Ipswich April 1714'. The Treaty of Utrecht in 1713, negotiated by the Tory government under Robert Harley (38), had ended the war with France.

78. William Harrison. *Poetical Miscellanies* (1714), ed. Richard Steele.

79–81. Thomas Parnell. **79.** *Poetical Miscellanies* (1714), ed. Richard Steele. **80–1.** *Poems on Several Occasions* (1722 [for 1721]).

82–91. John Gay. Texts from *Poetry and Prose*, ed. Vinton A. Dearing (2 vols., Oxford, 1974) and *Dramatic Works*, ed. John Fuller (2 vols., Oxford, 1983). **83.** The Thames was frozen (41–2) for three months in 1709–10 and for a shorter period in 1715–16. **85.** Atalanta (5) was presented by Meleager with the head of the Calydonian boar, which she had first wounded. Calisto (46) was a nymph ravished by Jupiter when he found her resting in a forest.

92–5. John Winstanley. **92.** *Poems Written Occasionally* (Dublin, 1742). As Winstanley's two collections contain poems by other hands, authorship of particular poems cannot be certain. This poem alludes to the collapse of the Tory government in 1714. **93.** *Gentleman's Magazine*, ii (April 1732). **94.** *Poems* (Dublin, 1742). **95.** *Poems*, vol. ii (Dublin, 1751). Joshua Ward (20) was a quack doctor, whose patent drop and pill claimed remarkable cures in the 1730s.

96–7. Mary Monck. *Poems and Translations upon Several Occasions* (1716). In **97**, the reference is to Madeleine de Scudéry's *Artamène: ou le Grand Cyrus* (Paris, 1649–53; English translation, 1653–5).

98–101. Henry Carey. **98–100.** Texts from *Poems on Several Occasions* (3rd edn., 1729). In **99**, one of the numerous satires on the versification of Ambrose Philips's poems about children (see poem 60), Andromache (22) refers to his *The Distrest Mother* (1712), translated from Racine's *Andromaque*. **101.** *The Musical Century*. vol. i (1737).

102. Capt. H——. *Poetical Miscellanies*, vol. vi (2nd edn., 1716).

103–4. Lady Mary Wortley Montagu. **103.** *Six Town Eclogues* (1747); text from *Essays and Poems*, eds. Robert Halsband and Isobel Grundy (Oxford, 1977). **104.** Dodsley's *Collection of Poems*, vol. iii (1748); this text preferred to the MS. printed by Halsband and Grundy.

105. Leonard Welsted. *The Free-Thinker*, no. 124 (29 May 1719); text from *Epistles, Odes &c. Written on Several Subjects* (1724). The poem imitates Horace, *Epistles*, I. v. and refers to the King's birthday.

106. Alexander Pennecuik. *Streams from Helicon: or, Poems on Various Subjects* (2nd edn., Edinburgh, 1720). The poem uses the canting language of thieves and beggars.

107. Edward Littleton. *A New Miscellany* (1720), ed. A. Hammond. The 'blooming maid' (4) is Arachne who was a Greek weaver turned by Athene into a spider.

108–11. Allan Ramsay. **108–9.** *Scots Songs* (Edinburgh, 1720); text from *Poems* (Edinburgh, 1721). **110.** *Poems* (Edinburgh, 1721). **111.** *The Tea-Table Miscellany*, vol. ii (Edinburgh, 1726); text from *Poems*, vol. ii (Edinburgh, 1729).

112. Thomas Tickell. *Works of . . . Joseph Addison* (1721), vol. i. Addison had married the Countess of Warwick in 1716; the poem is addressed to her son, the 7th Earl, and also mentions Addison's early patron, Charles Montagu, Earl of Halifax (22), and James Craggs (102), Addison's successor as one of the principal Secretaries of State.

113. Samuel Croxall. *The Fair Circassian* (2nd edn., 1721).

114. Charles Mordaunt, Earl of Peterborough. *The British Journal*, 28 Dec. 1723. For Mrs Howard, see notes to poems 14 and 69.

115. David Mallet. *William and Margaret. An Old Ballad* (Edinburgh, 1723?); text from *Poems on Several Occasions* (1743).

116–17. Elizabeth Tollet. **116.** *Poems on Several Occasions* (1724). **117.** *Poems on Several Occasions* (1755).

118–20. Henry Baker. **118–19.** *Original Poems, Serious and Humorous* (1725). **120.** *The Second Part of Original Poems* (1726).

121–2. Hetty Wright. **121.** Samuel Wesley, *Poems on Several Occasions* (1862), ed. J. Nichols. Mehetabel was the elder sister of Charles and John Wesley, unhappily married to William Wright, a Lincoln plumber. **122.** *Gentleman's Magazine*, iii (Oct. 1733).

123–6. John Dyer. **123.** *Poetical Works of Akenside and Dyer* (1855), ed. R. A. Willmott. **124.** *Miscellaneous Poems, By Several Hands* (1726), ed. David Lewis; text from *Poems* (1761). **125.** *Poetical Works* (1855), ed. Willmott.

127. George Berkeley. *A Miscellany, Containing Several Tracts on Various Subjects* (Dublin, 1752). In 1725, Berkeley had published his proposal to establish a college in Bermuda to further Christian education in the colonies.

128–9. Jonathan Richardson. *Morning Thoughts: or Poetical Meditations, Moral, Divine and Miscellaneous* (1776), ed. Jonathan Richardson the Younger. Richardson is better known as a portrait-painter, theorist of painting and friend of Pope.

130–2. Samuel Wesley. **130.** *Miscellaneous Poems, By Several Hands* (1726), ed. David Lewis. A monument to Samuel Butler (1612–80), the author of *Hudibras* (1663–78), had been erected in 1721. **131.** *Miscellaneous Poems*, vol. ii (1730), ed. David Lewis. **132.** *Poems on Several Occasions* (1736).

133–7. James Thomson. **133.** *Winter. A Poem* (1726). The text is that of the 1st edn.: the poem was later greatly expanded. Thomson's heroes (266–92) are ancient Greek and Roman philosophers, orators, lawgivers, leaders in war and poets. **134.** *A Poem Sacred to the Memory of Sir Isaac Newton* (1727); text from *The Seasons* (1730), with corrections from the *Works* (1738). **135.** *Miscellaneous Poems by Several Hands* (1729), ed. James Relph; text from Dodsley's *Collection of Poems*, vol. iii (1748). The Countess of Hertford (23), prominent at Court as Lady of the Bedchamber to the Queen, was an early and influential patron of Thomson. **136.** *Alfred: A Masque* (1740).

138. John Wright. *Spiritual Songs for Children* (1727).

139. Christopher Pitt. *Poems and Translations* (1727).

140. Francis Hawling. Text from *A Miscellany of Original Poems on Various Subjects* [1752?].

141. Anonymous. *A Collection of Epigrams* (1727).

142–4. William Somervile. **142–3.** *Original Poems, Translations, Fables, Tales* (1727).

145–9. John Byrom. **145.** *A Collection of Epigrams* (1727). There was much rivalry in the London operatic world between these composers, or at least between their supporters, in 1720–7. **146.** *A Select Collection of Poems*, vol. vii (1782), ed. J. Nichols. Nicolas Malebranche (1638–1715), French theologian and philosopher, author of *Recherche de la vérité* (1674–8), translated as *The Search after Truth* (1694), had enthusiastic followers in England in the first half of the century. Byrom mentions his purchase at Lord Cadogan's sale in a letter to his wife, 9 March 1727. There are several references in the poem to Byrom's system of shorthand, which he taught in London and Cambridge. *Cato* (9) is Addison's tragedy (1713). A bill for improving the navigation of the River Weaver (15) in Cheshire (Byrom came from Manchester) had a first reading in the House of Commons on 9 March 1727, the day of the sale. **147.** *The Chester Courant* (25 Nov. 1746); text from *Miscellaneous Poems* (Manchester, 1773), vol. i. The poem refers to the Young Pretender's invasion of England in the autumn of 1745. **148–9.** *Miscellaneous Poems* (Manchester, 1773), vols. i and ii.

150. Richard Savage. Some corrections from the text in *Gentleman's Magazine*, vii (Feb. 1737) have been adopted. Savage's belief that he was the illegitimate and unacknowledged son of the Earl Rivers and the Countess of Macclesfield is well known from Johnson's biography of his friend (1744).

151. Edward Chicken. From *The Collier's Wedding* (Newcastle, 173–?); text from the edition by W.C. (Newcastle, 1829) based on the MS. then in the editor's possession.

152. Anonymous. *Miscellaneous Poems by Several Hands* (1729), ed. James Relph. The visit to London of the four Iroquois 'Kings' (33) in April 1710 and their reaction to St. Paul's are described in *Spectator* no. 50 (27 April 1711).

153–4. James Bramston. **153.** William Pinkethman, the comic actor (8), had died in 1725. The maypole in the Strand (10) had been finally removed in 1718. **154.** Priscian (31) was a Roman grammarian. Sir Richard Blackmore (45) was the author of numerous, usually derided, epic poems. Richard Bentley (46), distinguished classical scholar, had published a pedantic edition of *Paradise Lost* in 1732.

155. Andrew Brice. From *Freedom: A Poem, Written in Time of Recess from the Rapacious Claws of Bailiffs, and Devouring Fangs of Gaolers* (Exeter, 1730). In 1727 Brice, an Exeter printer, published an article in his *Weekly Journal* criticizing the treatment of a prisoner in the town gaol. Threatened with prosecution, he went into hiding and wrote the long poem excerpted here. Valglin (66) is an anagram of Glanvill, the name of the prison-keeper.

156. Stephen Duck. *Poems on Several Subjects* (1730).

157–60. Hildebrand Jacob. **157.** *A New Miscellany* (1730); text from *Works* (1735). **158–60.** *Works* (1735).

161. Colley Cibber. *The Merry Musician*, vol. iv (1731?).

162. Charles Woodward. *The Kingston Atalantis: or, Woodward's Miscellany* (1731). Polly Peachum (59) is a character in Gay's *Beggar's Opera* (1728).

163–4. Mary Barber. **163.** *The Flower-Piece. A Collection of Miscellany Poems by Several*

Hands (1731), ed. Matthew Concanen; text from *Poems on Several Occasions* (1734). **164.** *Poems* (1734).

165–72. Alexander Pope (continued). Texts from *The Twickenham Edition of the Poems* (7 vols., 1939–61, revised 1953–63). **165.** For 'Sancho's dread doctor' (62) see *Don Quixote*, ch. 47. **167.** Dr John Arbuthnot, an early friend of Pope and of Swift (see poems 9 and 14), was Pope's physician; he died less than two months after the publication of this poem. Throughout the poem Pope's friendship with Arbuthnot and with John Gay (256–60), who had died in 1731, and the encouragement he had received as a young man from his earliest literary and aristocratic friends (135–42), are contrasted with the malice, hypocrisy and selfishness he attributes to the contemporary literary world. Too many minor writers, critics and booksellers are mentioned to make detailed identification possible. Some of them, such as Colley Cibber, Ambrose Philips and Leonard Welsted, appear in this anthology as poets; for others, also referred to by Swift, see headnote to poem 14. The most celebrated passages are the descriptions of Joseph Addison (193–214) and Lord Hervey, the courtier (305–33). At 299–300, Pope refers to malicious identifications of allusions in his *Epistle to Burlington* (poem 165). **168.** The poem is addressed to Martha Blount, one of Pope's oldest friends (see poem 65). 'Sappho' (24–8) is Lady Mary Wortley Montagu (see poem 68), whose relationship with Pope had deteriorated. 'Atossa' (115–50) has been identified as the Duchess of Buckinghamshire. Lines 63–4 refer to Jeremy Taylor's frequently reprinted *Holy Living and Holy Dying* and to John Foxe's celebrated sixteenth-century martyrology; and to Philip, Duke of Wharton and Francis Chartres (see headnote to poem 14). Line 198 refers to a Turkish servant of George I and Stephen Hales, clergyman and physiologist. **172.** (i) Colley Cibber and Charles Fleetwood (52) were managers of Drury Lane Theatre and, like Sir Henry Jansen, gamblers as well. (ii) Bishop Wilkins (56), a founder of the Royal Society, had envisaged the possibility of flight to the moon. (iii) Dr John Gilbert (30) was to become Archbishop of York. 'Palinurus' (36) refers to Sir Robert Walpole, the Prime Minister.

173. Robert Dodsley. *A Muse in Livery: or, The Footman's Miscellany* (1732).

174–80. George Farewell. *Farrago* (1733). The British Library copy is inscribed 'Writ by Mr Farewell at Bulloigne in France'. In the Stationers' Register the copyright is ascribed to 'Geo. Farewell'.

181. Samuel Bowden. *Poetical Essays on Several Occasions*, vol. i (1733).

182. Anonymous. *Gentleman's Magazine*, iii (June 1733).

183–4. John Bancks. **183.** *Poems on Several Occasions* [1733]; text from *Miscellaneous Works in Verse and Prose* (1738), vol. i. **184.** *Miscellaneous Works* (1738), vol. i.

185–8. Philip Dormer Stanhope, Earl of Chesterfield. **185.** *Weekly Register*, 12 May 1733. William Sherlock's *A Practical Discourse Concerning Death* (1689) reached a 22nd edn. in 1735. **186.** *Gentleman's Magazine*, vi (Nov. 1736). **187.** *Gentleman's Magazine*, xi (Feb. 1741). Richard 'Beau' Nash was for many years Master of Ceremonies at Bath. **188.** Dodsley's *Collection of Poems*, vol. i (2nd edn., 1748).

189. Robert Tatersal. *The Bricklayer's Miscellany: or, Poems on Several Subjects* (2nd edn., 1734).

190. Jean Adams. *Miscellany Poems* (Glasgow, 1734). A teacher and later a hawker, she died in Glasgow Workhouse in 1765.

191. Anonymous. *The Honey-Suckle*, no. 3 (1734).

193. Anonymous. *London Magazine*, iv (June 1735).

194–5. Matthew Green. **194.** Text from Dodsley's *Collection of Poems*, vol. i (1748). Robert Barclay published his *Apology for the True Christian Divinity, as the Same is set forth and preached by the people called in scorn Quakers* in 1678. For King Agrippa (76), see Acts 26: 28: 'Then Agrippa said unto Paul, Almost thou persuadest me to be a Christian'. The 'honoured prophet' (107) is Elijah (I Kings 17: 4–6).

196–7. Moses Browne. **196.** *Gentleman's Magazine*, vi (Oct. 1736); this text is preferred to the revision in *Poems on Various Subjects* (1739). **197.** *Poems* (1739).

198–9. John Armstrong. **199.** The excerpts are from books i, ii, and iv.

200. Henry Taylor. *Gentleman's Magazine*, vii (Jan. 1737); text from *London Magazine*, xxix (Jan. 1760).

201. Anonymous. *The Art of Wenching* (Dublin, 1737).

203–5. Aaron Hill. *Works* (1753), vol. iii.

206–9. William Shenstone. **206.** Text from *Poems upon Various Occasions* (Oxford, 1737); the poem was expanded for separate publication (1742), and further expanded and revised in Dodsley's *Collection of Poems*, vol. i (1748). **207–8.** *Works in Verse and Prose* (1764), vol. i. **209.** Dodsley's *Collection of Poems*, vol. v (1758); text from *Works* (1764), vol. i, but retaining stanza 5 from Dodsley.

210. John Wesley. *Psalms and Hymns* (1738). A translation from the German of Tersteegen (1729).

211. E. Dower. *The Salopian Esquire: or, The Joyous Miller . . . To which are added, Poems* (1738). The New River was an artificial stream brought in the early 17th century from Amwell through Islington to the New River Head or reservoir, whence it was piped underground to other parts of London.

212–17. Samuel Johnson. Texts from *Poems*, ed. D. N. Smith and E. L. McAdam, (revised edn., Oxford, 1974). **214.** Several farces and pantomimes about Faustus (36) had been performed since the 1720s. At 42 Johnson refers to Aphra Behn, Restoration dramatist and novelist, and to Thomas D'Urfey, dramatist and humorous poet (see poem 2). At 46 Johnson refers to Edward Hunt, pugilist, and Mahomet, a rope-dancer. **215.** Johnson refers to many ill-fated careers, including those of Cardinal Wolsey (99–128); George Villiers, Duke of Buckingham, assassinated in 1628, Thomas Wentworth, Earl of Strafford, executed in 1641, and Edward Hyde, Earl of Clarendon, banished in 1667 (129–34); Thomas Lydiat, mathematician and biblical scholar, who died in poverty in 1646 (164); Charles XII of Sweden, defeated by Peter the Great at Pultowa in 1709 (191–222); Xerxes, King of Persia, defeated at Salamis in 480 BC (223–40). The 'bold Bavarian' (241) and 'fair Austria' (245) are Charles Albert, Elector of Bavaria and Maria Theresa, claimants in the recent War of the Austrian Succession. 'Lydia's monarch' (313) was Croesus. Anne Vane and Catherine Sedley (321–2) had both been royal mistresses. **216.** The poem concerns Sir John Lade, who duly squandered his fortune. **217.** Levett was the physician who lived for many years in Johnson's house.

219. John Gambold. *Hymns and Sacred Poems* (1739), ed. John and Charles Wesley.

220. Sir Charles Hanbury Williams. *Gentleman's Magazine*, xxxv (Jan. 1765); text from MS. in *Works* (1822), vol. i. Appearing in the poem are the Duchess of Manchester, widow of the 2nd Duke; Richard Bateman, brother of Lord Viscount Bateman; General Charles Churchill, nephew of the Duke of Marlborough, who had an illegitimate son by Anne Oldfield, the actress (43); and Charles Stanhope, MP, elder brother of the 1st Earl of Harington. Margus's (82) was a fashionable warehouse for Indian goods. Martin Folkes, antiquary, was President of the Royal Society 1741–52; and John Theophilus Desaguliers, lecturer on experimental philosophy, had been FRS since 1714 (122–3). The Royal Society then met at Crane Court (128).

221. Richard Glover. Text from *The Champion*, 27 May 1740. During Vice-Admiral Francis Hosier's blockade of Porto Bello in 1726, several thousand sailors died of fever, a disaster attributed by the Opposition to the inactivity imposed on Hosier by the Government. In 1739 Admiral Edward Vernon successfully attacked Porto Bello: the *Burford* (22) was his flagship.

222. Sarah Dixon. *Poems on Several Occasions* (Canterbury, 1740).

223. Anonymous. *Gentleman's Magazine*, x (Jan. 1740).

224–7. Charles Wesley. **224–5.** *Hymns and Sacred Poems* (1740). **226.** *Hymns and Sacred Poems* (1742). **227.** *Short Hymns* (1762).

228. Anonymous. Anxious about its safety at the beginning of the War of the Austrian Succession, George II spent several months during 1741 in his Electorate of Hanover. The publisher believed that the author of this poem was 'really disorder'd in his Intellect'.

229. William Dunkin. *Select Poetical Works*, vol. ii (Dublin, 1770). From May 1742 Swift was protected by a committee of guardians.

230. Nicholas James. *Poems on Several Occasions* (Truro, 1742).

231. Edward Young. The excerpts are from *Night* i (1742), vii (1744) and ix (1745); text from *Works* (1757), vols. i-ii.

232–42. Thomas Gray. Texts from *Poetical Works*, ed. Roger Lonsdale (Oxford, 1977). **233.** Eton was founded by Henry VI (4). **234.** Richard West, Gray's schoolfriend, had died on 1 June 1742 at the age of 25. **236.** Tophet is Henry Etough, Rector of Therfield, Herts., disliked at Cambridge for his interference in university affairs and religious hypocrisy. **238.** The last three stanzas refer to Shakespeare, Milton, Dryden, and Gray himself. **239.** The Bard denounces Edward I and his army, who had supposedly slaughtered the Welsh bards during the subjugation of Wales in 1283. The ghosts of the bards prophesy the fate of the Plantagenet kings down to Richard III, before the Bard himself foretells the return of the House of Tudor and its accompanying poetic revival. **241.** From the sixth-century Welsh poem, the *Gododdin*. **242.** Henry Fox, Lord Holland, Paymaster-General 1757–65, had been deserted by his political colleagues (17–18) and had retired to ornament his estate near Margate with mock ruins.

244. Josiah Relph. *A Miscellany of Poems* (Glasgow, 1747).

248–9. Anonymous. **248.** *London Magazine*, xiii (June 1744); **249.** *Gentleman's Magazine*, xiv (July 1744).

250–6. William Collins. Texts from *Poetical Works*, ed. Roger Lonsdale (Oxford, 1977). **251.** The 'Epode' refers to Aeschylus and to Sophocles' *Oedipus at Colonus*. **252.** Lines 1–16 refer to Spenser, *Faerie Queene*, IV. iv–v, the episode of Florimel's magic girdle. **256.** Addressed to John Home, Scottish dramatist. This posthumously published poem survives only in a fragmentary draft. Collins refers to *Macbeth* (176–82), Tasso's *Gerusalemme Liberata*, and Edward Fairfax's English translation in 1600 (188–99), and to Ben Jonson's visit to Drummond of Hawthornden near Edinburgh in 1619 (211–12).

257–9. Joseph Warton. **257.** Text from Dodsley's *Collection of Poems*, vol. iii (1748). Aegeria (21) was the Roman goddess of fountains and childbirth. According to legend, she used to counsel Numa, King of Rome, by night at her sacred spring. **258.** *Odes on Various Subjects* (1746); text from 2nd edn., 1747. **259.** Dodsley's *Collection of Poems*, vol. vi (1758).

260–2. Mark Akenside. **260.** Book iv was first published in *Poems* (1772), in which Akenside's revised text of the whole poem was entitled *The Pleasures of the Imagination.* Excerpts (i) and (ii) are from book iii, excerpt (iii) from book iv. **261–2.** Dodsley's *Collection of Poems*, vol. vi (1758).

263–4. Sneyd Davies. **263.** In John Whaley, *A Collection of Original Poems and Translations* (1745). **264.** *Gentleman's Magazine*, xlviii (Dec. 1778). The poem was written not later than 1745, since John Whaley (like Sneyd Davies and Charles Pratt (100), a Fellow of King's College, Cambridge) died in that year. Also appearing in the poem are Styan Thirlby, Fellow of Jesus College, Cambridge, critic and theologian, and John Dodd of Swallowfield, Berkshire, MP for Reading. Whaley's father (16) had been a Norwich shopkeeper.

265. Anonymous. *London Magazine*, xiv (March 1745).

266. Isaac Hawkins Browne. John Carteret, Earl of Granville, an unpopular politician, had resigned as Secretary of State in 1744. When he attempted to regain power in 1746, the occasion of this poem, he was unable to form a government.

267. John Dobson. *Gentleman's Magazine*, xvi (Nov. 1746). Dobson was a naval officer. The poem refers (71–2) to the Duke of Cumberland's campaign against the Jacobite invasion in 1746.

268. Tobias Smollett. *The Land of Cakes*, bk. i (1746); text from *The Union* (Oxford, 1753). After the Jacobite rebellion, the Duke of Cumberland ruthlessly repressed the Scottish clans.

269–71. Mary Leapor. **269.** *Poems upon Several Occasions*, vol. ii (1751). She was the daughter of a Northamptonshire gardener. Her poems were published posthumously, after her death at the age of twenty-four. **270–1.** *Poems upon Several Occasions* (1748).

272. John Ellis. *Chester Courant*, 10 Nov. 1747; text from *The Chester Miscellany* (Chester, 1750). A longer version , perhaps expanded by another hand, was printed in the *European Magazine*, xxi (1792).

273. Anonymous. *The Poets Petitions; an Essay on Modern Wit* (Dublin, 1747).

274–5. William Whitehead. **274.** *Gentleman's Magazine*, xvii (Sept. 1747). Holben (43) refers to the sixteenth-century woodcuts of the Dance of Death attributed to Hans Holbein. **275.** *Poems on Several Occasions* (1754). The 'sages of the Samian school' (68) were followers of Pythagoras, vegetarians.

276–8. Thomas Warton. Text from Dodsley's *Collection of Poems*, vol. iv (1755). **277.** *Poems* (1777). **278.** Text from 2nd edn., 1782.

279–80. Robert Nugent. Dodsley's *Collections of Poems*, vol. ii (1748).

281. Thomas Edwards. Dodsley's *Collection of Poems*, vol. ii (2nd edn., 1748).

283–93. Christopher Smart. **283–4.** *London Magazine*, xvii (Dec. 1748); text from *Poems on Several Occasions* (1752). **285.** The illness described in this poem may have been the beginning of Smart's mental breakdown. **286.** First published as *Rejoice in the Lamb* in 1939, *Jubilate Agno* was written between 1758 and 1763 while Smart was confined in a private madhouse. No attempt has been made here to elucidate the extraordinary range of his autobiographical, biblical and scientific references, for which see his *Poetical Works*, vol. i (Oxford, 1980), ed. Karina Williamson, the source of the present text which is unmodernized. **287.** *A Song to David* (1763), sts. xlix–lxxxvi; text from *A Translation of the Psalms of David* (1765). **288.** *Ode to . . . the Earl of Northumberland, with some other Pieces* (1764). **289–90.** *A Translation of the Psalms of David* (1765). **291–3.** *Hymns for the Amusement of Children* (1771 [for 1770]).

294. Henry Brooke. *The Songs in Jack the Gyant Queller. An Antique History* (Dublin, 1749); text from *A Collection of the Pieces Formerly Published* (1778), vol. iv.

295. Anonymous. *Gentleman's Magazine*, xix (Nov. 1749).

296. Catherine Jemmat. *Gentleman's Magazine*, xx (Nov. 1750); preferred to the revised text in her *Miscellanies in Prose and Verse* (1766).

297. Anonymous. *Fables and Tales for the Ladies* (1750). The volume may be basically by John Rockall, but this poem appears in a section 'by another hand'.

298. Philip Doddridge. *Hymns* (Shrewsbury, 1755).

299. Anonymous. *Gentleman's Magazine*, xxi (March 1751).

300–1. Soame Jenyns. **301.** *Poems* (1752).

302. John Brown. From 'Dedication' to Richard Cumberland, *Odes* (1776).

303–4. Anonymous. *The Merry Lad: A Choice Collection of Songs* (Sheffield, 1753).

305. Anonymous. *Gentleman's Magazine*, xxiii (Oct. 1753).

306. Anonymous. *Gentleman's Magazine*, xxiv (June 1754). An Act to allow naturalization of Jews (10) in 1753 had been immediately repealed after widespread popular protest.

307. John Dalton. The ladies addressed were the Misses Lowther. The Lowther family had developed Whitehaven harbour to cope with the growing volume of coal-shipping. Thomas Savery (71) was the inventor of an early steam-powered machine for raising water from mines.

308–10. Robert Lloyd. **308.** *The Connoisseur*, no. 135 (26 Aug. 1756); text from *Poems* (1762). William Halfpenny (108) was an architect and author of such books as *Rural Architecture in the Chinese Taste* (1750). **309.** Text from *Poems* (1762). In Tasso's *Gerusalemme Liberata* Armida (35) lured Christian knights to her enchanted garden. **310.** *St. James's Magazine*, i (Oct. 1762).

311. Kenrick Prescot. *Poems* ([Cambridge], 1772). Prescot was Master of St. Catherine's College, Cambridge 1741–79, and Rector of Balsham, Cambridgeshire, from 1752.

312–13. Robert Andrews. *Eidyllia: or, Miscellaneous Poems* (Edinburgh, 1757); texts from *Odes* (Birmingham, 1766). In **313** line 6, adopted from *Paradise Lost*, III. 35, refers to Thamyris, the Thracian bard blinded by the Muses, and Homer.

314. Anonymous. *Gentleman's Magazine*, xxvii (May 1757). Sternhold (24) was the author of the sixteenth-century metrical version of the Psalms still in use in the eighteenth century. Adjustment to the Gregorian Calendar (New Style) (60) in 1752 had involved the disappearance of eleven days. George Parker, Earl of Macclesfield (59), the astronomer, was mainly responsible for this unpopular change.

315. Anonymous. *Gentleman's Magazine*, xxviii (Aug. 1758); text and the attribution to 'J.T.' from *Gentleman's Magazine*, lxvi pt. ii (Sept. 1796). The chaplain had evidently been ordained by Bishop Benjamin Hoadly (56). The author may have been James Townley (1714–78), author of the popular farce *High Life Below Stairs* (1759), later headmaster of Merchant Taylors' School, who had himself been ordained by Hoadly in 1736.

316. David Garrick. Performed in *Harlequin's Invasion* (1759); text from the setting by William Boyce (1759?). There was widespread fear of a French invasion in 1759.

317. Frances Greville. *Edinburgh Chronicle*, 19 April 1759; text from *Poetical Calendar*, vi (June 1763).

318. John Maclaurin, Lord Dreghorn. *Essays in Verse* ([Edinburgh], 1769). The *Love Elegies* (1743) of James Hammond (1) had popularized the use of the quatrain for elegies.

319. James Macpherson. *Fragments of Ancient Poetry* (Edinburgh, 1760).

320. Anonymous. *Gentleman's Magazine*, xxx (Aug. 1760).

321–3. William Woty. **321.** *Gentleman's Magazine*, xxx (May 1760). The poem describes a popular tea-garden in Islington. For Francis (37) see *1 Henry IV*, II. iv. **322.** *Poetical Works* (1770), vol. i. **323.** *Poetical Amusements* (Nottingham, 1789).

324. James Cawthorn. *Poems* (1771).

325. Francis Fawkes. *Original Poems and Translations* (1761).

326. John Cunningham. *Day and Other Pastorals* (Edinburgh, 1761); text from *Poems Chiefly Pastoral* (Newcastle, 1766).

327. Thomas Morris. *Monthly Magazine*, i (Feb. 1796). Morris served in America with the 17th Foot under General Bradshaw and was the elder brother of Charles Morris (see **483–4**). The poem is an imitation of Horace, *Odes*, II. xvi.

328. Emanuel Collins. *Miscellanies in Prose and Verse* (Bristol, 1762).

329. Thomas Mozeen. *A Collection of Miscellaneous Essays* (1762).

330. Anonymous. *Gentleman's Magazine*, xxxii (April 1762). The 'expedition fleet' was probably that which sailed for Havana from Spithead under Admiral Pocock and Lord Albemarle in March 1762.

331. James Eyre Weeks. *British Magazine*, iii (Dec. 1762); text from *Poetical Calendar*, vi (June 1763).

332–4. George Alexander Stevens. **332.** *Beauties of All the Magazines*, i (Aug. 1762); text from *Songs, Comic, and Satyrical* (Oxford, 1772). **333–4.** *Songs* (Oxford, 1772).

335. John Collier. *Tim Bobbin's Toy-Shop open'd Or, His Whimsical Amusements* (Manchester, 1763). The British had captured Guadeloupe (3) in the West Indies in 1759, but returned it to the French at the Peace of Paris in 1763.

336. Anonymous. *Poetical Calendar*, v (May 1763). Robert Dodsley (16) had been for more than two decades the most successful publisher of fashionable poetry.

337–9. Charles Churchill. Texts from *Poetical Works*, ed. Douglas Grant (Oxford, 1956). **337.** This passage was added to *The Rosciad* (1761) in 1763. The critic was Thady Fitzgerald, who had recently attacked David Garrick. **338.** Churchill refers to William Mason (9) and George, Lord Lyttelton (13), both fashionable poets. *Gisbal* (12), a parody of Ossian published in 1762, was a satire on the Earl of Bute's administration. **339.** (ii) Churchill refers to William Whitehead, the Poet Laureate (46) and Francis Hayman (125), the painter. Lines 107–10 refer to the adjustment of the calendar in 1752: see note to poem 314.

340. James Grainger. The passages are from books i and iv. Grainger, a physician, spent the last years of his life on St. Christopher in the West Indies.

341–5. Oliver Goldsmith. Texts from *Collected Works*, ed. Arthur Friedman (Oxford, 1966), vol. iv. **344.** Altama (344) is a river in Georgia; Torno (418) is a river in Sweden, and Pambamarca (418) a mountain in Ecuador, then in Peru. **345.** (i) Thomas Townshend (6) was MP for Whitchurch. (ii) Goldsmith refers (23) to William Kenrick, miscellaneous writer; Henry Kelly, dramatist; and William Woodfall, journalist.

346. Leonard Howard. *Miscellaneous Pieces in Verse and Prose* (1765). An eccentric and improvident clergyman, at one time Chaplain to the Dowager Princess of Wales, Howard was more than once imprisoned in the King's Bench. Prisoners who could purchase the privilege of the Rules could walk outside the prison, which was a self-contained community in which alcohol was easily available.

347. Thomas Percy. *Reliques of Ancient English Poetry* (1765), vol. i.

350. Frederick Forrest. *A Rattle for Grown Children. By Young D'Urfey* (1766).

351. Anonymous. *Gentleman's Magazine*, xxxvi (May 1766).

352. Richard Jago. Text of 1st edn. preferred to the revision in *Poems, Moral and Descriptive* (1784).

353–4. Michael Bruce. *Poems on Several Occasions* (Edinburgh, 1770).

355. Anonymous. *Gentleman's Magazine*, xxxvii (Sept. 1767).

356. William Julius Mickle. *Ancient and Modern Scots Songs* (Edinburgh, 1769), ed. David Herd; text from *Poetical Works* (1806), ed. J. Sim. Mickle may only have revised and expanded the poem, which has also been attributed to Jean Adams (see poem 190).

357. Thomas Moss. *Poems on Several Occasions* (Wolverhampton, 1769).

358. John Gerrard. *Poems by John Gerrard, Curate of Withycombe in the Moor, Devon* (1769). *Northern* (100) alludes to Lord North, the Prime Minister.

359. Anonymous. *New Foundling Hospital for Wit*, pt. iii (1769). Schemes for regulating the affairs of the East India Company (17–24) and for limiting the profits from its activities in Bengal were much debated during 1769.

360–2. Thomas Chatterton. Texts from *Complete Works*, ed. Donald S. Taylor (2 vols., Oxford, 1971). The glosses are Chatterton's own, except those with a square bracket, which derive from *Poems* (1777).

363–4. Gilbert White. **363.** *The Natural History and Antiquities of Selborne* (1789). **364.** *Gentleman's Magazine*, liv (April 1784); text from *A Naturalist's Calendar* (1795), ed. John Aikin.

365. George Smith. *Six Pastorals* (1770). Smith was one of three brothers in Chichester, all well-known painters.

367. William Mason. Mason printed Gray's journal of his 1769 tour of the Lake District in his *Memoirs* of the poet in 1775.

369. Lady Anne Lindsay. *Ancient and Modern Scottish Songs* (2nd edn., Edinburgh, 1776), vol. ii, ed. David Herd; text from the authorized edition by Sir Walter Scott (Edinburgh, 1825).

370. George Keate. *Poetical Works* (1781), vol. ii. Sir John Fielding (31), brother of the novelist, was a prominent London magistrate; John Wilkes (32) had been the radical hero of the 1760s.

371. Charles Jenner. *Town Eclogues* (1772).

372. James Graeme. *Poems on Several Occasions* (Edinburgh, 1773). A farmer's son, educated at Edinburgh University, Graeme was a tutor in a gentleman's family before his death of consumption at the age of twenty-two.

373–5. Robert Fergusson. The poems were first published at Edinburgh in the *Weekly Magazine* on 2 Jan. and 15 Oct. 1772, and 8 April 1773; texts from *Poems* (Edinburgh, 1773). In **373** *Tulloch Gorum* (48) was a popular song by John Skinner.

376–7. Horace Walpole. *Works* (1798), vol. iv.

378–92. William Cowper. Texts from *Poetical Works*, revised edn. by Norma Russell (Oxford, 1967). **380.** Abiram (16) in Numbers 16 was one of the rebels with Korah against Moses, who were swallowed up when the earth opened beneath them. **381.** Cowper had visited Ramsgate in 1763, a few months before his mental breakdown. **382.** Selkirk, the supposed prototype of Robinson Crusoe, had lived alone on Juan Fernandez 1704–9. **385.** The extracts are from books i, ii, iv and v. (ii) Presumably a reference to Lord Mansfield's judgement in 1772 that West Indian planters could not hold slaves in England, since slavery was contrary to English law. **386.** An Act imposing some restrictions on the traffic of slaves was passed in the House of Lords in 1788. **388.** Cowper's mother had died when he was almost six. **389.** The oak was in Yardley Chase, near Cowper's home in Weston Underwood. At 156–60 Cowper quotes his own translation of *Iliad*, bk. vi. **390.** Mary Unwin, with whom Cowper had lived since 1765, was seven years older than the poet and had had a stroke in 1791. **391.** Cowper and Mrs Unwin were moving from Weston, near Olney, to East Anglia under the care of his cousin. **392.** Based on an incident in Richard Walters, *Voyage Round the World . . . by George Anson* (1748).

393. Phillis Wheatley. *Poems on Various Subjects, Religious and Moral* (1773). She was brought as a slave to Boston from Africa in 1761, aged about seven, and bought by John Wheatley, a tailor. Her *Poems* were published in London during a visit in 1773 to England with her master's son.

394. Anonymous. *Simplicity: or, Domestic Poems* (1773). The Pantheon (68) was a much admired place of entertainment, opened in 1772, for assemblies, masquerades and, later, opera.

395. John Langhorne. The extracts are from books i (1774) and ii (1775). (i) For John Wilkes (3) see note to poem 370. For Gay's Marian (24) see 82. (ii) The vagrant poor were entitled to relief only in their own parishes. Since a bastard child would be entitled in the parish in which it was born, pregnant paupers were often ruthlessly moved on (81–2). David Teniers (10) was a seventeenth-century Flemish painter of genre scenes. For Sternhold (96) see note to poem 314.

396–400. Charles Dibdin. **396–7.** *The Waterman: or, The First of August* (1774). **398.** *Songs*, vol. i (1790); text from *The Professional Life of Mr. Dibdin* (1803), vol. iii. **399–400.** *A Tour to Land's End* (1798); texts from *Professional Life* (1803), vol. iv.

401. Thomas Penrose. *Flights of Fancy* (1775), with a correction from *Poems* (1781).

402–3. Anonymous. *Modern Midnight Conversation, or Matrimonial Dialogues, Adapted to the Times* (1775).

404–5. Richard Brinsley Sheridan. Texts from *Dramatic Works*. ed. Cecil Price (Oxford, 1973), vol. i.

406. Augustus Montagu Toplady. *Gospel Magazine*, iii (March 1776).

407. Anonymous. *Gentleman's Magazine*, xlvi (March 1776). Since the battle of Bunker Hill in June 1775, the British army had been besieged in Boston. News that General Howe had evacuated his forces in the month this poem appeared would not yet have reached England.

408. Anonymous. *London Magazine*, xlv (April 1776).

409. Anonymous. *Gentleman's Magazine*, xlvi (May 1776). Thetis' son (17) was Achilles. The Nemean fair (28) refers to one of the four ancient panhellenic festivals.

410. Anonymous. *London Magazine*, xlv (Sept. 1776).

411. Susanna Blamire. *Poetical Works* (Edinburgh, 1842). For 'old style' (131) see note to poem 314.

412–15. John Codrington Bampfylde. *Sixteen Sonnets* (1778). The son of a Devon landowner and educated at Cambridge, Bampfylde was later confined in a private madhouse.

416–17. John Newton. *Olney Hymns* (1779).

418. J. Wilde. *Songs and Verses* ([Newcastle?], 1779).

419. 'Brian Bendo'. *The Matrimonial Museum; or, Meritorious Monitor* (Newcastle, 1779).

420–1. John Hawthorn. *Poems, By John Hawthorn, Light Dragoon in the Inniskilling Regiment* (Salisbury, 1779). Born in Bainbridge, Northern Ireland, Hawthorn was a linen-weaver before enlisting in 1778.

422–4. John Freeth. **422.** *The Warwickshire Medley* (Birmingham, [1780?]). The British army had won a costly victory over American forces at Bunker Hill near Boston in June 1775. **423.** *Modern Songs on Various Subjects* (Birmingham, 1782). **424.** *New London Magazine*, iii (1786, Supplement); text from *The Political Songster* (6th edn., Birmingham, 1790). The decision to colonize Botany Bay, New South Wales, had been taken in Aug. 1786 and the first convicts were transported there in 1787. Major James George Semple (27), a notable adventurer, was sentenced to transportation in Sept. 1786, but later released on condition that he leave England. The 'White Boys' (36) were members of an Irish agrarian association, who had recently renewed disturbances in Munster (Sept. 1785).

425. Anonymous. *Gentleman's Magazine*, li (Oct. 1781). A collection of the poems of Dafydd ap Gwilym (*fl.* 1340–70) was to be published in 1789, eds. Owen Jones and William Owen Pughe.

426. John Scott. *Poetical Works* (1782).

427. Samuel Henley. *European Magazine*, i (April 1782); preferred to the revised text in *The Story of Al Raoui* (1799), though one emendation has been adopted.

428. —— O'Brien. *O'Brien's Lusorium* (1782). Attributions to William O'Brien, the actor and dramatist, are unlikely. The *European Magazine*, ii (Nov. 1782), described the author as frequenting and sometimes presiding over 'all the lower order of clubs in the metropolis . . . where the fun of the night is not interrupted by any chastening of wisdom, or recollection of decency'. The 'Morniment' (10) is the Monument, erected by Wren to commemorate the Great Fire of London.

429–31. Edward Thompson. *Nauticks; or, Sailor's Verses* (2 vols., 1783). Thompson was a naval officer who, when on half-pay, published poetry and edited such poets as Oldham and Marvell. In 1778 he commanded the *Hyaena*, a small frigate which he took to the West Indies, returning with a convoy. In 1780–1 he was sent to the West Indies again to establish and defend the colonies of Demerara and Essequibo.

433. Anonymous. *London Magazine, Enlarged and Improved*, i (Dec. 1783). Islington Spa (26) was an afternoon tea-garden, patronized by tradesmen. Bagnigge Wells (26) was a popular resort for drinking the waters and breakfasting.

434–40. Thomas Holcroft. **434.** *British Magazine*, iii (Aug. 1783); text from *Wit's Magazine*, i (April 1784). Voltaire had repeatedly criticized Shakespeare's ignorance of the laws of dramatic art. **435–7.** *Songs . . . in The Noble Peasant* (1784); but emendations in **437** are adopted from its reappearance in *Songs . . . in The Choleric Fathers* (1785). **438.** *European Magazine*, vii (April 1785). **439.** *The Adventures of Hugh Trevor: A Novel* (1794), vol. iii. **440.** *Morning Chronicle*, 12 Sept. 1794. Haydn made highly successful visits to London in 1791 and 1794–5.

441–60. William Blake. Texts from *Writings*, ed. G. E. Bentley, Jr. (2 vols., Oxford, 1978).

461. Thomas Maurice. *European Magazine*, vi (Oct. 1784). Since the 1750s British forces had been fighting to gain control of the sub-continent, in particular against the Mahrattas and Hyder Ali. There were growing protests in Britain against such imperialism, but Fox's attempt to introduce a bill for the reform of the East India Company in Nov. 1783 had been defeated and had led to the collapse of the Fox–North coalition. Nadir Shah (11), ruler of Iran, had invaded India in 1739 and ordered the massacre of 30,000 people in Delhi.

462. Sir George Dallas. *The India Guide; Or, Journal of a Voyage to the East Indies in 1780* (Calcutta, 1785).

463–74. Robert Burns. Texts from *Poems and Songs*, ed. James Kinsley (3 vols., Oxford, 1968). **463.** 'Holy Willie' was William Fisher, elder of Mauchline, the village near which Burns was a tenant farmer. The censure by the Kirk Session of Gavin Hamilton (67), Burns's landlord and friend, had been rejected by the more liberal Presbytery of Ayr. Also mentioned are William Auld (89), the parish minister, and Robert Aiken (85), an Ayr solicitor, patron and friend of Burns. **464.** The child was born on 22 May 1785 to Elizabeth Paton, who had been a servant in the Burns household. **468.** The leader (34) was General James Wolfe, who died after the famous scaling of the Heights of Abraham and capture of Quebec from the French in 1759. The Moro (37) was the fortress guarding the harbour of Santiago, Cuba, stormed by the British in 1762. Admiral Curtis (38) had defended Gibraltar against French and Spanish forces in 1782, when General Eliott had destroyed the Spanish floating batteries (40).

475. Robert Merry. *European Magazine*, x (Dec. 1786).

476. John Carr. The poem refers to the River Derwent in Durham. Lilly (28) was William Lilly (1468?–1522), whose Latin grammar was still used in schools.

477. Henry James Pye. *Poems on Various Subjects* (1787), vol. i. The first ascent in Britain had been made by Lunardi in Sept. 1784.

478. John Frederick Bryant. *Verses* (1787). He is described on the titlepage as 'Late Tobacco-Pipe Maker at Bristol'.

479. Ann Yearsley. *Poems on Various Subjects* (1787). She sold milk from door to door in Bristol and was the mother of six children, before being patronized by Hannah More. Yearsley and More had quarrelled, however, by the time this, her second, collection of poems was published.

480. L. Ker. *Minor Poems; Or Poetical Pieces . . . Collected by L. Ker, M.B.* (1787).

481–2. John O'Keeffe. **481.** *The Farmer* (1787), II. iii. **482.** *A Father's Legacy to his Daughter* (1834).

483–4. Charles Morris. **483.** *A Complete Collection of Songs, by Captain Morris* (5th edn., 1787). **484.** *A Collection of Political and Other Songs* (14th edn., 1797).

485–91. John Wolcot ('Peter Pindar'). *Instructions to a Celebrated Laureat* (1787); text from *Works*, vol. ii (1794). Samuel Whitbread began his career as a clerk in a brewery, eventually becoming its owner and MP for Bedford. The Royal visit took place on 26 May 1787. **486.** *A Rowland for an Oliver* (1790). **487.** *Odes of Importance* (1792). Charles Lennox, Duke of Richmond (15) still benefited from the duty on coal shipped in the Tyne, granted to his ancestor, the first Duke, by Charles II. James Cecil, Marquis of Salisbury (16) was Lord Chamberlain, and Charles Jenkinson, Lord Hawkesbury, a politician. **488.** *Odes to Kien Long, the Present Emperor of China* (1792). **489.** *Pindariana* (1794). **490–1.** *The Royal Tour, and Weymouth Amusements* (1795). In **490** 'M[oo]re' (27) is John Moore, Archbishop of Canterbury. In **491**, the 'Huntingdonian Priest' (9) is Rowland Hill, preacher, and first Chairman of the Religious Tract Society, who had been Chaplain to Selina Hastings, Countess of Huntingdon, a famous Methodist.

492. William Crowe. *Lewesdon Hill* (Oxford, 1788).

493. Thomas Russell. *Sonnets and Miscellaneous Poems* (Oxford, 1789). Hephaestus, the Greek god of fire, was hurled from Olympus by Zeus when he took the part of his mother Hera in a quarrel. He dropped on the island of Lemnos in the Aegean, breaking his leg, and remained lame thereafter. (There are variant versions of the myth.)

494. Anonymous. *County Magazine*, iii (Salisbury, July 1788). Calpe is Gibraltar (see note to **468**).

495–8. Anna Seward. **495.** Bodleian MS. Pigott d. 12, pp. 11–12; *European Magazine* xxii (Oct. 1792); text from *Llangollen Vale, With Other Poems* (1796). She had been born at Eyam, Derbyshire, while her father was Rector there. **496.** *Gentleman's Magazine*, lix (March 1789). **497.** Bodleian MS. Pigott d.12, pp. 13–17, dated August 1790; text from *Poetical Works* (Edinburgh, 1810), vol. ii. **498.** Bodleian MS. Eng. poet. c.51, pp. 155–6; text from *Gentleman's Magazine*, lxii (April 1792).

499. Charlotte Smith. *Elegiac Sonnets* (5th edn., 1789).

500. John Williams. *Poems: By Anthony Pasquin* (1789), vol. i.

501. Sir Samuel Egerton Brydges. *Sonnets and other Poems* (new edn., 1789).

502. Anonymous. *Asylum for Fugitive Pieces*, vol. iii (1789).

503–4. William Lisle Bowles. *Fourteen Sonnets, Elegiac and Descriptive, Written During a Tour* (Bath, 1789); texts from *Sonnets and Other Poems* (4th edn., Bath, 1796).

505–6. Erasmus Darwin. **505.** *European Magazine*, xvi (Dec. 1789), where the verses are described as 'on some Medallions made by Mr Wedgwood from a Specimen of Clay from Sydney Cove, presented to him by Sir Joseph Banks'. **506.** From *The Botanic Garden*, pt. ii: *The Loves of the Plants* (Lichfield, 1789) and pt. i: *The Economy of Vegetables* (1791). In (i) Darwin refers to Henry Fuseli's 'The Nightmare', exhibited at the Royal Academy in 1782. In (ii) 'Mona' (17) refers to the Earl of Uxbridge's copper mines on Anglesey; Darwin goes on to describe Matthew Boulton's steam-operated coining-machine at Soho near Birmingham, on which four boys aged 10 or 12 could strike thirty thousand guineas an hour.

507. Andrew Macdonald. *Miscellaneous Works* (1791).

508. William Sotheby. *Poems: Consisting of a Tour Through Parts of North and South Wales* (Bath, 1790).

509–12. Joanna Baillie. *Poems; Wherein it is Attempted to Describe Certain Views of Nature and of Rustic Manners* (1790). This, her first book of verse, seems not previously to have been identified.

513. Samuel Bishop. *Poetical Works* (1796), vol. ii.

514. John Aikin. *Poems* (1791).

515. Richard Polwhele. *The Influence of Local Attachment*, bk. vii (expanded edn., 1798). Polwhele spent his childhood in St. Clement, near Truro in Cornwall.

516. Laurence Hynes Halloran. *Poems on Various Occasions* (Exeter, 1791). Franz Anton Mesmer, who anticipated the techniques of modern hypnotism, fled to England after the French Revolution, but his disciples had already been active in London in the 1780s. The poem describes Mesmer, or one of his followers, attempting to induce a fit or trance by running his fingers over the patient's body, seeking the small 'magnets' which compose the great 'magnet' of the body as a whole.

517. John Taylor. *Norfolk Chronicle*, 16 July 1791; text from *Hymns and Miscellaneous Poems* (1863).

518. John Learmont. *Poems Pastoral, Satirical, Tragic and Comic* (Edinburgh, 1791). Learmont was a gardener in Dalkeith.

519. Anonymous. *Miscellanies in Prose and Verse* (Edinburgh, 1791). Some of the prose is by Francis Garden, Lord Gardenstone, but the authorship of the verse is uncertain: a likely contributor is James Thomson Callender (d. 1803), who escaped to America after being arrested for sedition in 1793.

520. William Shepherd. *Monthly Magazine*, iii (March 1797). The embassy to Peking under George, Earl Macartney, embarked in Sept. 1792 and returned two years later.

521–2. Joseph Mather. *A Collection of Songs, Poems, Satires, &c.* (Sheffield, 1811). Mather's verses were written down by others, as he could not read or write. An emendation in **521** is adopted from the text in *Songs* (Sheffield, 1862), ed. J. Wilson. In **522** 'Birmingham' (11) probably refers to the riots there in July 1791 by the 'Church and King' faction against supporters of the French Revolution. Thomas Paine's *The Rights of Man* appeared in two parts in 1791–2.

523. Richard Graves. *Senilities; or, Solitary Amusements: in Prose and Verse* (1801). Mary Wollstonecraft's *A Vindication of the Rights of Woman* was published in Jan. 1792.

524. Edward Rushton. *A Tribute to Liberty. Or, A New Collection of Patriotic Songs* (1793), ed. R. Thompson. Rushton lost his sight while mate on a slaving expedition to Guinea in 1774. He became a tavern-keeper, journalist and bookseller in Liverpool, and recovered his sight in 1807 after thirty-three years of blindness.

525. John Parrish. *Three Short Political Poems, Addressed to the Society for Preserving Liberty and Property against Levellers and Republicans* (1793). The 'test' (41) refers to recent attempts to modify the Test and Corporation Acts to legalize the participation of dissenters in civil government. The 'fighting Jew' (82) was Daniel Mendoza, the pugilist.

526. Thomas Cole. *The Life of Hubert: A Narrative, Descriptive and Didactic Poem*, bk. i (1795).

527. James Woodhouse. *Life and Poetical Works* (1896), ed. R. I. Woodhouse, vol. i. A Staffordshire shoemaker by trade, Woodhouse was patronized by Shenstone and enjoyed brief celebrity in the London literary world after the publication of his *Poems* (1764). He was later steward to Mrs Elizabeth Montagu and eventually a bookseller in London.

528. James Kennedy. *Treason!!! Or, Not Treason !!! Alias The Weaver's Budget* [1795]. Kennedy had been assistant secretary to the British Convention of the Friends of the People at Edinburgh in Nov. 1793. Several delegates were arrested and sentenced to transportation to Botany Bay.

529. George Galloway. *Poems* (2nd edn., Edinburgh, 1795). When France declared war on Britain in Feb. 1793, the Duke of York had been sent with an expeditionary force to defend Holland. The campaign was unsuccessful. Admiral Sir Edward Pellew (18) was frequently in action against the French navy in the early 1790s.

530. Joseph Fawcett. *The Art of War* (1795); preferred to the revised text in *Poems* (1798). Lines 10–12 and 15–17 are adapted from *King John*, III. iii. 35–8.

531. Hannah More. Published in the Cheap Repository Tracts distributed to the lower classes, the poem supposedly stopped a riot by colliers near Bristol.

532. William Parsons. Bodleian MS. Don.d.123 ff.59–60, dated 15 July 1795; there is another version in *Thraliana*, ed. K. C. Balderston (Oxford, 1942), vol. ii. On 13 July 1795 there had been an anti-war riot which moved from Charing Cross to Downing Street and St. George's Fields before being dispersed by soldiers.

533. William Taylor. *The Cabinet. By a Society of Gentlemen* (Norwich, 1795), vol. ii.

534. Annabella Plumptre. *The Cabinet* (Norwich, 1795), vol. iii.

535–6. John Thelwall. **535.** *Poems Written in Close Confinement* (1795). A prominent radical, Thelwall had been arrested in May 1794 and imprisoned first in the Tower and later in Newgate. Along with Thomas Hardy and Horne Tooke, he was acquitted in Dec. 1794 after a famous trial. **536.** *Poems Chiefly Written in Retirement* (Hereford, 1801). Thelwall had been visiting Coleridge at Nether Stowey near Bridgwater. The Wordsworths (55–7) had recently moved to Alfoxden, 4 miles away. Coleridge dissuaded Thelwall from settling in the neighbourhood.

537–8. Anna Laetitia Barbauld. **537.** *Works* (1825), vol. i. **538.** *Monthly Magazine*, vii (April 1799). Coleridge had visited her in Bristol in Aug. 1797.

539. Anonymous. *European Magazine*, xxx (July 1796).

540. Edmund Gardner. *European Magazine*, xxx (Aug. 1796); preferred to the revised text in *Miscellanies in Prose and Verse* (Bristol, 1798), vol. ii.

541. George Colman the Younger. *My Night-Gown and Slippers; or Tales in Verse* (1797). The poem was intended as a parody of the German legendary tales fashionable in the 1790s. Lines 50–1 quote *Macbeth*, II. i. 49–51.

542. Charles Newton. *Poems* (Cambridge, 1797).

543. Robert Southey. *Poems* (Bristol, 1797).

544–6. George Canning, John Hookham Frere and George Ellis. **544.** *The Anti-Jacobin, or Weekly Examiner*, no. 2 (27 Nov. 1797); text from 4th edn., 1799. **545.** *The Anti-Jacobin*, no. 30 (4 June 1798); text from 4th edn., 1799. A burlesque of such German drama as Schiller's *The Robbers*. **546.** *The Anti-Jacobin*, no. 36 (9 July 1798); text from 4th edn., 1799. The poem was a valedictory attack on fashionable and subversive ideas. The Marquis de Condorcet (30), author of numerous works in favour of social reform and scientific enlightenment, was influential in the early stages of the French Revolution. The references to Loire and Lyons (76 and 77) allude to the mass executions in Nantes and Lyons in 1793 of opponents, or suspected opponents, of the Revolution. Rome had fallen to Napoleon in Feb. 1798, leading to the expulsion of Pope Pius VI (99).

547–8. Mary Alcock. *Poems* (1799). She was the sister of Richard Cumberland the dramatist. The poems may date from the 1780s. **548.** For the White Boys (26) see note to poem 424.

550. James Plumptre. Richard Cumberland (21) had celebrated the Lake District in his *Odes* (1776); Joseph Farington (22) had published a collection of engravings of the Lakes in 1789.

551. Anonymous. *European Magazine*, xxxv (April 1799). The plays of Schiller and August von Kotzebue enjoyed a considerable vogue in the 1790s. The poem parodies Gray's 'Ode to Adversity'.

552. James Bisset. *A Poetic Survey Round Birmingham* (Birmingham, [1800]).

POSTSCRIPT

Since the anthology went to press, I have realized that poem 304 is a revised version of 'A Song' in Thomas D'Urfey's *Wit and Mirth*, vol. i (1719).

INDEX OF FIRST LINES

The references are to the numbers of the poems

INDEX OF AUTHORS

The references are to the numbers of the poems